J2EE™:
The Complete Reference

About the Author

Jim Keogh teaches courses on Java Application Development, including J2EE, at Columbia University and is a member of the Java Community Process Program. He developed the first e-commerce track at Columbia and became its first chairperson. Jim spent more than a decade developing advanced systems for major Wall Street firms. Jim introduced PC programming nationally in his Popular Electronics Magazine column in 1982, 4 years after Apple Computer started in a garage. He was also a team member who built one of the first Windows applications by a Wall Street firm, featured by Bill Gates in 1986. Jim is the author of 54 books, several best-selling computer books. He is also a faculty member, Graduate School, Saint Peter's College, Jersey City, NJ.

About the Technical Editors

Richard V. Dragan is a member of the faculty of Columbia University where he helped developed and teaches the Java Application Development lab course. This course is where advanced students build a working J2EE application as part of their graduation requirement. Dragan is also a Java consultant and frequent contributor to PC Magazine and Computer Shopper (where he wrote a programming column for four years) and has published over 120 articles and reviews over the past seven years. Currently, he also is a contributing editor for programming books for amazon.com where he writes a monthly electronic mailing of recommended programming titles. He is completing his Ph.D. at CUNY and writes fiction and plays classical guitar in his spare time.

Ken Davidson uses J2EE to develop mission critical systems for the Pepsi Business Support Group. He is on the faculty of Columbia University where he teaches course in J2EE technologies including EJB, JMS, and JNDI. Davidson was a senior member of the development team and design and implement the live auction site for eBay using Java technology.

Richard Weiss is a member of the faculty of Columbia University where he has spent several years teaching Java in the Electronic Commerce Track. Weiss has more than 10 years experience and is director of support for a software development company in New York City. Previously he directed technology projects for an airline and for NYU Medical Center that included WAN/LAN technologies, programming/application projects, and Web design and architecture projects. Weiss received his B.S. in applied physics from SUNY Binghamton in 1989.

J2EE™:
The Complete Reference

Jim Keogh

McGraw-Hill/Osborne
New York Chicago San Francisco
Lisbon London Madrid Mexico City
Milan New Delhi San Juan
Seoul Singapore Sydney Toronto

McGraw-Hill/Osborne
2600 Tenth Street
Berkeley, California 94710
U.S.A.

To arrange bulk purchase discounts for sales promotions, premiums, or fund-raisers, please contact **McGraw-Hill**/Osborne at the above address. For information on translations or book distributors outside the U.S.A., please see the International Contact Information page immediately following the index of this book.

J2EE™: The Complete Reference

1234567890 CUS CUS 0198765432

ISBN 0-07-222472X

Publisher
   Brandon A. Nordin

Vice President & Associate Publisher
   Scott Rogers

Acquisitions Editor
   Wendy Rinaldi

Project Editor
   Julie M. Smith

Acquisitions Coordinator
   Athena Honore

Technical Editors
   Richard V. Dragan
   Ken Davidson
   Richard Weiss

Copy Editor
   Dennis Weaver

Proofreader
   Stefany Otis

Indexer
   Valerie Perry

Computer Designers
   Apollo Publishing Services,
   Mickey Galicia, Melinda Moore Lytle

Illustrators
   Michael Mueller, Lyssa Wald

Series Design
   Peter F. Hancik

This book was composed with Corel VENTURA™ Publisher.

Dedicated to Amber-Leigh Christine, the light of our lives

Contents

Part I

J2EE Basics

Part II

J2EE Databases

Part III

J2EE Foundation

Part IV

J2EE Interconnectivity

Part V

Web Services

Part VI

Appendixes

Acknowledgments

S pecial thanks go to Kenneth E. Davidson, Rich Dragon, and Richard Weiss who formed a team of advisers from the Columbia University faculty whose expert opinions and suggestions have made this book possible.

Introduction

Java technology has evolved from a programming language designed to create machine independent embedded systems into a robust, vendor-independent, machine-independent server-side technology, enabling the corporate community to realize the full potential of web-centric applications.

Java began with the release of the Java Development Kit (JDK). It was obvious from the start that Java was on a fast track to becoming as a solution to many corporate systems problems. More interfaces and libraries were extended the JDK, as the corporate world demanded—and received—application programming interfaces (API) that addressed real world situations.

JDK API extensions fully integrated into the JDK with the release of the Java 2 Standard Edition (J2SE). J2SE contains all the APIs needed to build industrial strength Java applications. However, the corporate world felt J2SE lacked the strength required for developing enterprise-wide applications.

Again the corporate pushed Sun Microsystems, Inc. to revise Java technology to address needs of an enterprise. Sun then launched the Java Community Program (JCP), which brought together corporate users, vendors, and technologists to develop a standard for enterprise Java APIs. The result is the Java 2 Platform, Enterprise Edition commonly referred to as Java 2 Enterprise Edition (J2EE).

Enterprise systems are traditionally designed using the client/server model where client-side systems request processing from service-side systems. However, enterprise systems were undergoing their own evolution. A new model called web services gradually replaced the client/server model in corporations.

Application programmers assembled applications from an assortment of processing components called web services. Each web service was independent from other web services and independent from applications. Client-side application communicates with a middle-tier, server-side application, which in turns interacts with the necessary web services that are also located on the server-side.

With the adoption of the web services model in corporations, the JCP realized that J2EE must also go through another evolutionary cycle. With the introduction of J2EE 1.4, the Java community has merged J2EE technology with web services technology.

What's Inside

This book covers in detail all aspect of J2EE and Web services. The book is divided into these five parts:

- Part I J2EE Basics
- Part II Java Databases
- Part III J2EE Foundation
- Part IV Java Interconnectivity
- Part V Web Services
- Part VI Appendixes

Part one provides a comprehensive discussion of J2EE basics. In this part you receive an overview of J2EE and the foundation of the J2EE architecture and framework. You are also presented with the best practices for designing and developing a J2EE application.

Database technology is a critical component of every J2EE application. In the second part of the book you learn about database concepts and Java data object and how to incorporate basic and advanced JDBC techniques to build even the most complex and challenging J2EE applications.

As you'll discover as you read chapters of this book, J2EE embraces many existing Java technologies. These include Java API of XML Processing (JAXP), Java API for XML Messaging (JAXM), Java Servlets, Java ServerPages, and Enterprise JavaBeans. Each of these technologies is detailed in Par III J2EE Foundation.

Part IV of this book covers Java Interconnectivity, which shows you how to communicate to Web services, objects, and other applications through the use of an assortment of Java technologies. These include Java Mail, Java IDL/CORBA Common

Object Request Broker Architecture, Java Remote Method Invocation, Java Messaging Service (JMS), Java Security, and Java Naming and Directory Interface.

It is in Part V of the book where you learn web services technology and how to incorporate web services technology into your J2EE application. Topics include SOAP, Universal Description, Discovery, Integration (UDDI), Electronic Business XML (EbXML), Java API for XML Registries (JAXR), and the Web Service Description Language (WSDL).

Part VI is a handy reference guide that I've provided for those moments when you need some quick information to get you back on track, but don't want to re-read the theory you learned in the main part of the book. If you want quick, succinct information on J2EE classes, methods, and interfaces, look no further.

A Book for All Programmers

J2EE: The Complete Reference is designed for all Java programmers, regardless of their experience level. It does assume, however, a reader is able to create at least a time Java program. If you are just learning Java this book will make an excellent companion to any Java tutorial and serve as a source of answers to your specific questions. Experienced Java and J2EE pros will find the coverage of the many new web services features very helpful.

Don't Forget: Code On The Web

Remember, the source code for all of programs in this book is available free of charge on the Web at http://www.osborne.com. Downloading this code prevents you from having to type in the examples.

The
Complete
Reference

J2EE

Part I

J2EE Basics

The new web-centric corporation is changing the way in which it delivers highly efficient, enterprise-wide distributive systems. The old way of building enterprise systems won't solve today's corporate IT requirements. To meet the round-the-clock instantaneous demand expected by thousands of concurrent users, developers will have to evolve.

Technologists at Sun Microsystems, Inc. and the Java Community Program rewrote the way developers build large-scale, web-centric distributive systems by using Java 2, Enterprise Edition (J2EE). J2EE addresses complex issues faced by programmers who develop these systems.

The first part of this book introduces you to the basic concepts used in both J2EE and web services technology. These concepts are split into four areas of interest, beginning with an overview and definition of J2EE, as well as an illustration of its role in the evolutionary process of computer programming.

Next we'll take a look at J2EE architecture. Here you'll roll up your sleeves and get your hands into the guts of J2EE, allowing you to see how J2EE works within the web services infrastructure.

At first glance, you might feel overwhelmed by the power of J2EE—but luckily that feeling should be short-lived. The third concept-area illustrates J2EE best practices, including commonly used design principles used by J2EE programmers to build advanced J2EE web-centric distributive systems.

Part I concludes with a look at the J2EE design patterns used to solve common programming problems that crop up during the development of a J2EE application. After reading Part I you'll have a solid foundation on which to to build your own J2EE applications.

Chapter 1

Java 2 Enterprise Edition Overview

Throughout the course of history there have been periods where disruptive technology revolutionized everyday life and forced the scientific, political, and economic communities to rethink their practices. Electricity, the telegraph, telephone, radio, television, automobile, airplanes, satellites, and cable television are technologies that radically altered the status quo to become a demarcation between old and new. Generations define themselves by these radical changes in technology.

The Internet is the most recent technology to change the way we interact with each other and change the way we do business. Transactions and communication occur online and are nearly instantaneous. Overnight mail has been replaced by email sent at almost the speed of light. Junk mail has been replaced by spam. Most banking is handled at home or at work. And buying a special gift is a few keystrokes away.

Disruptive technologies spawn supportive technologies that become its integral component and make the disruptive technology operate more effectively. Java 2 Enterprise Edition is a supportive technology that is closely associated with the Internet. This is because Java 2 Enterprise Edition enables software engineers and programmers to create an industrial-strength software infrastructure that makes web-based applications cost-effective to build and reliable to use in any mission-critical system.

Although Java 2 Enterprise Edition seems to be rooted with the Internet, it is really the next growth spurt in the evolution of programming languages. In this chapter, I'll take you on a brief tour of the genealogy of Java 2 Enterprise Edition, which will piece together the puzzle of how forerunner programming languages became the foundation for today's Java 2 Enterprise Edition (J2EE).

The ABC of Programming Languages

Over the years there have been numerous attempts to make it easy for programmers to write instructions that are processed by computers. And it seems that a single letter of the alphabet identifies some of these early languages. One of the earliest programming languages is assembly language. Assembly language requires a programmer to use rather abstract symbols to represent machine instructions that direct a central processing unit (CPU) to move and manipulate bytes of information inside the computer.

Programmers can write highly efficient programs using assembly language because assembly language syntax gives a programmer direct low-level access to hardware. For example, a programmer can specify a specific memory address or a specific register within the CPU to store data, which is not possible in many other languages.

Although assembly language can produce efficient programs, assembly language is difficult to learn, difficult to use effectively, and a nightmare to debug. These drawbacks became the impetus for the creation of more programmer-friendly languages such as FORTRAN, COBOL, and BASIC. Instead of using abstract symbols as found in assembly language, these languages use English-like words and punctuation to create computer instruction.

FORTRAN, COBOL, and BASIC had their strengths and weaknesses, too. FORTRAN was designed to write efficient scientific applications, but lacked the power necessary to produce system code. COBOL was the choice for writing business applications. However, it too couldn't be used to generate system code. And both languages weren't as easy to learn as BASIC. BASIC was an all-purpose programming language that was intuitive to learn, but lacked the efficiency necessary to build industrial-strength applications.

And all three of these languages failed to follow structured principles for controlling the flow of a program. This resulted in the creation of countless code segments that were linked together by conditional branches and caused a typical program to jump from code segment to code segment, creating an organization widely known as spaghetti code.

The Pascal programming language is another early programming language that was originally used to teach students how to program and later found an unsuccessful trek into industry. The Pascal programming language successfully gave structure to programming, something that was lacking in other languages. However, early Pascal syntax lacked features that were key to the creation of system code and application programs—and therefore the Pascal programming language wasn't widely adopted by programmers.

FORTRAN, COBOL, BASIC, and Pascal were programming languages developed prior to the computer revolution of the early 1970s. Until then, system-level programming was kept away from most programmers. But that was to change as technologists focused on developing a computer language that was easy to learn, well structured, and could be used to build both industrial-strength system code and application code.

The B and C of Programming Languages

Technologists from the Cambridge University computer lab joined with colleagues from London University in the early 1960s to design a programming language that made it easy for computers to be programmed. Their efforts resulted in the Cambridge Programming Language (CPL). CPL (sometimes referred to as the Combined Programming Language) was a complex language, which probably inhibited its wide adoption.

Towards the end of that decade, Martin Richards (who worked at Cambridge University) simplified CPL. Richards called his version of CPL Basic CPL (BCPL), which was designed to program the IBM 370 computer. In BCPL, the type of an object is inferred from the context in which the object is used rather than defined by a data type within the program. Listing 1-1 is a sample of BCPL. You can read more about BCPL in *BCPL: The Language and Its Compiler* by Martin Richards and Colin Whitby-Strevens. BCPL was used in Cambridge University until the late 1980s when the Cambridge University computer lab moved to C.

Listing 1-1
A sample of
BCPL.

```
LET START () BE $(
     LET F(N) = N=0 -> 1, N*F(N-1)
     FOR I = 1 TO 10 DO WRITEF(""F(%N), = %N*N"", I, F(I))
     FINISH
$)
```

A paper describing BCPL was published in the proceeding of the 1969 AFIPS spring Joint Computer Conference. In the same year, Ken Thompson (with assistance from Dennis Ritchie) set out to develop the UNIX operating system written in PDP-7 assembler. Thompson felt UNIX needed a high level language for UNIX to provide a beneficial computing service. He looked towards FORTRAN as the solution.

Thompson used a language called TMG, developed by Doug McIlroy, to create a flavor of FORTRAN for UNIX. But that only lasted about a week. Instead of FORTRAN, Thompson defined a new language that was greatly influenced by BCPL. He called the language B. The B programming language was used to program the PDP-7 and subsequently the PDP-11. Listing 1-2 illustrates a function written in the B programming language. A major difference between BCPL and the B programming language is that BCPL is a typeless programming language and the B programming language is a single-type programming language where a word was only type.

Listing 1-2
A sample
of the B
programming
language.

```
infact (n)
{
    auto f, i, j;
    extrn fact;
     f = 1;
    i = 0;
    for (i=0; i <= n; ++i) {
        fact[i] = f = #* j;
        i =#+ 1;
    }
    return (f);
}
```

The B programming language sufficed for a couple of years, but it gradually became inefficient. And an attempt to embellish the language with the creation of the NB language (New B) fell short of its mark. However, Dennis Ritchie's effort succeeded in the early 1970s. He called the new language the C programming language.

Ritchie was able to create the C programming language without the drawbacks found in previous programming languages. Many believe that Ritchie's success was strongly influenced by the fact that Ritchie was a practicing programmer and designed the C programming language to conform to the way he and other programmers develop software. That is, programmers divide a program into its functionality and create code segments called *functions* to define the functionality.

This approach was a radical departure from the traditional ways in which programming languages were developed. Up to that time, committees of academics designed programming languages, which typically lacked features professional programmers needed to create effective and efficient programs.

The C programming language was designed by a programmer for professional programmers and had the power and structure that is necessary to build industrial-strength programs. It was these factors that caused programmers to rapidly embrace the C programming language. The C programming language revolutionized the way programs were designed and written.

The C programming language was distributed with UNIX and soon became the de facto standard for writing UNIX programs. In 1990 the American National Standards Institute (ANSI) formally adopted a standard for the C programming language.

Taking Programming Languages Up a Notch

The computer revolution of the 1970s increased the demand for sophisticated computer software to take advantage of the ever-increasing capacity of computers to process data. The C programming language became the linchpin that enabled programmers to build software that was just as robust as the computer it ran on.

As the decade of the 1980s approached, programmers were witnessing another spurt in the evolution of programming language. Computer technology advanced to a point beyond the capabilities of the C programming language. The problem wasn't new. It occurred previously and caused the demise of generations of programming languages. Simply stated, the problem was that programs were becoming too complicated to design, write, and manage to keep up with the capabilities of computers.

The number of lines of code contained in the program measures a program's complexity. Early computers were programmed by toggling switches to encode machine instructions with binary values. Only a couple of hundred instructions could practically be programmed. Advances in computer technology drove demand for increasingly complex programs. The programming community responded with the creation of assembly language, which could handle hundreds of lines of code.

The need for more complex software continued. While assembly language and subsequent programming language could technically process thousands of lines of code, it was the human element that became a barrier from building more complex software. That is, thousands of lines of code are difficult to comprehend and manage.

And this too affected the C programming language. A C program that consists of 50,000 lines of code is impractical to maintain. This meant that the C programming language that once radically altered the way software was written was also developing a weakness, which sent technologists looking for a better way to design and write programs.

It was the early 1980s when a new design concept moved programming to the next evolutionary step. This was the period when object-oriented programming (OOP) took programmers by storm, and with it a new programming language called C++.

Object-oriented programming changed the way in which programmers designed applications. The C programming language required programmers to divide an application into data and functionality, called functions, that weren't bound together by program instructions. Object-oriented programming enabled programmers to divide an application into objects that resembled real-life objects all too familiar to programmers and users of the application.

The real world is built from objects, and objects are built from one or more other objects. For example, a house is an object that is comprised of other objects such as doors, windows, walls, ceilings, and floors.

Each object has data associated with it and functionality. For example, data associated with a window consists of height, width, length, and style among other characteristics. A window's functionality includes opening and closing the window.

In an object-oriented program both data and functionality are directly bound to an object without program instructions. This is a startling contrast to C programming, where data and functionality are naturally disassociated from each other. This meant that while the C programming language could be used to create objects, the language lacked the features that would naturally bind data and functionality to an object.

In 1979, Bjarne Stroustrup of Bell Laboratories in New Jersey enhanced the C programming language to include object-oriented features. He called the language C++. (The ++ is the incremental operator in the C programming language.) C++ is truly an enhancement of the C programming language, and began as a preprocessor language that was translated into C syntax before the program was processed by the compiler.

Stroustrup introduced the concept of a class from which instances of objects are created. A class contains data members and member functions that define an object's data and functionality. He also introduced the concept of inheritance that enabled a class to inherit some or all data members and member functions from one or more other classes—all of which complements the concepts of object-oriented programming. By 1998, ANSI officials standardized Stroustrup's C++ specification.

The Beginning of Java

Just as C++ was becoming the language of choice for building industrial-strength applications, another growth spurt in the evolution of programming language was budding, fertilized by the latest disruptive technology—the World Wide Web.

The Internet had been a well-kept secret for decades before the National Science Foundation (which oversaw the Internet) removed barriers that prevented the Internet's commercialization. Until 1991, when it was opened to commerce, the Internet was the exclusive domain of government agencies, the academic community, and anyone else able to connect.

Once the commercialize barrier was lifted, the World Wide Web, one of the several services offered on the Internet, became a virtual community center where visitors could get free information about practically anything and browse through thousands of virtual stores.

Browsers power the World Wide Web. A browser interprets ASCII text files written in HTML into an interactive display that can be interpreted on any machine. The browser must be compatible with the correct version of HTML and HTTP implementation. This meant any computer could use the same file without the programmer having to modify the file, which was something unheard of at the time. Programs written in C or C++ were machine dependent and could not run on a different machine unless the program was recompiled.

There has always been a compatibility problem with the client machine, one that (among other reasons) was caused by the use of binary protocols used to communicate between client machines and servers. Binary protocols are inflexible and are operating system specific. However, protocols used to exchange data between client and server are ASCII text based. This means that Internet protocols are not operating system dependent.

It didn't take long before information technology departments of corporations realized that substantial cost savings could be gained by adopting Internet technology for internal use in the form of an intranet. An intranet is basically a corporation's exclusive Internet that can be accessed over a corporation's internal computer network.

There was always interest in developing a machine-independent programming language that enabled corporations and software manufacturers to build one application that could run without modification on every computer. However, attempts to develop such a versatile language always fell short of reaching its objectives. The programming language closest to reaching this goal was C and C++—where source code is written once, then compiled into an executable that was machine dependent.

Both C and C++ use a preprocessor that enables a programmer to quickly distinguish the target environment. This means that a programmer can use one version of source code to create executables for different machines. This is possible because C and C++ use conditional preprocessor directives in the source code, which tells the preprocessor to include specific statements in the source code before the source code is compiled. Listing 1-3 illustrates a preprocessor conditional directive that includes a comment in the source code if the target environment is WIN32. WIN32 is defined in the program as the operating system environment. Of course, the comment is replaced with environment-specific statements in the source code.

Listing 1-3
Here is a sample of a preprocessor condition directive.

```
#ifdef _WIN32
    //include WIN32 statements here
#endif
```

The success of the Internet gave renewed focus to developing a machine-independent programming language—the same year the Internet was commercialized, five technologists at Sun Microsystems, Inc. set out to develop a machine-independent programming language. James Gosling, Patrick Naughton, Chris Warth, Ed Frank, and Mike Sheridan spent 18 months developing the programming language that they called Oak, which was renamed Java when this new language made its debut in 1995.

Java had gone through numerous iterations between 1991 and 1995, during which time many other technologists at Sun Microsystems, Inc. made substantial contributions. These included Bill Joy, Arthur van Hoff, Jonathan Payne, Frank Yelin, and Tim Lindholm.

Although Java is closely associated with the Internet, Java was developed as a language for programming software that could be embedded into electronic devices regardless of the type of CPU used by the device, such as programs that run consumer appliances.

The Java team from Sun Microsystems, Inc. succeeded in creating a portable programming language, something that had eluded programmers since computers were first programmed. Their success, however, was far beyond their original dreams. The same concept used to make Java programs portable to electronic devices also could be used to make Java programs run on computers running Microsoft Windows, UNIX, and Macintosh.

Timing was perfect. The Internet/intranet had wetted corporate America's appetite for cost-effective portable programs that could replace mission-critical applications within the corporation. And Java had proven itself as being a programming language used to successfully develop machine-independent applications.

It was in the mid-1990s when the team from Sun Microsystems, Inc. realized that Java could be easily adapted to develop software for the Internet/intranet. Towards the turn of the century, many corporations embraced Java and began replacing legacy applications—many of which were written in C and C++—with Java Internet/intranet-enabled applications.

Java and C++

In keeping with the genealogical philosophy where only the dominant genes are passed on to the next generation, the Java development team at Sun Microsystems, Inc. incorporated the best of C++ into Java and left out features of C++ that were inefficient and not programmer friendly. The Java team also created new features that gave Java the dynamics necessary for Internet-based programming.

Many of the primitive constructs of the Java language are similar to, and at times exactly the same as, constructs in C++. For example, Java is an object-oriented programming language that uses classes to create instances of objects. Those classes have data members and member methods similar to classes found in C++.

However, Java doesn't have pointers, which is a cornerstone of the C++ (and C) programming language. Pointers, while efficient when used properly, can be difficult to master and can cause runtime errors when improperly used in a C++ program.

Java comes with automatic garbage collection, which is not found in C++ (and C). Garbage collection is a routine that recovers spent memory without the programmer having to write code to free previously reserved memory. You'll find a complete discussion on the features of Java in *Java 2: The Complete Reference*. The Java development team was wise to base Java on C++ because C++ programmers find transitioning to Java a straightforward process, which is why corporations that have a staff of C++ programmers look favorably on Java.

The close relationship between Java and C++ has led more than a few programmers to assume that the purpose of Java is to enhance the C++ programming language—and eventually replace C++. This isn't true. Both languages are designed to solve different problems. Java is designed for applications that must coexist on different kinds of machines—and frequently over an Internet-based infrastructure. In contrast, C++ is designed to run on a specific machine, although a C++ program can be recompiled to run on other machines.

Java Bytecode

Java programs are written similar to C++ programs in that the programmer writes source code that contains instructions into an editor or in an integrated development environment, and then the source code is compiled. However, that's where Java and C++ part ways. The compiling and linking process of a C++ program results in an executable that can be run on an appropriate machine. In contrast, the Java compiler converts Java source code into bytecode that is executed by the Java Virtual Machine (JVM).

The JVM is an interpreter of Java bytecode, which is a throwback to days when BASIC programs were converted to machine code at runtime rather than compile time. Very few, if any, modern programming languages except for Java are interpreted at runtime. Instead, programs are compiled and linked to the more efficient executable.

At first blush, one would expect a Java program to take a performance hit because an additional processing step is necessary at runtime to convert each instruction into machine code. However, performance degradation caused by runtime translation is minimized through optimization of the Java source code into bytecode at compile time. Furthermore, Java minimizes the number of instructions that must be translated by shifting many instructions to the JVM and by dividing instructions into function components.

Machine-specific instructions are not included in bytecode. Instead, they already reside in the JVM, which is machine specific. This means that the bytecode might contain fewer instructions that need to be translated than a comparable C++ program.

As you'll learn in the next chapter and throughout this book, a Java 2 Enterprise Edition program is typically designed around functional components, each of which might be a separate bytecode file. Therefore, instead of including all functionality in the program—which is the case with many C++ programs—a J2EE program could consist of several bytecode files each called and translated as needed by the program.

Therefore, although the Java compiler generates bytecode that must be interpreted by the JVM at runtime, the number of instructions that need translation is usually minimal and have already been optimized by the Java compiler.

Sun Microsystems, Inc. is sensitive to concerns that bytecode must be interpreted at runtime, and to alleviate these concerns they have included a Just In Time (JIT) compiler with the JVM in the Java 2 release. The JIT compiler converts bytecode into executable code at runtime, which in many cases boosts performance significantly.

JIT compiling occurs as needed by the JVM, rather than compiling the complete Java program into an executable. This is because the JVM performs certain checks at runtime that cannot be performed on the executable itself.

The Advantages of Java

The Java development team at Sun Microsystems, Inc. released Java at a perfect time, just when the Internet community was moving from passive data to dynamic programs. Internet users were wowed by the ability to click hyperlinks to display web pages that were filled with text and pictures. However, that thrill quickly lost its magic. Internet users wanted real-time interaction with web pages rather than receiving passive data that they simply read.

They wanted more personalized responses from web pages—and so did corporations that sought to bring electronic commerce to the Internet. Among other wishes, corporations needed a way to build dynamic catalogs and online shopping, and a way to make shopping at their virtual store an experience that kept customers coming back.

Static web pages couldn't offer the dynamics demanded by Internet users and corporations. Only an executable program could provide the power for customized interactions. Unfortunately, executable programs were machine dependent, and the Internet was machine independent. The door was opened for the new programming language to enter and provide the means to transform the passive Internet into a dynamic and alive cyberspace.

The Internet posed a programming challenge unlike previous challenges. This is because of the way the Internet operates. Typically, a user tells the operating system to run an executable. Both the request and the execution occur on the user's computer, commonly called a *client*. The executable is machine dependent. However, it works differently on the Internet. The web server initiates the program that is executed by the client, rather than the user, and therefore the executable must be portable and machine independent.

For example, when a user selects a hyperlink on a web page, the browser requests that the web server download to the client the web page associated with the selected hyperlink. Embedded in the web page might be a reference to run a small Java program called an *applet*. The browser reads the reference to the applet, then requests that the web server download the applet. Once the applet is received, the browser requests that the JVM execute the applet automatically without any additional interaction by the user.

Although applets are downloaded in the same way as images, applets contain the intelligence to personalize the user experience by reading tiny amounts of information, called *cookies*, that are stored on the client and interact directly with users through user input.

Applets

Java broke ground in a new direction by giving programmers a choice to create one of two types of executables. These are an applet or an application. An applet is a small program that can be efficiently downloaded over the Internet and is executed by a Java-compatible browser. An application is a program that is executed directly by the user. The Java programming language can be used to create both an applet and an application.

The Internet is founded on two important principals. First, information should be freely shared, and second, web pages and other files sent to clients are safe to download and use. Unfortunately, not everyone lives up to the second principal. Some programmers introduced malicious programs that can wreak havoc on a client's computer if downloaded from a server.

The Java team at Sun Microsystems, Inc. anticipated this potential security concern and created a barrier, sometimes referred to as a firewall, between an applet and the client's operating system. All applets are restricted to the Java environment (JVM) and are prohibited from interacting with the client's operating system. For example, an applet does not have disk drive access except to read and write cookies, and an applet can only make a network connection to the server that downloaded the applet to the browser.

Built for a Robust Environment

It has been said that the Sun Microsystems, Inc. Java development team created Java as a programmer's language much along the concepts developed by Ritchie and Stroustrup. They then built upon this concept to make Java easy to learn, robust, and reliable, and incorporated advanced concepts to meet the ever-growing demand for architecture-neutral programs that work efficiently in a distributive environment.

The Java development team adopted many features found in C and C++, rather than create an entirely new language. This subtle but important consideration made it easy for existing programmers to assimilate Java. Furthermore, the team streamlined Java to provide only a few ways of accomplishing a task. This is a critical factor when a programmer must create industrial-strength programs that can continually deliver high performance over networks with a global reach.

Mission-critical systems—and those not-so-mission-critical systems that help run modern corporations are accessible from practically anywhere in the world. Information that was once available only from the computer on an executive's desktop is now obtainable from an executive's home office or hotel room, and soon from the executive's airline seat.

Corporations have built a robust network infrastructure that links together clients and servers that directly or indirectly contain mission-critical information needed for executives to make business decisions.

The network is the highway that transports information from clients to servers and servers to clients. Networked programs make the transmission possible and provide the intelligence for the executives to make sense of the information received from servers.

A key element of networked programs is that a program must be able to do multiple tasks simultaneously so that many clients can interact with the program at the same time. The Java development team designed Java to be a multithreaded programming language where each thread is a process that can work independently from other processes and permit multiple access to the same program simultaneously.

Multithreaded programming changes the way a programmer conceptualizes a program. Rather than the programmer designing a program in functional subsystems, the programmer focuses on behaviors—each of which can become a thread.

Furthermore, Java uses intra-address-space messaging to access remote objects over the network. This is referred to as call to a remote method invocation, which is discussed in Chapter 15.

Built-in Reliability

The Java development team at Sun Microsystems, Inc. have taken extraordinary steps to beef up Java to prevent the most common reasons why programs fail at runtime. Two of these are error handling and memory management.

Java has stringent rules for error handling within a program. Error-handling routines must be located in the code near instructions that could cause errors. This means a programmer will find it difficult to inadvertently overlook writing error-handling routines.

Memory management is an aspect of programming that can lead to runtime errors. In some programming languages, the programmer is directly responsible for managing how the program uses memory. This means the programmer must write instructions to allocate memory and then release that allocated memory once the program no longer requires the memory. Once memory is freed, the program can reallocate memory for another portion of the program.

In complex programs, it is easy for a programmer to mismanage memory by releasing memory that is still being used by a portion of the program or by not freeing previously allocated memory. This can lead to an out-of-memory condition during runtime.

The Java development team made memory management automatic and removed memory management from the programmer's control. This process is called *garbage* collection, where Java allocates memory and releases memory as necessary based upon the needs of the program.

However, programmers still must test their programs for memory leaks, because in some cases the Java garbage collector may not recognize complex relationships between objects and memory management. Let's say class A references class B and class B is associated with a resource. When the Java garbage collector destroys class A, it will also destroy class B, but may not destroy the resource associated with class B. You can learn more about Java garbage collection in *Java 2: The Complete Reference*.

Besides error trapping and memory management, the Java development team also has Java double-check the code—once at compile time and another check at runtime by the JVM. This means that once a program passes both checks, a programmer is assured that the program will run predictably regardless of environmental conditions at either the client or server.

For example, a common nightmare for programmers and users alike occurs when changes are made to the operating system. There is always a lingering doubt of whether or not existing programs on the system will work properly. However, programs written in Java are secure because the JVM, and not the operating system, executes Java programs.

J2EE and J2SE

Java itself has undergone an evolution that has nearly taken on a life of its own. Originally designed for programs that controlled electronic devices, Java made waves in the Internet development community by providing a means to give intelligence to passive web pages. However, the Java development team's design has made Java the programming language of choice for programming enterprise-wide, web-centric applications.

Information technology departments had always sought ways to create cost-effective computer applications. One approach is client/server architecture, which uses a two-tier architecture where client-side software requests services from server-side software.

A traditional database application illustrates the two-tier architecture. Software running on the client captures a request for information from a user, then formats the request into a query that is sent over the network to the database server for processing. The database server then transmits the requested data to the client, where software presents data to the user.

Increasingly, backend systems and infrastructure grew as information technology departments streamlined operations to deliver information and technology services to the desktop. Client/server architecture exploded from a two-tier architecture to a multi-tier architecture, where a client's request to a server generates requests to other servers that are connected together through a backbone network.

This is very similar to you asking a travel agent to arrange your vacation. The travel agent contacts hotels, airlines, the car rental company, restaurants, and other vendors that are necessary to fulfill your request.

Although a multi-tier architecture provides services efficiently, it also makes it complex to design, create, debug, distribute, and maintain an application because a programmer must be assured that all tiers work together. However, the Java development team enhanced the capabilities of Java to dramatically reduce the complexity of developing a multi-tier application.

The Java development team grouped together features of Java into three editions, each having a software development kit (SDK). The original edition of Java is called the Java 2 Standard Edition (J2SE) and consists of application programming interfaces (APIs) needed to build a Java application or applet.

The Java 2 Mobile Edition (J2ME) contains the API used to create wireless Java applications. And the Java 2 Enterprise Edition, an enhanced version of the J2SE, has the API to build applications for a multi-tier architecture.

The Birth of J2EE

For the Internet to grow, web applications required a way to interact with backend services such as a database and dynamically generate web pages. Common Gateway Interface (CGI) technology was a solution that was adopted by many corporations. CGI technology consisted of a program that was callable by a browser whenever the appropriate hyperlink or submit action from a web form occurred.

In addition to calling a CGI program, the browser was also able to pass the CGI program data that was either entered by the user into a form on the web page or hard-coded in the hyperlink. The CGI program used this data to interact with components of the corporation's infrastructure, such as retrieving account information from a database. This information was then incorporated into a web page that the CGI program dynamically generated and sent to the browser for display.

CGI technology addressed the problem of interfacing web clients with the corporate infrastructure. However, a new set of problems appears as corporations increasingly move towards web-centric applications. CGI technology was resource intensive and not scalable to meet the dramatic increase in the number of clients who needed to access corporate resources through CGI programs.

The Java development team devised a solution to problems associated with CGI technology. Their solution was scalable and required fewer resources than CGI technology, and yet was capable of interfacing with the corporate infrastructure and generating dynamic web pages. Their solution was a Java servlet.

A Java servlet consists of Java classes, data, and methods, which are callable by a browser similar to how a browser calls a CGI program. You'll learn all about Java servlets in Chapter 10.

Although Java servlets improved upon the foundation laid by CGI technology, Java servlets suffered from a serious drawback. A Java servlet requires programmers to be knowledgeable about the Java programming language. Web programmers at that time were proficient in HTML and scripting languages such as JavaScript, but not comfortable with a full-featured programming language such as Java. Java was used for nearly all coding in a Java servlet and HTML code was used only in output statements that were sent to the browser.

This posed a problem for the Java development team. Java servlets had to be made easier to program before they'd be widely accepted by web programmers. Their solution was to create a new technology called JavaServer Pages (JSP). JSP programs could be written with little if any knowledge of Java, because most of the coding in a JSP program is written in HTML with snippets of Java code intermingled. A JSP program is then automatically translated into a Java servlet. You'll learn how to create JSP programs in Chapter 11.

Databases

Nearly every web-centric application requires access to a corporation's database so that clients can enter new information, recall existing information, and modify (if necessary) information the corporation has on file.

There are many database management system (DBMS) products on the market that are used to manage data. These include Oracle, DB2, Informix, Sybase, and others. Each DBMS product uses proprietary algorithms and software to manage data. This posed another dilemma for the Java development team, but one that was easily overcome by the standardization that had taken place in database technology.

The Java development team needed an API that would interface between commercial DBMS products and Java. It would have been a maintenance nightmare if programmers needed a different API for each database product, which had been the case in the early days of database programming.

By the time the Java development team turned their attention to a database API, the database community had already agreed on two major standards for DBMS products. These are a relational database structure and Structured Query Language (SQL).

A relational database structure applies normalization rules that, among other things, reduce redundancy in data by organizing data into groups that later take form as tables. A table consists of rows and columns, similar to a spreadsheet, and tables are related together using a common value in the rows of each table. The concept of a relational database is discussed in detail in Chapter 5.

SQL is similar to a programming language in that SQL consists of keywords and statements. However, SQL differs from a programming language in that instead of instructing the operating system or JVM to perform tasks, SQL instructs a DBMS to perform data management tasks.

The adoption of a relational database structure and SQL by the database community simplified the task of the Java development team. They could create one API that connected to the DBMS, formulated a SQL statement, sent the SQL statement to the DBMS, then received information from the DBMS, which consists of the requested data or a message. They called this the Java Database Connectivity (JDBC) API, which you'll learn how to use in Chapter 6.

The Maturing of Java

As previously mentioned, Java is an evolving programming language that began with the release of the Java Development Kit (JDK). During this evolutionary process, the Java development team included more interfaces and libraries as programmers demanded new APIs. These new features to the JDK were called *extensions*, APIs that were add-ons to the JDK. Sun Microsystems, Inc. incorporated these extensions into a new Java Development Kit called Java 2 Standard Edition.

Information technology departments of corporations look towards web-centric applications as a way to economize while offering streamlined services to employees and customers. An increased emphasis was placed on server-side programming and on development of vendor-independent APIs to access server-side systems.

Sun Microsystems, Inc. responded by creating the Java Community Program (JCP) that invited corporate users, vendors, and technologists to develop a standard for enterprise Java APIs. The JCP effort resulted in the Java 2 Platform, Enterprise Edition commonly referred to as Java 2 Enterprise Edition (J2EE).

Java Beans and Java Message Service

J2EE is a combination of several technologies that offers a cohesiveness to bond together server-side systems and services and produce an industrial-strength scalable environment within which web-centric applications can thrive.

A critical ingredient in the development of J2EE is the collaborative environment fostered by Sun Microsystems, Inc. within which vendors and technologists come together in the JCP to create and implement Java-based technologies.

Two of these promising technologies included in J2EE are Enterprise Java Beans (EJB) and the Java Message Service (JMS). EJB consists of specifications and APIs for developing reusable server-side business components designed to run on application servers. As you'll learn in Chapter 12, EJB facilitates the breadth of processing required by a business, including distributed transaction processing that is used in many web-centric applications. Manufacturers of application servers have joined the JCP to create a standard specification to implement EJB with their application servers.

For example, EJB is used to encode and share business logic among clients by using a session bean, entity bean, or message-driven bean. A stateful session bean retains data accumulated during a session with a client. The data is lost once the client no longer references the bean. A stateless session bean does not maintain any state between method calls. A message-driven bean is called by the JMS container. The message-driven bean deployment descriptor specifies the type of messages it wants to receive. An entity bean is used to collect and retain rows of data from a database, and survives as long as the data associated with the bean is viable.

JMS is a standard and an API used to provide vendor-independent communication with Message-Oriented Middleware (MOM). This means Java programs and middleware can transact using a common language. JMS is the first standard written for earlier technology. Until the arrival of JMS, vendors provided their own API for messaging.

Why J2EE?

With the onset of web-centric applications that grew more dependent than ever on server-side technologies such as middleware, information technology departments of corporations needed a sustainable way to develop applications and related middleware that were portable and scalable.

These applications needed to be designed to handle thousands of users simultaneously 24 hours a day, seven days a week, without any downtime. One of the major challenges to building such a complex application is to be able to design and test it. J2EE simplifies the creation of an enterprise-wide application, because functionality is encapsulated in components of J2EE. This enables designers and programmers to organize the application into functionality that is distributed across the server-side components built using J2EE.

Furthermore, the collaboration of industry leaders in the JCP results in J2EE as the industry standard enterprise environment within which all competitive products must operate. This means corporate clients are assured that server-side products they purchase are supported by J2EE. This also means that a corporation is no longer locked into one vendor. Instead, products from multiple vendors can be mixed and matched based on their cost-effectiveness while being bonded together with J2EE technology.

J2EE is a versatile technology because application components built using J2EE are able to communicate with each other behind the scenes using standard communications methods such as HTTP, SSL, HTML, XML, RMI, and IIOP.

All J2EE programs are written in Java, enabling a corporation to use its existing staff of Java programmers to create programs that work at each layer of the multi-tier infrastructure. Corporations no longer need to find programmers to write programs to interface with a vendor-specific component. This also shortens the development cycle for complex programs that require multithreading and synchronization, because J2EE contains all the interfaces and libraries that handle these complex issues.

Java Beans, Java Servlets and JavaServer Pages are core components of J2EE. In addition, J2EE consists of seven standard services, all of which are discussed throughout this book. These services are as follows.

CORBA Compliance

Sun Microsystems, Inc. built into J2EE two CORBA technologies that enable Java programs to communicate with any enterprise system that is compliant with CORBA technology and to interact with legacy systems. These technologies are JavaIDL and RMI-IIOP. JavaIDL is used to interconnect Java programs with CORBA-based systems. RMI-IIOP is a blend of Java Remote Method Invocation API (RMI) and the Internet Inter-ORB Protocol (IIOP) used with CORBA to link together Java programs and legacy systems.

JavaMail API

The Java development team needed an efficient way for customers and e-commerce sites to exchange information such as order confirmations. The solution is JavaMail API, which enables Java programmers to communicate by sending email messages to web users.

Java Message Service

The Java Message Service (JMS) API is used to build into Java programs a transmission link between components. This link enables fault-tolerant messages to be transmitted and received in asynchronous mode.

Java Naming and Directory Interface API

Objects can be located in various locations on servers linked to the infrastructure of a corporation. The Java development team required a method to enable Java programs to easily locate these objects. Their solution was to create standardized naming conventions and directories, and the Java Naming and Directory Interface (JNDI) API, so programmers can look up objects from within their Java programs.

Java Transaction API

One transaction can involve multiple components, and the Java development team needed a way for components to manage their own transactions. The team created the Java Transaction API (JTA) to enable Java programmers to build into components routines to handle transactions.

JDBC API

Many Java programs and components must access information contained in a database, as previously discussed in this chapter. The Java development team devised the JDBC API that enables a program to connect to and interact with practically any commercial DBMS.

XML Deployment Descriptors

Many corporations and some industries have adopted XML as a way to store, manipulate, and exchange textual information that appears in documents. The Java development team has included a set of descriptors in J2EE that enable programmers to create tools and components that can interact with XML documents. XML deployment descriptors define the environment and the functionality of components when they are deployed into the J2EE container. The J2EE container learns how and where to deploy components by reading the deployment descriptors. Components don't interact with deployment descriptors. Some of the more common activities of XML deployment descriptors are to

- Manage transactions between the container and Enterprise Java Beans
- Register a message-driven bean to a queue
- Define JNDI lookup names
- Manage stateful and stateless session beans

Looking Forward

The Java programming language is the foundation on which J2EE is built. This chapter provided you with a look back at the evolution of programming language that has culminated into the Java programming language. This evolution continues with introduction of J2EE by Sun Microsystems, Inc. J2EE is used to create a new breed of applications that are based on web services components. J2EE programmers don't write code in the traditional sense. Instead J2EE programmers assemble a J2EE application from web services components.

The remainder of this book introduces you to the concepts of web services, J2EE architecture and strategies for designing and building J2EE components that collectively form a J2EE application.

You'll learn database design, development, and how to access data from within a J2EE application using JDBC API and XML. You'll learn professional techniques for building your own web components using Java servlets, JavaServer Pages, and Enterprise Java Beans. And then you'll learn how to interconnect web components to form an industrial-strength J2EE application.

The
Complete
Reference

J2EE

Chapter 2

J2EE Multi-Tier Architecture

The expectation for instant gratification was ratcheted up a notch with the growth of the Internet and the maturity of corporate infrastructure. Executives and customers alike demand instant access to information any time, any place—24 hours a day, 7 days a week. Whether it's accessing the corporation online catalog, placing an online order, retrieving account information, or sending and receiving email, they want an immediate response.

Information technology departments of corporations had to devise a scheme to revamp their networks and systems to accommodate thousands of people who wanted to simultaneously access corporate resources. To meet these expectations, technologists rethought the way in which information is stored, accessed by, and delivered to clients.

Focus was directed at the technology architecture model used to provide services to desktop and remote computers. Many IT departments used a two-tier, client/server architecture model where desktop software called *clients* request information over the corporate network infrastructure to *servers* running software that fulfilled a client's request.

However, this two-tier architecture depends heavily on keeping client software updated, which is both difficult to maintain and costly to deploy in a large corporation that has several intranets and a workforce that consists of field representatives and other remote users. Web-based, multi-tier systems don't require client software to be upgraded whenever presentation and functionality of an application are changed.

The infrastructure had to be revamped. The two-tier, client/server architecture had to be abandoned and a new, multi-tier architecture had to be built in its place. The Java development team at Sun Microsystems, Inc. with the collaboration of the Java Community Program (JCP) developed the Java programming language to be used to build software for this new multi-tier architecture.

In this chapter you'll learn about multi-tier architecture and the role each Java 2 Enterprise Edition component plays in the redevelopment of corporate America's infrastructure—and how Java 2 Enterprise Edition is becoming a key component in web services technology.

Distributive Systems

The concept of multi-tier architecture has evolved over decades, following a similar evolutionary course as programming languages. The key objective of multi-tier architecture is to share resources amongst clients, which is the fundamental design philosophy used to develop programs.

As you learned in the previous chapter, programmers originally used assembly language to create programs. These programs employed the concept of software services that were shared with the program running on the machine.

Software services consist of subroutines written in assembly language that communicate with each other using machine registers, which are memory spaces within the CPU of a machine. Whenever a programmer required functionality provided by a software service, the programmer called the appropriate assembly language subroutine from within the program. Although the technique of using software services made creating programs efficient by reusing code, there was a drawback. Assembly language subroutines were machine specific and couldn't be easily replicated on different machines. This meant that subroutines had to be rewritten for each machine.

The introduction of FORTRAN and COBOL brought the next evolution of programming languages, and with it the next evolution of software services. Programs written in FORTRAN could share functionality by using functions instead of assembly language subroutines. The same was true of programs written in COBOL. A function is conceptually similar to a Java method, which is a group of statements that perform a specific functionality. The group is named, and is callable from within a program.

Although both assembly language subroutines and functions are executed in a single memory space, functions had a critical advantage over assembly language subroutines. A function could run on different machines by recompiling the function.

No longer were software services exclusive to a particular machine. However, software services were restricted to a machine. This meant programs and functions that comprise software services had to reside on the same machine. A program couldn't call a software service that was contained on a different machine.

Programs and software services were saddled with the same limitations that affected data exchange at that time. Magnetic tapes were used to transfer data, programs, and software services to another machine. There wasn't a real-time transmission system.

Real-Time Transmission

Real-time transmission came about with the introduction of the UNIX operating system. The UNIX operating system contains support for Transmission Control Protocol/Internet Protocol (TCP/IP), which is a standard that specifies how to create, translate, and control transmissions between machines over a computer network.

It was also around the same time when technologists developed the Remote Procedure Call (RPC). RPC defined a way to share functions written in any procedural language such as FORTRAN, COBOL, and the C programming language. This meant that software services were no longer limited to a machine. Furthermore, a programmer could now call a function that was created by a different program using a different procedural language that resided on an entirely different machine as long as that machine was connected to the same network.

Another important development in the evolution of distributive systems came with the development of eXternal Data Representation (XDR). While RPC enabled programmers to call preprogrammed functions that were available on the network using TCP/IP, there remained a need to exchange complex data structures between programs and functions— and between functions.

The solution came with the introduction of XDR. XDR specified how complex data structures could be exchanged among programs and software services. This became the linchpin that changed the way programmers and system designers conceived applications. Instead of limiting an application to one machine, an application became a collaborative development effort that utilized software services that were available throughout the network.

Software Objects

The next evolutionary step in programming language gave birth to object-oriented languages such as C++ and Java. Procedural languages focused on functionality, where a program was organized into functions that contained statements and data that were necessary to execute a task. Functions were either internal software services within a program or external software services called by RPC.

Programs written in an object-oriented language were organized into software objects—not by functionality. A software object resembles a real-world object in that a software object encapsulates data and functionality in the same way data and functionality are associated with a real-world object. A software object is a software service that can be used by a program.

Although objects and programs could use RPC for communication, RPC was designed around software services being functionally centric and not software-object-centric. This meant it was unnatural for programs to call software objects using RPC. A new protocol was needed that could naturally call software objects.

Simultaneously two protocols were developed to access software objects. These were Common Object Request Broker Architecture (CORBA) and Distributed Common Object Model (DCOM). CORBA was developed by a consortium that included Sun Microsystems, Inc., IBM, and Oracle among others. Microsoft developed DCOM.

As you probably suspect, CORBA and DCOM were incompatible. This resulted in confusion in the marketplace, which some technologists believe caused the lack of widespread adoption of either protocol. Companies that embraced distributive object technology had to adopt either CORBA or DCOM. Otherwise, companies had to use a protocol converter as a gateway between environments that used CORBA and DCOM.

Web Services

The Internet indirectly shed new light on the conflict between these competing protocols. The Internet is based on a set of open protocol standards that centered on the Hypertext Transport Protocol (HTTP) that is used to share information between machines. HTTP isn't a replacement for TCP/IP. Instead, HTTP is a high-level protocol that uses TCP/IP for low-level transmission.

The Internet solidified the direction of distributive systems by proving to corporations that they can greatly improve efficiency through better utilization of computer networks. But there was another hurdle to overcome. Internet technology lacked the capability to share software services that businesses needed to fully integrate large-scale business applications.

The next evolution of software services was born and was called web services. There is a common misnomer regarding web services. Some believe the "web" component of web services comes from the relationship web services has with the Internet. This isn't true. Web services is a web of services where services are software building blocks that are available on a network from which programmers can efficiently create large-scale distributive systems.

Three new standards were developed with the introduction of web services. These are Web Services Description Language (WSDL), Universal Description, Discovery, and Integration (UDDI), and Service Oriented Architecture Protocol (SOAP).

Programmers use WSDL to publish their web service, thereby making the web service available to other programmers over the network. A programmer uses UDDI to locate web services that have been published and uses SOAP to invoke a particular web service. You'll learn more about WSDL, UDDI, and SOAP in Part V of this book.

Many large-scale distributive systems and web services have something in common. They are written using J2EE because J2EE addresses the complex issues that a programmer faces when developing a large-scale distributive system. There are numerous web services used in a typical large-scale distributive system and each service is associated with a tier in the multi-tier architecture that is used to share resources over a corporate infrastructure.

The Tier

A tier is an abstract concept that defines a group of technologies that provide one or more services to its clients. A good way to understand a tier structure's organization is to draw a parallel to a typical large corporation (see Figure 2-1).

At the lowest level of a corporation are facilities services that consist of resources necessary to maintain the office building. Facilities services encompass a wide variety of resources that typically include electricity, ventilation, elevator services, computer network services, and telephone services.

The next tier in the organization contains support resources such as accounting, supplies, computer programming, and other resources that support the main activity of the company. Above the support tier is the production tier. The production tier has the resources necessary to produce products and services sold by the company. The highest tier is the marketing tier, which consists of resources used to determine the products and services to sell to customers.

Any resource is considered a client when a resource sends a request for service to a service provider (also referred to as a service). A service is any resource that receives and fulfills a request from a client, and that resource itself might have to make requests to other resources to fulfill a client's request.

Let's say that a product manager working at the marketing tier decides the company could make a profit by selling customers a widget. The product manager requests an accountant to conduct a formal cost analysis of manufacturing a widget. The accountant is on the support tier of the organization. The product manager is the client and the accountant is the service.

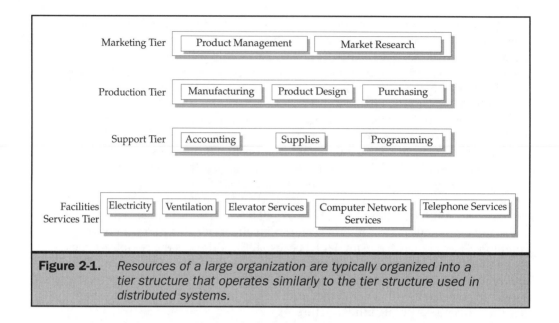

Figure 2-1. Resources of a large organization are typically organized into a tier structure that operates similarly to the tier structure used in distributed systems.

However, the accountant requires information from the manufacturing manager to fulfill the product manager's request. The manufacturing manager works on the production tier of the organization. The accountant is the client to the manufacturing manager who is the service to the accountant.

In multi-tier architecture, each tier contains services that include software objects, database management systems (DBMS), or connectivity to legacy systems. Information technology departments of corporations employ multi-tier architecture because it's a cost-efficient way to build an application that is flexible, scalable, and responsive to the expectations of clients. This is because the functionality of the application is divided into logical components that are associated with a tier. Each component is a service that is built and maintained independently of other services. Services are bound together by a communication protocol that enables a service to receive and send information from and to other services.

A client is concerned about sending a request for service and receiving results from a service. A client isn't concerned about how a service provides the results. This means that a programmer can quickly develop a system by creating a client program that formulates requests for services that already exist in the multi-tier architecture. These services already have the functionality built into them to fulfill the request made by the client program.

Services can be modified as changes occur in the functionality without affecting the client program. For example, a client might request the tax owed on a specific order. The request is sent to a service that has the functionality to determine the tax. The business logic for calculating the tax resides within the service. A programmer can modify the business logic in the service to reflect the latest changes in the tax code without having to modify the client program. These changes are hidden from the client program.

Clients, Resources, and Components

Multi-tier architecture is composed of clients, resources, components, and containers (see Figure 2-2). (In J2EE, the term "component" is used in place of the term "service," but both have the same philosophical meaning.) A *client* refers to a program that requests service from a component. A *resource* is anything a component needs to provide a service, and a *component* is part of a tier that consists of a collection of classes or a program that performs a function to provide the service. A *container* is software that manages a component and provides a component with system services.

The relationship between a container and a component is sometimes referred to as a contract, whose terms are governed by an application programming interface (API). An API defines rules a component must follow and the services a component will receive from the container.

A container handles persistence, resource management, security, threading, and other system-level services for components that are associated with the container. Components are responsible for implementation of business logic. This means programmers can focus on encoding business rules into components without becoming concerned about low-level system services.

This is an important concept in multi-tier architecture because modification can be made to low-level security, for example, without requiring any modification to a component. Only the container needs to be modified by the programmer.

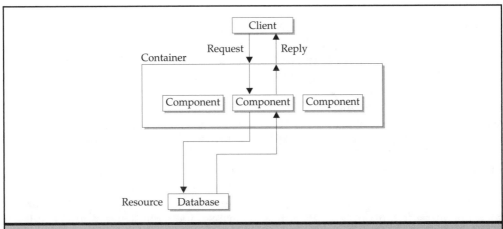

Figure 2-2.   *A multi-tier architecture consists of clients, resources, components, and containers that are used by a programmer to create a distributive system.*

The relationship between a component and a container is very similar to the relationship between a program and an operating system. The operating system provides low-level system services such as I/O to a program. Programs don't need to be modified if a new disk drive is installed in the computer. Instead, the operating system is reconfigured to recognize the new disk drive.

Accessing Services

A client uses a client protocol to access a service that is associated with a particular tier. A protocol is a standard method of communication that both a client and the tier/component/resource understand. There are a number of protocols that are used within a multi-tier infrastructure because each tier/component/resource could use different protocols.

One of the most commonly implemented multi-tier architectures is used in web-centric applications where browsers are used to interact with corporate online resources. A browser is a client and requests a service from a web server using HTTP.

In a typical enterprise-wide application, a browser requests services from other components within infrastructures such as a servlet. A servlet uses a resource protocol to access resources that are necessary for the servlet to fulfill the request. For example, a servlet will use the JDBC protocol to retrieve data from DBMS. You'll be introduced to specific protocols throughout this book as you learn to build components and use resources.

J2EE Multi-Tier Architecture

J2EE is a four-tier architecture (see Figure 2-3). These consist of the Client Tier (sometimes referred to as the Presentation Tier or Application Tier), Web Tier, Enterprise JavaBeans Tier (sometimes referred to as the Business Tier), and the Enterprise Information Systems Tier. Each tier is focused on providing a specific type of functionality to an application.

It's important to delineate between physical location and functionality. Two or more tiers can physically reside on the same Java Virtual Machine (JVM) although each tier provides a different type of functionality to a J2EE application. And since the J2EE multi-tier architecture is functionally centric, a J2EE application accesses only tiers whose functionality is required by the J2EE application.

It's also important to disassociate a J2EE API with a particular tier. That is, some APIs (i.e., XML API) and J2EE components can be used on more than one tier, while other APIs (i.e., Enterprise JavaBeans API) are associated with a particular tier.

The Client Tier consists of programs that interact with the user. These programs prompt the user for input and then convert the user's response into requests that are forwarded to software on a component that processes the request and returns results to the client program. The component can operate on any tier, although most requests from clients are processed by components on the Web Tier. The client program also translates the server's response into text and screens that are presented to the user.

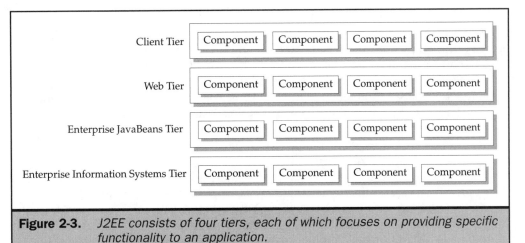

Figure 2-3. *J2EE consists of four tiers, each of which focuses on providing specific functionality to an application.*

The Web Tier provides Internet functionality to a J2EE application. Components that operate on the Web Tier use HTTP to receive requests from and send responses to clients that could reside on any tier. A client is any component that initiates a request, as explained previously in this chapter.

For example (see Figure 2-4), a client's request for data that is received by a component working on the Web Tier is passed by the component to the Enterprise JavaBeans Tier where an Enterprise Java Bean working on the Enterprise JavaBeans

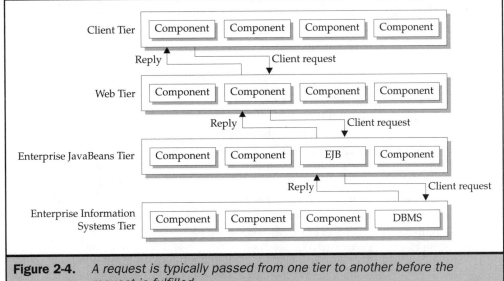

Figure 2-4. *A request is typically passed from one tier to another before the request is fulfilled.*

Tier interacts with DBMS to fulfill the request. Requests are made to the Enterprise JavaBeans by using the Java Remote Method Invocation (RMI) API. The requested data is then returned by the Enterprise JavaBeans where the data is then forwarded to the Web Tier and then relayed to the Client Tier where the data is presented to the user.

The Enterprise JavaBeans Tier contains the business logic for J2EE applications. It's here where one or more Enterprise JavaBeans reside, each encoded with business rules that are called upon indirectly by clients. The Enterprise JavaBeans Tier is the keystone to every J2EE application because Enterprise JavaBeans working on this tier enable multiple instances of an application to concurrently access business logic and data so as not to impede the performance.

Enterprise JavaBeans are contained on the Enterprise JavaBeans server, which is a distributed object server that works on the Enterprise JavaBeans Tier and manages transactions and security, and assures that multithreading and persistence are properly implemented whenever an Enterprise JavaBean is accessed.

Although an Enterprise JavaBean can access components on any tier, typically an Enterprise JavaBean accesses components and resources such as DBMS on the Enterprise Information System (EIS) Tier.

Access is made using an Access Control List (ACL) that controls communication between tiers. The ACL is a critical design element in the J2EE multi-tier architecture because ACL bridges tiers that are typically located on different virtual local area networks and because ACL adds a security level to web applications. Hackers typically focus their attack on the Web Tier to try to directly access DBMS. ACL prevents direct access to DBMS and similar resources.

The EIS links a J2EE application to resources and legacy systems that are available on the corporate backbone network. It's on the EIS where a J2EE application directly or indirectly interfaces with a variety of technologies, including DBMS and mainframes that are part of the mission-critical systems that keep the corporation operational. Components that work on the EIS communicate to resources using CORBA or Java connectors, referred to as J2EE Connector Extensions.

Client Tier Implementation

There are two components on the Client Tier that are described in the J2EE specification. These are applet clients and application clients. An applet client is a component used by a web client that operates within the applet container, which is a Java-enabled browser. An applet uses the browser as a user interface.

An application client is a Java application that operates within the application client container, which is the Java 2 Runtime Environment, Standard Edition (JRE). An application has its own user interface and is capable of accessing all the tiers in the multi-tier architecture depending how the ACLs are configured, although typically an application has access to only the web layer.

A rich client is a third type of client, but a rich client is not considered a component of the Client Tier because a rich client can be written in a language other than Java—and therefore J2EE doesn't define a rich client container.

A rich client is similar to an application client in that both are applications that contain their own user interface. And as with an application client, a rich client can access any tier in the environment, depending on the ACLs configuration, using HTTP, SOAP, ebXML, or an appropriate protocol.

Classification of Clients

Besides defining clients as an applet client, application client, or a rich client, clients are also classified by the technology used to access components and resources that are associated with each tier. There are five classifications: a web client, Enterprise JavaBeans client, Enterprise Information System (EIS) client, web service peers, and a multi-tier client.

A web client consists of software, usually a browser, that accesses resources located on the Web Tier. These resources typically consist of web pages written in HTML or XML. However, a web client can also access other kinds of information that is located on the Web Tier. Web clients communicate with Web Tier resources using either HTTP or the Hypertext Transmission Protocol Secured (HTTPS), which is used to transfer encrypted information.

Enterprise JavaBeans clients are similar to web clients in that an Enterprise JavaBeans client works on the Client Tier and interfaces the J2EE application with the user. However, an Enterprise JavaBeans client only accesses one or more Enterprise JavaBeans that are located on the Enterprise JavaBeans Tier rather than resources on the Web Tier.

This access is made possible by using the RMI API. RMI handles communication between the Enterprise JavaBeans client and the Enterprise JavaBeans Tier using either the Java Remote Method Protocol (JRMP) or the Internet Inter-ORB Protocol (IIOP).

EIS clients are the interface between users and resources located on the EIS Tier. These clients use Java connectors, appropriate APIs, or proprietary protocols to utilize resources such as DBMS and legacy data sources.

A web service peer is a unique type of client because it's also a service that works on the Web Tier. Technically, a web service peer forms a peer-to-peer relationship with other components on the Web Tier rather than a true client/server relationship. However, a web service peer is commonly referred to as a client because it requests service from other components on the Web Tier, although a web service peer can also access other tiers. Typically, a web service peer makes requests over HTTP using either electronic business XML or the Simple Object Access Protocol (SOAP).

Multi-tier clients are conceptually similar to a web service peer except a multi-tier client accesses components located on tiers other than the tier where the multi-tier client resides. Multi-tier clients typically use the Java Message Service (JMS) to communicate asynchronously with other tiers.

Web Tier Implementation

The Web Tier has several responsibilities in the J2EE multi-tier architecture, all of which is provided to the Client Tier using HTTP. These responsibilities are to act as an intermediary between components working on the Web Tier and other tiers and the Client Tier. Intermediary activities include

- Accepting requests from other software that was sent using POST, GET, and PUT operations, which are part of HTTP transmissions
- Transmit data such as images and dynamic content

There are two types of components that work on the Web Tier. These are servlets and JavaServer Pages (JSP), although many times they are proxied to the Application or EJB Tier. A servlet is a Java class that resides on the Web Tier and is called by a request from a browser client that operates on the Client Tier. A servlet is associated with a URL that is mapped by the servlet container.

A request for a servlet contains the servlet's URL and is transmitted from the Client Tier to the Web Tier using HTTP. The request generates an instance of the servlet or reuses an existing instance, which receives any input parameters from the Web Tier that are necessary for the servlet to perform the service. Input parameters are sent as part of the request from the client.

An instance of a servlet fulfills the request by accessing components/resources on the Web Tier or on other tiers as is necessary based on the business logic that is encoded into the servlet. The servlet typically generates an HTML output stream that is returned to the web server. The web server then transmits the data to the client. This output stream is a dynamic web page.

JSP is similar to a servlet in that a JSP is associated with a URL and is callable from a client. However, JSP is different than a servlet in several ways, depending on the container that is used. Some containers translate the JSP into a servlet the first time the client calls the JSP, which is then compiled and the compiled servlet loaded into memory. The servlet remains in memory. Subsequent calls by the client to the JSP cause the web server to recall the servlet without translating the JSP and compiling the resulting code. Other containers precompile a JSP into a .java file that looks like a servlet file, which is then compiled into a Java class.

Business logic used by JSP and servlets is contained in one or more Enterprise JavaBeans that are callable from within the JSP and servlet. The code is the same for both JSP and servlet, although the format of the code differs. JSP uses custom tags to access an Enterprise JavaBeans while servlets are able to directly access Enterprise JavaBeans. You'll learn how to create and use servlets in Chapter 10, JSPs in Chapter 11, and Enterprise JavaBeans in Chapter 12.

Enterprise JavaBeans Tier Implementation

J2EE uses distributive object technology to enable Java developers to build portable, scalable, and efficient applications that meet the 24-7 durability expected from an enterprise system. The Enterprise JavaBeans Tier contains the Enterprise JavaBeans server, which is the object server that stores and manages Enterprise JavaBeans.

The Enterprise JavaBeans Tier is a vital element in the J2EE multi-tier architecture because this tier provides concurrency, scalability, lifecycle management, and fault tolerance. The Enterprise JavaBeans Tier automatically handles concurrency issues that assure multiple clients have simultaneous access to the same object. The Enterprise JavaBeans Tier is the tier where some vendors include features that enable scalability of an application, because the tier is designed to work in a clustered environment. This assumes that vendor components that are used support clustering. If not, a Local Director is typically used for horizontal load balancing.

The Enterprise JavaBeans Tier manages instances of components. This means component containers working on the Enterprise JavaBeans Tier create and destroy instances of components and also move components in and out of memory.

Fault-tolerance is an important consideration in mission-critical applications. The Enterprise JavaBeans Tier is the tier where some vendors include features that provide fault-tolerant operation by making it possible to have multiple Enterprise JavaBeans servers available through the tier. This means backup Enterprise JavaBeans servers can be contacted immediately upon the failure of the primary Enterprise JavaBeans server.

The Enterprise JavaBeans server has an Enterprise JavaBeans container within which is a collection of Enterprise JavaBeans. As discussed in previous sections of this chapter, an Enterprise Java Bean is a class that contains business logic and is callable from a servlet or JSP.

Collectively the Enterprise JavaBeans server and Enterprise JavaBeans container are responsible for low-level system services that are required to implement business logic of an Enterprise Java Bean. These system services are

- Resource pooling
- Distributed object protocols
- Thread management
- State management
- Process management
- Object persistence
- Security
- Deploy-time configuration

A key benefit of using the Enterprise JavaBeans server and Enterprise JavaBeans container technology is that this technology makes proper use of a programmer's expertise. That is, a programmer who specializes in coding business logic isn't concerned about coding system services. Likewise, a programmer whose specialty is system services can focus on developing system services and not be concerned with coding business logic.

Any component, regardless of the tier where the component is located, can use Enterprise JavaBeans. This means that an Enterprise Java Bean client can reside outside the Client Tier. The protocol used to communicate between the Enterprise JavaBeans Tier and other tiers is dependent on the protocol used by the other tier.

Components on the Client Tier and the Web Tier communicate with the Enterprise JavaBeans Tier using the Java RMI API and either IIOP or JRMP. Sometimes software on other tiers, usually the middle tier, uses JMS to communicate with the Enterprise JavaBeans Tier. This communication isn't exclusively used to send and receive messages between machines. JMS is also used for other communication, such as decoupling tiers using the queue mechanism.

However, the Enterprise Java Bean that is used must be a message-driven bean (MDB). MDBs are commonly used to process messages on a queue that may or may not reside on the local machine. You'll learn more about MDB when Enterprise JavaBeans is discussed in detail in Chapter 12.

Enterprise Information Systems Tier Implementation

The Enterprise Information Systems (EIS) Tier is the J2EE architecture's connectivity to resources that are not part of J2EE. These include a variety of resources such as legacy systems, DBMS, and systems provided by third parties that are accessible to components in the J2EE infrastructure.

This tier provides flexibility to developers of J2EE applications because developers can leverage existing systems and resources currently available to the corporation and do not need to replicate them in J2EE.

Likewise, developers can utilize off-the-shelf software that is commercially available in the marketplace because the EIS Tier provides the connectivity between a J2EE application and non-J2EE software. This connectivity is made possible through the use of CORBA and Java Connectors or through proprietary protocols.

Java Connector technology enables software developers to create a Java Connector for legacy systems and for third-party software. The connector defines all the elements that are needed to communicate between the J2EE application and the non-J2EE software. This includes rules for connecting to each other and rules for conducting secured transactions. You'll learn more on how these connections are created in Part IV, Java Interconnectivity.

Challenges

Although J2EE enables programmers to design and build large-scale distributive systems that use web services connected together in a multi-tier architecture, there remain design considerations that could inhibit successful deployment of the system.

Let's begin with transactions. Typically, resources are locked until a transaction is completed, which is adequate for short-lived transactions. However, an issue occurs when a single transaction takes hours to complete and other components of the system require access to resources that are being used for the transaction. Programmers must build into an application a routine that correlates IDS and uses JMS to decouple tiers that are locked.

Reliability is another issue. The assumption is that a resource is always available and will provide optimal performance when called within a distributive system. However, the assumption is based on a false premise, as proven when a resource (i.e., database) within a corporate network environment is offline at the time a system requires database access. This situation is compounded when resources are outside the corporate network environment and become services that are provided by a third party.

This means that Java applications must provide proper error-handling routines. The compiler forces the developer to either catch or throw all exceptions except for RuntimeExceptions. It's up to the developer to provide a graceful response to an error condition. The developer must also be aware of possible RuntimeExceptions that may be thrown during the execution of a program. These can be a little subtler because the compiler does not require them to be caught or thrown.

Likewise, security becomes an issue. Even if access to resources is made using HTTP and Secured Sockets Layer (SSL), another security level is needed to assure that only authorized systems have access to the resource. SSL only protects data when it's en route between two systems. Similar security issues are successfully addressed in today's corporate infrastructure using a variety of techniques that include ACLs, IP filtering, and routing. However, security becomes complex in a web service multi-tier architecture application if resources used by the application are provided by organizations outside a corporation's infrastructure.

This leads to the issue of how to manage and test a large distributive system that uses web services. There are many resources used by such a system, and each resource must be acquired, integrated into the system, accessible, and accurately perform its function; otherwise, the system fails. A large distributive system can have numerous fail points that must be adequately tested.

Chapter 3

J2EE Best Practices

With the onset of Internet technology, systems designers and programmers faced challenges similar to those faced by the men and women who worked towards making space flight a reality. The game had changed. Old technology and design methods were no longer adequate to build the new, highly efficient systems needed to maintain a competitive edge.

The old way of designing and building systems lacked the wherewithal to deliver highly efficient, enterprise-wide distributive systems to meet the 24 hours, 7 days a week instant demand expected by thousands of concurrent users. Technologists at Sun Microsystems, Inc. and other technology organizations threw out the book and rewrote the rules for system development.

The J2EE is one of their initial steps towards devising a better technology to create advanced distributive systems. But J2EE only provides the framework within which to build these systems. New design and programming techniques were needed to address the demands of corporations. Once again technologists had to think out of the box and devise new ways of building a system. And once again new concepts in design were born.

These concepts fall within two general categories: best practices and patterns. Best practices are proven design and programming techniques used to build advanced enterprise distributive systems. Patterns are routines that solve common programming problems that occur in such systems. You'll learn best practices in this chapter and then learn patterns in Chapter 4.

Enterprise Application Strategy

Not too long ago information technology departments of many corporations viewed an application in the same way some of us view an automobile. That is, an application and an automobile both have a useful life, after which they are replaced. This throwaway philosophy has its merits in that the corporation will have different needs five years hence, and therefore it makes economic sense to design an application to meet those needs rather than retrofitting the existing application.

The throwaway philosophy works well for applications that services a small group of users such as applications focused on departmental needs. However, this philosophy loses its economical and practical sense when applied to an enterprise application.

An enterprise application is a mission-critical system whose continual successful operation determines the corporation's success. This means that an enterprise application is complex in nature and meets the needs of a diverse, constantly changing division of a corporation. The bottom line is that building an enterprise application is time-consuming, and once the enterprise application is implemented successfully, few in the corporation want to tinker with a critical application that works fine.

Corporations face the realities of an enterprise application about three years after the application becomes operational. The enterprise application starts to age. Corporate needs change to meet new challenges in the marketplace and so the enterprise application must change. These changes occur gradually with the creation of a few new reports, and then maybe the addition of new fields and tables in key databases.

These are relatively minor changes, especially when compared to creating a new enterprise application. However, as the application reaches its five-year anniversary these minor changes begin taking their toll, mainly because of a philosophy that seems to be prevalent among programmers whose job it is to maintain legacy applications. These programmers have one and only one objective—make sure change to the legacy works without negatively affecting the application.

Rather than tinker with code that was written by another program and is working fine, the programmer typically writes a routine separate from existing code and then calls the routine using a hook in the legacy application. This results in minimum changes to the existing application and the new routine can easily be shut off should problems arise after the new routine is implemented.

While this is a clever and successful technique that has been used by programmers for decades, this technique inadvertently creates an application that looks like a bowl of spaghetti. The application isn't maintainable, and it is for this reason that the corporation is practically forced to re-create the enterprise application. Simply said, it is less expensive to re-create the application than it is to pay a programmer to study and change spaghetti code.

Besides the maintenance nightmare of a legacy system, information technology departments also realize that departmental applications that once had a limited scope were useful to other departments throughout the company. These applications were cloned, which saved a corporation the cost of developing a similar application. However, cloning caused two additional problems. First, each clone was slightly modified to meet the needs of its users, and multiple programmers were maintaining the same basic application.

A New Strategy

Corporations have taken on a global strategy where business activities and applications that support those activities are dispersed to business units throughout the world. However, rather than working independently, these business units transfer knowledge among other business units within the corporation to give the whole corporation a competitive edge in the global market.

In addition, corporate management approaches business similar to how football team owners approach the game of football. Management sets the main objectives for the corporation and then assembles a team to reach the objectives. On the gridiron, players are hired, each having a specific role that helps the team reach its goal—win the game. In the corporate world, business units are the players. Business units are purchased, merged, and sold to come up with a cohesive organization to reach the corporate goal—earn profits.

All enterprise applications must interface with each other to assure that information can be shared amongst business units. That is, all applications and systems have to work together and have the flexibility built into the architecture so that an enterprise application is incrementally changed to meet new business demands without having to be reconstructed.

This eliminates the lag that occurs with the throwaway philosophy. No longer will business units need to suffer the pain that occurs when changes to the application are not made in a timely manner because the application is not maintainable. The new corporate information technology strategy is to employ an architecture within which enterprise applications can coexist and can be incrementally developed and implemented.

Information technology departments realize that many applications used by business units have the same functionality. This means that there is duplicate effort within the corporation to maintain those applications. The new strategy of making enterprise applications interoperable has led to a new concept used to build enterprise applications.

An enterprise application has become a collaborative effort that is divided into two roles—building functional components and assembling functional components into an enterprise application—which enables functional components to be shared amongst many enterprise applications.

The Enterprise Application

The term "enterprise application" is elusive since practically any application used by more than one person to conduct business could be considered an enterprise application. And yet looking at an application we can easily determine if it is an enterprise application or not by asking the question, "Does the application service the entire corporation or a small group of users within the corporation?"

It is important that there is a clear understanding of what is meant by the term "enterprise application" because techniques used to design and build an enterprise application may not be the best way to develop a smaller application. This is because an enterprise application must deal with performance, security, and other issues that are not found in other kinds of applications.

For the purpose of J2EE, consider an enterprise application to be one that

- Is concurrently used by more than a handful of users
- Uses distributive resources such as DBMS that are shared with other applications
- Delegates responsibility to perform functionality among distributive objects
- Uses web services architecture and J2EE technology to link together components (i.e., objects) that are dispersed throughout the corporate infrastructure

Unlike many smaller applications, an enterprise application is highly visible within a corporation whose success greatly depends on the application's successful operations. This results in corporate users having high expectations from an enterprise application. They want the enterprise application to

- Be available 24 hours a day, 7 days a week without any downtime
- Have an acceptable response time even in the face of increasing usage
- Have the flexibility to be modified quickly without requiring a redesign of the application
- Be vendor independent
- Be able to interact with existing systems
- Utilize existing system components (i.e., objects)

This means developers have to create an enterprise application that is available and scalable to adjust to increases and decreases in demand. The application must be extensible and maintainable so new business rules can be easily added to the application. In addition, the application must be portable so the company isn't locked into a specific vendor. Developers also must build in interoperability so the enterprise application interacts with other applications and is able to reuse existing code.

Clients

As discussed in the previous chapter, J2EE is organized into tiers, the first of which is the Client Tier. Software working on the Client Tier has several functions, many of which are easily developed by programmers. However, there are a few functions that are less intuitive to program and therefore pose a challenge to programmers. These functions are to

- Present the application's user interface to the person who is using the application
- Collect and validate information from the person using the application
- Control the client's access to resources
- Prevent clients from sending duplicate requests

Client Presentation

An enterprise application uses a thin client model where nearly all functionality associated with the application is contained on the server-side rather than with the client. Thin clients handle the user interface that presents information to the user and captures input from the user. There are two strategies for building presentation functionality into a client. These are to use a browser-based user interface or to create a rich client (i.e., applet or application) where a graphical user interface is programmed into the client. Each has its advantages and disadvantages.

A browser-based user interface is written in either the Hypertext Markup Language (HTML) or the Extensible Markup Language (XML), which is used by an XML-enabled browser to interact with the user. The browser runs on the client machine and interprets HTML or XML code into elements of a user interface.

The browser-based strategy enables easy implementation of the presentation layer of an enterprise application because details of presentation such as user interface controls and event handling are built into the browser. Furthermore, browsers provide a standardized user experience that incorporates elements that are intuitive to use. That is, little or no training is needed for a person to use a browser-based application.

However, the browser-based strategy has disadvantages too. First, the developer doesn't have exact control over presentation to the user. Instead, the developer suggests user interface elements to the browser, such as font, color, and position of text and images. The browser controls how these elements are displayed. Developers who use the browser-based strategy must test the enterprise application with various browsers and browser versions to be sure that the presentation is acceptable.

Another disadvantage of the browser-based strategy is the presentation is limited to interactions that can be implemented using a markup language or plug-ins, which limits the design of the user interface. That is, features that cannot be written in a markup language or provided by a plug-in cannot be implemented in the application.

Still another disadvantage is the presentation layer is server-side dependent. This means the application accesses the server more than if a richer client strategy was used to create the user interface. Practically each time an event occurs in a browser-based presentation, the browser must access the server, which might decrease performance and response time for the user.

A browser-based strategy typically uses the HTTP protocol. HTTP is a stateless protocol, so the developer must have a strategy for maintaining session state on the server. This situation can become complex if the system requires failover support. Most "out-of-the-box" technologies for managing session state do not replicate the session.

In contrast, the richer client strategy gives a developer total control over elements of the presentation and event trapping. That is, a developer can use WYSIWYG to create the presentation and isn't limited to only events that are trapped by the browser.

In addition, a richer client accesses a server only as needed and not in response to nearly every event that occurs in the presentation. This might result in fewer server interactions and increase response time because there are fewer messages sent to the server.

Best Practice—Developing a Client for Enterprise Application   *The best practice when developing a client for an enterprise application is to use the strategy that is most appropriate for each aspect of the presentation. That is, both strategies can be used for pieces of the presentation of an enterprise application. Use the browser-based strategy for simple presentations and the richer client strategy whenever more complex presentations are necessary that cannot be adequately handled directly by a browser.*

Client Input Validation

Information that is entered into a client by a user should be validated, depending on the nature of the information. Details of the validation process are application dependent; however, the developer has two places where validation can occur: with the client or on the server side.

A developer can implement three kinds of validation strategies (see Figure 3-1): syntactic, lexical, and semantic. Syntactic validation determines if information that consists of several related values is well formed, such as time that is composed of hours and minutes. Lexical validation looks at a single value to assure that the type of value corresponds to the type of data that is expected by the application. For example, an hour value must be an integer to pass a lexical validation. Semantic validation examines the meaning of the information to determine if the information is likely to be correct. Semantic validation determines if the value of the hour is less than 24 and greater than or equal to 0.

There are three fundamental factors that must be considered when designing validation procedures for an enterprise application. These are to avoid duplicating the validation procedure within the application, provide the user with immediate results from the validation process, and minimize the effect the validation process has on the server.

Duplication of the validation process can become a maintenance nightmare whenever rules for validation change. Ideally, validation rules should be applied by one object that is called whenever the validation process is needed. Duplication problems can occur if the validation process is built into client software because there might be many instances of the client software.

Users require nearly instantaneous feedback as to the validity of the data whenever they enter information into a client. Feedback should indicate that the data is valid or

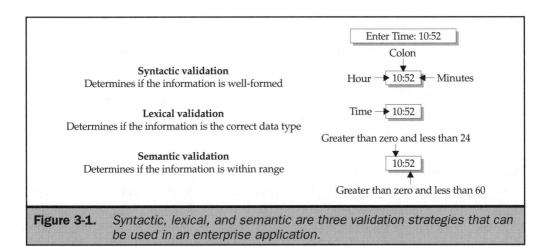

Figure 3-1.   *Syntactic, lexical, and semantic are three validation strategies that can be used in an enterprise application.*

invalid. Any delay providing feedback to the user can lead to a poor user experience with the application.

A common source of delay is when a developer uses a server-side validation process. This is because a conflict might arise if multiple applications concurrently call the object that validates data. A request to validate data might be queued (see "The Power of Threads" later in this chapter) until another application's data is validated. There are a host of other reasons for delays on the server side. These include heavy network traffic and slow hardware components such as the server itself.

However, if designed properly, you shouldn't have any threading or concurrency issues on the server. Validation is typically performed by regular expressions. The Pattern class in the JDK1.4 is also thread safe. This means you compile the pattern once and use it with any number of processes.

In this case, Pattern is declared as a static member of the validation class to ensure only one copy is compiled. Matcher classes are created as required to match against the Pattern.

Best Practice—Developing a Validation Strategy   *The best practice when developing a validation strategy is to perform as much (if not all) of the validation on the server side. Avoid validating on the client side because client-side validation routines frequently must be updated when a new version of the browser is released.*

Also, it is easy to bypass client-side scripts used in the validation process. Someone with minimal knowledge of protocols can save the page, delete the JavaScript, and then resubmit the form. Another concern is that validation scripts may never load because they are sometimes filtered by the company's firewall.

The second step of the validation process is to perform more sophisticated analysis of the information, such as verifying that a customer's account number is valid and that the customer is in good standing with the company. These validation rules are likely to change during the life of the enterprise application and therefore server-side software should perform this validation.

Best Practice—Reducing the Opportunity for User Error   *Another best practice is to reduce the opportunity for a user to enter incorrect information by using presentation elements that limit choices. These elements include radio buttons, check boxes, list boxes, and drop-down combo boxes. Information that is collected using those elements doesn't have to be validated because the application presents the user with only valid choices. There isn't any opportunity for the user to enter invalid data.*

Client Control

In practically every enterprise application, clients are restricted to resources based on the client's needs. The scope of resources a client can access is commonly referred to as a *client view*. A client view might consist of specific databases, tables, or rows and columns of tables. There are two ways for a client view to be defined: through embedding logic to define the view into the application, or by using a controller component that is known as a resource guard.

The resource guard (see Figure 3-2) is a component that resides outside of the application that receives requests for resources from all applications. A request for a resource contains a client ID that is compared to the client's configuration. Access is either granted or rejected based upon access rights within the client's configuration.

Another method that is useful whenever only database access is required is to group together users who have similar needs into a group profile, then assign permissions to the group. In this way, the DBMS manages security directly without you having to write your own security routines.

Best Practice—Using Security Measures   *The best practice is to use security measures that exist in DBMS or networks, where feasible. However, if this isn't the best alternative, use a resource guard rather than embed the definition of a client view into the application, unless only one client uses the resource. This is because multiple clients and applications can use the resource guard to access shared resources. In this way, the logic to define the client view isn't duplicated in multiple applications.*

As discussed previously in this chapter, requirements for an enterprise application are in constant change, even after the application is implemented. This means the application might be the sole user of a resource when the application is placed in production, but will need to share the resource at some point in the future.

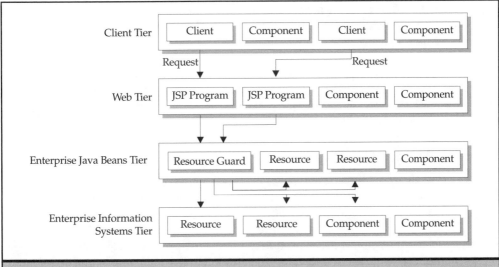

Figure 3-2.   *A resource guard is a component outside the application that manages access to restricted resources.*

Best Practice—Working with a Resource that Becomes Sharable   *The best practice to use when a resource becomes sharable is to remove the embedded logic that defines the client view from the application and place the logic into a resource guard. In this way, the logic is preserved while still providing flexibility to the application.*

A resource guard is a component that is shared with other applications. Therefore, the developer must construct a resource guard using one of the techniques used to share code within J2EE. Three of the more common ways are to build a resource guard using a JavaServer Page, a servlet, or Enterprise JavaBeans.

Best Practice—Using Resource Guards   *The best practice is to use an Enterprise JavaBean as the resource guard and use security mechanisms that are already in the web container and resource, rather than build the logic for the resource guard from scratch.*

Once the client view is defined, the developer must determine a strategy for implementing the client view. There are two commonly used strategies: the all-or-nothing strategy or the selective strategy. The all-or-nothing strategy requires the developer to write logic that enables or prevents a client from accessing the complete resources. Simply said, the client can either access all features of a resource or is prohibited from accessing the resource entirely.

In contrast, the selective strategy grants a client access to the resource, but restricts access to selected features of the resource based on the client's needs. For example, a client may have read access to the table that contains orders, but doesn't have rights to insert a new order or modify an existing order.

Best Practice—Using the Selective Strategy   *The best practice is to use the selective strategy because this strategy provides the flexibility to activate or deactivate features of a resource as required by each client. The all-or-nothing strategy doesn't provide this flexibility. This means the developer will need to replace the all-or-nothing strategy with the selective strategy after the application is in production, should a client's needs change. In addition, the selective strategy can also be used to provide the same features as provided by the all-or-nothing strategy. That is, the developer can grant a client total access to a resource or prohibit a client from accessing the resource.*

Duplicate Client Requests

A common problem with thin client applications is for the client to inadvertently submit a duplicate request for service, such as submitting a duplicate order. There are many ways a client can generate a duplicate request, but they all stem from the same source, which is the browser user interface.

A browser is the user interface used in a thin client application. However, the browser contains elements that can lead to a duplicate request being sent. Namely, the Back and Stop buttons. The Back button causes the browser to recall the previously displayed web page from the web server. The Stop button halts the implementation of a request. This means the browser processes some, but not all, of the requests.

Normally, the selection of these buttons has minimal consequence to the client because the browser either displays an unwanted page (previous page) or displays a partial page. In both cases, the user can easily correct the situation.

However, a problem might occur if the client is sending a web form such as an order form to the Web Tier. Let's say that the user submits the order form. The application generates a confirmation web page that the browser displays. The user then inadvertently selects the browser's Back button, which redisplays the order form. This might be confusing and cause the user to resubmit the order form, thinking that a snafu occurred. In reality, two orders are submitted.

Best Practice—Flushing the Session   *The best practice is to flush the session explicitly and updating the session object without waiting for the page to complete. The session is still available and checks can be made on the server to see if the form was previously submitted.*

Let's say the beginning of the JSP updates the session state to indicate the form was submitted and processed, but the server terminates the JSP before it completes. This can happen when the user hits the Stop button or the ESC key, causing the process on the server to be terminated. The session state object may not be updated. Explicitly updating the session object without waiting for the page to complete alleviates potential problems (Figure 3-3).

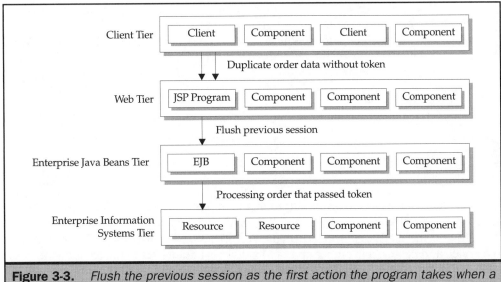

Figure 3-3.   *Flush the previous session as the first action the program takes when a new form is submitted. This avoids duplicate sessions from occurring.*

Sessions Management

A web service-based enterprise application consists of distributive services (i.e., components) located on J2EE tiers that are shared amongst applications. A client accesses components by opening a session with the Web Tier. The session begins with an initial request for service and ends once the client no longer requests services.

During the session, a client and components exchange information, which is called session state. Practically any kind of information can be a session state, including a client's ID, a client's profile, or choices a client makes in a web form.

A component is an entity whose sole purpose is to receive information from a client, process that information, and return information to the client when necessary. Information used by a component is retained until the request from the client is fulfilled. Afterwards, information is destroyed. A component lacks persistence. Persistence is the inherent capability of retaining information (session state) between requests.

This means that it is up to the enterprise application to devise a way to maintain session state until the session is completed. There are two common ways to manage session state: on the client side or server side on the Enterprise JavaBeans Tier.

Client-Side Session State

Session state can be maintained by the client rather than on the server using one or a combination of three techniques. These are by using a hidden field in an HTML form, by rewriting URLs, and by using cookies.

An enterprise application typically uses an HTML form to collect information from a user. An HTML form can contain many elements. The more commonly used elements are text, fields, and buttons. Text consists of characters that appear on the form such as the title of the form and instructions for completing the form.

A field is the place on the form where the user enters data. Each field has a field name that uniquely identifies the field and a value (see Listing 3-1). There are several kinds of fields, including drop-down combo boxes that list valid entries, radio buttons, check boxes, and free-form text fields. A button is an image selected by the user to submit or clear the form.

Listing 3-1
HTML code that creates a form that contains a field called FIRSTNAME.

```
<INPUT TYPE="TEXT" NAME="FIRSTNAME" SIZE="40">
<INPUT TYPE="SUBMIT" VALUE="SUBMIT">
<INPUT TYPE="RESET" VALUE="CLEAR">
```

When the user selects the Submit button, the browser extracts the field names and field values from the form and assembles them into a query string (see Listing 3-2). The browser then calls a component on the Web Tier, which is usually a JSP program or servlet, and passes field names and field values as parameters to the component.

The component then processes this information. Once processing is completed, the component dynamically generates a web page that may contain another form, depending on the nature of the application.

Listing 3-2
Here is a query string created when the browser extracts the field name and field value from Listing 3-1 assuming the value of the field is Jim Keogh.

```
www.mysite.com/jsp/myjsp.jsp?FIRSTNAME=JimKeogh
```

Hidden Field

The component can include in the HTML form a field that isn't displayed on the form. This field is called a hidden field. A hidden field is similar to other fields on the form in that a hidden field can hold a value. However, this value is assigned to the hidden field by the component rather than by the user.

A hidden field is treated the same as other fields on the form when a user selects the Submit button (see Listing 3-3). That is, the name of the hidden field and the value of the hidden field are extracted from the form along with the other fields by the browser and sent as a parameter to the component. This means that session state can be retained by assigning the session state as a value to one or more hidden fields on each form that is used during the session.

Listing 3-3
Here is the same HTML form as shown in Listing 3-1; however, a hidden field has been placed into the form.

```
<INPUT TYPE="HIDDEN" NAME="AccountNumber" VALUE="1234">
<INPUT TYPE="TEXT" NAME="FIRSTNAME" SIZE="40">
<INPUT TYPE="SUBMIT" VALUE="SUBMIT">
<INPUT TYPE="RESET" VALUE="CLEAR">
```

Best Practice—Using Hidden Fields   *The best practice for using a hidden field to maintain session state is to do so only when small amounts of string information need to be retained. Although using a hidden field is easy to implement, it can cause performance issues if large amounts session of state are required by the application. This is because the session state must be included with each page sent to the browser during the session regardless if the session state plays an active role on the page.*

In addition, hidden fields contain only string values and not numeric, dates, and other data types, which means the component might need to convert the string values into more appropriate values each time the page is sent to the component. Furthermore, session state is exposed during transmission. This means session state that contains sensitive information such as credit card numbers must be encrypted to secure the information during transmission.

URL Rewriting

URL rewriting is another strategy for managing session state. A URL is the element within the web page that uniquely identifies a component and is used by the browser to request a service. The browser can attach to the URL field names and field values that are passed to the component if the component requires this information to process the request. This is what happens when a user submits an HTML form, as discussed in the previous section.

URL rewriting simulates the routine the browser performs to extract field names and field values from an HTML form. That is, the developer places field names and field values into a query string as part of the URL statement (see Listing 3-4). When the user selects the hyperlink that is associated with the URL statement, the browser calls the component identified by the URL and passes the component field names and field values that are contained in the URL statement.

Listing 3-4
Sample of a
URL rewrite
that includes
a customer
ID placed in
the hyperlink
that calls a
JSP program.

```
<P> <A HREF = "http://www.mysite.com/jsp/myjsp.jsp?AccountNumber=1234>
Click to place a new order</A></P>
```

Best Practice—Using URL Rewriting   *The best practice is to use URL rewriting to retain session state whenever an HTML form is not used by the client. For example, the user might place an order using an HTML form. The order contains the user's account number along with other information.*

After the order is processed, a JSP program generates a confirmation page that is displayed by the browser. The confirmation page doesn't contain an HTML form, but does contain a hyperlink that is associated with a component that generates a new order form. The hyperlink asks the user if he or she wants to place another order. If the user selects the hyperlink, the browser calls the component and a new order form is displayed on the screen.

The developer might rewrite the URL that is associated with this hyperlink to include the name of the account field and the user's account number. In this way, the account number is automatically submitted to the component that generates a new order form when the user selects the hyperlink.

There are also several critical disadvantages of URL rewriting. The most important disadvantage is that maintaining session state depends on the client's machine. Problems with the client machine might cause the application to lose the session state. Also, including session state with every page requires the system to process and transmit more code than if cookies or server-side session state management were used.

Cookies

A cookie is a small amount of data (maximum of 4KB) that the enterprise application stores on the client's machine. A cookie can be used to store session state. The developer can create a JSP program that dynamically generates a page that writes and reads one or more cookies. In this way, session state persists between pages.

Best Practice—Using Cookies *The best practice is to use a cookie only to retain minimum data such as a client ID and use other techniques described in this section to retain large amounts of information. A developer must also implement a contingency routine should the user discard the cookie or deactivate the cookie feature.*

There are two major disadvantages of using cookies to retain session state. First, cookies can be disabled, thereby prohibiting the enterprise application from using a cookie to manage session state.

The other disadvantage is that cookies are shared amongst instances. This means a client might run two instances of a browser, creating two sessions. All instances access the same cookie and therefore share the same session state, which is likely to cause conflicts when processing information because the wrong session state might be processed. And of course, the user can always view the contents of the cookie using a basic text editor, making information stored in the cookie insecure.

Server-Side Session State

As discussed in the previous section, storing session state on the client side has serious drawbacks, most of which center on the dependency on the client's machine. That is, session state is lost if a client's machine fails.

An alternative to maintaining session state on the client side is to store session state on the server. Typically, the information technology department of a corporation goes to extremes to assure that the server and backup servers are available 24 hours a day, 7 days a week, which is not the treatment given to client machines.

Best Practice—Using the HttpSession Interface *The best practice is to maintain session state on the Enterprise JavaBeans Tier using an Enterprise JavaBean or on the Web Tier using the HttpSession interface. Each session state is assigned a session ID, which relates the session state with a particular client session. The session ID is used whenever the session state is written to or retrieved from the server.*

This provides the most reliable way to save and access session state and is scalable, thereby able to handle multiple sessions and various sizes of session state. It also decreases the vulnerability to someone inadvertently or covertly gaining unauthorized access to the session state.

Replication Servers

It is not uncommon for an enterprise application to use a cluster of replication servers where each server has the full complement of components. Whenever a request is received from a client, the request is routed to the next available server within the cluster. In this way, the infrastructure can maintain acceptable performance even if hundreds of requests are received simultaneously.

However, this can easily result in a problem if session state is maintained on the server side. Which server has the session state for the client? There are two strategies that are used to manage this problem. These are to replicate session state across all servers within the cluster or to route a client to the same server for the duration of the session.

However, keep in mind that clustering J2EE servers is vendor specific and is not part of the J2EE specifications. In addition, vendors typically replicate session on a primary and secondary server rather than on all the servers.

Best Practice—Maintaining a Sticky User Experience   *The best practice is to maintain a sticky user experience, depending on your business needs. This means the client always uses the same server during the session and the session state is stored on one server within the cluster. This also means that the session is lost should the server go down.*

Valid Session State

Another issue that is common with an enterprise application that stores session state on a server is whether or not the session state is valid. Session state automatically becomes invalid and removed when the session ends. However, there might be occasions when the session ungracefully terminates without removing the session state, such as during a communication failure that occurs during the session.

Best Practice—Setting a Session Timeout   *The best practice is to always set a session timeout, which automatically invalidates session state after time has passed and the session state has not been accessed. The actual length of time before the session automatically terminates will vary depending on the nature of the application. However, once time has expired, the session ends—and therefore the session state is removed.*

Web Tier and JavaServer Pages

The web tier contains components that directly communicate with clients. The Web Tier is also the location where JavaServer Pages (JSP) programs reside. JSPs are commonly proxy to an application server as implemented by Tomcat and Weblogic. Weblogic uses web server plug-ins in their implementation.

This is a particularly good technique to use when vertically scaling your application because it provides additional security. All executable processing resides below the web server and out of reach of an attack, which is usually focused on web servers. A JSP program is a component that provides service to a client. The nature of the service depends on the design of the application.

A JSP program is identified with a URL that is associated with a hyperlink built into a web page displayed on the client. When a user selects the hyperlink, the browser calls the JSP program, which executes JSP statements.

For example, a JSP program might receive order information (field names and field values) that a browser extracted from an HTML order form and passed to the JSP program. The JSP program uses information received from the browser to process the order by calling one or more Enterprise JavaBeans. Once processing is completed, the JSP program generates a dynamic web page that serves as a confirmation of the order.

Presentation and Processing

A JSP program can contain two components: the presentation component and the processing logic. The presentation component defines the content that is displayed by the client. Processing logic defines the business rules that are applied whenever the client calls the JSP program.

Although placing both the presentation and processing logic components in the same component seems to compartmentalize enterprise application, this technique can lead to nonmaintainable code. This is because of two reasons.

First, presentation and processing logic components tend to become complex and difficult to comprehend, especially when the code consists of a mixture of HTML code and Java scriptlets. That is, there is too much information in the program for the programmer to digest.

The other reason is that programmers with different skill sets typically write each component. A programmer who is proficient in HTML writes the presentation component. A Java programmer writes the processing logic component. This means that two programmers must work on the same JSP program, which can be inefficient.

Best Practice—Separating Code   *The best practice for writing a JSP program is to separate the presentation code and the processing code (see Figure 3-4). Place the presentation code in the JSP program and place the processing code in Enterprise JavaBeans. Have the JSP program call the Enterprise JavaBeans whenever the JSP program is required to process information. An alternative best practice is to simply include files that contain code to hide the code from the graphic artist.*

There are several benefits to using this strategy. First, the JSP program is easier for a programmer to comprehend since the processing logic no longer resides in the JSP program. That is, there are fewer lines of code for the programmer to digest, making the program maintainable.

The task is also divided along discipline lines. The HTML programmer can focus on creating the JSP program while the Java programmer builds the Enterprise JavaBeans, and both tasks can occur in parallel.

Another benefit is that the processing logic is sharable with other enterprise applications. This is because the Enterprise JavaBean that contains the processing logic can be called by other applications.

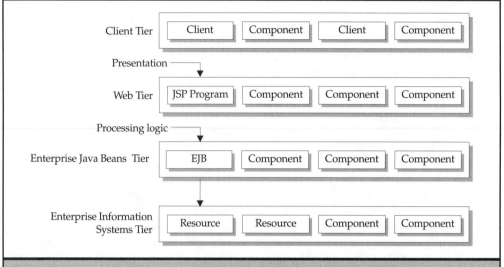

Figure 3-4. *A JSP program is used to create the presentation for an enterprise application while Enterprise JavaBeans are used to process information.*

The Inclusion Strategy

The designer of an enterprise application typically uses the same elements for all web pages of the user interface to provide continuity throughout the application. This means that the same code can appear in more than one web page, which is inefficient and a maintenance nightmare.

A further complication arises when multiple JSP programs generate web pages, because the developer must identify and change every JSP program that generates a web page each time a change is made to an element that is common to all pages.

Best Practice—Using the Inclusion Strategy *The best practice to avoid redundant code is to use the inclusion strategy, which uses either the include directive or include action to insert commonly used code into a JSP program. The JSP program include directive is used within the JSP program to specify the file whose content must be included in the JSP program. This file should contain shared code such as HTML statements that define common elements of web pages. The include action calls a JSP program within another JSP program. Commonly used code is contained in the called JSP program.*

The critical difference between the include action and the include directive is that the include action places the results generated by the called JSP program into the calling JSP program. In contrast, the include directive places source code into the JSP program rather than the results of running that source code.

Best Practice—Using the Include Directive   *The best practice is to use the include directive whenever variables are used in the JSP program. The include directive places the variable name in the calling JSP program and lets the calling JSP program resolve the variable. In contrast, the include action places the value of the variable in the calling JSP program.*

Style Sheets

It is important that an enterprise application's user interface is consistent throughout the application. Consistency helps the user become familiar with how to use the application. This means that the developer must write JSP programs that generate web pages having the same general appearance (i.e., same font style, font size, and color combination).

Consistency therefore requires that each web page contain redundant code that defines the web page style. And, as mentioned in the previous section, redundant code leads to maintenance headaches.

Best Practice—Enforcing Continuity with CSS   *The best practice to enforce continuity among web pages that comprise an application's user interface is to use Cascading Style Sheet (CSS). CSS is a file that describes the style of elements that appear on the web page.*

The developer tells the client (i.e., browser) to reference the CSS file by using a CSS directive in the web page. The browser then automatically applies the style defined in the CSS file to the web page that contains the CSS directive. The programmer can easily change the style of the user interface by modifying the CSS file. Those changes are automatically implemented as the client displays each web page.

Besides making the user interface maintainable, CSS also reduces the amount of storage space required for web pages. This is because code that is used to define the style is placed in a shared file rather than being replicated in all web pages that use the style.

Simplify Error Handling

An enterprise application should trap errors that can occur at runtime using techniques that are available in Java (see *Java 2: The Complete Reference*). However, it is important that the application translate raw error messages into text that is understood by the user of the application. Otherwise, the error message is likely to confuse and frustrate the user.

Although errors can occur throughout the application, a client should present to the user errors generated by a JSP program or by a servlet. This is true even if an Enterprise JavaBean called by the JSP program catches the error. Once the error is trapped, the Enterprise JavaBeans forwards the error message to the JSP program. The JSP program translates the error message into a message easily understood by a user and then displays the translated error message in a dynamically generated a web page.

Best Practice—Handling Errors *A best practice for handling errors is to generate a user-friendly error message that reflects the processing that was executing when the error occurred, session state (where applicable), and the nature of the error.*

Let's say that a user submitted an order form. The browser called a JSP program and passed order form information to the program. The JSP program called an Enterprise JavaBean that connects to a database and processes the order.

Suppose the Enterprise JavaBeans is unable to connect to the database. An error is thrown and caught by the Enterprise JavaBeans who forwards the error message to the JSP program. The error message "unable to connect to the database" is meaningless to the person who submitted the order, so it doesn't make sense to display this error message.

However, the JSP program evaluates the session state, which indicates the web page displayed an order form and that the order was being processed at the time the error occurred. The JSP program knows from the error message received from the Enterprise JavaB eans that connection to the order database failed. This means the JSP program could format an error message that says, "We experienced technical difficulties when processing your order. Please wait ten minutes and resubmit your order."

Best Practice—Saving Error Messages *Another best practice when handling errors is to have either the JSP program or the Enterprise JavaBeans save all error messages and related information (i.e. session state) to an error file, then notify technical support that an error was detected.*

Enterprise JavaBeans Tier

The Enterprise JavaBeans Tier contains Enterprise JavaBeans that provide processing logic to other tiers. Processing logic includes all code and data that is necessary to implement one or more business rules.

As discussed in the previous chapter, the purpose of creating an Enterprise JavaBean is to encapsulate code that performs one task very well and to make that code available to any application that needs that functionality.

Although the concept of using Enterprise JavaBeans is easily understood, there can be confusion when designing Enterprise JavaBeans into an application's specification. Simply stated, the developer must determine what functionality should be built into an Enterprise JavaBean.

Let's say that an online order entry application must determine if a customer is in good standing before the customer order is processed. The business logic requires the application to verify the customer's status is "good" before placing the order in the orders table. This means two database tasks must be performed. Should each task be in its own Enterprise JavaBeans? If so, then how are both Enterprise JavaBeans called? Should both tasks be included in one Enterprise JavaBean?

These questions reoccur many times during the development of an enterprise application, and answers to these questions can have either a negative or positive effect on the performance of the application.

Best Practice—Making JavaBeans Self-Contained   *The best practice is make each Enterprise JavaBeans self-contained and minimize the interdependence of Enterprise JavaBeans where possible. That is, avoid having a trail of Enterprise JavaBeans calling each other. Instead, design an individual Enterprise JavaBean to complete a specific task.*

In the previous example, a good design is to use three Enterprise JavaBeans. One verifies the customer's status. Another processes the order. And the remaining Enterprise JavaBeans takes on the role of a controller.

A controller is an Enterprise JavaBeans that is called by the JSP program. The controller calls the Enterprise JavaBeans that verifies the customer's status. Based on information returned to the controller by this Enterprise JavaBeans, the controller either calls the second Enterprise JavaBeans to process the order or returns to the JSP program an order rejection notice, which the JSP program sends to the client.

Entity to Enterprise JavaBeans Relationship

There is a tendency for developers to create a one-to-one relationship between entities defined in an application's entity relationship diagram and with Enterprise JavaBeans. That is, each entity has its own entity Enterprise JavaBeans that contains all the processing logic required by the entity.

While the one-to-relationship seems a logical implementation of the entity relationship diagram, there are drawbacks that might affect the efficient running of the application. Each time an Enterprise JavaBean is created, there is increased overhead for the network and for the Enterprise JavaBeans container. Creating a one-to-one relationship, as such, tends to generate many Enterprise JavaBeans and therefore is likely to increase overhead, which results in a performance impact. In addition, this also limits the scalability of the application.

Best Practice—Translating Entity Relationship Diagrams   *The best practice when translating an entity relationship diagram into Enterprise JavaBeans is to consolidate related processes that are associated with several entities into one session Enterprise JavaBeans. This results in the creation of fewer Enterprise JavaBeans while still maintaining the functionality required by the application.*

Efficient Data Exchange

A JSP program and Enterprise JavaBeans frequently exchange information while the enterprise application is executing. The JSP program might pass information received from the client to the Enterprise JavaBeans. Likewise, the Enterprise JavaBeans might return values to the JSP program once processing is completed.

There are two common ways in which information is exchanged between a JSP program and Enterprise JavaBeans. These are by individually sending and receiving each data element or by using a value object to transfer data in bulk.

Some developers intuitively use a value object only when bulk data needs to be transferred and send data individually when single values are exchanged. While this seems logical, there is a serious performance penalty—especially with enterprise applications that have many simultaneous clients. Transmitting individual data increases the network overhead.

Best Practice—Exchanging Information Between JSP and Enterprise   *The best practice when exchanging information between a JSP program and Enterprise JavaBeans is to use a value object. In this way, there is less stress on the network than sending individual data and the value objects retain the association among data elements.*

Enterprise JavaBeans Performance

While Enterprise JavaBeans provide an efficient way to process business rules in a distributed system, Enterprise JavaBeans remains vulnerable to bottlenecks that occur when Enterprise JavaBeans communicate with other components. Bottlenecks effectively decrease the efficiency of implementing Enterprise JavaBeans.

The primary cause of bottlenecks is remote communication—that is, communication that occurs between components over the network. This is sometimes referred to as Enterprise JavaBeans chatter. As mentioned previously in this chapter, by its nature Enterprise JavaBeans uses appreciable amounts of resources to communicate with remote components.

Therefore, the more communication that occurs between an Enterprise JavaBeans and other components, the higher the likelihood that bottlenecks will occur. This is especially prevalent when clients directly access Enterprise JavaBeans, although the Enterprise JavaBeans specification prohibits such direct interaction.

Best Practice—Placing Components in Communication   *The best practice is to keep remote communication to the minimum needed to exchange information and to minimize the duration and any communication. A common way to accomplish this objective is by placing components that frequently communicate with each other on the same server, where possible.*

Consider Purchasing Enterprise JavaBeans

There are entities and workflow common to many businesses. Information and processes used for both of these are encapsulated into entities Enterprise JavaBeans and session Enterprise JavaBeans, respectively. An entity Enterprise JavaBeans is modeled after an entity in the enterprise application's entity relationship diagram. A session Enterprise JavaBeans is modeled after processes common to multiple entities.

Many corporations have entities that use the same or very similar functionality. For example, many corporations use the same credit card approval process. Therefore, the same basic Enterprise JavaBeans is re-created in each corporation. This means corporations waste dollars by building something that is already available in the marketplace.

Best Practice—Surveying the Marketplace   *The best practice is to survey the marketplace for third-party Enterprise JavaBeans that meet some or all of the functionality that is required by an entity Enterprise JavaBeans or session Enterprise JavaBeans for an enterprise application. The Sun Microsystems, Inc. web site offers third-party Enterprise JavaBeans in their Solutions Marketplace.*

The Model-View-Controller (MVC)

Developing an enterprise application is a complex undertaking because the application must be capable of serving many diverse clients simultaneously over a distributed infrastructure. Furthermore, the application must be scalable so the application can continue to provide acceptable performance regardless of the increase in the number of clients who use the application.

Throughout this section you learned the best practices for making an application scalable and maintainable by incorporating processing logic into Enterprise JavaBeans. However, deciding which features of an application should be built into an Enterprise JavaBeans can be confusing.

Best Practice—Using the Model-View-Controller   *The best practice for simplifying the distribution of an application's functionality is to use the Model-View-Controller (MVC) strategy that is endorsed by Sun Microsystems, Inc. and which has its roots in the decades-old technology of Smalltalk.*

The MVC strategy basically divides applications into three broad components (see Figure 3-5). These are the model class, the view class, and the controller class. The model class consists of components that control data used by the application. The view class is composed of components that present data to the client. And the controller class is responsible for event handling and coordinating activities between the model class and the view class.

Enterprise JavaBeans are used to build components of the model class. Likewise, JSP programs and servlets are used to create view class components. And session Enterprise JavaBeans are used for controller class components.

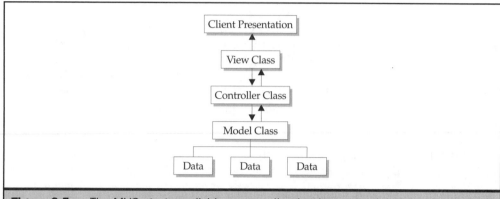

Figure 3-5. *The MVC strategy divides an application into a model class, a view class, and a controller class, which coordinates activities between the two other classes.*

The Myth of Using Inheritance

Inheritance is a cornerstone of the Java programming language, which itself is a feature inherited from the C++ programming language. There are three reasons for using inheritance in an enterprise application. First, inheritance enables functionality and data to be reused without having to rewrite the functionality and data several times in an application. Inheritance is also used to embellish both a functionality and data. That is, the class that inherits a functionality can modify the functionality without affecting the original functionality. Inheritance also provides a common interface based on functionality that is used by similar classes.

As you remember from when you learned of the Java programming language (see *Java 2: The Complete Reference*), there are two kinds of classes used in inheritance: the base class and the derived class. The base class contains methods and data some or all of which are inherited by a derived class. An object of the derived class has access to some or all of the data and methods of the base class and all the data and methods of the derived class.

A motor vehicle is a good example of inheritance. A motor vehicle is a base class and has an engine, drivetrain, wheels, and body, among other components. An automobile and a truck are two kinds of motor vehicles. They are derived classes and inherit an engine, drivetrain, wheels, body, and other components from the motor vehicle class.

However, the automobile class embellishes the engine, the drivetrain, wheels, and body to meet the needs of an automobile. Likewise, a truck class embellishes the same components to meet the needs of a truck.

The relationship between a base class and derived class is referred to as *coupling*. That is, there is a derived class bonded to a base class. A base class must exist for the derived class to exist. Both the automobile class and the truck class are coupled to the motor vehicle class.

Developers of enterprise applications are concerned with how to efficiently translate an entity relationship diagram into an application's class model. A common error is for the developer to rely heavily on inheritance, which results in an application built on coupled classes.

Best Practice—Using an Interface   *The best practice when translating an entity relationship diagram to an application's class model is to use an interface rather than use coupling, where possible. An interface is a class that adds functionality to a real-world object.*

Interfaces and Inheritance

An interface contains functionality that is used across unlike real-world objects. This is different from a base class in that a base class provides functionality that is fundamental to like real-world objects.

For example, an acceleration interface provides acceleration functionality to any real-world object regardless if the real-world object is a motor vehicle, aircraft, or a baseball that is hit into the outfield. In this way, unrelated real-world objects that have the same functionality can share the same data and methods of an interface.

A common mistake is to use an interface as a base class because intuitively this seems sensible, but an interface is too narrow in scope which means an interface consists of one of many functionalities that are used by real-world objects.

Best Practice—Identifying Functionality   *The best practice is to identify functionality that is common among real-world objects that are used by an application. Place these features into a base class. The remaining features that are unique to each of these objects are placed into a derived class. And where there is a function that is common to unlike real-world objects, place that function into an interface class.*

An interface (see "The Power of Interfaces" section) contains method signatures without specifying how those methods are implemented. This means an interface definition specifies the name of a method and the data type and position of the method's parameter list. The class that uses the interface defines code within the method. In this way, the application hides the implementation of the interface, which is an example of polymorphism.

Composition and Inheritance

A misnomer when designing an application that uses an interface is that designers cannot reuse the implementation of the interface—that is, the method that contains the interface signature can only be used with one object. This is untrue.

Best Practice—Creating a Delegate Class *The best practice is to create a delegate class. A delegate class contains implementations of interfaces that are commonly used by objects in an application. Let's say that the acceleration interface discussed previously in this section uses a standard formula to calculate the acceleration of an object. Therefore, the implementation of the acceleration interface is the same across unlike objects. A delegate class should be created that defines this implementation so the implementation can be used by other objects by calling the acceleration method of the delegate class.*

Using a delegate class is a keystone to the composition strategy, which is a way of extending the responsibilities of an object without inheritance. The composition strategy delegates responsibility to another object without the object being a derived class. This is a subtle but critical factor that differentiates composition from inheritance.

Inheritance extends the responsibilities of a base class by enhancing attributes and functionality of its derived class. Let's say the motor vehicle class should contain a method of installing a child seat in the vehicle.

Not all motor vehicles require this functionality, which means it doesn't make sense to include the functionality in the base class if the functionality isn't common to all motor vehicles. However, including the functionality in the automobile derived class can expand the functionality of the motor vehicle.

Best Practice—Using Composition *The best practice is to use composition whenever functionality needs to expand the responsibilities of unlike objects. Instead of incorporating the function in each object or in each of the object's base classes, the developer should delegate the responsibility to a delegate class that performs the functionality as required by the object.*

Potential Problems with Inheritance

While inheritance fosters strong coupling between similar objects and provides a mechanism for objects to share attributes and functionality, there are inherent problems that might occur that could have a negative impact on an enterprise application. One of these problems is called the *ripple effect*.

The ripple effect occurs whenever a change is made to the base class. Changes to a base class ripple down to all the derived classes and might negatively impact the implementation of attributes and functionality of the derived class.

This means that the developer who is responsible for maintaining a base class must examine the impact any change in the base class has on derived classes before making the change. Failure to assess the potential impact of a change could lead to errors in the derived class.

Another problem with inheritance happens as an application matures and requires frequent changes to both base and derived classes. These changes result in object transmute where data and methods of an existing class are moved to another class after the existing class is deleted.

This can lead to a number of issues such as lost data and methods and copying data and methods that are no longer necessary. And to further complicate the transition, the developer needs to assess the impact the object has on the derived class if the base class is replaced.

Best Practice—Minimizing the Use of Inheritance   *The best practice is to minimize the use of inheritance in an enterprise application. Only use inheritance when there is commonality among objects that is not functionality. Otherwise, use composition. That is, an object that is a "type of" should inherit commonality from a base class. An object that performs functionality "like" other classes should use composition to delegate responsibility.*

You should use the refactoring strategy whenever changes are made to a base class. The refactoring strategy requires that the developer divide changes into small modifications and then make each small modification, followed by thorough testing. At the successful conclusion of the test, make the next small modification. Repeat these steps until all the modifications are completed.

Maintainable Classes

Classes are a focal point of every enterprise application since classes form the nucleus of many components in the application. It is therefore critical that an application is developed so that its many classes are easily maintained; otherwise, any modification of the application might be difficult to accomplish and introduce processing errors.

There are two factors that determine if classes are maintainable. These are coupling and cohesion. Coupling occurs when there is a class dependent on another class. This is illustrated in the previous section where a derived class is dependent on a base class. Coupling also occurs when a class delegates responsibility to another class.

Before a change can be made to either the derived class or the base class, the developer must assess the impact on the coupled class. As previously discussed, changes to a base class might negatively impact a derived class. Changes to a derived class won't affect the base class, but could inadvertently modify functionality inherited from the base class. In either scenario, additional precautions must be taken by the developer to assure that the modification doesn't cause a negative impact.

Cohesion describes how well a class' functionality is focused. That is, a class that has broad functionality isn't as cohesive as a class that has a single functionality. For example, a class that validates account status and processes orders is less cohesive than a class that simply validates an account status.

Another design consideration is to avoid packages with cross dependencies. If package A has a class that depends on a class in package B, then the developer needs to ensure he or she doesn't introduce a class in B that depends on a class in A.

Best Practice—Designing an Enterprise Application *The best practice is to design an enterprise application with highly cohesive classes and minimum coupling. This strategy ensures that classes are optimally designed for maintenance. This is because a class that has few functions and isn't dependent on another class is less complicated to modify than a class with broad functionality that inherits from a base class.*

In reality, an enterprise application is built as a collaborative effort and by its nature must have a blend of cohesion and coupling. Therefore, let the application requirements dictate the mixture of cohesiveness and coupling that is used in the design of an enterprise application.

Performance Enhancements

Some developers have concerns over the performance of an enterprise Java application because of the nature in which the application is compiled into bytecode rather than native code. Although bytecode is optimized, as you learned in the previous chapter, bytecode still needs to be interpreted by the Java Virtual Machine (JVM). It is this overhead that detracts from the application's performance.

There are two ways to reduce or practically eliminate the amount of bytecode that is interpreted at runtime: by using HotSpot, new in the Just In Time compiler from Sun Microsystems, Inc., or by using a native compiler.

HotSpot tunes the performance of an application at runtime so the application runs at optimal performance. HotSpot analyzes both client- and server-side programs and applies an optimization algorithm that has the greatest performance impact for the application. An application that uses HotSpot typically has a quick startup.

The drawback of using HotSpot is that machine time and other resources are used to analyze and optimize bytecode while the application runs, rather than simply dedicating these resources purely to running the application.

Another concern about using HotSpot is the complexity of debugging runtime errors. Runtime errors occur in the optimized code and not necessarily in the bytecode. Therefore, it can be difficult to re-create the error.

Best Practice—Testing the Code *The best practice for achieving top performance is to test both the native compiled code with the bytecode of the program. Code compiled with a native compiler such as that offered by Tower Technology optimizes translated bytecode into an executable similar to how source code written in C++ and other programming languages is compiled into an executable.*

However, the executable code is larger than the original bytecode because the compiler reduces the number of memory references, assuming you optimized it for speed. Executable code provides an economical alternative to the acquisition of hardware to boost performance of a Java enterprise application only if the overhead of the executable doesn't cause its own performance bottleneck.

It goes without saying that the major drawback of compiling a Java enterprise application is the application becomes machine dependent and therefore lacks the flexibility that is inherent in noncompiled Java applications.

A new hybrid strategy is developing to increase performance of a Java application where an application is divided into static and dynamic modules. Static modules such as an Enterprise JavaBeans container are compiled into native libraries that are executables, and dynamic modules such as Enterprise JavaBeans are compiled into bytecode. Only dynamic modules are optimized at runtime.

The Power of Interfaces

Designing an enterprise application using interfaces provides built-in flexibility, known as *pluggability*, because an interface enables the developer to easily replace components. As mentioned previously in this chapter, an interface is a collection of method signatures. A method signature consists of the name and the number and type of parameters for a method.

A developer implements the interface by defining a method of a class that has the same method signature as the interface. The developer must also define the method by itself. This means that the developer controls the behavior of the method whose method signature is defined in the interface.

Let's say a developer is building an enterprise application that processes orders. However, there are two different processes. One processes for bulk sales and another for retail sales. Two classes are defined, called retailOrder and bulkOrder.

Also, an interface is created to make uniform the way in which components send orders. We'll keep the interface simple for this example by requiring an order to have an account number, order number, product number, and quantity. The interface defines a method signature used to send an order. The method signature is shown in Listing 3-5.

Listing 3-5
Here is an example of a method signature.

```
sendOrder(int, int, int, int);
```

The developer must define a method in the retailOrder and bulkOrder classes that have the same signature as the sendOrder method signature. Likewise, the developer must place code within these methods to receive and process the order.

The programmer who wants to write a routine that sends an order needs only to know the class name to use and that the class implements the interface. The programmer already knows the method to call to send the order because the method signature is defined in the interface.

If the programmer wants to send a retail order, the programmer creates an instance of the retailOrder class and then calls the sendOrder() method which passes it the order information. A similar process is followed to send a bulkOrder, except the programmer creates an instance of the bulkOrder class. The call is made to the same method.

Simply said, an interface defines a standard way to interact with classes that implement the interface. This enables a developer to replace a class with another class that implements the same interface, and only the statement that creates the instance of the class needs to be changed in the program that calls the method. The routine calls the same method and passes the method the same argument.

Best Practice—Handling Differing Behaviors   *The best practice is to create an interface whenever an application contains common behaviors where algorithms used to process the behaviors differ. Basically, the developer calls the method using the interface and passes the method information it needs and the method does everything else.*

Likewise, the developer whose method is called isn't concerned about the routine that called the method. Instead, the developer is only concerned about receiving and processing information.

The Power of Threads

Proper use of threads can increase the efficiency of running an enterprise application because multiple operations can appear to perform simultaneously. A thread is a stream of executing program statements. More than one thread can be executed within an enterprise application. This means that multiple statements can run parallel.

The thread class (see *Java 2: The Complete Reference*) is used to create a thread. Once the thread is created, the developer can specify the behavior of the thread (i.e., start, stop) and the point within the program where the thread begins execution.

A major benefit of using threads in an enterprise application is to be able to share processing time between multiple processes. Only one thread is processed at a time, although using multiple threads in an application gives the appearance of concurrent processing. Actually, the number of application threads being processed at one time is equal to or less than the number of CPUs on the machine.

The developer can assign a priority to each thread. A thread with a higher priority is processed before threads with lower priority. In this way, the developer is able to increase the response time of critical processes.

A simple example of using threads is when a client is printing a document while inputting data into the application. Typically, data entry has a higher priority than printing. Therefore, the data input thread priority is set as "high" and the printing thread is set as "low." Printing occurs while the application is waiting for the client to enter data. Once data is received from the client, the printing thread is temporarily suspended until the data input thread finishes processing—at which time the print thread resumes processing.

The use of threads in an enterprise application can be risky if methods executed by threads are not synchronized, because more than one thread might run within a method. Multiple threads that execute the same method share values, which can cause unexpected results.

However, synchronizing a method enables one thread at a time to run within the method. This practically locks the method and assures that values aren't shared. Other threads wanting to run within the method are queued until the executing thread finishes processing. However, the executing thread might be suspended if another thread executing elsewhere in the application has a higher priority than the executing thread.

Best Practice—Using Threads in an Enterprise Application   *There are several best practices to employ when using threads in an enterprise application. Avoid using threads unless multiple processes require access to the same resources concurrently. This is because using multiple threads incurs processing overhead that can actually decrease response time.*

Keep the number of threads to a minimum; otherwise, you'll notice a gradual performance degradation. If your application experiences a decrease in performance, prioritize threads. Assign a higher priority to critical processes.

Another method to increase performance when using multiple threads in an application is to limit the size of methods that are synchronized. The objective is to minimize the amount of time that a synchronized method locks out other threads.

Careful analysis of a synchronized method might reveal that only a block of code within the method affects values that must not be accessed by another thread until the process is completed. Other code in the method could be executed without conflicting with other threads.

If this is the case, place the block of code that affects value into a separate synchronized method. Typically, this reduces the amount of code that is locked when the thread executes and therefore shortens the execution time of the method.

Be on the alert for possible deadlocks when using too many synchronized methods in an application. A deadlock can occur when a synchronized method calls other methods that are also synchronized. The call to the method is a thread that might be queued because another thread is executing in the called method. And the called method might also call another synchronized method, causing a similar situation to occur.

Safe processing must be the top concern when implementing threads in an application. Synchronizing methods is one way to assure a thread processes safely. Another way is to have the object that is threaded determine when to suspend and stop the thread, instead of having other objects control the process.

Threading issues typically occur on multi-CPU machines and rarely on single-CPU machines. Therefore, it is critical that applications that use threads be tested on a multi-CPU machine to be assured that all threading issues are addressed.

Best Practice—Suspending or Stopping Threaded Objects   *The best practice is to design objects so that a request is made that a threaded object be either suspended or stopped, rather than directing the threaded object to suspend and stop. There is a subtle but important difference between a request and a directive. A directive causes an action to occur immediately. A request causes an action to occur at an appropriate time.*

The threaded object should have built-in logic that determines the point in the process when it is safe to suspend or stop the thread. This practice is safer than if another object issues the suspend command or stop command.

The Power of Notification

An enterprise application typically has many events that occur randomly. Each event might affect multiple objects within the application and therefore it is critical that a notification process be implemented within the application, so that changes experienced by an object can be transmitted to other objects that are affected by the change.

Let's say a developer built a stock-trading application that accepts real-time stock feeds from outside vendors. An object within the application is responsible for comparing an incoming stock price to the previous price for the same issue. If the incoming price deviates by 5 percent from the previous price, a notification of the change is made to another object that flashes the stock price on the display. This object also changes the color of the display to red, indicating a drop in price, or green, indicating an increase in price.

There are three ways in which objects are notified of changes: passive notification, timed notification, and active notification. Passive notification is the process whereby objects poll relative objects to determine the current state of the object. The current state is typically the value of one or more data members of the object.

Although passive notification is the easiest notification method to implement, this is also the notification method that has the highest processing overhead. This is because there could be many objects polling many other objects, and each poll consumes processing time.

An alternative to the passive notification method is timed notification. Timed notification suspends the thread that polls objects for a specific time period. Once time expires, the thread comes alive once more and polls relative objects to determine the current state of the object.

The drawback of both passive notification and timed notification is that each of these notification methods polls relative objects. This means that polling occurs even if there are no changes in status. This wastes processing time.

Best Practice—Using Active Notification   *The best practice is to use active notification. Active notification requires the object whose status changes to notify other relative objects that a change occurred. Objects that are interested in the status of the object must first register with the object. This registration process basically identifies the objects that need to be notified when a change occurs.*

The original active notification method was called the observable-observer method, which is also known as the publisher-scriber model. The publisher is the object that changes and the subscriber is the object that is interested in learning about these changes.

There are also other variations on the same theme. One such variation is the observable-repeater method, which is nearly identical to the observable-observer method except the observer forwards changes received from the observable to objects that have registered with the observer.

Best Practice—Creating Different Threads   *The best practice is to create different threads for each notification process and assign a priority to each thread based on the importance of the notification. Assign a high priority to those notifications that are critical to running the application, and assign a low priority to those less critical to the success of the application.*

Chapter 4

J2EE Design Patterns and Frameworks

Designing and building a J2EE application is a challenging proposition to say the least because a J2EE application distributes processing across multiple tiers, each consisting of many components—some of which reside on different Java Virtual Machines. Compounding the complexity of a J2EE application is the high expectation of performance—that it be available 24 hours a day, 7 days a week and be simultaneously accessed by multiple users.

Over time and through trial and error, J2EE developers have come up with the best way to solve complex J2EE programming problems. These techniques are called *patterns*. A pattern is a proven technique that is used to develop an efficient J2EE application. Professional developers use patterns to avoid making common mistakes when designing and building a J2EE application.

You can benefit from the experiences of professional J2EE developers by incorporating appropriate patterns in the design of your J2EE application. In this chapter, you'll learn about the concept of patterns and about commonly used patterns that help overcome many challenges that you'll face when developing a J2EE application.

The Pattern Concept

Nothing is more frustrating than trying to balance a checkbook. This is challenging, at least for some of us. It could take hours reconciling a bank statement to the check register, yet an accountant might do the same job in less than a minute. This is because the accountant is taught to use techniques that increase the efficiency of reconciling a bank statement.

Some of us recalculate the sum of both the check register and the bank statement, then compare each check and bank charge. However, an accountant subtracts balances then searches the check register and the bank statement for an item that is equal to the difference. This is because accountants learned from other accountants that the difference is equal to a check or bank charge that is typically missing from the check register or bank statement. This technique is called a pattern.

A pattern is a solution or technique that has solved a problem and therefore can be used to solve the same problem in the future. Professionals in every discipline use a common group of patterns to solve problems. Collectively this group is called a catalog of patterns. A new person to the profession avoids making errors of those who came before by using a pattern.

Programmers use the concept of abstraction to reduce complex problems to simpler problems that have simpler solutions. Developers have learned over the years that these simpler problems are common in many applications and that patterns can be applied to solve them. This means that solutions can be reused to solve repeating problems, without having to rethink through the problem to reach a solution.

The birth of patterns for system development originated in the architectural profession in the late 1970s when Christopher Alexander who was an architecture professor at the

University of California at Berkeley published a catalog of architectural design patterns. These patterns defined a set of proven solutions to common architectural design problems.

About a decade later, patterns started to make their way into the software development community and formally made its presence at the 1987 Object Oriented, Programming, System, Languages, and Applications (OOPSLA) Conference where Kent Beck and Ward Cunningham presented design patterns for Smalltalk. James Coplien saw the benefits of patterns in software development and wrote patterns for C++, which he published a few years after Beck's and Cunningham's presentation.

It wasn't until 1995 when a definitive work on patterns was developed by Erich Gamma, Richard Helm, Ralph Johnson, and John Vlissides in their book *Design Patterns: Elements of Reusable Object-Oriented Software*. Gamma, Helm, Johnson, and Vlissides became known as the Gang of Four, commonly referenced as GoF.

Besides creating patterns for their disciplines, Alexander and the GoF also defined a format for defining a pattern. The format defines topic areas used to describe a pattern. Many of today's pattern catalogs use a variation of the Alexander and the GoF format.

In this chapter, four categories are used to describe each pattern: pattern name, pattern objective, when to use the pattern, and the advantages and disadvantages of using the pattern. The pattern name uniquely identifies the pattern and the pattern objective describes the goal of the pattern. The pattern definition explains the concepts used in the pattern, and the topic "when to use the pattern" tells you the most appropriate times to implement the pattern in a J2EE application. The advantages and disadvantages of using the pattern explore factors that must be weighed to determine if a pattern is advantageous to use in a particular application.

Pattern Catalog

Patterns are grouped into a collection called a pattern catalog, which you can reference whenever you are designing a J2EE application. The following is a pattern catalog that contains many patterns that you'll find beneficial when designing your application. You can use this patterns catalog as the foundation for your own patterns catalog and then add new patterns to the catalog along the way.

Handle-Forward pattern

Pattern Objective

The objective of the handle-forward pattern is to create a handle or forward model infrastructure whereby a request is passed from one component to another component until the request reaches the component that can fulfill the request (see Figure 4-1).

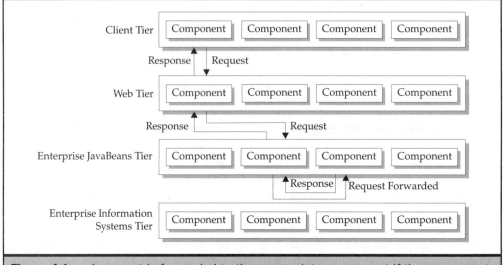

Figure 4-1. *A request is forwarded to the appropriate component if the component that initially receives the request is unable to fulfill the request.*

Pattern Definition

A developer creates a J2EE application by assembling appropriate web services components, each of which offers the developer a unique service. The developer must determine which of those services to use and then write code within the application to send a component a message requesting the service.

The developer determines the component to call based on the events encountered by the application. Each event might cause a call to a different component. However, calling components has two disadvantages.

First, calling a component is resource intensive and incurs system overhead. This means the more time an application calls a resource, the higher the load on the infrastructure. Another disadvantage is that calling components is a complex process. The developer must identify each component, determine if the service is required for the application, and then determine which event triggers a call to the component.

The handle-forward pattern reduces overhead and simplifies calling components by requiring each component to either process a request or forward a request to another component. In this way the application sends a request for service to one component and that component has the responsibility to process the request directly or indirectly by passing the request to the next appropriate component.

When to Use the Pattern

The handle-forward pattern is ideally suited for an application that implements an approval process such as when an order is received from a client. A company might refrain from processing the order until certain approvals are given. These include approval from the accounts receivable system, indicating that the client paid any outstanding charges. All orders above $100 might require approval from the credit department. Likewise, the credit department approval is required if the client has reached his or her maximum credit limit.

Each approval process applies different routines and is likely to be contained within different components. The handle-forward pattern groups together diverse and independent approval processes into one request instead of burdening the application with the task of requesting all the necessary approvals.

Advantages and Disadvantages of Using the Pattern

There are three major advantages of using the handle-forward pattern. First, this pattern simplifies the requests for service that are made by an application because the requests are always made to one component. Next, the application makes fewer requests for service, which decreases the overhead. This is because the component that receives the request from the application requests additional services directly from other components.

The last major advantage is flexibility. A process can easily be inserted or removed from the initial request without affecting the application. For example, an additional approval process can be implemented by changing the logic in the last component to forward the request for approval to a new component.

There are two major disadvantages to using the handle-forward pattern. The first is the message traffic that is generated by components forwarding messages to other components. A message might be passed to a number of components that can't process the message. Therefore, these transmissions are wasteful.

The other disadvantage is the delicate planning required to implement the handle-forward pattern. Each component that is used in the pattern must be identified and constructed in a way that a message is never dropped.

The best way to overcome these disadvantages is to limit the implementation of the handle-forward pattern to a small number of components that are necessary to collectively process a request.

Translator Pattern

Pattern Objective

The objective of the translator pattern is to provide a way for an application to convert a message written in one style to another style of message. A message can be a request for service that contains information necessary to fulfill the request. However, the request might not be in the format required by the component that processes the request. The translator pattern reformats the message appropriately and then retransmits the request to the appropriate component for fulfillment (see Figure 4-2).

Pattern Definition

The developer of a J2EE application is responsible for properly formatting requests for service and ensuring that the application provides proper information for a component to fulfill the request. A common problem is that components that provide similar but distinctly different services need information in their own formats.

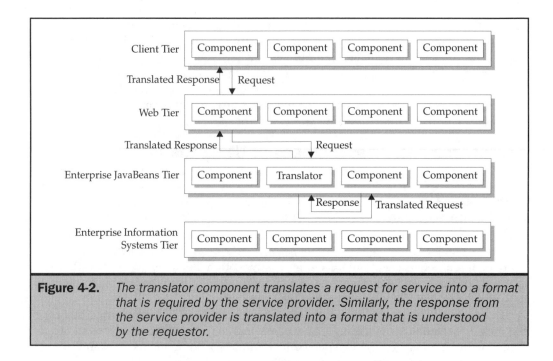

Figure 4-2. *The translator component translates a request for service into a format that is required by the service provider. Similarly, the response from the service provider is translated into a format that is understood by the requestor.*

This means that the developer must write the same reformatting code into every application that requires these services. Furthermore, this code must be rewritten every time a new component is introduced into the system that is needed by these applications.

The translator pattern transfers the responsibility for encoding various formats from application programmers to a component programmer. The component programmer designs a component to accept a single formatted message and use the message to provide one or more similar services.

The message describes the service or services requested as well as the information that is necessary to provide the service or services. The component implements the translator pattern, then (a) identifies the requested service, (b) translates the message into the message format required by the component that provides the service, and (c) calls the component and passes the reformatted message to the component.

When to Use the Pattern

Implement the translator pattern whenever an application requires similar kinds of service from components that use different messaging formats. The application will then be able to send the translator component a message that contains the type of service required and information required by the service to process the request. The translator component then reformats the message and information, and calls the proper service.

Advantages and Disadvantages of Using the Pattern

The major advantage of using the translator pattern is to concentrate translation routines into one component instead of having the same routines incorporated into multiple applications or multiple components. Translation routines can easily be maintained when they are located in one component. This means routines can be inserted, removed, or enhanced in one place and affect every application that requires translations.

The major disadvantage is that a translator can easily grow in size and become too complex to maintain and test. Therefore, it is best to use the translator pattern when a small number of translations are necessary by the application.

A common use of a translator is to process a credit card purchase. In this example, an XML message that contains purchase information is sent to an Enterprise JavaBean. The Enterprise JavaBean extracts from the XML message information needed to process the credit card purchase. This information is translated into a message format that is understood by the object that connects to the backend system to complete the credit card processing.

Distributor Pattern

Pattern Objective

The objective of the distributor pattern is to manage communication between components used by one or more applications. The distributor component receives a message from an application or another component and forwards the message to the appropriate component based on the context of the message (see Figure 4-3).

Pattern Definition

The distributor pattern has some of the basic characteristics found in the translator pattern in that messages are sent to one component and that component forwards the messages to other components. However, the distributor pattern differs from the translator pattern because the distributor component doesn't process the message.

The distributor component is similar to a network router that receives packets of data and forwards those packets to the appropriate network address. In the case of the distributor component, messages are comparable to packets and components are similar to network addresses.

The distributor pattern requires the developer to create an interface for the distributor component that identifies the destination component and contains an object required by the destination component to process the request, if necessary. The distributor component then receives and forwards the message to the destination component.

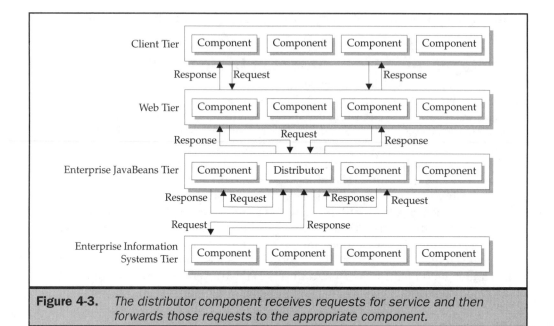

Figure 4-3.   *The distributor component receives requests for service and then forwards those requests to the appropriate component.*

When to Use the Pattern

The distributor pattern should be used to simplify communications whenever one or more applications and/or components need to process many messages to multiple components. For example, multiple applications might generate various requests for service. Instead of incorporating the communications details in each application, those details are contained in a distributor component.

Applications send requests to the distributor component. The distributor component then forwards the message to the appropriate component. Although the distributor pattern can be used across applications, it is usually specific to one application.

Advantages and Disadvantages of Using the Pattern

The advantage of using the distributor pattern is to foster a maintainable communication infrastructure. The communication details used to interact with destination components are located in one component rather than dispersed throughout applications. This means components can be added, removed, or modified within the distributor component. Likewise, applications and other components only need to reference the distributor component when there is a need to send a message to other components.

The disadvantages of using the distributor pattern are similar to the disadvantages of using the translator pattern. That is, the distributor component easily grows large and complex, making it difficult to maintain. Likewise, the developer must be sure that references to other components are correct within the distributor component; otherwise, messages will be forwarded to the wrong component.

Broadcaster Pattern

Pattern Objective

The objective of the broadcaster pattern is to receive messages from one or more applications or components, then distribute these messages to other components that have an interest in receiving those messages. The broadcaster pattern is similar to the translator pattern and the distributor pattern in that all three patterns receive and retransmit messages to other components. However, the broadcaster pattern differs in that components that receive the retransmission must register with the broadcaster component in order to receive messages (see Figure 4-4).

Pattern Definition

The broadcaster pattern has a similar functionality as satellite television. A program provider transmits a signal that contains the program to a satellite. The satellite retransmits the signal to all satellite receiving dishes that have subscribed to that programming channel.

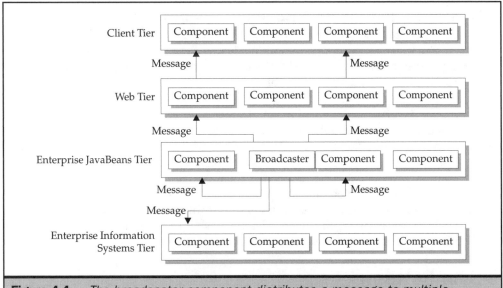

Figure 4-4. *The broadcaster component distributes a message to multiple components. Transmission of the broadcast is triggered by an event that may or may not be reacted to by components.*

In the case of the broadcaster pattern, the application or component that generated the message is similar to the program provider. The broadcaster component is the satellite, and components that receive the retransmission are the satellite receiving dishes.

In the real world, a message is generated based on events that occur, such as when the users of an application resize the application screen. The event typically triggers other components to react to the event. The application or component that causes the event to occur is referred to as the *observable component* and the component that receives the message from the observable component is called the *observer*.

Components that are notified when the event is occurred are called *listeners*. The observer communicates with listeners through a listener interface. That is, each listener has a method that is called by the observer when an event occurs.

When to Use the Pattern

The broadcaster pattern should be used whenever a message that is generated by one source must be shared with a selected number of components. A good example is when an order is received from a customer. The order is an event that triggers other actions to occur. Once the order passes credit approval and is accepted, order information in the form of a message is sent to a broadcaster component, which distributes the message to components that perform other processes. These processes include adjusting the customer's account, crediting the sales rep with the sale, generating a fulfillment order, and, of course, producing the invoice.

Advantages and Disadvantages of Using the Pattern

The major advantage of implementing the broadcaster pattern is to simplify communications among components. All the details needed to communicate with registered components are contained in one location, which is the broadcaster component. This means that only one component needs to be maintained whenever changes are made to listeners.

The major disadvantage is the format of the message. The information required for each listener to process might be unique. That is, some listeners may require more information than other listeners to react to the event. This could result in long messages being transmitted to several components that require only some of the information contained in the message in order to process the message.

The best approach to overcome this problem is to begin by using a message format that contains all the information each listener requires. If performance degradation occurs, consider overloading the listener interface by adjusting the message parameters to accommodate the variable message formats required by some listeners.

Zero Sum Pattern

Pattern Objective

The objective of the zero-sum pattern is to treat a group of independent processes as a single processing unit that collectively can succeed or fail. The unit succeeds only if all processes within the unit terminate successfully. However, the unit fails if even one process fails. This means that successfully terminated processes must be reversed whenever a process fails (see Figure 4-5).

Pattern Definition

The zero-sum pattern is named after the concept of a zero-sum game where a contestant can either win or lose, but there isn't a middle ground. The zero-sum pattern is implemented by creating a processing controller component that is responsible for initiating and directing the actions of unrelated but coordinated components that process information.

The processing controller component calls coordinated components whenever the processing controller component receives a message that is triggered by an event. The message may or may not be retransmitted to coordinated components, depending on the nature of the application.

Coordinated components are controlled through several interfaces. These are initialize, start, pause, stop, and reverse. Initialize is called by the processing controller component the first time processing begins. Subsequently pause is called to temporarily halt processing, which is resumed by calling start. The processing controller component calls stop whenever it wants the coordinated component to terminate processing, such as when another coordinated component process fails. Reverse is called to back out processing that has occurred since the last time initialize was called.

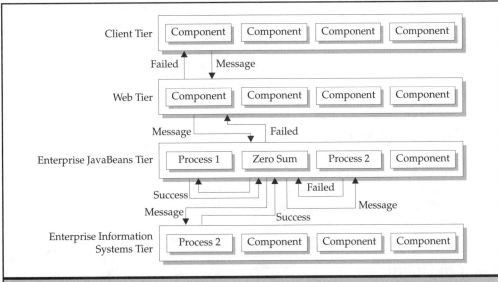

Figure 4-5.   *The zero sum component triggers a sequence of processes, all of which must terminate successfully for the entire transaction to be terminated successfully. If one process fails, the entire transaction fails.*

When to Use the Pattern

The zero-sum pattern is ideally used for any type of transaction processing that has multiple coordinated but independent components used to complete the transaction processing. Order processing is a good example of when to use the zero-sum pattern.

Order processing requires that components adjust the customer's account, credit the sales rep with the sale, generate a fulfillment order, adjust inventory, and produce the invoice, among other activities.

Each of these activities might be handled by separate components, each of which could fail during processing. Let's say that the company implemented a business rule that requires all processes to successfully complete; otherwise, the order is placed in the pending queue. The zero-sum pattern can be used to assure that the application conforms with the business rule.

Advantages and Disadvantages of Using the Pattern

The major advantage of the zero-sum pattern is that it makes it easy to maintain and coordinate the activities of independent components by using one component—the processing controller component. The developer can place new, independent components under the direction of the processing controller component whenever additional processing is required by the application.

The major disadvantage is that synchronization of independent components could waste resources, especially whenever there is frequent failure of at least one process. Resources must be used to reverse processes that have been completed. The resource is used again for reprocessing. Furthermore, the zero-sum pattern might cause a processing bottleneck to occur, especially when one coordinated component is unreliable and breaks down sporadically.

You can overcome these limitations by implementing the zero-sum pattern only in applications where there are a small number of reliable processes that need to be coordinated. This will reduce the number of points of failure and therefore reduce the amount of reprocessing.

Status Flag Pattern

Pattern Objective

The objective of the status flag pattern is to identify a status whose value determines the actions that are taken by one or more independent components. For example, the status flag pattern is typically used in conjunction with the zero-sum pattern to register whether or not any of the coordinated processing components have failed.

Pattern Definition

The status flag pattern uses an object to record the status of one or multiple actions. The value of the status depends on the nature of the application. The status is referenced before and during processing by a processing controller component or by other components to determine what, if any, actions should be taken.

A good example of an implementation of the status flag pattern is the illustration used in the zero-sum pattern description where an order is processed. It is the responsibility of the processing controller component to direct the actions of each coordinated component.

Before initializing a coordinated component, the processing controller component examines the status flag to determine if any previously called coordinated component processing has failed. If so, the next coordinated component isn't initialized.

The value of the status flag changes as each coordinated component terminates and returns the processing status to the processing controller component. In this example, the status flag has one of two values. They are pass or fail. Whenever the status flag value changes to fail, the processing controller component directs all coordinated components that have processed successfully to reverse their processing.

When to Use the Pattern

The status flag pattern should be used whenever multiple activities are dependent on a common status. The status can have one of multiple values, depending on the nature of the application. However, each value must be meaningful to components whose activities depend on the status.

For example, the status might be "processing." Each component that monitors the status must understand what the "processing" status means as related to the activity of the component; otherwise, the status is meaningless.

Advantages and Disadvantages of Using the Pattern

The major advantage of using the status flag pattern is to facilitate a common link between independent components that is used to change the behavior of these components. Each value assigned to the status flag should trigger a different action by components.

The disadvantage of using the status flag pattern is that processing by multiple components is hinged on the value of one status flag. That is, multiple processes stop if the status flag is unavailable or corrupted.

You can work around this disadvantage by building into components that reference the status flag contingency an action that is triggered whenever the status flag is unavailable. For example, the component might time out attempts to access the status flag and then take the least distributive action, which is usually to terminate processing and signal an error. Failure to implement contingency action might hang the component and thereby negatively impact the application.

Sequencer Pattern

Pattern Objective

The objective of the sequencer pattern is to sequentially access independent components from either an application or from a component (see Figure 4-6). Let's say that an application uses a group of independent components to process an order.

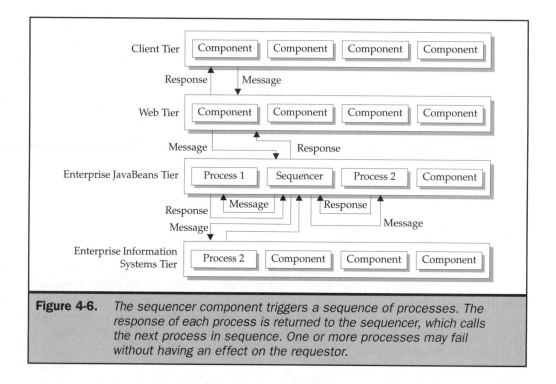

Figure 4-6. *The sequencer component triggers a sequence of processes. The response of each process is returned to the sequencer, which calls the next process in sequence. One or more processes may fail without having an effect on the requestor.*

Order processing requires that components adjust the customer's account, credit the sales rep with the sale, generate a fulfillment order, adjust inventory, and produce the invoice, among other activities.

Suppose each activity must be performed in a particular order. The developer could write the code to call each component in the application in the proper order. However, this means that the code is repeated in every application that places an order. A more efficient approach to address this issue is for the application to call a sequencer component that in turn calls other components in the proper sequence.

Pattern Definition

The sequencer pattern requires that a sequencer component be developed that receives a message from applications or components to trigger the sequential execution of a group of independent components. The message should contain any information those components need to process the request.

The sequencer component must contain logic to call components in sequence. The order in which these components are called can be fixed or vary, depending on the nature of the application. A fixed sequence is one where components are always called in the same order. A variable sequence is when conditional logic is used within the sequencer component to trigger which components are called and when they are called.

In a variable sequence, a call to a component is triggered by either a value contained in the message received from the application or originating component or by the results of a component that was previously called by the sequencer component.

For example, the sequencer component might call a component that sends a fulfillment request to the company's warehouse only if the warehouse has sufficient inventory to fill the order. This component returns to the sequencer component a value that indicates whether or not the warehouse can fill the order.

If the warehouse doesn't have sufficient inventory, the sequencer component will call a component that uses a local wholesaler to fill the order. However, this component is called only if the item is out of stock in the warehouse.

When to Use the Pattern

The sequencer pattern should be used whenever an application requires the use of multiple, independent web services and each of these web services must execute in a particular order.

Advantages and Disadvantages of Using the Pattern

The major advantage of using the sequencer pattern is to simplify maintenance of routines that call components. All rules that govern which components are called and when they are called are contained in one component that can be called from any application or component that needs to call a group of components.

A developer will find it easy to adapt to changes in these rules, because these changes are made in one place. This means that components can be added or removed from the sequence or called only when specific conditions exist.

The major disadvantage is that developers of applications or components that use the sequencer component assume that the underlying components are related in a particular order. The sequencer component hides the fact that the underlying components are independent.

Furthermore, the developer must take particular care to assure those rules for sequencing calls to components conform to the expectations of applications and components that use the sequencer. This becomes especially important when those rules are modified since the modification could affect many applications and components that are beyond the control of the programmer who developed the sequence component.

Behavior Separation Pattern

Pattern Objective

The objective of the behavior separation pattern is to provide a way to implement a behavior that is independent from an object that calls the behavior. The object-oriented design philosophy stipulates that behavior and data are encapsulated within an object. While the coupling of an object to behavior has value, there are times when a behavior is shared amongst dissimilar objects and therefore encapsulation works against the spirit of efficiency. The behavior separation pattern addresses this issue.

Pattern Definition

There is a tendency to speak in generalizations when it comes to some behaviors. For example, specifications for an application might require a collection of data to be sorted. At first the developer might consider sorting as one behavior that must be built into the application. But sorting consists of multiple behaviors since there are a number of sort algorithms that the developer can implement, depending on the nature of the application.

In the case of sorting, the developer needs to make serious design decisions. Which sort algorithm should be used? Should the application be able to switch among algorithms, depending on the data being sorted? Some sorting algorithms are more efficient than others, depending on the nature of the sort. Must the sorting behavior be encapsulated in every object that requires sorting, or can the behavior be shared amongst many objects, applications, and components?

Implementation of the behavior separation pattern resolves these issues by separating the behavior from the object, application, and components that require the behavior. The behavior separation pattern requires the development of a component that contains the independent behavior. In this example, the component contains one method for each sorting algorithm. The component then receives a message from the application or component that requires sorting. The message is formatted with the type of sort and reference to the collection that will be sorted.

When to Use the Pattern

The behavior separation pattern should be implemented whenever a behavior is shared amongst applications and components and when the behavior isn't similar to behaviors that are encapsulated with an object of an application or component. For example, sorting a list of catalog items is an ancillary behavior of an object that presents a catalog page to a client. Therefore, sorting is a candidate for implementation of the behavior separation pattern.

Advantages and Disadvantages of Using the Pattern

The benefit of implementing the behavior separation pattern is that common behaviors can extend the behavior of an object, application, or component without having to be encapsulated within it. That is, the behavior is shared and callable from multiple objects, applications, and components.

Another benefit of using the behavior separation pattern is it introduces behavior flexibility. A developer can easily add new behaviors, or modify and remove existing behaviors, because the behavior is located in one place rather than in many objects.

The disadvantage of using the behavior separation pattern is the need to identify those behaviors that are commonly used by multiple objects, applications, and components. The problem is that the developer must account for subtle differences in behavioral needs in what at first appears to be the same behavior.

The sorting example illustrates this point. Sorting is a behavior that is common to multiple objects, applications, and components. However, each of these might require a different sorting algorithm.

The developer must also design an interface used to call the behavior from objects, applications, and components. The interface design must include all the information necessary to carry out the behavior regardless of the subtle variation.

Consolidator Pattern

Pattern Objective

The objective of the consolidator pattern is to simplify accessing data that is dispersed throughout multiple resources. An application or component that needs data sends a request to a consolidator component, which contains the logic to retrieve and consolidate data from multiple sources and return the consolidated data to the requestor (see Figure 4-7).

Pattern Definition

Information is typically contained in many places within a distributive environment. The chore of locating, retrieving, and organizing this information into a presentable form is challenging to say the least. A developer can implement the consolidator

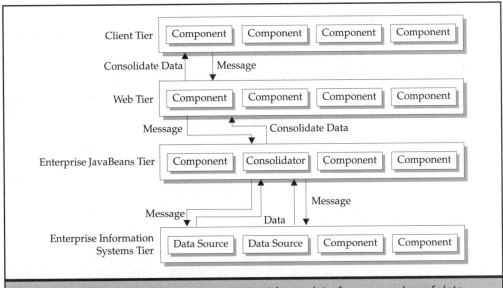

Figure 4-7. *The consolidator component retrieves data from a number of data sources and consolidates the data into one cohesive unit, which is returned to the requestor.*

pattern rather than build data-gathering logic into all the applications and components that require data.

Let's say that an application or component needs to retrieve information about an order. The application or component should simply submit the request along with the order number to a consolidator component and not be concerned about the location of data that comprises the order or how to retrieve this data.

The consolidator pattern is implemented by creating a consolidator component that contains the logic to receive a message for information from a requestor, process the request, and return the consolidated data to the requestor.

Processing is segmented into two general tasks. The first task is to translate the request into the appropriate format that is used to retrieve the data and then to send the reformatted request to resources that contain the information.

Typically, these resources are one or more database management systems (DBMS) and the reformatted request takes the form of a SQL query. You'll learn more about DBMS and SQL in Chapters 5, 6, and 7.

The other task is to consolidate data returned from these resources into a cohesive form that can easily be accessed by the requestor. The form of the returned data to the request is dependent on the nature of the application or component.

When to Use the Pattern

The consolidator pattern should be implemented whenever information required by an application or component is stored in various locations in a distributive system and when multiple applications and components need access to the consolidated information.

Avoid using this pattern if only one application or component requires the data and if the data is located in one location, such as in a single DBMS.

Advantages and Disadvantages of Using the Pattern

The advantage of using the consolidator pattern is to simplify the data gathering process. All code necessary to gather and consolidate data from multiple resources is contained in one component, which is the consolidator component.

A developer needs only to modify the consolidator component, should there be any changes in the source of the data. In addition to these advantages, the consolidator pattern also simplifies a request for data by an application or component. The developer of the application or component basically sends a message to the consolidator component saying, "give me order 1234." The developer doesn't need to know the details of retrieving the information.

The disadvantage of implementing the consolidator pattern is that the developer of the consolidator component must carefully define all the consolidations of data that might be requested. This analysis becomes increasingly complex as the number of different requestors grows. That is, each requestor might have unique needs that must be accommodated in the logic of the consolidator component.

Another disadvantage is that the consolidator component might become a bottleneck in an application's or component's need to retrieve information. Simply said, there might be more requests than can be handled by the consolidator component, and response time then becomes unreasonable.

These disadvantages can be avoided by restricting the variations of requests that are handled by a consolidator component, and in doing so limiting the number of applications and components that will call the consolidator component. If necessary, multiple consolidator components can be used, each retrieving and consolidating a particular set of data.

Simplicity Pattern

Pattern Objective

The objective of the simplicity pattern is to simplify implementing complex processing routines by requiring applications and components that need to call these routines to make a simple request to one component. That component translates the simple request into a call to the appropriate component, which fulfills the request.

Pattern Definition

The concept of the simplicity pattern is very similar to that of the consolidator pattern. Both are designed to handle the complexities of a task. However, the simplicity pattern receives a simple message from the requestor, which is then forwarded to another component.

Let's say that an application is designed to manage orders and needs to insert a new order, update an existing order, retrieve an order, and cancel an order. Each of these is a separate task that is performed by different components.

The simplicity pattern requires that the developer create one component that receives requests to execute various routines from multiple applications and components. For example, an application sends the component a message to insert a new order. The message identifies the task it wants performed and references the necessary information needed to perform the task.

The component calls the appropriate routine, which is likely to be contained in another component, and, if necessary, reformats the message into the format required by the called component.

When to Use the Pattern

The simplicity pattern should be implemented whenever there are many tasks, each of which requires a different format to execute and that can be executed by multiple applications and components.

Avoid using the simplicity pattern if there are few tasks, and if one application or component calls these tasks. This is because it is inefficient to build a component to handle calls that can be better handled directly by the application or component that requires that the task be performed.

Advantages and Disadvantages of Using the Pattern

The advantage of using the simplicity pattern is the developer can simplify the message format used to request service. That is, the message doesn't have to conform to the interface used by the underlying components that actually perform the task. The component that receives the request can transform the message into the interface as long as the simplified message format contains the necessary information to process the request.

Another advantage of using the simplicity pattern is that components that perform a task become pluggable. That is to say, components can be added and removed without requiring changes in applications or other components.

For example, suppose there was an enhanced way of inserting an order. The existing component that inserts orders can be de-referenced and replaced with reference to the new component. Applications and components that need to insert a new order continue to send the same simple message without being aware that the underlying component changed.

The disadvantage of using the simplicity pattern is the difficulty of creating a message format that is simply to be used in an application and component and yet has the necessary information required by the underlying component to carry out the task.

Stealth Pattern

Pattern Objective

The objective of the stealth pattern is to conceal the identity of the application or component that requests a service. Requests for service are made to the stealth component rather than directly to the component that provides the service.

The stealth component acts as a proxy for the requestor and uses its own identification to request service. The service provider assumes that the service is being provided to the stealth component and has no way of knowing the identity of the requestor.

Pattern Definition

There are scenarios when an application's or component's identify must be hidden for security reasons. One of the easiest ways to achieve this objective is to implement the stealth pattern, because the identity of the application or component is never revealed to the service provider.

Let's say that an application is used to investigate possible improprieties and requires information about a suspected account. It is important that the investigation remain confidential so the owner of the account isn't harmed if it later turns out that there are no improprieties.

A stealth component can be developed to hide the application that is used for the investigation. All transactions between the application and components within the infrastructure funnel through the stealth component.

The stealth component uses a filter-forward model where the requestor's identifying information is replaced with the stealth component's information, and then the filtered message is forwarded to the service provider. Messages from the service provider are forwarded directly to the requestor without any modification.

When to Use the Pattern

The stealth pattern should be implemented whenever a requestor's identity must be hidden from service providers.

Advantages and Disadvantages of Using the Pattern

The advantage of using the stealth pattern is it conceals the identity of a requestor while still enabling the requestor to access web services. This provides a level of security to applications and components whose identity must be concealed.

The disadvantage of using the stealth pattern is this causes a misleading audit trail of services. Typically, an infrastructure keeps a log of service requests. The log contains the date and time of the request and identifies the requestor and service provider, along with other information.

However, log entries show that the stealth component made requests for services. The original requestor's identity doesn't appear in the log. Therefore, the audit trail is misleading.

The Complete Reference

J2EE

Part II

J2EE Databases

At the center of nearly every J2EE application is a repository of information that is accessed and manipulated by service-side components such as web services and client-side applications. A repository is a database management system that stores, retrieves, and maintains the integrity of information stored in its databases.

A J2EE application uses Java data objects, JDBC, and other technology necessary in interacting with a database management systems, to provide information to the J2EE application.

In Part II you'll learn database concepts in relationship to Java data objects. You'll also explore the details of JDBC, which is used to connect to and interact with popular—and some not so popular—database management systems. And you'll also learn how to create and send requests for information and then integrate the results into your J2EE application.

Chapter 5

J2EE Database Concepts

A J2EE application is built by assembling components, many of which are shared with other applications, as you learned in Part I. Each component provides a J2EE application with a web service, and one of these is access to one or more databases.

A database is a collection of data that is managed by a database management system (DBMS). Many corporations use one of several commercially available DBMSs such as Oracle, DB2, Sybase, and Microsoft Access, which is used for small data collections.

Components that provide database access to a J2EE application interact with commercial DBMSs by using a combination of Java data objects that are defined in the Java Database Connection (JDBC) specification and by using the Structured Query Language (SQL). Java data objects form a communications link with a DBMS while SQL is the language used to construct the message (called a query) that is sent to the DBMS to request data, update data, delete data, and otherwise manipulate data in the DBMS.

This is the first of three chapters that show how to incorporate database interactions into a J2EE application. This first chapter covers database fundamentals, where you learn how to transform data elements of a business system into a relational database, which is a common task in development of J2EE applications. You can skip this chapter if you are familiar with this technique.

The next chapter focuses on Java data objects—what they are, how they work, and how to use them to communicate with a DBMS. The third chapter shows how to write and execute queries, and then interact with the results returned by the DBMS.

Data

You are probably familiar with the term "data" because you use data in everyday life, such as when you dial a telephone number or log into a computer network using a user ID and password. The telephone number, user ID, and password are types of data.

Yet the term "data" is commonly confused with the term "information." Although these terms have similar meaning in the vernacular, they are different when related to a DBMS. Information consists of one or more words that collectively infer a meaning, such as a person's address.

Data refers to an atomic unit that is stored in a DBMS and is sometimes reassembled into information. Examples of data are a person's street address, city, state, and ZIP code. Each of these is an atomic unit that is commonly found in a DBMS. A J2EE component can access one or multiple atomic units as is required by a J2EE application or another component. A database is an organization of data so a J2EE component can quickly find, retrieve, update, or delete one or more data elements.

Database

As mentioned previously in this chapter, a database in the purest sense is a collection of data. While you can use Java and Java's I/O classes to create your own database, you'll probably interact with a commercially available DBMS. A DBMS provides an industrial-strength solution to data management and uses proprietary and public domain algorithms to assure fast and secure interaction with data stored in the database.

There are many different DBMSs, most of which adhere to a widely accepted relational database model. A database model is a description of how data is organized in a database. In a relational database model, data is grouped into tables using a technique called normalization, which you'll learn about later in this chapter. Tables are grouped into a database.

Once a database and at least one table are created, a J2EE component can send SQL statements to the DBMS to

- Save data
- Retrieve data
- Update data
- Manipulate data
- Delete data

Tables

A table is the component of a database that contains data in the form of rows and columns, very similar to a spreadsheet. A row contains related data such as a client's name and address. A column contains like data, such as a clients' first names.

Each column is identified by a unique name, called a column name, that describes the data contained in that column. For example, client first name is a likely choice as the name of a column that contains clients' first names.

In addition, columns are defined by attributes. An attribute describes the characteristic of data that can be stored in the column. Attributes include size, data type, and format. You'll learn about these and other attributes later in this chapter.

Database name, table name, column name, column attributes, and other information that describes database components are known as metadata. Metadata is data about data. For example, the size of the client's first name column describes the data contained within the column and therefore is referred to as metadata.

Metadata is used by J2EE components to identify database components without needing to know details of a column, the table, or the database. For example, a J2EE component can request from the DBMS the data type of a specific column. The column type is used by a J2EE component to copy data retrieved from the DBMS into a Java collection.

Database Schema

A database schema (see Figure 5-1) is a document that defines all components of a database such as tables, columns, and indexes. A database schema also shows relationships between tables, which are used to join together rows of two tables. You'll learn about indexes and relating tables later in this chapter.

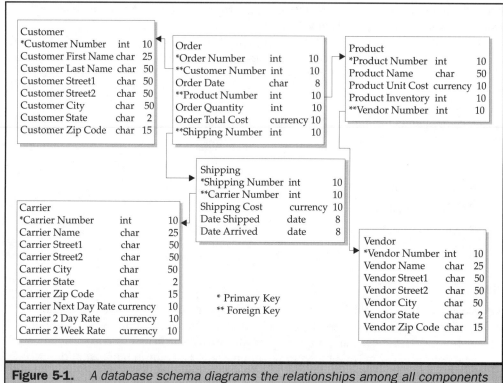

Figure 5-1. *A database schema diagrams the relationships among all components of a database.*

There are six steps that must be performed to create a database schema. These are

1. Identify information used in the existing system or legacy system that is being replaced by the J2EE application.

2. Decompose this information into data.

3. Define data.

4. Normalize data into logical groups.

5. Create primary and foreign keys.

6. Group data together into logical groups.

Identifying Information

The initial step to define a database schema is to identify all information that is used by the system that is being converted to J2EE technology. Information is associated with objects, also known as entities of the system.

An entity is, for example, an order form, a product, a customer, or a sales representative. Figure 5-2 illustrates the entities for an order system. Each entity is

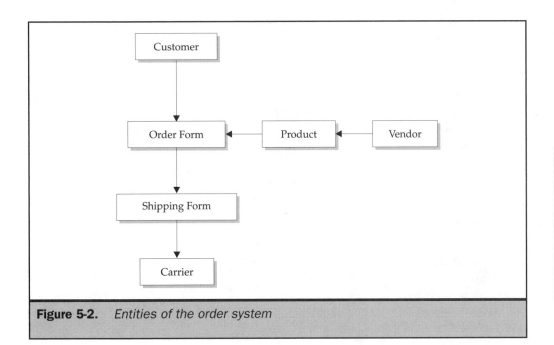

Figure 5-2.   *Entities of the order system*

defined by attributes. An attribute is information that describes an entity such as a customer name for a customer entity.

Don't confuse an entity attribute with data attributes, because an entity attribute can be different than data attributes. An entity attribute provides general information about an entity while a data attribute provides information about data that is used by the entity. Data, as you'll recall, is the atomic level of information. An attribute of an entity is at a more general level than the atomic level. For example, a customer name is an entity attribute, and a customer first name and customer last name are data attributes.

Identifying attributes is intuitive most times because an attribute is information commonly used to describe an entity. For example, a customer name and address are information normally used to describe a customer. Therefore, customer name and address are easily recognizable as attributes of a customer entity. Figure 5-3 contains attributes for entities in the order system. Notice how attributes of an entity uniquely identify the entity.

The best way to identify attributes of an entity is by analyzing instances of the entity. An entity is like an empty order form and an instance is an order form that contains order information. Looking at instances of an entity helps to identify attributes because you are viewing a real entity. That is, instead of looking at a blank order form you are looking at an order form that represents a real order. You'll find instances of an entity in the existing system.

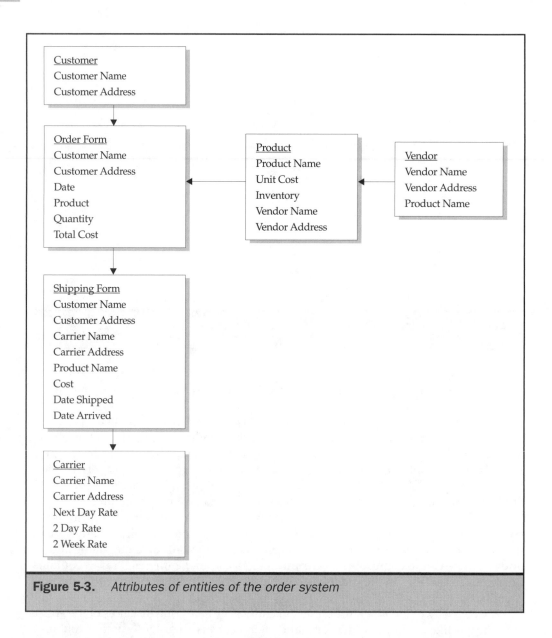

Figure 5-3. *Attributes of entities of the order system*

Once attributes are identified, you must describe the characteristics of each attribute (see Figure 5-4). Here are common characteristics found in many attributes.

- **Attribute name** The name of an attribute uniquely identifies the attribute from other attributes of the same entity. "First name" is an attribute name.

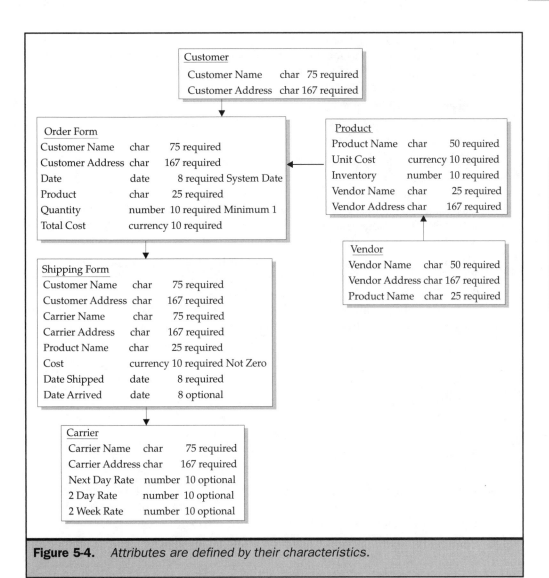

Figure 5-4. *Attributes are defined by their characteristics.*

Duplicate attribute names within the same entity are prohibited. However, two entities can use the same attribute name. That is, the customer entity and the sales representative entity both can have an attribute called first name.

■ **Attribute type**   An attribute type is nearly identical to the data type of a column in a table. Common attribute types include numeric, character, alphanumeric, date, time, Boolean, integer, float, and double, among other attribute types. However, unlike a data type for a column, you do not have to use precise terminology to describe an attribute type. That is, you might call an attribute type "sales in dollars, " which is not a valid Java data type but is sufficient to convey the type of information assigned to the entity. It is also advisable to include sample values that are assigned to the entity. This enables you to match the attribute with the most advantageous data type for the DBMS you are using when you create a table for the system.

- **Attribute size**   The attribute size describes the number of characters used to store values of the attribute. This is similar to the size of a column in a table.

- **Attribute range**   An attribute range is minimum and maximum values that can be assigned to an attribute. For example, the value of the "total amount" attribute of an order entity is likely to be greater than zero and less than 10,000 assuming that no order has ever been received that had a total amount of more than 9,999. This range is then used to throw an error should an order be received with a total amount outside of this range.

- **Attribute default value**   An attribute default value is the value that is automatically assigned to the attribute if the attribute isn't assigned a value by the J2EE application. For example, the J2EE component uses the default system's date for the date of an order if a sales representative fails to date the order. The system's date is the attribute default value.

- **Acceptable values**   An acceptable value for an attribute is one of a set of values established by the business unit and includes ZIP codes, country codes, methods of delivery, and simply yes or no.

- **Required value**   An attribute may require a value before the attribute is saved to a table. For example, an order entity has an order number attribute, which requires that an order number be assigned to the attribute.

- **Attribute format**   The attribute format consists of the way in which an attribute appears in the existing system, such as the format of the data.

- **Attribute source**   The attribute source identifies the origin of the attribute value. Common sources are from data entry and the J2EE component generated such as using the system's date as the value of the attribute.

- **Comments**   A comment is free-form text that is used to describe an attribute.

Decomposing Attributes to Data

Once attributes of entities are identified, attributes must be reduced to data elements. This process is called decomposing. For the most part, decomposing is an intuitive process because you can easily recognize whether or not an attribute is already at an atomic level, such as is illustrated in the customer name and customer address attributes. Both attributes are not atomic, however atomic level is obvious—first name, last name, city, state, and ZIP code.

However, decomposing other attributes might be less intuitive. For example, should a customer number attribute be decomposed? At first glance, the response is no because typically a customer number is already atomic.

Consider the following customer number that consists of three numbered segments: 12-24-1001. The first segment (12) represents the sales region within which the customer is located. The second segment (24) is the branch within the sales region that handles relationships with the customer. And the final segment (1001) is the number that identifies the customer within the branch and region.

Since the customer number is in three segments, should the customer number attribute be decomposed into each segment? This isn't an easy question to answer since in some systems it makes sense to further decompose the customer number attribute and in other systems no further decomposition of the customer number is necessary.

The nature of the system will determine whether or not additional decomposition is required for an attribute. For example, in this scenario the customer number probably should be further decomposed if the system references each segment of the customer number such as using the first segment to select customers of a particular region. Otherwise, the customer number should be treated as atomic.

How to Decompose Attributes

The process of decomposing attributes begins by analyzing the list of entities and its attributes. The list of attributes represents all the information used by the existing system. The objective is to reduce each attribute to a list of data that represents the atomic level of the attribute. Here's how to do this:

1. Look at each attribute and ask yourself if the attribute is atomic.

2. If the attribute isn't atomic, the attribute must be further decomposed. Create a list of data derived from the attribute below the attribute, as illustrated in Figure 5-5.

3. If the attribute is atomic, no further decomposition is necessary for that attribute. Place the name of the attribute on the data list.

4. Review the data list developed in step 2 and repeat the decomposition process until all attributes are atomic.

Tools for Analysis

Computer-aided software engineering (CASE) tools are designed to automate the process of analyzing a system. Oracle Designer/2000, Rational Rose, and Together J are three of the better CASE tools on the market.

A CASE tool transforms basic information that is entered into a CASE tool into entities, attributes, data, and relationships among entities. CASE tools are beyond the scope of this book. Visit the manufacturers' web sites for more information about CASE tools.

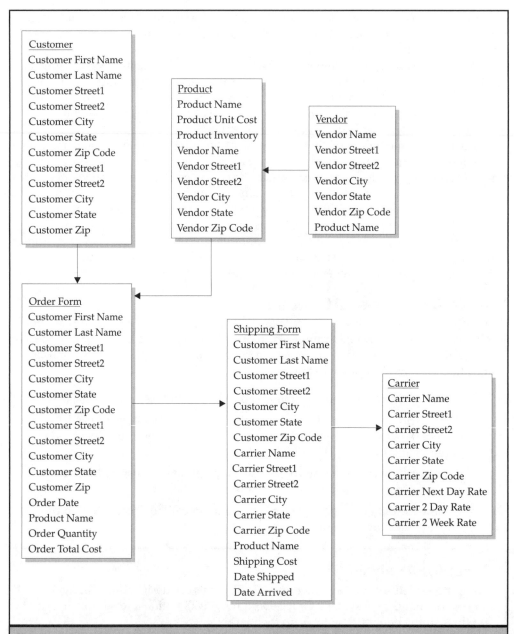

Figure 5-5. *Data elements for the customer name attribute*

Decomposing by Example

Let's work through an example of decomposing attributes using the customer address attribute of a customer entity. The following are attributes for the customer entity:

- Customer number
- Customer name
- Customer address
- Customer telephone number

Once the list of attributes is assembled, each attribute on the list must be decomposed. The customer address attribute is decomposed in this example. The same process can be applied to the other attributes.

Review the customer address attribute to determine if the attribute is atomic, which it isn't. Therefore, the customer address attribute must be decomposed into the following data elements:

- Street address 1
- Street address 2
- City
- State
- Country
- Country code
- Postal code
- Address type (that is, home or business)

Defining Data

Decomposing attributes results in the identification of data elements used by the existing system. Each data element must be defined using techniques similar to those used to describe an attribute. Here are common ways to define a data element:

- **Data name**   The unique name given to the data element, which should reflect the kind of data (see "The Art of Choosing a Name" section).

- **Data type**   A data type describes the kind of values that are associated with the data (see the "Data Types" section).

- **Data size**   The size of text data is the maximum number of characters required to represent values of the data. The size of numeric data is usually either the number of digits or the number of bytes for binary representation (that is, smallint in DB2 is 2 bytes).

The Art of Choosing a Name

Picking a name for a data element might seem intuitive, but it can easily become tricky when you realize the name must describe the data, it must be unique, and it may experience size and character limitations depending on the DBMS.

The nature of the data provides a hint to the data name, such as "first name" being used as the name for data that is associated with a person's first name. However, sometimes the obvious choice isn't the best choice. For example, intuitively one might select "telephone number" as the name of data that is associated with a telephone number. However, an entity such as a customer might have more than one telephone number, such as a home telephone number and business telephone number. This means the name of the data element that contains the telephone number must reflect that kind of telephone number, too.

Another twist in selecting a name comes when more than one entity contains similar data. In this example, there could be a customer entity and a sales representative entity, both of which have home and business telephone numbers. The solution is to use the name of the entity as part of the data element name, such as customer home telephone number and customer business telephone number since this clearly identifies the data.

Keep the length of the name reasonable. The names of data elements typically become column names in a table. Some DBMSs restrict the length of column names and the types of characters that can be used as a column name.

Names of data should have as few characters as possible to identify the data. There are two reasons for this. First, the data name will probably conform to any restrictions imposed by the DBMS. Second, a programmer won't need to type long column names in when interacting with the database.

A data name can be abbreviated using components of the name. For example, customer home telephone number can be shortened to cust home phone.

When abbreviating data names, make sure the same style of abbreviation is used for naming data. This means that cust is the abbreviation for customer and should be used in other data of the customer entity (that is, cust bus phone).

Be aware that some DBMSs prohibit spaces in column names. You can avoid this problem by removing spaces in the data name. However, doing so might make the name unreadable. Readability can be enhanced by capitalizing the first letter of each word in the name or separating these words with hyphens or underlines, such as

- CustHomePhone
- cust-home-phone
- cust_home_phone

Data Types

As previously mentioned in this chapter, a data type describes the characteristics of data associated with a data element. For example, a street address is likely to be an alphanumeric data type because a street address has a mixture of characters and numbers.

It is important to use care when selecting the data type of a data element at this stage in the analysis because the data type that you choose typically becomes the data type of the column in the table that contains the data.

Where possible, limit the choice of data types to those that are common to commercial DBMSs. Not all DBMSs use the same data type. Some DBMSs enhance the standard data type offering.

However, if you are unsure of the data type to describe a data element, then describe the type of data in your own words and include an example of data values that are associated with the data element. You can refine your choice to available data types in the DBMS when you create the table used to store the data element.

Many commercially available DBMSs adopted a common set of data types that center on the SQL set of data types, which you'll learn about in detail in the next chapter. However, some of these are listed here:

- **Character** Also referred to as text. Stores alphabetical characters and punctuation.
- **Alpha** Stores only alphabetical characters.
- **Alphanumeric** Stores alphabetical characters, punctuation, and numbers.
- **Numeric** Stores numbers only.
- **Date/Time** Stores date and time values.
- **Logical (Boolean)** Stores one of two values—true or false, 0 or 1, or yes or no.
- **LOB (Large object)** Stores large text fields, images, and other binary data.

Normalizing Data

Normalization is the process of organizing data elements into related groups to minimize redundant data and to assure data integrity. Redundant data elements occur naturally since multiple entities have the same data elements. For example, an order form and invoice are both entities that contain a customer name and address. Therefore, customer name and address are redundant.

For transactional databases, redundant data makes a database complex and inefficient, and exposes the database to problems referred to as anomalies when the DBMS maintains the database. Anomalies occur whenever new data is inserted into the database and when existing data is either modified or deleted and can lead to a breach in referential integrity of the database (see "Referential Integrity" later in this chapter). However, for reporting data, the redundancy rules are bent a little because redundant data is more efficient since it minimizes the number of joins and allows data to be summarized into logical groups.

Errors caused by redundant data are greatly reduced, and possibly eliminated, by applying the normalization process to the list of data elements that describe all the entities in a system. This is called normalizing the logical data model of a system.

The normalization process consists of applying a series of rules, called *normal forms*, to the list of data elements to

- Remove redundant data elements.
- Reorganize data elements into groups.
- Define one data element of the group (called a primary key) to uniquely identify the group. Often, two or more data elements make up the primary key, which is referred to as a composite key.
- Make other data elements of the group (called nonkey data elements) functionally dependent on the primary key.
- Relate one group to another using the primary key.

For example, a customer number is the primary key of a group that contains customer information. Other data contained in the group such as the customer first name and last name are referred to as nonkey data elements. Nonkey data elements are functionally dependent on the primary key. That is, a customer name, address, and related information cannot exist in the customer group without being assigned a customer number.

The Normalization Process

There are five normal forms. However, many industry leaders conclude that the fourth and fifth normal forms are difficult to implement and unnecessary. Therefore, we'll confine ourselves to the first three normal forms:

- First normal form (1NF) requires that information be atomic, as discussed previously in this chapter.
- Second normal form (2NF) requires data to be in the first normal form. In addition, data elements are organized into groups, eliminating redundant data. Each group contains a primary key and nonkey data, and nonkey data must be functionally dependent on a primary key.
- Third normal form (3NF) requires that data elements be in the second normal form and nonkey data must not contain transitive dependencies.

Grouping Data

A common way to organize data elements into groups is to first assemble a list of all data elements, as discussed previously in this chapter. When this is done, you'll notice that some data elements are duplicated because they are used by more than one entity. Duplicate data elements must be removed from the list. Although this is an intuitive process, you must be careful because not all data elements with similar sounding names are duplicates.

Let's say there are two data elements, one called zip code and the other postal code. At first glance these appear to have the same meaning. A ZIP code is another term for postal code—or is it?

A ZIP code is a specific kind of postal code used in the United States. A postal code is a general term that also applies to postal codes used by countries other than the United States.

The difference is subtle, but could have an impact if you assume zip code and postal code are the same. For example, many relational databases contain a table of ZIP codes where only valid ZIP codes are stored. The table also contains the city and state that corresponds to a ZIP code.

Postal code data may or may not be contained in a relational database table since it could be difficult to identify all the postal codes from every country—and maintain this list as postal codes are modified.

Figure 5-6 contains a list of all data elements before redundant data elements are removed. Figure 5-7 shows the same list after redundant data is removed. Notice that the number of data elements on the list has been dramatically reduced. Figure 5-8 organizes related data into groups.

Creating Primary Keys

As discussed previously in this chapter, a primary key is a data element that uniquely identifies a row of data elements within a group. The data selected to become the primary key may or may not exist in the data list generated as the results of analyzing entities. Sometimes a data element such as an order number is used as the primary key. Other times, the DBMS can be requested to automatically generate a primary key whenever a column in the group isn't suitable to be designated the primary key. Figure 5-8 indicates the primary key of each group with an asterisk.

Let's use a customer entity as an illustration. In the purest sense, a customer has a name and address as attributes. These attributes decompose to first name, last name, street, city, state, and ZIP code. However, none of these data elements are suited to become a primary key because individually and collectively none uniquely identify a customer.

Intuitively, the customer first name and last name seem to uniquely identify a customer, but upon closer analysis you'll see that more than one customer might have the same first name and last name. Likewise, there might be two people at the same address having the same name, although somewhat unlikely.

If neither a single data element nor a combination of data elements uniquely identifies a row, then you must create another data element to serve as the primary key of the table, which is what is required in the previous example. Alternatively you can request the DBMS automatically generate a primary key.

Nearly all commercial DBMSs can generate primary keys to make the database thread safe and reliable. In contrast, a J2EE component that generates a key must contain the logic to be sure that none of the components running on different servers accidentally generate the same key.

Customer First Name
Customer Last Name
Customer Street1
Customer Street2
Customer City
Customer State
Customer Zip Code
Customer Street1
Customer Street2
Customer City
Customer State
Customer Zip
Customer First Name
Customer Last Name
Customer Street1
Customer Street2
Customer City
Customer State
Customer Zip Code
Customer Street1
Customer Street2
Customer City
Customer State
Customer Zip
Order Date
Product Name
Order Quantity
Order Total Cost
Product Name
Product Unit Cost
Product Inventory
Vendor Name
Vendor Street1
Vendor Street2
Vendor City
Vendor State
Vendor Zip Code
Vendor Name
Vendor Street1
Vendor Street2
Vendor City

Vendor State
Vendor Zip Code
Product Name
Customer First Name
Customer Last Name
Customer Street1
Customer Street2
Customer City
Customer State
Customer Zip Code
Carrier Name
Carrier Street1
Carrier Street2
Carrier City
Carrier State
Carrier Zip Code
Product Name
Shipping Cost
Date Shipped
Date Arrived
Carrier Name
Carrier Street1
Carrier Street2
Carrier City
Carrier State
Carrier Zip Code
Carrier Next Day Rate
Carrier 2 Day Rate
Carrier 2 Week Rate

Figure 5-6.   *Here is a list of data elements from the entities shown in Figure 5-5.*

Customer First Name
Customer Last Name
Customer Street1
Customer Street2
Customer City
Customer State
Customer Zip Code
Order Date
Product Name
Order Quantity
Order Total Cost
Product Unit Cost
Product Inventory
Vendor Name
Vendor Street1
Vendor Street2
Vendor City
Vendor State
Vendor Zip Code
Carrier Name
Carrier Street1
Carrier Street2
Carrier City
Carrier State
Carrier Zip Code
Shipping Cost
Date Shipped
Date Arrived
Carrier Next Day Rate
Carrier 2 Day Rate
Carrier 2 Week Rate

Figure 5-7.   *Here is the list of data elements shown in Figure 5-6 after redundant data is removed.*

Functional Dependency

A functional dependency occurs when data depends on other data such as when nonkey data is dependent on a primary key. This means that all nonkey data has a functional dependency on the primary key within its group.

For example, order product quantity in the Orders group cannot exist unless there is an order number. The order number is the primary key of the group and the order

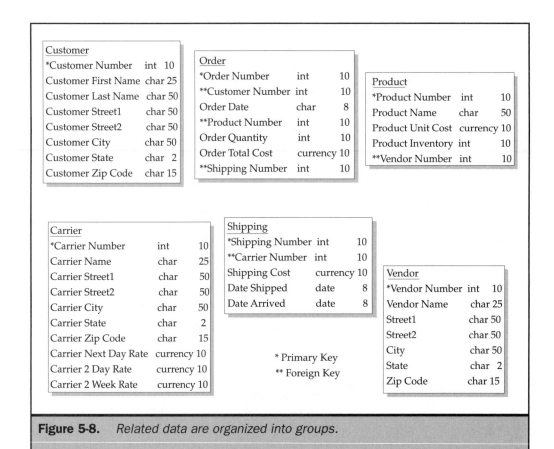

Figure 5-8. *Related data are organized into groups.*

product quantity is the nonkey data. You can say that order product quantity is functionally dependent on order number. This is noted by the expression order

```
product quantity -> order number.
```

Transitive Dependencies

A transitive dependency is a functional dependency between two or more nonkey data elements. This is difficult to understand at first, but an example will clearly illustrate transitive dependency.

The first grouping in Figure 5-9 shows the order entity with two data elements. These are sales rep number and region, which is the region to which the sales representative is assigned. Salesperson and region have a transitive dependency. The region is functionally dependent on the salesperson and the salesperson is functionally dependent on the order number. Since both salesperson and region are nonkey data, they are therefore functionally mutually dependent.

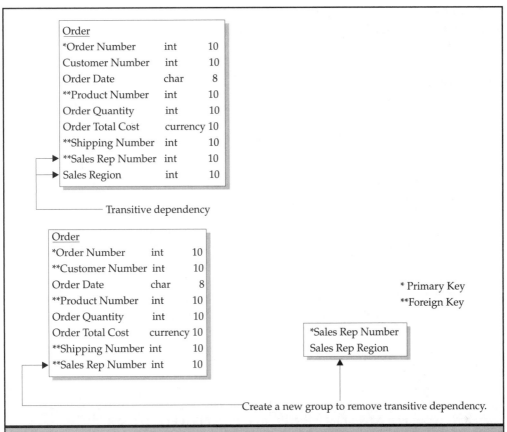

Figure 5-9. *Sales rep number and region (top) form a transitive dependency. Regrouping data elements (see bottom) resolves the transitive dependency problem.*

The problem lies with the fact that a salesperson cannot be relocated to a different region without having to modify the region data element in the order information group. Therefore, data elements must be regrouped to conform to the third normal form and eliminate transitive dependency.

The second grouping in Figure 5-9 illustrates the regrouping of the order entity to address the transitive dependency problem. Notice that a new group is formed that contains the sales rep number and the region.

The sales rep number and the region can be used as a composite key. A composite key, as you recall from an earlier discussion in this chapter, is a primary key that consists of two data elements.

In this example, the sales rep number and the region can be joined to form a composite key. If a sales representative is permitted to make sales in multiple regions, the composite key is used to associate the sales representative with one of many regions and a region to one of many sales representatives.

Identifying transitive dependencies is tricky. You have to carefully analyze the data elements once the list of data elements is in the second normal form to spot transitive dependencies.

Foreign Key

As you recall, a foreign key is a primary key of another group (see ** in Figure 5-8) used to draw a relationship between two groups of data elements. Relationships between two groups are made using the value of a foreign key and not necessarily the name of a foreign key.

Let's say there are two groups: one contains customer information and the other contains order information. The primary key in the customer information group is the customer number and the primary key in the order information group is the order number.

Each row in the order group contains the customer number of the customer who placed the order. The customer number in the order group is a foreign key. That is, the customer number in the order group is the primary key of the customer information group.

The DBMS is able to join information about a customer, along with information about orders placed by that customer, by joining together the customer number in both the customer information group and the order group.

Referential Integrity

The success of a relational database is based on the existence of primary keys and foreign keys of data groups to create relationships among groups. The existence of this relationship is called referential integrity, as is illustrated in Figure 5-10.

Referential integrity is enforced by imposing database constraints. This means the DBMS assures referential integrity by preventing primary and foreign keys from being modified or deleted. Likewise, database constraints prevent new rows from being inserted without maintaining referential integrity.

The Art of Indexing

An index is used to quickly locate information in a table similar to how information is located in a book. However, instead of page numbers, an index references the row number in the table that contains the search criteria.

Conceptually an index is a table that has two columns. One column is the key to the index and the other column is the number of the row in the corresponding table that contains the value of the key.

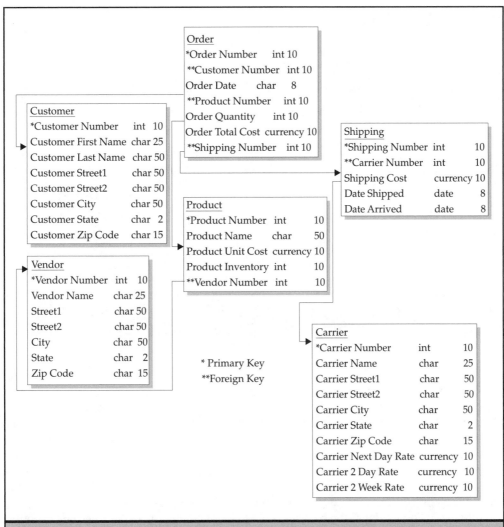

Figure 5-10. *Groups of data elements are related to other groups of data elements by using a combination of foreign keys and primary keys.*

Let's say that you created a table of customer information and use the customer number as the primary key to the table. Figure 5-11 contains such a table. An index is created using the primary key as the index key.

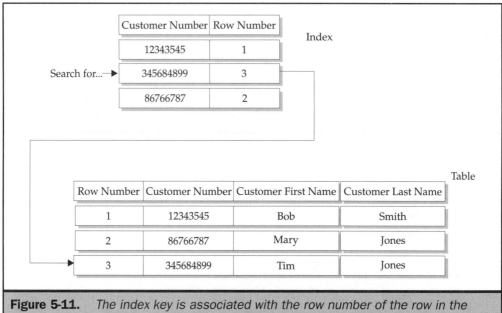

Figure 5-11. *The index key is associated with the row number of the row in the table that contains other information related to the index key.*

Notice that each row in the index corresponds to a row in the customer table. However, an index always has two columns regardless of the number of columns in the associated table. The number of columns plays a critical role in finding information quickly in a table because an index has less information for a DBMS to search than a table that contains all the data.

Indexed keys are sorted in alphabetical or numerical order depending on the value of the key. The DBMS begins at the center row of the index when searching for a particular key value. The search criteria is either an exact match to the key value of the center row of the index, is greater than the key value, or less than the key value.

If there is a match, then the row that corresponds to the key is retrieved. If the value is greater than the key, then the DBMS begins the next search at the center row of the lower half of the index. Likewise, if the value is less than the key, the search continues at the center row of the upper half of the index. The process is repeated until either a match is found or the search criteria cannot be found.

An Index in Motion

Unlike an index of a book, a table can be associated with multiple indexes each of which contains a different key. For example, a customer information table might have an index based on a ZIP code and another on a customer number. The designer of the database determines the number of indexes that are associated with a table, although some DBMSs create their own indexes to speed searches if an appropriate index doesn't exist.

A J2EE component sends the DBMS a query that contains search criteria for information required by the component. Instead of searching the table that contains the search criteria, the DBMS compares the search criteria to keys of indexes, looking for an index to use in the search.

Let's say that a J2EE component needs to retrieve information about a customer. The request for information, called a query, is sent to the DBMS along with the customer number. The DBMS recognizes that the request contains a customer number, then searches a catalog of indexes for an index that uses customer number as its key.

The DBMS always uses an index, if one exists, to locate search criteria. If an index doesn't match the search criteria, then the DBMS either creates a temporary index as part of the search or sequentially searches the table. The method used with your DBMS depends on how the manufacturer designed the DBMS.

Once an index is located or a temporary index is created, the DBMS compares the search criteria contained in the request to the index key. When a match is found, the DBMS notes the row number in the second column of the index and then opens the associated table and moves directly to the row that corresponds to the row number. The DBMS then selects columns from the row that contains customer information requested by the J2EE component.

Drawbacks Using an Index

An index offers an unparalleled advantage for finding information in a table quickly. However, there is a drawback when too many indexes are used with one table. That is, an unacceptable delay can occur whenever a row is inserted into or deleted from the table.

Once an index is built, the DBMS is responsible for automatically maintaining the index whenever a row is inserted or deleted from the table. This means that each index associated with a table must be modified whenever a row is inserted or deleted from the table, which can cause performance degradation if a table is associated with many indexes. The tradeoff of using multiple indexes is the time necessary for the DBMS to maintain each index.

Performance degradation can be minimized by using a publisher-consumer database design for applications where rows are frequently inserted, deleted, or modified, such as in an order processing system.

The publisher-consumer database design consists of two or more databases that contain the same information. One database, called the publisher, receives a request from the J2EE component to insert a new row, or modify or delete an existing row. J2EE components don't use the publisher to retrieve information; therefore, the publisher database isn't indexed.

A consumer database receives instructions to insert a new row, or modify or delete an existing row from the publisher. However, the consumer receives requests for information from a J2EE component. Therefore, the consumer database is indexed.

Once the publisher passes data to the consumer, the publisher is free to process the next incoming data, during which time the DBMS is updating the consumer's indexes. There are two major benefits to this design.

First, a bottleneck is avoided when many requests are received by the DBMS to insert new information or update existing information. This is because the publisher has two tasks to perform: insert or modify the database, then pass along those changes to the consumer.

The other benefit is that the database becomes scalable. This means that the database can be adjusted to handle an increased volume of requests. Let's say a company begins with the publisher and one consumer. Over time there is an increase in the number of requests for information, which can overwhelm the DBMS and cause performance degradation. This can be remedied by creating a second consumer and routing requests to one or the other consumer, reducing response time by half.

Clustered Keys

A clustered key is an index key whose value represents data contained in multiple columns of the corresponding table. Although there is only one column in the index to store the index key, that value can be a combination of data from multiple columns of the table.

Let's say a customer name is used as the index key. The customer name is composed of two data elements: the customer first name and the customer last name. Since there is only one column for the index key, the customer first name and the customer last name are concatenated into one value. That is, the DBMS takes one data element and places it behind the other data element to create a new data element that becomes the index key.

Let's say that the customer first name is Tom and last name is Jones. Here's what they look like when they are concatenated: **TomJones**. Notice there isn't a space between the first and last name. This is because concatenating places the character of the second value immediately following the last character of the first value.

Clustered keys add overhead to a DBMS because columns are delimited and the delimiter must be escaped if the delimiter appears in the data. This extra step might impede performance of the DBMS.

The DBMS treats the index key of a clustered index as it does any index key and uses a combination of trees and hashing algorithms to locate search criteria in the index.

Concatenating data elements

- Create an index key that uses two or more columns to uniquely identify rows in a table.
- Facilitate searching for values of multiple columns such as a customer name using one index.

Derived Keys

A derived key consists of a value that represents part of the value of a column rather than the entire value of the column. Let's say that an order number is comprised of three components. The first component represents the sales region within which the order was placed. The second component is the sales representative's number. And the last component is a unique number that identifies the order.

Although the order number appears in one column of the order table, a component of the order number can be used as an index key. For example, the DBMS can be instructed to derive an index key from the order number by using the first component. This means the index can be used to search for all orders placed within a region that is specified in the search criteria.

Selective Rows

Typically, all the rows in a table are represented in an index associated with that table. However, an index can be created that references a subset of rows in a table. The subset is determined when the index is created.

Let's return to the order number example used in the previous section to illustrate this feature. There might be tens of thousands of orders, each having a row in the order table and in indexes associated with the order table.

Suppose a J2EE component is used only to search for orders within a specified region. Never will there be an occasion for the component to search other than in the region. Indexes used for searches by the component can be limited to only rows of the table that contain orders placed within the region as identified by the first component of the order number. This means that the index does not contain any reference to rows in the order table that are outside the specified region.

There is a performance benefit that is realized by using an index that contains a subset of all the rows of the associated table. This is because rows that will never be searched are excluded from the index, thereby reducing the number of rows of the index that must be searched by the DBMS.

The boost in performance, however, is only realized in databases that contain huge numbers of rows. Little if any increase in performance is realized by creating a subset of rows in a typical database because many DBMSs have been optimized to search volumes of data without having to use a subset of rows in an index.

Using a conditional statement when creating an index, which you'll learn in the next two chapters, creates a subset. In the order number example, the conditional statement directs the DBMS to include rows in the index where the first component of the order number matches the conditional statement. All other rows are excluded from the index.

Exact Matches and Partial Matches

A DBMS can be instructed to use an index to find an exact or partial match to the search criteria. By default, the DBMS searches for exact matches whenever a query is received from a J2EE component. However, the programmer can construct the query to direct the DBMS to find partial matches, which you'll learn how to do in Chapter 7.

An exact match requires that all the characters of the search criteria match the index key. If a single character is mismatched, then the DBMS does not return data in the corresponding row of the table.

A partial match requires that some—not all—the characters of the index key match the search criteria. That is, if the first character of the search criteria and the index key are the same and the remaining characters are different, the DBMS stills considers it a match and returns data in the corresponding row of the table. Exact matches are used whenever a particular value and only that value is required, such as a specific customer number. Partial matches are used whenever someone is unsure of the exact value.

Let's say that a sales representative is looking for information about a customer, but she isn't sure if the customer last name is Johnson or Johnston. A search can be made using an index of customer names looking for any customer that has the first five letters of Johns and any other characters as their last name.

In this example, the customer name index is a concatenated index. The order in which values are concatenated plays a critical role when a DBMS searches for a partial match. This is because the DBMS begins matches left to right. Therefore, the most significant value must be placed first in the concatenated key.

The most significant value in the customer name is the customer last name because there are more people with the same first name than the same last name. Therefore, the index key is last name then first, such as **JohnstonMike**.

Searching for Phonetic Matches

Some DBMSs feature phonetic searches where the DBMS returns rows containing index keys that sound like the search value. This means that the DBMS stores both exact spelling and phonic spelling of the index key.

Phonetic searches are a valuable feature to look for in a DBMS, especially for use with databases used for customer service. Customer service typically must take bits and pieces of information provided by a customer, then assemble those pieces into meaningful search criteria.

Many times interactions with customers take place over the telephone where the customer service representative does not have access to printed materials (that is, invoices) that the customer has at hand.

This situation typically leads to miscommunication that aggravates a customer relationship. Although a phonetic search won't guarantee better communication between the customer service representative and the customer, it does give the customer service representative a tool with which to locate information necessary to properly respond to a customer.

Phonetic searches are made possible by an algorithm built in to the DBMS. The phonetic algorithm used by the DBMS defines each index key phonetically. Likewise, the DBMS converts the search criteria into its phonetic spelling before comparing the phonetic spelling of the search criteria to the phonetic spelling of the index key.

The Complete Reference

Chapter 6

JDBC Objects

Practically every J2EE application saves, retrieves, and manipulates information stored in a database using web services provided by a J2EE component. A J2EE component supplies database access using Java data objects contained in the JDBC application programming interface (API). Java data objects have methods that open a connection to a database management system (DBMS) and then transmit messages (queries) to insert, retrieve, modify, or delete data stored in a database.

The DBMS uses the same connection to send messages back to the J2EE component. These messages contain rows of data requested by the J2EE component or information indicating the status of the query being processed by the DBMS. Additional Java data objects are used to interact with data that is returned to the J2EE component by the DBMS.

This is the second of three chapters that focus on how to write a J2EE component to interact with a database. The previous chapter showed how to develop a database schema, which is the database design. This chapter shows how to use Java data objects to connect to the DBMS, send queries to the DBMS, and manipulate data returned by the DBMS. The next chapter shows how to use SQL to write queries that interact with DBMSs.

The Concept of JDBC

There are many industrial-strength DBMSs commercially available in the market. These include Oracle, DB2, Sybase, and many other popular brands. The challenge Sun Microsystems, Inc. faced in the late 1990s was to develop a way for Java developers to write high-level code that accesses all popular DBMSs.

One of the major obstacles for Sun Microsystems, Inc. to overcome was a language barrier. Each DBMS defined its own low-level way to interact with programs to access data stored in its databases. This meant low-level code written to communicate with an Oracle database might need to be rewritten to access a DB2 database.

Sun Microsystems, Inc. met the challenge in 1996 with the creation of the JDBC driver and the JDBC API. Both were created out of necessity, because until then Java wasn't considered an industrial-strength programming language since Java was unable to access DBMSs.

The JDBC driver developed by Sun Microsystems, Inc. wasn't a driver at all. It was a specification that described the detail functionality of a JDBC driver. DBMS manufacturers and third-party vendors were encouraged to build JDBC drivers that conformed to Sun Microsystems, Inc.'s specifications. Those firms that built JDBC drivers for their products could tap into the growing Java applications market.

The specifications required a JDBC driver to be a translator that converted low-level proprietary DBMS messages to low-level messages understood by the JDBC API, and vice versa.

This meant Java programmers could use high-level Java data objects defined in the JDBC API to write a routine that interacted with the DBMS. Java data objects convert the routine into low-level messages that conform to the JDBC driver specification and send them to the JDBC driver. The JDBC driver translates the routine into low-level messages that are understood and processed by the DBMS.

JDBC drivers created by DBMS manufacturers have to

- Open a connection between the DBMS and the J2EE component.
- Translate low-level equivalents of SQL statements sent by the J2EE component into messages that can be processed by the DBMS.
- Return data that conforms to the JDBC specification to the JDBC driver.
- Return information such as error messages that conforms to the JDBC specification to the JDBC driver.
- Provide transaction management routines that conform to the JDBC specification.
- Close the connection between the DBMS and the J2EE component.

The JDBC driver makes J2EE components database independent, which complements Java's philosophy of platform independence. Today there are JDBC drivers for nearly every commercial DBMS, and they are available from the Sun Microsystems, Inc. web site (www.sun.com) or from the DBMS manufacturer's web site.

Java code independence is also extended to implementation of the SQL queries. SQL queries are passed from the JDBC API through the JDBC driver to the DBMS without validation. This means it is the responsibility of the DBMS to implement SQL statements contained in the query.

JDBC Driver Types

JDBC driver specification classifies JDBC drivers into four groups. Each group is referred to as a JDBC driver type and addresses a specific need for communicating with various DBMSs. The JDBC driver types are as follows:

Type 1 JDBC-to-ODBC Driver

Microsoft was the first company to devise a way to create a DBMS-independent database program when they created the Open Database Connection (ODBC). ODBC is the basis from which Sun Microsystems, Inc. created JDBC. Both ODBC and JDBC have similar driver specifications and an API. The JDBC-to-ODBC driver, also called the JDBC/ODBC Bridge, is used to translate DBMS calls between the JDBC specification and the ODBC specification. The JDBC-to-ODBC driver receives messages from a J2EE component that conforms to the JDBC specification as discussed previously in this chapter. Those messages are translated by the JDBC-to-ODBC driver into the ODBC message format, which is then translated into the message format understood by the DBMS. However, avoid using the JDBC/ODBC Bridge in a mission-critical application because the extra translation might negatively impact performance.

Type 2 Java/Native Code Driver

The Java/Native Code driver uses Java classes to generate platform-specific code—that is, code only understood by a specific DBMS. The manufacturer of the DBMS provides both the Java/Native Code driver and API classes so the J2EE component can generate the platform-specific code. The obvious disadvantage of using a Java/Native Code driver is the loss of some portability of code. The API classes for the Java/Native Code driver probably won't work with another manufacturer's DBMS.

Type 3 JDBC Driver

The Type 3 JDBC driver, also referred to as the Java Protocol, is the most commonly used JDBC driver. The Type 3 JDBC driver converts SQL queries into JDBC-formatted statements. The JDBC-formatted statements are translated into the format required by the DBMS.

Type 4 JDBC Driver

Type 4 JDBC driver is also known as the Type 4 database protocol. This driver is similar to the Type 3 JDBC driver except SQL queries are translated into the format required by the DBMS. SQL queries do not need to be converted to JDBC-formatted systems. This is the fastest way to communicate SQL queries to the DBMS.

JDBC Packages

The JDBC API is contained in two packages. The first package is called `java.sql` and contains core Java data objects of the JDBC API. These include Java data objects that provide the basics for connecting to the DBMS and interacting with data stored in the DBMS. `java.sql` is part of the J2SE.

The other package that contains the JDBC API is `javax.sql`, which extends `java.sql` and is in the J2EE. Included in the `javax.sql` package are Java data objects that interact with Java Naming and Directory Interface (JNDI) and Java data objects that manage connection pooling, among other advanced JDBC features.

A Brief Overview of the JDBC Process

Although each J2EE component is different, J2EE components use a similar process for interacting with a DBMS. This process is divided into five routines. These include:

- Loading the JDBC driver
- Connecting to the DBMS
- Creating and executing a statement
- Processing data returned by the DBMS
- Terminating the connection with the DBMS

It is sometimes better to get a general understanding of how the process works before delving into the details of each routine of the process. Therefore, the next few sections of this chapter provide an overview of the process and each routine. A more detailed discussion of each routine is provided later in this chapter.

Loading the JDBC Driver

The JDBC driver must be loaded before the J2EE component can connect to the DBMS. The Class.forName() method is used to load the JDBC driver. Suppose a developer wants to work offline and write a J2EE component that interacts with Microsoft Access on the developer's PC. The developer must write a routine that loads the JDBC/ODBC Bridge driver called sun.jdbc.odbc.JdbcOdbcDriver. The driver is loaded by calling the Class.forName() method and passing it the name of the driver, as shown in the following code segment:

```
Class.forName( "sun.jdbc.odbc.JdbcOdbcDriver");
```

Connect to the DBMS

Once the driver is loaded, the J2EE component must connect to the DBMS using the DriverManager.getConnection() method. The java.sql.DriverManager class is the highest class in the java.sql hierarchy and is responsible for managing driver information.

The DriverManager.getConnection() method is passed the URL of the database, and the user ID and password if required by the DBMS. The URL is a String object that contains the driver name and the name of the database that is being accessed by the J2EE component.

The DriverManager.getConnection() method returns a Connection interface that is used throughout the process to reference the database. The java.sql.Connection interface is another member of the java.sql package that manages communication between the driver and the J2EE component. It is the java.sql.Connection interface that sends statements to the DBMS for processing. Listing 6-1 illustrates the use of the DriverManager.getConnection() method to load the JDBC/ODBC Bridge and connect to the CustomerInformation database.

Listing 6-1
Open a connection with a database.

```
String url = "jdbc:odbc:CustomerInformation";
String userID = "jim";
String password = "keogh";
Statement DataRequest;
private Connection Db;
try {
   Class.forName( "sun.jdbc.odbc.JdbcOdbcDriver");
   Db = DriverManager.getConnection(url,userID,password);
}
```

J2EE DATABASES

Create and Execute a SQL Statement

The next step, after the JDBC driver is loaded and connection is successfully made with a particular database managed by the DBMS, is to send a SQL query to the DBMS for processing. A SQL query consists of a series of SQL commands that direct the DBMS to do something such as to return rows of data to the J2EE component. You'll learn how to write queries in the next chapter.

The Connect.createStatement() method is used to create a Statement object. The Statement object is then used to execute a query and return a ResultSet object that contains the response from the DBMS, which is usually one or more rows of information requested by the J2EE component.

Typically, the query is assigned to a String object, which is passed to the Statement object's executeQuery() method, which is illustrated in the next code segment. Once the ResultSet is received from the DBMS, the close() method is called to terminate the statement. Listing 6-2 retrieves all the rows and columns from the Customers table.

Listing 6-2
Retrieves all the rows from the Customers table.

```
Statement DataRequest;
ResultSet Results;
try {
        String query = "SELECT * FROM Customers";
        DataRequest = Database.createStatement();
        DataRequest = Db.createStatement();
        Results = DataRequest.executeQuery (query);
        DataRequest.close();
  }
```

Process Data Returned by the DBMS

The java.sql.ResultSet object is assigned the results received from the DBMS after the query is processed. The java.sql.ResultSet object consists of methods used to interact with data that is returned by the DBMS to the J2EE component.

Later in this chapter you'll learn the details of using the java.sql.ResultSet object. However, the following code is an abbreviated example that gives you a preview of a commonly used routine used to extract data returned by the DBMS. Error-catching code is purposely removed from this example in order to minimize code clutter. You'll find the completed version of this routine later in this chapter and throughout Chapter 7.

Assume for Listing 6-3 that a J2EE component requested customers' first names and last names from a table. The result returned by the DBMS is already assigned to the ResultSet object called Results. The first time that the next() method of the ResultSet is called, the ResultSet pointer is positioned at the first row in the ResultSet and returns a boolean value that if false indicates that no rows are present in the ResultSet. The if statement in Listing 6-3 traps this condition and displays the "End of data" message on the screen.

However, a true value returned by the next() method means at least one row of data is present in the ResultSet, which causes the code to enter the do...while loop. The getString() method of the ResultSet object is used to copy the value of a specified column in the current row of the ResultSet to a String object. The getString() method is passed the name of the column in the ResultSet whose content needs to be copied, and the getString() method returns the value from the specified column.

You could also pass the number of the column to the getString() method instead of passing the column number. However, do so only if the columns are specifically named in the SELECT statement; otherwise, you cannot be sure of the order in which the columns appear in the ResultSet, especially because the table might be reorganized since the table was created and therefore the columns might be rearranged.

In Listing 6-3, the first column of the ResultSet contains the customer's first name and the second column contains the customer's last name. Both of these are concatenated in this example and assigned to the printrow String object, which is displayed on the screen. This process continues until the next() method, called as the conditional argument to the while statement, returns a false, which means the pointer is at the end of the ResultSet.

Listing 6-3
Retrieving data from the ResultSet.

```
ResultSet Results;
String FirstName;
String LastName;
String printrow;
boolean Records = Results.next();
if (!Records ) {
   System.out.println( "No data returned");
   return;
}
else
{
 do {
   FirstName = Results.getString (FirstName) ;
   LastName = Results.getString (LastName) ;
   printrow = FirstName + " " + LastName;
   System.out.println(printrow);
 } while ( Results.next() );
}
```

Terminate the Connection to the DBMS

The connection to the DBMS is terminated by using the close() method of the Connection object once the J2EE component is finished accessing the DBMS. The close() method throws an exception if a problem is encountered when disengaging the DBMS. You'll learn how to handle this exception later in this chapter. The following is an example of calling the close() method. Although closing the database connection automatically closes the ResultSet, it is better to close the ResultSet explicitly before closing the connection.

```
Db.close();
```

Database Connection

A J2EE component does not directly connect to a DBMS. Instead, the J2EE component connects with the JDBC driver that is associated with the DBMS. However, before this connection is made, the JDBC driver must be loaded and registered with the DriverManager as mentioned previously in this chapter.

The purpose of loading and registering the JDBC driver is to bring the JDBC driver into the Java Virtual Machine (JVM). The JDBC driver is automatically registered with the DriverManager once the JDBC driver is loaded and is therefore available to the JVM and can be used by J2EE components.

The Class.forName() method, as illustrated in Listing 6-4, is used to load the JDBC driver. In this example, the JDBC/ODBC Bridge is the driver that is being loaded. You can replace the JDBC/ODBC Bridge with the appropriate JDBC driver for the DBMS being used in your J2EE application.

The Class.forName() method throws a ClassNotFoundException if an error occurs when loading the JDBC driver. Errors are trapped using the catch{} block whenever the JDBC driver is being loaded.

Listing 6-4
Load the driver and catch any exceptions that might be thrown during the process.

```
try {
    Class.forName( "sun.jdbc.odbc.JdbcOdbcDriver");
}
catch (ClassNotFoundException error) {
    System.err.println("Unable to load the JDBC/ODBC bridge." + error.getMessage());
    System.exit(1);
}
```

The Connection

After the JDBC driver is successfully loaded and registered, the J2EE component must connect to the database. The database must be associated with the JDBC driver, which is usually performed by either the database administrator or the systems administrator. Some students who are learning JDBC programming prefer to use Microsoft Access as the DBMS because the DBMS is usually available on the student's local computer. The "Associating the JDBC/ODBC Bridge with the Database" section shows how to associate the JDBC/ODBC Bridge with a Microsoft Access database.

The data source that the JDBC component will connect to is defined using the URL format. The URL consists of three parts. These are

- ■ **jdbc**   which indicates that the JDBC protocol is to be used to read the URL.
- ■ **<subprotocol>**   which is the JDBC driver name.
- ■ **<subname>**   which is the name of the database.

The connection to the database is established by using one of three getConnection() methods of the DriverManager object. The getConnection() method requests access to the database from the DBMS. It is up to the DBMS to grant or reject access. A Connection object is returned by the getConnection() method if access is granted; otherwise, the getConnection() method throws a SQLException.

Sometimes the DBMS grants access to a database to anyone. In this case, the J2EE component uses the getConnection(String url) method. One parameter is passed to the method because the DBMS only needs the database identified. This is shown in Listing 6-5.

J2EE DATABASES

Listing 6-5
Connecting to a database using only the URL.

```
String url = "jdbc:odbc:CustomerInformation";
Statement DataRequest;
Connection Db;
try {
   Class.forName( "sun.jdbc.odbc.JdbcOdbcDriver");
   Db = DriverManager.getConnection(url);
}
catch (ClassNotFoundException error) {
    System.err.println("Unable to load the JDBC/ODBC bridge." + error);
    System.exit(1);
}
catch (SQLException error) {
    System.err.println("Cannot connect to the database." + error);
    System.exit(2);
}
```

Other databases limit access to authorized users and require the J2EE to supply a user ID and password with the request to access the database. In this case, the J2EE component uses the getConnection(String url, String user, String password) method as illustrated in Listing 6-6.

Listing 6-6
Connecting to a database using a user ID and password.

```
String url = "jdbc:odbc:CustomerInformation";
String userID = "jim";
String password = "keogh";
Statement DataRequest;
Connection Db;
try {
   Class.forName( "sun.jdbc.odbc.JdbcOdbcDriver");
```

```
        Db = DriverManager.getConnection(url,userID,password);
  }
catch (ClassNotFoundException error) {
      System.err.println("Unable to load the JDBC/ODBC bridge." + error);
      System.exit(1);
}
catch (SQLException error) {
      System.err.println("Cannot connect to the database." + error);
      System.exit(2);
}
```

There might be occasions when a DBMS requires information besides a user ID and password before the DBMS grants access to the database. This additional information is referred to as properties and must be associated with a Properties object, which is passed to the DBMS as a getConnection() parameter.

Typically, properties used to access a database are stored in a text file, the contents of which are defined by the DBMS manufacturer. The J2EE component uses a FileInputStream object to open the file and then uses the Properties object load() method to copy the properties into a Properties object. This is illustrated in Listing 6-7. Notice that the third version of the getConnection() method passes the Properties object and the URL as parameters to the getConnection() method.

Listing 6-7
Using properties to connect to the database.

```
Connection Db;
Properties props = new Properties ();
try {
FileInputStream propFileStream = new fileInputStream("DBProps.txt";);
props.load(propFileStream);
}
catch(IOException err) {
    System.err.print("Error loading propFile: ");
    System.err.println (err.getMessage());
    System.exit(1);
}
try {
    Class.forName( "sun.jdbc.odbc.JdbcOdbcDriver");
    Db = DriverManager.getConnection(url, props);
}
catch (ClassNotFoundException error) {
      System.err.println("Unable to load the JDBC/ODBC bridge." + error);
      System.exit(2);
}
catch (SQLException error) {
      System.err.println("Cannot connect to the database." + error);
      System.exit(3);
}
```

TimeOut

Competition to use the same database is a common occurrence in the J2EE environment and can lead to performance degradation of a J2EE application. For example, a J2EE application that needs database access requests service from an appropriate J2EE component. In turn, the J2EE component attempts to connect to the database.

However, the DBMS may not respond quickly for a number of reasons, which might include that database connections are not available. Rather than wait for a delayed response from the DBMS, the J2EE component can set a timeout period after which the DriverManager will cease to attempt to connect to the database.

The public static void DriverManager.setLoginTimeout(int seconds) method can be used by the J2EE component to establish the maximum time the DriverManager waits for a response from a DBMS before timing out.

Likewise, the public static int DriverManager.getLoginTimeout() method is used to retrieve from the DriverManager the maximum time the DriverManager is set to wait until it times out. The DriverManager.getLoginTimeout() method returns an int that represents seconds.

Associating the JDBC/ODBC Bridge with the Database

You use the ODBC Data Source Administrator to create the association between the database and the JDBC/ODBC bridge. Here's what you need to do:

1. Select Start | Settings, and then the Control Panel.

2. Select ODBC 32 to display the ODBC Data Source Administrator.

3. Add a new user by selecting the Add button.

4. Select the driver then select Finish. Use the Microsoft Access Driver if you are using Microsoft Access; otherwise, select the driver for the DBMS that you are using. If you don't find the driver for your DBMS on the list, you'll need to install the driver. Contact the manufacturer of the DBMS for more information on how to obtain the driver.

5. Enter the name of the database as the Data Source name in the ODBC Microsoft Access Setup dialog box. This is the name that will be used within your Java database program to connect to the DBMS.

6. Enter a description for the data source. This is optional, but will be a reminder of the kind of data that is stored in the database.

7. Click the Select button. You'll be prompted to browse the directory of each hard drive connected to your computer in order to define the direct path to the database. Click OK once you locate the database, and the directory path and the name of the database will be displayed in the ODBC Microsoft Access Setup dialog box.

8. Since this is your database, you can determine if a login name and password is required to access the database.

9. If so, then click the Advanced button to display the Set Advanced Options dialog box. This dialog box is used to assign a login name, also referred to as a user ID, and a password to the database. Select OK. If not, then skip this step.

10. When the ODBC Microsoft Access Setup dialog box appears, select OK.

11. Select OK to close the ODBC Data Source Administrator dialog box.

Connection Pool

Connecting to a database is performed on a per-client basis. That is, each client must open its own connection to a database and the connection cannot be shared with unrelated clients, which is a serous drawback in the J2EE environment.

For example, a client that needs to frequently interact with a database must either open a connection and leave the connection open during processing, or open or close and reconnect each time the client needs to access the database.

Leaving a connection open might prevent another client from accessing the database should the DBMS have available a limited number of connections. Connecting and reconnecting is simply time-consuming and causes performance degradation.

The release of the JDBC 2.1 Standard Extension API introduced connection pooling to address the problem. A connection pool is a collection of database connections that are opened once and loaded into memory so these connections can be reused without having to reconnect to the DBMS.

Clients use the DataSource interface to interact with the connection pool. The connection pool itself is implemented by the application server, which hides from the client details on how the connection pool is maintained.

There are two types of connections made to the database. The first is the physical connection, which is made by the application server using PooledConnection objects. PooledConnection objects are cached and reused.

The other type of connection is the logical connection. A logical connection is made by a client calling the DataSource.getConnection() method, which connects to a PooledConnection object that already has a physical connection to the database.

Listing 6-8 illustrates how to access a connection from a connection pool. A connection pool is accessible by using the Java Naming and Directory Interface (JNDI), which you'll learn about in Chapter 16. JNDI provides a uniform way to find and access naming and directory services independent of any specific naming or directory service.

First a J2EE component must obtain a handle to the JNDI context, which is illustrated in the first statement in this code segment. Next, the JNDI lookup() method is called and is passed the name of the connection pool, which returns the DataSource object called pool in this example. The getConnection() method of the DataSource object is then called, as illustrated earlier in this chapter. The getConnection() returns the logical connection to the database, which is used by the J2EE component to access the database.

The close() method of the DataSource object is called once when the J2EE component is finished accessing the database. The close() method closes the logical connection to the database and not the physical database connection. This means that the same physical connection can be used by the next J2EE component that needs access to the database.

Listing 6-8
Connecting
to a
database
using
a pool
connection.

```
Context ctext = new InitialContext();
DataSource pool = (DataSource)
ctext.lookup("java:comp/env/jdbc/pool");
Connection db = pool.getConnection();
// Place code to interact with the database here
db.close();
```

Statement Objects

Once a connection to the database is opened, the J2EE component creates and sends a query to access data contained in the database. The query is written using SQL, which you'll learn about in the next chapter.

One of three types of Statement objects is used to execute the query. These objects are Statement, which executes a query immediately; PreparedStatement, which is used to execute a compiled query; and CallableStatement, which is used to execute store procedures.

The Statement Object

The Statement object is used whenever a J2EE component needs to immediately execute a query without first having the query compiled. The Statement object contains the executeQuery() method, which is passed the query as an argument. The query is then transmitted to the DBMS for processing.

The executeQuery() method returns one ResultSet object that contains rows, columns, and metadata that represent data requested by query. The ResultSet object also contains methods that are used to manipulate data in the ResultSet, which you'll learn about later in this chapter.

The execute() method of the Statement object is used when there may be multiple results returned. A third commonly used method of the Statement object is the executeUpdate() method. The executeUpdate() method is used to execute queries that contain UPDATE and DELETE SQL statements, which changes values in a row and removes a row respectively. The executeUpdate() method returns an integer indicating the number of rows that were updated by the query. The executeUpdate() is used to INSERT, UPDATE, DELETE, and DDL statements.

Listing 6-9 is an enhanced version of Listing 6-2, used previously in this chapter to illustrate how to open a database connection. The enhancements are to create a query, execute the query, and return a ResultSet.

Two new objects are declared in Listing 6-9: a Statement object called DataRequest and a ResultSet object called Results. In the second try{ } block, the query is assigned to the String object query. The query requests the DBMS to return all the rows from the Customer table of the CustomerInformation database.

Next, the createStatement() method of the Connection object is called to return a Statement object. The executeQuery() method of the Statement object is passed the query and returns a ResultSet object that contains data returned by the DBMS. Finally, the close() method of the Statement object is called to close the statement.

The close() method closes all instances of the ResultSet object returned by the Statement. Failure to call the close() method might cause resources used by the Statement object to remain unavailable to other J2EE components until the garbage routine is automatically run. Java statements used to manipulate the ResultSet is placed between the call to the executeQuery() method and the close() method.

The executeQuery() method throws an SQLException should an error occur during the processing of the query. For example, the query may contain syntax not understood by the DBMS. In this case, the DBMS returns a SQL error message that is passed along to the J2EE component by the executeQuery() method.

Listing 6-9
Using the Statement object to execute a query.

```
String url = "jdbc:odbc:CustomerInformation";
String userID = "jim";
String password = "keogh";
Statement DataRequest;
ResultSet Results;
Connection Db;
try {
   Class.forName( "sun.jdbc.odbc.JdbcOdbcDriver");
   Db = DriverManager.getConnection(url,userID,password);
 }
catch (ClassNotFoundException error) {
    System.err.println("Unable to load the JDBC/ODBC bridge." + error);
    System.exit(1);
}
catch (SQLException error) {
    System.err.println("Cannot connect to the database." + error);
    System.exit(2);
}
try {
    String query = "SELECT * FROM Customers";
    DataRequest = Db.createStatement();
    Results = DataRequest.executeQuery (query);
    //Place code here to interact with the ResultSet
    DataRequest.close();
 }

catch ( SQLException error ){
    System.err.println("SQL error." + error);
```

```
        System.exit(3);
    }
    Db.close();
```

Listing 6-10 illustrates how to use the executeUpdate() method of the Statement object. You'll notice that Listing 6-10 is nearly identical to Listing 6-9. However, the query updates a value in the database rather than requesting that data be returned to the J2EE component. You'll learn more about how to write queries to update values in a database in the next chapter.

Three changes are made to Listing 6-9 to illustrate the executeUpdate() method of the Statement object. First, the declaration of the ResultSet object is replaced with the declaration of an int called rowsUpdated.

Next, the query is changed. The SQL UPDATE command directs the DBMS to update the Customers table of the CustomerInformation database. The value of the PAID column of the Customers table is changed to 'Y' if the value of the BALANCE column is zero.

Finally, the executeUpdate() method replaces the executeQuery() method and is passed the query. The number of rows that are updated by the query is returned to the executeUpdate() method by the DBMS and is then assigned to the rowsUpdated int, which can be used for many purposes within the J2EE component such as sending a confirmation notice to the J2EE application that requested database access.

Listing 6-10
Using the execute Update() method.

```java
String url = "jdbc:odbc:CustomerInformation";
String userID = "jim";
String password = "keogh";
Statement DataRequest;
Connection Db;
int rowsUpdated;
try {
    Class.forName( "sun.jdbc.odbc.JdbcOdbcDriver");
    Db = DriverManager.getConnection(url,userID,password);
 }
catch (ClassNotFoundException error) {
    System.err.println("Unable to load the JDBC/ODBC bridge." + error);
    System.exit(1);
}
catch (SQLException error) {
    System.err.println("Cannot connect to the database." + error);
    System.exit(2);
}
try {
    String query = "UPDATE Customers SET PAID='Y' WHERE BALANCE = '0';
    DataRequest = Db.createStatement();
    rowsUpdated = DataRequest.executeUpdate (query);
    DataRequest.close();
```

```
    }
catch ( SQLException error ){
    System.err.println("SQL error." + error);
    System.exit(3);
}
Db.close();
```

PreparedStatement Object

A SQL query must be compiled before the DBMS processes the query. Compiling occurs after one of the Statement object's execution methods is called. Compiling a query is an overhead that is acceptable if the query is called once. However, the compiling process can become an expensive overhead if the query is executed several times by the same instance of the J2EE component during the same session.

A SQL query can be precompiled and executed by using the PreparedStatement object. In this case, the query is constructed similar to queries that were illustrated previously in the chapter. However, a question mark is used as a placeholder for a value that is inserted into the query after the query is compiled. It is this value that changes each time the query is executed.

Listing 6-11 illustrates how to use the PreparedStatement object. Listing 6-11 is very similar to Listing 6-9 in the Statement object that returned information from the Customers table.

However, the query directs the DBMS to return all customer information where the customer number equals the customer number specified in the query. Notice that that query has a question mark as the value of the customer number. The question mark is a placeholder for the value of the customer number that will be inserted into the precompiled query later in the code.

The preparedStatement() method of the Connection object is called to return the PreparedStatement object. The preparedStatement() method is passed the query, which is then precompiled.

The setxxx() method of the PreparedStatement object is used to replace the question mark with the value passed to the setxxx() method. There are a number of setxxx() methods available in the PreparedStatement object, each of which specifies the data type of the value that is being passed to the setxxx() method (see the "Data Types" section later in this chapter). In Listing 6-11, the setString() method is used because the customer number is being passed as a string.

The setxxx() requires two parameters. The first parameter is an integer that identifies the position of the question mark placeholder and the second parameter is the value that replaces the question mark placeholder. In Listing 6-11, the first question mark placeholder is replaced with the value of the second parameter.

Next, the executeQuery() method of the PreparedStatement object is called. The executeQuery() statement doesn't require a parameter because the query that is to be executed is already associated with the PreparedStatement object.

The advantage of using the PreparedStatement object is that the query is precompiled once and the setxxx() method called as needed to change the specified values of the query without having to recompile the query. The PreparedStatement object also has an execute() method and an executeUpdate() method, as described in the previous section.

The precompiling is performed by the DBMS and is referred to as "late binding." When the DBMS receives the request, the DBMS attempts to match the query to a previously compiled query. If found, then parameters passed to the query using the setxxx() methods are bound and the query is executed. If not found, then the query is compiled and retained by the DBMS for later use.

The JDBC driver passes two parameters to the DBMS. One parameter is the query and the other is an array of late binding variables. Both binding and compiling is performed by the DBMS. The late binding is not associated with the specific object or code block where the preparedStatmenet() is declared.

Listing 6-11
Using the
Prepared
Statement
object.

```
String url = "jdbc:odbc:CustomerInformation";
String userID = "jim";
String password = "keogh";
ResultSet Results;
Connection Db;
try {
   Class.forName( "sun.jdbc.odbc.JdbcOdbcDriver");
   Db = DriverManager.getConnection(url,userID,password);
 }
catch (ClassNotFoundException error) {
      System.err.println("Unable to load the JDBC/ODBC bridge." + error);
      System.exit(1);
}
catch (SQLException error) {
      System.err.println("Cannot connect to the database." + error);
      System.exit(2);
}
try {
      String query = "SELECT * FROM Customers WHERE CustNumber = ?";
      PreparedStatement pstatement = Db.preparedStatement(query);
      pstatement.setString(1, "123");
      Results = pstatement.executeQuery ();
      //Place code here to interact with the ResultSet
      pstatement.close();
 }
catch ( SQLException error ){
     System.err.println("SQL error." + error);
      System.exit(3);
}
Db.close();
```

CallableStatement

The CallableStatement object is used to call a stored procedure from within a J2EE object. A stored procedure is a block of code and is identified by a unique name. The type and style of code depends on the DMBS vendor and can be written in PL/SQL, Transact-SQL, C, or another programming language. The stored procedure is executed by invoking the name of the stored procedure.

The CallableStatement object uses three types of parameters when calling a stored procedure. These parameters are IN, OUT, and INOUT. The IN parameter contains any data that needs to be passed to the stored procedure and whose value is assigned using the setxxx() method as described in the previous section.

The OUT parameter contains the value returned by the stored procedures, if any. The OUT parameter must be registered using the registerOutParameter() method and then is later retrieved by the J2EE component using the getxxx() method.

The INOUT parameter is a single parameter that is used to both pass information to the stored procedure and retrieve information from a stored procedure using the techniques described in the previous two paragraphs.

Listing 6-12 illustrates how to call a stored procedure and retrieve a value returned by the stored procedure. Listing 6-12 is similar to other listings used in this chapter, but has been modified slightly to call a stored procedure.

The first statement in the second try{} block creates a query that calls the stored procedure LastOrderNumber, which retrieves the most recently used order number. The stored procedure requires one parameter that is represented by a question mark placeholder. This parameter is an OUT parameter that will contain the last order number following the execution of the stored procedure.

Next, the preparedCall() method of the Connection object is called and is passed the query. This method returns a CallableStatement object, which is called cstatement. Since an OUT parameter is used by the stored procedure, the parameter must be registered using the registerOutParameter() of the CallableStatement object.

The registerOutParameter() method requires two parameters. The first parameter is an integer that represents the number of the parameter, which is 1—meaning the first parameter of the stored procedure. The second parameter to the registerOutParameter() is the data type of the value returned by the stored procedure, which is Types.VARCHAR.

The execute() method of the CallableStatement object is called next to execute the query. The execute() method doesn't require the name of the query because the query is already identified when the CallableStatement object is returned by the prepareCall() query method.

After the stored procedure is executed, the getString() method is called to return the value of the specified parameter of the stored procedure, which in this example is the last order number.

Listing 6-12
Calling a
stored
procedure.

```
String url = "jdbc:odbc:CustomerInformation";
String userID = "jim";
```

```
String password = "keogh";
String lastOrderNumber;
Connection Db;
try {
   Class.forName( "sun.jdbc.odbc.JdbcOdbcDriver");
   Db = DriverManager.getConnection(url,userID,password);
 }
catch (ClassNotFoundException error) {
    System.err.println("Unable to load the JDBC/ODBC bridge." + error);
    System.exit(1);
}
catch (SQLException error) {
    System.err.println("Cannot connect to the database." + error);
    System.exit(2);
}
try {
    String query = "{ CALL LastOrderNumber (?)}";
    CallableStatement cstatement = Db.prepareCall(query);
    cstatement.registerOutParameter(1, Types. VARCHAR);
    cstatement.execute();
                    lastOrderNumber = cstatement.getString(1);
    cstatement.close();
 }
catch ( SQLException error ){
    System.err.println("SQL error." + error);
    System.exit(3);
}
Db.close();
```

ResultSet

As you'll remember from previous sections in this chapter, a query is used to update, delete, and retrieve information stored in a database. The executeQuery() method is used to send the query to the DBMS for processing and returns a ResultSet object that contains data that was requested by the query.

The ResultSet object contains methods that are used to copy data from the ResultSet into a Java collection object or variable for further processing. Data in a ResultSet object is logically organized into a virtual table consisting of rows and columns. In addition to data, the ResultSet object also contains metadata such as column names, column size, and column data type.

The ResultSet uses a virtual cursor to point to a row of the virtual table. A J2EE component must move the virtual cursor to each row and then use other methods of the ResultSet object to interact with the data stored in columns of that row.

The virtual cursor is positioned above the first row of data when the ResultSet is returned by the executeQuery() method. This means that the virtual cursor must be moved to the first row using the next() method. The next() method returns a boolean true if the row contains data; otherwise, a boolean false is returned indicating that no more rows exist in the ResultSet.

Once the virtual cursor points to a row, the getxxx() method is used to copy data from the row to a collection, object, or variable. As illustrated previously in this chapter, the getxxx() method is data type specific. For example, the getString() method is used to copy String data from a column of the ResultSet. The data type of the getxxx() method must be the same data type as the column in the ResultSet.

The getxxx() method requires one parameter, which is an integer that represents the number of the column that contains the data. For example, getString(1) copies the data from the first column of the ResultSet.

Columns appear in the ResultSet in the order in which column names appeared in the SELECT statement in the query. Let's say a query contained the following SELECT statement: SELECT CustomerFirstName, CustomerLastName FROM Customer. This query directs the DBMS to return two columns. The first column contains customer first names and the second column contains customer last names. Therefore, getString(1) returns data in the customer first-name column of the current row in the ResultSet.

Reading The ResultSet

Listing 6-13 illustrates a commonly used routine to read values from a ResultSet into variables that can later be further processed by the J2EE component. Listing 6-13 is based on previous code segments in this chapter.

Once a successful connection is made to the database, a query is defined in the second try{} block to retrieve the first name and last name of customers from the Customers table of the CustomerInformation database.

The next() method of the ResultSet is called to move the virtual pointer to the first row in the ResultSet. If there is data in that row, the next() returns a true, which is assigned the boolean variable Records. If there isn't any data in that row, Records is assigned a false value. A false value is trapped by the if statement where the "End of data" message is displayed and the program terminates.

A true value causes the program to enter the do...while in the third try{} block where the getString() method is called to retrieve values in the first and second columns of the ResultSet, which corresponds to the first name and last name. These values are assigned to their corresponding String object, which is then concatenated and assigned the printrow String object and printed on the screen.

The next() method is called in the while statement to move the virtual cursor to the next row in the ResultSet and determine if there is data in that row. If so, statements within the do...while loop are executed again. If not, the program breaks out of the look and executes the close() statement to close the Statement object, as is discussed previously in this chapter.

Listing 6-13
Reading data from the ResultSet.

```
String url = "jdbc:odbc:CustomerInformation";
String userID = "jim";
```

```
String password = "keogh";
String printrow;
String FirstName;
String LastName;
Statement DataRequest;
ResultSet Results;
Connection Db;
try {
   Class.forName( "sun.jdbc.odbc.JdbcOdbcDriver");
   Db = DriverManager.getConnection(url,userID,password);
 }
catch (ClassNotFoundException error) {
      System.err.println("Unable to load the JDBC/ODBC bridge." + error);
      System.exit(1);
}
catch (SQLException error) {
      System.err.println("Cannot connect to the database." + error);
      System.exit(2);
}
try {
      String query = "SELECT FirstName,LastName FROM Customers";
      DataRequest = Db.createStatement();
      Results = DataRequest.executeQuery (query);
}
catch ( SQLException error ){
      System.err.println("SQL error." + error);
       System.exit(3);
}
boolean Records = Results.next();

if (!Records ) {
   System.out.println("No data returned");
   System.exit(4);
}
try {
  do {
     FirstName = Results.getString ( 1 ) ;
      LastName = Results.getString ( 2 ) ;

      printrow = FirstName + " " + LastName;
     System.out.println(printrow);

  } while (Results.next() );
  DataRequest.close();
}
catch (SQLException error ) {
   System.err.println("Data display error." + error);
   System.exit(5);
}
```

Scrollable ResultSet

Until the release of the JDBC 2.1 API, the virtual cursor could only be moved down the ResultSet object. But today the virtual cursor can be moved backwards or even positioned at a specific row. The JDBC 2.1 API also enables a J2EE component to specify the number of rows to return from the DBMS.

There are six methods of the ResultSet object that are used to position the virtual cursor in addition to the next() method discussed in the previous section. These are first(), last(), previous(), absolute(), relative(), and getRow().

The first() method moves the virtual cursor to the first row in the ResultSet. Likewise, the last() method positions the virtual cursor at the last row in the ResultSet. The previous() method moves the virtual cursor to the previous row. The absolute() method positions the virtual cursor at the row number specified by the integer passed as a parameter to the absolute() method.

The relative() method moves the virtual cursor the specified number of rows contained in the parameter. The parameter is a positive or negative integer where the sign represents the direction the virtual cursor is moved.

For example, a -4 moves the virtual cursor back four rows from the current row. Likewise, a 5 moves the virtual cursor forward five rows from the current row. And the getRow() method returns an integer that represents the number of the current row in the ResultSet.

The Statement object that is created using the createStatement() of the Connection object must be set up to handle a scrollable ResultSet by passing the createStatement() method one of three constants. These constants are TYPE_FORWARD_ONLY, TYPE_SCROLL_INSENSITIVE, and TYPE_SCROLL_SENSITIVE.

The TYPE_FORWARD_ONLY constant restricts the virtual cursor to downward movement, which is the default setting. The TYPE_SCROLL_INSENSITIVE, and TYPE_SCROLL_SENSITIVE constants permit the virtual cursor to move in both directions. The TYPE_SCROLL_INSENSITIVE constant makes the ResultSet insensitive to changes made by another J2EE component to data in the table whose rows are reflected in the ResultSet. The TYPE_SCROLL_SENSITIVE constant makes the ResultSet sensitive to those changes.

Listing 6-14 illustrates how to reposition the virtual cursor in the ResultSet. This listing is a modification of the previous code segments used as examples in this chapter that retrieve customers' first names and last names from the Customers table of the CustomerInformation database.

Since Listing 6-14 moves the virtual cursor in multiple directions, the TYPE_SCROLL_INSENSITIVE constant is passed to the createStatement(). This enables the use of virtual cursor control methods in the third try{} block. Initially, the virtual cursor moves to the first row of the ResultSet and then to the last row before being positioned at the second to last row of the ResultSet.

Next, the virtual cursor is positioned to the tenth row of the ResultSet using the absolute() method. Finally, the relative() method is called twice. The first time the relative() method is called, the virtual cursor is moved back two rows from the current row, which places the virtual cursor at row 8. The relative() method is again called to return the virtual cursor back to its original row by moving the virtual cursor two rows forward.

If you use any of these methods and end up positioning the cursor before the first record or beyond the last record, there won't be any errors thrown.

Listing 6-14
Using a scrollable virtual cursor.

```
String url = "jdbc:odbc:CustomerInformation";
String userID = "jim";
String password = "keogh";
String printrow;
String FirstName;
String LastName;
Statement DataRequest;
ResultSet Results;
Connection Db;
try {
   Class.forName( "sun.jdbc.odbc.JdbcOdbcDriver");
   Db = DriverManager.getConnection(url,userID,password);
 }
catch (ClassNotFoundException error) {
      System.err.println("Unable to load the JDBC/ODBC bridge." + error);
      System.exit(1);
}
catch (SQLException error) {
      System.err.println("Cannot connect to the database." + error);
      System.exit(2);
}
try {
      String query = "SELECT FirstName,LastName FROM Customers";
      DataRequest = Db.createStatement(TYPE_SCROLL_INSENSITIVE);
      Results = DataRequest.executeQuery (query);
}

catch ( SQLException error ){
      System.err.println("SQL error." + error);
       System.exit(3);
}

boolean Records = Results.next();
if (!Records ) {
   System.out.println("No data returned");
   System.exit(4);
}
try {
  do {
```

```
        Results.first();
        Results.last();
        Results.previous();
        Results.absolute(10);
        Results.relative(-2);
        Results.relative(2);
         FirstName = Results.getString ( 1 ) ;
         LastName = Results.getString ( 2 ) ;
         printrow = FirstName + " " + LastName;
        System.out.println(printrow);
      } while (Results.next() );
    DataRequest.close();
  }
  catch (SQLException error ) {
      System.err.println("Data display error." + error);
      System.exit(5);
  }
```

Not All JDBC Drivers Are Scrollable

Although the JDBC API contains methods to scroll a ResultSet, some JDBC drivers may not support some or all of these features and therefore are unable to return a scrollable ResultSet. Listing 6-15 can be used to test whether or not the JDBC driver in use supports a scrollable ResultSet.

<table>
<tr>
<td>

Listing 6-15

Testing whether a driver supports a scrollable ResultSet.

</td>
<td>

```
boolean forward, insensitive, sensitive;
DataBaseMetaData meta = Db.getMetaData();
forward = meta.supportsResultsSetType(ResultSet.TYPE_FORWARD_ONLY);
insensitive = meta.supportsResultsSetType(ResultSet. TYPE_SCROLL_INSENSITIVE);
sensitive = meta.supportsResultsSetType(ResultSet. TYPE_SCROLL_SENSITIVE);
System.out.println("forward: " + answer);
System.out.println("insensitive: " + insensitive);
System.out.println("sensitive: " + sensitive);
 (h2) Specify Number Of Rows To Return
```

</td>
</tr>
</table>

When the J2EE component requests rows from the ResultSet, some rows are fetched into the driver and returned at one time. Other times, all rows requested may not be retrieved at the same time. In this case, the driver returns to the DBMS and requests another set of rows that are defined by the fetch size, and then discards the current set of rows. This process continues until the J2EE retrieves all rows.

Although the Statement class has a method for setting maximum rows, the method may not be effective since the driver does not implement it. In addition, the maximum row setting is for rows in the ResultSet and not for the number of rows returned by the DBMS. For example, the maximum rows can be set to 100. The DBMS might return

500 rows, but the ResultSet object silently drops 400 of them. This means all 500 rows are still pumped over the network.

The fetch size is set by using the setFetchSize() method, which is illustrated in Listing 6-16. However, all DBMS vendors may not implement the fetch size. Consult the driver documentation to determine if fetch size is supported. If fetch size isn't supported, the methods will compile and execute, but have no effect.

Don't become overly concerned about setting the fetch size, because fetch size is in the area of performance tuning—which is handled by the database administrator or the network engineer.

Listing 6-16 illustrates how to set the maximum number of rows that are returned by the DBMS. The second try{} block in Listing 6-16 calls the createStatement() method of the Connection object and then sets the maximum number of rows to 500 using the setFetchSize() method of the Statement object.

Listing 6-16
Setting the maximum number of rows returned in a ResultSet.

```
String url = "jdbc:odbc:CustomerInformation";
String userID = "jim";
String password = "keogh";
String printrow;
String FirstName;
String LastName;
Statement DataRequest;
ResultSet Results;
Connection Db;
try {
    Class.forName( "sun.jdbc.odbc.JdbcOdbcDriver");
    Db = DriverManager.getConnection(url,userID,password);
 }
catch (ClassNotFoundException error) {
    System.err.println("Unable to load the JDBC/ODBC bridge." + error);
    System.exit(1);
}
catch (SQLException error) {
    System.err.println("Cannot connect to the database." + error);
    System.exit(2);
}
try {
    String query = "SELECT FirstName,LastName FROM Customers";
    DataRequest = Db.createStatement(TYPE_SCROLL_INSENSITIVE);
    DataRequest.setFetchSize(500);
    Results = DataRequest.executeQuery (query);
}

catch ( SQLException error ){
    System.err.println("SQL error." + error);
     System.exit(3);
}
```

Updatable ResultSet

Rows contained in the ResultSet can be updatable similar to how rows in a table can be updated. This is made possible by passing the createStatement() method of the Connection object the CONCUR_UPDATABLE. Alternatively, the CONCUR_READ_ONLY constant can be passed to the createStatement() method to prevent the ResultSet from being updated.

There are three ways in which a ResultSet can be changed. These are updating values in a row, deleting a row, and inserting a new row. All of these changes are accomplished by using methods of the Statement object.

Update ResultSet

Once the executeQuery() method of the Statement object returns a ResultSet, the updatexxx() method is used to change the value of a column in the current row of the ResultSet. The xxx in the updatexxx() method is replaced with the data type of the column that is to be updated.

The updatexxx() method requires two parameters. The first is either the number or name of the column of the ResultSet that is being updated and the second parameter is the value that will replace the value in the column of the ResultSet.

A value in a column of the ResultSet can be replaced with a NULL value by using the updateNull() method. The updateNull() method requires one parameter, which is the number of the column in the current row of the ResultSet. The updateNull() doesn't accept the name of the column as a parameter.

The updateRow() method is called after all the updatexxx() methods are called. The updateRow() method changes values in columns of the current row of the ResultSet based on the values of the updatexxx() methods.

Listing 6-17 illustrates how to update a row in a ResultSet. In this example, customer Mary Jones was recently married and changed her last name to Smith before processing the ResultSet. The updateString() method is used to change the value of the last name column of the ResultSet with 'Jones'. The change takes effect once the updateRow() method is called; however, this change only occurs in the ResultSet. The corresponding row in the table remains unchanged until an update query is run, which is discussed in the next chapter.

Listing 6-17
Updating the ResultSet.

```
String url = "jdbc:odbc:CustomerInformation";
String userID = "jim";
String password = "keogh";
Statement DataRequest;
ResultSet Results;
Connection Db;
try {
   Class.forName( "sun.jdbc.odbc.JdbcOdbcDriver");
   Db = DriverManager.getConnection(url,userID,password);
 }
```

```
catch (ClassNotFoundException error) {
      System.err.println("Unable to load the JDBC/ODBC bridge." + error);
      System.exit(1);
}
catch (SQLException error) {
      System.err.println("Cannot connect to the database." + error);
      System.exit(2);
}
try {
      String query = "SELECT FirstName,LastName FROM Customers WHERE
FirstName = 'Mary' and LastName = 'Smith'";
      DataRequest = Db.createStatement(ResultSet.CONCUR_UPDATABLE);
      Results = DataRequest.executeQuery (query);
}

catch ( SQLException error ){
    System.err.println("SQL error." + error);
      System.exit(3);
}

boolean Records = Results.next();
if (!Records ) {
   System.out.println("No data returned");
   System.exit(4);
}
try {
       Results.updateString ("LastName", "Smith");
      Results.updateRow();
      DataRequest.close();
}
catch (SQLException error ) {
   System.err.println("Data display error." + error);
   System.exit(5);
}
```

Delete Row in the ResultSet

The deleteRow() method is used to remove a row from a ResultSet. Sometimes this is advantageous when processing the ResultSet because this is a way to eliminate rows from future processing. For example, each row of a ResultSet may have to pass three tests. Those that fail to pass the first test could be deleted from the ResultSet, thereby reducing the number of rows in the ResultSet that have to be evaluated for the second test. This also deletes it from the underlying database.

The deleteRow() method is passed an integer that contains the number of the row to be deleted. A good practice is to use the absolute() method described previously in the chapter to move the virtual cursor to the row in the ResultSet that should be deleted. However, the value of that row should be examined by the program to assure it is the proper row before the deleteRow() method is called. The deleteRow() method is then passed a zero integer indicating that the current row must be deleted, as shown in the following statement:

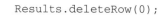

```
Results.deleteRow(0);
```

Insert Row in the ResultSet

Inserting a row into the ResultSet is accomplished using basically the same technique as is used to update the ResultSet. That is, the updatexxx() method is used to specify the column and value that will be placed into the column of the ResultSet.

The updatexxx() method requires two parameters. The first parameter is either the name of the column or the number of the column of the ResultSet. The second parameter is the new value that will be placed in the column of the ResultSet. Remember that the data type of the column replaces the xxx in the method name.

The insertRow() method is called after the updatexxx() methods, which causes a new row to be inserted into the ResultSet having values that reflect the parameters in the updatexxx() methods. This also updates the underlying database.

Listing 6-18 illustrates how to insert a new row in a ResultSet. In this example, the query returns the first name and last name of all customers. The name Tom Smith is inserted into the ResultSet in the third try{} block using the updateString() method. Remember that columns are numbered based on the order that the column names appear in the SELECT statement of the query. The new row is added to the ResultSet after the insertRow() method is called.

Listing 6-18
Inserting a
new row
into the
ResultSet.

```
String url = "jdbc:odbc:CustomerInformation";
String userID = "jim";
String password = "keogh";
Statement DataRequest;
ResultSet Results;
Connection Db;
try {
    Class.forName( "sun.jdbc.odbc.JdbcOdbcDriver");
    Db = DriverManager.getConnection(url,userID,password);
 }
catch (ClassNotFoundException error) {
    System.err.println("Unable to load the JDBC/ODBC bridge." + error);
    System.exit(1);
}
catch (SQLException error) {
    System.err.println("Cannot connect to the database." + error);
    System.exit(2);
}
try {
    String query = "SELECT FirstName,LastName FROM Customers";
```

```
        DataRequest = Db.createStatement(CONCUR_UPDATABLE);
        Results = DataRequest.executeQuery (query);
}

catch ( SQLException error ){
     System.err.println("SQL error." + error);
      System.exit(3);
}

boolean Records = Results.next();
if (!Records ) {
    System.out.println("No data returned");
   System.exit(4);
}
try {
     Results.updateString (1, "Tom");  // updates the ResultSet
     Results.updateString (2, "Smith"); // updates the ResultSet
     Results.insertRow(); // updates the underlying database
     DataRequest.close();
}
catch (SQLException error ) {
   System.err.println("Data display error." + error);
   System.exit(5);
}
```

Transaction Processing

A transaction may involve several tasks similar to the tasks that are required to complete a transaction at a supermarket. In a supermarket transaction, each item purchased must be registered, the transaction must be totaled, and the customer must tender the amount of the purchase. The transaction is successfully completed only if each task is completed successfully. If one task fails, the entire transaction fails. Previously completed tasks must be reversed if the transaction fails. For example, goods that were registered must be removed from the register and returned to the shelf.

A database transaction consists of a set of SQL statements, each of which must be successfully completed for the transaction to be completed. If one fails, SQL statements that executed successfully up to that point in the transaction must be rolled back.

A database transaction isn't completed until the J2EE component calls the commit() method of the Connection object. All SQL statements executed prior to the call to the commit() method can be rolled back. However, once the commit() method is called, none of the SQL statements can be rolled back.

The commit() method must be called regardless if the SQL statement is part of a transaction or not. This means that the commit() method must be issued in the previous examples used in this chapter. However, the commit() method was automatically called in these examples because the DBMS has an AutoCommit feature that is by default set to true.

If a J2EE component is processing a transaction, the AutoCommit feature must be deactivated by calling the setAutoCommit() method and passing it a false parameter. Once the transaction is completed, the setAutoCommit() method is called again—this timing passing it a true parameter, reactivating the AutoCommit feature.

Listing 6-19 illustrates how to process a transaction. The transaction in this example consists of two SQL statements, both of which update the Street address of rows in the Customer table. Each SQL statement is executed separately and then the commit() method is called. However, should either SQL statement throw an SQL exception, the catch{} block reacts by rolling back the transaction before displaying the exception on the screen.

Listing 6-19
Executing a database transaction.

```
String url = "jdbc:odbc:CustomerInformation";
String userID = "jim";
String password = "keogh";
Statement DataRequest1, DataRequest2 ;
Connection Database;
try {
      Class.forName( "sun.jdbc.odbc.JdbcOdbcDriver");
      Database = DriverManager.getConnection(url,userID,password);
}
catch (ClassNotFoundException error) {
    System.err.println("Unable to load the JDBC/ODBC bridge." + error);
    System.exit(1);
}
catch (SQLException error) {
    System.err.println("Cannot connect to the database." + error);
    System.exit(2);
 }
try {
  Database .setAutoCommit(false)
  String query1 = "UPDATE Customers SET Street = '5 Main Street' " +
          "WHERE FirstName = 'Bob'";
  String query2 = "UPDATE Customers SET Street = '10 Main Street' " +
          "WHERE FirstName = 'Tim'";
  DataRequest1= Database.createStatement();
  DataRequest2= Database.createStatement();
  DataRequest.executeUpdate (query1 );
  DataRequest.executeUpdate (query2 );
  Database.commit();
  DataRequest1.close();
  DataRequest2.close();
  Database.close();
  }
  catch(SQLException ex) {
   System.err.println("SQLException: " + ex.getMessage());
```

```
   if (con != null) {
     try {
       System.err.println("Transaction is being rolled back ");
       con.rollback();
     }
   catch(SQLException excep) {
         System.err.print("SQLException: ");
         System.err.println(excep.getMessage());
     }
   }
 }
(h2) Savepoints
```

A transaction may consist of many tasks, some of which don't need to be rolled back should the entire transaction fail. Let's say there are several tasks that occur when a new order is processed. These include updating the customer account table, inserting the order into the pending order table, and sending a customer a confirmation email.

Technically, all three tasks must be completed before the transaction is considered completed. Suppose the email server is down when the transaction is ready to send the customer a confirmation email. Should the entire transaction be rolled back? Probably not since it is more important that the order continue to be processed (i.e., delivered). The confirmation notice can be sent once the email server is back online.

The J2EE component can control the number of tasks that are rolled back by using savepoints. A savepoint, introduced in JDBC 3.0, is a virtual marker that defines the task at which the rollback stops. In the previous example, the task before the email confirmation notice is sent can be designated as a savepoint.

Listing 6-20 illustrates how to create a savepoint. This is the same code segment as Listing 6-19, but a savepoint is created after the execution of the first update SQL statement.

There can be many savepoints used in a transaction. Each savepoint is identified by a unique name. The savepoint name is then passed to the rollback() method to specify the point within the transaction where the rollback is to stop.

In this example, there is one savepoint called sp1. The name "sp1" is the parameter to the rollback() method in the catch{} block. The purpose of this example is to illustrate how to set and release a savepoint and how to use the savepoint name in the rollback() method. Of course, for commercial applications more rigorous code is necessary that identifies the executeUpdate() method that threw the exception among other error-checking routines. The releaseSavepoint() method is called to remove the savepoint from the transaction. The name of the savepoint that is to be removed is passed to the releaseSavepoint() method.

Listing 6-20
Using
savepoints
in a
transaction.

```
String url = "jdbc:odbc:CustomerInformation";
String userID = "jim";
String password = "keogh";
```

J2EE DATABASES

```
Statement DataRequest1, DataRequest2 ;
Connection Database;
try {
       Class.forName( "sun.jdbc.odbc.JdbcOdbcDriver");
       Database = DriverManager.getConnection(url,userID,password);
}
catch (ClassNotFoundException error) {
    System.err.println("Unable to load the JDBC/ODBC bridge." + error);
    System.exit(1);
}
catch (SQLException error) {
    System.err.println("Cannot connect to the database." + error);
    System.exit(2);
 }
try {
  Database .setAutoCommit(false)
  String query1 = "UPDATE Customers SET Street = '5 Main Street' " +
          "WHERE FirstName = 'Bob'";
  String query2 = "UPDATE Customers SET Street = '10 Main Street' " +
          "WHERE FirstName = 'Tim'";
  DataRequest1= Database.createStatement();
  Savepoint s1 = Database.setSavepoint ("sp1");
  DataRequest2= Database.createStatement();
  DataRequest.executeUpdate (query1);
  DataRequest.executeUpdate (query2);
  Database.commit();
  DataRequest1.close();
  DataRequest2.close();
  Database.releaseSavepoint ("sp1");
  Database.close();
}
catch ( SQLException error ){
   try {
     Database.rollback(sp1);
   }
   catch ( SQLException error ){
      System.err.println("rollback error." + error.getMessage());
      System.exit(3);
   }
    System.err.println("SQL error." + error. getMessage());;);
   System.exit(4);
}
 (h2) Batch Statements
```

Another way to combine SQL statements into a transaction is to batch together these statements into a single transaction and then execute the entire transaction. You can do this by using the addBatch() method of the Statement object. The addBatch() method receives a SQL statement as a parameter and places the SQL statement in the batch.

Once all the SQL statements that comprise the transaction are included in the batch, the executeBatch() method is called to execute the entire batch at the same time. The executeBatch() method returns an int array that contains the number of SQL statements that were executed successfully.

The int array is displayed if a BatchUpdateException error is thrown during the execution of the batch. The batch can be cleared of SQL statements by using the clearBatch() method. The transaction must be committed using the commit() method. Make sure that setAutoCommit() is set to false before executing the batch, as discussed in the previous section.

Listing 6-21 illustrates how to batch SQL statements. In this example, two SQL statements are created as discussed previously in this chapter. Each SQL statement is added to the batch using the addBatch() method.

Once both SQL statements are added to the batch, the executeBatch() method is called to execute each of the SQL statements. The commit() method is then called to commit the changes created by the SQL statement. Until the commit() method is called, the transaction can be rolled back as described in the previous section.

Listing 6-21
Batching SQL statements into a transaction.

```
String url = "jdbc:odbc:CustomerInformation";
String userID = "jim";
String password = "keogh";
Statement DataRequest;
Connection Database;
try {
      Class.forName( "sun.jdbc.odbc.JdbcOdbcDriver");
      Database = DriverManager.getConnection(url,userID,password);
}
catch (ClassNotFoundException error) {
    System.err.println("Unable to load the JDBC/ODBC bridge." + error);
    System.exit(1);
}
catch (SQLException error) {
    System.err.println("Cannot connect to the database." + error);
    System.exit(2);
 }
try {
  Database .setAutoCommit(false)
  String query1 = "UPDATE Customers SET Street = '5 Main Street' " +
          "WHERE FirstName = 'Bob'";
  String query2 = "UPDATE Customers SET Street = '10 Main Street' " +
          "WHERE FirstName = 'Tim'";
  DataRequest= Database.createStatement();
  DataRequest.addBatch(query1);
  DataRequest.addBatch(query2);
```

```
    int [ ] updated = DataRequest.executeBatch ();
    Database.commit();
    DataRequest1.close();
    DataRequest2.close();
    Database.close();
}
catch(BatchUpdateException error) {
   System.out.println("Batch error.");
   System.out.println("SQL State: " + error.getSQLState());
   System.out.println("Message: " + error.getMessage());
   System.out.println(Vendor: " + error.getErrorCode());
   int [ ] updated  = error.getUpdatecount();
   int count = updated.length();
   for int - i = 0; i < count; i++) {
       System.out.print (updated[i]);
   }
   SQLException sql = error;
   While (sql != null)
      {
          System.out.println("SQL error " + sql);
          sql = sql.getnextException();
      }
   try{
      DataRequest.clearBatch();
   }
   catch(BatchUpdateException error) {
       System.out.println("Unable to clear the batch: " + error.getMessage());
   }
}
```

ResultSet Holdability

Whenever the commit() method is called, all ResultSet objects that were created for the transaction are closed. Sometimes a J2EE component needs to keep the ResultSet open even after the commit() method is called.

You can control whether or not ResultSet objects are closed following the call to the commit() method by passing one of two constants to the createStatement() method. These constants are HOLD_CURSORS_OVER_COMMIT and CLOSE_CURSORS_AT_COMMIT.

The HOLD_CURSORS_OVER_COMMIT constant keeps ResultSet objects open following a call to the commit() method and CLOSE_CURSORS_AT_COMMIT closes ResultSet objects when the commit() method is called.

RowSets

The JDBC RowSets object is used to encapsulate a ResultSet for use with Enterprise Java Beans (EJB). A RowSet object contains rows of data from a table(s) that can be used in a disconnected operation.

That is, an EJB can interact with a RowSet object without having to be connected to a DBMS, which is ideal for J2EE components that have PDA clients. You'll learn more about EJB and RowSets in Chapter 12.

Auto-Generated Keys

It is common for a DBMS to automatically generate unique keys for a table as rows are inserted into the table. The getGeneratedKeys() method of the Statement object is called to return keys generated by the DBMS.

The getGeneratedKeys() returns a ResultSet object. You can use the ResultSet.getMetaData() method to retrieve metadata relating to the automatically generated key, such as the type and properties of the automatically generated key. You can learn more about retrieving metadata in the next section of this chapter.

Metadata

Metadata is data about data, as discussed previously in this chapter. A J2EE component can access metadata by using the DatabaseMetaData interface. The DatabaseMetaData interface is used to retrieve information about databases, tables, columns, and indexes among other information about the DBMS.

A J2EE component retrieves metadata about the database by calling the getMetaData() method of the Connection object. The getMetaData() method returns a DatabaseMetaData object that contains information about the database and its components.

Once the DatabaseMetaData object is obtained, an assortment of methods contained in the DatabaseMetaData object are called to retrieve specific metadata. Here are some of the more commonly used DatabaseMetaData object methods:

- **getDatabaseProductName()**   Returns the product name of the database.
- **getUserName()**   Returns the username.
- **getURL()**   Returns the URL of the database
- **getSchemas()**   Returns all the schema names available in this database.
- **getPrimaryKeys()**   Returns primary keys.
- **getProcedures()**   Returns stored procedure names.
- **getTables()**   Returns names of tables in the database.

ResultSet Metadata

There are two types of metadata that can be retrieved from the DBMS. These are metadata that describes the database as mentioned in the previous section and metadata that describes the ResultSet. Metadata that describes the ResultSet is retrieved by calling the getMetaData() method of the ResultSet object. This returns a ResultSetMetaData object, as is illustrated in the following code statement:

```
ResultSetMetaData rm = Result.getMetaData()
```

Once the ResultSet metadata is retrieved, the J2EE component can call methods of the ResultSetMetaData object to retrieve specific kinds of metadata. The more commonly called methods are as follows:

- **getColumnCount()** Returns the number of columns contained in the ResultSet.
- **getColumnName(int number)** Returns the name of the column specified by the column number.
- **getColumnType(int number)** Returns the data type of the column specified by the column number.

There are many other methods used to retrieve practically any information you need to know about a database and the ResultSet—these are more methods than can be described in this chapter. You can obtain detailed information about each of these methods by visiting Sun Microsystems, Inc.'s web site at java.sun.com.

Data Types

The setxxx() and getxxx() methods are used throughout this chapter to set a value of a specific data type and to retrieve a value of a specific data type. The xxx in the names of these methods is replaced with the name of the data type.

Table 6-1 contains a list of data types and their Java equivalents. You can use this list to determine the proper data name to use to replace the xxx in the setxxx() and getxxx() methods.

SQL Type	Java Type
CHAR	String
VARCHAR	String
LONGVARCHAR	String
NUMERIC	java.math.BigDecimal
DECIMAL	java.math.BigDecimal
BIT	Boolean
TINYINT	Byte
SMALLINT	Short
INTEGER	Integer
BIGINT	Long
REAL	float
FLOAT	float
DOUBLE	double
BINARY	Byte[]
VARBINARY	Byte[]
LONGVARBINARY	byte[]
BLOB	java.sql.Blob
CLOB	java.sql.Clob
ARRAY	java.sql.Array
STRUCT	java.sql.Struct
REF	java.sql.Ref
DATALINK	java.sql.Types
DATE	java.sql.date
TIME	java.sql.Time
TIMESTAMP	java.sql.Timestamp

Table 6-1. *A List of Data Types for Use with the setxxx() and getxxx() Methods*

Exceptions

There are three kinds of exceptions that are thrown by JDBC methods. These are SQLExceptions, SQLWarnings, and DataTruncation. SQLExceptions commonly reflect a SQL syntax error in the query and are thrown by many of the methods contained in the java.sql package. Hopefully, the syntax errors in your code get resolved quickly. In production, this exception is most commonly caused by connectivity issues with the database. It can also be caused by subtle coding errors like trying to access an object that's been closed. For example, you try to roll back a transaction in a catch clause and don't check first if the database connection is still valid. The getNextException() method of the SQLExceptions object is used to return details about the SQL error or a null if the last exception was retrieved. The getErrorCode() method of the SQLException object is used to retrieve vendor-specific error codes.

The SQLWarning throws warnings received by the Connection from the DBMS. The getWarnings() method of the Connection object retrieves the warning and the getNextWarning() method of the Connection object retrieves subsequent warnings.

Whenever data is lost due to truncation of the data value, a DataTrunction exception is thrown.

Quick Reference Guide

JDBC classes and interface contain many methods. This quick reference guide (encompassed in the following Tables 6-2 through 6-12) provides a brief overview of the more commonly used methods. Full details of these methods and all the JDBC classes and interfaces are available at java.sun.com.

Syntax	Descriptions
public void registerOutParameter(int parameterIndex, int sqlType) throws SQLException	Registers the OUT parameter.
public void registerOutParameter(int parameterIndex, int sqlType, int scale) throws SQLException	Registers the OUT parameter.
public boolean wasNull() throws SQLException	Determines an OUT parameter value is null.

Table 6-2.   *java.sql Package* Public Interface CallableStatement

Syntax	Descriptions
set by name	
public void setURL(String parameterName, URL val) throws SQLException	Sets a parameter to a java.net.URL object.
Descriptions	Syntax
public void setNull(String parameterName, int sqlType) throws SQLException	Sets a parameter to a null value.
public void setBoolean(String parameterName, boolean x) throws SQLException	Sets a parameter to a Java boolean value.
public void setByte(String parameterName, byte x) throws SQLException	Sets a parameter to a Java byte value.
public void setShort(String parameterName, short x) throws SQLException	Sets a parameter to a Java short value.
public void setInt(String parameterName, int x) throws SQLException	Sets a parameter to a Java int value.
public void setLong(String parameterName, long x) throws SQLException	Sets a parameter to a Java long value.
public void setFloat(String parameterName, float x) throws SQLException	Sets a parameter to a Java float value.
public void setDouble(String parameterName, double x) throws SQLException	Sets a parameter to a Java double value.
public void setBigDecimal(String parameterName, BigDecimal x) throws SQLException	Sets a parameter to a java.math.BigDecimal value.
public void setString(String parameterName, String x) throws SQLException	Sets a parameter to a Java String value.
public void setBytes(String parameterName, byte[] x) throws SQLException	Sets a parameter to a Java array of bytes.
public void setDate(String parameterName, Date x) throws SQLException	Sets a parameter to a java.sql.Date value.

Table 6-2. *java.sql Package* Public Interface CallableStatement (continued)

Syntax	Descriptions
public void setTime(String parameterName, Time x) throws SQLException	Sets a parameter to a java.sql.Time value.
public void setTimestamp(String parameterName, Timestamp x) throws SQLException	Sets a parameter to a java.sql.Timestamp value.
public void setBinaryStream(String parameterName, InputStream x, int length) throws SQLException	Sets the designated parameter to the given input stream, which will have the specified number of bytes.
public void setObject(String parameterName, Object x, int targetSqlType, int scale) throws SQLException	Sets a parameter with the given object.
public void setObject(String parameterName, Object x, int targetSqlType) throws SQLException	Sets a parameter with the given object.
public void setObject(String parameterName, Object x) throws SQLException	Sets a parameter with the given object.
public void setDate(String parameterName, Date x, Calendar cal) throws SQLException	Sets a parameter to a java.sql.Date value.
public void setTime(String parameterName, Time x, Calendar cal) throws SQLException	Sets a parameter to a java.sql.Time value.
public void setTimestamp(String parameterName, Timestamp x, Calendar cal) throws SQLException	Sets a parameter to a java.sql.Timestamp value.
public void setNull(String parameterName, int sqlType, String typeName) throws SQLException	Sets a parameter to a null value.
get by index	
public String getString(int parameterIndex) throws SQLException	Determines the value of the designated JDBC CHAR, VARCHAR, or LONGVARCHAR parameter.
public boolean getBoolean(int parameterIndex) throws SQLException	Determines the value of the designated JDBC BIT parameter.

Table 6-2.   *java.sql Package* Public Interface CallableStatement (continued)

Syntax	Descriptions
public byte getByte(int parameterIndex) throws SQLException	Determines the value of the designated JDBC TINYINT parameter.
public short getShort(int parameterIndex) throws SQLException	Determines the value of the designated JDBC SMALLINT parameter.
public int getInt(int parameterIndex) throws SQLException	Determines the value of the designated JDBC INTEGER parameter.
public long getLong(int parameterIndex) throws SQLException	Determines the value of the designated JDBC BIGINT parameter.
public float getFloat(int parameterIndex) throws SQLException	Determines the value of the designated JDBC FLOAT parameter.
public double getDouble(int parameterIndex) throws SQLException	Determines the value of the designated JDBC DOUBLE parameter.
public BigDecimal getBigDecimal(int parameterIndex, int scale) throws SQLException	Determines the value of the designated JDBC NUMERIC parameter.
public byte[] getBytes(int parameterIndex) throws SQLException	Determines the value of the designated JDBC BINARY or VARBINARY parameter.
public Date getDate(int parameterIndex) throws SQLException	Determines the value of the designated JDBC DATE parameter.
public Time getTime(int parameterIndex) throws SQLException	Determines the value of the designated JDBC TIME parameter.
public Timestamp getTimestamp(int parameterIndex) throws SQLException	Determines the value of the designated JDBC TIMESTAMP parameter.

Table 6-2.   *java.sql Package* Public Interface CallableStatement (continued)

J2EE DATABASES

Syntax	Descriptions
public Object getObject(int parameterIndex) throws SQLException	Determines the value of the designated parameter.
public BigDecimal getBigDecimal(int parameterIndex) throws SQLException	Determines the value of the designated JDBC NUMERIC parameter.
public Object getObject(int i, Map map) throws SQLException	Returns an object representing the value of the OUT parameter.
public Ref getRef(int i) throws SQLException	Determines the value of the designated JDBC REF parameter.
public Blob getBlob(int i) throws SQLException	Determines the value of the designated JDBC BLOB parameter.
public Clob getClob(int i) throws SQLException	Determines the value of the designated JDBC CLOB parameter.
public Array getArray(int i) throws SQLException	Determines the value of the designated JDBC ARRAY parameter.
public Date getDate(int parameterIndex, Calendar cal) throws SQLException	Determines the value of the designated JDBC DATE parameter.
public Time getTime(int parameterIndex, Calendar cal) throws SQLException	Determines the value of the designated JDBC TIME parameter.
public Timestamp getTimestamp(int parameterIndex, Calendar cal) throws SQLException	Determines the value of the designated JDBC TIMESTAMP parameter.
public void registerOutParameter(int paramIndex, int sqlType, String typeName) throws SQLException	Registers the designated output parameter.

Table 6-2.   *java.sql Package* *Public Interface CallableStatement* (continued)

Syntax	Descriptions
public void registerOutParameter(String parameterName, int sqlType) throws SQLException	Registers the OUT parameter named parameterName.
public void registerOutParameter(String parameterName, int sqlType, int scale) throws SQLException	Determines the parameter named parameterName.
public void registerOutParameter(String parameterName, int sqlType, String typeName) throws SQLException	Determines the designated output parameter.
public URL getURL(int parameterIndex) throws SQLException	Determines the value of the designated JDBC DATALINK parameter.

get by name

public String getString(String parameterName) throws SQLException	Determines the value of a JDBC CHAR, VARCHAR, or LONGVARCHAR parameter.
public boolean getBoolean(String parameterName) throws SQLException	Determines the value of a JDBC BIT parameter.
public byte getByte(String parameterName) throws SQLException	Determines the value of a JDBC TINYINT parameter.
public short getShort(String parameterName) throws SQLException	Determines the value of a JDBC SMALLINT parameter.
public int getInt(String parameterName) throws SQLException	Determines the value of a JDBC INTEGER parameter.
public long getLong(String parameterName) throws SQLException	Determines the value of a JDBC BIGINT parameter.
public float getFloat(String parameterName) throws SQLException	Determines the value of a JDBC FLOAT parameter.
public double getDouble(String parameterName) throws SQLException	Determines the value of a JDBC DOUBLE parameter.
public byte[] getBytes(String parameterName) throws SQLException	Determines the value of a JDBC BINARY or VARBINARY parameter.

Table 6-2.   *java.sql Package* Public Interface CallableStatement (continued)

Syntax	Descriptions
public Date getDate(String parameterName) throws SQLException	Determines the value of a JDBC DATE parameter.
public Time getTime(String parameterName) throws SQLException	Determines the value of a JDBC TIME parameter.
public Timestamp getTimestamp(String parameterName) throws SQLException	Determines the value of a JDBC TIMESTAMP parameter.
public Object getObject(String parameterName) throws SQLException	Determines the value of a parameter as an Object.
public BigDecimal getBigDecimal(String parameterName) throws SQLException	Determines the value of a JDBC NUMERIC parameter.
public Object getObject(String parameterName, Map map) throws SQLException	Returns an object representing the value of the OUT parameter.
public Ref getRef(String parameterName) throws SQLException	Determines the value of a JDBC REF parameter.
public Blob getBlob(String parameterName) throws SQLException	Determines the value of a JDBC BLOB parameter.
public Clob getClob(String parameterName) throws SQLException	Determines the value of a JDBC CLOB parameter.
public Array getArray(String parameterName) throws SQLException	Determines the value of a JDBC ARRAY.
public Date getDate(String parameterName, Calendar cal) throws SQLException	Determines the value of a JDBC DATE parameter.
public Time getTime(String parameterName, Calendar cal) throws SQLException	Determines the value of a JDBC TIME parameter.
public Timestamp getTimestamp(String parameterName, Calendar cal) throws SQLException	Determines the value of a JDBC TIMESTAMP parameter.
public URL getURL(String parameterName) throws SQLException	Determines a URL.

Table 6-2. *java.sql Package* Public Interface CallableStatement (continued)

Syntax	Descriptions
Syntax	**Descriptions**
public void close() throws SQLException	Closes a connection.
public boolean isClosed() throws SQLException	Determines if a Connection object is closed.
public DatabaseMetaData getMetaData() throws SQLException	Retrieves a DatabaseMetaData.
public void setReadOnly(boolean readOnly) throws SQLException	Places a connection in read-only.
public boolean isReadOnly() throws SQLException	Determines if a Connection object is in read-only.
public String getCatalog() throws SQLException	Determines a connection's catalog name.
Warnings	
public SQLWarning getWarnings() throws SQLException	Retrieves the first warning reported.
public void clearWarnings() throws SQLException	Clears all warnings reported.
Holdability	
public void setHoldability(int holdability) throws SQLException	Changes the holdability of ResultSet objects.
public int getHoldability() throws SQLException	Determines the holdability of a ResultSet.
Transactions	
public Savepoint setSavepoint() throws SQLException	Creates an unnamed savepoint.
public Savepoint setSavepoint(String name) throws SQLException	Creates a named savepoint.
public void rollback(Savepoint savepoint) throws SQLException	Reverses all changes made after a savepoint was set.
public void releaseSavepoint(Savepoint savepoint) throws SQLException	Removes the Savepoint object.
public void commit() throws SQLException	Makes all changes permanent.

Table 6-3. *java.sql Package* Public Interface Connection Interface

J2EE DATABASES

Syntax	Descriptions
public void rollback() throws SQLException	Reverses changes made to a transaction and releases any database locks.
public void setAutoCommit(boolean autoCommit) throws SQLException	Sets the auto-commit mode.
public boolean getAutoCommit() throws SQLException	Determines if the auto-commit mode is set.

CallableStatement

Syntax	Descriptions
public CallableStatement prepareCall(String sql, int resultSetType, int resultSetConcurrency, int resultSetHoldability) throws SQLException	Creates a CallableStatement object that generates a ResultSet.
public CallableStatement prepareCall(String sql, int resultSetType,int resultSetConcurrency) throws SQLException	Creates a CallableStatement object that generates a ResultSet.
public CallableStatement prepareCall (String sql) throws SQLException	Creates a CallableStatement object.

Statement

Syntax	Descriptions
public Statement createStatement(int resultSetType, int resultSetConcurrency, int resultSetHoldability) throws SQLException	Creates a Statement object that will generate a ResultSet.
public Statement createStatement(int resultSetType, int resultSetConcurrency) throws SQLException	Creates a Statement object that generates a ResultSet.
public Statement createStatement() throws SQLException	Creates a Statement object.

PrepareStatement

Syntax	Descriptions
public PreparedStatement prepareStatement (String sql) throws SQLException	Creates a PreparedStatement object.
public PreparedStatement prepareStatement (String sql, int resultSetType,int resultSetConcurrency, int resultSetHoldability) throws SQLException	Creates a PreparedStatement object that will generate a ResultSet.

Table 6-3. *java.sql Package* Public Interface Connection Interface (continued)

Synatx	Descriptions
public PreparedStatement prepareStatement (String sql, int[] columnIndexes) throws SQLException	Creates a PreparedStatement object that returns auto-generated keys.
public PreparedStatement prepareStatement (String sql, int resultSetType, int resultSetConcurrency) throws SQLException	Creates a PreparedStatement object that generates a ResultSet.
public PreparedStatement prepareStatement (String sql, String[] columnNames) throws SQLException	Creates a PreparedStatement object that returns auto-generated keys.

Table 6-3. *java.sql Package* Public Interface Connection Interface (continued)

J2EE DATABASES

Syntax	Descriptions
public Connection getConnection() throws SQLException	Retrieves the connection that produced metadata.
public boolean supportsSavepoints() throws SQLException	Determines if a database supports savepoints.
public boolean supportsNamedParameters() throws SQLException	Determines if a database supports named parameters to callable statements.
public boolean supportsMultipleOpenResults() throws SQLException	Determines if it is possible to have multiple ResultSet objects returned from a CallableStatement simultaneously.
public int getMaxUserNameLength() throws SQLException	Determines the maximum number of characters in a username.
public boolean supportsTransactions() throws SQLException	Determines if a database supports transactions.
public int getJDBCMajorVersion() throws SQLException	Determines the major JDBC version number of a driver.

Table 6-4. *java.sql Package* Public Interface DatabaseMetaData

Synatx	Descriptions
public int getJDBCMinorVersion() throws SQLException	Determines the minor JDBC version number of a driver.
Database	
public String getURL() throws SQLException	Retrieves the URL for a DBMS.
public String getDatabaseProductName() throws SQLException	Determines the name of a DBMS.
public String getDatabaseProductVersion() throws SQLException	Determines the version number of a DBMS.
public ResultSet getSchemas() throws SQLException	Determines the schema names.
public ResultSet getCatalogs() throws SQLException	Determines the catalog names.
public ResultSet getTypeInfo() throws SQLException	Retrieves a description of standard SQL types supported by a database.
public int getDatabaseMajorVersion() throws SQLException	Determines the major version number of a database.
public int getDatabaseMinorVersion() throws SQLException	Determines the minor version number of a database.
Columns and Rows	
public int getMaxColumnNameLength() throws SQLException	Determines the maximum number of characters allowed in a column name.
public int getMaxColumnsInGroupBy() throws SQLException	Determines the maximum number of columns allowed in a GROUP BY clause.
public int getMaxColumnsInIndex() throws SQLException	Determines the maximum number of columns allowed in an index.
public int getMaxColumnsInOrderBy() throws SQLException	Determines the maximum number of columns allowed in an ORDER BY clause.

Table 6-4. *java.sql Package* Public Interface DatabaseMetaData (continued)

Synatx	Descriptions
public int getMaxColumnsInSelect() throws SQLException	Determines the maximum number of columns allowed in a SELECT list.
public int getMaxColumnsInTable() throws SQLException	Determines the maximum number of columns allowed in a table.
public int getMaxConnections() throws SQLException	Determines the maximum number of concurrent connections that are possible to a database.
public int getMaxIndexLength() throws SQLException	Determines the maximum number of bytes allowed for an index.
public int getMaxRowSize() throws SQLException	Determines the maximum number of bytes allowed in a row.
public ResultSet getColumns(String catalog, String schemaPattern, String tableNamePattern, String columnNamePattern) throws SQLException	Retrieves a description of table columns.
public ResultSet getColumnPrivileges (String catalog, String schema, String table, String columnNamePattern) throws SQLException	Determines access rights for columns.

Statement

public int getMaxStatementLength() throws SQLException	Determines the maximum number of characters permitted in a SQL statement.
public int getMaxStatements() throws SQLException	Determines the maximum number of active statements that can be open at the same time.
public boolean supportsBatchUpdates() throws SQLException	Determines if a database supports batch updates.

Table 6-4. *java.sql Package* Public Interface DatabaseMetaData (continued)

Syntax	Descriptions
Table	
public int getMaxTableNameLength() throws SQLException	Determines the maximum number of characters in a table name.
public int getMaxTablesInSelect() throws SQLException	Determines the maximum number of tables allowed in a SELECT statement.
public ResultSet getTables(String catalog, String schemaPattern, String tableNamePattern, String[] types) throws SQLException	Determines tables available in a catalog.
public ResultSet getTablePrivileges(String catalog, String schemaPattern, String tableNamePattern) throws SQLException	Determines access rights for each table.
Keys	
public ResultSet getPrimaryKeys(String catalog, String schema, String table) throws SQLException	Retrieves a description of a table's primary key.
public ResultSet getIndexInfo(String catalog, String schema, String table, boolean unique, boolean approximate) throws SQLException	Retrieves a description of table's indices and statistics.
public boolean supportsGetGeneratedKeys() throws SQLException	Determines if auto-generated keys can be retrieved.
Procedure	
public ResultSet getProcedureColumns (String catalog, String schemaPattern, String procedureNamePattern, String columnNamePattern) throws SQLException	Determines a catalog's stored procedure parameter and result columns.
public ResultSet getProcedures(String catalog, String schemaPattern, String procedureNamePattern) throws SQLException	Determines the stored procedures available in a catalog.

Table 6-4. *java.sql Package* Public Interface DatabaseMetaData (continued)

Syntax	Descriptions
Holdability	
public boolean supportsResultSetHoldability(int holdability) throws SQLException	Determines whether a database supports holdability.
public int getResultSetHoldability() throws SQLException	Determines the default holdability of a ResultSet.

Table 6-4.   *java.sql Package* Public Interface DatabaseMetaData (continued)

Syntax	Descriptions
public static Connection getConnection(String url, Properties info) throws SQLException	Opens a connection to a database.
public static Connection getConnection (String url, String user, String password) throws SQLException	Opens a connection to a database.
public static Connection getConnection (String url) throws SQLException	Opens a connection to a database.
Timeout	
public static void setLoginTimeout (int seconds)	Sets the maximum time in seconds before the login to the database times out.
public static int getLoginTimeout()	Determines the maximum time in seconds before the login to the database times out.

Table 6-5.   *java.sql Package* Public Class DriverManager

Syntax	Descriptions
Syntax	**Descriptions**
public ResultSetMetaData getMetaData() throws SQLException	Retrieves a ResultSetMetaData object.
public ParameterMetaData getParameterMetaData() throws SQLException	Determines the metadata for a PreparedStatement's parameters.
public void addBatch() throws SQLException	Adds a parameter to a PreparedStatement batch of commands.
Execute	
public ResultSet executeQuery() throws SQLException	Executes a query in a PreparedStatement and returns a ResultSet.
public int executeUpdate() throws SQLException	Executes the SQL statement that contains an INSERT, UPDATE, or DELETE statement in a PreparedStatement.
public boolean execute() throws SQLException	Executes an SQL statement in a PreparedStatement.
Parameters	
public void setNull(int parameterIndex, int sqlType) throws SQLException	Sets the parameter to a null value.
public void setString(int parameterIndex, String x) throws SQLException	Sets the String value.
public void setDate(int parameterIndex, Date x) throws SQLException	Sets the java.sql.Date value.
public void setTime(int parameterIndex, Time x) throws SQLException	Sets the java.sql.Time value.
public void setTimestamp(int parameterIndex, Timestamp x) throws SQLException	Sets the java.sql.Timestamp value.

Table 6-6. *java.sql Package* Public Interface PreparedStatement

Syntax	Descriptions
public void clearParameters() throws SQLException	Clears the current parameter values.
public void setNull(int paramIndex, int sqlType, String typeName) throws SQLException	Sets a parameter to a null value.

Table 6-6. *java.sql Package* Public Interface PreparedStatement (continued)

Syntax	Descriptions
public void close() throws SQLException	Closes a ResultSet.
public ResultSetMetaData getMetaData() throws SQLException	Retrieves metadata.
public Statement getStatement() throws SQLException	Retrieves the Statement object.
Warnings	
public SQLWarning getWarnings() throws SQLException	Retrieves the first warning reported on a ResultSet.
public void clearWarnings() throws SQLException	Clears all warnings reported on a ResultSet.
Virtual Cursor Movement	
public boolean next() throws SQLException	Moves the virtual cursor down one row.
public boolean isFirst() throws SQLException	Determines if the virtual cursor is on the first row.
public boolean isLast() throws SQLException	Determines if the virtual cursor is on the last row.

Table 6-7. *java.sql Package* Public Interface ResultSet

Syntax	Descriptions
public boolean first() throws SQLException	Moves the virtual cursor to the first row.
public boolean last() throws SQLException	Moves the virtual cursor to the last row.
public int getRow() throws SQLException	Determines the current row number.
public boolean absolute(int row) throws SQLException	Moves the virtual cursor to the row.
public boolean relative(int rows) throws SQLException	Moves the virtual cursor a relative number of rows.
public boolean previous() throws SQLException	Moves the virtual cursor to the previous row.
Fetch Size	
public void setFetchSize(int rows) throws SQLException	Gives the database driver a hint as to how many rows should be fetched when more rows are needed for this ResultSet.
public int getFetchSize() throws SQLException	Determines the fetch size for this ResultSet.
Rows	
public boolean rowUpdated() throws SQLException	Determines if a row has been updated.
public boolean rowInserted() throws SQLException	Determines if a row has had an insertion.
public boolean rowDeleted() throws SQLException	Determines if a row is deleted.
public void updateNull(int columnIndex) throws SQLException	Inserts a null into a column.

Table 6-7.   *java.sql Package* Public Interface ResultSet (continued)

Syntax	Descriptions
public void insertRow() throws SQLException	Inserts a row into a ResultSet and into the database.
public void updateRow() throws SQLException	Updates the underlying database with the row of this ResultSet.
public void deleteRow() throws SQLException	Deletes a row from a ResultSet and from the database.
public void refreshRow() throws SQLException	Refreshes the current row with the current value in the database.
public void cancelRowUpdates() throws SQLException	Cancels updates.

Table 6-7. *java.sql Package* Public Interface ResultSet (continued)

Syntax	Descriptions
public int getColumnCount() throws SQLException	Retrieves the number of columns in a ResultSet object.
public boolean isCaseSensitive(int column) throws SQLException	Determines if a column is case sensitive.
public boolean isSearchable(int column) throws SQLException	Determines if a column can be used in a WHERE clause.
public boolean isCurrency(int column) throws SQLException	Determines if a column is a cash value.
public int isNullable(int column) throws SQLException	Determines if a null value can be placed in the column.
public boolean isSigned(int column) throws SQLException	Determines if values are signed numbers.

Table 6-8. *java.sql Package* Public Interface ResultSetMetaData

Syntax	Descriptions
Columns	
public int getColumnDisplaySize(int column) throws SQLException	Retrieves the column's maximum width in characters.
public String getColumnLabel(int column) throws SQLException	Retrieves the column's label.
public String getColumnName(int column) throws SQLException	Retrieves the column's name.
public int getPrecision(int column) throws SQLException	Retrieves the column's precision.
public int getColumnType(int column) throws SQLException	Retrieves the data type of the column.
public String getColumnTypeName (int column) throws SQLException	Retrieves the name of the column data type.
public boolean isReadOnly(int column) throws SQLException	Indicates if a column is read-only.
public boolean isWritable(int column) throws SQLException	Indicates if a column is writable.

Table 6-8. *java.sql Package* Public Interface *ResultSetMetaData* (continued)

Syntax	Descriptions
public int getSavepointId() throws SQLException	Retrieves a savepoint ID.
public String getSavepointName() throws SQLException	Retrieves a savepoint name.

Table 6-9. *java.sql Package* Public Interface *Savepoint*

Syntax	Descriptions
public void close() throws SQLException	Releases a Statement object.
public ResultSet getResultSet() throws SQLException	Retrieves the current ResultSet object.
public int getUpdateCount() throws SQLException	Determines the number of rows that were updated.
public Connection getConnection() throws SQLException	Retrieves a Connection object.
public ResultSet getGeneratedKeys() throws SQLException	Retrieves auto-generated keys.

Timeout

public int getQueryTimeout() throws SQLException	Determines the maximum number of seconds for a Statement object to execute.
public void setQueryTimeout(int seconds) throws SQLException	Sets the maximum number of seconds for a Statement object to execute.

Rows

public int getMaxRows() throws SQLException	Retrieves the maximum number of rows for a ResultSet object.
public void setMaxRows(int max) throws SQLException	Sets the maximum number of rows for a ResultSet object.
public void setFetchSize(int rows) throws SQLException	Gives database a hint for how many rows to retrieve when more rows are needed for the ResultSet.
public int getFetchSize() throws SQLException	Determines the number of rows for the fetch size.

Warnings

public SQLWarning getWarnings() throws SQLException	Retrieves the first warning on a Statement object.
public void clearWarnings() throws SQLException	Clears all the warnings reported on a Statement object.

Table 6-10. *java.sql Package* Public Interface Statement

Syntax	Descriptions
Execute	
public boolean execute(String sql) throws SQLException	Executes a SQL statement.
public ResultSet executeQuery (String sql) throws SQLException	Executes a SQL statement and returns a ResultSet object.
public int executeUpdate(String sql) throws SQLException	Executes a SQL statement that contains INSERT, UPDATE, or DELETE statements or DDL statements.
Batch	
public void addBatch(String sql) throws SQLException	Adds a SQL statement to a batch.
public void clearBatch() throws SQLException	Empties a batch of SQL statements.
public int[] executeBatch() throws SQLException	Executes a batch of SQL statements.

Table 6-10. *java.sql Package* Public Interface Statement (continued)

Syntax	Descriptions
public Connection getConnection() throws SQLException	Opens a connection to a data source.
public Connection getConnection (String username, String password) throws SQLException	Opens a connection to a data source.

Table 6-11. *javaxsql Package* Public Interface DataSource

Syntax	Descriptions
public void setUrl(String url) throws SQLException	Sets the URL a RowSet.
public boolean isReadOnly()	Determines if a RowSet object is read-only.
public void setReadOnly(boolean value) throws SQLException	Sets a RowSet object to read-only.
public int getMaxFieldSize() throws SQLException	Determines the maximum number of bytes that can be placed in a column.
public int getMaxRows() throws SQLException	Determines the maximum number of rows that can be in a RowSet.

DataSource

public String getDataSourceName()	Determines the logical name of the data source for a RowSet.
public void setDataSourceName(String name) throws SQLException	Sets the data source name for a RowSet.

Username and Password

public String getUsername()	Determines the username used to create a database connection for a RowSet.
public void setUsername(String name) throws SQLException	Sets the username for a RowSet.
public String getPassword()	Determines the password used to create a database connection.
public void setPassword(String password) throws SQLException	Sets the database password for a RowSet.

Table 6-12. *javaxsql Package* Public Interface RowSet

Syntax	Descriptions
Timeout	
public int getQueryTimeout() throws SQLException	Determines the maximum time the driver will wait for a statement to execute.
public void setQueryTimeout(int seconds) throws SQLException	Sets the maximum time the driver will wait for a statement to execute.

Table 6-12. *javaxsql Package* Public Interface RowSet (continued)

The Complete Reference

J2EE

Chapter 7

JDBC and Embedded SQL

A J2EE component interacts with a database management system (DBMS) using Java data objects and SQL statements that are embedded into the J2EE component and are executed by the Java data objects.

Java data objects are discussed in the previous chapter. This chapter continues with a detailed look at how to create a SQL statement, execute the SQL statement, and interact with rows of data returned to the J2EE component by the DBMS in response to the request for data.

SQL is presented in this chapter using a practical approach. Each section of the chapter focuses on common tasks that are used in a J2EE component, rather than on SQL keywords. This means you can quickly locate a routine in the chapter and then incorporate the routine directly into your J2EE component.

Model Programs

There are many programming styles that can be used to write the data access portion of a J2EE component. Two programming styles are used in this chapter to illustrate how a J2EE component can interact with a DBMS. These are referred to as "Model A program" and "Model B program."

The Model A program style is used to execute SQL requests that use the execute() or executeUpdate() methods (see Chapter 6) and don't return a ResultSet. The Model B program style is used to execute SQL requests that use the executeQuery() method, which returns a ResultSet. Each of these is described in detail in the next two sections of this chapter.

Both program styles are designed to minimize the code clutter in this chapter. Code clutter occurs whenever many lines of code are used in code examples, but only a few lines of code change between examples.

In an effort to reduce code clutter, each complete program model is presented at the beginning of the chapter. One or two comments are used to indicate where within the program model to place code segments that are used to illustrate SQL routines throughout the rest of the chapter.

These code segments are contained either within a try { } block or within the DownRow() method. The try { } block is where the SQL statement is created and executed. The DownRow() method is where the J2EE component interacts with the ResultSet.

Let's say that you want to update a row in a database. As you'll remember from the last chapter, the executeUpdate() method is used to execute the query and no ResultSet is returned. Therefore, you can replace the second try { } block in the Model A program with the code segment contained in the section of this chapter that shows how to update a row in the database. As you'll see in the next section, the Model A program does not contain a DownRow() method because no ResultSet is returned.

Suppose that you want to retrieve data from the database. The executeQuery() method is used in this scenario. The Model B program is used for this purpose because a ResultSet is returned. In this case, the section of this chapter that shows how to retrieve data from a database contains two code segments. The first code segment contains the query and replaces the second try { } block in the Model B program. The other code segment replaces the DownRow() method of the Model B program and interacts with the ResultSet.

The next two sections of this chapter explain how each model program works. Other sections of this chapter discuss commonly used tasks and show how to incorporate those tasks into a J2EE component. Each of these sections also indicates which program model to use with the task.

Model A Program

The Model A program shown in Listing 7-1 is designed to execute queries that do not return a ResultSet. The Model A program is organized into the ModelA() constructor and the main(). The main() creates an instance of the ModelA object called sql1, which causes the execution of the constructor.

The constructor begins by creating three String objects. These are url, userID, and password. The url is assigned the URL of the database. In this example, the JDBC/ODBC bridge is used to connect to the CustomerInformation database. Of course, the URL used in your J2EE component replaces the URL in Model A and will represent the JDBC driver and database that is specific to your J2EE component. Likewise, the database used with your J2EE component may or may not require a user ID and password. If these are required, they will undoubtedly be different than the user ID and password used in Model A.

The first try { } block in Model A uses the Class.forName() method to load the JDBC driver into the Java Virtual Machine (JVM). You will probably need to replace the driver used in Model A with the appropriate JDBC driver for your J2EE component.

Once the JDBC driver is loaded, the getConnection() method is called to open a connection to the database using the url, userID, and password String objects. The getConnection() method returns a Connection object called database, which is declared above the definition of the constructor.

Two catch { } blocks follow the first try { } block and are used to trap exceptions that occur while the driver is loaded and a connection is established with the database. You can change the text of messages shown in Model A, which are displayed when an exception is caught, to a message that is more conducive to your programming style and J2EE requirements.

The second try { } block in Model A contains a comment. You should replace this try { } block with the try { } that appears in the section of this chapter that describes the task that you want performed by the J2EE component. You'll notice as you read through this chapter that the try { } block within each section references a Statement object called DataRequest, which is declared as a private member of the ModelA class.

The second try { } block is followed by a catch { } block that traps SQL exceptions that occur during the execution of the query in the second try { } block.

Anytime a database connection is closed, you should first check for a null value on the Connection object. If the connection is no longer valid, the close() method will throw a NullPointerException.

```
import java.sql.*;
public class ModelA
{
  private Connection Database;
  private Statement DataRequest;
  public ModelA ()
  {
    String url = "jdbc:odbc:CustomerInformation";
    String userID = "jim";
    String password = "keogh";
    try {
      Class.forName( "sun.jdbc.odbc.JdbcOdbcDriver");
      Database = DriverManager.getConnection(url,userID,password);
    }
    catch (ClassNotFoundException error) {
      System.err.println("Unable to load the JDBC/ODBC bridge." + error);
      System.exit(1);
    }
    catch (SQLException error) {
      System.err.println("Cannot connect to the database. "+ error);
      if(Database != null) {
        try {
          Database.close();
        }
        catch(SQLException er){}
        }
      System.exit(2);
    }
    try {
      // insert example code here
    }
    catch ( SQLException error ) {
      System.err.println("SQL error." + error);
      if(Database != null) {
        try {
          Database.close();
        }
        catch(SQLException er){}
        }
      System.exit(3);
      }
      if(Database != null) {
        try {
          Database.close();
        }
        catch(SQLException er){}
```

```
        }
      }
  public static void main ( String args [] )
  {
    final ModelA sql1 = new ModelA ();
    System.exit ( 0 ) ;
  }
}
```

Model B Program

The Model B program shown is in Listing 7-2 is designed for use by J2EE components that retrieve information from a database. Notice that the Model B program is similar to the Model A program in that the constructor definition (except for the name of the constructor) and the main() are identical. Therefore, refer to the previous section for a description of the constructor and main().

The second try { } block in Model B is where you place the try { } block contained in sections of this chapter that discuss how to retrieve information from a database. This try { } executes a query and returns a ResultSet object called Results, which is declared as a private member of the ModelB class.

Model B also contains DisplayResults() and DownRow(). DisplayResults() is passed the ResultSet returned in the second try { } block, which is used to move the virtual cursor to the first row of the ResultSet using the next() method (see Chapter 6). The next() returns a boolean value that is assigned to the Records variable. The if statement evaluates the value of Records and displays a "No data returned" message if Records contains a false value indicating that there isn't any data in the row.

However, a true value causes the do...while loop to execute, which is where a call to DownRow() is made, passing it the ResultSet. Then, DownRow() retrieves data stored in columns of the ResultSet and assigns those values to variables. Each section of this chapter that discusses a task that retrieves data from a database has its own DownRow(). Therefore, you need to replace the DownRow() in Model B with the DownRow() that is associated with the task that you want performed by the J2EE component.

After DownRow() extracts data from the current row of the ResultSet, control returns to DisplayResults() where the next() method is called and the results are evaluated by the while. If the next() method returns a true value, then DownRow() is recalled; otherwise, the do...while loop is exited and control returns to the constructor.

DisplayResults() also contains a catch { } block that traps errors thrown by statements within the try { } block.

Listing 7-2
A model J2EE component that retrieves information from a database.

```
import java.sql.*;
public class ModelB
{
   private Connection Database;
   private Statement DataRequest;
   private ResultSet Results;
   public ModelB ()
```

```
{
  String url = "jdbc:odbc:CustomerInformation";
  String userID = "jim";
  String password = "keogh";
  try {
    Class.forName( "sun.jdbc.odbc.JdbcOdbcDriver");
    Database = DriverManager.getConnection(url,userID,password);
  }
  catch (ClassNotFoundException error) {
    System.err.println("Unable to load the JDBC/ODBC bridge." + error);
    System.exit(1);
  }
  catch (SQLException error) {
    System.err.println("Cannot connect to the database." + error);
    System.exit(2);
  }
  try {
    // Enter example code here
  }
  catch ( SQLException error ){
    System.err.println("SQL error." + error);
    if(Database != null) {
      try {
        Database.close();
      }
      catch(SQLException er){}
      }
    System.exit(3);
  }
  if(Database != null) {
    try {
      Database.close();
    }
    catch(SQLException er){}
    }
  }
  private void DisplayResults (ResultSet DisplayResults) throws SQLException
  {
    boolean Records = DisplayResults.next();
    if (!Records ) {
      System.out.println( "No data returned");
      return;
    }
    try {
      do {
        DownRow( DisplayResults) ;
      } while ( DisplayResults.next() );
    }
    catch (SQLException error ) {
```

```
          System.err.println("Data display error." + error);
          if(Database != null) {
            try {
              Database.close();
            }
            catch(SQLException er){}
          }
          System.exit(4);
      }
  }
  private  void DownRow ( ResultSet DisplayResults ) throws SQLException
  {
     //Enter new DownRow() code here
  }
  public static void main ( String args [] )
  {
     final ModelB sql1 = new ModelB ();
     System.exit ( 0 ) ;
  }
}
```

Tables

Chapter 5 showed how to design a database. A database design is used as the basis for building tables and indexes that comprise a database. Tables and indexes are created using a query written using SQL. Typically, the database administrator writes and executes the query that creates tables and indexes, although it is possible to have a J2EE component or a Java application execute the same query to create tables and indexes.

The following sections demonstrate various techniques that are used in a query to create a table. Later in this chapter, techniques are presented to create indexes. These queries can be executed from within the Model A program, as discussed previously in this chapter, or executed outside of a Java program using an interface such as ISQL that is supplied with a DBMS.

The user ID that is used to log onto the DBMS and execute the query must have rights to create and drop tables. Dropping a table removes the table from the database, which is discussed later in this chapter.

Depending on the policies of your IT department, developers are commonly given rights to create and drop tables in the development environment. Only the database administrator has these rights to do the same in the production environment.

Creating a Table

You create a table by formatting a SQL query. The query contains the CREATE TABLE SQL statement that contains the name of the table, which is called CustomerAddress in Listing 7-3 because the table will contain address information on customers.

Following the table name are the column definitions, which are enclosed within parentheses. The first column is called CustomerNumber. The data type of the column and the column size follows the column name. A comma separates each column.

The CustomerAddress table contains four columns. These are as follows:

- **CustomerNumber** The customer number is a string of a maximum of 30 characters.

- **CustomerStreet** The customer street is a string of a maximum of 30 characters.

- **CustomerCity** The customer city is a string of a maximum of 30 characters.

- **CustomerZip** The customer ZIP code is a string of a maximum of 30 characters.

All the SQL commands are enclosed in double quotations and assigned to a String object called query. Next, the program creates a SQL statement using the createStatement() method of the Connection object (see Chapter 6). This method returns the handle to the DBMS to the DataRequest object, which is an object of the Statement class.

The query is sent to the DBMS using the executeQuery() method. If successful, the DBMS creates the table. If unsuccessful, the table isn't created and the DBMS returns an error message. The SQL statement is then closed using DataRequest.close().

Listing 7-3
Creating a table.

```
try {
   String query = "CREATE TABLE CustomerAddress (" +
      " CustomerNumber CHAR(30), " +
      " CustomerStreet CHAR(30), " +
      " CustomerCity CHAR(30), " +
      " CustomerZip CHAR(30))";
   DataRequest = Database.createStatement();
   DataRequest.execute(query);
   DataRequest.close();
}
```

Requiring Data in a Column

There are business rules that require a value in specific columns of a row such as the columns that contain a customer's name. You can require the DBMS to reject rows that are missing a value in specific columns by using the NOT NULL clause in the query when the table is created. Listing 7-4 illustrates how the NOT NULL clause is used in a query.

In this example, a CustomerAddress table is being created that contains the same four columns that are used in Listing 7-3 except all of these columns require a value. That is, a row that is missing a value in any of these columns is rejected by the DBMS and will not be inserted into a table.

Listing 7-4
Requiring
a value be
placed in
a column
of a table.

```
try {
  String query = "CREATE TABLE CustomerAddress ( " +
    "CustomerNumber CHAR(30) NOT NULL," +
    "CustomerStreet CHAR(30) NOT NULL," +
    "CustomerCity CHAR(30) NOT NULL," +
    "CustomerZip CHAR(30) NOT NULL)";
  DataRequest = Database.createStatement();
  DataRequest.execute (query );
  DataRequest.close();
}
```

Setting a Default Value for a Column

The DBMS can enter a default value into a column automatically if the column is left
empty whenever a new row is inserted into the table. You determine the value entered
by the DBMS by creating a default value when you create the table. Any value can be
used as the default value as long as the value conforms to the data type and size of
the column.

Let's say most of your customers reside within the 07660 ZIP code. Some customers
living in the area fail to give their sales representative their ZIP code when placing their
first order. They assume that since the ZIP code is the same as your business, you already
know the ZIP code.

A default value is assigned to a column when you create the table by using the
DEFAULT clause. The DEFAULT clause is followed in the query by the value the DBMS
will place in the column if the column is empty in the incoming row. Listing 7-5 illustrates
how to set a default value for a column when you create a table.

Listing 7-5
Creating a
default
value for
a column.

```
try {
  String query = "CREATE TABLE CustomerAddress ( " +
    "CustomerNumber CHAR(30) NOT NULL," +
    "CustomerStreet CHAR(30) NOT NULL," +
    "CustomerCity CHAR(30) NOT NULL," +
    "CustomerZip CHAR(30) NOT NULL DEFAULT '07660')";
  DataRequest = Database.createStatement();
  DataRequest.executeUpdate (query );
  DataRequest.close();
}
```

Dropping a Table

A developer may have the right to remove a table, but this is usually reserved for the
development environment only. The decision to drop a table shouldn't be made lightly

because once a table is dropped you are unable to recover the table. Instead, the table must be re-created and the data must be reinserted into the table.

In addition to losing data elements stored in the table, dropping a table may also affect the integrity of the database and tables that relate to values in the dropped table.

Using the Drop Table statement in the query drops a table. As illustrated in Listing 7-6, the Drop Table statement contains the name of the table that is to be dropped.

Listing 7-6
Dropping
a table.

```
try {
    String query = new String ("DROP TABLE CustomerAddress");
    DataRequest = Database.createStatement();
    DataRequest. execute(query);
    DataRequest.close();
}
```

Indexing

The database schema describes indexes along with tables that are used in the database. Writing a query, as is illustrated in the next section, creates an index. Likewise, a query is used to remove an existing index, which is referred to as "dropping an index."

Developers are typically permitted to create or drop tables within the development environment and only the database administrator has rights to do the same in the production environment, although these rights may vary according to IT department policy.

Executing the query to create or drop an index follows similar procedures as used to create and drop a table. That is, the query can be executed within or outside a J2EE component or Java application as is described in the earlier "Tables" section. Listings in the following sections should be used with the Model A program since no ResultSet is returned when the query is executed.

Creating an Index

An index is created by using the CREATE INDEX statement in a query, as is illustrated in Listing 7-7. The CREATE INDEX statement contains the name of the index and any modifier that describes to the DBMS the type of index that is to be created. In addition, the CREATE INDEX statement uses the ON clauses to identify the name of the table and the name of the column whose value is used for the index.

Listing 7-7 creates an index called CustNum that contains values in the CustomerNumber column of the CustomerAddress table. The CustNum index doesn't have duplicate key values and therefore the UNIQUE modifier is used in the CREATE INDEX statement to prohibit duplicate key values from being included in the index.

Listing 7-7
Creating a
unique
index.

```
try {
    String query = "CREATE UNIQUE INDEX CustNum " +
```

```
                "ON CustomerAddress (CustomerNumber)";
    DataRequest = Database.createStatement();
    DataRequest.execute (query);
    DataRequest.close();
}
```

Designating a Primary Key

A primary key (see Chapter 5) can be designated when a table is created by using the Primary Key modifier as is illustrated in Listing 7-8. This example contains a query that creates a table, as described previously in this chapter, and one column within the table is designated the primary key.

You'll remember that the primary key uniquely identifies each row in a table. Therefore, the column or columns chosen as the primary key must have unique values. That is, the column cannot contain duplicate values.

As shown in Listing 7-8, the OrderNumber column is used as the primary key and is identified in the PRIMARY KEY modifier. Once a column is designated as the primary key, the DBMS prevents duplicate and null values from being placed in the column.

Listing 7-8
Designating a primary key for a table.

```
try {
    String query = "Create Table Orders ( " +
       "OrderNumber CHAR(30) NOT NULL, " +
       "CustomerNumber CHAR(30),   " +
       "ProductNumber CHAR(30), " +
       "CONSTRAINT ORDERS_PK PRIMARY KEY (OrderNumber))";
    DataRequest = Database.createStatement();
    DataRequest. execute(query);
    DataRequest.close();
}
```

Creating a Secondary Index

A secondary index is created by using the CREATE INDEX statement in a query without the use of the UNIQUE modifier as is described previously in this chapter. This means that a secondary index can have duplicate values.

Listing 7-9 illustrates how to create a secondary index. In this example, the index is called CustZip whose key is the CustomerZip column of the CustomerAddress table.

Listing 7-9
Creating a secondary index.

```
try {
    String query = new String ("CREATE INDEX CustZip " +
       "ON CustomerAddress (CustomerZip) ");
    DataRequest = Database.createStatement();
```

```
        DataRequest. execute(query);
        DataRequest.close();
    }
```

Creating a Clustered Index

A clustered index is an index whose key is created from two or more columns of a table as you learned in Chapter 5. For example, combining a customer's last name with a customer first name is a typical key for a clustered index.

Listing 7-10 shows how to create a clustered index. This example creates an index called CustName and uses the LastName and FirstName columns of the Customers table as the key for the index.

It is important to realize that the order in which column names appear in the ON clause plays a critical role in the index. As you remember from Chapter 5, the value of the second column is concatenated to the value of the first column that appears in the query. This means that the key in this key would be KeoghJim, assuming Jim Keogh is a value in the FirstName and LastName columns of the table.

Therefore, the DBMS may not be able to find a search a criterion that is JimKeogh if the key to the clustered index is KeoghJim. Of course, this assumes that the DBMS uses the clustered index for the search.

Listing 7-10
Creating a clustered index.

```
try {
    String query = "CREATE INDEX CustName " +
      " ON Customers (LastName, FirstName)";
    DataRequest = Database.createStatement();
    DataRequest.execute (query);
    DataRequest.close();
}
```

Dropping an Index

An existing index can be removed from the database by using the DROP INDEX statement. The DROP INDEX statement is similar in construction to the DROP TABLE statement, discussed previously in this chapter.

Listing 7-11 shows how to create a query that removes an index. In this example, the CustName index that is associated with the Customers table is dropped.

Listing 7-11
Dropping an index.

```
try {
    String query = new String("DROP INDEX CustName ON Customers ");
    DataRequest = Database.createStatement();
    DataRequest. execute(query);
    DataRequest.close();
}
```

 # Inserting Data into Tables

Once a database, tables, and indexes are created, a J2EE component can insert a new row into a table. In the next several sections of this chapter, you'll learn the technique for writing a query that inserts data into all or some of the columns of a new row.

As you learned in Chapter 6, the executeUpdate() method is used to execute a query that, among other tasks, inserts a row. The executeUpdate() method does not return a ResultSet; therefore, you should use the Model A program with code segments shown in this section that inserts a row into a table.

These code segments insert a row into the Customers table that is defined next. Make sure that you create this table in the CustomerInformation database, using techniques described previously in this chapter, before attempting to insert a new row.

- CustomerNumber, Numeric
- FirstName, VARCHAR, 50
- LastName, VARCHAR, 50
- DateOfFirstOrder, Date

Inserting a Row

The INSERT INTO statement is used to insert a new row into a table. This is illustrated in Listing 7-12. The INSERT INTO statement contains the name of the table into which the row is to be inserted and the name of the columns in which values are inserted. The VALUES clause is used to define the values that are to be placed into the row.

Although the column names are optional, you should always use column names because it is a bad practice to assume that columns appear in a particular order in the table. This is because the table might be restructured by the database administrator without your knowledge.

Each value is placed in the VALUES clause in the same order as the corresponding column's name. In Listing 7-12, a new row is being inserted into the Customers table. The first value in the VALUES clause is the customer number and is followed by the customer's first name, last name, and date of the first order placed by the customer. This order is the same order of the columns names.

You can exclude a value from appearing in a column by excluding the column from the query. For example, you could have removed the LastName column and corresponding value, and the LastName column will be employed for that row.

Be careful that you don't exclude a value that is required by the table; otherwise, the DBMS rejects the row—causing an exception to be thrown.

Listing 7-12
Inserting a row into a table.

```
try {
    String query = "INSERT INTO Customers   " +
        " (CustomerNumber, FirstName, LastName, DateOfFirstOrder) " +
        " VALUES (1,'Mary','Smith','10/10/2001') ";
```

J2EE DATABASES

```
    DataRequest = Database.createStatement();
    DataRequest.executeUpdate (query);
    DataRequest.close();
}
```

Inserting the System's Date into a Column

Sometimes business rules require that the current date be placed into a column of a new row. For example, the system's date is usually used as the date of a new order. You can place the system's date into a column by calling the CURRENT_DATE function. This is not implemented in all versions of DBMS. If you're using Microsoft Access for your DBMS, then you use NOW. Oracle uses SYSDATE. DB2 uses CURRENT DATE (no underscore).

The CURRENT_DATE function directs the DBMS to use the system's date of the server as the value for the column. This is illustrated in Listing 7-13. In this example, the CURRENT_DATE function is called to provide the value for the DateOfFirstOrder column in the new row of the Customers table.

Listing 7-13
Inserting the system's date into a column.

```
try {
    String query = new String ("INSERT INTO Customers (CustomerNumber ,FirstName, "+
      " LastName, DateOfFirstOrder )" +
      " VALUES ( 4,'Mary','Jones', CURRENT_DATE)");
    DataRequest = Database.createStatement();
    DataRequest.executeUpdate (query );
    DataRequest.close();
}
```

Inserting the System Time into a Column

Call the CURRENT_TIME() function whenever a column requires the current time. The CURRENT_TIME() function is called by the DBMS when the query is processed and returns the current time of the server. Listing 7-14 illustrates how to call the CURRENT_TIME() function within a query.

 Caution *A word of caution: Implementation of dates and time functions has not been standardized among vendors. This means that some or all date and time functions discussed in this section may not work with all DBMSs. You should consult with your database administrator or DBMS vendor to determine the proper date and time functions to use with your DBMS.*

Listing 7-14
Inserting the current time into a column.

```
try {
    String query = new String ("INSERT INTO Customers (CustomerNumber ,FirstName, "+
      " LastName, TimeOfFirstOrder ) " +
```

```
        " VALUES ( 2,'Bob','Jones', CURRENT_TIME() )") ;
    DataRequest = Database.createStatement();
    DataRequest.executeUpdate(query );
    DataRequest.close();
}
```

Inserting a Timestamp into a Column

A timestamp consists of both the current data and time and is used in applications where both date and time are critical to the operation of the business. For example, Wall Street firms timestamp orders as they arrive, and this is used to correlate with the market price of stocks at precisely the date and time the order was processed.

Caution *A word of caution: Not all DBMSs support timestamp. Therefore, consult with your database administrator or DBMS vendor for comparable functionality if examples in this section do not work with your DBMS.*

You can place the timestamp into a column by calling the TIMESTAMP() function, as is illustrated in Listing 7-15. The server's system date and time is returned by the function and placed into the column.

Listing 7-15
Inserting a timestamp into a column.

```
try {
    String query = new String ("INSERT INTO Customers (CustomerNumber ,FirstName, "+
        " LastName, FirstOrder ) )" +
        " VALUES ( 2,'Bob','Jones', CURRENT_TIMESTAMP() ) ";
    DataRequest = Database.createStatement();
    DataRequest.executeUpdate (query );
    DataRequest.close();
}
```

Selecting Data from a Table

Retrieving information from a database is the most frequently used routine of J2EE components that interact with a database. Some developers feel that retrieving information is one of the most complex routines to write because there are various ways information can be retrieved.

The following sections of this chapter illustrate the various techniques that can be used to retrieve data using the executeQuery() method. As you learned in Chapter 6, the executeQuery() method returns a ResultSet. Therefore, you'll need to use the Model B program with these code segments.

Each section contains a try { } block and a DownRow() method, which replace the second try { } block in the Model B program and the DownRow() method in the Model B program as described previously in this chapter.

Code segments illustrated in these sections retrieve data from the Customers table. Here are the columns that comprise the Customers table, which you should create before executing the code segments:

- FirstName, VARCHAR, 50
- LastName, VARCHAR, 50
- Street, VARCHAR, 50
- City, VARCHAR, 50
- State, VARCHAR, 2
- ZipCode, VARCHAR, 12

Make sure that you insert rows into the Customers table before trying to execute code segments that appear in the following sections. Table 7-1 contains rows of data that you can use in the Customers table.

Selecting All Data from a Table

The SELECT statement is used to retrieve data from a table, as illustrated in Listing 7-16. In this example, all the columns of all the rows of the Customers table are returned in the ResultSet by the DBMS after the query is processed.

As you'll see in the next few sections, names of columns that you want retrieved from the table are included in the SELECT statement. The executeQuery() method is used to execute the query and returns a ResultSet object. The ResultSet object is passed to the DisplayResults() method, which is defined in the Model B program at the beginning of this chapter. The DisplayResults() method is responsible for moving through the ResultSet and displaying the contents of the ResultSet on the screen.

FirstName	LastName	Street	City	State	ZipCode
Bob	Jones	5 First Street	New York City	NY	07555
Mary	Smith	8 Third Street	Dallas	TX	75553
Bob	Jones	5 First Street	New York City	NY	07555
Mark	Russell	3 Sixth Street	Los Angeles	CA	82272
Susan	Allen	18 Fifth Street	Chicago	IL	45003
Mark	Russell	3 Sixth Street	Los Angeles	CA	82272

Table 7-1.   *Rows That Need to Be Inserted into the Customers Table*

As you'll recall from the beginning of this chapter, the DisplayResults() method calls the DownRow() method, which extracts data from the current row of the ResultSet and displays the row on the screen.

Listing 7-17 contains the DownRow() method for Listing 7-18. In this example, the DownRow() method is passed the ResultSet object from the DisplayResults() method, as described at the beginning of this chapter.

The DownRow() method then declares String objects that are assigned the value of each column in the ResultSet. There is also a String object called printrow, which is assigned all the other String objects and is used to display the values on the screen.

The getString() method is called to gather the value of a specific column in the ResultSet. Using the number of the column, as described in Chapter 6, specifies the column in the getString() method. The getString() method returns the value of the column, which is assigned to a String object. Remember, the getString() method is really the getxxx() method discussed in Chapter 6. The data type of the column replaces the xxx.

Listing 7-16
Selecting all data from a table.

```
try {
   String query = new String ("SELECT " +
      " FirstName, LastName, Street, City, State, ZipCode " +
      " FROM Customers");
   DataRequest = Database.createStatement();
   Results = DataRequest.executeQuery (query);
   DisplayResults (Results);
   DataRequest.close();
}
```

Listing 7-17
Copying values from the ResultSet.

```
private  void DownRow ( ResultSet DisplayResults ) throws SQLException
{
   String FirstName= new String();
   String LastName= new String();
   String Street= new String();
   String City = new String();
   String State = new String();
   String ZipCode= new String();
   String printrow;
   FirstName = DisplayResults.getString ( 1 ) ;
   LastName = DisplayResults.getString ( 2 ) ;
   Street = DisplayResults.getString ( 3 ) ;
   City = DisplayResults.getString ( 4 ) ;
   State = DisplayResults.getString ( 5 ) ;
   ZipCode = DisplayResults.getString ( 6 ) ;
   printrow = FirstName + " " + LastName + " " +
      City + " " + State +  " " + ZipCode;
   System.out.println(printrow);
}
```

Requesting One Column

You can specify a column that you want returned from the table by using the column name in the SELECT statement, as illustrated in Listing 7-18. In this example, the LastName column of all the rows in the Customers table is returned in the ResultSet. Listing 7-19 contains the DownRow() method that is used to retrieve data from the ResultSet that is returned by Listing 7-18.

Listing 7-18
Selecting
one column
to be
retrieved
from
a table.

```
try {
    String query = new String ("SELECT LastName FROM Customers");
    DataRequest = Database.createStatement();
    Results = DataRequest.executeQuery (query);
    DisplayResults (Results);
    DataRequest.close();
}
```

Listing 7-19
Copying
values
from the
ResultSet.

```
private  void DownRow ( ResultSet DisplayResults )throws SQLException
{
    String LastName= new String();
    LastName = DisplayResults.getString ( 1 ) ;
    System.out.println(LastName);
}
```

Requesting Multiple Columns

Multiple columns can be retrieved by specifying the names of the columns in the SELECT statement, similar to the way you select one column in Listing 7-18. This is illustrated in Listing 7-20 where the FirstName and LastName columns for all the rows in the Customers table are returned in the ResultSet. Listing 7-21 shows the DownRow() method that is used to copy and display values from the ResultSet.

Listing 7-20
Copying
values
from the
ResultSet.

```
try {
    String query = new String ("SELECT FirstName, LastName FROM Customers");
    DataRequest = Database.createStatement();
    Results = DataRequest.executeQuery (query);
    DisplayResults (Results);
    DataRequest.close();
}
```

Listing 7-21
Copying
values
from the
ResultSet.

```
private  void DownRow ( ResultSet DisplayResults )throws SQLException
{
    String FirstName= new String();
    String LastName= new String();
```

```
String printrow;
FirstName = DisplayResults.getString ( 1 ) ;
LastName = DisplayResults.getString ( 2 ) ;
printrow = FirstName + " " + LastName;
System.out.println(printrow);
}
```

Requesting Rows

Specific rows can be retrieved from a column by using the WHERE clause in conjunction with the SELECT statement. The WHERE clause contains an expression that is used by the DBMS to identify rows that should be returned in the ResultSet. Any logical expression can be used to include or exclude rows based on values in columns of a row, which is discussed later in this chapter.

Listing 7-22 illustrates how to use the WHERE clause to specify rows. In this example, the SELECT statement retrieves all the columns of rows in the Customers table where the LastName column has the value 'Jones'. You can use the DownRow() method in Listing 7-17 to copy and display values in the ResultSet that is returned by Listing 7-22.

Listing 7-22
Selecting particular rows from a table.

```
try {
    String query = new String ("SELECT "  +
        " FirstName, LastName, Street, City, State, ZipCode " +
        " FROM Customers " +
        " WHERE LastName = 'Jones' ");
    DataRequest = Database.createStatement();
    Results = DataRequest.executeQuery (query);
    DisplayResults (Results);
    DataRequest.close();
}
```

Requesting Rows and Columns

A query can select less than all the columns and all the rows of a table by using a combination of techniques shown previously in this chapter, which is illustrated in Listing 7-23. In this example, the FirstName and LastName of rows in the Customers table are returned in the ResultSet as long as the value of the LastName column is 'Jones'. You can use the DownRow() method shown in Listing 7-21 to copy and display values of the ResultSet returned by Listing 7-23.

Listing 7-23
Retrieving specific columns and rows.

```
try {
    String query = new String("SELECT FirstName, LastName " +
        " FROM Customers " +
        " WHERE LastName = 'Jones' ");
```

```
      DataRequest = Database.createStatement();
      Results = DataRequest.executeQuery (query);
      DisplayResults (Results);
      DataRequest.close();
    }
```

AND, OR, and NOT Clauses

The WHERE clause in a SELECT statement can evaluate values in more than one column of a row by using the AND, OR, and NOT clauses to combine expressions in the WHERE clause. As you'll learn in the next three sections, compound expressions in the WHERE clause are individually evaluated, then the results of these evaluations are further evaluated based on the AND, OR, and NOT clauses that are used in the WHERE clause.

For example, the AND clause requires that both expressions in the compound expression evaluate to true before the WHERE clause expression evaluates true and includes a specified row in the ResultSet.

The OR clause requires that at least one of the expressions in the compound expression evaluate to true before the WHERE clause expression evaluates true. And the NOT clause is used to reverse the logic, changing an expression that evaluates true to a false. Each of these clauses is illustrated in the next three sections.

AND Clause

The purpose of the AND clause is to join two subexpressions together to form one compound expression. The AND clause tells the DBMS that the boolean value of both subexpressions must be true for the compound expression to be true. If the compound expression is true, then the current row being evaluated by the DBMS is returned to your program.

Listing 7-24 illustrates the use of the AND clause in the WHERE clause. In this example, the FirstName and LastName columns of rows from the Customers table are returned in the ResultSet only if the value of the LastName column is 'Jones' and the value of the FirstName column is 'Bob'. You can use the DownRow() method shown in Listing 7-21 to copy and display values of the ResultSet returned by Listing 7-24.

Listing 7-24
Using the AND clause to form a compound expression in the WHERE clause.

```
try {
    String query = new String ("SELECT FirstName, LastName " +
       " FROM Customers " +
       " WHERE LastName = 'Jones' " +
       " AND FirstName = 'Bob'");
    DataRequest = Database.createStatement();
    Results = DataRequest.executeQuery (query);
    DisplayResults (Results);
    DataRequest.close();
}
```

OR Clause

The OR clause is used to create a compound expression using two subexpressions, nearly identical to the way the AND clause joins subexpressions. However, the OR clause tells the DBMS that the compound expression evaluates to a boolean true if either of the two subexpressions evaluate to a boolean true.

Listing 7-25 illustrates the use of the OR clause in the WHERE clause. In this example, the FirstName and LastName columns of rows from the Customers table are returned in the ResultSet only if the value of the FirstName column is 'Mary' or the value of the FirstName column is 'Bob'. Listing 7-21 contains the DownRow() method that you can use with Listing 7-25.

Listing 7-25
Using the OR clause to form a compound expression in the WHERE clause.

```
try {
   String query = new String ("SELECT FirstName, LastName " +
      " FROM Customers " +
      " WHERE FirstName = 'Mary' " +
      " OR FirstName = 'Bob'");
   DataRequest = Database.createStatement();
   Results = DataRequest.executeQuery (query);
   DisplayResults (Results);
   DataRequest.close();
}
```

NOT Clause

The NOT clause reverses the logic of the subexpression contained in the NOT clause. If the subexpression evaluates to a boolean true value, then the NOT clause reverses the logic to return a boolean false value.

In contrast, if the subexpression evaluates to a boolean false value, then the compound expression evaluates to a boolean true value.

Listing 7-26 illustrates the use of the NOT clause. In this example, only rows that don't contain the value 'Mary' in the FirstName column are returned. Listing 7-21 contains the DownRow() method that can be used with Listing 7-26.

Listing 7-26
Using the NOT clause to form a compound expression in the WHERE clause.

```
try {
   String query = new String( "SELECT FirstName, LastName " +
      "FROM Customers " +
      "WHERE NOT FirstName = 'Mary' " );
   DataRequest = Database.createStatement();
   Results = DataRequest.executeQuery (query);
   DisplayResults (Results);
   DataRequest.close();
}
```

J2EE DATABASES

Joining Multiple Compound Expressions

The AND and OR clauses are used to link together two or more subexpressions as discussed previously in this chapter. This results in a compound expression. There can be multiple compound expressions within a WHERE clause expression.

Let's say that you want information about Bob Smith, but you are unsure whether he is in Department 42 or Department 45. You can format a query that uses both the AND clause and the OR clause to retrieve this information. Here's how the WHERE clause might be formatted in this scenario.

Caution *A word of caution: The AND clause has a higher precedence than the OR clause, so the OR clause must be placed within parentheses in this example.*

```
WHERE FirstName = 'Bob' AND LastName = 'Smith AND (Dept = '42' OR Dept = '45')
```

Although the WHERE clause may appear confusing, you can simplify the WHERE clause expression by identifying subexpressions and compound expressions. From reading the previous section, you probably identified the first compound expression and its subexpressions, which is

```
FirstName = 'Bob' AND LastName = 'Smith'
```

The second compound expression is

```
Dept = '42' OR Dept = '45'
```

The second AND clause in the WHERE clause links together these two compound expressions. You can use the AND, OR, and the NOT clauses to create complex selection expressions. The number of compound expressions that you can use in the WHERE clause expressions is practically endless, although some DBMSs establish a limit. This is because of processing time that is necessary to evaluate a complex WHERE clause expression. Contact your database administrator or the manufacturer of your DBMS to determine the limitations of the DBMS that you are using for your system.

Equal and Not Equal Operators

The equal and not equal operators are used to determine if the value in the WHERE clause expression is or isn't in the specify column. You've been using the equal operator throughout examples in this chapter. The next section illustrates the use of the not equal operator.

Before running the query in the next section, modify the Customers table by inserting a Sales column into the table. The Sales column is a long data type. After making the modification, place values in the Sales column of the Customers table as shown in Table 7-2.

FirstName	LastName	Street	City	State	ZipCode	Sales
Bob	Jones	5 First Street	New York City	null	07555	50000
Mary	Smith	8 Third Street	Dallas	TX	75553	20000
Bob	Jones	5 First Street	New York City	null	07555	50000
Mark	Russell	3 Sixth Street	Los Angeles	null	82272	30000
Susan	Allen	18 Fifth Street	Chicago	IL	45003	40000
Mark	Russell	3 Sixth Street	Los Angeles	CA	82272	30000

Table 7-2.   *Insert These Values into the Customers Table*

Not Equal Operator

The not equal operator is used in a WHERE clause expression or subexpression to identify rows that should not be returned by the DBMS. Listing 7-27 illustrates the use of the not equal operator.

In this example, all columns of rows in the Customers table are returned where the values in the Sales column are not equal to 50000. Listing 7-28 contains the DownRow() method that is used to copy and display values in the ResultSet.

Listing 7-27
Excluding rows from the ResultSet using the not equal operator.

```
try {
   String query = new String ("SELECT   " +
     "FirstName, LastName, Street, City, State, ZipCode, Sales " +
     "FROM Customers " +
     "WHERE NOT Sales = 50000 " );
   DataRequest = Database.createStatement ();
   Results = DataRequest.executeQuery (query);
   DisplayResults (Results);
   DataRequest.close ();
   Database.close ();
}
```

Listing 7-28
Copying values from the ResultSet.

```
private  void DownRow ( ResultSet DisplayResults )throws SQLException
{
   String FirstName= new String ();
   String LastName= new String ();
   String Street= new String ();
   String City = new String ();
```

J2EE DATABASES

```
    String State = new String();
    String ZipCode= new String();
    long Sales;
    String printrow;
    FirstName = DisplayResults.getString ( 1 ) ;
    LastName = DisplayResults.getString ( 2 ) ;
    Street = DisplayResults.getString ( 3 ) ;
    City = DisplayResults.getString ( 4 ) ;
    State = DisplayResults.getString ( 5 ) ;
    ZipCode = DisplayResults.getString ( 6 ) ;
    Sales = DisplayResults.getLong ( 7 ) ;
    printrow = FirstName + " " + LastName + " " +
      City + " " + State +  " " + ZipCode + " " + Sales;
    System.out.println(printrow);
}
```

Less Than and Greater Than Operators

The less than and greater than operators direct the DBMS to assess whether or not the value in the specified column of the current row is less than or greater than the value in the WHERE clause expression.

Keep in mind that a value in a column that equals the value in the WHERE clause expression is evaluated as a boolean false. Therefore the row containing that value isn't returned in the ResultSet. The value in the column must be less than or greater than, but not equal to, the value in the WHERE clause expression.

Less Than Operator

Listing 7-29 illustrates the user of the less than operator in the WHERE clause. In this example, all the columns of rows from the Customers table are returned as long as the value of the Sales column is less than 50000.

Listing 7-28 contains the DownRow() method that should be used to copy and display the ResultSet returned by Listing 7-29.

Listing 7-29
Using the less than operator in the WHERE clause expression.

```
try {
   String query = new String ("SELECT  " +
     "FirstName, LastName, Street, City, State, ZipCode, Sales " +
     " FROM Customers " +
     " WHERE Sales < 50000 " );
   DataRequest = Database.createStatement();
   Results = DataRequest.executeQuery (query);
   DisplayResults (Results);
   DataRequest.close();
}
```

Greater Than Operator

The greater than operator is used similar to the less than operator except the value in the column must be greater than the value in the WHERE clause expression for the row to be returned in the ResultSet.

Listing 7-30 illustrates the use of the greater than operator. In this example, all the columns of rows in the Customers table are returned in the ResultSet if the value of the Sales column is greater than 40000. Listing 7-28 contains the DownRow() method that should be used to copy and display the ResultSet returned by Listing 7-30.

Listing 7-30
Using the greater than operator in the WHERE clause expression.

```
try {
   String query = new String ("SELECT   " +
     "FirstName, LastName, Street, City, State, ZipCode, Sales " +
     "FROM Customers " +
     "WHERE Sales > 40000 " );
   DataRequest = Database.createStatement();
   Results = DataRequest.executeQuery (query);
   DisplayResults (Results);
   DataRequest.close();
}
```

Less Than Equal To and Greater Than Equal To

A drawback of using the less than and greater than operators is that rows containing the value of the WHERE clause expression are not returned in the ResultSet. Alternatively, the less than equal to or the greater than equal to operators include rows that contain the WHERE clause expression. This is illustrated in the next two sections.

Less Than Equal To

Listing 7-31 illustrates how to use the less than operator in the WHERE clause. In this example, all columns of rows in the Customers table are returned if the value of the Sales column of the row is less than or equal to 50000.

Listing 7-28 contains the DownRow() method that should be used to copy and display the ResultSet returned by Listing 7-31.

Listing 7-31
Using the less than equal to operator in the WHERE clause expression.

```
try {
   String query = new String ("SELECT   " +
     "FirstName, LastName, Street, City, State, ZipCode, Sales " +
     "FROM Customers " +
     "WHERE Sales <= 50000 " );
   DataRequest = Database.createStatement();
   Results = DataRequest.executeQuery (query);
```

```
        DisplayResults (Results);
        DataRequest.close();
    }
```

Greater Than Equal To

As illustrated in Listing 7-32, the greater than equal to operator is used similar to the less than equal to operator. In this example, all the columns in rows of the Customers table are returned in the ResultSet if the value of the Sales column in the row is greater than or equal to 50000.

Listing 7-28 contains the DownRow() method that should be used to copy and display the ResultSet returned by Listing 7-32.

Listing 7-32
Using the greater than equal to operator in the WHERE clause expression.

```
try {
    String query = new String ("SELECT   " +
      "FirstName, LastName, Street, City, State, ZipCode, Sales " +
      "FROM Customers " +
      "WHERE Sales >= 50000 ");
    DataRequest = Database.createStatement();
    Results = DataRequest.executeQuery (query);
    DisplayResults (Results);
    DataRequest.close();
}
```

BETWEEN

The BETWEEN operator is used to define a range of values that is to be used as the value of the selection expression. The range must consist of a sequential series of values such as from 100 to 200. The BETWEEN operator must follow the name of the column in the WHERE clause. The AND operator is used to join the lower and upper values of the range. All values in the range, including the first and last values, are considered when the DBMS evaluates the value of the column specified in the selection expression.

Listing 7-33 illustrates the use of the BETWEEN operator. In this example, all the columns in rows of the Customers table are returned in the ResultSet if the value of the Sales column in the row is between 20000 and 39999.

Listing 7-28 contains the DownRow() method that should be used to copy and display the ResultSet returned by Listing 7-33.

Listing 7-33
Using the BETWEEN operator in the WHERE clause expression.

```
try {
    String query = new String("SELECT   " +
      "FirstName, LastName, Street, City, State, ZipCode, Sales " +
```

```
      "FROM Customers " +
      "WHERE Sales BETWEEN 20000 AND 39999 " );
   DataRequest = Database.createStatement();
   Results = DataRequest.executeQuery (query);
   DisplayResults (Results);
   DataRequest.close();
}
```

LIKE

The LIKE operator directs the DBMS to return a row in the ResultSet if a value in a specified column partially matches the value of the WHERE clause expression. The WHERE clause expression must include a character that must be an exact match and a wildcard character that is used to match any other character.

Caution *A word of caution: The LIKE operator is very convenient and powerful to use; however, it also uses a lot of database overhead and therefore should be used with discretion.*

Here are the wildcards that are used with the LIKE operator:

■ **Underscore (_)**   A single character wildcard character. For example, if you are unsure if the customer's last name is Anderson or Andersen, you use the underscore in place of the character that is in question such as Anders_n.

■ **Percent (%)**   A multicharacter wildcard character used to match any number of characters. For example, Smi% is used to match a value of a column where the first three characters are Smi and any other character that follows Smi.

Listing 7-36 illustrates the use of the LIKE operator. In this example, all the columns in rows of the Customers table are returned in the ResultSet if the value of the LastName column in the row has the first three characters Smi and any other characters.

Listing 7-28 contains the DownRow() method that should be used to copy and display the ResultSet returned by Listing 7-34.

Listing 7-34
Using the
LIKE
operator in
the
WHERE
clause
expression.

```
try {
   String query = new String ("SELECT    " +
      "FirstName, LastName, Street, City, State, ZipCode, Sales " +
      "FROM Customers " +
      "WHERE LastName LIKE 'Smi%' ");
   DataRequest = Database.createStatement();
   Results = DataRequest.executeQuery (query);
   DisplayResults (Results);
   DataRequest.close();
}
```

IS NULL Operator

The IS NULL operator is used to determine if a specified column does not contain any value. You'll find it useful to use the IS NULL operator whenever you need to identify rows that are missing information in a column.

It is important to understand that the number zero or a space are not NULL values. For example, a zero value in the sales column of a table is a real value. Likewise, a column that contains a space isn't NULL, because a space is a valid ASCII character. NULL is void of any value and occurs when a row is inserted into a table without having a value or the value is explicitly set to NULL.

Listing 7-35 illustrates the use of the IS NULL operator. In this example, all the columns in rows of the Customers table are returned in the ResultSet if the value of the State column in the row is NULL.

Listing 7-28 contains the DownRow() method that should be used to copy and display the ResultSet returned by Listing 7-35.

Listing 7-35
Using the
IS NULL
operator in
the WHERE
clause
expression.

```
try {
   String query = new String ("SELECT  " +
      "FirstName, LastName, Street, City, State, ZipCode, Sales " +
      "FROM Customers " +
      "WHERE State IS NULL ");
   DataRequest = Database.createStatement();
   Results = DataRequest.executeQuery (query);
   DisplayResults (Results);
   DataRequest.close();
}
```

DISTINCT Modifier

The SELECT statement returns all rows in a table unless a WHERE clause is used to exclude specific rows. However, the ResultSet includes duplicate rows unless a primary index is created for the table or only unique rows are required in the table, as you learned previously in this chapter.

There will be occasions when you want to exclude all but one copy of a row from the ResultSet. You can do this by using the DISTINCT modifier in the SELECT statement, as illustrated in Listing 7-36. The DISTINCT modifier tells the DBMS not to include duplicate rows in the ResultSet.

You'll find this useful whenever data from multiple sources are combined into one table, as is the case of a mailing list. The DISTINCT modifier filters repeating rows that contain the same name and address.

 A word of caution: This technique requires a lot of system overhead and therefore should be used with discretion. An alternative approach to using this is to write a WHERE clause expression that returns the same results as using the DISTINCT modifier.

In this example, all the columns in rows of the Customers table are returned in the ResultSet exclusive of duplicate rows. Listing 7-28 contains the DownRow() method that should be used to copy and display the ResultSet returned by Listing 7-36.

Listing 7-36
Using the
DISTINCT
modifier.

```
try {
   String query = new String ("SELECT DISTINCT   " +
      "FirstName, LastName, Street, City, State, ZipCode, Sales " +
      "FROM Customers ");
   DataRequest = Database.createStatement();
   Results = DataRequest.executeQuery (query);
   DisplayResults (Results);
   DataRequest.close();
}
```

IN Modifier

The IN modifier is used to define a set of values used by the DBMS to match values in a specified column. The set can include any number of values and appear in any order.

Let's say that you wanted a list of customers who purchase three products. You'd place the three product identification numbers in a set, then tell the DBMS to search the order table for orders that contain product numbers that are in the set. If the product numbers match, then customer information associated with the row is returned to your program.

The IN modifier is used in the WHERE clause to define the list of values in the set. This is demonstrated in Listing 7-37 where the DBMS is told to compare values in the Sales column with the three values in the group clause. If any of these three values are found in the Sales column of the current row, the row is returned to the program. Listing 7-28 contains the DownRow() method that should be used to copy and display the ResultSet returned by Listing 7-37.

Listing 7-37
Using the IN
modifier in
the WHERE
clause.

```
try {
   String query = new String ("SELECT   " +
      "FirstName, LastName, Street, City, State, ZipCode, Sales " +
      " FROM Customers " +
      " WHERE Sales IN (20000, 30000, 40000) " );
   DataRequest = Database.createStatement();
   Results = DataRequest.executeQuery (query);
   DisplayResults (Results);
   DataRequest.close();
}
```

NOT IN Modifier

The NOT IN modifier is similar to the IN modifier explained in the previous section except the NOT IN modifier reverses the logic of the previous selection expression. That is, the NOT IN modifier identifies a set of values that shouldn't match rows returned to the program.

Listing 7-38 shows how the NOT IN modifier is used in a program. In this example, all columns of rows in the Customers table where the value of the Sales column isn't 20000, 30000, or 40000 are returned in the ResultSet. Rows with sales of 20000, 30000, or 40000 are not returned. Listing 7-28 contains the DownRow() method that should be used to copy and display the ResultSet returned by Listing 7-38.

Listing 7-38
Using the NOT IN modifier in the WHERE clause.

```
try {
    String query = new String ("SELECT " +
        "FirstName, LastName, Street, City, State, ZipCode, Sales " +
        " FROM Customers " +
        " WHERE Sales NOT IN (20000, 30000, 40000) " );
    DataRequest = Database.createStatement();
    Results = DataRequest.executeQuery (query);
    DisplayResults (Results);
    DataRequest.close();
}
```

Metadata

Metadata is data that describes data, which you learned about in Chapter 6. Metadata is returned with the ResultSet object and can be extracted from the ResultSet object by creating a ResultSetMetaData using techniques that are described in the next several sections of this chapter.

Metadata can be used in a J2EE component for various purposes such as to display the column name of a column and determine the data type of a column among other metadata. The most commonly used metadata are

- Column name
- Column number
- Column data type
- Column width

Number of Columns in ResultSet

Listing 7-39 contains the DownRow() method that illustrates how to determine the number of columns that are in the ResultSet. The getMetaData() method is called to extract metadata from the ResultSet. The getMetaData() method returns a ResultSetMetaData object, which is called metadata in this example.

The ResultSetMetaData object contains several methods that are used to copy specific metadata from the ResultSet. In this example, the getColumnCount() method is called to retrieve the number of columns contained in the ResultSet, which is then assigned to the NumberOfColumns variable and printed on the screen using the println() method. This doesn't work with all drivers.

The DownRow() method in Listing 7-39 can replace the DownRow() method in the Model B program and used in any version of the Model B program that is presented in this chapter. Of course, the DownRow() method must be modified to copy and display data contained in the ResultSet, as shown previously in this chapter.

Listing 7-39
Determining the number of columns in a ResultSet.

```
private  void DownRow ( ResultSet DisplayResults )throws SQLException
{
   ResultSetMetaData metadata = DisplayResults.getMetaData ();
   int NumberOfColumns;
   String printrow;
   NumberOfColumns = metadata.getColumnCount ();
   System.out.println("Number Of Columns: " + NumberOfColumns);
}
```

Data Type of a Column

Listing 7-40 illustrates how to determine the data type of a column. You'll notice that this technique is very similar to the technique described in the previous section that retrieved the number of columns in the ResultSet.

In this example, the getColumnTypeName() method is called to copy the data type from column nine of the ResultSet to the ColumnType object. Any valid column number in the ResultSet can be passed to the getColumnTypeName() method. You can use the data type returned by the getColumnTypeName() method to determine the proper getxxx() method to use to copy data from the ResultSet. The type is returned as the native type, not the SQL type.

Listing 7-40
Determining the date type of columns in a ResultSet.

```
private  void DownRow ( ResultSet DisplayResults ) throws SQLException
{
   ResultSetMetaData metadata = DisplayResults.getMetaData ();
   String ColumnType = new String();
   String printrow;
   ColumnType = metadata.getColumnTypeName ( 9 );
   System.out.println("Column Type: " + ColumnType );
}
```

Name of a Column

Retrieving the column name from the metadata uses a process similar to that used to copy the data type of a column from the metadata and is illustrated in Listing 7-41. In this example, the getColumnLabel() method is used to copy the column name from a specific column and assign the column name to the String object ColumnName. The number of the column in the ResultSet is passed to the getColumnLabel() method.

```
private  void DownRow ( ResultSet DisplayResults ) throws SQLException
{
   ResultSetMetaData metadata = DisplayResults.getMetaData ();
   String ColumnName = new String();
   String printrow;
   ColumnName = metadata.getColumnLabel (9) ;
   System.out.println("Column Name: " + ColumnName);
}
```

Column Size

The column size of a column, also referred to as the column width, is called the display size and represents the number of characters that are necessary to display the maximum value that might be stored in the column.

You retrieve the display size by using the getColumnDisplaySize() method as is illustrated in Listing 7-42. This listing is similar to the other listings discussed in metadata sections of this chapter.

The getColumnDisplaySize( ) is called and passed the number of the column whose display size is to be retrieved from the ResultSet. The display size is then shown on the screen.

```
private  void DownRow ( ResultSet DisplayResults ) throws SQLException
{
   ResultSetMetaData metadata = DisplayResults.getMetaData ();
   int ColumnWidth;
   String printrow;
   ColumnWidth = metadata.getColumnDisplaySize ( 9 ) ;
   System.out.println("Column Width:" + ColumnWidth);
}
```

Updating Tables

Modifying data in a database is one of the most common functionalities included in every J2EE component that provides database interactions. Generally, any information that is retrievable is also changeable depending on access rights and data integrity issues, which are discussed in Chapter 5.

The next several sections illustrate techniques that are used to update rows in a table of a database. Code segments described in these sections use the executeUpdate()

method to process queries. As you recall from Chapter 6, the executeUpdate() method does not return a ResultSet. Therefore, the Model A program described earlier in this chapter should be used with code segments in these sections.

Before executing code segments presented in these sections, you'll need to create a Customers table as defined here, then insert the rows of data that are contained in Table 7-3.

- FirstName, VARCHAR, 50

- LastName, VARCHAR, 50

- Street, VARCHAR, 50

- City, VARCHAR, 50

- State, VARCHAR, 2

- ZipCode, VARCHAR, 12

- Discount, long

Updating a Row and Column

The UPDATE statement is used to change the value of one or more columns in one or multiple rows of a table. The UPDATE statement must contain the name of the table that is to be updated and a SET clause. The SET clause identifies the name of the column and the new value that will be placed into the column, overriding the current value. The UPDATE statement may have a WHERE clause if a specific number of rows are to be updated. If the WHERE clause is omitted, all rows are updated based on the value of the SET clause.

FirstName	LastName	Street	City	State	Zipcode	Discount
Bob	Jones	5 First Street	New York City	NY	07555	10
Mary	Smith	8 Third Street	Dallas	TX	75553	20
Tom	Jones	5 First Street	New York City	NY	07555	11
Mark	Russell	23 Eighth Street	Los Angeles	CA	82272	16
Susan	Allen	18 Fifth Street	Chicago	IL	45003	15
Kelly	Russell	32 Fourth Street	Los Angeles	CA	82272	15

Table 7-3. *Insert These Values into the Customers Table*

Listing 7-43 illustrates how to update one column. In this example, the value of the Street column of the Customers table is changed to '5 Main Street'. However, the change occurs only where the value of the FirstName column is 'Bob'.

Listing 7-43
Updating a
row and
column.

```
try {
    String query = new String("UPDATE Customers " +
        "SET Street = '5 Main Street' " +
        " WHERE FirstName = 'Bob'");
    DataRequest = Database.createStatement();
    DataRequest.executeUpdate (query);
    DataRequest.close();
}
```

Updating Multiple Rows

Multiple rows of a table can be updated by formatting the WHERE clause expressions to include criteria that qualify multiple rows for the update. There are four common WHERE clause expressions that are used to update multiple rows of a table. These are

- **The IN test**   The WHERE clause expression contains multiple values in the IN clause that must match the value in the specified column for the update to occur in the row.

- **The IS NULL test**   Rows that don't have a value in the specified column are updated when the IS NULL operator is used in the WHERE clause expression.

- **The comparison test**   The WHERE clause expression contains a comparison operator, as described previously in this chapter, that compares the value in the specified column with a value in the WHERE clause expression.

- **All rows**   A query can direct the DBMS to update the specified column in all rows of a table by excluding the WHERE clause in the query.

Always be cautious whenever you execute a query that updates multiple rows, because the query has the potential to affect all the information contained in a table. An error in a query is multiplied by the number of rows in a table whenever the query updates more than one row.

IN Test

The IN clause provides two or more values that are compared to the value of the designed column in the IN clause. Rows whose columns contain one of these values are then updated by the UPDATE statement.

Listing 7-44 illustrates how the IN test is used to update rows of the Customers table. In this example, the value of the Discount column is changed to 25 if the current value of the Discount column is either 12 or 15.

J2EE DATABASES

Listing 7-44
Updating a
row using
the IN test.

```
try {
  String query = new String ("UPDATE Customers " +
    "SET Discount = 25 " +
    "WHERE Discount IN (12,15)");
  DataRequest = Database.createStatement();
  DataRequest.executeUpdate (query);
. DataRequest.close();
}
```

IS NULL Test

The IS NULL test evaluates the value of a column designated in the test to determine if the column is NULL. That is, the column is empty of any value. If so, then the IS NULL test returns a true and the UPDATE statement updates the column specified in the SET clause.

Listing 7-45 illustrates how to use the IS NULL test in the UPDATE statement. In this example, the IS NULL test determines if the LastName column is NULL. If so, then a zero is placed in the Discount column. If not, then the value of the Discount column remains unchanged.

Listing 7-45
Updating a
row using
the IS
NULL test.

```
try {
  String query = new String ("UPDATE Customers " +
    "SET Discount = 0 " +
    "WHERE LastName IS NULL  ");
  DataRequest = Database.createStatement();
  DataRequest.executeUpdate (query);
  DataRequest.close();
}
```

Updating Based on Values in a Column

An expression in the WHERE clause can be used to identify rows that are to be updated by the UPDATE statement. All the WHERE clause expressions discussed previously in the SELECT statement also apply to the UPDATE statement. Review the SELECT statement section for details on how to properly formulate the WHERE clause expression.

Listing 7-46 illustrates how to identify a row to update. In this example, rows in the Customers table that have a Discount greater than 20 will have the value of the Discount changed to 20.

Listing 7-46
Updating a
row based
on a value in
a designated
column.

```
try {
  String query = new String ("UPDATE Customers " +
```

```
      "SET Discount = 20 " +
      "WHERE Discount > 20 ");
   DataRequest = Database.createStatement();
   DataRequest.executeUpdate (query);
   DataRequest.close();
}
```

Updating Every Row

All rows in a table can be updated by excluding the WHERE clause in the UPDATE
statement. This technique is illustrated in Listing 7-47. In this example, the value of
the Discount column in all rows in the Customers table is changed to zero.

Listing 7-47
Updating
every row in
the table.

```
try {
   String query = new String ("UPDATE Customers " +
      "SET Discount = 0 ");
   DataRequest = Database.createStatement();
   DataRequest.executeUpdate (query);
   DataRequest.close();
}
```

Updating Multiple Columns

Multiple columns of rows can be updated simultaneously by specifying the column names
and appropriate values in the SET clause of the query. Listing 7-48 illustrates this
technique. In this example, rows in the Customers table where the LastName column
has the value 'Jones' are updated. The SET clause contains the column names and the
new values that override the current values of those columns. In this case, the value of
the Discount column is changed to 12 and the value of the Street column is changed to
'Jones Street'.

Listing 7-48
Updating
multiple
columns
of a table.

```
try {
   String query = new String ("UPDATE Customers " +
      "SET Discount = 12, Street = 'Jones Street'" +
      "WHERE LastName = 'Jones'");
   DataRequest = Database.createStatement();
   DataRequest.executeUpdate (query);
   DataRequest.close();
}
```

Updating Using Calculations

The value that replaces the current value in a column does not have to be explicitly defined in the SET clause if the value can be derived from a value in another column of the same row.

Let's say that a row contains the retail price of an item purchased by a customer. The customer is granted a percentage discount based on the how well the customer is valued by the business. The UPDATE statement can calculate the discounted price and place the discount price in the DiscountPrice column of the row. The value of the discount price doesn't need to be included in the SET clause. Instead, the discount price can be calculated.

Listing 7-49 illustrates how to use the results of a calculation to update a value of a column in a table. In this example, the value that is placed in the DiscountPrice column is calculated by using values in the Price column and in the Discount column. The results of this calculation override the current value in the DiscountPrice column.

Before running this query, you'll need to create a new Customers table or modify the existing Customers table to reflect the following columns. You'll also need to insert the data shown in Table 7-4 into the Customers table.

- FirstName, VARCHAR, 50
- LastName, VARCHAR, 50
- Street, VARCHAR, 50
- City, VARCHAR, 50
- State, VARCHAR, 2
- ZipCode, VARCHAR, 12
- Discount, long
- Price, long
- DiscountPrice, long

Listing 7-49
Updating a column using a calculation.

```
try {
   String query = new String ("UPDATE Customers " +
      "SET DiscountPrice = Price * ((100 - Discount) / 100) ");
   DataRequest = Database.createStatement();
   DataRequest.executeUpdate (query);
   DataRequest.close();
}
```

FirstName	LastName	Street	City	State	Zipcode	Discount	Price
Bob	Jones	5 First Street	New York City	NY	07555	10	100
Mary	Smith	8 Third Street	Dallas	TX	75553	20	200
Tom	Jones	5 First Street	New York City	NY	07555	20	300
Mark	Russell	23 Eighth Street	Los Angeles	CA	82272	10	400
Susan	Allen	18 Fifth Street	Chicago	IL	45003	15	500
Kelly	Russell	32 Fourth Street	Los Angeles	CA	82272	15	600

Table 7-4.   *Insert These Values into the Customers Table*

Deleting Data from a Table

Deleting rows is necessary to purge erroneous information from the database and to remove information that is no longer needed. However, you must build safeguards in to assure that critical information isn't inadvertently deleted from the database. Before you delete a row from a table, you must be certain that other tables are not negatively affected.

The next section of this chapter illustrates the technique for removing a row from a table by using the DELETE FROM statement. Multiple rows can be deleted by including a WHERE clause in the DELETE FROM statement as described in detail in the earlier "Updating Tables" section of this chapter.

The query that contains the DELETE FROM statement is executed using the executeQuery() method. As you learned in Chapter 6, the executeQuery() method doesn't return a ResultSet. Therefore, use the Model A program with the code segment described in the next section.

Deleting a Row from a Table

A row is deleted from a table by using the DELETE FROM statement. The DELETE FROM statement includes the name of the table and a WHERE clause that contains an expression that identifies the row or rows to remove from the table.

Listing 7-50 illustrates how to use the DELETE FROM statement. In this example, rows from the Customers table are being deleted where the value of the LastName column is 'Jones' and the value of the FirstName column is 'Tom'. Make sure you have a row that contains these values in the Customers table before running this code segment.

Listing 7-50
Deleting
a row.

```
try {
    String query = new String ("DELETE FROM Customers " +
      "WHERE LastName = 'Jones' and FirstName = 'Tom'");
    DataRequest = Database.createStatement();
    DataRequest.executeUpdate (query);
    DataRequest.close();
}
```

Joining Tables

In Chapter 5, you learned about normalization and how rows of data elements that are placed in tables are related to each other by linking rows using a common value in each row of two tables. Linking rows is called joining tables.

Tables are joined in a query using a two-step process. First, both tables that are being joined must be identified in the FROM clause where tables are listed one after the other and are separated by a comma.

Next, an expression is created in the WHERE clause that identifies the columns that are used to create the join. Let's say that an Orders table is joined to the Customers table using the customer number. The customer number in the Orders table is in the CustomerNumber column and the customer number in the Customers table is the CustNum column. The following line contains a WHERE clause expression that joins these tables:

```
WHERE CustomerNumber = CustNum
```

The joined tables create a logical table that has all the columns of both tables. All the tasks performed on a single table previously in this chapter can also be applied to join tables.

Joining too many tables can cause performance degradation and bring response time to a crawl. Typically, five is the maximum number of tables that are joined. However, the actual number may vary depending on the DBMS, so consult with your database administrator or DBMS manufacturer for the maximum number of tables permitted to be joined using your DBMS.

Before you try examples in this chapter, you'll need to create a Customers table, ZipCode table, Store table, Products table, and Orders table. These tables are defined next. Insert the rows described in Tables 7-5 through 7-9 into the appropriate tables before running codes segments described in the following sections of this chapter.

- **Customers Table**
  - CustNumber, Number, Primary Key
  - FirstName, VARCHAR, 50
  - LastName, VARCHAR, 50
  - Street, VARCHAR, 50
  - Zip, VARCHAR, 12
- **ZipCode Table**
  - ZipCode, VARCHAR, 12, Primary Key
  - City, VARCHAR, 50
  - State, VARCHAR, 2
- **Store Table**
  - StoreNumber, Number, Primary Key
  - ZipCode, VARCHAR, 12
- **Products Table**
  - ProductNumber, Number, Primary Key
  - ProductName, VARCHAR, 50
  - UnitPrice, Long
- **Orders Table**
  - OrderNumber, Number, Primary Key
  - ProdNumber, Number
  - CustomerNumber, Number
  - StoreNumber, Number
  - Quantity, Number
  - SubTotal, Long

CustNumber	FirstName	LastName	Street	Zip
591	Anne	Smith	65 Cutter Street	04735
721	Bart	Adams	15 W. Spruce	05213
845	Tom	Jones	35 Pine Street	07660
901	Mary	Smith	5 Maple Street	08513

Table 7-5.   *Insert These Values into the Customers Table*

ZipCode	City	State
04735	Woodridge	TX
05213	River Ville	CA
07660	West Town	NJ
08513	SunnySide	NY

Table 7-6.   *Insert These Values into the ZipCode Table*

StoreNumber	ZipCode
278	08513
345	07660
547	05213
825	04735

Table 7-7.   *Insert These Values into the Store Table*

ProductNumber	ProductName	Unit Price
1052	CD Player	100
3255	VCR	250
5237	DVD Player	325
7466	50-inch TV	532

Table 7-8. *Insert These Values into the Products Table*

Joining Two Tables

Listing 7-51 illustrates the technique used to join two tables. In this example, the Customers table and the ZipCode table are identified in the FROM clause. These are the tables that are being joined.

The WHERE clause expression identifies the Zip column from the Customers table and the ZipCode column from the ZipCode table. The equal operator directs the DBMS to join rows in both the Customers table and the ZipCode table where values of the Zip column and the ZipCode column have the same value. Rows whose columns don't match are excluded from the join (see the "Inner and Outer Joins" section later in this chapter). If both columns used for the join have the same name, then a column name qualifier is used to associate the column with each table, which is discussed later in this chapter. It's usually considered good practice to always use a table name or alias.

OrderNumber	ProdNumber	CustomerNumber	StoreNumber	Quantity	SubTotal
122	5237	591	345	1	325
334	3255	901	278	1	250
365	3255	901	278	4	1000
534	7466	591	825	3	1596
587	5237	845	345	1	325
717	1052	721	825	2	200
874	7466	721	825	1	532

Table 7-9. *Insert These Values into the Orders Table*

Once the Customers and ZipCode tables are joined, the SELECT statement references column names of both tables to return in the ResultSet. In this example, City, State, and ZipCode columns are in the ZipCode table and the FirstName and LastName columns are in the Customers table.

The query in Listing 7-51 uses the executeQuery() method to execute the query. Therefore, you'll need to use the Model B program to run this example. Listing 7-52 contains the DownRow() method that extracts and displays data from the ResultSet.

Listing 7-51
Joining two
tables.

```
try {
  String query = new String ("SELECT FirstName, LastName, City, State, ZipCode " +
    "FROM Customers, ZipCode " +
    "WHERE Zip = ZipCode");
  DataRequest = Database.createStatement();
  Results = DataRequest.executeQuery (query);
  DisplayResults (Results);
  DataRequest.close();
}
```

Listing 7-52
The
DownRow()
method
used when
joining
two tables.

```
private  void DownRow ( ResultSet DisplayResults )
     throws SQLException
{
  String FirstName= new String();
  String LastName= new String();
  String Street= new String();
  String City = new String();
  String State = new String();
  String ZipCode= new String();
  String printrow;
  FirstName = DisplayResults.getString ( 1 ) ;
  LastName = DisplayResults.getString ( 2 ) ;
  Street = DisplayResults.getString ( 3 ) ;
  City = DisplayResults.getString ( 4 ) ;
  State = DisplayResults.getString ( 5 ) ;
  ZipCode = DisplayResults.getString ( 6 ) ;
  printrow = FirstName + " " + LastName + " " +
    City + " " + State +  " " + ZipCode + " " + Sales + " " + Profit;
  System.out.println(printrow);
}
```

Parent/Child Join

A parent/child join is used to join tables that have a parent/child relationship where rows in the parent table must exist for rows in the child table to exist, which is illustrated in Listing 7-53.

In this example, two tables are joined together using the product number value. These are the Products table and the Orders table. Only rows that have a matching product number in both tables are placed in the virtual table that consists of rows from both tables.

The Products table is the parent table in this relationship because an order cannot be placed without a product appearing in the Products table. Basically, a customer cannot order a product that doesn't exist in the Products table.

Listing 7-53 is executed using the executeQuery() method and therefore returns a ResultSet. This means that you must use the Model B program to run this code segment. Listing 7-54 contains the DownRow() method that retrieves and displays values from the ResultSet.

Listing 7-53
The parent/
child join.

```
try {
    String query = new String (" SELECT OrderNumber, ProductName " +
        " FROM Orders, Products " +
        " WHERE ProdNumber = ProductNumber");
    DataRequest = Database.createStatement();
    Results = DataRequest.executeQuery (query);
    DisplayResults (Results);
    DataRequest.close();
}
```

Listing 7-54
The
DownRow()
method
used with a
parent/
child join.

```
private  void DownRow ( ResultSet DisplayResults )
        throws SQLException
{
    int OrderNum, ProdNum;
    String printrow = new String();
    OrderNum = DisplayResults.getInt ( 1 ) ;
    ProdNum = DisplayResults. getInt ( 2 ) ;
    printrow = OrderNum + " " + ProdNum;
    System.out.println(printrow);
}
```

Multiple Comparison Join

The WHERE clause expression used to join together tables can be a compound expression. A compounded expression consists of two or more subexpressions, each of which is evaluated separately, as is described previously in this chapter.

A compound expression is used to specify more than one selection criteria used to join two tables, which is illustrated in Listing 7-55. In this example, the DBMS is directed to join together rows of the Products table and rows of the Orders table.

There are two components of the subexpression in this example. The first requires the DBMS to match product numbers in both tables. The other subexpression requires that the value in the Quantity column be greater than 2.

The AND operator is used to join together both subexpressions. This means that both subexpressions must evaluate true for the DBMS to join rows of both tables. That is, only a row where the product number matches in both tables and the quantity of the order is greater than 2 is included in the temporary table. If either subexpression evaluates as false, then the row is not included in the virtual table.

Listing 7-55 is executed using the executeQuery() method and therefore returns a ResultSet. This means that you must use the Model B program to run this code segment. Listing 7-56 contains the DownRow() method that retrieves and displays values from the ResultSet.

Listing 7-55
The multiple comparison join.

```
try {
    String query = " SELECT OrderNumber, ProductName, Quantity " +
        " FROM Orders, Products " +
        " WHERE ProdNumber = ProductNumber " +
        " AND Quantity > 2";
    DataRequest = Database.createStatement();
    Results = DataRequest.executeQuery (query);
    DisplayResults (Results);
    DataRequest.close();
}
```

Listing 7-56
The DownRow() method used with a multiple comparison join.

```
private  void DownRow ( ResultSet DisplayResults )
       throws SQLException
{
    int OrderNum, ProdNum, Quantity;
    String printrow = new String();
    OrderNum = DisplayResults.getInt ( 1 ) ;
    ProdNum = DisplayResults. getInt ( 2 ) ;
    Quantity = DisplayResults. getInt ( 3 ) ;
    printrow = OrderNum + " " + ProdNum + " " + Quantity;
    System.out.println(printrow);
}
```

Multitable Join

More than two tables can be joined together by using the name of each table in the join in the FROM clause and by defining the join with the appropriate column names in the WHERE clause expression.

Listing 7-57 shows you how to create a multitable join. There are three tables joined in this example. These are the Customers table, the Orders table, and the Products table, as shown in the WHERE clause.

Notice that all three tables don't need to have a common value used to join them. Each pair of tables has a value common to both of them. Customer numbers that are common between the tables join the Customers table and the Orders table. The Orders table and the Products table are joined by the product number.

You'll need to use the Model B program with this code segment because a ResultSet is returned. Listing 7-58 contains the DownRow() method to use to retrieve and display values in the ResultSet.

Listing 7-57
The multiple table join.

```
try {
    String query = new String (" SELECT FirstName,
LastName, OrderNumber, ProductName, Quantity " +
        " FROM Customers, Orders, Products " +
        " WHERE ProdNumber = ProductNumber " +
        " AND CustNumber = CustomerNumber");
    DataRequest = Database.createStatement ();
    Results = DataRequest.executeQuery (query);
    DisplayResults (Results);
    DataRequest.close ();
}
```

Listing 7-58
The DownRow() method used with a multiple table join.

```
private  void DownRow ( ResultSet DisplayResults )
    throws SQLException
{
    int OrderNum, Quantity;
    String FirstName = new String();
    String LastName = new String();
    String ProductName = new String();
    String printrow = new String();
    FirstName = DisplayResults.getString ( 1 ) ;
    LastName = DisplayResults.getString ( 2 ) ;
    OrderNum = DisplayResults.getInt ( 3 ) ;
    ProductName = DisplayResults.getString ( 4 ) ;
    Quantity = DisplayResults. getInt ( 5 ) ;
    printrow = FirstName + " " + LastName + " " + OrderNum + " " + ProductName + " "
+ Quantity ;
    System.out.println(printrow);
}
```

Creating a Column Name Qualifier

Column names should reflect the kind of data element stored in the column, as you learned in Chapter 5. However, there is likely to be a conflict when two or more tables use the same column name to store the data element. This is the case where both the Products table and the Orders table contain product numbers.

Conflicts with column names can be resolved in a join by using a column name qualifier. A column name qualifier identifies the table that contains the column name. Listing 7-59 illustrates how to use a column name qualifier. In this example, assume that the name of the Customers table and the name of the Orders table both have a column called CustomerName. Therefore, the name of the CustomerName column must be prefaced with the name of the table.

Listing 7-59 returns a ResultSet. The DownRow() method shown in Listing 7-60 is used along with the Model B program to copy and display values from the ResultSet.

Listing 7-59
Creating a column name qualifier.

```
try {
    String query = new String ("SELECT Customers.CustNumber, " +
        " FirstName, LastName, OrderNumber, " +
        " ProductName, Quantity " +
        " FROM Customers, Orders, Products " +
        " WHERE ProdNumber = ProductNumber " +
        " AND Customers.CustomerNumber = Orders.CustomerNumber");
    DataRequest = Database.createStatement();
    Results = DataRequest.executeQuery (query);
    DisplayResults (Results);
    DataRequest.close();
}
```

Listing 7-60
The DownRow() method used with a column name qualifier.

```
private  void DownRow ( ResultSet DisplayResults )
        throws SQLException
{
    int CustomerNumber, OrderNum, Quantity;
    String FirstName = new String();
    String LastName = new String();
    String ProductName = new String();
    String printrow = new String();
    CustomerNumber = DisplayResults. getInt ( 1 ) ;
    FirstName = DisplayResults.getString ( 2 ) ;
    LastName = DisplayResults.getString ( 3 ) ;
    OrderNum = DisplayResults.getInt ( 4 ) ;
    ProductName = DisplayResults.getString ( 5 ) ;
    Quantity = DisplayResults. getInt ( 6 ) ;
    printrow = CustomerNumber + " " + FirstName + " " + LastName + " " + OrderNum +
 " " + ProductName + " " + Quantity ;
    System.out.println(printrow);
}
```

Creating a Table Alias

A query can be made readable by using table aliases. A table alias is an abbreviation for the name of the table, and is used in place of the table name in the join and in the SELECT statement. Listing 7-61 shows you how to create and use a table alias in a query.

Following each table name in the FROM clause is a letter, used as the table alias for the table. The table alias is used in place of the table name in the column name qualifier.

Any letter or combination of letters can be used as a table alias; however, you should make the table alias

- With as few letters as possible to save space in the query string

- Representative of the table name, such as the first letter(s) of the table name

- Unique, and not a duplicate of another table name, table alias, or column name

The DownRow() method shown in Listing 7-60 is used with Listing 7-61 to extract and display values of the ResultSet.

Listing 7-61
Creating a
table alias.

```
try {
    String query = new String ("SELECT c.CustNumber , " +
        " c.FirstName, c.LastName, o.OrderNumber, " +
        " p.ProductName, o.Quantity " +
        " FROM Customers c, Orders o, Products  p" +
        " WHERE o.ProdNumber = p.ProductNumber " +
        " AND c.CustomerNumber = o.CustomerNumber");
    DataRequest = Database.createStatement();
    Results = DataRequest.executeQuery (query);
    DisplayResults (Results);
    DataRequest.close();
}
```

Inner and Outer Joins

The joins shown in previous sections of this chapter link together rows that have matching values in the column specified in the join. A row in a table that doesn't match is excluded from the join.

There are two kinds of joins, each of which either excludes or includes rows in both tables of the join that don't match. These are

- **Inner join**   An inner join excludes rows of either table that don't have a matching value.

- **Outer join**   An outer join includes rows of either table that don't have a matching value.

The following sections in this chapter discuss each type of join in detail. However, some DBMSs may not adhere to the SQL syntax for some or all joins, and use their own syntax. Therefore, consult with your database administrator or DBMS manufacturer for the proper syntax for joins if examples in this book don't work with your DBMS. Code segments used in these sections are executed using the executeQuery() method. Therefore, you'll need to use the Model B program. Remember that joins can also be used with the UPDATE and DELETE statements, in which case the Model A program is used.

Inner Join

Joins discussed previously in this chapter use an inner join to include only rows of both tables that have matching values. Unmatched rows are excluded, and therefore those rows are not returned in the ResultSet.

Listing 7-62 demonstrates the use of an inner join by joining the Orders table and the Products table using product number and joining the Orders table and the Customers table using the customer number. Listing 7-63 contains the DownRow() method used with Listing 7-62 to copy and display the contents of the ResultSet.

Listing 7-62
Creating an inner join.

```
try {
    String query = new String (" SELECT FirstName, LastName, OrderNumber,
ProductName, Quantity " +
        " FROM Customers,Orders, Products " +
        " WHERE ProdNumber = ProductNumber " +
        " AND Customers.CustNumber = Orders.CustomerNumber");
    DataRequest = Database.createStatement();
    Results = DataRequest.executeQuery (query);
    DisplayResults (Results);
    DataRequest.close();
}
```

Listing 7-63
The DownRow() method used with an inner join.

```
private  void DownRow ( ResultSet DisplayResults )
        throws SQLException
{
    int OrderNum, Quantity;
    String FirstName = new String();
    String LastName = new String();
    String ProductName = new String();
    String printrow = new String();
    FirstName = DisplayResults.getString ( 1 ) ;
    LastName = DisplayResults.getString ( 2 ) ;
    OrderNum = DisplayResults.getInt ( 3 ) ;
    ProductName = DisplayResults.getString ( 4 ) ;
    Quantity = DisplayResults. getInt ( 5 ) ;
    printrow = FirstName + " " + LastName + " " + OrderNum + " " + ProductName + " "
+ Quantity ;
    System.out.println(printrow);
}
```

Outer Join—Left, Right, Full

An outer join occurs when matching and no matching rows of either or both tables are contained in the join. There are three kinds of outer joins:

- **Left outer join**   All matched and unmatched rows of the first table and matched rows of the second table are included in the join.

- **Right outer join**   Matched rows of the first table and matched and unmatched rows of the second table are included in the join.

- **Full outer join**   Matched and unmatched rows of both tables are included in the join.

Left Outer Join   Listing 7-64 shows you how to create a left outer join. This example creates a join between the Customers table and the Orders table using the customer number. The *= operator is used in the WHERE clause to create a left outer join. Think of the asterisk as a wildcard that tells the DBMS to use any row in the first table.

Before running Listing 7-64, you need to insert the row shown in Table 7-10 into the Orders table; otherwise, there will not be unmatched rows because all the rows in both tables currently have matching values. Listing 7-65 contains the DownRow() method that is used with Listing 7-64.

Listing 7-64
Creating a left outer join.

```
try {
    String query = new String (" SELECT FirstName, LastName,OrderNumber " +
        "  FROM Customers LEFT JOIN Orders " +
        "  ON Customers.CustNumber = Orders.CustomerNumber");
    DataRequest = Database.createStatement();
    Results = DataRequest.executeQuery (query);
    DisplayResults (Results);
    DataRequest.close();
}
```

Listing 7-65
The DownRow() method used with an inner join.

```
private  void DownRow ( ResultSet DisplayResults )
    throws SQLException
{
    int, OrderNum;
    String FirstName = new String();
    String LastName = new String();
    String printrow = new String();
    FirstName = DisplayResults.getString ( 1 ) ;
    LastName = DisplayResults.getString ( 2 ) ;
    OrderNum = DisplayResults.getInt ( 3 ) ;
    printrow = FirstName + " " + LastName + " " + OrderNum;
    System.out.println(printrow);
}
```

OrderNumber	ProdNumber	CustomerNumber	StoreNumber	Quantity	SubTotal
733	7466	999	825	1	532

Table 7-10.   *Insert These Values into the Orders Table*

Right Outer Join   Listing 7-66 illustrates how to create a right outer join. In this example, the Customers table and the Orders table are joined using the customer number. All rows in the Orders table are used in the join regardless if the customer number in the Orders table has a corresponding customer number in the Customers table.

The WHERE clause contains the right outer join operator (=*), which is similar to the left outer join operator except the asterisk is positioned to the right of the equivalent operator.

Before running Listing 7-66 you need to insert the row shown in Table 7-11 into the Orders table; otherwise, there will not be unmatched rows because all the rows in both tables currently have matching values. Listing 7-65 contains the DownRow() method that is used with Listing 7-66.

Listing 7-66
Creating
a right
outer join.

```
try {
   String query = new String (" SELECT FirstName, LastName,OrderNumber" +
      " FROM Customers c, Orders o" +
      " WHERE c.CustNumber =* o.CustomerNumber");
   DataRequest = Database.createStatement();
   Results = DataRequest.executeQuery (query);
   DisplayResults (Results);
   DataRequest.close();
}
```

Full Outer Join   A full outer join uses all the rows of both tables regardless if they match. Listing 7-67 shows how to create a full outer join. The full outer join operator (*=*) is a combination of the left outer join operator and the right outer join operator, although

OrderNumber	ProdNumber	CustomerNumber	StoreNumber	Quantity	SubTotal
555	1052	999	278	14	1400

Table 7-11.   *Insert These Values into the Orders Table*

some DBMSs use FULL JOIN or other syntax to create a full join. Consult with your database administrator or the DBMS manufacturer for the syntax used by your DBMS. Listing 7-65 contains the DownRow() method that is used with Listing 7-67.

Listing 7-67
Creating a full outer join.

```
try {
    String query = new String("SELECT FirstName, LastName,OrderNumber " +
        " FROM Customers c, Orders o" +
        " WHERE c.CustNumber *=* o.CustomerNumber");
    DataRequest = Database.createStatement();
    Results = DataRequest.executeQuery (query);
    DisplayResults (Results);
    DataRequest.close();
}
```

Calculating Data

The DBMS can calculate values in a table and return the result of the calculation in the ResultSet by using one of the five built-in calculation functions. There are five kinds of built-in calculation functions that are discussed in the following sections. These are

- **SUM()** Tallies values in a column that is passed to the built-in function.
- **AVG()** Averages values in a column that is passed to the built-in function.
- **MIN()** Determines the minimum value in a column that is passed to the built-in function.
- **MAX()** Determines the maximum value in a column that is passed to the built-in function.
- **COUNT()** Determines the number of rows in a column that is passed to the built-in function.

Before you try examples in this chapter, you'll need to create an Orders table, Sales table, and Customers table. These tables are defined next. Insert the rows described in Tables 7-12 through 7-14 into the appropriate tables before running the code segments described in the following sections of this chapter.

- **Orders Table**
  - OrderNumber, Number, Primary Key
  - ProdNumber, Number
  - CustomerNumber, Number
  - StoreNumber, Number
  - Quantity, Number
  - SubTotal, Long

OrderNumber	ProdNumber	CustomerNumber	StoreNumber	Quantity	SubTotal
122	5237	591	345	1	325
334	3255	901	278	1	250
365	3255	901	278	4	1000
534	7466	591	825	3	1596
587	5237	845	345	1	325
717	1052	721	825	2	200
874	7466	721	825	1	532

Table 7-12. *Insert These Values into the Orders Table*

- **Sales Table**
  - StoreNumber, Number, Primary Key
  - Sales, Number
  - Estimate, Number
- **Customers Table**
  - CustNumber, Number, Primary Key
  - FirstName, VARCHAR
  - LastName, VARCHAR
  - Street, VARCHAR
  - Zip, VARCHAR

StoreNumber	Sales	Estimate
6245	500	450
8644	650	700

Table 7-13. *Insert These Values into the Sales Table*

CustNumber	FirstName	LastName	Street	Zip
591	Anne	Smith	65 Cutter Street	04735
721	Bart	Adams	15 W. Spruce	05213
845	Tom	Jones	35 Pine Street	07660
901	Mary	Smith	5 Maple Street	08513

Table 7-14.   *Insert These Values into the Customers Table*

Sum()

The SUM() built-in function calculates the sum of the values in the column that is passed to the function. Listing 7-68 illustrates how to use the SUM() built-in function. In this example, values in the Quantity column in the Orders table are passed to the SUM() built-in function.

Listing 7-68 uses the executeQuery() method to execute the query. Therefore, the Model B program should be used with this listing. Listing 7-69 contains the DownRow() method that is used with Listing 7-68.

Listing 7-68
Determining the sum of values in a column.

```
try {
   String query = new String ("SELECT SUM(Quantity) " +
      "FROM Orders ");
   DataRequest = Database.createStatement();
   Results = DataRequest.executeQuery (query);
   DisplayResults (Results);
   DataRequest.close();
}
```

Listing 7-69
The DownRow() method used with the SUM() built-in function.

```
private  void DownRow ( ResultSet DisplayResults )
      throws SQLException
{
   long ReturnValue;
   ReturnValue = DisplayResults.getLong ( 1 ) ;
   System.out.println(ReturnValue);
}
```

AVG()

The AVG() built-in function calculates the average value in the column that is passed to the function. The average is returned in the ResultSet. Listing 7-70 illustrates how to use the AVG() built-in function to calculate the average of the values in the Quantity column of the Orders table. This code segment is used with the Model B program and Listing 7-69 contains the DownRow() method to use with Listing 7-70 to retrieve and display the average from the ResultSet.

Listing 7-70
Determining the average of values in a column.

```
try {
   String query = new String ("SELECT AVG(Quantity) " +
      "FROM Orders ");
   DataRequest = Database.createStatement();
   Results = DataRequest.executeQuery (query);
   DisplayResults (Results);
   DataRequest.close();
}
```

MIN()

The MIN() built-in function returns the lowest value contained in the column passed to the MIN() built-in function. Listing 7-71 shows how to use the MIN() built-in function to determine the minimum value in the Quantity column of the Orders table. This code segment is used with the Model B program and Listing 7-69 contains the DownRow() method to use with Listing 7-71 to retrieve and display the minimum value from the ResultSet.

Listing 7-71
Determining the minimum value in a column.

```
try {
   String query = new String ("SELECT MIN(Quantity) " +
      "FROM Orders ");
   DataRequest = Database.createStatement();
   Results = DataRequest.executeQuery (query);
   DisplayResults (Results);
   DataRequest.close();
}
```

MAX()

The MAX() built-in function returns the highest value contained in the column passed to the MAX() built-in function. Listing 7-72 shows how to use the MAX() built-in function to determine the maximum value in the Quantity column of the Orders table. This code segment is used with the Model B program and Listing 7-69 contains the DownRow() method to use with Listing 7-72 to retrieve and display the value from the ResultSet.

Listing 7-72
Determining the maximum value in a column.

```
try {
   String query = new String ("SELECT MAX(Quantity) " +
      "FROM Orders ");
   DataRequest = Database.createStatement();
```

J2EE DATABASES

```
        Results = DataRequest.executeQuery (query);
        DisplayResults (Results);
        DataRequest.close();
    }
```

COUNT()

Counting the number of rows or values in a table is a very common calculation. The COUNT() built-in function returns the number of rows in a column. Listing 7-73 uses the COUNT() built-in function to determine the number of values that appear in the Quantity column of the Orders table. The result is returned in the ResultSet.

Rows without values in the column are excluded from the count. This means the value returned does not necessarily represent the total number of rows in the table. The return value represents the total number of rows in the table containing values for every row.

This code segment is used with the Model B program and Listing 7-69 contains the DownRow() method to use with Listing 7-73 to retrieve and display the value from the ResultSet.

Listing 7-73
Counting
the number
of values
in a column.

```
try {
    String query = new String ("SELECT COUNT(Quantity) " +
        "FROM Orders ");
    DataRequest = Database.createStatement();
    Results = DataRequest.executeQuery (query);
    DisplayResults (Results);
    DataRequest.close();
}
```

Counting All Rows in a Table

The COUNT() built-in function as described in the previous section is also used to return the number of rows in a table. This is accomplished by passing the COUNT() built-in function an asterisk rather than the name of a column. Listing 7-74 illustrates this technique.

This code segment is used with the Model B program and Listing 7-69 contains the DownRow() method to use with Listing 7-74 to retrieve and display the value from the ResultSet.

Listing 7-74
Counting
the number
of rows.

```
try {
    String query = new String ("SELECT COUNT(*) " +
        "FROM Orders ");
    DataRequest = Database.createStatement();
```

```
    Results = DataRequest.executeQuery (query);
    DisplayResults (Results);
    DataRequest.close();
}
```

Retrieving Multiple Counts

Multiple counts can be returned in the ResultSet by using more than one COUNT()
built-in function in the SELECT statement. This is illustrated in Listing 7-75 where the
ResultSet contains the total number of rows in the Orders table and the number of rows
from the Orders table that contain values in the Quantity column.

This code segment is used with the Model B program and Listing 7-76 contains the
DownRow() method to use with Listing 7-75 to retrieve and display values from
the ResultSet.

Listing 7-75
Retrieving
multiple
counts.

```
try {
   String query = new String ("SELECT COUNT(*), COUNT(Quantity) " +
      "FROM Orders ");
   DataRequest = Database.createStatement();
   Results = DataRequest.executeQuery (query);
   DisplayResults (Results);
   DataRequest.close();
}
```

Listing 7-76
The
DownRow()
method used
with multiple
calls to the
COUNT()
built-in
function.

```
private  void DownRow ( ResultSet DisplayResults )
    throws SQLException
{  long TotalRows, TotalValues;
   TotalRows = DisplayResults.getLong ( 1 ) ;
   TotalValues = DisplayResults.getLong ( 2 ) ;
   System.out.println("Rows: " + TotalRows + "\nValues: " + TotalValues);
}
```

Calculating a Subset of Rows

You can restrict the scope of a built-in calculation function by using a WHERE clause
expression to specify the criteria for a row to be included in a calculation. Any valid
WHERE clause expression can be used to filter rows to be excluded from the calculation.
Likewise, the WHERE clause expression is used to include rows in the calculation. WHERE
clause expressions are discussed earlier in this chapter.

Listing 7-77 illustrates how to restrict the scope of a built-in calculation function by
using a WHERE clause expression. In this example, the DBMS is told to count the number
of values in the OrderNumber column of the Orders table and to average and total the

value of the Quantity column of the Orders table. The WHERE clause contains an expression that joins together the Customers table and the Orders table using the customer number as the common value between these tables. This means the calculations are performed only on rows that are in the join. Rows whose customer numbers don't appear in both the Customers table and Orders table are excluded from the calculations.

This code segment is used with the Model B program and Listing 7-78 contains the DownRow() method to use with Listing 7-77 to retrieve and display values from the ResultSet.

Listing 7-77
Calculating a subset of rows.

```
try {
   String query = new String (" SELECT COUNT(OrderNumber), AVG(Quantity),
SUM(Quantity) " +
      " FROM Orders o, customers c " +
      " WHERE o.CustomerNumber = c.CustNumber");
   DataRequest = Database.createStatement();
   Results = DataRequest.executeQuery (query);
   DisplayResults (Results);
   DataRequest.close();
   }
```

Listing 7-78
Here is the DownRow() method to be used when calculating a subset of rows.

```
private  void DownRow ( ResultSet DisplayResults )
      throws SQLException
{
   long Orders;
   long Average;
   long Sum;
   Orders = DisplayResults.getLong ( 1 ) ;
   Average = DisplayResults.getLong ( 2 ) ;
   Sum = DisplayResults.getLong ( 3 ) ;
   System.out.println("Total Orders = " + Orders);
   System.out.println("Average Qty  = " + Average);
   System.out.println("Total Qty  = " + Sum);
}
```

NULLs and Duplicates

Two common problems that occur when using built-in functions are columns that don't contain a value and rows that contain duplicate values in the same column. Many times, you don't want empty columns and duplicate rows included in the calculation.

You can use the DISTINCT modifier to exclude duplicate rows from the calculation. Likewise, problems posed by NULL columns can be avoided by using the IS NULL operator along with the NOT operator in a selection expression. Both of these are discussed earlier in this chapter.

Calculating Without Using Built-In Functions

Although built-in calculation functions are very useful, the DBMS can perform calculations that are defined in the SELECT statement.

Listing 7-79 illustrates how to do this. In this example, the DBMS is directed to return to the program the value of the StoreNumber column and the difference between the value in the Sales column and the value in the Estimate column. Neither the Sales column nor the Estimate column data is returned. Instead, only the difference between these two columns is returned. Any arithmetic expression can be used in the SELECT statement, along with the appropriate names of columns that contain data elements used in the calculation.

This code segment is used with the Model B program and Listing 7-80 contains the DownRow() method to use with Listing 7-79 to retrieve and display values from the ResultSet.

Listing 7-79
Calculating without built-in functions.

```
try {
   String query = new String ("SELECT StoreNumber, Sales - Estimate " +
     " FROM Sales ");
   DataRequest = Database.createStatement();
   Results = DataRequest.executeQuery (query);
   DisplayResults (Results);
   DataRequest.close();
}
```

Listing 7-80
Here is the DownRow() method to be used when calculating without built-in functions.

```
private  void DownRow ( ResultSet DisplayResults )
    throws SQLException
{
   String Store;
   long Difference;
   Store = DisplayResults.getString ( 1 ) ;
   Difference = DisplayResults.getLong ( 2 ) ;
   System.out.println("Store = " + Store);
   System.out.println("Difference = " + Difference);
}
```

Grouping and Ordering Data

Columns are returned in the ResultSet in the order the column names appear in the SELECT statement of the query. The order in which rows appear in the ResultSet can be grouped into similar values or sorted in ascending or descending order by using the GROUP BY clause or the ORDER BY clause, which are discussed in the next few sections of this chapter.

Grouping is the task of organizing rows of data according to similar values within the same column. Let's say that you want to see sales for each store. The ResultSet can be grouped by store number.

Sorting is the task of organizing rows of data in either alphabetical or numerical order according to the value of a column in the ResultSet. A DBMS is capable of creating simple and complex sorting. A simple sort is when the values in a single column are used for the sort. A complex sort is when multiple columns are used for the sort, such as sorting rows by last name—and within last names, by first names.

Code segments in these sections return a ResultSet; therefore, the Model B program should be used to execute these code segments. Before executing these code segments, create a Sales table as defined next and then insert rows of data contained in Table 7-15 into the Sales table.

- Sales Table
  - StoreNumber, Number, Primary Key
  - Sales, Number
  - Estimate, Number
  - SalesRepNumber, Number

Group By

The GROUP BY clause specifies the name of the column whose values are used to group rows in the ResultSet. Listing 7-81 illustrates this technique. In this example, the

StoreNumber	Sales	Estimate	SalesRepNumber
123	300	200	4
223	450	500	3
123	322	200	4
345	56	30	8
345	125	100	5
223	76	50	2
345	200	156	5

Table 7-15.   *Insert These Values into the Sales Table*

StoreNumber column and the sum of the values in the Sales column from the Sales table are returned.

The GROUP BY clause organizes the ResultSet by the value in the StoreNumber column. This means that the ResultSet contains the sum of the Sales column for each StoreNumber. Listing 7-82 contains the DownRow() method that is used to retrieve and display values from the ResultSet.

Listing 7-81
Grouping the ResultSet.

```
try {
    String query = new String (" SELECT StoreNumber, SUM(Sales) " +
        " FROM Sales " +
        " Group By StoreNumber");
    DataRequest = Database.createStatement();
    Results = DataRequest.executeQuery (query);
    System.out.println("Store     Sales");
    System.out.println("-----     -----");
    DisplayResults (Results);
    DataRequest.close();
}
```

Listing 7-82
Here is the DownRow() method to be used when grouping the ResultSet.

```
private  void DownRow ( ResultSet DisplayResults )
        throws SQLException
{
    long Store;
    long Sum;
    Store = DisplayResults.getLong ( 1 ) ;
    Sum = DisplayResults.getLong ( 2 ) ;
    System.out.println(Store + "          " + Sum);
}
```

Grouping Multiple Columns

The DBMS can create a subgroup within a group in the ResultSet. A subgroup is a grouping within another grouping. For example, the business unit may want to see orders organized by store—and within each store, orders organized by product.

A subgroup is created by placing the name of the column used for the subgroup as the second column name in the GROUP BY clause of the query. Any number of subgroups can be created, depending on the limitations established by the manufacturer of the DBMS that is used by your program. Column names in the GROUP BY clause must be separated with a comma.

Listing 7-83 illustrates how to create a subgroup. In this example, the ResultSet is grouped by store number, and within each store number group a subgroup is created using the sales representative number. Listing 7-84 contains the DownRow() method that is used to retrieve and display values from the ResultSet.

Listing 7-83
Creating groupings and subgroupings in the ResultSet.

```
try {
    String query = new String (" SELECT StoreNumber,SalesRepNumber, SUM(Sales) " +
        " FROM Sales " +
        " Group By StoreNumber, SalesRepNumber");
    DataRequest = Database.createStatement();
    Results = DataRequest.executeQuery (query);
    System.out.println("Store   SalesRep    Sales");
    System.out.println("-----   --------    -----");
    DisplayResults (Results);
    DataRequest.close();
}
```

Listing 7-84
Here is the DownRow() method to be used when grouping and subgrouping the ResultSet.

```
private  void DownRow ( ResultSet DisplayResults )
    throws SQLException
{
    long StoreNumber;
    long SalesRepNumber;
    long Sum;
    StoreNumber = DisplayResults.getLong ( 1 ) ;
    SalesRepNumber = DisplayResults.getLong ( 2 ) ;
    Sum = DisplayResults.getLong ( 3 ) ;
    System.out.println(StoreNumber + "      " + SalesRepNumber + "     " + Sum);
}
```

Conditional Grouping

The number of rows that are included in a group can be limited by including a conditional expression in the query. A conditional expression is similar to the WHERE clause expression discussed previously in this chapter.

The DBMS uses the conditional expression to qualify whether or not the current row should be included in any group of the ResultSet. Only rows that meet the condition are returned. A row that doesn't meet the condition is excluded. The conditional expression is placed in the HAVING clause of the query. The HAVING clause sets the criteria for a row to be included in a group.

Listing 7-85 demonstrates the use of the HAVING clause in a query. In this example, the value of the StoreNumber column and the total sales for each store from the Sales table are grouped by store number. The HAVING clause excludes from the group stores that have total sales of less than $401. Listing 7-86 contains the DownRow() method used to retrieve and display values in the ResultSet.

Here are the requirements for using a conditional expression in the HAVING clause:

- The expression must result in a single value.

- The result must appear in every column named in the expression.

- The expression can include a built-in calculation function.

J2EE DATABASES

Listing 7-85
Conditional
grouping
the
ResultSet.

```
try {
  String query = new String ("SELECT StoreNumber, SUM(Sales) " +
    " FROM Sales " +
    " Group By StoreNumber" +
    " HAVING SUM(Sales) > 400");
  DataRequest = Database.createStatement();
  Results = DataRequest.executeQuery (query);
  System.out.println("Store   Sales");
  System.out.println("-----   -----");
  DisplayResults (Results);
  DataRequest.close();
}
```

Listing 7-86
Here is the
DownRow()
method
to be
used when
conditionally
grouping the
ResultSet.

```
private  void DownRow ( ResultSet DisplayResults )
    throws SQLException
{
  long StoreNumber;
  long Sum;
  StoreNumber = DisplayResults.getLong ( 1 ) ;
  Sum = DisplayResults.getLong ( 2 ) ;
  System.out.println(StoreNumber + "          " + Sum);
}
```

Working with NULL Columns

Columns that are empty can create unexpected results when you execute a query. This is because sometimes the empty column is included or excluded from the operation depending on the nature of the query.

As you learned previously in this chapter, the DBMS includes empty columns when calculating average values and counting rows, but excludes empty columns when calculating the minimum or maximum value within a column.

The DBMS may include or exclude a row in a group depending on the conditional expression. Here's how this works:

- A row is included in a group if the empty column isn't used to group rows or used in the conditional expression in the HAVING clause.

■ A row is excluded from the group if the empty column is used in the conditional expression and the conditional expression normally excludes empty columns from the calculation (i.e., MIN(), MAX()).

■ A row is included in the group if the empty column is used in the conditional expression and the conditional expression normally includes empty columns from the calculation (i.e., AVG(), COUNT()).

■ A row is included in the group if the empty column is used to group rows. Rows containing the empty column are placed in their own group.

Sorting Data

The ResultSet can be placed in alphabetical or numerical order by using the ORDER BY clause in the query. Listing 7-87 shows how to use the ORDER BY clause. In this example, values in the StoreNumber column and values in the Sales column from the Sales table are returned in the ResultSet. The ORDER BY clause specifies the StoreNumber column, which sorts the value of the StoreNumber column in ascending numerical order. Listing 7-88 contains the DownRow() method that is used to retrieve and display values from the ResultSet.

Listing 7-87
Sorting the ResultSet.

```
try {
    String query = new String ("SELECT StoreNumber, Sales " +
        " FROM Sales " +
        " ORDER BY StoreNumber");
    DataRequest = Database.createStatement();
    Results = DataRequest.executeQuery (query);
    System.out.println("Store  Sales");
    System.out.println("-----  -----");
    DisplayResults (Results);
    DataRequest.close();
}
```

Listing 7-88
Here is the DownRow() method to be used when sorting the ResultSet.

```
private  void DownRow ( ResultSet DisplayResults )
    throws SQLException
{
    long StoreNumber;
    long Sales;
    StoreNumber = DisplayResults.getLong ( 1 ) ;
    Sales = DisplayResults.getLong ( 2 ) ;
    System.out.println(StoreNumber + "          " + Sales);
}
```

Major and Minor Sort keys

You can create a sort within a sort by specifying more than one column to be sorted, such as sorting rows by customer last name—and then within last name, sorting by customer first name.

The first column specified in the ORDER BY clause is called the major sort key and is the initial value used to sort rows. The second and subsequent columns in the ORDER BY clause are called minor sort keys. A comma must separate each column name.

Listing 7-89 illustrates how to sort the ResultSet using major and minor sort keys. In this example, the StoreNumber column and Sales column from the Sales table are returned in the ResultSet.

The ORDER BY clause sorts the ResultSet by values in the StoreNumber column. Within each StoreNumber value, the value in the Sales column is sorted. Both sorts are ascending numerical sorts. Listing 7-88 contains the DownRow() method that is used to retrieve and display the ResultSet returned by Listing 7-89.

Listing 7-89
Sorting the ResultSet using major and minor sort keys.

```
try {
    String query = new String ("SELECT  StoreNumber, Sales " +
       " FROM Sales " +
       " ORDER BY StoreNumber, Sales");
    DataRequest = Database.createStatement();
    Results = DataRequest.executeQuery (query);
    System.out.println("Store  Sales");
    System.out.println("-----  -----");
    DisplayResults (Results);
    DataRequest.close();
}
```

Descending Sort

In addition to choosing the column to sort, you can also select the direction of the sort by using the ASC or DESC modifier. Listing 7-90 shows how to use the DESC modifier in the ORDER BY clause to specify a descending sort. By default the sort is ascending, although you can use the ASC modifier to explicitly direct that the sort be in ascending order.

The ASC or DESC modifier must appear after the column name in the ORDER BY clause, as illustrated in this example. The ASC or DESC modifier can be used for major and minor sort keys.

Listing 7-88 contains the DownRow() method that is used to retrieve and display the ResultSet returned by Listing 7-90.

Listing 7-90
Sorting the ResultSet in descending order.

```
try {
    String query = new String ("SELECT StoreNumber, Sales "
```

```
        " FROM Sales " +
        " ORDER BY StoreNumber DESC ");
    DataRequest = Database.createStatement();
    Results = DataRequest.executeQuery (query);
    System.out.println("Store   Sales");
    System.out.println("-----   -----");
    DisplayResults (Results);
    DataRequest.close();
  }
```

Sorting Using Derived Data

Derived data is data that doesn't exist in a table but can be derived from data in a table, such as the calculation that was discussed previously in "Calculating Data." As illustrated in Listing 7-91, placing the calculation that derives the data in the SELECT statement creates derived data.

Listing 7-91 returns the store number and the difference between the value in the Sales column and the value in the Estimate column from the Sales table. The difference is derived data.

Derived data doesn't have a column name. This means that you are unable to include a column name in the ORDER BY clause to designate the derived data as the major or minor sort key for the sort.

However, you can use the column number of the derived data in place of a column name to sort the derived data. The column number of the derived data corresponds to the position of the derived data in the SELECT statement.

In this example, the calculation expression that produces the derived data is the second data referenced in the SELECT statement. Therefore, the derived data appears in the second column of the ResultSet. Use 2 in place of the column name in the ORDER BY clause. Listing 7-88 contains the DownRow() method that is used to retrieve and display the ResultSet returned by Listing 7-91.

Listing 7-91
Sorting
derived
data.

```
try {
    String query = new String ("SELECT StoreNumber, (Sales-Estimate) " +
        " FROM Sales " +
        " ORDER BY 2 ");
    DataRequest = Database.createStatement();
    Results = DataRequest.executeQuery (query);
    System.out.println("Store   Sales");
    System.out.println("-----   -----");
    DisplayResults (Results);
    DataRequest.close();
  }
```

Subqueries

In the real world, you'll find that you need to create queries that are more complex than simply requesting columns be returned from the database. Instead, you might request columns based on the result of another query.

You can direct the DBMS to query the result of a query by creating a subquery within the query. A subquery joins together two queries to form one complex query, which efficiently identifies data to be included in the ResultSet.

A subquery is a query that is formatted very similar to a query. However, rows that are selected as a result of the subquery are not returned to your program. Instead, selected rows are queried by another query. Rows chosen by the second query are returned in the ResultSet.

A subquery resembles the format of a query. Each has a SELECT statement and a FROM clause, and can also include a WHERE clause and a HAVING clause to qualify rows to return. The WHERE clause and the HAVING clause are used to express a condition that must be met for a row to be included in the ResultSet.

There are also differences between a query and a subquery. The most noticeable difference is with the ResultSet. The ResultSet of a query is returned to the J2EE component. In contrast, the ResultSet of a subquery is returned to a temporary table, which is then used by a query or another subquery to further extract rows.

This means the J2EE component never sees the result of a subquery. Instead, the subquery result is an intermediate step working towards the final selection of data from the database.

There are two rules that you must follow when using a subquery in your program. These rules are

- **Return one column from the subquery**   The purpose of a subquery is to derive a list of information from which a query can choose appropriate rows. Only a single column needs to be included in the list.

- **Don't sort or group the result from a subquery**   Since the ResultSet of the subquery isn't going to be returned in the ResultSet of the query, there isn't a need to sort or group data in the ResultSet of a subquery.

The next several sections illustrate how to create a subquery. These sections can be run using the Model B program, as described previously in this chapter. Before attempting to run these code segments, create the following tables and insert rows shown in Table 7-16 and Table 7-17 into the appropriate tables.

- Sales Table
    - StoreNumber, Number, Primary Key
    - Estimate, Number
    - SalesRepNumber, Number

StoreNumber	Estimate	SalesRepNumber
345	200	4
278	500	3
825	200	2

Table 7-16.   *Insert These Values into the Sales Table*

- Orders Table
  - OrderNumber, Number, Primary Key
  - ProdNumber, Number
  - CustomerNumber, Number
  - StoreNum, Number
  - Amount, Number

Creating a Subquery

A subquery is a query whose results are evaluated by an expression in the WHERE clause of another query, as is illustrated in Listing 7-92. In this example, the subquery is defined below the first WHERE clause. The subquery joins rows of the Sales table and the Orders table by store number value, as is shown in the second WHERE clause. Once joined, the subquery totals the value of the Amount column for each store number and returns the results to a temporary table.

OrderNumber	ProdNumber	CustomerNumber	StoreNum	Amount
122	5237	591	345	200
334	3255	901	278	321
365	3255	901	278	433
534	7466	591	825	523
555	1052	999	278	23
717	1052	721	825	75
874	7466	721	825	354

Table 7-17.   *Insert These Values into the Orders Table*

The query then returns a ResultSet that contains store numbers where the value of the Estimate column in the Sales table is equal to the total number of the Amount column returned by the subquery. Listing 7-93 contains the DownRow() method that retrieves and displays the ResultSet from Listing 7-92.

Listing 7-92
Creating a
subquery.

```
try {
  String query = new String (" SELECT StoreNumber " +
    " FROM Sales "+
    " WHERE Estimate = (SELECT SUM(Amount) " +
    " FROM Orders, Sales " +
    " WHERE StoreNum = StoreNumber) ");
  DataRequest = Database.createStatement();
  Results = DataRequest.executeQuery (query);
  System.out.println("Store");
  System.out.println("-----");
  DisplayResults (Results);
  DataRequest.close();
}
```

Listing 7-93
The
DownRow()
method
used with a
subquery.

```
private  void DownRow ( ResultSet DisplayResults )
      throws SQLException
{
  long Store;
  Store = DisplayResults.getLong ( 1 ) ;
  System.out.println(Store);
}
```

Conditional Testing

Any conditional expression, as discussed previously in this chapter, can be used to evaluate a relationship between a query and the results of the subquery. There are four types of conditional tests that you can use with a subquery. These are

- **Comparison test**   This is a test that uses comparison operators to compare values in the temporary table with values in the table used by the query.

- **Existence test**   This test determines if a value in the current row of the table used by the query also exists in the temporary table.

- **Set membership test**   This test is similar to the existence test in that the DBMS is directed to determine if a value in the current row of the table used by the query also exists in the temporary table.

- **Qualified test**   This test consists of either the Any test or the All test and determines if a value in the current row of the table used by the query is in one row of the temporary table or all rows of the temporary table.

The comparison test is illustrated earlier in this chapter. The next several sections show how to perform the other tests. Before executing code segments in these sections, insert rows shown in Table 7-18 in the Sales table.

The Existence Test

The existence test is used whenever you need to return rows in the ResultSet where a value in a column is present in the results of the subquery. The existence test requires that you place the EXISTS modifier between the query and the subquery.

Listing 7-94 gives a good example of how to use an existence test. The DBMS is told to return a single instance of store numbers from the Sales table only if the store number is in the Orders table. The store number isn't returned if the store hasn't placed an order. Listing 7-93 contains the DownRow() method that can be used with Listing 7-94.

Listing 7-94
Performing the existence test.

```
try {
    String query = new String (" SELECT DISTINCT StoreNumber " +
        " FROM Sales  "+
        " WHERE EXISTS " +
        " (SELECT StoreNum " +
        " FROM Orders " +
        " WHERE StoreNum = StoreNumber) ");
    DataRequest = Database.createStatement();
    Results = DataRequest.executeQuery (query);
    System.out.println("Store");
    System.out.println("-----");
    DisplayResults (Results);
    DataRequest.close();
}
```

Membership Test

The IN modifier is used to determine if a value in the table that is being queried is a member of the results produced by the subquery. If the value appears in both tables

StoreNumber	Estimate	SalesRepNumber
345	150	5
278	300	6
825	230	7

Table 7-18. *Insert These Values into the Sales Table*

and results of the subquery, then the conditional test is evaluated as true and the row that contains the value is returned in the ResultSet; otherwise, the row is skipped.

The IN modifier is used in Listing 7-95. In this example, the subquery returns store numbers from the Orders table where the value in the Estimate column of the corresponding row in the Sales table is less than the value in the Amount column of the Orders table.

The IN modifier is used to determine if the store number in the Sales table is returned in the results of the subquery. If so, then the sales representatives number from the Sales table is returned in the ResultSet; otherwise, the sales representative number in the current row of the Sales table is skipped. Listing 7-93 contains the DownRow() method that can be used with Listing 7-95.

Listing 7-95
Performing the membership test.

```
try {
   String query = new String (" SELECT SalesRepNumber " +
     " FROM Sales   "+
     " WHERE StoreNumber IN " +
     " (SELECT StoreNum " +
     " FROM Orders " +
     " WHERE Estimate < Amount) ");
   DataRequest = Database.createStatement();
   Results = DataRequest.executeQuery (query);
   System.out.println("Store");
   System.out.println("-----");
   DisplayResults (Results);
   DataRequest.close();
}
```

ANY Test

The ANY test determines if the value specified in the query is in any of the rows returned by the subquery. If there is at least one match, the row is returned in the ResultSet; otherwise, the row is ignored.

Listing 7-96 shows how to construct an ANY test. The objective of this program is to return the store number from the Sales table for any store where the estimate is greater than the amount of any of the store's orders in the Orders table.

The ANY test tells the DBMS to include the store number in the ResultSet if the value of the Estimate column for the store in the Sales table is greater than any value in the Amount column for that store in the temporary table. Listing 7-93 contains the DownRow() method that can be used with Listing 7-96.

Rules for the ANY Test

■ The ANY test fails if the subquery produces an empty result. Therefore, the query doesn't return any rows in the ResultSet.

- A NULL value returned by the subquery causes the query to return a NULL value. This is because the query is unsure if the value of the table in the query is in the results of the subquery.

- No value is returned in the ResultSet if the value in the table being queried is not in the results of the subquery.

Listing 7-96
Performing
the ANY
test.

```
try {
    String query = new String (" SELECT DISTINCT StoreNumber " +
        " FROM Sales  "+
        " WHERE Estimate  > ANY  " +
        " (SELECT Amount" +
        " FROM Orders " +
        " WHERE StoreNumber = StoreNum) ");
    DataRequest = Database.createStatement();
    Results = DataRequest.executeQuery (query);
    System.out.println("Store");
    System.out.println("-----");
    DisplayResults (Results);
    DataRequest.close();
}
```

ALL Test

The ALL test is similar to the ANY test in that the value of the table specified in the query is compared to values returned by the subquery. However, these tests differ in that the ANY test requires at least one match for the row to be included in the ResultSet. The ALL test requires that the values in the table specified in the query match all the values returned by the subquery.

Listing 7-97 illustrates how to implement the ALL test. In this example, the store number joins together the Sales table and the Orders table. Once the tables are joined, the subquery is processed, which returns the value in the Amount column for each store in the Orders table.

Next, the value in the Estimate column of the Sales table is compared with each Amount value returned by the subquery. If the Amount value for each row returned by the subquery is less than the value in the Estimate column, the row in the Sales table is placed in the ResultSet. Otherwise, the row in the Sales table is skipped. The ALL test follows the same rules that apply to the ANY test (see the previous section). Listing 7-93 contains the DownRow() method that can be used with Listing 7-97.

Listing 7-97
Performing
the ALL
test.

```
try {
    String query = new String (" SELECT DISTINCT Store " +
        " FROM Sales  "+
        " WHERE Estimate  > ALL  " +
```

```
     " (SELECT Amount" +
     " FROM Orders " +
     " WHERE StoreNumber = StoreNum) ");
  DataRequest = Database.createStatement();
  Results = DataRequest.executeQuery (query);
  System.out.println("Store");
  System.out.println("-----");
  DisplayResults (Results);
  DataRequest.close();
}
```

VIEW

You can reduce the complexity of your J2EE component by creating one or more VIEW of the database for each user ID that is passed to the J2EE component for data access. A VIEW is similar to creating a table that contains only the data the user ID is permitted to access. A VIEW limits columns and rows that can be queried to specific information that pertains to a user ID. A VIEW is like a filter that hides information from a user ID.

Each VIEW is uniquely identified with a name and contains selection criteria for columns and rows that appear in the VIEW when the VIEW is used by a J2EE component. Once a VIEW is created, the J2EE component references a VIEW the same way that a table is referenced in a query.

Rules for Using VIEWs

- Create as many VIEWs as necessary to simplify access to a database.
- Restrict access to a table on a need to know basis.
- Work with the owner of the data to establish reasonable restrictions.
- Classify users into groups that have similar access requirements to information.
- Create a VIEW for each classification of user, rather than for each user.
- More than one column can be used in a VIEW.
- More than one table can be used in a VIEW.
- A VIEW is treated as a table in a query regardless of the number of columns and tables that are used to create the VIEW.
- Use a VIEW whenever your program accesses some columns in many tables. The VIEW simplifies the number of tables that a J2EE component needs to directly access. Beware of data security restrictions that affect the underlying columns and tables used to create the VIEW. A VIEW inherits data security restrictions from tables used to create the VIEW. Therefore, if the user ID doesn't have rights to information in a table, the VIEW also has the same restrictions.

The following sections illustrate how to create and use a VIEW. You can execute code segments within each section using the Model A program. However, before doing so, create the following tables and insert into those tables the rows shown in Table 7-19 and Table 7-20.

- Orders Table
    - OrderNumber, Number, Primary Key
    - ProdNumber, Number
    - CustomerNumber, Number
    - StoreNum, Number
    - Amount, Long
- Products Table
    - ProductNumber, Number, Primary Key
    - ProductName, VARCHAR
    - UnitPrice, Long

Creating a VIEW

A VIEW is created by using the CREATE VIEW statement, as is illustrated in Listing 7-98. In this example, the CREATE VIEW statement contains the name of the VIEW, which is Store278. Any unique name can be used as the name of a VIEW.

The AS modifier contains the query whose results form the rows and column that are contained in the VIEW. In this example, all the columns and rows of the Orders table

OrderNumber	ProdNumber	CustomerNumber	StoreNum	Amount
122	5237	591	345	200
334	3255	901	278	321
365	3255	901	278	433
534	7466	591	825	523
555	1052	999	278	23
717	1052	721	825	75
874	7466	721	825	354

Table 7-19. *Insert These Values into the Orders Table*

ProductNumber	ProductName	UnitPrice
1052	CD Player	100
3255	VCR	250
5237	DVD Player	325
7466	50-inch TV	532

Table 7-20. *Insert These Values into the Products Table*

where the value of the StoreNum column is 278 are placed in the VIEW. Only rows that pertain to store 278 are contained in the VIEW. Data from all other stores are excluded.

Listing 7-98
Creating
a VIEW.

```
try {
    String query = new String (" CREATE VIEW Store278 AS " +
      " SELECT  *  " +
      " FROM Orders  " +
      " WHERE StoreNum  = 278");
    DataRequest = Database.createStatement();
    DataRequest.execute(query);
    DataRequest.close();
}
```

Selecting Columns to Appear in the VIEW

You can include or exclude any column in a VIEW. Columns excluded from a VIEW remain in underlying tables used to create the VIEW. However, those columns are hidden from the J2EE component.

Listing 7-99 illustrates how to include columns in a VIEW. This example creates a VIEW called StoreProd. The SELECT statement contains column names from the Orders table that are included in the VIEW. All other columns of the Orders table are excluded from the VIEW.

Listing 7-99
Selecting
columns to
appear in
a VIEW.

```
try {
    String query = new String (" CREATE VIEW StoreProd AS " +
      " SELECT StoreNum, ProdNumber " +
      " FROM Orders  ");
    DataRequest = Database.createStatement();
    DataRequest.executeQuery (query);
    DataRequest.close();
}
```

Creating a Horizontal VIEW

There are two kinds of VIEWs. These are a vertical VIEW and a horizontal VIEW. A vertical VIEW includes all rows of the underlying table and includes some, but not all, columns of the table. This is illustrated in Listing 7-99. A horizontal VIEW contains all columns in the underlying table, but only some rows of the table. This means some rows are excluded from the VIEW and cannot be accessed.

Listing 7-100 shows how to create a horizontal VIEW. In this example, a VIEW called cust901 is created that contains all rows in the Orders table where the value of the CustomerNumber column is 901. Horizontal VIEWs are ideal for situations where access to all columns of a table(s) is required, but access to all rows is not required.

Listing 7-100
Creating a horizontal VIEW.

```
try {
    String query = new String (" CREATE VIEW cust901 AS " +
        " SELECT  *  " +
        " FROM Orders" +
        " WHERE CustomerNumber = 901");
    DataRequest = Database.createStatement();
    Results = DataRequest.execute(query);
    DataRequest.close();
}
```

Creating a Multitable VIEW

A multitable VIEW is created similar to how a single table VIEW is created, as illustrated in previous sections of this chapter. Tables used in the VIEW must be joined. Listing 7-101 shows how this is done. Notice that a vertical VIEW is created and contains three columns from the Orders table and the Products table. The Orders table and the Products table are joined together in the WHERE clause using the product number. Although columns in the VIEW come from two tables, columns are treated as if they are from the same table in a query that uses the VIEW.

Listing 7-101
Creating a multitable VIEW.

```
try {
    String query = new String (" CREATE VIEW ProdDesc AS " +
        " SELECT  StoreNum, ProdNumber, ProductName " +
        " FROM Orders, Products  " +
        " WHERE ProdNumber = ProductNumber");
    DataRequest = Database.createStatement();
    Results = DataRequest.execute(query);
    DataRequest.close();
}
```

Grouping and Sorting VIEW

Rows in a VIEW can be grouped and sorted when the VIEW is created, rather than grouping or sorting rows in a query that uses the VIEW. A VIEW can be grouped or sorted by using the GROUP BY clause and/or the ORDER BY clause, as discussed previously in this chapter.

Listing 7-102 shows how to sort rows in the VIEW. In this example, a VIEW called GroupProdDesc is created based on the underlying Orders table and Products table, which are joined together by product number. The GroupProdDesc VIEW consists of the store number, product number, and product name that are sorted by the value in the ProdNumber column.

Listing 7-102
Grouping and
sorting
VIEWs.

```
try {
  String query = new String (" CREATE VIEW GroupProdDesc AS " +
    " SELECT  StoreNum, ProdNumber, ProductName " +
    " FROM Orders, Products   " +
    " WHERE ProdNumber = ProductNumber" +
    " ORDER BY ProdNumber  ");
  DataRequest = Database.createStatement();
  Results = DataRequest.execute(query);
  DataRequest.close();
}
```

Modifying a VIEW

A VIEW can be modified and those modifications affect the underlying tables that are used to create the VIEW. There are three ways in which a VIEW can be modified. These are

- **Update**   Values in one or more columns of a VIEW are changed to values supplied by the query.
- **Insert**   A new row is added to the VIEW and indirectly to the underlying table(s) used to create the VIEW.
- **Delete**   A row is removed from the VIEW and from the underlying table(s) used to create the VIEW.

Rules for Updating a VIEW

Calculation, expressions, and built-in column functions cannot be used in the SELECT statement of the VIEW. Instead, only names of columns can be used.

- Exclude the GROUP BY clause and HAVING clause from the VIEW.
- Duplicate rows must be included in the modification. You cannot use the DISTINCT modifier in the VIEW if values of the VIEW are going to be modified.

■ The user ID used in your program must have rights to modify the underlying tables that comprise the VIEW.

■ Subqueries cannot be used in a VIEW if rows of the VIEW are to be modified.

Updating a VIEW

You can replace values in a VIEW by using the UPDATE statement, as discussed previously in this chapter. Listing 7-103 illustrates how this is done. In this example, the Store278 VIEW is referenced in the UPDATE statement. The SET clause specifies the Amount column, which is to be updated, and the value that will override the current value in the Amount column. This means the number 700 replaces whatever value is in the column.

The WHERE clause is used to identify rows in the VIEW that are to be updated. Rows that have 334 as the value in the OrderNumber column will have 700 inserted into the Amount column.

Listing 7-103
Updating
a VIEW.

```
try {
   String query = new String (" UPDATE Store278 " +
      " SET Amount = 700 " +
      " WHERE OrderNumber  = 334 ");
   DataRequest = Database.createStatement();
   Results = DataRequest.execute(query);
   DataRequest.close();
}
```

Inserting a Row into a VIEW

A new row can be inserted into the underlying tables that comprise a VIEW by using the INSERT INTO statement and referencing the name of the VIEW, as shown in Listing 7-104. In this example, a new row is inserted in the Store278 VIEW using the same technique as described previously in this chapter to insert a row into a table.

Listing 7-104
Inserting a
row into
a VIEW.

```
try {
   String query = new String (" INSERT INTO Store278 " +
      " (OrderNumber, ProdNum, CustomerNumber, StoreNum, Amount) " +
      " VALUES (325, 9545 ,301 ,278 ,400) ");
   DataRequest = Database.createStatement();
   Results = DataRequest.execute(query);
   DataRequest.close();
}
```

Deleting a Row from a VIEW

You can remove a row from a VIEW by using the DELETE FROM statement. The DELETE FROM statement requires the name of the VIEW from which the row or rows are to be deleted.

Listing 7-105 illustrates how to delete a row from a VIEW. In this example, one or more rows from Store278 are deleted. Rows designated to be deleted are identified in the WHERE clause. In this case, rows that have the value 555 in the OrderNumber column are removed from the Orders table, which is the underlying table of the Store278 VIEW.

Listing 7-105
Deleting a row from a VIEW.

```
try {
    String query = new String (" DELETE FROM Store278 " +
      " WHERE OrderNumber = 555  ");
    DataRequest = Database.createStatement();
    Results = DataRequest.execute(query);
    DataRequest.close();
}
```

Dropping a VIEW

A VIEW can be removed by using the DROP VIEW statement. The DROP VIEW statement requires the name of the VIEW that is to be dropped. There are two modifiers that are used with the DROP VIEW statement. These are

- **CASCADE**   Removes all VIEWs that depend on the VIEW specified in the DROP VIEW statement, and removes the specified VIEW.

- **RESTRICT**   Removes only the VIEW specified in the DROP VIEW statement. All dependent VIEW remain intact.

A dependent VIEW is a VIEW that has another VIEW as one of its underlying components, rather than a table. Listing 7-106 shows you how to drop a VIEW. In this example, the Store278 VIEW and all of its dependent VIEWs are dropped, although there aren't any dependent VIEWs. Some DBMSs use DROP TABLE instead of DROP VIEW.

Listing 7-106
Dropping a VIEW.

```
try {
    String query = new String (" DROP VIEW  Store278 CASCADE");
    DataRequest = Database.createStatement();
    Results = DataRequest.DataRequest.execute(query);
    DataRequest.close();
}
```

J2EE DATABASES

The Complete Reference

Part III

J2EE Foundation

A J2EE application is centered on core Java technologies that provide both client-side and server-side functionality to a J2EE application. In this part you'll learn about these technologies and how you can implement them in your J2EE application.

You begin with HTML, XML, and XHTML, which are markup languages used in a light client application and for transmitting information between web services and other applications. Once you developed a solid foundation in these markup languages, you are shown how to implement them using Java API for XML Processing and Java API for XML Messaging.

Your focus is then directed to three critical Java technologies. These are Java servlets, Java ServerPages, and Enterprise JavaBeans. Java servlets and Java ServerPages are used to create server-side components that directly interact with a light client application. Enterprise JavaBeans is used to create processing components of a J2EE application and web services.

The Complete Reference

Chapter 8

HTML, XML, and XHTML

This chapter is the first of five chapters that discuss technologies that form the foundation of a J2EE application. The concepts of these technologies were introduced in the first part of this book and include Java servlets, JavaServer Pages (JSP), Enterprise Java Beans (EJB), and the Hypertext Markup Language (HTML), the Extensible Markup Language (XML), and the Extensible Hypertext Markup Language (XHTML).

A user interacts with a J2EE application through a user interface that is created using HTML. The user interface relays a user's request to components built using Java servlets and/or JSP. Sometimes these components need web services built using EJB to fulfill the user's request, which typically results in the Java servlet or JSP dynamically generating another user interface page created using HTML.

XML is a language used to create documents that are shared within systems of a corporation and within an industry. There is an increasing requirement for components built using Java servlets, JSP, and EJB to manipulate data organized into an XML document such as those used to generate an online catalog.

Therefore, we begin the discussion of the J2EE foundation technologies with a look at HTML, XML, and XHTML. XHTML is the reformulation of HTML. This knowledge, along with techniques illustrated in the other chapters of this part, enables you to create J2EE components that dynamically generate a user interface and manipulate the latest form of electronic documents.

HTML

It is a fair assumption that you know what a web page is and how to navigate hyperlinks that appear on the page. And it might also be safe to assume that you already know something about HTML, the language used to create a web page. Knowledge of HTML is important before you create J2EE components using JSP because, as you'll learn in later chapters, the majority of JSP is written using HTML.

Skip this section and proceed to the XML section if you are fluent in HTML. However, continue reading if HTML is new to you or if you need to brush up on your HTML skills. The purpose of this section is not to thoroughly cover HTML, because there just isn't enough room in this book to do so.

The purpose of this section is to introduce you to some general concepts of HTML and focus on two features of the language that are commonly encountered when using HTML in a JSP to dynamically build a web page. These features are HTML forms and HTML tables.

HTML forms are commonly used in a JSP to generate a web page that collects information from a user, which is then submitted to a JSP or Java servlet for processing. For example, an HTML form is used as a data entry form. Data received by the JSP or Java servlet from the form is typically forwarded to a component built using an EBJ that interfaces with a DBMS.

An HTML table is a spreadsheet-like grid that is produced dynamically by the JSP or Java servlet to display data that is retrieved from the DBMS. HTML code in the JSP or Java servlet creates each table component and places labels and data within cells of the table before transmitting the HTML web page to the browser for display. Tables are also used for other purposes, such as to define a page layout.

The user interface for your J2EE application is created by either writing HTML code yourself or using an HTML development tool to do so, then modifying the HTML code produced by the HTML development tool as needed. This section focuses on HTML topics that you'll find useful when creating dynamically generated web pages. You should read *HTML: The Complete Reference* for a more thorough discussion of HTML.

Basic Concepts of HTML

As the name describes, HTML is a markup language that is used to define how text should be displayed in a browser or other software that is capable of interpreting HTML, such as some word processors. Tags are used to specify how text is to be displayed. Consider a tag as a command to the browser.

Most tags come in pairs, called the opening tag and the closing tag. An opening tag consists of the tag name contained within angled brackets. A closing tag is similar in appearance to the opening tag except the closing tag has a forward slash (/) before the tag name within the angled brackets. Text that appears between the opening and closing tag is displayed according to the definition of the tag. For example, the following tag pair causes text between the tags to appear in bold. The <B> is the HTML tag for bold.

```
<B>First Name:</B>
```

Many tags offer a variety of options that refine the display of text that appears between the tags. One or more attributes define these options each of which is assigned a value. Attributes and their values are placed within the opening tag before the closed angle bracket.

The next code segment illustrates how to use attributes and values when setting the FONT tag for text. The opening FONT tag contains the attribute SIZE, which is assigned the value 7. Text that appears between the opening and closing tags is displayed in type size 7. Values can appear within quotation marks, although quotation marks are optional if the value contains only letters, digits, a hyphen, or a period. However, all formatting is typically defined in a style sheet (see *HTML: The Complete Reference*).

```
<FONT SIZE="7">First Name:</FONT>
```

Placing one pair of tags within another pair can nest pairs of tags. However, it is critical that the order of nesting be followed. That is, the inner nested pair must have an open and closed tag within the outer pair of tags. This is shown in the next code segment where the <B> tag pair is placed within the <FONT> tag pair:

```
<FONT SIZE="7"><B>First Name: </B></FONT>
```

HTML consists of many tags. Practically all the tags, attributes, and values that you'll need to construct a user interface for your J2EE application are automatically placed into the HTML page by the development tool. However, you'll still find it necessary to edit HTML code directly to assure that the web page works with all browsers.

The following sections discuss the tags that you'll frequently use for web pages that you'll generate using JSP or Java servlets. Table 8-1 at the end of the HTML section contains a listing of commonly used tags. You can refer to these if you ever need to read HTML code, although typically you'll let the development tool read the code for you.

The Skeleton of a Web Page

All tags on a web page are contained within the HTML tag, although some browsers will interpret a web page even if the HTML tag is omitted. A web page is divided into two sections within the HTML tag. These are the HEAD and the BODY.

The HEAD contains tags that affect the entire web page, such as the TITLE tag, FONT, and background color for the page. Text that appears in the TITLE tag is displayed on the title bar of the browser window or centered at the top of the screen, depending on the browser. The TITLE is also used in search indexes, browser history lists, and bookmarks. The BODY tag contains other tags that define the web page.

Another option used component is a web page is the document type tag that appears above the HTML tag. The document type tag defines the web page as being an HTML document type. Listing 8-1 contains the typical skeleton for a web page. A web page development tool automatically creates the skeleton for web pages created using the tool. You'll have to write the web page skeleton into your JSP or Java servlets that dynamically generate a web page. You'll see how this is done in later chapters of this book.

Listing 8-1
The skeleton
of a web
page.

```
<!DOCTYPE HTML PUBLC "-//W3C//DTD HTML 4.0 TRANSITIONAL//EN"
<HTML>
<HEAD><TITLE>My J2EE</TITLE></HEAD>
<BODY>
</BODY>
</HTML>
```

Creating a Form

An HTML form is used to collect data from a user, as discussed previously in this chapter. There are two components to an HTML form. These are the shell of the form and the processing of the form. The shell of the form consists of form elements such as fields, labels, and buttons that are used to enter information into the form. The form is placed within the BODY tag of the web page.

Processing is conducted by a server-side component, which is built using JSP or servlet technology in the case of a J2EE application. The next few sections focus on the shell of the form, while processing is discussed in detail in the Chapter 11 JSP and Chapter 10 servlet chapters.

The FORM tag is used to create an HTML form and is placed within the <BODY> tag of the web page. Tags that create the contents of the form—such as fields, labels, and buttons—are placed within the form tag, as is seen in later sections of this chapter.

The FORM tag has two attributes. These are METHOD and ACTION. METHOD is an optional attribute. If it's not specified, GET is the default value of METHOD. The value of the METHOD attribute describes how data collected in the form is sent to the server. The value of the ACTION attribute defines the server-side component that is called to process the form. This is typically a JSP or servlet.

One of two values can be assigned to the METHOD attribute. These are GET and POST. The GET value tells the browser to append field names and data collected in the form to the URL of the server-side component that will process the form. The field names and data are automatically assigned to the QUERY_STRING environment variable on the server where the processing component breaks down the appended data collection into individual data for processing. The GET method limits the amount of data that can be appended to the URL, which means that some data might be truncated.

The POST value transmits a data file that contains data collected in the form to the server. The processing component receives the file from standard input and proceeds to parse the data. There isn't any size limitation to the data file.

Listing 8-2 contains the shell of an HTML form. In this example, the POST method is used to send data from the form to the processing component. The processing component is called form1.jsp and is assigned to the ACTION attribute. Of course, you can expand the name of the processing component to include the full URL.

You can use any combination of fields, labels, and buttons in a form to collect data from a user. The next several sections discuss each of these in detail.

Listing 8-2
The shell of an HTML form.

```
<FORM METHOD=POST ACTION="form1.jsp">
</FORM>
```

Creating Text Boxes

A text box is an element in a form where the user enters text data. Using the INPUT tag creates a text box. The INPUT tag is a single tag and doesn't have a close tag. There are two attributes that can be used to create a text box. These are TYPE and NAME.

The value of the TYPE attribute is "text." This tells the browser that the field is a text box. Other fields are also created using the INPUT tag, but the value of their TYPE attribute defines the field as other than a text box, which you'll see later in this chapter.

The value of the NAME attribute is the field name. The field name is used to identify data that is entered into the field when the data is sent to the processing component. The processing component then extracts the data from the field name.

Let's say that a form contains two text boxes whose NAME attribute values are fname and lname and the user entered **Jim Keogh** into each respective text box.

Furthermore, let's assume that the GET method is used to send data to the form1.jsp component. Here's how the query string, which is the URL and appended data, appears:

```
form1.jsp?fname=Jim&lname=Keogh
```

Notice that a question mark separates the URL from the data. Each data element is paired with the field name and an ampersand separates each field name/data element pair. Just the field name and the data element are used in the file transmitted if the POST method is employed.

Two optional attributes are commonly used with a text box. These are SIZE and MAXLENGTH. The value of the SIZE attribute is the number of characters wide the text box appears on the form. The value of the MAXLENGTH attribute is the maximum number of characters that a user can enter into the text box. Listing 8-3 creates a paragraph on the form (<P>) that contains the text First Name: followed by a text box. The text First Name: is the label for the text box. The closing paragraph tag (</P>) is optional.

Listing 8-3
Creating a
text box.

```
<P> First Name: <INPUT TYPE="text" NAME="fname" SIZE="20" MAXLENGTH="20"> </P>
```

Creating a Password Box

A password box is a kind of text box in that a user is able to enter free-form text into the text box. However, characters entered into a password box are replaced on the screen with either bullets or asterisks, although characters that are actually entered by the user are assigned to the field name defined in the NAME attribute. Listing 8-4 illustrates how to construct a password box.

Characters entered into a password box appear in the query string and file when the data from the form is transmitted to the processing component. That is to say, data that is associated with a password box is not encrypted.

Listing 8-4
Creating a
password
box.

```
<P>
Password: <INPUT TYPE="password" NAME="password" SIZE=20 MAXLENGTH="20">
</P>
```

Creating a Larger Text Area

Sometimes a J2EE application requires a user to enter multiple lines of free-formed text, such as when asking the user to make a comment. A TEXTAREA is used to capture large amounts of free-formed text. A TEXTAREA is also used to display a block of text outside of a form.

A TEXTAREA is created by using the TEXTAREA tag, which requires both an opening and closing tag. The TEXTAREA tag may use the NAME attribute, whose value is the field name for the data collected in the TEXTAREA if the TEXTAREA is used in a form.

There are three other attributes that are commonly used with the TEXTAREA tag. These are ROWS, COLS, and WRAP. The WRAP attribute may not work with all browsers. The value of the ROWS attribute defines the height of the TEXTAREA on the form. The default value is four rows. The value of the COLS attribute defines the width of the TEXTAREA in characters. The default value might be 40 characters, depending on the browser. The WRAP attribute doesn't contain a value and tells the browser to wrap text around to the next line as the user enters data into the TEXTAREA. Some browsers automatically wrap text in the TEXTAREA. Scroll bars appear whenever the user enters more text than what can appear within the TEXTAREA.

Listing 8-5 illustrates how to create a TEXTAREA. In this example, the TEXTAREA is five rows high. The user can enter more than five rows, but only five rows are shown in the TEXTAREA. The user needs to use scroll bars to view text that is contained beyond the fifth row.

Listing 8-5
Creating a
TEXTAREA.

```
<TEXTAREA NAME="comments" ROWS="5" COLS="20" WRAP> </TEXTAREA>
```

Creating Radio Buttons

A radio button is one of a set of radio buttons that are used by a person to choose one of a set of options. Each radio button is associated with an option. Whenever a radio button within the set is selected by the user, all the other radio buttons within the set are unselected.

An INPUT tag (as discussed earlier to create a text box) is also used to create a radio button. There are three attributes that are used for a radio button. These are TYPE, NAME, and VALUE. The value of the TYPE attribute is "radio" to tell the browser that a radio button is to be displayed. The value of the NAME attribute is the name given to the set of radio buttons. Each radio button in the set must have the same name because it is the value of the NAME attribute that defines the set to which a radio button belongs. The value of the VALUE attribute is the data that is paired with the value of the NAME attribute when the data is sent to the processing component.

Each radio button is defined with its own INPUT tag and related attributes. This is illustrated in Listing 8-6. In this example, there is one set of radio buttons that consists of two radio buttons. You can select one of the radio buttons within the set as the default selection by using the CHECKED attribute, as shown in Listing 8-6. The CHECKED attribute does not have an associated value. Text that appears outside the INPUT tags is displayed on the form.

Caution *The value of the NAME attribute may be treated as case sensitive by some browsers.*

Listing 8-6
Creating
radio
buttons.

```
<H1>Please choose one:</H1>
<INPUT TYPE="radio" NAME="gender"VALUE="female" CHECKED>Female
<INPUT TYPE="radio" NAME="gender "VALUE="male">Male
```

Creating Check Boxes

A check box is similar in concept to a radio button in that both are used to display and record options that are available to a user. Check boxes are also grouped into sets and are created using the INPUT tag and the TYPE, NAME, VALUE, and CHECKED attributes that are discussed in the previous section.

However, check boxes differ from radio buttons in that the value of the TYPE attribute is "checkbox" and a user can select multiple check boxes within the same group. Likewise, multiple check boxes can be a default selection by using the CHECKED attribute.

Listing 8-7 illustrates how to create a check box. In this example, the user can select one or more ways he or she commutes to work. The default selection is Car. All the values selected by the user are associated with the field name "commute" when the data is sent to the processing component. Let's say that the user selected Car and Train. The browser sends commute=car&commute=train.

Listing 8-7
Creating check boxes.

```
<H2>How do you commute to work?</H2>
<INPUT TYPE="checkbox" NAME="commute"VALUE="car" CHECKED>Car
<INPUT TYPE="checkbox" NAME=" commute "VALUE="train" >Train
<INPUT TYPE="checkbox" NAME=" commute "VALUE="plane" >Plane
<INPUT TYPE="checkbox" NAME=" commute "VALUE="boat" >Plane
```

Creating Menus

A menu is a component of a form that contains a drop-down list of options from which the user can choose. A menu is created using a combination of the SELECT tag, which requires an opening and closing tag, and the OPTION tag, which requires only an opening tag.

The SELECT tag should contain a NAME attribute whose value is the field name. The SELECT tag also has the SIZE attribute, which is the number of visible rows of the menu in characters. The OPTION tag may have one attribute, which is the VALUE. The value of the VALUE attribute is the data that is associated with the option. If the VALUE tag is not specified in the OPTION tag, the default text defined in the OPTION tag becomes the text of the option. Text that appears on the form is placed to the right of the OPTION tag. Any OPTION can be selected as default by using the SELECTED attribute in the OPTION tag. The SELECTED attribute does not have a value.

Listing 8-8 illustrates how to create a menu. In this example, the menu is called "commute" and has four options with the "car" option selected as default. After the user selects an option and submits the form, the value of selected options are associated with the field name "commute" and sent to the processing component.

Listing 8-8
Creating a menu.

```
<H2>How do you commute to work?</H2>
<SELECT NAME="commute" SIZE="5" >
<OPTION SELECTED VALUE="car">Car
```

```
<OPTION VALUE="train">Train
<OPTION VALUE="plane">Plane
<OPTION VALUE="boat">Boat
</SELECT>
```

Options that appear in a menu can be grouped using the OPTGROUP tag. The OPTGROUP tag requires an opening and closing tag and LABEL attributes. The value of the LABEL attribute is the text that appears in the menu to describe the group of options. Listing 8-9 shows how to create groupings within a menu. Groupings are also referred to as submenus and require that the attribute MULTIPLE be placed in the SELECT tag. There isn't a value for the MULTIPLE attribute. The MULTIPLE attribute enables the user to select more than one item using the SHIFT or CTRL key, but may not work with all browsers.

Listing 8-9
Creating menu groupings.

```
<H2>How do you commute to work?</H2>
<SELECT NAME="commute" SIZE="5" MULTIPLE>
  <OPTGROUP LABEL="Traditional">
    <OPTION SELECTED VALUE="car">Car
    <OPTION VALUE="train">Train
  </OPTGROUP>
  <OPTGROUP LABEL="Non-Traditional">
    <OPTION VALUE="plane">Plane
    <OPTION VALUE="boat">Boat
  </OPTGROUP>
</SELECT>
```

Creating Hidden Elements

As discussed in Part I, a common problem with a J2EE application is to retain data during a session. There are a number of techniques that are available to do this, which will be discussed in the Chapter 12 Enterprise Java Beans chapter. One of those techniques is to use a hidden field in a form that is generated dynamically by the processing component, although this method is not as efficient as other methods discussed later in this book.

A hidden field is very similar to a text field, discussed previously in this chapter, except the field doesn't appear on the form. A hidden field is created using the INPUT tag and requires three attributes. These are TYPE, NAME, and VALUE. The value of the TYPE attribute is "hidden" and the value of the NAME attribute is the field name. The value of the VALUE attribute is the data.

Although a hidden field isn't displayed on the form, the field name and value of the VALUE attribute are sent to the processing component along with other fields on the form.

There is no difference between data from a hidden field and data from visible fields on the form. Listing 8-10 illustrates how to create a hidden field.

Listing 8-10
Creating a
hidden field.

```
<INPUT TYPE="hidden" NAME="userID" VALUE="123">
```

Creating the Submit Button

A Submit button, when selected by a user, is the button that causes the browser to extract the field name and data from the form and send them to the processing component, as discussed previously in this chapter.

A Submit button is created using the INPUT tag and requires the TYPE attribute whose value is "submit." The VALUE attribute is optional. The value of the VALUE attribute is the text that appears on the Submit button. The default value is Submit Query although the actual default is browser dependent. Listing 8-11 illustrates how to create the Submit button.

Listing 8-11
Creating a
Submit
button.

```
<INPUT TYPE="submit" VALUE="Submit Form">
```

Using the Reset Button

A form typically has a Reset button, which resets fields to their values when the form was originally displayed on the web page. This means that data entered by the user is removed from all the fields if the Reset button is selected, and fields return to their default values.

A Reset button is created similar to how a Submit button is created, using the INPUT tag as illustrated in Listing 8-12. However, the value of the TYPE attribute is "reset" and the value of the VALUE tag can be any text that is to appear on the button. The default value for the VALUE tag is Reset.

Listing 8-12
Creating a
Reset
button.

```
<INPUT TYPE="reset" VALUE="Reset Form">
```

Organizing Components on the Form

Components can be organized on the form into groups where the group is identified by a label. This is a clever way to prevent component clutter on the form. The FIELDSET tag is used to create a group on the form. The FIELDSET group requires an open and close tag and a LEGEND open and close tag.

Fields, labels, and buttons that are in the same group are placed within the FIELDSET open and close tag. The LEGEND tag is also placed within the FIELDSET tag and is used to name the group. Listing 8-13 illustrates how to organize components on a form.

Listing 8-13
Creating
groups of
components
on a form.

```
<FIELDSET>
  <LEGEND>Customer Information</LEGEND>
  First Name:<INPUT TYPE="text" NAME="firstname" SIZE=15>
  Last Name:<INPUT TYPE="text" NAME="lastname" SIZE=15>
</FIELDSET>
```

Setting the Tab Order

Typically a person moves from field to field within a form by pressing the TAB key. The order in which fields are selected using the TAB key is determined either by the order in which the fields are placed on the form or by setting the TABINDEX attribute value.

The TABINDEX attribute is used for every field on the form and tells the browser where to move the cursor on the form when the user selects the TAB key. The value of the TABINDEX is a number that corresponds to the order in which the field is to be selected. The first field to be selected is number 1. The second field is 2, and so on.

Listing 8-14 illustrates how to set the TABINDEX value for a field. Each field should also contain an ID attribute whose value uniquely identifies the field on the form. In this example, the value of the NAME attribute is also used as the value of the ID attribute, but these fields can have different values.

Listing 8-14
Setting the
TABINDEX
value for
a field.

```
<INPUT TYPE="text" NAME="firstname" ID="firstname" SIZE=20 TABINDEX=2>
```

Keeping Elements from Being Changed

There are occasions when the processing component places values in a field in a form that it dynamically generates. For example, this is common when a customer is completing a multipage form and each page appears on a different web page. The design might require that information such as the customer name be entered on the first page by the customer, then carried forward to subsequent pages by the processing component.

Typically, information carried forward from the previous page appears as a value assigned to the VALUE attribute of a field by the processing component. While this technique displays previously entered data, it causes a problem. The user might alter the information in the field. For example, the customer might change the value of the customer name fields that appear on subsequent pages of the form.

You can prevent the user from changing values in a field by using the READONLY attribute with the field. The READONLY attribute is illustrated in Listing 8-15.

Caution *A user can save the HTML form locally, modify the value by changing the code, then submit the form.*

Listing 8-15
Preventing a
user from
changing a
value of a field
on the form.

```
<INPUT TYPE="text" NAME="firstname" VALUE="Bob" READONLY>
```

Tables

A feature common to many J2EE applications is for a user to recall information that is stored in a database. Typically, a web page is displayed that contains a form, which is used to collect search criteria from a user. The search criteria is sent to the processing component by the browser when the user selects the Submit button, as described in the previous section.

The processing component parses the search criteria from the form and passes this to a web services component such as a EJB, which retrieves the data from the DBMS using techniques described in Part II of this book.

Data is then returned through the web services component to the processing component where the data is properly formatted into a web page using HTML. Many times the data is presented in tabular format and requires the processing component to dynamically create the table using HTML.

Previous sections of this chapter illustrate how to create a form that, among other things, captures search criteria. Part II of this book showed you how to use Java data objects to interact with the DBMS. The next few sections show how to dynamically build a table in HTML. You'll use this method in conjunction with JSP or Java servlets, which are discussed later in this book.

Creating a Table

Using the TABLE tag, the TR tag, the TH tag, and the TD tag creates a table. The TABLE tag requires an open tag and close tag to define the body of the table. Within the TABLE tag are the other tags that create a grid within the table.

The TR tag defines a row and requires an opening and closing tag. The TH tag and the TD tag define a column. Both of these tags also require an opening and closing tag. The TH tag defines a cell header and the TD tag defines a data cell. Headings and data that appear in a cell of the table are placed between the opening and closing TH tag and TD tag. The closing tags for TR, TD, and TH are optional.

Listing 8-16 illustrates how to create a table. In this example, the table contains two rows and three columns. The first row contains column headers that identify the contents of the column. The second row contains data.

Listing 8-16
Creating
a table.

```
<TABLE>
 <TR>
   <TH>Sales For Store 1</TH>
   <TH>Sales For Store 2</TH>
   <TH>Sales For Store 3</TH>
 </TR>
 <TR>
   <TD>$500</TD>
   <TD>$300</TD>
   <TD>$200</TD>
 </TR>
</TABLE>
```

Adding a Caption to the Table

The caption of a table describes the kind of information that the table contains. Using the CAPTION tag placed within the TABLE tag above the first row creates a caption. The CAPTION tag requires an open tag and close tag. Text that appears between the open tag and close tag is the caption that appears above the table.

The caption can be positioned above, below, to the right, or to the left of the table by using the ALIGN attribute. The value of the ALIGN attribute is top, bottom, left, or right. The top value is the default value, which places the caption at the top center of the table. However, ALIGN is typically defined in a style sheet.

Keep in mind that the ALIGN attribute conveys to the browser the desired location of the caption. The browser determines the absolute position of the caption on the web page. Listing 8-17 illustrates how to create a caption for a table.

Listing 8-17
Creating a caption for the table.

```
<CAPTION ALIGN=bottom> Store Sales</CAPTION>
```

Adding a Border to the Table

A border can be placed around a table by using the BORDER attribute. The BORDER attribute tells the browser to use a border around the table. You can specify the thickness of the boarder in pixels by assigning the thickness to the BORDER attribute. For example, BORDER="5" creates a border that is 5 pixels thick. The browser uses the default border thickness if you don't specify a pixel value. Listing 8-18 illustrates how to create a border for a table.

Listing 8-18
Creating a border for a table.

```
<TABLE BORDER=6">
```

Choosing Border Style

By default, the BORDER tag causes a frame to appear around the entire table and around each cell within the table. You can control where the border appears by using the FRAME attribute and the RULES attribute.

The FRAME attribute is used to define where the frame appears around the sides of the board. The values of the FRAME attribute are described here:

- **void**   No external frame.
- **above**   A single frame on top.
- **below**   A single frame on bottom.
- **bsides**   A frame on both the top and bottom sides.
- **vsides**   A frame on both the right and left sides.
- **rbs**   A single frame on the right side.
- **lbs**   A single frame on the left side.
- **box or border**   A frame on all sides (default).

The values of the RULES attribute define the style of frame used within the table to highlight the cells. The values of the RULES attribute are described here. Listing 8-19 illustrates how to create a border and apply a frame style outside and inside the table.

- ■ **none**   No internal rules.
- ■ **rows**   Horizontal rules between each row.
- ■ **cols**   Vertical rules between each column.
- ■ **groups**   Rules between column groups and horizontal sections as defined by column groups.
- ■ **all**   Rules between each row and columns in the table (default).

Listing 8-19
Creating a
border style
outside
and inside
the table.

```
<TABLE BORDER FRAME=vsides RULES=cols >
```

Merging Two Cells

Sometimes the design of a table requires that two cells merge. Although many word processors and spreadsheets refer to this as merging cells, technically one cell spans the space of two cells. This is commonly used when a column header references more than one column.

You can span a cell across multiple columns by using the COLSPAN attribute for either the TH tag or the TD tag. The value of the COLSPAN attribute is a number that represents the number of columns over which the cell spans. Listing 8-20 illustrates this technique.

Listing 8-20
Spanning
columns.

```
<TH COLSPAN=2> Store 1 </TH>
```

Spanning a Cell Across Two or More Rows

A cell can span multiple adjacent rows by using the ROWSPAN attribute with either the TH tag or the TD tag. The value of the ROWSPAN attribute is a number that represents the number of rows over which the cell spans. Listing 8-21 illustrates how to span rows.

Listing 8-21
Spanning
rows.

```
<TH ROWSPAN=2> Store 1 </TH>
```

Changing a Table's Width and Height

The size of a table on the web page can be altered from the default size by using the WIDTH and HEIGHT attributes of the TABLE tag. The value of both attributes can be a number that reflects the absolute size in pixels or a percentage. A percentage defines the width and height of the table as a percentage of the full window size so that the table remains proportional to the browser window. Listing 8-22 illustrates how to control the size of the table.

Listing 8-22
Changing
the size of
a table.

```
<TABLE WIDTH=50% HEIGHT=90%>
```

Changing the Size of a Cell

The WIDTH and HEIGHT attributes are also used to change the size of a cell using the same metric as the attributes used for a table. However, these attributes are used with the TH tag or the TD tag rather than the TABLE tag, as is illustrated in Listing 8-23.

Listing 8-23
Changing
the size
of a cell.

```
<TD WIDTH=200 HEIGHT=100>
```

Aligning the Contents of Cells

The contents within a cell can be aligned horizontally and vertically by using the ALIGN and VALIGN attributes in either the TH tag or TD tag. The value of the ALIGN attribute can be left, center, right, or justify, which causes the contents to be flush with both sides of the cell. The default value of the ALIGN attribute in the TH tag is center and with the TD tag is left.

The value of the VALIGN can be top, middle, bottom, or baseline. The baseline value aligns the context of the cell with the first line of text that appears in the cell or is the same as value top if no text is in the cell. The default value of the VALIGN tag is middle. Listing 8-24 illustrates how to align the contents of a cell.

Listing 8-24
Aligning the
contents
of a cell.

```
<TD VALIGN=top ALIGN=left>
```

Changing the Background Color of a Cell

The background color of a cell can be changed from the default color chosen by the browser by using the BGCOLOR attribute with the TH tag or the TD tag. The value of the BGCOLOR attribute is the name of the background color, as is illustrated in Listing 8-25. However, background color is typically defined in a style sheet.

Listing 8-25
Changing the
background
color of
a cell.

```
<TD BGCOLOR=yellow>
```

Spacing and Padding the Cells

The size of a cell can be fine-tuned by adjusting the spacing and padding of the cell. Cell spacing adjusts the space between cells and is set by using the CELLSPACING

J2EE FOUNDATION

attribute for the TABLE tag. The value of the CELLSPACING attribute is a number that defines the number of pixels that appear between each cell. The default value for cell spacing is 2.

Cell padding adjusts the spacing between the contents of the cell and the cell wall. The CELLPADDING attribute is used with the TABLE tag to set the cell padding to a desired number of pixels. The default value for cell padding is 1. The BORDER attribute, as discussed previously in this chapter, can also be used with the TABLE tag. Listing 8-26 illustrates how to set the spacing and padding of cells in a table.

Listing 8-26
Setting the spacing and padding of cells.

```
<TABLE BORDER CELLSPACING=15 CELLPADDING=15>
```

Controlling Line Breaks in a Cell

A browser typically divides lines of text within a cell, depending on the size of the column and row. This means there is always the risk that data within a cell might appear on multiple lines if there isn't room to place the data on one line. The browser can be forced to keep data on one line by using the NOWRAP attribute with either the TH tag or the TD tag. The NOWRAP attribute doesn't require a value. Listing 8-27 illustrates how to use the NOWRAP attribute, and Table 8-1 contains a listing of commonly used tags.

Listing 8-27
Setting the NOWRAP attribute.

```
<TD NOWRAP>
```

Tag	Definition
A	Anchor
APPLET	Java applet
AREA	Client-side image map area
B	Bold text style
BASE	Document base URI
BASEFONT	Base font size
BLOCKQUOTE	Long quotation
BODY	Document body

Table 8-1. *HTML Tags*

Tag	Definition
BR	Forced line break
BUTTON	Push button
CAPTION	Table caption
CENTER	Shorthand for DIV align=center
CITE	Citation
CODE	Computer code fragment
COL	Table column
COLGROUP	Table column group
DD	Definition description
DEL	Deleted text
DFN	Instance definition
DIR	Directory list
DIV	Generic language/style container
DL	Definition list
DT	Definition term
EM	Emphasis
FIELDSET	Form control group
FONT	Local change to font
FORM	Interactive form
FRAME	Subwindow
FRAMESET	Window subdivision
H1	Heading
H2	Heading
H3	Heading
H4	Heading
H5	Heading
H6	Heading
HEAD	Document head
HR	Horizontal rule

J2EE FOUNDATION

Table 8-1.   *HTML Tags* (continued)

Tag	Definition
HTML	Document root element
I	Italic text style
IFRAME	Inline subwindow
IMG	Embedded image
INPUT	Form control
ISINDEX	Single line prompt
KBD	Text to be entered by the user
LABEL	Form field label text
LEGEND	Fieldset legend
LI	List item
LINK	A media-independent link
MAP	Client-side image map
MENU	Menu list
OL	Ordered list
OPTGROUP	Option group
OPTION	Selectable choice
P	Paragraph
PARAM	Named property value
PRE	Preformatted text
Q	Short inline quotation
S	Strikethrough text style
SCRIPT	Script statements
SELECT	Option selector
SMALL	Small text style
SPAN	Generic language/style container
STRIKE	Strikethrough text
STRONG	Strong emphasis
SUB	Subscript
SUP	Superscript

Table 8-1. *HTML Tags* (continued)

Tag	Definition
TABLE	Create a table
TBODY	Table body
TD	Table data cell
TEXTAREA	Multiline text field
TFOOT	Table footer
TH	Table header cell
THEAD	Table header
TITLE	Document title
TR	Table row
TT	Teletype or monospaced text style
U	Underlined text style
UL	Unordered list

Table 8-1. *HTML Tags* (continued)

XML

The Extensible Markup Language (XML) is a language used to create other languages that define components of a document. You probably don't realize as you read this book that it is composed of elements that give the text the look and feel of a book.

These elements include the title page, table of contents, the index, and chapters, each of which conforms to a specific style. Each element is considered data, similar to names and addresses that you might save to a table of a database.

In a relational database, data is described using metadata such as a column name, column data type, and column size. The language that you create using XML is used to create metadata that describes elements in a document (that is, book).

XML is similar in concept to the Hypertext Markup Language (HTML) in that an element is defined using tags and attributes. Tags and attributes are comparable to the metadata of a relational database.

Why Use XML?

There are a number of reasons why XML has been adopted as a standard in companies that need to manage documents:

- **Simplifies data exchange** XML provides a standard data definition for information that is commonly shared electronically amongst members of an industry. For example, a company might want to electronically extract from a vendor's product catalog the product number and unit price of selected items. The selection of product numbers and unit prices is simplified if the vendor uses an industry-accepted set of XML tags to describe product number and unit price elements of the catalog.

■ **Organizes a document** XML enables a company to easily identify components of a document that can be recalled by using XML tags. For example, online booksellers typically receive selected information about a book from a publisher, which is displayed on the catalog page of the bookseller's web site. This includes the table of contents, author's biography, back cover copy, the preface, and maybe a sample chapter. The publisher can easily provide an online bookseller with these components because the publisher organizes components of a book using XML tags.

■ **Reusable document elements** A company can create a new document from elements of an existing document by referencing the XML tags of those elements. Let's say that a company wants to create a holiday sales catalog. Product information can be easily assembled into the company's special sales catalog by referencing selected XML tags from their general sales catalog.

■ **Standardizing display of information** Each element of a document that is created using an XML-based language includes rules for displaying the element. For example, the display format of pricing information of a product is associated with the XML tag that describes pricing information. Therefore, XML provides consistency in display of information.

■ **Browser readable** An XML document can be displayed by Internet Explorer 5 (for both Macintosh and Windows) and Netscape 6 browsers.

The XML Flow

There is a two-step process used to create an XML-based document. The first step is to create an XML Schema, which is a document you create that contains the definition of the language that describes your document.

The language consists of a definition of a customized set of tags. These tags are very similar to HTML tags, except you create tag names and attributes of these tags. You'll see how to do this later in this chapter.

You can think of the XML Schema as a dictionary that defines tags used to describe elements of your document. The XML Schema is referenced whenever the document is accessed, such as when a vendor shares catalog information electronically with a client.

The second step is for you to create the document using elements defined in the XML Schema. For example, you might define a tag called RetailPrice in the XML Schema. You'll enclose the retail price element of your document with the retail price tag as shown here:

```
<RetailPrice>$15.95</RetailPrice>
```

There is a growing trend to standardize XML Schemas throughout a company and within an industry, to facilitate an efficient method of exchanging information. This is especially prevalent in industries where documents tend to consist of the same elements.

The book publishing industry is a good example. Practically every book has the same basic set of elements, as described in the previous section. Therefore, the book publishing industry has standardized on a XML Schema that contains tags to describe every possible element that could appear in a book.

In an ideal world, this means that all companies involved in the manufacturing and selling of a book properly interpret elements of an XML-based book by referencing the industry adopted XML Schema. In the real world, it is difficult to create an XML Schema standard that is agreeable to everyone in the industry and is broad enough to encompass all the nuances that could exist in all books, but various industry groups are attempting to do just that.

XML Parsers

An XML parser is a program that transforms an XML document into a structure that allows programmatic access to a document's content. During the transformation process, the XML parser reads the XML document and examines XML syntax, then reports any syntax errors that are encountered. Common syntax errors occur because of unbalanced start and end tags, improper use of quotations for attribute values, and improper use of capitalization. XML is case sensitive.

There are two parses used to access a document's content. These are using the Document Object Model (DOM) and the Simple API for XML (SAX), which is used by Java, C, and other programming languages to programmatically use the content of an XML document.

XML parsers that use DOM generate a tree structure of the XML document's content, which is stored in memory. In contrast, a SAX parser generates events when components of an XML document are encountered such as a tag and content, which sends the related content from the XML document to the program that is accessing the XML document.

DOM parsers enable the contents of the XML document to be accessed quickly and enable the XML document to be modified by adding and removing nodes. However, SAX parsers, without the memory overhead, provide greater performance than DOM parsers provide. As a general rule, a DOM parser is used whenever an XML document needs to be modified; otherwise, a SAX parser is preferred.

An XML parser is included in Internet Explorer 5 and Netscape 6 browsers. However, these browsers display both tags and content of an XML document, rather than content defined by those tags. This is because, unlike HTML tags, the browser is unable to translate XML tags to display the content. However, a browser can translate the XML document into an HTML document if an Extensible Style Sheet is defined, which I'll show you how to do later in this chapter.

There are many XML parsers available for free on the Internet. These are stand-alone XML parsers (that is, not related to Internet Explorer 5 and Netscape 6). You will find an XML parser that can be used to access an XML document with Java (JAXP) on the Sun Microsystems's web site (www.sun.com).

Browsers and XML

The reality is that a browser cannot read an XML-based document. This is because a browser reads HTML documents that contain HTML tags and not XML tags. XML tags are literally displayed by a browser as if tags are part of the text that is displayed on the screen.

However, a browser can convert an XML-based document to an HTML document by using an XML style sheet referred to as Extensible Stylesheet Language Transformation (XSLT). An XSLT contains rules a browser uses to translate each element of the XML-based document into tags on an HTML page. You can create an XSLT style sheet. I'll show you how to do this later in this chapter.

Why use XML when a browser must translate the XML document into an HTML document? Why not simply use HTML? Creating a document using HTML makes the document browser readable, but doesn't accurately describe elements of the document. For example, you might place the retail price of an item in an HTML paragraph such as

```
<P>$15.95</P>
```

However, the paragraph tag doesn't describe the text as being the retail price. It simply tells the browser that text appearing between the paragraph tags should be displayed in a paragraph.

In contrast, the RetailPrice tag, as described in the previous section, defines the text as a retail price. This enables other programs that read the document to properly process the text as a retail price. In addition to using the RetailPrice tag, you might create an XSLT for the document that further states that text displayed within the RetailPrice tag should be displayed in a paragraph.

The Design of an XML Document

An XML-based document is defined in a file you created in a text editor and consists of XML tags that are nested within each other, similar to the structure of an HTML web page. The outermost element of the XML document is called the root element, within which other elements are placed that represent components of the document.

Although a book is used in this section to illustrate an XML document, the same design concept applies to any XML document—only the names of the elements are different than the elements of a book.

The root element of a book contains all other elements of the book. Typically, the tag name describes the type of information that is contained in the element, although you are free to use any name for a tag that conforms to the XML naming rule.

Names must begin with a letter, underscore, or colon, and names may contain letters, digits, underscores, hyphens, periods, and colons. XML is case sensitive.

The root element tag in this example is called book, as shown next. Each element must have an open tag and a close tag, which is similar to HTML. That is, the name of an open and close tag is enclosed within an angle bracket and the second character of a closed tag must be a forward slash.

```
<book>
</book>
```

Tags used to identify other elements follow the same naming convention as the root element, except each element has a unique tag name as defined in the XML Schema. Let's assume for now that the XML Schema for the book is already defined.

You can use the same element multiple times within the document, as is illustrated in Listing 8-28 where the <Chapter> tag is used to identify two chapters in the book. The <Chapter> tag is defined once in the XML Schema. This is similar to defining a word in a dictionary, then using the word multiple times in a book.

Listing 8-28 contains other elements of an XML-based book. Text for each element of the book is placed within the appropriate open and close tag set.

Listing 8-28
Elements
of an
XML-based
book.

```
<book>
   <TitlePage>
   </TitlePage>
   <CopyWritePage>
   </CopyWritePage>
   <TableOfContents>
   </TableOfContents>
   <Preface>
   </Preface>
   <Chapter>
   </Chapter>
   <Chapter>
   </Chapter>
</book>
```

Nesting Elements

You've seen in the previous section how the root element contains other elements. This is referred to as *nesting*, where elements within the root element are considered nested elements. You can have any number of nested elements as required by the design of the document.

Any element can have nested elements. There are three new elements in Listing 8-29 that are nested with elements of the book. These new elements are called <Header>, <Footer>, and <PageNumber>.

The <Header> describes the text that appears at the top of the page. The <Footer> describes text that appears at the bottom of the page. <PageNumber> describes the page number element.

Each element in the book contains the <Header> and <Footer> elements as nested elements. Furthermore, each <Footer> element contains the <PageNumber> element as a nested element.

You'll notice that each nested element is indented to make it easier to read. However, newline characters and whitespace characters are treated as text elements. You can write a program to ignore newline characters and whitespace characters as long as the document is properly formed. You'll learn how this is done in the next chapter.

Listing 8-29
How to nest elements.

```
<book>
  <TitlePage>
    <Header>
    </Header>
    <Footer>
      <PageNumber>
      </PageNumber>
    </Footer>
  </TitlePage>
  <CopyWritePage>
    <Header>
    </Header>
    <Footer>
      <PageNumber>
      </PageNumber>
    </Footer>
  </CopyWritePage>
  <TableOfContents>
    <Header>
    </Header>
    <Footer>
      <PageNumber>
      </PageNumber>
    </Footer>
  </TableOfContents>
  <Preface>
    <Header>
    </Header>
```

```
      <Footer>
        <PageNumber>
        </PageNumber>
      </Footer>
    </Preface>
    <Chapter>
      <Header>
      </Header>
      <Footer>
        <PageNumber>
        </PageNumber>
      </Footer>
    </Chapter>
    <Chapter>
      <Header>
      </Header>
      <Footer>
        <PageNumber>
        </PageNumber>
      </Footer>
    </Chapter>
  </book>
```

Processing Instructions

Besides tags that identify elements of a document, XML also has a tag called a processing instruction. A processing instruction either declares information that is necessary to process the document or directs the program that processes the document to perform a specific function.

A processing instruction tag begins with a <? and ends with a ?>. All XML documents begin with a processing instruction that declares the version of XML used by the document.

Other processing instructions are illustrated as new features are introduced throughout this chapter. Listing 8-30 shows how a processing instruction is used to declare the XML version used in the document.

Listing 8-30
How to declare the XML version for the document.

```
<?xml version="1.0"?>
<book>
</book>
```

Attributes

An XML attribute is similar to an HTML attribute that you used previously in this chapter to describe an element of a document. An attribute is declared within the opening tag of an element by specifying the attribute name and the attribute's value.

Any name can be used for an attribute as long as the name conforms to the XML naming rules and the name is unique within an element. An attribute is local to an element. This means that two elements can have the same attribute name, but the attribute only affects the element that declared the attribute.

The value of an attribute can be any secondary information that is needed to enhance information contained in the element. However, the value of XML attributes must be enclosed within double or single quotations, which is unlike HTML where quotations are optional.

If the value itself contains single quotations, enclose the value with double quotations. This assures that the single quotations will be considered as text. Likewise, use single quotations to enclose a value that contains double quotations or escape with ' and ".

Let's say that you created a personnel document that, among other elements, contains a photograph of an employee. You might create an XML tag called <Photo> and an attribute called source whose value is the name of the file that contains the employee's picture. Here's how the element is written in an XML-based document:

```
<Photo source="emp12345.jpg"> John Smith </Photo>
```

Some elements may require an attribute value, but not require text within the element. For example, the <Photo> element may not require the text John Smith because John Smith might be identified elsewhere in another element of the document such as <EmployeeFirstName> and <EmployeeLastName>. In this scenario, you'd simply leave the element empty of text. This is referred to as an empty element.

There are characters that have a special meaning to the XML processor that processes an XML document. These are the ampersand, greater than character, and less than character. XML uses abbreviations that can be substituted for those characters. Table 8-2 lists them. Use the abbreviation instead of the character in values and text of elements within the XML-based document.

Create a Document Type Definition (DTD)

A forerunner of an XML Schema is a document type definition (DTD), which is still used with some XML documents. This section provides a brief introduction to DTD because focus has switched from DTD to XML Schema, which is covered in more depth in the next section. You can learn more about DTD from *XML: The Complete Reference*.

A DTD defines tags that can be used with an XML document and like an XML Schema is used to standardize a particular set of tags for a company or industry. A

Character	Abbreviation
Ampersand (&)	&amp;
Greater than (>)	&gt;
Less than (<)	&lt;
Single quotation (')	&apos;
Double quotation (")	&quot;

Table 8-2.   *Abbreviations for Special XML Characters*

DTD, as with an XML Schema, is optional and therefore you can create an XML document without referencing either a DTD or XML Schema.

Excluding these from an XML document means that any tag can be used in the document. In contrast, a DTD or XML Schema requires tags in the XML document to be defined in the DTD or XML Schema; otherwise, the XML document is not considered well formed.

A DTD requires that elements be defined using the <!ELEMENT> declaration. The <!ELEMENT> declaration must contain the name of the element and the content type. Here's how a Customer element is defined:

```
<!DOCTYPE CUSTOMER [
   <!ELEMENT CustomerFirstName (#PCDATA)>
]>
```

The previous example is a document type definition file called CUSTOMER. The file extension is .dtd. This DTD defines one element called CustomerFirstName and the element has a content type of #PCDATA, which is called parsed character data because characters are translated using the characters listed in Table 8-2.

The DTD is referenced on the first line of an XML document by using the following directive. This states that the program that processes the XML document will find the customer.dtd file located on the URL mywebsite.com. Of course, you replace mywebsite.com with the URL that contains the DTD:

```
<!DOCTYPE CUSTOMER SYSTEM "http://mywebsite.com/customer.dtd">
```

Create an XML Schema

An XML Schema defines elements and attributes of the language that you create using XML and it replaces a document type definition (DTD), which is another method of defining tags for use in the XML document. An XML Schema is a kind of dictionary that is used by an XML processor to transform the XML document into another kind of document, which can itself be another XML document. The output of an XML processor is dependent on the nature of the processor.

For example, a common use of an XML processor is to transform an XML document into an HTML document that can be displayed by a browser. You'll see how this is done in the "Create an XSLT" section later in this chapter.

All elements and attributes that you use in an XML document must be defined in the XML Schema; otherwise, the XML processor is unable to process the XML document.

An XML document that conforms to an XML Schema is considered a well-formed document. That is, the XML document does not contain any errors. The XML processor determines if the XML document is well formed by applying the XML Schema rules to the XML document. The XML processor displays an error message if an element or attribute in the XML document is either not defined in the XML Schema or doesn't obey rules defined in the XML Schema.

Let's say that you defined an element in the XML Schema called age with an integer data type. An XML processor will display an error if a string is entered as text for the age element in an XML document. This is because the element requires an integer value. For example, "33" might be entered as the value for age. This is acceptable as long as you didn't narrow the scope of the value using a regular expression, which is discussed later in this chapter. However, an error is thrown if "Joe" is entered.

Defining an XML Schema

An XML Schema is a file that you create using any text editor. The file must have the file extension .xsd and the contents of the file must conform to the XML Schema language.

An XML Schema begins by declaring the XML Schema namespace. A *namespace* is a prefix that identifies your XML Schema from another XML Schema, which is critical whenever your XML document is combined with another XML document.

Both XML documents might use the same name for an element, but have different definitions for the element. Therefore, the namespace prefix is used to distinguish elements of different documents whenever these documents are combined.

Here's how you begin an XML Schema:

```
<?xml version="1.0" ?>
<xsd:schema xmlns:xsd="http://www.w3.org/2000/10/XMLSchema">
</xsd:schema>
```

The <?xml version="1.0" ?> defines the XML version that is used in the XML Schema. The xsd:schema defines the namespace used by the XML Schema and the corresponding XML document, which is xsd. The URL identifies the version of the XML Schema language that is used to create the XML Schema. This is located on the w3 organization's web site, which is the group responsible for defining XML standards.

Defining an Element

There are two types of elements defined in an XML Schema. These are simple elements and complex elements. A simple element is an element that contains only text. A complex element is an element that contains other elements or attributes.

The definition of a simple element consists of three components. First is the XML Schema language syntax that identifies to the XML processor that you are defining an element (xsd:element). Next is the name of the element (name=) and the last component is the data type of the element (type=). Listing 8-31 is a definition of a simple element that defines the FirstName element as being of the string data type. You'll notice that the <xsd:schema> uses the abbreviation closing tag, which is a forward slash immediately preceding the closing angle bracket. The traditional closing tag is not necessary if the abbreviation closing is used.

Listing 8-31
How to define a simple element.

```
<?xml version="1.0" ?>
<xsd:schema xmlns:xsd="http://www.w3.org/2000/10/XMLSchema">
  <xsd:element name="FirstName" type="xsd:string" />
</xsd:schema>
```

Here is how the FirstName element is used in an XML document:

```
<FirstName>Bob</FirstName>
```

Complex Element Types

There are four kinds of complex types of elements. These are as follows:

- Elements that contain other elements and optional attributes
- Elements that contain other elements and text and optional attributes
- Elements that contain only text and optional attributes
- Elements that are empty and optional attributes

Listing 8-32 is a definition of a complex element called Person that contains two elements. These are FirstName and LastName, both of which are of the string data type. Data types are introduced later in this chapter.

Listing 8-32
How to define a complex element.

```
<?xml version="1.0"?>
<xsd:schema xmlns:xsd="http://www.w3.org/2000/10/XMLSchema">
  <xsd:complexType name="Person">
    <xsd:sequence>
      <xsd:element name="FirstName" type="xsd:string"/>
```

```
        <xsd:element name="LastName" type="xsd:string"/>
      </xsd:sequence>
    </xsd:completeType>
  </xsd:schema>
```

In this example, the definition of a complex element type begins by using the xsd:complexType syntax followed by the name of the complex element type, which is Person. The xsd:sequence tells the XML processor that elements within the complex element type must appear in the sequence these elements appear within the definition of the complex element type. The next two lines define two simple element types called FirstName and LastName. Listing 8-33 is how the Person element is used in an XML document.

Listing 8-33
How previously defined elements are used in an XML document.

```
<Person>
  <FirstName>Bob</FirstName>
  <LastName>Smith</LastName>
</Person>
```

Predefine the Content of an Element

There might occasions when you require an element to contain a predefined value such as using the name of your company in an XML document. You can have the XML Schema insert the company name instead of requiring the person who creates the XML document to enter the company name.

A predefined content is created when you define an element in the XML Schema by using either the fixed or default attribute followed by the content that will be included when the element is used in an XML document. This is illustrated here:

- <sxd:element name="Company" type="xsd:string" fixed="My Company"/> is used to assign the value "My Company" to the "Company" element. If the "Company" element isn't included in the XML document, the "Company" element doesn't contain any value.

- <sxd:element name="Company" type="xsd:string" default-="My Company"/> is used to assign the value "My Company" to the "Company" element. If the "Company" element isn't included in the XML document, the "Company" element is automatically assigned the content "My Company".

Setting a Set of Acceptable Values

You can restrict the content of an element to one of a series of values by setting the xsd:enumeration tag when you define the element in the XML Schema. Each xsd:enumeration tag is assigned an acceptable value that can appear as the element's content.

Listing 8-34 illustrates how to create a list of acceptable content for an element. The element is called state and a few abbreviations for states are listed to show how to use the xsd:enumeration tag.

The XML document is considered well formed only if one of the values listed in the definition element is included as content for the element, if the element is used in the XML form.

Listing 8-34
How to create a list of acceptable content for an element.

```
<xsd:element name="state">
  <xsd:simpleType>
    <xsd:restriction base="xsd:string">
      <xsd:enumeration value="CA"/>
      <xsd:enumeration value="NJ"/>
      <xsd:enumeration value="TX"/>
    </xsd:restriction>
  </xsd:simpleType>
</xsd:element>
```

Data Types

A data type of an element restricts the kind of data that can be contained by an element to only data that conforms to the specified data type. For example, an element that defines a serial number is an integer data type. This means the content of the element must be an integer. Content other than an integer (for example, a person's name) causes the XML processor to display an error message when the document is processed.

You can specify the data type of an element by assigning one of the several predefined data types to the type attribute of the xsd:element definition. Here are commonly used data types. The entire list of data types is available from http:// www.w3.org/TR/xmlschema-2/#built-in-datatypes.

- **xsd:boolean**   An element must contain a Boolean value.

- **xsd:date**   An element must contain a date using yyyy-mm-dd with (optionally) time zone indicator—time zone affects sorting rules.

- **xsd:decimal**   An element that contains a decimal value, but can also contain an integer. A total of 18 digits is the minimum number of digits available in a processor that conforms to the XML standard.

- **xsd:string**   An element must contain character data, including whitespace and punctuation.

- **xsd:time**   An element must contain a time value, which is hh:mm:ss.sss with (optionally) time zone indicator—time zone affects sorting.

- **xsd:uri**   An element must contain a URI.

In addition to predefined data types, you can create customized data types that are based on predefined data types. This is a way to extend a predefined data type to include restrictions such as a range of dates. You'll see how this is done later in this chapter.

Dates and Time

The XML Schema language contains a variety of predefined date and time data types that enable you to control date and time content that is contained in an element of your XML document.

Table 8-3 contains date and time data types along with the format in which the data and/or time content must appear within element. The table also illustrates the proper declaration of the data type in the XML Schema and includes an example on how date and/or time are entered as content in an element.

Date Type	Format	Declaration	Example in XML Document
xsd:timeDuration	PnYnMnDTnHnMnS P1Y3M10D = 1 year 3 months 10 days T4H25M30S = 4 hours 25 minutes 30 seconds	`<xsd:element name="LenEmployment" type="xsd:timeDuration"/>`	< LenEmployment > P1Y3M10D </ LenEmployment >
xsd:time	hh:mm:ss.sss 15:30:00.000 = 3:30 p.m.	`<xsd:element name="MeetTime" type="xsd:time"/>`	< MeetTime >15:30 </ MeetTime >
xsd:timeInstance	A moment in time. ccyy-mm-ddThh:mm:ss.sss 2003-10-18T14:43:22.543 = Oct. 18, 2003 2:43:22.543 PM	`<xsd:element name="TradeReceived" type="xsd:timeInstant"/>`	< TradeReceived > 2003-10-18T14:43:22.543 </ TradeReceived >
xsd:date	ccyy-mm-dd 2003-10-18 = Oct. 18, 2003	`<xsd:element name="TradeDate" type="xsd:date"/>`	< TradeDate > 2003-10-18 </ TradeDate >
xsd:month	ccyy-mm 2003-10 = Oct. 2003	`<xsd:element name="TradeMonth" type="xsd:month"/>`	< TradeMonth > 2003-10 </ TradeMonth >
xsd:year	ccyy 2003= 2003	`<xsd:element name="TradeYear" type="xsd:year"/>`	< TradeYear >2003 </ TradeYear >
xsd:century	cc 20= 2000	`<xsd:element name="TradeCentury" type="xsd:century"/>`	< TradeCentury > 2000 </ TradeCentury >

Table 8-3. *Date and Time Data Types*

Date Type	Format	Declaration	Example in XML Document
xsd:recurringDay	Whenever content of the element should represent a day of the month with regard to year and century. ---15 = the 15th day of the month	<xsd:element name= "RegMeeting" type= "xsd:recurringDate"/>	< RegMeeting >---15 </ RegMeeting >

Table 8-3.   *Date and Time Data Types* (continued)

Time isn't time zone dependent if the time zone indicator (Z) is excluded from the date/time declaration. However, the time is adjusted for the time zone if the time zone indicator is used as the last character in the content.

The XML Schema language uses the Coordinated (Universal) Time (UTC), which is the local time in London and commonly referred to as Greenwich mean time. The element requires a particular format where a minus or plus sign precedes the time difference between local time and GMT.

For example, eastern standard time is UTC-5, or five hours earlier than it is in London (Greenwich mean time). Pacific standard time is UTC-8. Western Europe is UTC+1, with some exceptions.

You indicate UTC time by using the Z symbol in the data type, or you can use the plus and minus signs to indicate the time difference between the time in the XML document and Greenwich mean time. For example, a -5 indicates eastern standard time or five hours before Greenwich mean time.

Numeric Data Types

You can specify that the content of an element be a numeric data type by using one of the several predefined numeric data types that exist in the XML Schema language. Table 8-4 illustrates each data type.

Keep in mind that defining an element as having a numeric data type does not prevent a person from entering non-numeric values as content in the element.

Content that is of a different data type than the data type you specify in the XML Schema causes the XML processor to consider the XML document not well formed and prevents the XML document from being processed.

Customized Data Types

A customized data type is a data type that you create based on a predefined XML Schema data type. The purpose of creating your own data type is to enhance the data typing capabilities of existing data.

Data Type	Format	Declaration	Example in XML Document
xsd:decimal	Content can contain a decimal value. n.n = 10.95	<xsd:element name= " price" type="xsd: decimal "/>	<price> 10.95</price>
xsd:integer	Content must be an integer. n = 34	<xsd:element name= " age" type="xsd: integer "/>	< age > 34</ age >
xsd:positiveInteger	Content must be a positive integer. n = 34	<xsd:element name= " age" type="xsd: positiveInteger "/>	< age > 34</ age >
xsd:negativeInteger	Content must be a negative integer. -n = -30	<xsd:element name= " countdown" type= "xsd: negativeInteger "/>	< countdown > -30 </ countdown >
xsd:nonPositiveInteger	Content must be a nonpositive integer. -n = -30 nonPositive and nonNegative include 0	<xsd:element name= " countdown" type= "xsd: negativeInteger "/>	< countdown > -30 </ countdown >
xsd:nonNegativeInteger	Content must be a nonnegative integer. n = 34	<xsd:element name= " age" type="xsd: positiveInteger "/>	< age > 34</ age >
xsd:float	Content can be a 32-bit floating-point value. n.nnnnnnn = 1.5647834 Can also use exponential notation, such as 1.234e-3. In addition, the following modifiers can be used: INF—Positive infinity. -INF—Negative infinity. 0—Positive zero. -0—Negative zero. NaN—Not a number (important for parsers).	<xsd:element name= " size" type="xsd: float "/>	<size > 1.5647834 </ size >

Table 8-4. *Numeric Data Types*

Data Type	Format	Declaration	Example in XML Document
xsd:double	Content can be a 64-bit floating-point value. n.nnnnnnnnnnnnnnn =1.564783445673967 Can also use exponential notation, such as 1.234e-3. In addition, the following modifiers can be used: INF—Positive infinity. -INF—Negative infinity. 0—Positive zero. -0—Negative zero. NaN—Not a number (important for parsers).	<xsd:element name= " size" type="xsd: double "/>	<size > 1.564783445673967 </ size >

Table 8-4. *Numeric Data Types* (continued)

J2EE FOUNDATION

Let's say that you define an element whose content is a ZIP code. A ZIP code element is usually declared as a string data type. However, a string data type accepts any combination of characters and numbers, which means an XML document could have a ZIP code element that contains a value other than a ZIP code, such as a 20 digit number.

You can create a custom data type that restricts the content of an element such as a ZIP code element. In that way any extraneous characters entered as content causes the XML document not to be well formed.

There are two kinds of custom data types. These are simpleType and complexType. A simpleType does not contain other elements or attributes. A complexType can contain other elements and attributes, and these are discussed later in this chapter.

SimpleType   You define a simpleType by using the xsd:simpleType tag in the XML Schema and include a unique name to identify the data type. Listing 8-35 shows how to define a custom data type that is a simpleType, which is called PostalCodeType.

After the xsd:simpleType tag defines the name of the custom data type, the xsd:restriction tag is used to define the base data type for the custom data type. The base data type is the predefined data type that is enhanced by the custom data type. The PostalCodeType enhances the xsd:string data type.

Next, the xsd:pattern tag is used to describe characters and/or numbers that are acceptable to the custom data type. That is, content entered into an element that is defined as the PostalCodeType is limited to characters and/or numbers that match the value of the xsd:pattern tag.

The pattern is defined using a regular expression language that is similar to the regular expression language used in Perl. The content of an element that is defined as the custom data type must match the pattern to conform to a well-formed XML document.

Table 8-5 lists the symbols for a regular expression. You can combine regular expression symbols to create sophisticated limitations to entries made into an element.

In the PostalCodeType example (see Listing 8-35), the xsd:pattern tag is used and the value attribute is assigned a pattern. This means that the content for the PostalCodeType element must have five digits followed by an optional dash and four digits. The [0-9] can be replaced with "\d" to represent a digit.

Symbol	Definition
. (Period)	Any character
\d	Any digit
\D	Any nondigit
\s	Any whitespace
\S	Any nonwhitespace character
x*	Zero or more occurrences of x where x can be any character or pattern. You can evaluate the number of occurrences of the pattern by placing x in parentheses such as (abc)* where the string "abc" appears from zero times to many times in x.
x?	Zero or one occurrence of the character where x can be any character or pattern (see above).
x+	One or more occurrences of the character where x can be any character or pattern (see above). The plus sign means one or more occurrences.

Table 8-5. *Symbols Used to Create a Pattern*

Symbol	Definition
(xyz){3}	A pattern is defined within the parentheses and the value within the French braces indicates the number of times the pattern appears in the string. This means xyz appears three times in the string. Square brackets are used for character sets.
[0-9]	Defines a character set where the value must match one of the values in the character set. The dash is used to define a range of sequential values such as: [0-9A-Za-z] matches any alphanumeric character. [0-9 A-Za-z] is the same as above except it also matches a space character (0x20). [0-9] is equivalent to [0123456789] or [0987654321]. [0-9\-] matches digits and the dash character.
x{4}	Must have exactly four x's in a row where x can be any character or pattern defined using the parentheses (see above).
x{4,}	Must have at least four x's in a row where x can be any character or pattern.
x{4,9}	Must have at least four and at most nine x's in a row where x can be any character or pattern.
'abcd'	This means that the string contains 'abcd'.
'^abcd'	This means that the string starts with 'abcd'.
'abcd$'	This means that the string ends with 'abcd'.
'^abcd$'	This means that the string equals with 'abcd'.
\$	The backslash matches the literal value of any special that follows the backslash character. In this example, it matches a $.

Table 8-5.   *Symbols Used to Create a Pattern* (continued)

Once a value is assigned to the xsd:pattern tag, you must insert a close xsd.restriction tag and a close xsd:simpleType tag into the XML Schema.

Listing 8-35
How to create a pattern for a custom data type.

```
<xsd:simpleType name="PostalCodeType">
  <xsd:restriction base = "xsd:string">
    <xsd:pattern value="\[0-9]{5}(-[0-9]{4})?" />
  </xsd:restriction>
</xsd:simpleType>
```

Setting a Range of Values

In addition to creating a pattern for a custom data type, you can also specify a range of values that must be contained in an element. There are four ways to specify a value range. These are by using maximum and minimum and inclusive and exclusive tags:

- **<xsd:maxInclusive value="3500"/>** Requires that the value be less than or equal to the value assigned to value.

- **<xsd:maxExclusive value="3500"/>** Requires that the value be less than the value assigned to value.

- **<xsd:minInclusive value="3500"/>** Requires that the value be equal to or greater than the value assigned to value.

- **<xsd:minExclusive value="3500"/>** Requires that the value be greater than the value assigned to value.

Setting Length of Contents

You can limit the length of characters in a custom data type by using one of three length tags. Each tag is used to set the minimum, maximum, and exact length for the content of an element that is defined using the custom data type.

Here are the length tags:

- **<xsd:length value="15"/>** Specifies that the content of an element must be 15 characters in length for the XML document to be well formed.

- **<xsd:maxLength value="15"/>** Specifies that the content of an element must have no more than 15 characters in length for the XML document to be well formed.

- **<xsd:minLength value="15"/>** Specifies that the content of an element must have at least 15 characters in length for the XML document to be well formed.

Setting Precision and Scale

You can limit the number of digits that are entered into an element and limit the number of digits to the right of the decimal by using the precision and scale tags in a custom data type definition:

- ***<xsd:precision value="6"/>** Sets the maximum number of digits that appear in an element for the XML document to be well formed. The entered number, including the decimal value but excluding the decimal itself, must be no more than six digits.

- ***<xsd:scale value="3"/>** Sets the maximum number of digits that appear to the right of the decimal in an element for the XML document to be well formed. No more than three digits can appear to the right of the decimal in this example.

Complex Data Types

In the previous sections you learned how a simpleType custom data type is defined. A simpleType is used for elements that don't contain other elements or attributes. Many of the XML documents that you create will have elements that contain other elements or attributes, and therefore defining a custom data type that is a simpleType is inappropriate.

Therefore, you need to define a custom data type that is a complexType. A complexType custom data type is designed for elements that contain other elements or attributes.

Listing 8-36 shows how to declare a complexType that contains two elements. You can have as many elements as is required by your document by inserting the definition of elements within the complexType definition as shown in Listing 8-36.

The complexType is called "Person" and the two elements are the person's "FirstName" and "LastName". This means that an element in the XML document that is defined as a "Person" data type must contain two elements that are called "FirstName" and "LastName". An XML document isn't considered well formed if the element of a "Person" data type doesn't contain these two elements.

Furthermore, these elements must appear in the same sequence as defined in the "Person" data type. This is because the xsd:sequence tag is used in the definition. You could enable these elements to appear in any order by replacing the xsd:sequence tag with the <xsd:all> tag.

If you replace the xsd:sequence tag with the <xsd:all> tag , the XML document will be considered well formed if the element defined as a "Person" type contains both elements and those elements could be in reverse order as they are defined in the "Person" data type definition.

Listing 8-36
How to
declare a
complexType.

```
<xsd:complexType name="Person">
  <xsd:sequence>
    <xsd:element name="FirstName" type="xsd:string"/>
    <xsd:element name="LastName" type="xsd:string"/>
  </xsd:sequence>
</xsd:complexType>
```

Defining Attributes

An attribute is additional information used by an element besides the element's content. You've seen attributes used previously in this chapter with HTML tags. You define an attribute for an XML element by using the xsd:attribute tag in the XML Schema. The attribute requires a name that is unique to the element and a data type that can be a predefined data type or a custom data type.

Listing 8-37 illustrates how to define an attribute. The attribute is called "Gender" and is used by the "Employee" element to identify the gender of an employee.

The element and attribute are used in an XML document by writing <Employee Gender="Female" />. An attribute is optional unless you make the attribute required. That is, a person can use the "Employee" element, exclude the attribute, and the XML document is still considered well formed.

You can require the attribute by assigning the "required" value to the use attribute such as <xsd:attribute name="Gender" type="xsd:string" use="required"/>.

Listing 8-37
How to
define an
attribute.

```
<xsd:element name="Employee">
  <xsd:complexType>
    <xsd:complexContent>
      <xsd:extension base="xsd:anytype">
        <xsd:attribute name="Gender" type="xsd:string"/>
      </xsd:extension>
    </xsd:complexContent>
  </xsd:complexType>
</xsd:element>
```

The value of an attribute can be predefined by using fixed or default, similar to how these are used to predefine the content of an element. Declaring the predefined value as fixed means the predefined value is assigned to the attribute only if the element appears in the XML document. The attribute isn't assigned the predefined value if the element isn't used in the XML document.

In contrast, an attribute that has a predefined value as default is always assigned the predefined value even if the element doesn't appear in the XML document.

Listing 8-38 creates a predefined value for the "Gender" attribute as assigned "fixed" and the value attribute is assigned the predefined value "Female". You can make the attribute default by replacing the "fixed" with "default".

Listing 8-38
How to
create a
predefined
value for
an attribute.

```
<xsd:element name="Employee">
  <xsd:complexType>
    <xsd:complexContent>
      <xsd:extension base="xsd:anytype">
        <xsd:attribute name="Gender" type="xsd:string" use="fixed" value="Female"/>
      </xsd:extension>
    </xsd:complexContent>
  </xsd:complexType>
</xsd:element>
```

Referencing an XML Schema

You link an XML document to an XML Schema by referencing the XML Schema file in the root tag of the XML document. Let's say that XML Schema is stored in a file called myXMLSchema.xsd. Listing 8-39 shows how you reference the XML Schema inside the XML document.

Listing 8-39
How to reference the XML Schema inside the XML document.

```
<?xml version="1.0" ?>
<root xmlns :xsi="http://www.w3.org/2000.10.XMLSchema-instance"
xsi:noNamespaceSchemaLocation="http://www.jimkeogh.com/ns/
myXMLSchema/myXMLSchema.xsd">
```

The xsi:schemaLocation attribute of the root tag declares the namespace, which points to the location of the file that contains the XML Schema for the XML document.

Create an XSLT

An XSLT is used by an XML-enabled browser (that is, Internet Explorer 5 and Netscape 6) to transform an XML document into an HTML document so the contents of an XML document can be displayed in a browser.

Here's the process that occurs when an XSLT is used to transform an XML document. First, an XSLT processor analyzes the XML document and translates components (that is, tags, attributes, and content) into a hierarchical representation of the XML document, which is referred to as a node tree. A *node* is a component of an XML document.

Next, the XSLT processor matches each node with a template in the XSLT style sheet. A template contains a two-part instruction. The first part is a label that matches a node in the XML document. The second part is the transformation that takes place when the node is encountered by the XSLT processor.

The transformation part of the instruction is where HTML code is inserted into the XSLT style sheet file that has the extension xsl. This HTML code is displayed or saved to a file whenever that XSLT processor finds a node in the XML document that matches the label of the instruction.

XSLT Defined

An XSLT style sheet consists of one or more template definitions that are processed by the XSLT processor when the template label matches a component in the XML document.

The template definition consists of code that will be output by the XSLT processor. The kind of code that you use in the template definition depends on the program that will use the output.

J2EE FOUNDATION

For example, HTML code is used in the template definition if the output is going to be displayed by a browser. The output is automatically sent to the browser if the browser uses an XSLT processor; otherwise, the XSLT processor sends the output to a file, which can then be read by a browser.

Listing 8-40 shows a short XML document followed by an XSLT style sheet (see Listing 8-41) that contains templates. The XML document has an element called Employee and it contains an attribute called Dept. There are two other elements, which are FirstName and LastName.

The XSLT style sheet begins with the namespace declaration and version identifier. If you're using the Internet Explorer 5 XSLT processor, you'll need to replace the namespace declaration with <xsl:stylesheet xmlns:xsl="http://www.w3.org/TR/WD-xsl">.

The template is defined in the XSLT style sheet and begins with the <xsl:template> tag that contains the match attribute. The value of the match attribute is the name of the XML document component that is transformed by the template.

The content of an element is referenced from within a template definition by using the <xsl:value-of select="   "/> tag. The value of the select is specific to each element and must be enclosed within quotations as illustrated in Listing 8-41. The XSLT processor replaces the tag with the contents of the element.

Make sure that you properly use double quotations and single quotations when referencing the attribute of an XML document element. The value of the match attribute must be enclosed in double quotations. The value of the XML document attribute must be enclosed in single quotes within the square brackets.

The template must have a closed </xsl:template> tag. Listing 8-42 illustrates the output of the HTML document.

Listing 8-40
A sample XML document saved in Employee.xml, in the same directory as Employee.xsl.

```xml
<?xml version="1.0"?>
<?xml-stylesheet type="text/xsl" href="Employee.xsl" ?>
<MyDocument title="My test page">
  <Employee Dept="52">
    <FirstName>Jane</FirstName>
    <LastName>Smith</LastName>
  </Employee>
  <Employee Dept="59">
    <FirstName>Henry</FirstName>
    <LastName>Hudson</LastName>
  </Employee>
</MyDocument>
```

Listing 8-41
An XSLT style sheet saved in Employee.xsl.

```xml
<?xml version="1.0"?>
<xsl:stylesheet xmlns:xsl="http://www.w3.org/1999/XSL/
      Transform" version="1.0">
```

```
    <xsl:template match="MyDocument">
    <html>
      <head>
        <title><xsl:value-of select="@title"/></title>
      </head>
      <body>
        Employee list:<br/>
        <xsl:for-each select="Employee">
          First name: <xsl:value-of select="FirstName"/><br/>
          Last name: <xsl:value-of select="LastName"/><br/>
          Dept: <xsl:value-of select="@Dept"/><br/><br/>
        </xsl:for-each>
      </body>
    </html>
    </xsl:template>
    </xsl:stylesheet>
```

Listing 8-42
Open
Employee.xml
IE5 or higher
and the following
should be
displayed and
the title bar in
the browser
should say "My
test page".

```
Employee list:
First name: Jane
Last name: Smith
Dept: 52

First name: Henry
Last name: Hudson
Dept: 59
```

Planning an XML Database Program

An XML document has some of the characteristics of a database in that the XML document is a collection of data identified by metadata and stored in a file. In a relational database, data is stored in columns that are identified by a column name. In an XML document, data is stored in elements that are identified by tags.

Data stored in both an XML document and a relational database can be manipulated by a program and exchanged with data from other applications. However, data in a relational database is more efficiently manipulated than data in an XML document because of the way data is organized and managed by a DBMS.

You can blend the simplicity of an XML document with the efficient data management capabilities of a relational database by storing an XML document into a relational database and using a DBMS to manage the XML document.

Concepts of an XML Database Program

Many corporations that need to manage large amounts of information stored in documents have embraced the advantages of XML. XML is intuitive and flexible, and enables information to be organized in an advantageous way for corporations and industry to exchange information.

An industry group can agree on a standard XML Schema for a particular type of document, such as a book. This standard enables participants in the industry to share and manipulate a document economically. For example, a printer is able to accept XML files of a manuscript to transform the files into a finished book.

However, XML is a fledgling technology that isn't as robust and mature as other data collection and management tools such as relational DBMS. An XML document is stored in a text file, also known as a flat file, that doesn't lend itself to efficient data management.

A text file consists of a long series of characters, some of which represent XML tags while others represent data. There isn't an easy way to distinguish between a tag and data. This means that a program must search each character of the text file looking for data.

Let's say that you wanted an employee's name and you used the employee's number to locate the employee in the following XML document. Listing 8-43 illustrates how to locate the employee information.

Listing 8-43
Locating employee information in an XML document.

```
<?xml version="1.0"?>
<root xmlns:xsi="http?//www.w3.org/2000.10.XMLSchema-instance"
xsi:noNamespaceSchemaLocation="http://www.jimkeogh.com/ns/
myXMLSchema/myXMLSchema.xsd">
<Person EmpNumber="1234">
   <FirstName>Bob</FirstName>
   <LastName>Smith</LastName>
</Person>
```

A program starts by reading the first line of the XML document and compares the contents of the line with elements defined in the XML Schema. That is, the program looks for the line that contains the Person tag.

When the line is found, the program searches the line for the EmpNumber attribute and then compares the value of the attribute with the employee number of the search criteria. If the employee numbers don't match, the program continues to reach subsequent lines until either the Person tag is located or the program reaches the end of the XML document.

If the employee numbers match, the program reads the following lines to retrieve the first name and last name of the employee. However, each of those lines contains an open and close tag (that is, <FirstName> and </FirstName>) and the employee's name. Therefore, the program must parse the employee's name from the line to complete the search process.

In contrast, a DBMS doesn't need to read through all possible metadata and data to locate a particular employee number. Instead, a DBMS typically uses an index (see Part II) that contains the employee number (the key) and a reference to related employee information in a table.

Using XML to organize and manage a database can become unattractive when compared to other forms of data management (for example, a relational database). This is especially true when information is contained in many XML documents.

Let's say that XML is used to organize personnel data. Employees complete a personal form when a company hires them. The personal form could be stored as an XML document. This means that a company that has 1,000 employees has 1,000 XML documents to store and manage, which is a cumbersome task unless XML documents are blended with a relational database.

Objectives of an XML Database

An XML database is a blend of XML technology and DBMS technology that provides companies the best of both technologies. The result is a blend of technologies that enables companies to efficiently manage XML documents.

By blending these technologies, companies are able to

- Store and retrieve XML documents
- Search multiple XML documents for specific data
- Search and replace element tags and/or data stored in an XML document
- Modify an XML document
- Delete components of an XML document or delete the entire XML document

This means information can be organized according to an industry- or enterprise-wide accepted XML Schema and be managed by a DBMS. Also, SQL queries can be used to insert, retrieve, modify, and delete both metadata and data in an XML document.

Types of XML Database Schemas

In essence, an XML database is a relational database that contains one or multiple XML documents. That is, any relational database product (for example, Oracle, mySQL, or DB2) can be used as an XML database.

An XML database uses a different database schema than is commonly used in other relational databases (see Part II). This is because an XML database is used to store components of an XML document rather than simply storing data contained in the document.

For example, the XML document described in the previous section has three elements (Person, FirstName, LastName), one attribute (EmpNumber), and three pieces of information (1234, Bob, Smith).

A traditional database schema could be used to store data contained in the XML document, if only the data was to be stored in the database. A single table of three columns—Employee Number, First Name, and Last Name—could be used. Each row of the table would contain an employee number and employee name.

However, an XML database must store data contained in elements of the XML document and other components of the XML document (that is, tag name, attribute name, open tags, and close tags).

XML database designers use one of three database schemas to store an XML document in a relational database. I'll briefly introduce each here and then explain them later in this chapter:

- **Coarse-grained**   The database consists of one table that contains two columns. One column identifies the XML document and the other column is used to store the entire XML document.

- **Medium-grained**   The XML document is divided into slices and each slice is placed in a row of a table.

- **Fine-grained**   Individual components of the XML document are stored in columns of multiple tables in the database.

Coarse-Grained XML Relational Database

The coarse-grained style requires that the XML document be stored in the database as an entire document, rather than decomposing documents into document elements. At first glance, you might consider the coarse-grained style nothing more than a document stored in a flat file rather than in a database. This is because a program that retrieves the document must parse the data from the document line by line, similar to how data is extracted from a document in a flat file.

As you'll recall from Part II of this book, information in an entity, which a document is, is decomposed into atomic components called data. Data is then organized into rows and columns of a table, and an index is used to locate data.

Therefore, you are probably wondering what the benefits are of storing an XML document in its entirety into a database instead of storing data components of the document in the database. The benefits of using the coarse-grained style are

- XML documents can be referenced quickly using the capabilities of a DBMS.

- DBMS provides an efficient means of protecting documents through the use of security and data recovery features.

- The coarse-grained style provides an intermediate step from moving from a flat file XML document system to an XML document system that is decomposed and normalized into tables.

- XML is often used for transmitting data between partner companies or within a company. The data can be preformatted into XML and stored in the database; then, the query simply selects all the unsent records and sends them to their destination in XML form.

The database schema for the coarse-grained style consists of one table that has three columns. The columns are

- DocumentID, Number, Primary Key
- DocumentName, VARCHAR
- Document, CLOB

An XML document is inserted into the table and retrieved from the table using a query and Java data objects (see Part II). Let's assume that the XML document contains customer information and the XML document name is CustNum123, which is the customer's number. The XML document is recalled from the database by using the query in Listing 8-44. The ResultSet contains one column, which is the XML document, and is retrieved by using the getCLOB() method (see Chapter 6).

Listing 8-44
A query to
retrieve
an XML
document.
from a
database.

```
SELECT Document
FROM XMLTable
WHERE DocumentName = 'CustNum123'
```

Medium-Grained XML Relational Database

The major disadvantage of using the coarse-grained style as described in the previous section is that the J2EE component that retrieves the XML document from the database must parse data from the XML document before being able to use the data.

The medium-grained style provides finer granularity than that found in the coarse-grained style—but not the finest granularity, as is seen in the fine-grained style, which is discussed later in this chapter.

The medium-grained style requires that the XML document be sliced into subsections. These subsections are then stored using the coarse-grained technique. Let's say that an XML document contains a book. The entire book would be stored in a row of a database if the coarse-grained technique were used.

However, the XML document that contains the book can easily be sliced into subsections where each subsection is a chapter of the book. This means that each chapter is contained in one row of the table.

The coarse-grained style is similar to a book that doesn't have a table of contents or an index. This means you must look line by line through the book trying to locate the information that you need.

The medium-grained style is similar to a book that has a table of contents. The table of contents slices the book into medium chunks that help you identify the general area of the book to look at to locate information that you need. The fine-grained style is similar to a book that has an index. That is, the book is sliced into the finest elements of the book, which are words.

Let's say that you wanted to create an XML database that uses the medium-grained style to store chapters of a book. The following is a likely database schema. The primary key for the table is the ChapterID, which together uniquely identifies each row in the table. Listing 8-45 contains the query used to retrieve a chapter from the database. The chapter is returned in the ResultSet and copied from the ResultSet using the getCLOB() method.

- ChapterID, Number, Primary Key
- DocumentID, Number, Foreign Key
- DocumentName, VARCHAR

J2EE FOUNDATION

- ChapterName, VARCHAR
- Chapter, CLOB

Listing 8-45
A query to
retrieve
an XML
document
from a
database.

```
SELECT Chapter
FROM XMLTable
WHERE DocumentName = 'ISBN1234' and ChapterName = 'Introduction'
```

Fine-Grained XML Relational Database

The fine-grained style requires that an XML document be decomposed into elements, attributes, and character data regions—each of which are grouped together into a table. There is also another table that is used to store parent/child relationships between elements, subelements, and character data.

The advantage of using a fine-grained style is that each element, attribute, and character data region can be easily accessed, modified, or deleted without affecting other components of the document. For example, data that is associated with an element can be modified by changing the value of the column that contains the data, rather than having to parse the data from the XML document, change the data, then reconstruct the XML document.

The major disadvantage of using the fine-grained style is the time necessary to decompose and regenerate the entire XML document. Each time an XML document is stored in a database, a J2EE component must parse the XML document into elements, attributes, and character data region as well as recording parent/child relationships between elements, subelements, and character data. You would probably perform parsing and a series of inserts using a stored procedure, rather than in the J2EE component. Many developers avoid using the fine-grained style and instead prefer the medium-grained style.

A J2EE component must reconstruct the XML document from elements, attributes, and character data regions retrieved from the database, which is time-consuming. The following is the database schema for the fine-grained style.

Listing 8-46 illustrates how to retrieve data stored from a fine-grained style database. In this example, the query retrieves the document name, attribute value, and the element value from the XML document. An entire XML document can be reconstructed by using the ParentID in the Elements table to determine the parent/child relationships between elements and subelements.

- Documents Table
  - DocumentID, Number, 8 digits, Primary Key
  - DocumentName, VARCHAR, 128 characters, Not Null
- Elements Table

- DocumentID, Number, 8 digits, Primary Key, Foreign Key references documents.documentID
- ElementID, Number, 8 digits, Primary Key
- ParentID, Number, 8 digits, Foreign Key references elements.elementID (nullable because of the root node)
- ElementName, VARCHAR, 32 characters, Not Null
- ElementValue, VARCHAR, Not Null

- Attributes Table (the DocumentID and AttributeID combined create the Primary Key)
    - AttributeID, Number, 8 digits, Primary Key
    - ElementID, Number, 8 digits, Not Null, Foreign Key references elements.elementID
    - AttributeName, VARCHAR, 32 characters, Not Null
    - AttributeValue, VARCHAR, 255 characters, Not Null

Listing 8-46
Retrieving the document name, customer number, and the customer last name from an XML document.

```
Select D.DocumentName, A.AttributeValue, E.ElementValue
FROM Documents D, Attributes A, Elements E
WHERE D.DocumentName = 'Customers' and D.DocumentID = A.DocumentID and
A.AttributeName = 'CustomerNumber' and A.AttributeValue = '123467' and
E.DocumentID = D.DocumentID and E.Element = 'FirstName' and A.ElementID = E.
ElementID
```

XHTML

XHTML is the next major generation of HTML and incorporates many aspects of XML. This section is not designed to teach you XHTML. For that, you should pick up a copy of *HTML: The Complete Reference*, which contains all you need to know about HTML and XHTML.

XHTML uses practically all of the HTML elements. However, XHTML imposes new rules that require you to tweak your HTML syntax to make your HTML documents XHTML compliant. This section illustrates the tweaking:

- XHTML is case sensitive. This means all HTML syntax must be in lowercase. For example, <FORM> must be changed to <form>.
- Every open tag must have a closing tag. For example, a paragraph is inserted into a document using the <P> tag. Although the document should also contain a </P> tag, most browsers don't require it. This is no longer the situation with XHTML-compliant browsers.

■ A shortcut can be used for tags such as <br> that usually don't have a closing tag.
 is a line break. The shortcut is to use <br />. Notice there is a space between the last letter of the tag and the forward slash. Attributes are placed btween the last letter of the tag name and the close angle bracket, such as <img src="my.jpg" />. If this is used as the opening tag, you don't need a closing tag to be XHTML compliant.

■ Values of all attributes must be enclosed with double quotations. This is optional in HTML.

Chapter 9

Java and XML

Information management is key to the success of most businesses. For many companies information is managed at the atomic level in the form of data by using a database management system, as discussed in Part II.

However, information used by some industries such as publishing and pharmaceuticals need to manage information at a coarser level in the form of a document. Documents are composed of components such as forward, preface, and chapters. XML technology enables a company to identify each document component using tags and attributes to create an XML document. XML works well because XML is platform independent and is extendable with little or no impact to existing systems.

An XML document can be created, read, and manipulated by using a J2EE component that is built using Java application program interfaces that are especially designed for use with an XML document. This chapter shows you how to build these J2EE components.

Generating an XML Document

A J2EE application can generate an XML document based on business rules that are encoded into one or more J2EE components. Typically, these J2EE components are either a Java servlet, a Java ServerPage (JSP), Enterprise JavaBeans (EJB), or a Java Message Service component.

Sending strings that contain XML tags and directives as output from either a JSP or Java servlet generates an XML document. Output from a Java servlet and a JSP is directed to the HTTP connection that invoked the Java servlet or a JSP, which is typically associated with a browser.

Java servlets and a JSP are discussed in detail later in this book; however, the following sections provide a brief overview of each and show how they can be used to produce an XML document.

Java Servlet

A Java servlet is a web server extension that provides a web service to a J2EE application. A Java servlet is similar to a Java program in that a Java servlet is a self-contained program that can perform a specific task and is called from another J2EE component such as the J2EE application user interface.

There are two ways in which a Java servlet is executed, which are briefly mentioned here and discussed in detail later in the book:

- Specifying the URL of the Java servlet as the value of the ACTION attribute of an HTML form (see Chapter 8) such as "http://www.myURL.com/servlets/myservlet." You can also place the URL path directly in the location bar of the browser.

- Chaining is another way to call a Java servlet. This enables a Java servlet to automatically be called based on the MIME type of a data stream and is configured by the web server administrator.

Listing 9-1 illustrates a Java servlet that generates an XML document. This document contains elements of a book and is the same document as is discussed in Listing 8-28 in Chapter 8. This is a simplified XML document that illustrates the technique used to create the document using a Java servlet. A real-world XML document contains many more elements than are illustrated here.

The web server calls the doGet() method or the doPost() of a Java servlet to invoke the Java servlet depending on whether the GET or POST method is used to transmit the request (see Chapter 8). Two parameters are used in these methods. These are the HttpServletRequest object (called input in this example) and the HttpServletResponse object (called output in this example). The HttpServletResponse object is used to return the output from the Java servlet to the web server.

The initial task of the Java servlet is to set the content type of information that is generated by the Java servlet by calling the setContentType() method of the HttpServletResponse object and passing the method "text/xml" string.

Next, a PrintWriter object is created using the getWriter() method of the HttpServletResponse object. In this example, the PrintWriter object is called out. The println() method of the PrintWriter object is then used to send strings that contain XML tags and directives to the web server. The tags and directives are processed according to the rules built into the requesting J2EE component—or in this example, rendered by the browser.

In this example, the XML document contains a template for a book. Only the <TitlePage> tag contains text. There are, of course, many more tags and directives used in a real-world XML document used for a book, and all those tags contain text.

J2EE FOUNDATION

Listing 9-1
Creating an XML document using a Java servlet.

```java
import java.io.*;
import javax.servlet.http.*;
import javax.servlet.*;
public class BookTemplate extends HttpServlet
{
  public void doGet(HttpServletRequest input, HttpServletResponse output)
    throws ServletException, IOException
  {
    output.setContentType("text/xml");
    PrintWriter out = output.getWriter();
    out.println("<?xml version=\"1.0\" ?>");
    out.println("<book>");
    out.println("<TitlePage>");
    out.println("J2EE, The Complete Reference");
    out.println("</TitlePage>");
    out.println("<CopyWritePage>");
    out.println("</CopyWritePage>");
    out.println("<TableOfContents>");
    out.println("</TableOfContents>");
    out.println("<Preface>");
    out.println("</Preface>");
    out.println("<Chapter>");
```

```
        out.println("</Chapter>");
        out.println("<Chapter>");
        out.println("</Chapter>");
        out.println("</book>");
    }
}
```

JavaServer Pages

As you'll learn in the JSP chapter later in this book, JSP was developed to make it easier for developers to create programs that generate dynamic HTML pages. Prior to the introduction of JSP, developers used Java servlets to generate dynamic web pages.

Java servlets are written using the Java programming language. HTML code is placed in output strings that are passed to methods such as println(). This meant that developers needed to be proficient Java programmers as well as HTML programmers.

In contrast, JSP is written mainly in HTML code with directives and other JSP constructs interspersed in the HTML. This means that an HTML developer could write a JSP program without being proficient in Java programming. JSP directives and other JSP constructs provide flow control within the JSP and are used to insert data into HTML code, among other things. JSP is translated into a Java servlet before the code is executed. You'll learn more on how this works later in the book.

Although JSP was originally designed to generate dynamic HTML pages, JSP is also used to dynamically generate an XML document. This is illustrated in Listing 9-2. In this example, the JSP is generating the same book template XML document that is created by the Java servlet in Listing 9-1.

Notice that Listing 9-2 doesn't contain any output methods such as println(), which is used in the Java servlet. This is because the entire content of the JSP is output except for JSP directives and other JSP constructs.

The first line of the JSP is the only directive used in this example. The directive <%@ page contentType="text/xml" %> sends an HTTP header that tells the browser what type of content to expect. The content type identifies the markup language used in the document. The default content type is "text/html." This means that a directive isn't necessary to change the content type if the JSP is generating an HTML page. However, the content type must be explicitly set since this JSP is generating an XML document.

Listing 9-2
Creating
an XML
document
using a JSP.

```
<%@ page contentType="text/xml" %>
<?xml version="1.0"?>
<book>
   <TitlePage>
   J2EE, The Complete Reference
   </TitlePage>
   <CopyWritePage>
   </CopyWritePage>
   <TableOfContents>
```

```
    </TableOfContents>
    <Preface>
    </Preface>
    <Chapter>
    </Chapter>
    <Chapter>
    </Chapter>
</book>
```

Parsing XML

An XML document contains information and tags that identify information, as you learned in the previous chapter. Any application that reads an XML document must parse information from the document in order to access information contained in the document.

Writing an application that parses a document is challenging and time-consuming. However, there are parsers available that are designed to parse an XML document and are accessible through an application programming interface (API). The parser API consists of Java classes that provide easy access to elements of an XML document.

There are two types of XML parsers. These are the Document Object Model (DOM) and the Simple API for XML (SAX). The DOM parser reads the entire XML document, which makes it easy to navigate the document. Although the DOM parser can be used with any size XML documents, the DOM parser is ideal for working with smaller XML documents. Larger documents can be slow to process using a DOM parser.

The SAX parser uses an event strategy. A J2EE component that interacts with a SAX parser to manipulate an XML document must contain event-handler classes that listen for specific events sent by the SAX parser as the SAX parser reads the XML document. Events are triggered whenever the SAX parser encounters an XML tag. The SAX parser is ideal for large XML documents, although the J2EE component might experience difficulties navigating a complex XML document because the SAX parser is event driven. The J2EE component doesn't have control of the parsing once the SAX parser is invoked. That is, the J2EE component must wait until the SAX parser has completed processing the XML document before the J2EE component can search the document.

In the real world, DOM is generally used to build and alter XML documents and SAX is used to read XML documents.

XML parsers can be used to parse any valid XML document, but are inappropriate for parsing non-XML documents such as a DTD (see Chapter 8). In this chapter, you'll learn how to parse an XML document using both DOM and SAX. Listing 9-4 contains the XML document that will be parsed in this chapter. Listing 9-3 is the DTD used for the XML document.

Listing 9-3
The book.dtd used for the book.htm.

```
<!ELEMENT book (chapter+)>
<!ELEMENT chapter (chapNum,chapTitle)>
```

```
<!ELEMENT chapNum (#PCDATA)>
<!ELEMENT chapTitle (#PCDATA)>
```

Listing 9-4
The book.xml
that is being
parsed.

```
<?xml version="1.0"?>
<!DOCTYPE book SYSTEM "book.dtd">
<book>
<chapter>
<chapNum>One</chapNum>
<chapTitle>Introduction to J2EE</chapTitle>
</chapter>
</book>
```

Document Object Model (DOM)

The DOM parser uses five classes that are used to navigate and parse elements of an XML document. These classes are the Node class, Document class, Element class, CharacterData class, and Attr class. These classes are introduced in this section and are illustrated in Listing 9-5.

A node is an object of the XML document and is not necessarily associated with an XML tag, such as text nodes. The Node class is a superclass so objects can share some common functionality. The values of a node name, node value, and attributes vary according to the node type. Table 9-1 lists the description of node names, node values, and attributes.

Interface	Name	Value	Attributes
Attr	Name of attribute	Value of attribute	null
CDATASection	"#cdata-section"	Content of the CDATASection	null
Comment	"#comment"	Content of the comment	null
Document	"#document"	null	null
DocumentFragment	"#document-fragment"	null	null
DocumentType	Document type name	null	null

Table 9-1. *Node Names, Node Values, and Attributes*

Interface	Name	Value	Attributes
Element	Tag name	null	NamedNode Map
Entity	Entity name	null	null
EntityReference	Name of entity referenced	null	null
Notation	Notation name	null	null
ProcessingInstruction	Target	Entire content excluding the target	null
Text	"#text"	Content of the text node	null

Table 9-1.   *Node Names, Node Values, and Attributes* (continued)

A node can have a value that is either the text of the node or the value of an attribute, depending on the nature of the node. The node text is the characters that appear between the open and close XML tags.

There are different kinds of objects within an XML document as you learned in Chapter 8. Each object has an associated note type. There are a number of standard node types that are identified by constants. These are shown in Table 9-2.

Constant	Node
static short ATTRIBUTE_NODE	The node is an Attr.
static short CDATA_SELECTION_NODE	The node is a CDATASection.
static short COMMENT_NODE	The node is a Comment.
static short DOCUMENT_FRAGMENT_NODE	The node is a DocumentFragment.

Table 9-2.   *The Commonly Used Node Constants*

Constant	Node
static short DOCUMENT_NODE	The node is a Document.
static short DOCUMENT_TYPE_NODE	The node is a DocumentType.
static short ELEMENT_NODE	The node is an Element.
static short ENTITY_NODE	The node is an Entity.
static short ENTITY_REFERENCE_NODE	The node is an EntityReference.
static short NOTATION_NODE	The node is a Notation.
static short PROCESSING_INSTRUCTION_NODE	The node is a ProcessingInstruction.
static short TEXT_NODE	The node is a Text node.

Table 9-2.   *The Commonly Used Node Constants* (continued)

There are three commonly used methods of the Node class that are used to parse information about a node. These are getNodeName(), getNodeValue(), and getNodeType(). Refer to Table 9-1 to determine the return value from each of these methods. The node type is returned as a short integer from the getNodeType() method. The short integer is equal to a node constant (see Table 9-2). The getNodeValue() method throws DOMExceptions.

Navigating The XML Document

Nodes in an XML document appear in a parent/child relationship. For example, a <Chapter> node contains <chapNum> and <chapTitle> nodes, which are child nodes of the <Chapter> node.

A NodeList can be retrieved by using the getChildNodes() method of the NodeList class. The list of child nodes is returned in a construct that is similar to an iterator. The getLength() method is called to determine the number of child nodes on the list. The getLength() method returns an int. The item() method is called to return a specific node, which is identified by the node's int position on the node list. For example, item(4) returns the fifth node on the list.

You can return a node without knowing the item number of the node by using one of a variety of methods. The getFirstChild() and getLastChild() methods return the first and last child node, respectively. The getNextSibling() and getPreviousSibling() methods return the next and previous nodes that have the same parent node as the current node. And you can retrieve the parent node of the current node by using the getParentNode() method, and retrieve the attribute of a node by using the getAttributes() method.

Modifying the Node List

The node list can be modified by using methods that insert, remove, and replace a child node. There are two methods used to insert a child node. You can also use importNode() from the Document class. These are the appendChild() and insertBefore() methods. The appendChild() method requires one argument, which is the node that is appended to the parent nodes.

The insertBefore() method requires two arguments, both of which are nodes. The first argument is the node that is being inserted into the XML document and the other argument is the node ahead of which the new node will be inserted. If the second argument is null, the node will be appended.

Let's say that you wanted to insert the <ChapNum> node above the <ChapTitle> node. The first argument in the insertBefore() method is the <ChapNum> node and the second argument is the <ChapTitle> node.

A node can be removed or replaced by using the removeChild() method and the replaceChild() method. The removeChild() method requires one argument, which is the node that is to be removed. The replaceChild() method requires two arguments. The first argument is the new child node that will replace the existing child node. The second argument is the existing child node that is being replaced.

| **Caution** | *The underlying NodeList is modified if you ran a method that returns a NodeList and then you started adding and removing nodes. Let's say that NodeList nl contains elements that are children of Element called ele. You could try to remove the children by using the following code segment, but only half the children will be removed because the getLength() method returns a different value in each iteration:* |

```
for(int i=0; i<nl.getLength(); i++)
{
        e.removeChild(nl.item(i));
}
```

You can reference a node by name using the getNamedItem() and setNamedItem() methods. The getNamedItem() method has one argument, which is a String that contains the name of the item, and returns the node. The setNamedItem() is used to append a new node. The setNamedItem() requires one argument, which is the new item. A node can be removed by using the removeNamedItem() where the node that is being removed is the argument to the removeNamedItem() method.

Document-Level Manipulations

A J2EE component can create and retrieve components of an XML document by using the Document class, which is derived from the Node class. You create a new element in the XML document by using the createElement() method. The createElement() method requires one argument, which is a String that contains the name of the element's tag.

You can create an attribute, comment, text node, and CDATA section using methods in the Document class. These are createAttribute(), createComment(), createTextNode(), and createCDATASection(). Each of these methods requires one argument, which is a String that contains the attribute name, the comment, text for the text node, and text for the CDATASection. Furthermore, createAttribute() and createCDATASection() methods throw a DOMException.

Two of the more commonly used methods to retrieve information from an XML document are getElementsByTagName() and getDocumentElement(). The getElementsByTagName() method requires one argument, which is a String that contains the name of the element. The getDocumentElement() method returns an Element that is the root element of the document.

Element- and Attribute-Level Manipulations

Element-level manipulations involve interacting with attributes of an element. There are three tasks that are commonly performed using an attribute. These are to retrieve the value of an attribute, to change the value of an attribute, and to remove the value of an attribute.

The value of an attribute is retrieved by using the getAttribute() method. The getAttribute() method requires one argument, which is a String that contains the name of the attribute. The value of the attribute is returned as String from the getAttribute() method.

The setAttribute() method is used to change the value of an attribute. Two arguments are required by the setAttribute() method. The first argument is a String that contains the name of the attribute whose value is being changed. The second argument is a String that contains the new value of the attribute. If an attribute with that name already exists, the attribute's value is changed to the new value.

The value of an attribute can be removed by using the removeAttribute() method. The removeAttribute() method requires one argument, which is a String that contains the name of the attribute whose value is to be removed. If the attribute has a default value, an attribute immediately appears with the default value. The setAttribute() and removeAttribute() methods throw a DOMException.

Attributes can also be manipulated by using the Attr class. The Attr class contains the getValue() method to retrieve the value of an attribute and a setValue() method to replace the value of an attribute. The setValue() method has one argument, which is a String that contains the new value of the attribute. You don't need to specify the attribute in these methods because the attribute is identified when the instance of the Attr class is created.

Two other commonly used methods of the Attr class are the getName() method and the getSpecified() method. The getName() method returns a String that contains the name of the attribute. The getSpecified() method returns a Boolean value that indicates if the attribute value is the default value specified in the DTD (see Chapter 8) or a value that is explicitly entered into the attribute. A Boolean true indicates the attribute is explicitly set.

Data-Level Manipulations

Data contained in elements of an XML document are treated as character sequences that are accessed by using the CharacterData class. The CharacterData class contains methods that enable you to determine the length of data and to retrieve data, append data, insert data, replace data, and remove data from the element. All these methods throw a DOMException.

The length of the data is determined by calling the getLength() method. The getLength() method returns an int that represents the number of characters contained in the data. Data can be retrieved from the XML document by using the getData() method for the substringData() method.

The getData() method returns a String that contains the entire sequence of characters in the data. The substringData() method is used to retrieve a portion of data. Two arguments are required by the substringData() method. The first argument is an int that represents the character offset of the first character that is to be retrieved from the data. The second argument is an int that represents the number of characters from the character offset that are to be retrieved. The substringData() method returns a String that contains the substring of the data.

There are four ways in which to place new data into an element. These are to append data, insert data, replace some data, and replace all the data. The appendData() method is used to append data to data that is currently in the element. The appendData() method requires one argument, which is a String that contains the data that will be appended to the existing data.

The insertData() method is used to place data within the existing data. Two arguments are required by the insertData() method. The first argument is an int that represents the character offset where the new data is to be inserted. The second argument is a String that contains that data to be inserted. Let's say that the new data is to be inserted after the fifth character of the current data. The first argument of the insertData() method is 5 and, of course, the second argument is the new data.

The replaceData() method is used to replace some data in an element. The replaceData() method requires three arguments. The first argument is an int that represents the character offset where the new data is to be inserted. The second argument is an int that represents the number of characters that are being replaced. And the third argument is a String that contains data that replaces a portion of the existing data. If you want to replace the entire data of an element, then you'll need to use the setData() method. The setData() method requires one argument, which is a String that contains the new data.

All or some of the data can be removed from an element by using the deleteData() method. The deleteData() method requires two arguments. The first argument is an int that represents the character offset of the first character that is to be removed from the data. The second argument is an int that represents the number of characters from the character offset that are to be removed.

DOM Parsing in Action

Listing 9-5 illustrates the technique used to parse an XML document using DOM. In this example, the book.xml document shown in Listing 9-4 is being parsed. The program begins by creating an instance of the DocumentBuilderFactory, which is called fact1 and uses the setValidating() method to have the DocumentBuilderFactory object create a parse that validates the XML document. The setIgnoringElementContentWhitespace() method is called and passed a Boolean true so whitespace characters won't cause a validation error.

Next, an instance of a DocumentBuilder is created called build1. This is basically the parser. A String object is declared and assigned the name of the XML document that will be parsed, which is book.xml. The String is passed to the File() method that returns the handle to the book.xml file to the parse() method. The parse() method retrieves the XML document and returns an instance of the Document object, which is called bookDoc. The bookDoc is the reference to the book.xml document and is used with methods that manipulate the document.

The first step after the book.xml is accessed is to retrieve the root element of the document. This is accomplished by using the getDocumentElement() method that returns an instance of the Element object called bookEle.

All other elements of the XML document are child nodes to the root element. This means the remaining elements can be retrieved by using the getChildNodes() method that returns an instance of the NodeList object called bookNodes.

The program steps through the node list by using a for loop. The total number of items in the node list, as returned by the getLength() method, is used to terminate the for loop. Each item is retrieved using the item() method that returns an instance of the Element object, which is called chapter. The program then displays the name of the node.

Next, the program calls the getElementsByTagName() method, passing it the chapNum tag name. This method returns a NodeList called numberList. The getFirstChild() method is then called to return the first child. The getData() method is then called to return the value of the first child, which is displayed by the program. This same process is used with the chapTitle tag. Any errors that occur during the execution of these methods are trapped by the catch{ } block.

Listing 9-5
Parsing the book.xml using DOM.

```
import java.io.*;
import javax.xml.parsers.*;
import org.w3c.dom.*;
public class DOMBookParser
{
  public static void main(String[] args)
  {
   try
   {
     DocumentBuilderFactory fact1= DocumentBuilderFactory.newInstance();
     fact1.setValidating(true);
     fact1.setIgnoringElementContentWhitespace(true);
     DocumentBuilder build1 = fact1.newDocumentBuilder();
```

```
      String book1 = "book.xml";
      Document bookDoc = build1.parse(new File(book1));
      Element bookEle = bookDoc.getDocumentElement();
      NodeList chapterNodes = bookEle.getChildNodes();
      for (int i=0; i < chapterNodes.getLength(); i++)
      {
        Element chapter = (Element) chapterNodes.item(i);
        System.out.print("Value: " + chapter.getNodeName() + " ");
        NodeList numberList = chapter.getElementsByTagName("chapNum");
        Text number = (Text) numberList.item(0).getFirstChild();
        System.out.print(number.getData() + " ");
        NodeList titleList = chapter.getElementsByTagName("chapTitle");
        Text title = (Text) titleList.item(0).getFirstChild();
        System.out.println(title.getData());
      }
    }
  }
  catch (Exception error)
  {
    System.err.println("Error parsing:" + error.getMessage());
    System.exit(1);
  }
  }
}
```

Simple API for XML (SAX)

The SAX parser is event driven, as mentioned previously in this chapter. This means that a J2EE component that uses the SAX parser must contain an event handler that listens to events generated by the SAX parser. An event is generated each time the SAX parser encounters a component of the XML document. The event handler must be able to react to events that you want to handle.

Listing 9-6 illustrates how to parse the book.xml (see Listing 9-4). This example begins by creating Boolean and StringBuffer data members of the SAXBookParser class. Each pair is used for elements that are to be parsed from the book.xml document.

The try{} block in main() begins similar to the try{} block in the DOM parser example in that a factory is created, the factory is designated as a validating parser, and then an instance of the SAXParser is created.

The factory is established by creating an instance of the SAXParserFactory class, which is called fact1. Then an instance of the SAXParser called build1 is declared, which is the SAXParser. A String object is declared called book1 and is assigned the name of the XML document that will be parsed, which is book.xml.

The similarities between the DOM parser and the SAX parser differ at this point in the program. In the SAX parser example, the program creates an event listener called event, which is an instance of the DefaultHandler. The event listener is associated with the SAXBookParser class.

Next, the program starts the parser by calling the parse() method. The parse() method requires two arguments. The first argument is the handle to the XML document, which is returned by the File() method. The second argument is the event listener that will respond to events generated by the SAX parser.

The program reacts to three events. These are the start of an Element, characters that are associated with anything that inherits from CharacterData, and the end of an element. You must define methods only for events that you want to handle. The SAX parser also generates an event at the beginning and end of the document. These are handled by the startDocument() and endDocument() methods, respectively. These methods are defined in a program if there is a need to implement procedures at the beginning and end of a document, which is not the case in Listing 9-6.

The startElement() method is automatically called when the parser encounters the beginning of an element in the XML document. Four String arguments are passed to the startElement() method. The first argument is the URI, the second argument is the local name, the third argument is the qName, and the last argument contains the attributes.

The startElement() method must contain logic to address specific elements. Listing 9-6 addresses the chapter, chapTitle, and chapNum elements that are found in the book.xml document.

If the SAX parser encounters the beginning of a parent element such as a chapter element, the StringBuffers for the parent and children are set to null, simply removing the content stored from the previous chapter element.

If the SAX parser encounters the beginning of a chapTitle element, the Boolean value of pChapterTitle is set to true indicating that a new chapTitle element is detected and a new StringBuffer is created.

Likewise, a similar process occurs if the SAX parser encounters the beginning of a chapNum element. In this case, the boolean value of pChapNum is set to true and a new StringBuffer is created.

The characters() method is called by the parser whenever text of an element is encountered. There are three arguments passed to the characters() method. The first argument is a character array that contains the text of the element. The second argument is an integer that represents the starting position of the text within the character array. And the third argument is an integer that represents the number of characters of the text.

The characters() method in Listing 9-6 appends the text to the StringBuffer of the appropriate element. The characters() method evaluates the value of Boolean data members (that is, pChapTitle, pChapNum) to determine the proper StringBuffer to append. Arguments passed to the characters() method are then passed to the append() method of the respective StringBuffer. Data is appended because the characters() method might be called multiple times for the same data stream. You shouldn't assume that the entire character stream is passed by one method call.

The endElement() method is called whenever the parser generates the end of element event, which occurs when a closing tag is read from the XML document. The endElement() method in Listing 9-6 is passed three String objects. The first String object is the namespace URI. The second String object is the local name, and the last String object is the qName.

The endElement() method converts the StringBuffer to a String and then displays the String if the name of the element passed to the endElement is the parent element, which is chapter in this example. However, if the element name isn't the parent, then the parse encountered the end of one of the parent's children. Therefore, the value of the Boolean data member for this child is reset to false.

Listing 9-6
Parsing the
book.xml
using SAX.

```java
import java.io.*;
import javax.xml.parsers.*;
import org.xml.sax.*;
import org.xml.sax.helpers.*;
public class SAXBookParser extends DefaultHandler
{
  protected boolean pChapNum;
  protected boolean pChapTitle;
  protected StringBuffer cChapNum;
  protected StringBuffer cChapTitle;
  public static void main(String[] args)
  {
    try
    {
      SAXParserFactory fact1 = SAXParserFactory.newInstance();
      fact1.setValidating(true);
      SAXParser build1 = fact1.newSAXParser();
      String book1= "book.xml";
      SAXBookParser event = new SAXBookParser();
      build1.parse(new File(book1), event);
    }
    catch (Exception error)
    {
      System.err.println("Error parsing: " + error.getMessage());
      System.exit(1);
    }
  }
  public void startElement(String uri, String localName, String qName, Attributes attributes)
  {
    if (qName.compareTo("chapter") == 0)
    {
      cChapTitle = null;
      cChapNum = null;
    }
    else if (qName.compareTo("chapNum") == 0)
    {
      pChapNum = true;
      cChapNum = new StringBuffer();
    }
    else if (qName.compareTo("chapTitle") == 0)
    {
      pChapTitle = true;
      cChapTitle = new StringBuffer();
```

```
      }
   }
   public void characters(char[] cha, int start, int length)
   {
     if (pChapTitle)
     {
       cChapTitle.append(cha, start, length);
     }
     else if (pChapNum)
     {
       cChapNum.append(cha, start, length);
     }
   }
   public void endElement(String namespaceURI, String localName, String qName)
   {
     if (qName.compareTo("chapter") == 0)
     {
       System.out.print("Chapter ");
       if (cChapNum != null)
       {
         System.out.print(cChapNum.toString());
         System.out.print(" ");
       }
       if (cChapTitle != null)
       {
         System.out.print(cChapTitle.toString());
       }
       System.out.println();
     }
     else if (qName.compareTo("chapTitle") == 0)
     {
       pChapTitle = false;
     }
     else if (qName.compareTo("chapNum") == 0)
     {
       pChapNum = false;
     }
   }
}
```

Quick Reference Guide

Java classes and interfaces used to interact with an XML document have many methods, the most common of which are discussed in this chapter. This quick reference guide provides a brief overview of other methods that can be used. Full details of these methods and all Java classes and interfaces designed to be used with an XML document are available at java.sun.com. DOM and SAX are both contained in JDK 1.4.

Note *The HandlerBase has been depreciated.*

Syntax	Descriptions
public void parse(InputStream is, HandlerBase hb) throws SAXException, IOException	Parse the content of the given InputStream instance as XML.
public void parse(InputStream is, HandlerBase hb, String systemId) throws SAXException, IOException	Parse the content of the given InputStream instance as XML using the specified HandlerBase.
public void parse(InputStream is, DefaultHandler dh) throws SAXException, IOException	Parse the content of the given InputStream instance as XML using the specified DefaultHandler.
public void parse(DefaultHandler InputStream is, DefaultHandler dh, DefaultHandler String systemId) throws SAXException, IOException	Parse the content of the given InputStream instance as XML using the specified DefaultHandler.
public void parse(String uri, DefaultHandler dh) throws SAXException, IOException	Parse the content described by the giving Uniform Resource Identifier (URI) as XML using the specified DefaultHandler.
public void parse(File f, DefaultHandler dh) throws SAXException, IOException	Parse the content of the file specified as XML using the specified DefaultHandler.
public void parse(InputSource is, DefaultHandler dh) throws SAXException, IOException	Parse the content given InputSource as XML using the specified DefaultHandler.
public abstract Parser getParser() throws SAXException	Returns the SAX parser that is encapsulated by the implementation of this class.
public abstract XMLReader getXMLReader() throws SAXException	Returns the XMLReader that is encapsulated by the implementation of this class.
public abstract boolean isNamespaceAware()	Indicates whether or not this parser is configured to understand namespaces.
public abstract boolean isValidating()	Indicates whether or not this parser is configured to validate XML documents.

Table 9-3. *javax.xml.parsers Public Abstract Class SAXParser*

Syntax	Descriptions
public abstract void setProperty(String name, Object value) throws SAXNotRecoginzedException, SAXNotSupportedException	Sets the particular property in the underlying implementation of XMLReader.
public abstract Object getProperty(String name) throws SAXNotRecoginzedException, SAXNotSupportedException	Returns the particular property requested in the underlying implementation of XMLReader.

Table 9-3. *javax.xml.parsers Public Abstract Class SAXParser* (continued)

Syntax	Descriptions
public String getName()	Returns the name of this attribute.
public boolean getSpecified()	If this attribute was explicitly given a value in the original document, this is true; otherwise, it is false.
public String getValue()	On retrieval, the value of the attribute is returned as a string.
public void setValue(String value) throws DOMException	On retrieval, the value of the attribute is returned as a string. Character and general entity references are replaced with their values.
public Element getOwnerElement()	The Element node this attribute is attached to, or null if this attribute is not in use.

Table 9-4. *org.w3c.dom Public Interface Attr*

Syntax	Descriptions
public Documenttype getDoctype()	The document type declaration associated with this document.
public DOMImplementation getImplementation()	The DOMImplementation object that handles this document.
public Element getDocumentElement()	This is a convenience attribute that allows direct access to the child node that is the root element of the document.
public Element createElement(String tagName) throws DOMException	Creates an Element with the specified name. Note that the instance returned implements the Element interface, so attributes can be specified directly on the returned object.
public DocumentFragment createDocumentFragment()	Creates an empty DocumentFragment object.
public Text createTextNode (String data)	Creates a Text node given the specified string.
public Comment createComment(String data)	Creates a Comment node given the specified string.
public CDATASection createCDATASection(String data) throws DOMException	Creates a CDATASection node whose value is the specified string.
public ProcessingInstruction createProcessingInstruction (String target, String data) throws DOMException	Creates a ProcessingInstruction node given the specified name and data strings.
public Attr createAttribute (String name) throws DOMException	Creates an Attr of the given name. Note that the Attr instance can then be set on an Element using the setAttributeNode method.

Table 9-5.   *org.w3c.dom **public interface Document***

Syntax	Descriptions
public EntityReference createEntityReference(String name) throws DOMException	Creates an EntityReference object. In addition, if the referenced entity is known, the child list of the EntityReference node is made the same as that of the corresponding Entity node.
public NodeList getElementsByTagName (String tagname)	Returns a NodeList of all the Elements with a given tag name in the order in which they are encountered in a preorder traversal of the Document tree.
public Node importNode(Node importedNode, boolean deep) throws DOMException	Imports a node from another document to this document. The returned node has no parent (parentNode is null).
public Element createElementNS(String namespaceURI, String qualifiedName) throws DOMException	Creates an element of the given qualified name and namespace URI.
public Attr createAttributeNS(String namespaceURI, String qualifiedName) throws DOMException	Creates an attribute of the given qualified name and namespace URI.
public NodeList getElementsByTagNameNS (String namespaceURI, String localName)	Returns a NodeList of all the Elements with a given local name and namespace URI in the order in which they are encountered in a preorder traversal of the Document tree.
public ElementgetElementById (String elementId)	Returns the Element whose ID is given by elementId. If no such element exists, returns null.

Table 9-5. *org.w3c.dom **public interface Document*** (continued)

Syntax	Descriptions
public String getTagName()	The name of the element.
public String getAttribute(String name)	Retrieves an attribute value by name.
public void setAttribute(String name, String value) throws DOMException	Adds a new attribute.
public void removeAttribute(String name) throws DOMException	Removes an attribute by name.
public Attr getAttributeNode (String name)	Retrieves an attribute node by name.
public Attr setAttributeNode(AttrnewAttr) throws DOMException	Adds a new attribute node.
public Attr removeAttributeNode(AttroldAttr) throws DOMException	Removes the specified attribute node.
public NodeList getElementsByTagName (String name)	Returns a NodeList of all descendant Elements with a given tag name, in the order in which they are encountered in a preorder traversal of this Element tree.
public String getAttributeNS(String namespaceURI, String localName)	Retrieves an attribute value by local name and namespace URI.
public void setAttributeNS(DOMException String namespaceURI, DOMException String qualifiedName, DOMException String value) throws DOMException	Adds a new attribute.
public void removeAttributeNS(String namespaceURI, String localName) throws DOMException	Removes an attribute by local name and namespace URI.
public Attr getAttributeNodeNS(String namespaceURI, String localName)	Retrieves an Attr node by local name and namespace URI.

Table 9-6. *org.w3c.dom Public Interface Element*

J2EE FOUNDATION

Syntax	Descriptions
public Attr setAttributeNodeNS(Attr newAttr) throws DOMException	Adds a new attribute.
public NodeList getElementsByTagNameNS(String namespaceURI, String localName)	Returns a NodeList of the entire descendant Elements with a given local name and namespace URI in the order in which they are encountered in a preorder traversal of this Element tree.
public boolean hasAttribute (String name)	Returns true when an attribute with a given name is specified on this element or has a default value, and false otherwise.
public boolean hasAttributeNS(String namespaceURI, String localName)	Returns true when an attribute with a given local name and namespace URI is specified on this element or has a default value, and false otherwise.

Table 9-6. *org.w3c.dom Public Interface Element* (continued)

Syntax	Descriptions
String getNodeName()	Returns the name of a node.
String getNodeValue() throws DOMException	Returns the value of a node.
public void setNodeValue(String nodeValue) throws DOMException	The value of a node.
public short getNodeType()	Returns an int of the node type.
public Node getParentNode()	Returns the parent node.
public NodeList getChildNodes()	Returns children nodes.
public Node getFirstChild()	Returns the first child of a node.
public Node getLastChild()	Returns the last child of a node.

Table 9-7. *org.w3c.dom Public Interface Node*

J2EE FOUNDATION

Syntax	Descriptions
public Node getPreviousSibling()	Returns the node immediately preceding a node.
public Node getNextSibling()	Returns the node immediately following a node.
public NameNodeMap getAttributes()	Returns the NamedNodeMap containing the attributes of a node (if it is an Element), or null otherwise.
public Document getOwnerDocument()	Returns the Document object associated with a node.
public Node insertBefore(Node newChild, Node refChild) throws DOMException	Inserts the node newChild before the existing child node refChild.
public Node replaceChild(Node newChild, Node oldChild) throws DOMException	Replaces the child node oldChild with newChild in the list of children, and returns the oldChild node.
public Node removeChild(Node oldChild) throws DOMException	Removes the child node indicated by oldChild from the list of children, and returns it.
public Node appendChild(Node newChild) throws DOMException	Adds the node newChild to the end of the list of children of this node.
public boolean hasChildNodes()	Returns whether this node has any children.
public Node cloneNode(boolean deep)	Returns a duplicate of this node and serves as a generic copy constructor for nodes.
public void normalize()	Places Text nodes in the full depth of the subtree underneath this Node, including attribute nodes, into a "normal" form where only structure separates Text nodes.
public String getNamespaceURI()	Returns the namespace URI of this node, or null if it is unspecified.

Table 9-7. *org.w3c.dom Public Interface Node* (continued)

Syntax	Descriptions
public String getPrefix()	Returns the namespace prefix of this node, or null if it is unspecified.
public void setPrefix(String prefix) throws DOMException	Returns the namespace prefix of this node, or null if it is unspecified.
public String getLocalName()	Returns the local part of the qualified name of this node.
public boolean hasAttributes()	Returns whether this node (if it is an element) has any attributes.

Table 9-7. *org.w3c.dom Public Interface Node* (continued)

Syntax	Descriptions
public int getLength()	Return the number of attributes in the list.
public String getURI(int index)	Look up an attribute's namespace URI by index.
public String getLocalName (int index)	Look up an attribute's local name by index.
public String getQName(int index)	Look up an attribute's XML 1.0 qualified name by index.
public String getType(int index)	Look up an attribute's type by index.
public String getValue(int index)	Look up an attribute's value by index.
public int getIndex(String uri, String localPart)	Look up the index of an attribute by namespace name.
public int getIndex(String qName)	Look up the index of an attribute by XML 1.0 qualified name.
public String getType(String uri, String localName)	Look up an attribute's type by namespace name.
public String getType(String Name)	Look up an attribute's type by XML 1.0 qualified name.

Table 9-8. *org.xml.sax Public Interface Attributes*

Syntax	Descriptions
public String getValue(String uri, String localName)	Look up an attribute's value by namespace name.
public String getValue(String Name)	Look up an attribute's value by XML 1.0 qualified name.

Table 9-8. *org.xml.sax Public Interface Attributes* (continued)

Syntax	Descriptions
public void setDocumentLocator(Locator locator)	Receive an object for locating the origin of SAX document events.
public void startDocument() throws SAXException	Receive notification of the beginning of a document.
public void endDocument() throws SAXException	Receive notification of the end of a document.
public void startPrefixMapping(String prefix, String uri) throws SAXException	Begin the scope of a prefix-URI namespace mapping.
public void endPrefixMapping(String prefix) throws SAXException	End the scope of a prefix-URI mapping.
public void startElement(String namespaceURI, String localName, String Name, Attributes atts) throws SAXException	Receive notification of the beginning of an element.
public void endElement(String namespaceURI, String localName, String Name) throws SAXException	Receive notification of the end of an element.
public void characters(char[] ch, int start, int length) throws SAXException	Receive notification of character data.

Table 9-9. *org.xml.sax Public Interface ContentHandler*

Syntax	Descriptions
public void ignorableWhitespace(char[] ch, int start, int length) throws SAXException	Receive notification of ignorable whitespace in element content.
public void processingInstruction(String target, String data) throws SAXException	Receive notification of a processing instruction.
public void skippedEntity(java.lang.String name) throws SAXException	Receive notification of a skipped entity.

Table 9-9.   *org.xml.sax Public Interface ContentHandler* (continued)

Syntax	Descriptions
public boolean getFeature(String name) throws SAXNotRecognizedException, SAXNotSupportedException	Look up the value of a feature.
public void setFeature(String name, boolean value) throws SAXNotRecognizedException, SAXNotSupportedException	Set the state of a feature.
Object getProperty(String name) throws SAXNotRecognizedException, SAXNotSupportedException	Look up the value of a property.
public void setProperty (String name, Object value) throws SAXNotRecognizedException, SAXNotSupportedException	Set the value of a property.
public void setEntityResolver(EntityResolver resolver)	Allow an application to register an entity resolver.

Table 9-10.   *org.xml.sax Public Interface XMLReader*

Syntax	Descriptions
public EntityResolver getEntityResolver()	Return the current entity resolver.
public void setDTDHandler (DTDHandler handler)	Allow an application to register a DTD event handler.
public DTDHandler getDTDHandler()	Return the current DTD handler.
public void setContentHandler (ContentHandler handler)	Allow an application to register a content event handler.
public ContentHandler getContentHandler()	Return the current content handler.
public void setErrorHandler (ErrorHandler handler)	Allow an application to register an error event handler.
public ErrorHandler getErrorHandler()	Return the current error handler.
public void parse(InputSource input) throws java.io.IOException, SAXException	Parse an XML document.
public void parse(String systemId) throws java.io.IOException, SAXException	Parse an XML document from a system identifier (URI).

Table 9-10.   *org.xml.sax Public Interface XMLReader* (continued)

Syntax	Descriptions
public DefaultHandler()	constructor
public InputSource resolveEntity(String publicId, String systemId) throws SAXException	Resolve an external entity.
public void notationDecl(String name, String publicId, String systemId) throws SAXException	Receive notification of a notation declaration.
public void unparsedEntityDecl(String name, String publicId, String systemId, String notationName) throws SAXException	Receive notification of an unparsed entity declaration.

Table 9-11.   *org.xml.sax.helpers Public Class DefaultHandler*

Syntax	Descriptions
public void setDocumentLocator (Locator locator)	Receive a Locator object for document events.
public void startDocument() throws SAXException	Receive notification of the beginning of the document.
public void endDocument() throws SAXException	Receive notification of the end of the document.
public void startPrefixMapping(String prefix, String uri) throws SAXException	Receive notification of the start of a namespace mapping.
public void endPrefixMapping(String prefix) throws SAXException	Receive notification of the end of a namespace mapping.
public void startElement(String uri, String localName, String qName, Attributes attributes) throws SAXException	Receive notification of the start of an element.
public void endElement(String uri, String localName, String qName) throws SAXException	Receive notification of the end of an element.
public void characters(char[] ch, int start, int length) throws SAXException	Receive notification of character data inside an element.
public void ignorableWhitespace(char[] ch, int start, int length) throws SAXException	Receive notification of ignorable whitespace in element content.
public void processingInstruction(String target, String data) throws SAXException	Receive notification of a processing instruction.
public void skippedEntity(String name) throws SAXException	Receive notification of a skipped entity.
public void warning(SAXParseException e) throws SAXException	Receive notification of a parser warning.
public void error(SAXParseException e) throws SAXException	Receive notification of a recoverable parser error.
public void fatalError(SAXParseException e) throws SAXException	Report a fatal XML parsing error.

Table 9-11. *org.xml.sax.helpers Public Class DefaultHandler* (continued)

Syntax	Descriptions
public ParserAdapter() throws SAXException	Create a new parser adapter.
public ParserAdapter(Parser parser)	Create a new parser adapter.
public void setFeature(String name, boolean state) throws SAXNotRecognizedException, SAXNotSupportedException	Set a feature for the parser.
public boolean getFeature(java.lang.String name) throws SAXNotRecognizedException, SAXNotSupportedException	Check a parser feature.
public void setProperty(java.lang.String name, java.lang.Object value) throws SAXNotRecognizedException, SAXNotSupportedException	Set a parser property.
public java.lang.Object getProperty(String name) throws SAXNotRecognizedException, SAXNotSupportedException	Returns a parser property.
public void setEntityResolver(EntityResolver resolver)	Set the entity resolver.
public EntityResolver getEntityResolver()	Returns the current entity resolver.
public void setDTDHandler(DTDHandler handler)	Set the DTD handler.
public DTDHandler getDTDHandler()	Returns the current DTD handler.
public void setContentHandler(ContentHandler handler)	Set the content handler.
public ContentHandler getContentHandler()	Returns the current content handler.

Table 9-12. *org.xml.sax.helpers Public Class ParserAdapter*

Syntax	Descriptions
public void setErrorHandler(ErrorHandler handler)	Set the error handler.
public ErrorHandler getErrorHandler()	Return the current error handler.
public void parse(String systemId) IOException, SAXException	Parse an XML document.
public void parse(InputSource input) throws IOException, SAXException	Parse an XML document.
public void setDocumentLocator(Locator locator)	Adapt a SAX1 document locator event.
public void startDocument() throws SAXException	Adapt a SAX1 start document event.
public void endDocument() throws SAXException	Adapt a SAX1 end document event.
public void startElement(java.lang.String qName, AttributeList Atts) throws SAXException	Adapt a SAX1 start element event.
public void endElement(java.lang.String qName) throws SAXException	Adapt a SAX1 end element event.
public void characters(char[] ch, int start, int length) throws SAXException	Adapt a SAX1 characters event.
public void ignorableWhitespace (char[] ch, int start, int length) throws SAXException	Adapt a SAX1 ignorable whitespace event.
public void processingInstruction (String target, String data) throws SAXException	Adapt a SAX1 processing instruction event.

Table 9-12. *org.xml.sax.helpers Public Class ParserAdapter* (continued)

Syntax	Descriptions
public XMLReaderAdapter() throws SAXException	Create a new adapter.
public XMLReaderAdapter(XMLReader xmlReader)	Create a new adapter.
public void setLocale(java.util.Locale locale) throws SAXException	Set the locale for error reporting.
public void setEntityResolver(EntityResolver resolver)	Register the entity resolver.
public void setDTDHandler(DTDHandler handler)	Register the DTD event handler.
public void setDocumentHandler(DocumentHandler handler)	Register the SAX1 document event handler.
public void setErrorHandler(ErrorHandler handler)	Register the error event handler.
public void parse(String systemId) throws IOException, SAXException	Parse the document.
public void parse(InputSource input) throws IOException, SAXException	Parse the document.
public void setDocumentLocator(Locator locator)	Set a document locator.
public void startDocument() throws SAXException	Start document event.
public void endDocument() throws SAXException	End document event.
public void startPrefixMapping(String prefix, String uri)	Adapt a SAX2 start prefix-mapping event.
public void endPrefixMapping (String prefix)	Adapt a SAX2 end prefix-mapping event.

Table 9-13.   *org.xml.sax.helpers Public Class XMLReaderAdapter*

Syntax	Descriptions
public void startElement(String uri, String localName, String qName, Attributes atts) throws SAXException	Adapt a SAX2 start element event.
public void endElement(String uri, String localName, String qName) throws SAXException	Adapt a SAX2 end element event.
public void characters(char[] ch, int start, int length) throws SAXException	Adapt a SAX2 characters event.
public void ignorableWhitespace(char[] ch, int start, int length) throws SAXException	Adapt a SAX2 ignorable whitespace event.
public void processingInstruction(java.lang.String target, java.lang.String data) throws SAXException	Adapt a SAX2 processing instruction event.
public void skippedEntity(java.lang.String name) throws SAXException	Adapt a SAX2 skipped entity event.

Table 9-13. *org.xml.sax.helpers Public Class XMLReaderAdapter* (continued)

Chapter 10

Java servlets

A J2EE application is a compilation of components, each of which provides a particular service to the application, as discussed in Part I. The user interface is the highest level and most visible component, and is used to provide a person with an intuitive means for calling services.

The user interface gathers a request from a person who uses the J2EE application and forwards the request to a component for processing. The component that processes a request is built using either a Java servlet or a JavaServer Page.

A Java servlet is a server-side program that is called by the user interface or another J2EE component and contains the business logic to process a request. A Java ServerPage is also a server-side program that performs practically the same duties as a Java servlet using a different technique. Both a Java servlet and a Java ServerPage call other components that handle processing details.

This chapter focuses on Java servlets and how to build a J2EE component using Java servlet technology. The next chapter shows you how to create a J2EE component using Java server Pages.

Java servlets and Common Gateway Interface Programming

J2EE applications use a lightweight client, typically a browser, that contains little or no processing logic. A middle-layer program based on the web server handles all processing. Originally a server-side program handled client requests by using the Common Gateway Interface (CGI), which was programmed using Perl or other programming languages. Java servlets is Sun Microsystems, Inc.'s initial efforts to replace CGI programming.

Although Java servlet technology replaces CGI, Java servlets technology and CGI both provide the same basic functionality. That is, explicit and implicit data is sent from a client to a server-side program in the form of a request that is processed and another set of explicit implicit data is returned.

Explicit data is information received from the client that is typically either entered by the user into the user interface or generated by the user interface itself (see Chapter 8). For example, user ID and password are explicit data that can be generated by a browser, applet, or custom client.

Implicit data is Hypertext Transmission Protocol (HTTP) information that is generated by the client (that is, browser) rather than the user. HTTP information contains data about the request such as the compression scheme, cookies, and media types. HTTP information is used by the Java servlet (and by the client when the Java servlet returns the results) to learn about the request itself. A complete discussion of HTTP and HTTP information is presented later in this chapter.

Processing a request takes on many different forms that include calling a Java servlet, an Enterprise JavaBean, and possibly a legacy system. Let's say that a request is

made to display product information (see Figure 10-1). The user enters the product
number, such as an ISBN used to uniquely identify a book into the user interface. The
user interface calls a Java servlet, passing the Java servlet the product number. The Java
servlet might call an Enterprise JavaBean to retrieve product information from a
database, and returns this information to the Java servlet.

The result of processing a request is returned to the client as explicit data. Typically,
this information is returned in the form of an HTML page that is dynamically generated
by the Java servlet. The Java servlet also generates implicit HTTP information such as the
type of document that is being returned to the client.

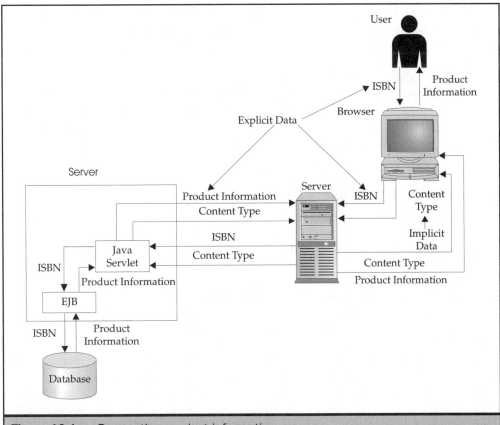

Figure 10-1. *Requesting product information*

Benefits of Using a Java servlet

Sun Microsystems, Inc. designed Java servlet technology to be more efficient and use less environment overhead than CGI. A new process begins each time a request is made to a CGI program. Starting a new process is time-consuming, but acceptable as long as the execution time of the CGI program is longer than the time that is necessary to begin the new process. However, executing a CGI program becomes unacceptable if the CGI program has a shorter execution time than beginning the new process.

Let's say that 100 instances of an application require a CGI program to process their requests simultaneously. The CGI program must be loaded into memory 100 times. That is to say, there are 100 copies of the CGI program in memory. Each instance must begin a new process, meaning 100 new processes are started—which is inefficient.

Also a CGI program isn't persistent. Once a CGI program terminates, all data used by the process is lost and cannot be used by other CGI programs.

Java servlet technology avoids inefficiencies. First, only one copy of a Java servlet is loaded into the Java Virtual Machine no matter the number of simultaneous requests made to the Java servlet. Each request begins a thread to the Java servlet rather than a new process, which saves memory usage on the server and increases response time because only one copy of the Java servlet needs to be loaded into memory. servlets generally run in the same process space as the servlet container—each copy of the servlet is a thread. There will be multiple copies of the servlet.

A Java servlet has persistence. This means that the Java servlet remains alive after the request is fulfilled. Data used by the Java servlet can be retained between calls to the Java servlet, if necessary to the business requirements of the J2EE application.

A Simple Java servlet

A Java servlet is a Java class that reads requests sent from a client and responds by sending information to the client. The Java class must extend Httpservlet and override the Httpservlet's doGet() and/or doPost() methods. The doGet() method is used to interact with a request sent using the METHOD="GET" attribute from an HTML form or when passing parameters on the URL like a hyperlink (see Chapter 8). The doPost() method is used for requests sent using the METHOD="POST".

Both the doGet() and doPost() methods require two arguments. The first argument is an HttpservletRequest object and the other argument is an HttpservletResponse object. The HttpservletRequest object contains incoming information and the HttpservletResponse object is used by the Java servlet to send outgoing information to the client. Both methods throw a servletException and IOException.

Incoming data includes explicit data and implicit data. Explicit data is supplied by a user and is contained in a query string that contains data from a form. Implicit data is HTTP information such as request headers, which are discussed later in this chapter.

Outgoing data is explicit data and implicit data that are generated by the Java servlet. Outgoing data is sent by using a PrintWriter object using the println() method and is forwarded to the client that made the request. The format of the data sent to the client is client dependent. For example, data takes the format of an HTML or XML page if the client is a browser.

The println() method is used in conjunction with a PrintWriter to send outgoing explicit data such as text that appears on a web page. Methods of the HttpservletResponse object are used to send implicit data.

Listing 10-1 illustrates a basic Java servlet that outputs both explicit and implicit data. The println() method is used to send explicit data in the format of a simple web page. The setContentType() method is used to set the value for the ContentType HTTP header information. ContentType identifies the type of document that is being sent explicitly. In this example, text/html is the ContentType passed to the setContentType() method. This identifies the explicit data as being in an HTML format.

You compile a Java servlet using the same process as you compile a Java program. Make sure that the CLASSPATH in your environment contains these entries: ".", javax.servlet (the JAR files containing the Java servlet classes), and the directory that contains the source code for the Java servlet. Once the Java servlet is compiled into a .class file, you must move the .class file into the directory where Java servlets are installed in your environment. Typically, this directory is install_dir/.../WEB-INF/ classes. You call the Java servlet by using the URL http://host/servlet/myservlet where myservlet is the name of the Java servlet. The URL can be placed as the value of the ACTION attribute of a form or as the URL of a web page link.

Listing 10-1
A basic
Java servlet.

```
import java.io.*;
import javax.servlet.*;
import javax.servlet.http.*;
public class js1 extends Httpservlet {
public void doGet(HttpservletRequest request, HttpservletResponse response)
    throws servletException, IOException {
  response.setContentType("text/html");
  PrintWriter out = response.getWriter();
  out.println("<!DOCTYPE HTML PUBLIC \"~//W3C//DTD HTML 4.0 " +
    "Transitional//EN\">\n" +
    "<HTML>\n" +
    "<HEAD><TITLE>Java servlet</TITLE></HEAD>\n" +
    "<BODY>\n" +
    "  <P>My A basic Java servlet </P>\n" +
    "</BODY>\n" +
    "</HTML>");
  }
}
```

Anatomy of a Java servlet

A Java servlet consists of at least four methods, each of which is called during the life cycle of the Java servlet. These methods are init(), service(), the appropriate request method, and destroy().

The init() method is called automatically when the Java servlet is created. You can override the init() method to include statements that are executed once during the life of the Java servlet and not for each request to use the Java servlet. The init() method is similar in concept to the init() method of an applet and is used to initialize variables and objects that are used throughout the Java servlet. The init() method doesn't require an argument, returns a void, and throws a servletException.

In the real world, the init() method is used to read server-specific initialization parameters such as performance parameters and database settings. The J2EE programmer customizes the functionality of a Java servlet based on the values of server-specific initialization parameters.

Listing 10-2 illustrates how to override the init() method to read server-specific initialization parameters. The servletConfig object contains the methods necessary to interact with server-specific initialization parameters. In this example, an instance of the servletConfig object is created and is called con. Next, the getInitParameter() method is called to retrieve the first initialization parameters, which is returned as a String object called p1. Server-specific initialization parameters are used with the deployment descriptor to control the behavior of the Java servlet and Java Server Pages, which is discussed later in this chapter.

Listing 10-2
Using the init() method to read server-specifi c initialization parameters

```
public void init() throw servletException {
    servletConfig con = getservletConfig();
    String p1 = con.getInitParameter("parameter1");
}
```

The service() method is called whenever a request for the Java servlet is made to the web server. A request spawns a new thread or an unused thread from the thread pool. There can be simultaneous calls to the service() method. The service() method examines the HTTP request type and then calls the appropriate request method such as doGet() and doPost().

Simultaneous calls to the service() method result in multiple concurrent threads of either doGet(), doPost(), or other request methods. This means shared data must be synchronized to prevent inadvertent changes to the data. Each thread owns its own object—you need to be careful if you're referencing static data.

Conflicts arising from shared data can be eliminated by preventing multiple threads of the Java servlet. This is accomplished by implementing the SingleThreadModel interface when the Java servlet is created. This results in the creation of one thread for the instance of the Java servlet. Other requests for the Java servlet are queued and invoked only when the active thread terminates.

Caution *Implementing the SingleThreadModel interface prevents instance variables of the Java servlet from being accessed simultaneously, but class variables and shared data outside the Java servlet must still be synchronized. Minimize the use of the SingleThreadModel interface; otherwise, you might experience performance latency, as the server becomes idle while the Java servlet pauses for I/O.*

The destroy() method is the last method to be called right before the Java servlet terminates, such as when an instance of a Java servlet is removed from memory. You can override the destroy() method with statements that release resources, such as closing a database connection.

 Caution *The destroy() method is not called when an abnormal occurrence such as a system malfunction causes the Java servlet to abruptly terminate.*

Deployment Descriptor

The deployment descriptor is a file located in the WEB-INF directory that controls the behavior of a Java servlet and Java Server Pages. The file is called the web.xml file and contains the XML header, DOCTYPE, and a web-app element. The web-app element should contain a servlet element with three subelements. These are servlet-name, servlet-class, and init-param.

The servlet-name element contains the name used to access the Java servlet. The servlet-class is the class name of the Java servlet and the init-param is the name of an initialization parameter that is used whenever a request is made to the Java servlet.

Listing 10-3 illustrates a simple web.xml deployment descriptor file. In this example, the name of the Java servlet within the web.xml file is MyJavaservlet. The class name of the Java servlet is myPackage.MyJavaservletClass. The name of the initialization parameter is parameter1 whose value is 735.

Listing 10-3
An example of the deployment descriptor file.

```
<?xml version="1.0" encoding-"ISO-8859=1"?>

<!DOCTYPE web-app PUBLIC "~//Sun Microsystems, Inc.//DTD Web Application2.2//EN"
"http://java.sun.com/j2ee/dtds/web-app_2_2.dtd">
<web-app>
  <servlet>
    <servlet-name>MyJavaservlet</servlet-name>
    <servlet-class>myPackage.MyJavaservletClass</servlet-class>
    <init-param>
      <param-name>parameter1</param-name>
      <param-value>735</param-value>
    </init-param>
```

J2EE FOUNDATION

```
    <servlet-mapping>
      <servlet-name> MyJavaservlet</servlet-name>
      <url-pattern>MyJavaservlet</url-pattern>
    </servlet-mapping>
    </servlet>
<web-app>
```

Reading Data from a Client

A client uses either the GET or POST Method to pass information to a Java servlet as described in Chapter 8. The doGet() or doPost() method is called in the Java servlet depending on the method used by the client.

Data sent by a client is read into a Java servlet by calling the getParameter() method of the HttpservletRequest object that instantiated in the argument list of the doGet() and doPost() methods. The getParameter() method requires one argument, which is the name of the parameter that contains the data sent by the client. The getParameter() method returns a String object. The String object contains the value of the parameter, if the client assigns a value to the parameter. An empty String object is returned if the client didn't assign a value to the parameter. Also, a null is returned if the parameter isn't received from the client.

As you learned in Chapter 8, an HTML form can contain a set of check boxes or other form objects that have the same data name but different values. This means that data received from a client might have multiple occurrences of the same parameter name.

You can read a set of parameters that have the same name by calling the getParameterValues() method. The getParameterValues() method has one argument, which is the name of the parameter, and returns an array of String objects. Each element of the array contains a value of the set of parameters. The getParameterValues() method returns a null if data received from the client doesn't contain the parameter named in the argument.

Caution *Parameter names are case sensitive.*

You can retrieve all the parameters by calling the getParameterNames() method. The getParameterNames() method does not require an argument and returns an Enumeration. Parameter names appear in any order and can be cast to a String object and used with the getParameter() and getParameterValues() methods.

Listing 10-4 contains an HTML form that prompts a user to enter an email address. When the user selects the Submit button, the browser calls the js2.class Java servlet and sends the email address as data. Listing 10-5 illustrates the js2.class Java servlet that reads data sent by this form. Listing 10-5 is a modification of Listing 10-1.

In this example, the getParameter() method is called and passed the parameter name email as an argument. The getParameter() method returns a string that is assigned to the email String object called email. The value of the email String object is then returned to the browser in the form of an HTML page.

Listing 10-4
An HTML form that calls a Java servlet.

```
<FORM ACTION="/servlet/myservlets.js2">
Enter Email Address: <INPUT TYPE="TEXT" NAME="email">
<INPUT TYPE="SUBMIT">
</FORM>
```

Listing 10-5
Reading data sent by a client using a Java servlet.

```
import java.io.*;
import javax.servlet.*;
import javax.servlet.http.*;
public class js2 extends Httpservlet {
  public void doGet(HttpservletRequest request, HttpservletResponse response)
     throws servletException, IOException {
   String email;
   email = request.getParameter("email");
   response.setContentType("text/html");
   PrintWriter out = response.getWriter();
   out.println("<!DOCTYPE HTML PUBLIC \"~//W3C//DTD HTML 4.0 " +
     "Transitional//EN\">\n" +
     "<HTML>\n" +
     "<HEAD><TITLE>Java servlet</TITLE></HEAD>\n" +
     "<BODY>\n" +
     "  <P>My Email Address: " + email + "</P>\n" +
     "</BODY>\n" +
     "</HTML>");
  }
}
```

Reading HTTP Request Headers

A request from a client contains two components. These are data (explicit data) sent by the client, such as the email address in Listing 10-5. The other component is a set of HTTP request headers sent by the browser that made the request (implicit data).

An HTTP request header (see Listing 10-6) contains information that describes the data component of the request. A Java servlet can read HTTP request headers and use the value of HTTP request headers to process the data component of the request. The more commonly used HTTP request headers are shown in Table 10-1.

Listing 10-6
A typical set
of HTTP
request
headers.

```
Accept: image/jpg, image/gif, */*
Accept-Encoding: Zip
Connect: Keep-Alive
Cookie: CustNum-12345
Host: www.mywebsite.com
Referer: http://www.mywebsite.com/index.html
```

HTTP Request Header	Description
Accept	Identifies the Multipurpose Internet Mail Extension (MIME) type (see Table 10-2) of data that can be handled by the browser that made the request. The Java servlet can read the Accept HTTP request header and avoid returning data in a data format that cannot be processed by the browser. Table 10-2 contains a list of MIME types. Some browsers such as Explorer 5 send the Accept header correctly for the original request, but incorrectly when the request is reloaded by the browser.
Accept-Charset	Identifies the character sets that can be used by the browser that made the request. The Accept-Encoding HTTP request header indicates the type of encoding handled by the browser. For example, the Java servlet might return data to the browser in a compressed format in an effort to reduce transmission time. The value of the Accept-Encoding HTTP request header tells the Java servlet the type of compression formats that the browser can process.
Accept-Language	Specifies the preferred languages that are used by the browser.
Authorization	Used by a browser to identify the client to the Java servlet whenever a protected web page is being processed.

Table 10-1. *HTTP Request Headers*

HTTP Request Header	Description
Connection	Identifies whether a browser can retrieve multiple files using the same socket, which is referred to as persistence. Persistence reduces transmission time by eliminating the need for the browser to open a connection for each file that is being transmitted. Connection varies between HTTP 1.0 and HTTP 1.1. For more information about HTTP visit www.w3.org/Protocols.
Content-Length	Contains the size of data in bytes that are transmitted using the POST method.
Cookie	Returns cookies to a server. The server originally sent these cookies to the browser. This HTTP request header is rarely read directly in a real-word application.
Host	Contains the host and port of the original URL; however, this is optional.
If-Modified-Since	Signifies that the browser's requests should be fulfilled only if the data has changed since a specified date. For example, a browser may request the Java servlet send a specific catalog page to the browser only after the date specified in the header.
If-Unmodified-Since	Signifies that the browse's requests should be fulfilled only if the data is older than a specified date.
Referer	Contains the URL of the web page that is currently displayed in the browser. This is useful to learn where requests are coming from. The value of the Referer HTTP request header can be spoofed and therefore its value is not reliable. Also note the spelling of this HTTP request header. It is Referer and not Referrer.
User-Agent	Identifies the browser that made the request.

Table 10-1. *HTTP Request Headers* (continued)

J2EE FOUNDATION

MIME Types	Description
application/msword	Microsoft Word file
application/octet-stream	Unrecognized or binary data
application/pdf	Acrobat file
application/postscript	Postscript file
application/vnd.lotus-notes	Lotus Notes file
application/vnd.ms-excel	Microsoft Excel file
application/vnd.ms-powerpoint	Microsoft PowerPoint file
application/x-gzip	Gzip archive
application/x-java-archive	JAR file
application/x-java-serialized-object	Serialized Java object
applciation/x-java-vm	Java bytecode (.class) file
application/zip	Zip file
audio/basic	Sound file in .au or .snd format
audio/mdid	MIDI sound file
audio/x-aiff	AIFF sound file
audio/x-wav	MS Windows sound file
image/gif	GIF image
image/jpeg	JPEG
image/png	PNG image
image/tiff	TIFF image
image/x-xbitmap	X Windows bitmap image
text/css	HTML Cascading Style Sheet
text/html	HTML document
text/plain	Plain text
text/xml	XML
video/mpeg	MPEG video clip
video/quicktime	QuickTime video clip

Table 10-2. *MIME Types*

A Java servlet can read an HTTP request header by calling the getHeader() method of the HttpservletRequest object. The getHeader() requires one argument, which is the name of the HTTP request header that is to be read. The HTTP request header name isn't case sensitive. The getHeader() function returns a String object that contains the value of the specified HTTP request header.

HTTP connections can be told to open or close a connection based on HTTP request. The type of request used depends on the version of HTTP used for the connection. HTTP 1.0 requires you to set the Connection header to Keep-Alive in order to keep the connection open as illustrated here:

```
Connection: Keep-Alive
```

Caution   *This heading is meaningless to a client or server that is using HTTP 1.0.*

HTTP 1.1 version also uses the Keep-Alive message to keep a connection open. You can also explicitly set the Connection header to close in order to close the connection after servicing the request. This is illustrated here:

```
Connection: close
```

Caution   *There is no guarantee that the connection will remain open. The Connection header is a request, not a command, and therefore only the client or the server can open and close a connection. For more information about HTTP, visit www.w3.org/Protocols.*

Let's say that you wanted to read the Connection HTTP request header in Listing 10-6. You place the following statement in the Java servlet. The String object is null if the set of HTTP request headers doesn't have the specified HTTP request header.

```
String conHeader = request.getHeader("Connection");
```

Besides the getHeader() method, the HttpservletRequest object has a variety of methods that are used to read specific kinds of HTTP request headers. The "HttpservletRequest Class" section of the Quick Reference Guide at the end of this chapter contains a listing of HttpservletRequest methods.

Sending Data to a Client and Writing the HTTP Response Header

A Java servlet responds to a client's request by reading client data and the HTTP request headers, then processing information based on the nature of the request. For example, a client request for information about merchandise in an online product catalog requires the Java servlet to search the product database to retrieve product information and then format the product information into a web page, which is returned to the client.

There are two ways in which a Java servlet replies to a client request. These are by sending information (explicit data) to the response stream and by sending information in the HTTP response header (implicit data). The HTTP response header is similar to the HTTP request header except the contents of the HTTP response header are generated by the web server that responds to the client's request.

Information is sent to the response stream by creating an instance of the PrintWriter object and then using the println() method to transmit the information to the client. This technique is discussed at the beginning of this chapter and illustrated in Listing 10-1.

An HTTP response header contains a status line, response headers, and a blank line, followed by the document. This is illustrated in Listing 10-7. There are three components to the status line. These are the HTTP version number, a status code, and a brief message associated with the status code.

In the example in Listing 10-7, the HTTP version number is 1.1 and the status code is 200, indicating that everything is fine with the request that was received from the client. OK is the message that is associated with the status code. This example contains one HTTP response header, which is Content-Type that identifies the document MIME (see Table 10-2) type as plain text. The document contains the expression "My response".

Listing 10-7
An HTTP response header.

```
HTTP/1.1 200 OK
Content-Type: text/plain

My response
```

A Java servlet can write to the HTTP response header by calling the setStatus() method of the HttpservletResponse object. The setStatus() method requires one argument, which is an integer that represents the status code. Table 10-3 contains a list of HTTP status codes. The argument can take the form of the int itself or a predefined constant that represents the int. The setStatus() method automatically inserts the status code and the short message associated with the status code into the HTTP response header.

For example, the following statement writes the status code 100 to the HTTP response header informing the client to send a follow-up request:

```
response.setStatus(100);
```

Status Code	Short Message	Constant	Description
100	Continue	SC_CONTINUE	Can the client send an attached document in a follow-up request? Respond with a status 100 if the answer is yes or 417 Expectation Failed if the answer is no.
200	OK	SC_OK	Everything is fine.
202	Accepted	SC_ACCEPTED	The request is being acted upon, but processing is not yet complete.
204	No Content	SC_NO_CONTENT	Continue to display the previous document because no new document is available.
205	Reset Content	SC_RESET_CONTENT	No new document. Reset the document view.
301	Moved Permanently	SC_MOVED_PERMANENTLY	The document is elsewhere. Supply new URL for the document in the Location HTTP response header.
302	Found	SC_FOUND	Interpret the URL given in the Location HTTP response header as a temporary replacement, not a permanent replacement.
303	See Other	SC_SEE_OTHER	Similar to 301 and 302 if the original request is POST; retrieve the new document with GET.
304	Not Modified	SC_NOT_MODIFIED	The client should use the cached version.
307	Temporary Redirect	No constant defined	The client is temporarily redirected to another URL.

Table 10-3. *HTTP 1.1 Status Codes*

Status Code	Short Message	Constant	Description
400	Bad Request	SC_BAD_REQUEST	Bad syntax in the client request.
401	Unauthorized	SC_UNAUTHORIZED	Attempt to access a password-protected page without identifying information in the Authorization HTTP response header.
403	Forbidden	SC_FORBIDDEN	Server refuses access to the resource usually because of bad file or directory permissions on the server.
404	Not Found	SC_NOT_FOUND	Resource not found.
405	Method Not Allowed	SC_METHOD_NOT_ALLOWED	Request method not allowed for resource.
415	Unsupported Media Type	SC_UNSUPPORTED_MEDIA_TYPE S	Server doesn't know how to handle attached document type.
500	Internal Server Error	SC_INTERNAL_SERVER_ERROR	Generic error caused by CGI programs or servlets failure.
501	Not Implemented	SC_NOT_IMPLEMENTED	The server cannot respond because of maintenance or overloading.
503	Service Unavailable	SC_SERVICE_UNAVAILABLE	The server is unable to process the request.
505	HTTP Version Not Supported	SC_HTTP_VERSION_NOT_SUPPROTED HTTP	Version not supported by server.

Table 10-3. *HTTP 1.1 Status Codes* (continued)

There are two other methods that developers use in a Java servlet to write the HTTP response header. These are sendError() and sendRedirect(). Both of these methods throw an IOException exception and return a void.

The sendError() method is used to notify the client that an error has occurred. Two arguments are required by the sendError() method. The first argument is an int that represents the status code, which is typically status code 404. The other argument is a String object that contains the short message. The short message is formatted automatically.

The sendRedirect() method transmits a location header to the browser. The browser uses the location header to connect to the URL specified in the location header. The location header is similar to the content-type: text/html except the location header looks like location:someURL.html. If you write to the response object after sending the location header, the response object fails. The browser terminates the connection as soon as the location header is received, which may cause the server to terminate the Java servlet and a JSP.

An HTTP response header is used to give the client directions on how to process the response document and provides additional information such as a cookie, which is discussed later in this chapter.

There are a number of HTTP response headers that can be set by a Java servlet. Table 10-4 contains a listing of commonly used HTTP response headers. Each HTTP response header is set from within a Java servlet by calling an appropriate method of the HttpservletResponse before the Java servlet writes the response document.

J2EE FOUNDATION

HTTP Response Header	Description
Allow	Specifies the request method (that is, GET, POST) supported by the server.
Cache-Control	Identifies conditions when the response document can safely be cached. One of the following possible values must be used: public Document is cacheable. private Store in private nonshared caches. no-cache Do not cache. no-store Do not cache. Do not store in a temporary location on disk. must-revalidate Revalidate document with original server. proxy-revalidates Same as must-revalidate. Applies only to shared caches. max-age=xxx Document is stale after xxx seconds. s-max-age=xxx Shared caches consider the document stale after xxx seconds.
Connection	Instructs to use or not to use persistence.

Table 10-4.   *HTTP 1.1 Response Headers*

HTTP Response Header	Description
Close	This is a parameter for the Connection header. If you don't want persistent connection, you tell the server http1.0.
Content-Encoding	Indicates page encoding.
Content-Language	Indicates the language of the document.
Content-Length	Indicates the number of bytes in the message before any character encoding is applied.
Content-Type	Indicates the MIME type of the response document.
Expires	Specifies the time in milliseconds when document is out of date (long tenMinutes = 18*60*1000).
Last-Modified	Indicates the last time the document was changed.
Location	The location of the document. This gets sent with sendRedirect().
Refresh	Indicates the number of seconds to wait before asking for a page update.
Retry-After	Indicates the number of seconds to wait before requesting service, if the service is unavailable.
Set-Cookie	Identifies the cookie for the page.
WWW-Authenticate	Indicates the authorization type (that is, BASIC, DIGEST).

Table 10-4. *HTTP 1.1 Response Headers* (continued)

The "HttpservletResponse Class" section of the Quick Reference Guide at the end of this chapter contains a list of methods that are used to write an HTTP response header.

Working with Cookies

A cookie is a small amount of data that is saved on the client's machine and can be created by and referenced by a Java servlet using the Java servlet cookie API. A cookie is composed of two pieces. These are the cookie name and the cookie value, both of which are created by the Java servlet. The cookie name is used to identify a particular cookie from among other cookies stored at the client. The cookie value is data associated with the cookie. Any character can be used except the following: [] () =," / ? @ : ;. However, version 1.0 can use these characters.

A Java servlet writes a cookie by passing the constructor of the Cookie object two arguments. The first argument is a String object that contains the name of the cookie. The other argument is a String object that contains the value of the cookie.

The following statement illustrates how a cookie is created when the instance of the Cookie object called myCookie is declared. In this example, a cookie called userID is being created and assigned the value 123:

```
Cookie myCookie = new Cookie("userID", "123");
```

Once a cookie is created, the Java servlet must insert the cookie into the HTTP response header by calling the addCookie() method of the HttpservletResponse object. The addCookie() method requires one argument, which is the name of the instance of the Cookie object. The addCookie() method must be called before the Java servlet writes the response document.

The following statement shows how to add a cookie to the HTTP response header. In this example, the instance of the Cookie object called myCookie, which is declared in the previous statement, is passed as the argument to the addCookie() method. Listing 10-8 contains a complete Java servlet that writes this cookie and sends a response document to a client.

```
response.addCookie(myCookie);
```

You can read a cookie by calling the getCookies() method of the HttpservletRequest object. The getCookies() method returns an array of Cookie objects. The Java servlet can step through the array of Cookie objects and retrieve attributes of each cookie by calling the getXXX() method where XXX represent the name of the attribute that you want to retrieve. Name and value are two commonly requested attributes. Table 10-5 lists all the cookie attributes and the "Cookie Class" section of the Quick Reference Guide at the end of this chapter contains a list of getXXX() methods.

Typically, a Java servlet steps through the array of Cookie objects comparing the desired cookie name with the name attribute of each cookie in the array. Once a match is found, the Java servlet then retrieves other attributes of that cookie as required by the J2EE application. Listing 10-9 illustrates how to read a cookie.

The addCookie() method does not affect cookies that already exist on the client. The cookie is limited to 4KB and most browsers limit the total space to 2MB for cookies, so addCookie() may cause others to be deleted. The expiration date is only a suggestion. The browser decides when to delete cookies, depending on storage space considerations. Instead, the addCookie() method appends a new cookie to the existing cookies. A Java servlet can modify the value of an existing cookie by using the setValue() method of the Cookie object, and modify other attributes of the cookie by using the appropriate setXXX() method that corresponds to the getXXX() method. These methods are also listed

Attribute	Description
Comment	The comment about the cookie
Domain	The domain of the cookie
MaxAge	The maximum length of time the cookie remains valid
Name	The name of the cookie
Path	The path of the cookie
Secure	The Boolean value that indicates whether or not the cookie should be transmitted only over an encrypted connection
Value	The value of the cookie
Version	The version of the cookie

Table 10-5. *Cookie Attributes*

in the "Cookie Class" section of the Quick Reference Guide at the end of this chapter. The following statement illustrates how to modify the value attribute of myCookie:

```
myCookie.setValue("456");
```

Listing 10-8
Writing a
cookie.

```
import java.io.*;
import javax.servlet.*;
import javax.servlet.http.*;
public class SetCookies extends Httpservlet {
  public void doGet(HttpservletRequest request, HttpservletResponse response)
      throws servletException, IOException {
    Cookie myCookie = new Cookie("userID", "123");
    response.addCookie(myCookie);
    response.setContentType("text/html");
    PrintWriter out = response.getWriter();
    out.println ("<!DOCTYPE HTML PUBLIC \"~//W3C//DTD HTML 4.0 " +
     "Transitional//EN\">\n" +
     "<HTML>\n" +
     "<HEAD><TITLE> My Cookie </TITLE></HEAD>\n" +
     "<BODY>\n" +
     "  <H1>" + My Cookie + "</H1>\n" +
     "  <P> Cookie written</P>\n" +
     "</BODY></HTML>");
  }
}
```

Listing 10-9
Reading a
cookie.

```
import java.io.*;
import javax.servlet.*;
import javax.servlet.http.*;
public class ShowCookies extends Httpservlet {
  public void doGet(HttpservletRequest request, HttpservletResponse response)
      throws servletException, IOException {
    response.setContentType("text/html");
    PrintWriter out = response.getWriter();
    out.println ("<!DOCTYPE HTML PUBLIC \"~//W3C//DTD HTML 4.0 " +
    "Transitional//EN\">\n" +
     "<HTML>\n" +
     "<HEAD><TITLE> My Cookie </TITLE></HEAD>\n" +
     "<BODY>\n" +
     "<H1>" + My Cookie + "</H1>\n" +
     "<P>" +
     Cookie[] cookies = request.getCookies();
     if (cookies == null)
     {
       out.println("No cookies");
     }
     else
     {
       Cookie MyCookie;
       for(int i=0; i< cookie.length(); i++)
       {
         MyCookie = cookies[i];
         out.println(myCookies.getName() + "=" + MyCookie.getValue());
       }
     }
  }
}
```

Tracking Sessions

A session is created each time a client requests service from a Java servlet. The Java servlet processes the request and responds accordingly, after which the session is terminated. Many times the same client follows with another request to the same Java servlet, and the Java servlet requires information regarding the previous session to process the request. However, HTTP is a stateless protocol, meaning that there isn't any holdover from previous sessions. Therefore, there is no way to track sessions using HTTP.

A Java servlet is capable of tracking sessions by using the HttpSession API. The HttpSession API uses the HttpSession object that is associated with the HttpservletRequest to determine if the request is a continuation from an existing session or is a new session.

A Java servlet calls the getSession() method of the HttpservletRequest object, which returns an HttpSession object if it is a new session. The getSession() method requires one argument, which is a boolean true. The getSession() returns a null if the user doesn't already have a session underway; otherwise, a new HttpSession object is created. The following statement illustrates how this is written: If the getSession() method doesn't use an argument, then, the getSession() method returns either the existing session or the getSession() method creates a new session and returns the session object. If the getSession() method takes a boolean true as an argument, the getSession() method returns the current session as a session object. If the current session doesn't exist, the getSession() method creates a new session and returns a session object.

If the getSession() method takes a boolean false as an argument, the getSession() method returns the current session as a session object. If the current session doesn't exist, the getSession() method returns a null.

```
HttpSession s1 = request.getSession(true);
```

An HtppSession object contains a data structure that is used to store keys and a value associated with each key. A key is an attribute of the session. You can read a value of an attribute by calling the HttpSession object's getAttribute() method, and you can modify the value of an attribute by calling the setAttribute() method.

The getAttribute() method requires one argument, which is a String object that contains the name of the attribute whose value you want to retrieve. The getAttribute() returns the value of the attribute, which is an object. The type of object depends on the nature of the attribute. For example, the value of an attribute can be a String object or an object that is defined in the Java servlet. Listing 10-10 illustrates how to read a session attribute. In this example, the session ID is read and returned to the client, where the session ID is displayed on the screen.

The setAttribute() method requires two arguments. The first argument is a String object that contains the name of the attribute. The other argument is an object similar to an object returned by the getAttribute() method.

The HttpSession API contains an assortment of methods that can be used to retrieve and manipulate information that enables a Java servlet to track a session. The "HttpSession Class" section of the Quick Reference Guide located at the end of the chapter lists these methods.

Listing 10-10
Reading a
session
attribute.

```
import java.io.*;
import javax.servlet.*;
import javax.servlet.http.*;
import java.net.*;
import java.util.*;
public class ShowSession extends Httpservlet {
  public void doGet(HttpservletRequest request, HttpservletResponse response)
      throws servletException, IOException {
```

```
response.setContentType("text/html");
PrintWriter out = response.getWriter();
HttpSession s1 = request.getSession(true);
String s1ID = s1.getId();
out.println ("<!DOCTYPE HTML PUBLIC \"~//W3C//DTD HTML 4.0 " +
 "Transitional//EN\">\n" +
 "<HTML>\n" +
 "<HEAD><TITLE> Session ID</TITLE></HEAD>\n" +
 "<BODY>\n" +
 "  <H1">Session ID</H1>\n" +
 "  <P>" + s1ID + "</P>\n" +
 "</BODY></HTML>");
    }
}
```

Quick Reference Guide

This Quick Reference Guide provides a brief overview of Java classes used to by a Java servlet to interact with HTTP. Full details of these classes and all Java classes and interfaces are available at java.sun.com.

J2EE FOUNDATION

Syntax	Descriptions
Object clone()	Overrides the standard clone method to return a copy of this cookie.
String getComment()	Returns the comment for the cookie.
String getDomain()	Returns the domain name set for this cookie.
int getMaxAge()	Returns the maximum age of the cookie, specified in seconds. By default, a -1 cookie persists until the browser shuts down.
String getName()	Returns the name of the cookie.
String getPath()	Returns the path on the server to which the browser returns this cookie.

Table 10-6.   *javax.servlet.http Cookie Class*

Syntax	Descriptions
boolean getSecure()	Returns true if cookie must be sent by (unspecified) secure means or false if not required to be sent over (unspecified) secure means.
String getValue()	Returns the value of the cookie.
int getVersion()	Returns the version of the protocol of the cookie.
void setComment(String purpose)	Specifies a comment of a cookie.
void setDomain(String pattern)	Specifies the domain of the cookie.
void setMaxAge(int expiry)	Sets the maximum age of the cookie in seconds.
void setPath(String uri)	Specifies a path for the cookie.
void setSecure(boolean flag)	Indicates cookie should only be sent using secure means.
void setValue(String newValue)	Assigns a new value to a cookie.
void setVersion(int v)	Sets the version of the cookie protocol.

Table 10-6. *javax.servlet.http Cookie Class* (continued)

Syntax	Descriptions
String getAuthType()	Returns the name of the authentication scheme.
String getContextPath()	Returns the context of the request.
Cookie[] getCookies()	Returns an array containing all of the cookies sent with this request.
long getDateHeader(String name)	Returns the value of the request header as a long value that represents a Date object.

Table 10-7. *javax.servlet.http HttpservletRequest Class*

Syntax	Descriptions
String getHeader(String name)	Returns the value of the s request header as a String.
Enumeration getHeaderNames()	Returns an enumeration of all the header names.
Enumeration getHeaders(String name)	Returns all the values of a request header as an Enumeration.
int getIntHeader(String name)	Returns the value of the specified request header as an int.
String getMethod()	Returns the HTTP method (GET, POST, or PUT).
String getPathInfo()	Returns any extra path.
String getPathTranslated()	Returns any extra path information after the servlet name.
String getQueryString()	Returns the query string in the request URL after the path.
String getRemoteUser()	Returns the user login if authenticated, or null if it has not been authenticated.
String getRequestedSessionId()	Returns the session ID.
String getRequestURI()	Returns the URI of the URL.
StringBuffer getRequestURL()	Reconstructs the URL.
String getservletPath()	Returns the path of the URL.
HttpSession getSession()	Returns the current session, or creates a session if there isn't a session.
HttpSession getSession(boolean create)	Returns the current HttpSession. If there is no session, a new session is created if the parameter is true—otherwise, returns null.

Table 10-7.   *javax.servlet.http HttpservletRequest Class* (continued)

J2EE FOUNDATION

Syntax	Descriptions
Principal getUserPrincipal()	Returns a Principal object containing the current authenticated user.
boolean isRequestedSessionIdFromCookie()	Determines if the session ID is part of a cookie.
boolean isRequestedSessionIdFromURL()	Determines if the session ID is part of the request URL.
boolean isRequestedSessionIdValid()	Determines if session ID is valid.
boolean isUserInRole(String role)	Returns a Boolean indicating whether the authenticated user is specified.

Table 10-7. *javax.servlet.http HttpservletRequest Class* (continued)

Syntax	Descriptions
void addCookie(Cookie cookie)	Adds a cookie.
void addDateHeader(String name, long date)	Adds a response header with the given name and date-value.
void addHeader(String name, String value)	Adds a response header with the given name and value.
void addIntHeader(String name, int value)	Adds a response header with the given name and integer value.
boolean containsHeader(String name)	Returns a Boolean indicating if the named response header is set.
String encodeRedirectURL(String url)	Encodes the specified URL for use in the sendRedirect() method by including the session ID.
String encodeURL(String url)	Encodes the specified URL by including the session ID.

Table 10-8. *javax.servlet.http HttpservletResponse Class*

Syntax	Descriptions
void sendError(int sc)	Sends an error response using the status code.
void sendError(int sc, String msg)	Sends an error response using the status code and message.
void sendRedirect(String location)	Sends a temporary redirect to the client using the redirect location URL.
void setDateHeader(String name, long date)	Sets a response header with the given name and date-value.
void setHeader(String name, String value)	Sets a response header by name and value.
void setIntHeader(String name, int value)	Sets a response header by name and value.
void setStatus(int sc)	Sets the status code.

Table 10-8. *javax.servlet.http HttpservletResponse Class* (continued)

J2EE FOUNDATION

Syntax	Descriptions
SC_ACCEPTED	Status code (202) Request was accepted, but processing was not completed.
SC_BAD_GATEWAY	Status code (502) The HTTP server received an invalid response from a server when acting as a proxy or gateway.
SC_BAD_REQUEST	Status code (400) The request was syntactically incorrect.
SC_CONFLICT	Status code (409) The request was not completed because of a conflict with the resource.

Table 10-9. *HttpservletResponse Class Constants (Fields)*

Syntax	Descriptions
SC_CONTINUE	Status code (100) The client can continue.
SC_CREATED	Status code (201) The request succeeded. New resource created on the server.
SC_EXPECTATION_FAILED	Status code (417) Expectation failed in the Expect request header.
SC_FORBIDDEN	Status code (403) The server refused to fulfill the request.
SC_GATEWAY_TIMEOUT	Status code (504) The upstream server did not send a timely response.
SC_GONE	Status code (410) The resource is no longer available. No forwarding address is known.
SC_HTTP_VERSION_NOT_ SUPPORTED	Status code (505) The server does not support the HTTP protocol version.
SC_INTERNAL_SERVER_ERROR	Status code (500) An error inside the HTTP server prevents the request from being fulfilled.
SC_LENGTH_REQUIRED	Status code (411) The request cannot be handled without a *Content-Length*.
SC_METHOD_NOT_ALLOWED	Status code (405) The method specified in the *Request-Line* is not allowed.
SC_MOVED_PERMANENTLY	Status code (301) The resource has permanently moved to a new location. Don't use the original URI to access the resource.
SC_MOVED_TEMPORARILY	Status code (302) The resource has temporarily moved to another location. Still use the original URI to access the resource.

Table 10-9.   *HttpservletResponse Class Constants (Fields)* (continued)

Syntax	Descriptions
SC_MULTIPLE_CHOICES	Status code (300) The requested resource corresponds to any one of a set of resources.
SC_NO_CONTENT	Status code (204) The request succeeded, but no new information to return.
SC_NON_AUTHORITATIVE_ INFORMATION	Status code (203) The meta information did not originate from the server.
SC_NOT_ACCEPTABLE	Status code (406) The resource identified by the request is only capable of generating response entities that have content characteristics not acceptable according to the accept headers sent in the request.
SC_NOT_FOUND	Status code (404) The requested resource is not available.
SC_NOT_IMPLEMENTED	Status code (501) The HTTP server does not support the functionality.
SC_NOT_MODIFIED	Status code (304) A conditional GET operation found is available and not modified.
SC_OK	Status code (200) The request succeeded.
SC_PARTIAL_CONTENT	Status code (206) The server has fulfilled the partial GET request.
SC_PAYMENT_REQUIRED	Status code (402) Reserved for future use.
SC_PRECONDITION_FAILED	Status code (412) The precondition of a request-header field evaluated to false when it was tested.

Table 10-9. *HttpservletResponse Class Constants (Fields)* (continued)

Syntax	Descriptions
SC_PROXY_AUTHENTICATION_REQUIRED	Status code (407) The client must authenticate with the proxy.
SC_REQUEST_ENTITY_TOO_LARGE	Status code (413) Process refused due to the request entity size.
SC_REQUEST_TIMEOUT	Status code (408) Request was not produced within the time limit.
SC_REQUEST_URI_TOO_LONG	Status code (414) Refused because of the size of the *Request-URI.*
SC_REQUESTED_RANGE_NOT_SATISFIABLE	Status code (416) The server cannot serve the requested byte range.
SC_RESET_CONTENT	Status code (205) The agent should reset the document view.
SC_SEE_OTHER	Status code (303) The response to the request is under a different URI.
SC_SERVICE_UNAVAILABLE	Status code (503) The HTTP server is temporarily overloaded.
SC_SWITCHING_PROTOCOLS	Status code (101) The server is switching protocols according to Upgrade header.
SC_TEMPORARY_REDIRECT	Status code (307) The requested resource is temporarily under a different URI.
SC_UNAUTHORIZED	Status code (401) The request requires HTTP authentication.
SC_UNSUPPORTED_MEDIA_TYPE	Status code (415) Request refused because the entity format is not supported.
SC_USE_PROXY	Status code (305) The requested resource must be accessed through the proxy identified in the Location.

Table 10-9.   *HttpservletResponse Class Constants (Fields)* (continued)

Syntax	Descriptions
Object getAttribute(String name)	Returns the object associated with the attribute, or null if attribute name is not found.
Enumeration getAttributeNames()	Returns an Enumeration of String objects containing the names of all the attributes.
long getCreationTime()	Returns the time when this session was created, measured in milliseconds since midnight January 1, 1970 GMT.
String getId()	Returns a String object that contains the unique identifier that identifies the session.
long getLastAccessedTime()	Returns the last time the client sent a request in the session, as the number of milliseconds since midnight January 1, 1970 GMT, and marked by the time the container received the request.
int getMaxInactiveInterval()	Returns the maximum time, in seconds, that the session remains open between client accesses.
servletContext getservletContext()	Returns the servletContext of the session.
void invalidate()	Invalidates this session.
boolean isNew()	Returns true if the client is unaware of the session or if the client doesn't join the session.
void removeAttribute(String name)	Removes the object associated with the attribute.
void setAttribute(String name, Object value)	Writes an object to the attribute.
void setMaxInactiveInterval(int interval)	Specifies a time in seconds after which the session is invalidated.

Table 10-10.   *javax.servlet.http HttpSession*

The Complete Reference

J2EE

Chapter 11

Java ServerPages

A Java ServerPage (JSP) is a server-side program that is similar in design and functionality to a Java servlet, which is described in the previous chapter. A JSP is called by a client to provide a web service, the nature of which depends on the J2EE application. A JSP processes the request by using logic built into the JSP or by calling other web components built using Java servlet technology or Enterprise JavaBean technology, or created using other technologies. Once the request is processed, the JSP responds by sending the results to the client.

However, a JSP differs from a Java servlet in the way in which the JSP is written. As you'll recall from Chapter 9, a Java servlet is written using the Java programming language and responses are encoded as an output String object that is passed to the println() method. The output String object is formatted in HTML, XML, or whatever formats are required by the client.

In contrast, JSP is written in HTML, XML, or in the client's format that is interspersed with scripting elements, directives, and actions comprised of Java programming language and JSP syntax. In this chapter you'll learn how to create a JSP that can be used as a middle-level program between clients and web services.

JSP

A JSP is simpler to create than a Java servlet because a JSP is written in HTML rather than with the Java programming language. This means that the JSP isn't cluttered with many println() methods as found in a Java servlet. However, a JSP offers basically the same features found in a Java servlet because a JSP is converted to a Java servlet the first time that a client requests the JSP.

There are three methods that are automatically called when a JSP is requested and when the JSP terminates normally. These are the jspInt() method, the jspDestroy() method, and the service() method. These methods can be overridden, although the jspInt() method and jspDestroy() methods are commonly overridden in a JSP to provide customized functionality when the JSP is called and terminates.

The jspInt() method is identical the init() method in a Java servlet and in an applet. The jspInt() method is called first when the JSP is requested and is used to initialize objects and variables that are used throughout the life of the JSP.

The jspDestroy() method is identical to the destroy() method in a Java servlet. The destroy() method is automatically called when the JSP terminates normally. It isn't called if the JSP abruptly terminates such as when the server crashes. The destroy() method is used for cleanup where resources used during the execution of the JSP are released, such as disconnecting from a database.

The service() method is automatically called and retrieves a connection to HTTP.

Installation

Once a JSP is created, you place the JSP in the same directory as HTML pages. This differs from a Java servlet, which must be placed in a particular directory that is included in the CLASSPATH. You don't need to set the CLASSPATH to reference a JSP.

However, there are three factors that you must address when installing a JSP. First, web services called by a JSP must be installed properly. For example, a Java servlet called by a JSP must be placed in the designated directory for Java servlets and referenced on the CLASSPATH. The development environment used to create the J2EE application determines the designated directory.

The second factor to be addressed is to avoid placing the JSP in the WEB-INF or META-INF directories. The development environment prohibits this. The last factor is that the directory name used to store a JSP mustn't have the same name as the prefix of the URL of the web application.

JSP Tags

A JSP program consists of a combination of HTML tags and JSP tags. JSP tags define Java code that is to be executed before the output of the JSP program is sent to the browser.

A JSP tag begins with a <%, which is followed by Java code, and ends with %>. There is also an Extendable Markup Language (XML) version of JSP tags, which are formatted as <jsp:TagID> </JSP:TagID>.

JSP tags are embedded into the HTML component of a JSP program and are processed by a JSP virtual engine such as Tomcat, which is discussed later in this chapter. Tomcat reads the JSP program whenever the program is called by a browser and resolves JSP tags, then sends the HTML tags and related information to the browser.

Java code associated with JSP tags in the JSP program is executed when encountered by Tomcat, and the result of that process is sent to the browser. The browser knows how to display the result because the JSP tag is enclosed within an open and closed HTML tag. You'll see how this works in the next section.

There are five types of JSP tags that you'll use in a JSP program. These are as follows:

- **Comment tag**   A comment tag opens with <%-- and closes with --%>, and is followed by a comment that usually describes the functionality of statements that follow the comment tag.

- **Declaration statement tags**   A declaration statement tag opens with <%! and is followed by a Java declaration statement(s) that define variables, objects, and methods that are available to other components of the JSP program.

- **Directive tags**   A directive tag opens with <%@ and commands the JSP virtual engine to perform a specific task, such as importing a Java package required by objects and methods used in a declaration statement. The directive tag closes with %>. There are three commonly used directives. These are import, include, and taglib. The import tag is used to import Java packages into the JSP program. The include tag inserts a specified file into the JSP program replacing the include tag. The taglib tag specifies a file that contains a tag library. Here are examples of each tag. The first tag imports the java.sql package. The next tag includes the books.html file located in the keogh directory. And the last tag loads the myTags.tld library.

```
<%@ page import=" import java.sql.*"; %>
<%@ include file="keogh\books.html" %>
<%@ taglib uri="myTags.tld" %>
```

- ■ **Expression tags** An expression tag opens with <%= and is used for an expression statement whose result replaces the expression tag when the JSP virtual engine resolves JSP tags. An expression tags closes with %>.

- ■ **Scriptlet tags** A scriptlet tag opens with <% and contains commonly used Java control statements and loops. A scriptlet tag closes with %>.

Variables and Objects

You can declare Java variables and objects that are used in a JSP program by using the same coding technique as used to declare them in Java. However, the declaration statement must appear as a JSP tag within the JSP program before the variable or object is used in the program.

Listing 11-1 shows a simple JSP program that declares and uses a variable. In this example, the program declares an int called age and initializes the variable with the number 29. The declaration statement is placed within JSP tag.

You'll notice that this JSP tag begins with <%!. This tells the JSP virtual engine to make statements contained in the tag available to other JSP tags in the program. You'll need to do this nearly every time you declare variables or objects in your program unless they are only to be used within the JSP tag where they are declared.

The variable age is used in an expression tag that is embedded within the HTML paragraph tag <P>. A JSP expression tag begins with <%=, which is followed by the expression.

The JSP virtual engine resolves the JSP expression before sending the output of the JSP program to the browser. That is, the JSP tag <%=age%> is replaced with the number 29; afterwards, the HTML paragraph tag and related information is sent to the browser.

Listing 11-1
Declaring
and using a
variable.

```
<HTML>
  <HEAD>
    <TITLE> JSP Programming </TITLE>
  </HEAD>
  <BODY>
    <%! int age=29; %>
    <P> Your age is: <%=age%> </P>
  </BODY>
</HTML>
```

Any Java declaration statement can be used in a JSP tag similar to how those statements are used in a Java program. You are able to place multiple statements within a JSP tag by extending the close JSP tag to another line in the JSP program. This is illustrated in Listing 11-2 where three variables are declared.

Listing 11-2
Declaring multiple variables within a single JSP tag.

```
<HTML>
  <HEAD>
    <TITLE> JSP Programming </TITLE>
  </HEAD>
  <BODY>
    <%! int age=29;
      float salary;
      int empnumber;
    %>
  </BODY>
</HTML>
```

Besides variables, you are also able to declare objects, arrays, and Java collections within a JSP tag using techniques similar to those used in a Java program. Listing 11-3 shows how to declare an object and an array.

In Listing 11-3, the JSP program creates three String objects, the first two declarations implicitly allocate memory, and the third declaration explicitly allocates memory. In addition, this JSP program creates arrays and a Vector.

Listing 11-3
Declaring objects and arrays within a single JSP tag.

```
<HTML>
  <HEAD>
    <TITLE> JSP Programming </TITLE>
  </HEAD>
  <BODY>
    <%! String Name;
      String [ ] Telephone = {"201-555-1212", "201-555-4433"};
      String Company = new String();
      Vector Assignments = new Vector();
      int[ ]  Grade = {100,82,93};
    %>
  </BODY>
</HTML>
```

Methods

JSP offers the same versatility that you have with Java programs, such as defining methods that are local to the JSP program. A method is defined similar to how a method is defined in a Java program except the method definition is placed within a JSP tag.

You can call the method from within the JSP tag once the method is defined. Listing 11-4 illustrates how this is done. In this example, the method is passed a student's grade and then applies a curve before returning the curved grade.

The method is called from within an HTML paragraph tag in this program, although any appropriate tag can be used to call the method. Technically, the method is called from within the JSP tag that is enclosed within the HTML paragraph tag.

The JSP tag that calls the method must be a JSP expression tag, which begins with <%=. You'll notice that the method call is identical to the way a method is called within a Java program. The JSP virtual engine resolves the JSP tag that calls the method by replacing the JSP tag with the results returned by the method, which is then passed along to the browser that called the JSP program.

Listing 11-4
Defining
and calling
a method.

```
<HTML>
  <HEAD>
    <TITLE> JSP Programming </TITLE>
  </HEAD>
  <BODY>
    <%! boolean curve (int grade)
        {
          return 10 + grade;
        }
    %>
    <P> Your curved grade is: <%=curve(80)%> </P>
  </BODY>
</HTML>
```

A JSP program is capable of handling practically any kind of method that you normally use in a Java program. For example, Listing 11-5 shows how to define and use an overloaded method.

Both methods are defined in the same JSP tag, although each follows Java syntax structure for defining a method. One method uses a default value for the curve, while the overload method enables the statement that calls the method to provide the value of the curve.

Once again, these methods are called from an embedded JSP tag placed inside two HTML paragraph tags.

Listing 11-5
Defining
and calling
a method
and an
overloaded
method.

```
<HTML>
  <HEAD>
    <TITLE> JSP Programming </TITLE>
  </HEAD>
  <BODY>
    <%! boolean curve (int grade)
        {
         return 10 + grade;
        }
        boolean curve (int grade,int curveValue)
        {
          return curveValue + grade;
        }
    %>
    <P> Your curved grade is: <%=curve(80, 10)%> </P>
    <P> Your curved grade is: <%=curve(70)%> </P>
  </BODY>
</HTML>
```

Control Statements

One of the most powerful features available in JSP is the ability to change the flow of the program to truly create dynamic content for a web page based on conditions received from the browser.

There are two control statements used to change the flow of a JSP program. These are the if statement and the switch statement, both of which are also used to direct the flow of a Java program.

The if statement evaluates a condition statement to determine if one or more lines of code are to be executed or skipped (as you probably remember from when you learned Java). Similarly, a switch statement compares a value with one or more other values associated with a case statement. The code segment that is associated with the matching case statement is executed. Code segments associated with other case statements are ignored.

The power of these controls comes from the fact that the code segment that is executed or skipped can consist of HTML tags or a combination of HTML tags and JSP tags. That is, these code segments don't need to be only Java statements or Java tags.

Listing 11-6 shows how to intertwine HTML tags and JSP tags to alter the flow of the JSP program. You'll notice that this program is confusing to read because the if statement and the switch statement are broken into several JSP tags. This is necessary because HTML tags are interspersed within these statements.

The if statement requires three JSP tags. The first contains the beginning of the if statement, including the conditional expression. The second contains the else statement, and the third has the closed French brace used to terminate the else block.

Two HTML paragraph tags contain information that the browser displays, depending on the evaluation of the conditional expression in the if statement. Only one of the HTML paragraph tags and related information are sent to the browser.

The switch statement also is divided into several JSP tags because each case statement requires an HTML paragraph tag and related information. And, as with the if statement, only one HTML paragraph tag and related information associated with a case statement that matches the switch value are returned to the browser.

Listing 11-6 contains simple examples of the if statement and switch statement. You can create more complex statements, such as nesting if statements, by using techniques illustrated in this example. Any flow control statements that you use in Java can also be incorporated into a JSP program. However, you must be careful to separate JSP tags from HTML tags and information that will be executed when the program's flow changes.

Listing 11-6
Using an if statement and a switch statement to determine which HTML tags and information are to be sent to the browser.

```
<HTML>
  <HEAD>
    <TITLE> JSP Programming </TITLE>
  </HEAD>
<BODY>
  <%! int grade=70;%>
  <% if (grade > 69) { %>
      <P> You passed! </P>
  <% } else { %>
  <P> Better luck next time. </P>
  <% } %>
  <% switch (grade) {
      case 90 : %>
        <P> Your final grade is a A </P>
  <%      break; %>
      case 80 : %>
        <P> Your final grade is a B </P>
  <%      break;
      case 70 : %>
        <P> Your final grade is a C </P>
  <%      break;
      case 60 : %>
        <P> Your final grade is an F </P>
  <%      break;
      }
  %>
  </BODY>
</HTML>
```

Loops

JSP loops are nearly identical to loops that you use in your Java program except you can repeat HTML tags and related information multiple times within your JSP program without having to enter the additional HTML tags.

There are three kinds of loops commonly used in a JSP program. These are the for loop, the while loop, and the do…while loop. The for loop repeats, usually a specified number of times, although you can create an endless for loop, which you no doubt learned when you were introduced to Java.

The while loop executes continually as long as a specified condition remains true. However, the while loop may not execute because the condition may never be true. In contrast, the do…while loop executes at least once; afterwards, the conditional expression in the do…while loop is evaluated to determine if the loop should be executed another time.

Loops play an important role in JSP database programs because loops are used to populate HTML tables with data in the result set. However, Listing 11-7 shows a similar routine used to populate three HTML tables with values assigned to an array.

All the tables appear the same, although a different loop is used to create each table. The JSP program initially declares and initializes an array and an integer, and then begins to create the first table.

There are two rows in each table. The first row contains three column headings that are hard coded into the program. The second row also contains three columns each of which is a value of an element of the array.

The first table is created using the for loop. The opening table row tag <TR> is entered into the program before the for loop begins. This is because the for loop is only populating columns and not rows.

A pair of HTML table data cell tags <TD> are placed inside the for loop along with a JSP tag that contains an element of the array. The JSP tag resolves to the value of the array element by the JSP virtual program.

The close table row </TR> tag and the close </TABLE> tag are inserted into the program following the French brace that closes the for loop block. These tags terminate the construction of the table.

A similar process is used to create the other two tables, except the while loop and the do…while loop are used in place of the for loop.

Listing 11-7
Using the for loop, while loop, and the do…while loop to load HTML tables.

```
<HTML>
  <HEAD>
    <TITLE> JSP Programming </TITLE>
  </HEAD>
  <BODY>
```

```
<%! int[ ]  Grade = {100,82,93};
    int x=0;
%>
<TABLE>
  <TR>
    <TD>First</TD>
    <TD>Second</TD>
    <TD>Third</TD>
  </TR>
  <TR>
    <% for (int 1; i<3; i++) { %>
        <TD><%=Grade[i]%> </TD>
    <%   } %>
  </TR>
</TABLE>
<TABLE>
  <TR>
    <TD>First</TD>
    <TD>Second</TD>
    <TD>Third</TD>
  </TR>
  <TR>
    <% while (x<3){ %>
        <TD><%=Grade[x]%> </TD>
        <%    x++;
      } %>
  </TR>
</TABLE>
<TABLE>
  <TR>
    <TD>First</TD>
    <TD>Second</TD>
    <TD>Third</TD>
  </TR>
  <TR>
    <% x=0;
        do{ %>
            <TD><%=Grade[x]%></TD>
          <%x++;
          } while (x<3) %>
```

```
        </TR>
      </TABLE>
    </BODY>
</HTML>
```

Tomcat

JSP programs are executed by a JSP Virtual Machine that runs on a web server. Therefore, you'll need to have access to a JSP Virtual Machine to run your JSP program. Alternatively, you can use an integrated development environment such as JBuilder that has a built-in JSP Virtual Machine or you can download and install a JSP Virtual Machine.

One of the most popular JSP Virtual Machines is Tomcat, and it is downloadable at no charge from the Apache web site. Apache is also a popular web server that you can also download at no cost.

You'll also need to have the Java Development Kit (JDK) installed on your computer, which you probably installed when you learned Java programming. You can download the JDK at no charge from the www.sun.com web site.

Here's what you need to do to download and install Tomcat:

1. Connect to jakarta.apache.org.

2. Select Download.

3. Select Binaries to display the Binary Download page.

4. Create a folder from the root directory called tomcat.

5. Download the latest release of jakarta-tomcat.zip to the tomcat folder.

6. Unzip jakarta-tomcat.zip. You can download a demo copy of WinZip from www.winzip.com if you don't have a zip/unzip program installed on your computer.

7. The extraction process should create the following folders in the tomcat directory: bin, conf, doc, lib src, and webapps.

8. Use a text editor such as Notepad and edit the JAVA_HOME variable in the tomcat.bat file, which is located in the \tomcat\bin folder. Make sure the JAVA_HOME variable is assigned the path where the JDK is installed on your computer.

9. Open a DOS window and type **\tomcat\bin\tomcat** to start Tomcat.

10. Open your browser. Enter **http://localhost:8080**. The Tomcat home page is displayed on the screen verifying that Tomcat is running.

Request String

The browser generates a user request string whenever the Submit button is selected. The user request string consists of the URL and the query string, as you learned at the beginning of this chapter. Here's a typical request string:

```
http://www.jimkeogh.com/jsp/myprogram.jsp?fname="Bob"&lname="Smith"
```

Your program needs to parse the query string to extract values of fields that are to be processed by your program. You can parse the query string by using methods of the JSP request object.

The getParameter(Name) is the method used to parse a value of a specific field. The getParameter() method requires an argument, which is the name of the field whose value you want to retrieve.

Let's say that you want to retrieve the value of the fname field and the value of the lname field in the previous request string. Here are the statements that you'll need in your JSP program:

```
<%! String Firstname = request.getParameter(fname);
    String Lastname = request.getParameter(lname);
%>
```

In the previous example, the first statement used the getParameter() method to copy the value of the fname from the request string and assign that value to the Firstname object. Likewise, the second statement performs a similar function, but using the value of the lname from the request string. You can use request string values throughout your program once the values are assigned to variables in your JSP program.

There are four predefined implicit objects that are in every JSP program. These are request, response, session, and out. The previous example used the request object's getParameter() method to retrieve elements of the request string. The request object is an instance of the HttpServletRequest (see Chapter 9). The response object is an instance of HttpServletResponse, and the session object is an instance of HttpSession. Both of these are described in detail in Chapter 9. The out object is an instance of the JspWriter that is used to send a response to the client.

Copying a value from a multivalued field such as a selection list field can be tricky since there are multiple instances of the field name, each with a different value. However, you can easily handle multivalued fields by using the getParameterValues() method.

The getParameterValues() method is designed to return multiple values from the field specified as the argument to the getParameterValues(). Here is how the getParameterValues() is implemented in a JSP program.

In this example, we're retrieving the selection list field shown in Listing 11-8. The name of the selection list field is EMAILADDRESS, the values of which are copied into an array of String objects called EMAIL. Elements of the array are then displayed in JSP expression tags.

Listing 11-8
Selecting
a listing
of fields.

```
<%! String [ ] EMAIL = request.getParameterValues("EMAILADDRESS ") ; %>
<P> <%= EMAIL [0]%> </P>
<P> <%= EMAIL [1]%> </P>
```

You can parse field names by using the getParameterNames() method. This method returns an enumeration of String objects that contains the field names in the request string. You can use the enumeration extracting methods that you learned in Java to copy field names to variables within your program.

The Quick Reference Guide in Chapter 9 contains a list of other commonly used HttpServletRequest class methods that you'll find useful when working with parameters.

Parsing Other Information

The request string sent to the JSP by the browser is divided into two general components that are separated by the question mark. The URL component appears to the left of the question mark and the query string is to the right of the question mark.

In the previous section you learned how to parse components of the query string, which are field names and values using request object methods. These are similar to the method used to parse URL information.

The URL is divided into four parts, beginning with the protocol. The protocol defines the rules that are used to transfer the request string from the browser to the JSP program. Three of the more commonly used protocols are HTTP, HTTPS (the secured version of HTTP), and FTP, which is a file transfer protocol.

Next is the host and port combination. The host is the Internet Protocol (IP) address or name of the server that contains the JSP program. The port number is the port that the host monitors. Usually the port is excluded from the request string whenever HTTP is used because the assumption is the host is monitoring port 80. Following the host and port is the virtual path of the JSP program. The server maps the virtual path to the physical path.

Here's a typical URL. The http is the protocol. The host is www.jimkeogh.com. There isn't a port because the browser assumes that the server is monitoring port 80. The virtual path is /jsp/myprogram.jsp.

```
http://www.jimkeogh.com/jsp/myprogram.jsp
```

User Sessions

A JSP program must be able to track a session as a client moves between HTML pages and JSP programs as discussed in Chapter 9. There are three commonly used methods to track a session. These are by using a hidden field, by using a cookie, or by using a JavaBean, which is discussed in the next chapter.

A hidden field is a field in an HTML form whose value isn't displayed on the HTML page, as you learned in Chapter 8. You can assign a value to a hidden field in a JSP program before the program sends the dynamic HTML page to the browser.

Let's say that your JSP database system displays a dynamic login screen. The browser sends the user ID and password to the JSP program when the Submit button is selected where these parameters are parsed and stored into two memory variables (see the "Request String" section).

The JSP program then validates the login information and generates another dynamic HTML page once the user ID and password are approved. The new dynamically built HTML page contains a form that contains a hidden field, among other fields. And the user ID is assigned as the value to the hidden field.

When the person selects the Submit button on the new HTML page, the user ID stored in the hidden field and information in other fields on the form are sent by the browser to another JSP program for processing.

This cycle continues where the JSP program processing the request string receives the user ID as a parameter and then passes the user ID to the next dynamically built HTML page as a hidden field. In this way, each HTML page and subsequent JSP program has access to the user ID and therefore can track the session.

The Quick Reference Guide in Chapter 9 contains a list of other commonly used HttpSession class methods that you'll find useful when working with a session.

Cookies

As you learned in Chapter 9, a cookie is a small piece of information created by a JSP program that is stored on the client's hard disk by the browser. Cookies are used to store various kinds of information, such as user preferences and an ID that tracks a session with a JSP database system.

You can create and read a cookie by using methods of the Cookie class and the response object as illustrated in Listing 11-9 and in Listing 11-10. Listing 11-9 creates and writes a cookie called userID that has a value of JK1234.

The program begins by initializing the cookie name and cookie value and then passes these String objects as arguments to the constructor of a new cookie. This cookie is then passed to the addCookie() method, which causes the cookie to be written to the client's hard disk.

Listing 11-10 retrieves a cookie and sends the cookie name and cookie value to the browser, which displays these on the screen. This program begins by initializing the

MyCookieName String object to the name of the cookie that needs to be retrieved from the client's hard disk. I call the cookie userID.

Two other String objects are created to hold the name and value of the cookie read from the client. Also I created an int called found and initialized it to zero. This variable is used as a flag to indicate whether or not the userID cookie is read.

Next an array of Cookie objects called cookies is created and assigned the results of the request.getCookies() method, which reads all the cookies from the client's hard disk and assigns them to the array of Cookie objects.

The program proceeds to use the getName() and getValue() methods to retrieve the name and value from each object of the array of Cookie objects. Each time a Cookie object is read, the program compares the name of the cookie to the value of the MyCookieName String object, which is userID.

When a match is found, the program assigns the value of the current Cookie object to the MyCookieValue String object and changes the value of the found variable from 0 to 1.

After the program reads all the Cookie objects, the program evaluates the value of the found variable. If the value is 1, the program sends the value of the MyCookieName and MyCookieValue to the browser, which displays these values on the screen.

The Quick Reference Guide in Chapter 9 contains a list of other commonly used Cookie class methods that you'll find useful when working with cookies.

J2EE FOUNDATION

Listing 11-9
How to create a cookie.

```
<HTML>
  <HEAD>
    <TITLE> JSP Programming </TITLE>
  </HEAD>
  <BODY>
    <%! String MyCookieName = "userID";
        String MyCookieValue = "JK1234";
        response.addCookie(new Cookie(MyCookieName, MyCookieValue));
    %>
  </BODY>
</HTML>
```

Listing 11-10
How to read a cookie.

```
<HTML>
  <HEAD>
    <TITLE> JSP Programming </TITLE>
  </HEAD>
  <BODY>
    <%! String MyCookieName = "userID";
        String MyCookieValue;
        String CName, CValue;
```

```
      int found=0;
      Cookie[] cookies = request.getCookies();
      for(int i=0; i<cookies.length; i++) {
        CName  = cookies[i].getName();
        CValue = cookies[i].getValue();
        if(MyCookieName.equals(cookieNames[i])) {
          found = 1;
          MyCookieValue = cookieValue;
        }
      }
      if (found ==1) { %>
        <P> Cookie name = <%= MyCookieName %> </P>
        <P> Cookie value = <%= MyCookieValue %> </P>
  <%}%>
 </BODY>
</HTML>
```

Session Objects

A JSP database system is able to share information among JSP programs within a session by using a session object. Each time a session is created, a unique ID is assigned to the session and stored as a cookie.

The unique ID enables JSP programs to track multiple sessions simultaneously while maintaining data integrity of each session. The session ID is used to prevent the intermingling of information from clients.

In addition to the session ID, a session object is also used to store other types of information, called *attributes*. An attribute can be login information, preferences, or even purchases placed in an electronic shopping cart.

Let's say that you built a Java database system that enables customers to purchase goods online. A JSP program dynamically generates catalogue pages of available merchandise. A new catalogue page is generated each time the JSP program executes.

The customer selects merchandise from a catalogue page, then jumps to another catalogue page where additional merchandise is available for purchase. Your JSP database system must be able to temporarily store purchases made from each catalogue page; otherwise, the system is unable to execute the checkout process. This means that purchases must be accessible each time the JSP program executes.

There are several ways in which you can share purchases. You might store merchandise temporally in a table, but then you'll need to access the DBMS several times during the session, which might cause performance degradation.

A better approach is to use a session object and store information about purchases as session attributes. Session attributes can be retrieved and modified each time the JSP program runs.

Listing 11-11 illustrates how to assign information to a session attribute. In this example, the program creates and initializes two String objects. One String object is assigned the name of the attribute and the other String object is assigned a value for the attribute. Next, the program calls the setAttribute() method and passes this method the name and value of the attribute.

Listing 11-12 reads attributes. The program begins by calling the getAttributeNames() method that returns names of all the attributes as an Enumeration.

Next, the program tests whether or not the getAttributeNames() method returned any attributes. If so, statements within the while loop execute, which assigns the attribute name of the current element to the AtName String object. The AtName String object is then passed as an argument to the getAttribute() method, which returns the value of the attribute. The value is assigned to the AtValue String object. The program then sends the attribute name and value to the browser.

The Quick Reference Guide in Chapter 9 contains a list of other commonly used HttpSession class methods that you'll find useful when working with a session.

Listing 11-11
How to create a session attribute.

```
<HTML>
  <HEAD>
    <TITLE> JSP Programming </TITLE>
  </HEAD>
  <BODY>
    <%! String AtName = "Product";
        String AtValue = "1234";
        session.setAttribute(AtName, AtValue);
    %>
  </BODY>
</HTML>
```

Listing 11-12
How to read session attributes.

```
<HTML>
  <HEAD>
    <TITLE> JSP Programming </TITLE>
  </HEAD>
  <BODY>
    <%! Enumeration purchases = session.getAttributeNames();
        while(purchases.hasMoreElements()){
          String AtName = (String)attributeNames.nextElement();
          String AtValue = (String)session.getAttribute(AtName); %>
          <P> Attribute Name <%= AtName %> </P>
          <P> Attribute Value <%= AtValue %> </P>
      <% } %>
  </BODY>
</HTML>
```

Quick Reference Guide

Syntax	Descriptions
void _jspService(HttpServletRequest request, HttpServletResponse response)	Corresponds to the body of the JSP page.

Table 11-1. *public interface HttpJspPage extends JspPage*

Sytax	Descriptions
void jspDestroy()	Automatically invoked when a JSP page is to be destroyed.
void jspInit()	Automatically invoked when the JSP page is initialized.

Table 11-2. *public interface JspPage extends Servlet*

Syntax	Descriptions
abstract Object findAttribute(String name)	Returns the value of an attribute.
abstract Object getAttribute(String name)	Returns an object associated with the name.
abstract Object getAttribute(String name, int scope)	Returns an object associated with the name.
abstract Enumeration getAttributeNamesInScope(int scope)	Returns all attributes of a scope.
abstract int getAttributesScope(String name)	Returns the scope based on name.
abstract ExpressionEvaluator getExpressionEvaluator()	Provides programmatic access to the ExpressionEvaluator.
abstract JspWriter getOut()	Determines if out object value of a JspWriter.

Table 11-3. *public abstract class JspContext extends java.lang.Object*

Syntax	Descriptions
abstract Map peekPageScope()	Peeks at the top of the page scope stack.
abstract Map popPageScope()	Removes a page scope from the stack.
abstract void pushPageScope(Map scopeState)	Places a page scope on the stack.
abstract void removeAttribute(String name)	Uses all scopes to delete an object reference associated with a name.
abstract void removeAttribute(String name, int scope)	Delete an object by name.
abstract void setAttribute(String name, Object attribute)	Registers a name associated with an object that has page scope semantics.
abstract void setAttribute(String name, Object o, int scope)	Registers a name associated with an object and scope.

Table 11-3. *public abstract class JspContext* **extends java.lang.Object** (continued)

Syntax	Descriptions
abstract String getSpecificationVersion()	Returns the version number of JSP

Table 11-4. *public abstract class JspEngineInfo* **extends Object**

Syntax	Descriptions
static JspFactory getDefaultFactory()	Returns the default JSP factory.
abstract JspEngineInfo getEngineInfo()	Returns information about the JSP engine.

Table 11-5. *public abstract class JspFactory* **extends Object**

J2EE FOUNDATION

Syntax	Descriptions
abstract PageContext getPageContext(Servlet servlet, ServletRequest request, ServletResponse response, String errorPageURL, boolean needsSession, int buffer, boolean autoflush)	Returns an instance of a PageContext.
abstract void releasePageContext (PageContext pc)	Releases an allocated PageContext object.
static void setDefaultFactory (JspFactory deflt)	Sets the default factory.

Table 11-5. *public abstract class JspFactory extends Object* (continued)

Syntax	Descriptions
abstract void clear()	Resets a buffer.
abstract void clearBuffer()	Resets a buffer.
abstract void close()	Closes and flushes a stream.
abstract void flush()	Flushes a stream.
int getBufferSize()	Returns the size of the buffer used by the JspWriter.
abstract int getRemaining()	Returns the number of unused bytes in the buffer.
boolean isAutoFlush()	Determines if a JspWriter is autoFlushing.
abstract void newLine()	Writes a line separator.

Table 11-6. *public abstract class JspWriter extends Writer*

Syntax	Descriptions
abstract void print(boolean b)	Prints a boolean value.
abstract void print(char c)	Prints a character.
abstract void print(char[] s)	Prints an array of characters.
abstract void print(double d)	Prints a double-precision floating-point number.
abstract void print(float f)	Prints a floating-point number.
abstract void print(int i)	Prints an integer.
abstract void print(long l)	Prints a long integer.
abstract void print(Object obj)	Prints an object.
abstract void print(String s)	Prints a string.
abstract void println()	Writes a line separator string to terminate a line.
abstract void println(boolean x)	Prints a boolean value with a terminated line
abstract void println(char x)	Prints a character with a terminated line.
abstract void println(char[] x)	Prints an array of characters with a terminated line
abstract void println(double x)	Prints a double-precision floating-point number with a terminated line.
abstract void println(float x)	Prints a floating-point number with a terminated line.
abstract void println(int x)	Prints an integer with a terminated line.
abstract void println(long x)	Prints a long integer with a terminated line.
abstract void println(Object x)	Prints an Object with a terminated line.
abstract void println(String x)	Prints a String with a terminated line.

Table 11-6. *public abstract class JspWriter **extends Writer*** (continued)

J2EE FOUNDATION

Syntax	Descriptions
abstract void forward(String relativeUrlPath)	Redirects the ServletRequest and ServletResponse to another active component in the application.
abstract Exception getException()	Returns the value of the exception object.
abstract Object getPage()	Returns the value of the page object.
abstract ServletRequest getRequest()	Returns the value of the response object.
abstract ServletResponse getResponse()	Returns the value of the response object.
abstract ServletConfig getServletConfig()	Returns the instance of the ServletConfig.
abstract ServletContext getServletContext()	Returns the instance of the ServletContext.
abstract HttpSession getSession()	Returns the value of the session object.
abstract void handlePageException (Exception e)	Redirects an unhandled page level exception to an error page.
abstract void handlePageException (Throwable t)	Makes an unhandled page level exception Throwable.
abstract void **include**(String relativeUrlPath)	Processes the resource as part of the current ServletRequest.
abstract void initialize(Servlet servlet, ServletRequest request, ServletResponse response, String errorPageURL, boolean needsSession, int bufferSize, boolean autoFlush)	Initializes an uninitialized PageContext.
JspWriter popBody()	Updates the page scope "out" attribute of the PageContext; and returns the previous JspWriter "out" saved by the matching pushBody().
BodyContent pushBody()	Saves the current "out" JspWriter; updates the page scope "out" attribute of the PageContext; and returns a new BodyContent object.
abstract void release()	Resets the internal state of a PageContext, for potential reuse.

Table 11-7.   *public abstract class PageContext extends JspContext*

Syntax	Descriptions
Object evaluate(String attributeName, String expression, Class expectedType, Tag tag, PageContext pageContext)	Evaluates the expression contained in a request.
String validate(String attributeName, String expression)	Validates an expression at translation time.

Table 11-8.   *public interface **ExpressionEvaluator***

Syntax	Descriptions
Object resolveVariable(String pName, Object pContext)	Resolves a variable within the given context.

Table 11-9.   *public interface **VariableResolver***

Syntax	Descriptions
void doInitBody()	Prepares to evaluate the body.
void setBodyContent(BodyContent b)	Sets the bodyContent property.

Table 11-10.   *public interface BodyTag extends IterationTag*

Syntax	Descriptions
void setDynamicAttribute(String uri, String localName, Object value)	Sets a dynamic attribute that is not declared in the Tag Library Descriptor.

Table 11-11.   *public interface DynamicAttributes*

J2EE FOUNDATION

Syntax	Descriptions
int doAfterBody()	Processes the body content.

Table 11-12. *public interface IterationTag* ***extends Tag***

Syntax	Descriptions
void invoke(Writer out, Map params)	Executes the fragment and directs all output to a Writer.

Table 11-13. *public interface* ***JspFragment***

Syntax	Descriptions
int doTag()	Processes a tag.
Object getParent()	Returns the parent of a tag.
void setJspBody(JspFragment jspBody)	Sets the body of a tag as a JspFragment object.
void setJspContext(JspContext pc)	Set a page context in the protected jspContext field.
void setParent(Object parent)	Sets a parent of a tag.

Table 11-14. *public interface* ***SimpleTag***

Syntax	Descriptions
int doEndTag()	Processes an end tag.
int doStartTag()	Processes a start tag.
Tag getParent()	Returns the parent for a tag.
void release()	Instructs a Tag handler to release state.
void setPageContext(PageContext pc)	Sets a page context.
void setParent(Tag t)	Sets the parent of a tag handler.

Table 11-15. *public interface* ***Tag***

Syntax	Descriptions
void doCatch(Throwable t)	Executes when a Throwable exception happens while the body is being evaluated.
void doFinally()	Executes after doEndTag().

Table 11-16. *public interface* ***TryCatchFinally***

The
Complete
Reference

Chapter 12

Enterprise JavaBeans

The J2EE architecture consists of components that together enable developers to build a robust, industrial-strength J2EE application that takes advantage of the efficiencies of distributive, web services technology.

Part I of this book introduced you to the J2EE architecture and presented an overview of J2EE components. Three of these components form the nucleus of a J2EE application. These are Java servlets, JavaServer Pages (JSP), and Enterprise JavaBeans (EJB).

Typically, a J2EE application uses a browser-based user interface composed of a web page. An HTML form collects information from a user and formulates a request for web services, which is passed along to a server-side component. The server-side component is written in either Java servlet or JSP technology. A Java servlet and a JSP perform an intermediary function, as you learned in Chapters 10 and 11.

As an intermediary between a client and web services, a Java servlet and JSP receive a request for a web service from a client and fulfill the request by calling other server-side components that contain the business logic needed to comply with part or all of the request. The results are returned to the Java servlet or JSP, which responds to the client.

Many of the server-side components called by a Java servlet and JSP are written using EJB technology. In this chapter, you'll learn about EJB technology and how to create your own EJB. You'll also learn how to call an EJB from with a Java servlet and JSP.

Enterprise JavaBeans

An Enterprise JavaBean (EJB) is a component of the J2EE architecture that primarily provides business logic to a J2EE application and interacts with other server-side J2EE components. The nature of the business logic and the interactions with other server-side J2EE components are dependent on the J2EE application.

Let's say that a user of a J2EE application needs to display a catalog page that contains merchandise information. The J2EE application displays a web page that contains an HTML form where the user can enter the identification number of the merchandise. The browser then calls a JSP program. The JSP program parses the product number of the merchandise from the query string sent by the browser. The product number is then passed to an EJB, which interacts with a database to extract information about the merchandise. This information is returned to the JSP program, which formats the information into a web page and sends the web page to the browser for display.

An EJB is written in the Java programming language. This means that an EJB is operating system and platform independent, provided you're not using any native code. The developer of an EJB class focuses on writing business logic to respond to requests for web services and does not focus on system-level services unless required by the specifications for the EJB. The EJB server handles system-level services such as threading, security, transactions, and persistence if the EJB tells the server how to handle them or the EJB can handle them itself.

The EJB Container

An EJB container is a vendor-provided entity located on the EJB server that manages system-level services for EJB. The EJB container is one of several containers, each of which handles a J2EE component such as Java servlets and JSP.

An EJB container provides a reusable pool of distributed components. Each EJB must be installed in an EJB container. Typically, an EJB container contains many EJBs. There can also be multiple EJB containers. However, an EJB must be installed in only one EJB container.

A client's request for web services is made to a web server, which forwards the client's request to the appropriate server. Typically, either the Java servlet server or the JSP server receives the client's request, depending on which is used for the J2EE application.

The Java servlet or JSP uses JNDI (see Chapter 16) to look up the EJB resource. The EJB object is returned and is used to get the EJB's home class. The home class is used to reference the bean class through the EJB's remote class.

EJB Classes

There are three kinds of EJB types. These are the Entity JavaBean class, the Session Java Bean class and the Message-Driven JavaBean class. These are commonly referred to as an entity bean, a session bean, and a message-driven bean.

An entity bean is used to represent business data. A session bean is used to model a business process. And a message-driven bean is used to receive messages from a JMS resource—either a Queue or Topic, which are discussed later in this chapter.

EJB Interfaces

The session and entity beans must have two interfaces. These are the Home interface and the Remote interface. Both interfaces are declared by the developer of the EJB and are implemented by the EJB container.

Figure 12-1 illustrates the relationships that exist in an EJB environment. At the center of the EJB environment is the EJB that contains the logic necessary to provide service to a client. The EJB is wrapped by the EJB container, which handles the EJB's life-cycle requirements as described previously in this chapter. The EJB container handles communications between the EJB and other components in the EJB environment using the Home interface and the Remote interface.

The local clients that are on the same Java Virtual Machine as the EJB interact with the EJB using the Home interface. The Remote interface is used by remote clients that are capable of accessing the EJB container from an application that is compliant with RMI and IIOP. The Remote and Home interfaces can be used to access the EJB either remotely (outside the container that the EJB resides in) or locally within the same container. Local and LocalHome are part of the EJB 2.0 specification and are used to access the EJB within the same container. Local is used much like the Remote interface

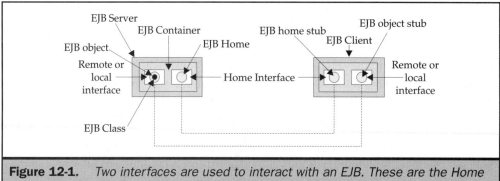

Figure 12-1. *Two interfaces are used to interact with an EJB. These are the Home interface and the Remote interface.*

and LocalHome is used in the same manner as the Home interface. The methods you expose in the Local interface have to match business methods in the bean class; however, the methods exposed through Local don't have to match Remote—you can expose a different set of methods if you choose to do so. This includes CORBA-based applications and non-Java programs. The Remote interface provides the client's view of the EBJ and has the prototype of each business method in the EJB. The EJB implements business methods and all the housekeeping methods.

Listing 12-1 illustrates a Home interface. The Home interface must extend the EJBHome interface. In this example, the interface is called myHome and declares one method, which is create(). The create() method returns myEJB object, which is the EJB that is used with the myHome interface. The create() method is defined in the EJB.

Listing 12-1
A simple Home interface for the myEJB EJB.

```
import javax.ejb.*;
import java.rmi.RemoteException;
public interface MyEJBHome extends EJBHome
{
  public MyEJB create() throws CreateException, RemoteException;
}
```

Listing 12-2 illustrates a Remote interface. The Remote interface is written using Java Remote Method Invocation syntax and declares methods that can be accessed by a remote client. The Remote interface extends the EJBObject. One method is declared in this example, which is called myMethod(). The definition of myMethod() is contained in the EJB bean class. There would be many more methods declared in the Remote interface in a real-world J2EE application. A method's signature is identical in the remote and bean classes except that the Remote interface declares a RemoteException.

Listing 12-2
A simple
Remote
interface for
myEJB EJB.

```
import java.rmi.RemoteException;
import javax.ejb.*;
public interface MyEJB extends EJBObject{
public String myMethod() throws RemoteException;
}
```

Deployment Descriptors

A deployment descriptor describes how EJBs are managed at runtime and enables the customization of EJB behavior without modification to the EJB code such as describing runtime attributes of transactional context. The behavior of an EJB can be modified within the deployment descriptor without having to modify the EJB class or the EJB interfaces.

A deployment descriptor is written in a file using XML syntax. Many times, an integrated development environment (IDE) used to create the EJB has a graphical user interface a developer can use to set deployment descriptor attributes. The IDE then generates the deployment descriptor file. A developer can also create a deployment descriptor file using an editor.

The deployment descriptor file is packaged in the Java Archive (JAR) file along with the other files that are required to deploy the EJB. These include classes and component interfaces that are necessary for each EJB in the package.

An EJB container references the deployment descriptor file to understand how to deploy and manage EJBs contained in the package. The deployment descriptor identifies the types of EJBs that are contained in the package as well as other attributes, such as how transactions are managed. The EJB container continues to reference the deployment descriptor after deployment.

Deployment descriptors are used in EJB 1.1 and EJB 2.0 and are nearly the same except the EJB 2.0 deployment descriptor has two elements that are not found in the EJB 1.1 deployment descriptor (<local> and <local-home>) and a different version is declared in the <!DOCTYPE>.

Listings 12-3 and 12-4 illustrate a skeleton of a deployment descriptor. Listing 12-3 is a deployment descriptor for EJB 1.1 and Listing 12-4 is a deployment descriptor for EJB 2.0. You'll notice that both deployment descriptors use XML elements similar to those you learned about in Chapter 8.

The deployment descriptor begins with the <!DOCTYPE> element that defines the URL for the document type definition (DTD) and the organization that defines the DTD. The DTD defines the structure of the XML document.

Next is the <ejb-jar> element, which is the root element of the deployment descriptor. Every deployment descriptor must contain an <ejb-jar> element and all other EJB elements must be nested with the <ejb-jar> element.

The first element within the <ejb-jar> element is the <enterprise-beans> element. It is here where the EJB is declared. There are three elements that can be contained within the <enterprise-beans> element. These are <entity>, <session>, and <message-driven>, each of which describes a type of EJB. However, the <message-driven> element is used only in EJB 2.0 and is not supported in EJB 1.1.

The <entity> element is used in Listing 12-3 and Listing 12-4 since the deployment descriptor describes an entity EJB, which you'll learn about later in this chapter. The <entity> element contains subelements that describe the entity EJB.

These include the <ejb-name> element that contains a descriptive name for the entity EJB. The <home> element describes the home interface that provides access to the entity EJB to remote clients. The <home> element must contain the fully qualified class name of the remote home interface. The <ejb-name> field is used to tie the two descriptors together and also used within the same descriptor to reference other attributes.

The <remote> element describes the fully qualified class name of the Remote interface, which defines the entity EJB's business methods to remote clients. The <local-home> element is used in EJB 2.0 deployment descriptors to describe the fully qualified class name of the local home interface. The local home interface identifies the entity EJB to co-locate EJB. Likewise, the <local> element is also used in EJB 2.0 deployment descriptors. The <local> element describes the fully qualified class name of the local interface. The local interface defines the entity EJB's business methods to other co-located EJB.

The <ejb-class> element describes the fully qualified class name of the EJB class, which implements the entity EJB's business methods. The <prim-key-class> element describes the fully qualified class name of the entity EJB's primary key that is used to locate data in a database.

The <persistence-type> element defines how the entity EJB manages persistence. As you'll learn later in this chapter, an entity EJB manages persistence through either container-managed persistence or bean-managed persistence. Therefore, the value for the <persistence-type> element must be either Container or Bean.

The <reentrant> element declares whether or not an entity EJB can be looped back without throwing an exception. A true value permits a look back, while a false value causes an exception to be thrown.

Listing 12-3
Deployment
descriptor
for EJB 1.1.

```
<!DOCTYPE ejb-jar PUBLIC "~//Sun Microsystems, Inc. //DTD EnterpriseJavaBeans
1.1//EN" "http://java/sun/com/dtd/ejb-jar_1_1/dtd">
<ejb-jar>
  <enterprise-beans>
    <entity>
     <ejb-name>myEJB</ejb-name>
     <home>com.jimkeogh.ejb.MyEJBHome</home>
```

```
        <remote>com.jimkeogh.ejb.MyEJBRemote</remote>
        <ejb-class>com.jimkeogh.ejb.MyEJB</ejb-class>
        <peristence-type>Container</persistence-type>
        <prim-key-class>java.lang.String</prim-key-class>
        <reentrant>False</reentrant>
      </entity>
    </enterprise-beans>
</ejb-jar>
```

Listing 12-4
Deployment
descriptor
for EJB 2.0.

```
<!DOCTYPE ejb-jar PUBLIC "~//Sun Microsystems, Inc. //DTD EnterpriseJavaBeans
2.0//EN" "http://java/sun/com/dtd/ejb-jar_2_0/dtd">
<ejb-jar>
  <enterprise-beans>
    <entity>
      <ejb-name>myEJB</ejb-name>
      <home>com.jimkeogh.ejb.MyEJBHome</home>
      <remote>com.jimkeogh.ejb.MyEJBRemote</remote>
      <local-home>com.jimkeogh.ejb.MyEJBHomeLocal</local-home>
      <local>com.jimkeogh.ejb.MyEJBLocal</local>
      <ejb-class>com.jimkeogh.ejb.MyEJB</ejb-class>
      <peristence-type>Container</persistence-type>
      <prim-key-class>java.lang.String</prim-key-class>
      <reentrant>False</reentrant>
    </entity>
  </enterprise-beans>
</ejb-jar>
```

The Anatomy of a Deployment Descriptor

The deployment descriptor skeleton provides a very brief overview of elements that are used in a typical deployment descriptor. There are many other elements that can be use to specify various deployment requirements and options for an EJB.

The root element of every standard deployment descriptor is the <ejb-jar> element. The <ejb-jar> element contains several subelements—some of which are required, while others are optional. Table 12-1 lists the subelements for the <ejb-jar> element. Some vendors require their own root element for vendor-specific deployment descriptors.

The <enterprise-beans> subelement contains its own set of subelements, three of which are the <session>, <entity>, and <message-driven> subelements. Each of these is used to describe a specific type of EJB, which you'll learn about later in this chapter.

The <session> subelement and the <entity> subelement contain other subelements that specify the deployment configuration for a session EJB and an entity EJB, respectively. These subelements are described in Table 12-2.

Table 12-3 lists subelements for the <message-driven> subelement. The <message-driven> subelement defines how a message-driven bean is to be deployed.

J2EE FOUNDATION

Subelement	Required/ Optional	Description
<description>	Optional	Describes the deployment descriptor.
<display-name>	Optional	Describes the JAR file and individual EJB components.
<small-icon>	Optional	Describes a small icon within the JAR file that is used to represent the JAR file.
<large-icon>	Optional	Describes a large icon within the JAR file that is used to represent the JAR file.
<enterprise-beans>	Required	Describes one or more enterprise beans contained in a JAR file. Only one <enterprise-beans> element is permitted in a deployment descriptor.
<ejb-client-jar>	Optional	Describes the path of the client JAR and is used by the client to access EJBs described in the deployment discriptor.
<assembly-descriptor>	Optional	Describes how EJBs are used in the J2EE application.

Table 12-1.   *<ejb-jar> Subelements*

Subelement	Required/ Optional	Description
<description>	Optional	Describes the session or entity EJB.
<display-name>	Optional	Describes the JAR file and individual EJB components.
<small-icon>	Optional	Describes a small icon within the JAR file that is used to represent the session or entity EJB.

Table 12-2.   *<session> and <entity> Elements*

Subelement	Required/ Optional	Description
<large-icon>	Optional	Describes a large icon within the JAR file that is used to represent the session or entity EJB.
<ejb-name>	One required	Describes the name of the session or entity EJB.
<home>	EJB 1.1 One required EJB 2.0 Optional	Describes the fully qualified class name of the session or entity EJB remote home interface.
<remote>	EJB 1.1 One required EJB 2.0 Optional	Describes the fully qualified class name of the session or entity EJB remote interface.
<local-home>	EJB 2.0 Optional	Describes the fully qualified class name of the session or entity EJB local home interface.
<local>	EJB 2.0 Optional	Describes the fully qualified class name of the session or entity EJB local interface.
<ejb-class>	One required	Describes the fully qualified class name of the session or entity EJB class.
<primkey-field>	Entity bean only, optional	Describes the primary key field for entity beans that use container-managed persistence.
<prim-key-class>	Entity bean only, one required	Describes the primary key class for entity beans.
<persistence-type>	Entity bean only, one required Values Container or Bean	Specifies either container-managed persistence or bean-managed persistence.

Table 12-2.   *<session> and <entity> Elements* (continued)

J2EE FOUNDATION

Subelement	Required/ Optional	Description
<reentrant>	Entity bean only, one required Values true or false	Specifies that back (reentrant invocations) is allowed or not.
<cmp-version>	EJB 2.0 Optional EJB containers must support both EJB 2.0 CMP and EJB 1.1.	Specifies the version of container-managed persistence.
<abstract-schema-name>	EJB 2.0 Optional	Specifies entity beans in a JAR file.
<cmp-field>	Entity bean only, zero or more Must exist for each container-managed field in the entity EJB class. Must include a <field-name> element.	For entity beans with container-managed persistence.
<env-entry>	Optional - zero or more	Specifies an environment entry available through JNDI ENC.
<ejb-ref>	Optional - zero or more	Specifies a remote EJB reference available through the JNDI ENC.
<ejb-local-ref>	Optional - zero or more - EJB 2.0	Specifies a local EJB reference available through the JNDI ENC.
<resource-ref>	Optional - zero or more	Specifies reference to connection factory available through the JNDI ENC.
<resource-env-ref>	Optional - zero or more - EJB 2.0	Specifies required administered objects.
<security-role-ref>	Optional - zero or more	Specifies security roles.

Table 12-2.   *<session> and <entity> Elements* (continued)

Subelement	Required/ Optional	Description
<security-identity>	Optional - EJB 2.0	Describes the principal for a method.
<session-type>	One required - session bean Value Stateful or Stateless	Specifies a session bean is either stateful or stateless.
<transaction-type>	One required - session bean Value Bean or Container	Specifies that a session bean manages transactions or the container manages transactions.
<query>	Optional - zero or more - EJB 2.0	Contains an EJB QL statement bound to a find or select method.

Table 12-2.   *<session> and <entity> Elements* (continued)

Subelement	Required/ Optional	Description
<description>	Optional	Describes the session or entity EJB.
<display-name>	Optional	Describes the JAR file and individual EJB components.
<small-icon>	Optional	Describes a small icon within the JAR file that is used to represent the message-driven bean EJB.
<large-icon>	Optional	Describes a large icon within the JAR file that is used to represent the message-driven bean EJB.

Table 12-3.   *<message-driven> Element*

Subelement	Required/ Optional	Description
<ejb-name>	One required	Describes the name of the message-driven bean EJB.
<ejb-class>	One required	Describes the fully qualified class name of the message-driven bean EJB class.
<transaction-type>	One required - session bean Value Bean or Container	Specifies that a message-driven bean manages transactions or the container manages transactions.
<security-identity>	Optional - EJB 2.0	Describes the principal for a method.
<env-entry>	Optional - zero or more	Specifies an environment entry available through JNDI ENC.
<ejb-ref>	Optional - zero or more	Specifies a remote EJB reference available through the JNDI ENC.
<ejb-local-ref>	Optional - zero or more - EJB 2.0	Specifies a local EJB reference available through the JNDI ENC.
<resource-ref>	Optional - zero or more	Specifies reference to connection factory available through the JNDI ENC.
<resource-env-ref>	Optional - zero or more - EJB 2.0	Specifies required administered objects.
<message-selector>	Optional Caution: Can cause problems with XML process. See CDATA	Specifies a conditional expression using Boolean logic to choose messages that are received from a topic or queue and delivered to a client.

Table 12-3. *<message-driven> Element* (continued)

Subelement	Required/ Optional	Description
<acknowledge-mode>	Required Only if EJB manages transactions. Value Auto-acknowledge or Dups-ok-acknowledge	Specifies the type of acknowledgement used when a message is received.
<message-driven-destination>	Required Values jacax.jms.Queue or javax.jms.Topic	Specifies the type of destination subscribed or listened to by the message-driven bean.

Table 12-3.   *<message-driven>* Element (continued)

J2EE FOUNDATION

CDATA

Special characters used in a <message-selector> subelement and the <ejb-ql> subelement can cause parsing errors to occur when the deployment descriptor is processed. The problem is that special characters might be considered XML syntax, such as the less than and greater than signs.

You can avoid this problem by using a CDATA section within the <message-selector> or the <ejb-ql>, as is illustrated in Listing 12-5. The CDATA section tells the XML processor not to translate the special characters as XML syntax. Instead, these characters are treated as literal.

Listing 12-5
Inserting a
CDATA
section into a
<message-
selector>
subelement.

```
<message-selector>
<![CDATA[
grade > 70 AND grade < 80);]]>
```

Environment Elements

The <env-entry> element is used in the deployment descriptor to define values that an EJB can use to customize the EJB's behavior. There are four subelements that can be used within the <env-entry> element. Some of these are required and others are optional.

The subelements are the <description>, <env-entry-name>, <env-entry-type>, and <env-entry-value>. The <description> subelement is optional and consists of text that describes the <env-entry>. The <env-entry-name> subelement is required and specifies the name of the <env-entity> element.

The <env-entry-type> subelement is also required and specifies the type of <env-entry-value> subelement. Finally, the <env-entry-value> subelement is optional and contains the value of the environment entry.

Listing 12-6 illustrates how to define an <env-entry> element in a deployment descriptor. Keep in mind that you need to place this code segment into a fully defined deployment descriptor, as discussed previously in this chapter.

This example creates an environment entry called PassingGrade that is an Integer type and has a value of 75. Listing 12-7 contains a code segment that illustrates how to access an environment entry from an EJB. In this example, a JNDI lookup is conducted to locate the PassingGrade environment entry.

Listing 12-6
Defining an <env-entry> element in a deployment descriptor.

```
<env-entry>
  <env-entry-name>PassingGrade</env-entry-name>
  <env-entry-type>java.lang.Integer</env-entry-type>
  <env-entry-value>75</env-entry-value>
</env-entry>
```

Listing 12-7
Accessing the <env-entry> element from a deployment descriptor.

```
InitialContext jc = new InitialContext();
Integer pGrade = (Integer) jc.lookup("java:comp/env/PassingGrade");
```

Referencing EJB

The deployment descriptor can specify that an EJB can reference another EJB either locally or remotely by using the <ejb-local-ref> element or <ejb-ref> element. This is possible in EJB 2.0. These references are only remote in EJB 1.1.

The <ejb-local-ref> element is used to declare a local reference to EJBs that are co-located in the same container and should be deployed in the same EJB JAR file, although they could reside in different JAR files. The <ejb-local-ref> element must follow the <ejb-ref> element in the deployment descriptor.

Listing 12-8 illustrates how to define an <ejb-local-ref> element. In this example, the <ejb-local-ref> definition contains the EJB type (Entity) and the names of the local component interfaces. The <ejb-link> subelement is used to explicitly link the EJB to other co-located EJBs. The name specified in the <ejb-link> subelement must be the name of the appropriate EJB in the same JAR file. That is, the <ejb-link> subelement value must be the same as a value for the <ejb-name> subelement in the JAR file. The value of the <ejb-local_ref> elements are mapped to co-located EJBs at deployment time but using a tool provided in the EJB container. Listing 12-9 illustrates how to access the reference using a JNDI lookup.

Listing 12-8
Defining the
<ejb-local-ref
> element.

```
<ejb-local-ref>
  <ejb-ref-name>ejb/myEJBHomeLocal</ejb-ref-name>
  <ejb-ref-type>Entity</ejb-ref-type>
  <local-home>com.myejb.myEJBHomeLocal</local-home>
  <local>com.myejb.myEJBLocal</local>
  <ejb-name>myEJB</ejb-name>
</ejb-local-ref>
<ejb-local-ref>
  <ejb-ref-name>ejb/yourEJBHomeLocal</ejb-ref-name>
  <ejb-ref-type>Entity</ejb-ref-type>
  <local--home>com.yourejb.yourEJBHomeLocal</local-home>
  <local>com.yourejb.yourEJBLocal</local>
  <ejb-name>yourEJB</ejb-name>
</ejb-local-ref>
```

Listing 12-9
Looking up
the local
reference.

```
InitialContext jc = new InitialContext();
myEJBHomeLocal myEJBHomeLocal  = (myEJBHomeLocal)
jc.lookup("java:comp/env/ejb/myEJBHomeLocal");
```

Reference to a remote EJB is made by using the <ejb-ref> element. The <ejb-ref> element has several required and optional subelements. The <description> subelement contains a textual description of the <ejb-ref> element and is optional. The <ejb-ref-name> subelement specifies the name of the reference and is a required subelement—as is the <ejb-ref-type> subelement, which specifies the type of the EJB.

Next are the required <remote> subelement and the <home> subelement. These specify the remote and home interfaces, respectively. The last subelement is <ejb-link>, which is optional and is used to explicitly link the EJB to the remote EJB.

Listing 12-10 illustrates how to define a remote reference. In this example, reference is made to myEJBHome, which is a session EJB. Listing 12-11 illustrates how to access the reference.

Listing 12-10
Defining a
remote
reference.

```
<ejb-ref>
  <ejb-ref-name>ejb/myEJBHome</ejb-ref-name>
  <ejb-ref-type>Session</ejb-ref-type>
  <home>com.myEJB.myEJBHome</home>
  <remote>com.myEJB.myEJBHome</remote>
  <ejb-link>myEJB</ejb-link>
</ejb-ref>
```

Listing 12-11
Accessing a
remote
reference.

```
InitialContext jc = new IntitalContext():
Object obj = jc.lookup("java:comp/env/ejb/myEJBHome");
myEJBHome myEJBhome = (myEJBHome)
PortableRemoteObject.narrow(obj, myEJBHome.class);
```

Reference Other Resources

The deployment descriptor is also used to describe references to external resources such as a database that can be accessed by an EJB. External references are specified by using the <resource-ref> element.

The <resource-ref> element contains several subelements. These are an optional <description> subelement, a required <res-ref-name>, a required <res-type>, and a required <res-auth>.

The <description> is used to describe the external resource and the <res-ref-name> is a name assigned to the external resource for use within the deployment descriptor. The <res-type> subelement specifies the type of resource and the <res-auth> subelement indicates the service responsible for login. This can either be the container or the application.

Listing 12-13 illustrates how to define a reference to an external resource. The resource in this example is a database called myDB. The type of the resources is javax.sql.DataSource. And the container handles all the login chores. Listing 12-14 shows how to access the external resource.

Listing 12-13
Defining an
external
resource.

```
<resource-ref>
   <Description>myDatabase</description>
   <res-ref-name>jdbc/myDB</res-ref-name>
   <res-type>javax.sql.DataSource</res-type>
   <res-auth>Container</res-auth>
</resource-ref>
```

Listing 12-14
Accessing an
external
resource.

```
InitialContext jc = new Initialcontext();
DataSource myDB = (DataSource) jc.lookup("java:comp/env/jdbc/myDB");
```

Sharing Resources

In the real world, EJBs work together to complete a transaction. Many times these EJBs interact with the same resource, such as a database. By default, EJB containers share resources. This means that EJBs that work on the same transaction use the same connection to access the common resources. Without sharing, each EJB opens its own connection. However, sometimes sharing resources can have a negative impact on the operations of the EJB. Therefore, you can explicitly activate or deactivate shared resources within the deployment descriptor.

Resource sharing is specified in the deployment descriptor by using the <res-sharing-scope> subelement within the <resource-ref> element. The <res-sharing-scope> subelement has one of two values. These are Shareable or Unshareable.

Security Elements

The <security-role-ref> element is used to specify an EJB's security role. There are three subelements within the <security-role-ref> element. These are <description>, <role-name>, and <role-link>.

The <description> subelement is optional and is used to provide a textual description for the <security-role-ref>. The <role-name> subelement is required. The value of the <role-name> subelement must be the same as the role name used in the EJBContext.isCallerInRole() method in the EJB.

The <role-link> subelement is optional and is used to map the EJB's role name to a logical role contained in the <security-role> element of the <assembly-descriptor> element in the deployment descriptor. The <security-role-ref> element is matched to the environment security role if the <role-link> subelement is not specified in the <security-role-ref> element.

Listing 12-15 illustrates how to define the <security-role> element in the deployment descriptor. In this example, the <role-name> is Supervisor and the <security-role-ref> subelement is matched to an environment security role. Listing 12-16 shows how the EJBContext.isCallerInRole() method is called within the EJB and matches the <role-name> in the deployment descriptor.

Listing 12-15
Defining the <security-role> element.

```
<security-role-ref>
   <description>myEBJ security role </description>
    <role-name>Supervisor</role-name>
</security-role-ref>
```

Listing 12-16
Verifying the role name from within an EJB.

```
boolean supervisor = context.isCallerInRole("Supervisor");
   if (!supervisor) {
      throw new AccessDeniedException();
   }
```

Query Element

A <query> element is used in a deployment descriptor to specify a query method and a QL statement that is used as the criteria for selecting data from a relational database. The <query> element has two subelements. These are <query-method> and <ejb-ql>.

The <query-method> subelement specifies the method that is invoked to execute the QL statement. The <ejb-ql> subelement defines the search criteria.

The <query-method> subelement itself has two subelements. These are the <method-name> subelement and the <method-params> subelement. The <method-name> subelement specifies the name of the method and the <method-params> subelement identifies parameters, if any, that are passed to the method. Each parameter is described by type in the <method-param> subelement.

The <ejb-ql> subelement of the <query> element contains a SQL statement that is used to retrieve information from the database. A question mark is used as a placeholder for a parameter passed to the method, if a parameter is passed to the method.

Listing 12-17 illustrates how to define a <query> element that specifies a method that does not have a parameter. In this example, RetrieveRoster is the name of the method. The <method-params> subelement does not contain a value because the RetrieveRoster method doesn't receive a parameter. The <ejb-ql> subelement contains the QL statement that retrieves the roster from the Rosters table.

Listing 12-18 shows how to define a <query> element that specifies a method that receives one parameter. In this example, the findbyCompany method receives a String as a parameter. The parameter then replaces the question mark in the <ejb-ql> subelement's QL statement. The QL statement retrieves the company object from the vendor table where the company matches the parameter.

Listing 12-17
Defining a
<query>
element
without a
parameter.

```
<query>
   <query-method>
      <method-name>RetrieveRoster</method-name>
      <method-params></method-params>
   </query-method>
   <ejb-ql>
      SELECT OBJECT(r) FROM Rosters As r
   </ejb-ql>
</query>
```

Listing 12-18
Defining a
<query>
element with
a parameter.

```
<query>
   <query-method>
      <method-name>findbyCompany</method-name>
      <method-params>
         <method-param>java.lang.String</method-param>
      </method-params>
   </query-method>
   <ejb-ql>
      SELECT OBJECT (v) FROM vendor v WHERE v.company = ?
   </ejb-ql>
</query>
```

Relationship Elements

An entity bean can model relationships similar to those found in the relational database model (see Part II). Relationships are divided into two groups. These are cardinality and directional. There are four types of cardinality relationships. These are

- One-to-one
- One-to-many
- Many-to-one
- Many-to-many

Each of these cardinality relationships has one of two directions, which are unidirectional or bidirectional. A unidirectional relationship is one where the relationship flows in one direction. For example, a customer places an order. The order doesn't place a customer; therefore, the customer-to-order relationship is unidirectional.

In contrast, a bidirectional relationship is one where the relationship flows in both directions. This is the case between a customer and a sales representative. A customer initiates contact with a sales representative and a sales representative can initiate contact with a customer.

The relationships are defined in the deployment descriptor using the <relationships> element, which is illustrated in Listing 12-19. In this example, the deployment descriptor defines a bidirectional, one-to-one relationship between myEJB and yourEJB. Keep in mind that a real-word deployment descriptor would have more statements than those shown in this example, to specify how one or more EJBs are to be deployed.

This example begins by defining two enterprise beans using the <enterprise-beans> element and <entity> subelement. Once the EJBs are defined, the deployment descriptor uses the <ejb-relationship> element to define the relationship between these EJBs. Two relationship roles are defined, which are myEJB to yourEJB and yourEJB to myEJB.

The first of these relationship roles are defined using the <ejb-relationship-role> element. There are three subelements in the <ejb-relationship-role> element. These are the <ejb-relationship-role-name>, <multiplicity>, the <ejb-relationship-role-source>, and the <cmr-field> subelements.

The <ejb-relationship-role-name> subelement specifies the name for the relationship role that is being defined. The first relationship role is named myEJB-one-yourEJB. The <multiplicity> subelement is used to define the relationship. The value of the <multiplicity> subelement is either One or Many, which reflects one of the cardinality relationships.

The <ejb-relationship-role-source> subelement identifies the EJB that is initiating the relationships, which is myEJB in the first relationship role and, later, yourEJB in the second relationship role. The <cmr-field> subelement contains the <cmr-field-name> element. The <cmr-field-name> element identifies the field name common to both EJBs that is used to create the relationship between the EJBs. In this example, homeID is the common field.

If the relationship is unidirectional, a second relationship role doesn't need to be defined in the deployment descriptor. However, this example is bidirectional and therefore the yourEJB-to-myEJB relationship role is defined.

```
<ejb-jar>
   <enterprise-beans>
      <entity>
      <ejb-name>myEJB</ejb-name>
      <local-home>com.ejb.myejb.myEJBHomeLocal</local-home>
      <local>com.ejb.myejb.myEJBLocal</local>
      </entity>
      <entity>
      <ejb-name>yourEJB</ejb-name>
      <local-home>com.ejb.yourejb.yourEJBHomeLocal</local-home>
      <local>com.ejb.yourejb.mathGrade.yourEJBLocal</local>
      </entity>
   </enterprise-beans>
   <relationships>
      <ejb-relation>
        <ejb-relation-name>myEJB-yourEJB</ejb-relation-name>
        <ejb-relationship-role>
        <ejb-relationship-role-name>myEJB-one-yourEJB</ejb-relationship-role-name>
         <multiplicity>One</multiplicity>
         <ejb-relationship-role-source>
           <ejb-name>myEJB</ejb-name>
         </ejb-relationship-role-source>
         <cmr-field>
          <cmr-field-name>homeID</cmr-field-name>
         </cmr-field>
        </ejb-relationship-role>
        <ejb-relationship-role>
        <ejb-relationship-role-name>yourEJB-one-myEJB</ejb-relationship-role-name>
         <multiplicity>One</multiplicity>
         <ejb-relationship-role-source>
           <ejb-name>yourEJB</ejb-name>
         </ejb-relationship-role-source>
        </ejb-relationship-role>
      </relationships>
    </ejb-relation>
  </ejb-jar>
```

Assembly Elements

The <assembly-descriptor> element is the second major section of the <ejb-jar> element. The first is the <enterprise-beans> element, which was discussed previously in this chapter. The <assembly-descriptor> element specifies method permissions, logical security roles, and transaction attributes. The <assembly-descriptor> element contains three subelements. These are <method-permission>, <security-role>, and <container-transactions>.

The <method-permission> is an optional subelement that describes security roles that can call an EJB's method. There are three subelements in the <method-permission> subelement. These are <description>, <role-name>, and <method>. The <description> subelement is the only one of the three subelements that is optional.

The <security-role> subelement is also optional and is used to define the security role that is used when accessing an EJB. There are two subelements within the <security-role> subelement. These are <description> and <role-name>. The <description> subelement is optional and the <role-name> subelement, is used to define the security role.

The <container-transactions> subelement is optional and is used to specify transaction attributes that apply to a method. There are three subelements contained within the <container-transactions> subelement. These are <description>, <method>, and <trans-attribute>. The <description> subelement is optional, and there must be at least one <method> subelement and only one <trans-attribute>. Session EJBs do not require a <container-transactions> subelement if the session EJB manages its own transactions; otherwise, a <container-transactions> subelement is necessary. All remote and home interface methods of an entity EJB must have a <container-transaction> subelement.

Method Permissions

Security roles and method permissions work together to specify that a role can invoke an EJB method. A role defines permissions a group of users have to call a method. As mentioned previously in this chapter, each security role has a <role-name> subelement that identifies the security role. The value associated with the <role-name> subelement is considered a label that has no relationship to security role names used in an environment.

For example, a <role-name> might have the value "Manager," but there isn't a "Manager" security role name in the environment's security mechanism. That is, the environment doesn't have a user group called "Manager" that is assigned specific rights.

However, you can assign values to the <role-name> subelement that correspond to security role names used in the environment's security mechanism, although there isn't a direct connection between them.

The <method-permission> subelement maps security roles to methods in the EJB's home interface and remote interface. Listing 12-20 illustrates how to define security roles and map them to method permissions.

This example specifies two method permissions. The first maps the Director security role to all the methods of the myEJB EJB. The asterisk is used in the <ejb-name> subelement as a wildcard indicating all methods of the EJB. The second maps the Faculty security role to a single method of the myEJB EJB. This is the getRoster method, as indicated in the <method-name> subelement.

This means that anyone having the Director security role can access all the methods of the myEJB EJB, including the getRoster method. However, those with the Faculty security role can access the getRoster method only.

Listing 12-20
Defining
security roles
and method
permissions.

```
<method-permission>
  <role-name>Director</role-name>
  <method>
    <ejb-name>myEJB</ejb-name>
    <method-name>*</method-name>
  </method>
</method-permission>
<method-permission>
  <role-name>Faculty</role-name>
  <method>
    <ejb-name>myEJB</ejb-name>
    <method-name>getRoster</method-name>
  </method>
</method-permission>
```

Security permissions are normally validated before access is given to a method. However, EJB 2.0 enables you to activate or deactivate this validation process by placing the <unchecked/> subelement in the <method-permission> subelement. Notice that <unchecked/> is an empty element. That is, the open and close tags are one.

Listing 12-21 illustrates how the <unchecked/> subelement is specified. Only the methods within the <method-permission> subelement are affected by the <unchecked/> subelement.

Listing 12-21
Defining
security roles
and method
permissions.

```
<method-permission>
  <role-name>Director</role-name>
  <method>
    <ejb-name>myEJB</ejb-name>
    <method-name>*</method-name>
  </method>
</method-permission>
<method-permission>
  <unchecked/>
  <role-name>Faculty</role-name>
  <method>
    <ejb-name>myEJB</ejb-name>
    <method-name>getRoster</method-name>
  </method>
</method-permission>
```

EJB 2.0 reintroduced the <runas> element that was originally included in EJB 1.0 but abandoned in EJB 1.1 because the vendor had a difficult time implementing it. The <runas> element is a subelement within the <security-identity> element.

The <runas> specifies the security identity that the EJB must run under. This is illustrated in Listing 12-22. In this example, myEJB runs under the Director security role.

Listing 12-22
Specifying <run-as> subelement in the <security-identity> element.

```
<entity>
   <ejb-name>myEJB</ejb-name>
   <security-identity>
     <run-as>
       <role-name>Director</role-name>
     </run-as>
   </security-identity>
</entity>
```

Transaction Elements

Many EJBs are designed to perform a transaction. A transaction is to execute a unit of work that may involve multiple tasks. However, the unit of work isn't completed unless all the tasks are successfully executed. If one task fails, the transaction fails and all successfully completed tasks of the transaction must be rolled back.

An EJB developer can declare a transaction using the deployment descriptor rather than explicitly controlling each task of the transaction within the EJB. This means that the developer can control the behavior of a transaction without modifying the business logic of the EJB.

Tasks of a transaction are defined as EJB methods. More than one EJB can take part in a transaction. Then, every EJB that participates in a transaction is considered to be within the transaction scope. The thread of execution of a transaction follows the transaction scope.

Let's say an order is placed. There is a four-step transaction used to process the order. First, the order message is read from the queue of incoming messages. Next, the J2EE application sends an email confirmation to the JMS queue notifying the customer that the order has been received and is being processed.

The third step in the transaction is to record the order by entering the order into the database. The final step is to send a JMS shipping order message to the warehouse to fulfill the order. If any of these steps fail, completed steps can be rolled back, which leaves the order message on the queue ready to be processed again.

Caution *In the real world, rolling back portions of a transaction that are processed by different vendors might be troublesome. For example, the JMS queue and the database are typically implemented by different vendors and therefore depend on the vendor's implementation of transactions for a rollback to be successful. Always load test a J2EE application that uses transactions to be sure that various vendor implementations don't cause problems with transactions.*

J2EE FOUNDATION

Any EJB method involved in the transaction can throw an exception that may or may not cause a rollback of the transaction. A rollback occurs only if a task needs to be reversed. Let's say that the credit card company doesn't approve the authorization in our example. Should the previous task, which examines the customer credit rating, be rolled back?

Of course not, because the examination didn't change the data in the customer's account. However, the EJB method could have posted the transaction to the customer's account at the same time as the credit check. In this scenario, a rollback is necessary to remove the transaction from the customer's account.

EJB Transaction Attributes   An EJB server will manage a transaction based on the EJB's transaction attribute when the EJB is deployed. This is referred to as Container managed. A transaction attribute can apply at the EJB level or the method level. All methods of the EJB are affected by the transaction attribute at the EJB level, while only specified methods are affected at the method level.

An EJB's transaction attribute is defined in the deployment descriptor by assigning one of the following values to the transaction attribute. Table 12-4 lists the transaction context the Container passes to the business method and resource managers based on the function of the transaction.

- **Mandatory**   The EJB must be within the transaction scope of the calling EJB (or client). A TransactionRequiredException (remote client) or TransactionRequiredLocalException (local client) is thrown if the calling EJB (or client) is not in the scope of a transaction.

- **Never**   The EJB must not be within a transaction scope. The EJB throws a RemoteException (remote client) or an EJBException (local client) if the calling EJB (or client) is involved in a transaction.

- **NotSupported**   The EJB and EJBs it calls are not within the transaction scope. The transaction is suspended while the EJB executes, and resumes once the EJB's execution is completed.

- **Required**   The EJB must be invoked within a transaction. The EJB can be part of another transaction or create its own transaction when called. The new transaction scope contains the EJB and EJBs it calls.

- **RequiresNew**   A new transaction is started when the EJB is called regardless if the calling EJB (or client) is part of an existing transaction. An existing transaction is suspended if it exists until the new transaction is completed.

- **Supports**   The EJB is included in the transaction scope. The EJB and EJBs it calls are part of the transaction. The EJB can interact with clients and EJBs that are not part of the transaction.

| Caution | *The EJB must be able to function with or without a transaction.* |

Transaction Attribute	Client	Associated with Business Method	Associated with Resource Managers
NotSupported	None	None	None
NotSupported	Passed with Client Request	None	None
Required	None	Initiated by Container	Initiated by Container
Required	Passed with Client Request	Passed with Client Request	Passed with Client Request
Supports	None	None	None
Supports	Passed with Client Request	Passed with Client Request	Passed with Client Request
RequiresNew	None	Initiated by Container	Initiated by Container
RequiresNew	Passed with Client Request	Initiated by Container	Initiated by Container
Mandatory	None	Error	Not Available
Mandatory	Passed with Client Request	Passed with Client Request	Passed with Client Request
Never	None	None	None
Never	Passed with Client Request	Error	Not Available

Table 12-4. *Transaction Context Passed by the Container to Business Method and Resource Managers*

Listing 12-23 illustrates how to set the transaction attribute in the deployment descriptor. This example contains only an abbreviated deployment descriptor. A typical deployment descriptor contains many more statements than appear here, as you learned in the deployment descriptor section of this chapter.

A transaction is defined in the <container-transaction> element of the deployment descriptor, which is a subelement of the <assembly-descriptor>. There are two general components of the <container-transaction> element. These are defined in the <method> subelement and the <trans-attribute> subelement.

The <method> subelement identifies the EJB and the EJB's method whose transaction attribute is being set. The <ejb-name> subelement identifies the name of the EJB and the <method-name> subelement identifies the method. The <trans-attribute> subelement identifies the value of the transaction attribute.

Two transaction attributes are set in Listing 12-23. The first one is set for all the methods of the myEJB EJB. The transaction attribute is set to Never, which means none of the methods in myEJB can be within a transaction scope.

The other transaction attribute is for the myMethod of the yourEJB. Here, the transaction attribute is set to NotSupported, which means that the myMethod and EJB and methods it calls are not within the transaction scope.

This is all assuming you specified container-managed transactions in the <transaction-type> attribute of the EJB.

Listing 12-23
Setting the transaction attribute.

```
<ejb-jar>
  <assembly-descriptor>
    <container-transaction>
      <method>
        <ejb-name>myEJB</ejb-name>
          <method-name>*</method -name>
      </method>
      <trans-attribute>Never</trans-attribute>
    </container-transaction>
    <container-transaction>
      <method>
        <ejb-name>yourEJB</ejb-name>
          <method-name>myMethod</method -name>
      </method>
      <trans-attribute>NotSupported</trans-attribute>
    </container-transaction>
  <assembly-descriptor>
</ejb-jar>
```

Transaction Limitations Container-managed persistence (CMP) entity beans should only use either the Mandatory, Required, or RequiresNew transaction attributes to assure proper database access during the transaction. Some EJB container/server vendors may offer support for Never, Supports, and NotSupported transaction attribute values for CMP entity beans.

CMP entity beans also restrict access to collections within a transaction. A Collection object of a transaction cannot be used by another transaction. However, the Collection object can be used by another bean if the bean obtains and accesses the same transaction context.

Message-driven beans should only use either NotSupported or Required transaction attribute values since other transaction values apply only to client transactions. As you'll learn later in this chapter, message-driven beans are not called by clients.

Exclude List Element

EJB 2.0 introduced another way to disable access to a method—by using the <exclude-list> element. The <exclude-list> element specifies methods that are uncallable. Attempts to invoke a method that is uncallable requires clients to receive either a java.rmi.RemoteException or javax.ejb.AccessLocalException, depending on whether a remote client or local client attempted to invoke the method.

Listing 12-24 illustrates how to specify the <exclude-list> element. The <exclude-list> element is a subelement within the <assembly-descriptor> element. The <exclude-list> element requires the <method> element and related subelements within the <method> element. One of these is the <ejb-name> subelement, which identifies the EJB that contains the method(s) being excluded. Also required is the <method-name> element, which is used to specify the name of the method that is being excluded.

In this example, myMethod of the myEJB EJB is contained within the <exclude-list> element, which means that the myMethod is not callable. You can place as many methods within the <exclude-list> as is necessary according to the business rules of the J2EE application.

Listing 12-24
Specifying methods that are not to be called.

```
<ejb-jar>
  <enterprise-beans>
    <entity>
      <ejb-name>myEJB</ejb-name>
    </entity>
  </enterprise-beans>
  <assembly-descriptor>
    <exclude-list>
     <method>
      <ejb-name>myEJB</ejb-name>
      <method-name>myMethod</method-name>
     </method>
    </exclude-list>
  </assembly-descriptor>
</ejb-jar>
```

J2EE FOUNDATION

Session Java Bean

A session bean contains business logic used to provide a service to a client and exists for the duration of the client server session. A session bean terminates once the session with the client server terminates.

A session bean can be stateless or stateful. A stateless session bean doesn't retain state between method calls and typically performs business logic that doesn't require data to be maintained during the session. This means that a client server can call any instances of a stateless session bean. It is common for an EJB container to create a pool of instances of a stateless session bean. The pool size is controlled by the deployment descriptor.

A stateful session bean retains data (state) between method calls with a client during a session. When calls are made to multiple methods, the stateful session bean is able to retain state between calls. This means the second method call between the client and the session bean can access data from its first method call.

The session bean can implement the SessionSynchronization interface, which makes the container notify the session bean of transaction-related events. Multiple instances of a session bean can exist; however, the state of each session bean is exclusive to an instance, and therefore each instance accesses its own state. Implementing SessionSychronization is optional. Simply stated, if you implement SessionSychronization, the container will notify the bean of three transactional events: beforeBegin(), beforeCompletion(), and afterCompletion(boolean committed).

Although a stateful bean retains state during a session, a session bean by its nature is not persistent. That is, transitional state is maintained for the life of the session. Once the session terminates, the EJB container removes the handle to the session bean and in effect removes any record of the session bean's identity. This means there isn't any way for the session bean developer to retrieve the instance of the session bean and its state after the session is completed.

Stateless vs. Stateful

Before creating a session bean, you must determine if the session bean should be stateless or stateful. Stateless session beans are generally more resource efficient than a stateful session bean because a stateless session bean can be used by the EJB container to service another request instead of waiting for the next method call.

A stateless session bean is shared amongst clients. In contrast, a stateful session bean is dedicated to a client. The more clients that use the stateful session bean, the more resources that are necessary to support those clients, and stateful session beans must be moved in and out of memory if there is insufficient memory to hold all instances of the stateful session bean.

Although a stateless session bean utilizes resources more efficiently than a stateful session bean, a stateless session bean can participate in a transaction the same way a stateful one can. If a stateless session bean needs to share data between calls, you should make a stateful session bean. Both deal with transactions the same way.

Creating a Session Java Bean

A session bean is a Java class that implements the SessionBean interface. The SessionBean interface requires that five methods be defined in the session bean class. These are ejbActivate(), ejbPassivate(), ejbRemove(), setSessionContext(SessionContext), ejbCreate(), and methods that contain business logic. The EJB container calls each of these methods at an appropriate time during the life of the session bean.

Listing 12-25 contains a skeleton of a session bean class. Although each method in this listing simply displays a brief message, they would normally execute appropriate statements in a real-world session bean class.

The ejbActivate() method is called whenever the session bean is removed from the pool and is referenced by a client. You should place routines in the ejbActivate() method that reacquire resources that were released when the session bean entered the passive state. A passive state occurs between method calls during a session.

The ejbPassivate() method is called before the instance enters the "passive" state when the session bean is returned to the object pool and should contain routines that release resources. Those resources can be required when the ejbActivate() method is called

The ejbRemove() method is called just before the bean is available for garbage collection. This is when the session bean is removed from the object pool (removed from memory). You should place routines in this method that release resources that were encumbered during the life of the session bean. The setSessionContext(SessionContext ctx) method is called before any business methods are called. This is where transactions are managed and accessed. The SessionContext object contains a variety of methods such as getEnvironment(), which returns a Properties objects. The Quick Reference Guide at the end of this chapter contains a complete listing of SessionContext methods.

The create() in the Home interface obtains a reference to a session bean from the EJB container. The session bean could be from the object pool or a new instance. The ejbCreate() method is used to initialize fields of the EJB instances and must have parameters that match the create() method in the Home interface.

The ejbCreate() method should take the form of ejbCreateSuffix(), where Suffix represents the action of the method. For example, the suffix ByCustomerID can be used in the name of the ejbCreate() method as ejbCreateByCustomerID().

| **Caution** | *The ejbCreateSuffix() cannot be used in EJB 1.1. This convention is used in EJB 2.0.* |

The myMethod() method is a method that contains business logic that is customized to the service provided by the EJB. You can replace myMethod() with one or multiple methods as required by the J2EE application. However, be sure to declare those methods in the Remote interface. Once the session bean is defined, you must reference the session bean in the deployment descriptor, as discussed previously in this chapter.

Listing 12-25
A code skeleton of a session bean.

```
import javax.ejb.*;
public class MyEJBBean implements SessionBean {
    public void ejbActivate()
    {
        System.out.println("Called ejbActivate()");
    }
    public void ejbRemove()
```

```
{
    System.out.println("Called ejbRemove()");
}
public void ejbPassivate()
{
    System.out.println("Called ejbPassivate()");
}
public void setSessionContext(SessionContext ctx)
{
    System.out.println("Called setSessionContext()");
}
public void ejbCreate ()
{
  System.out.println("Called ejbCreate()");
}
public String myMethod ()
{
  return("Called myMethod()");
}
}
```

Entity Java Bean

An entity bean is considered the powerhouse of a J2EE application because an entity bean is used to manage a collection of data retrieved from a database and stored in memory. An entity bean inserts, updates, and removes data while maintaining the integrity of the data.

Data collected and managed by an entity bean is referred to as *persistent data* and is managed in one of two ways: using Bean-Managed Persistence (BMP) or Container-Managed Persistence (CMP). BMP requires the bean to manage persistence and CMP requires the container to do the same. The EJB container synchronizes data stored in memory by the entity bean with the database. An entity bean is considered light on business logic and heavy on data management.

The entity bean developer uses JDBC API (see Part II) within the entity bean to interact with a relational database or uses other methods to access nonrelational databases. Alternatively, the entity bean developer can call a data access object to access data. Multiple clients can share an entity bean simultaneously.

An entity bean can have a remote interface, a local interface, or both interfaces. A remote interface enables remote clients to access the entity bean while the local interface provides access to clients running within the same environment. Typically, a remote interface is used by a client not located in the EJB container and Local is used by clients within the same EJB container. Local calls to an entity bean reduce the overhead commonly occurring in remote method invocations.

Container-Managed Persistence

A CMP entity bean is heavily dependent on support from the EJB container. The EJB container synchronizes the state of the entity bean with the database. However, EJB container support varies by vendor. Most vendors support automatic persistence between the entity bean and a relational database. A few vendors support more sophisticated object-to-relational mapping, which is where objects are automatically synchronized to a relational database.

There are three groups of methods that are typically contained in an entity bean. These are creation methods, business methods, and callback methods. Here's how the creation methods operate. The client calls the EJBHome client method, which causes the EJB container to call the ejbCreate() method. The default values are then set by the CMP entity bean, and the EJB container extracts field values from the CMP entity bean. Next, the EJB container creates both a representation in the database and a new Remote object, commonly referred to as a *wrapper*. Once this is completed, the EJB container calls the ejbPostCreate() method and the primary key becomes valid. The CMP entity bean performs any additional initialization that is required and the EJB container creates a new EJB instance before the remote reference is returned to the client.

Business methods are methods that are unique to the J2EE application. There are two general types of business methods in an entity bean. These are getXXX and setXXX, where XXX is the type of object that is either being retrieved from a database or written to a database. For example, the getProduct() method retrieves product information from a database. Likewise, the setProduct(Product prod) method writes a Product object to the database.

Callback methods are invoked in response to events that occur. There are seven commonly used callback methods. These are setEntityContext(EntityContext), unsetEntityContext(), ejbLoad(), ejbStore(), ejbActivate(), ejbPassivate(), and ejbRemote().

The setEntityContext(EntityContext ctx) method is called immediately following the creation of the instance and sets the context that is associated with the entity. The unsetEntityContext() method is called when the instance terminates.

A container invokes the ejbLoad() method to instruct the instance to synchronize its state by loading its state from the underlying database. The ejbStore() method is invoked by a container to instruct the instance to synchronize its state by storing it to the underlying database.

The ejbActivate() method is called whenever the instance of the entity bean is activated from its "passive" state. You should place routines in the ejbActivate() method that reacquire resources that were released when the entity bean entered the passive state. A passive state occurs between calls to the entity bean.

J2EE FOUNDATION

The ejbPassivate() method is called before the instance enters the "passive" state and should contain routines that release resources. Those resources can be required when the ejbActivate() method is called.

The ejbRemove() method is called immediately before the entity terminates by either the client or by the EJB container. You should place routines in this method that release resources that were encumbered during the life of the entity bean.

Listing 12-26 illustrates the skeleton of an entity bean. In this example, there are only two business methods, which are getProduct() and setProduct(Product prod). These retrieve product information and write product information to the underlying database. A real-world entity bean will have more than two business methods, based on the requirements of the J2EE application.

Listing 12-26
A skeleton of an entity bean.

```
import javax.ejb.EntityBean;
import javax.ejb.EntityContext;
public class myEJB implements EntityBean {
  int ID;
  private Product myProduct;
  public void ejbPostCreate()
  {
  }
  public Product getProduct()
  {
    return myProduct;
  }
  public void setProduct(Product prod)
  {
    myProduct = prod;
  }
  public void setEntityContext(EntityContext cntx)
  {
  }
  public void unsetEntityContext()
  {
  }
  public void ejbLoad()
  {
  }
  public void ejbStore()
  {
  }
  public void ejbActivate()
  {
```

```
    }
    public void ejbPassivate()
    {
    }
    public void ejbRemove()
    {
    }
}
```

The CMP entity bean does not provide database access. Database access is made available through an EJB container vendor tool. The tool is used to map instance fields in the CMP entity bean to a database. There are two instance fields in this example. These are int and the dependent object Product. Listing 12-27 defines the Product object. These fields are referred to as *container-managed fields* since the EJB container synchronizes the database with the state of these fields.

A CMP entity bean can contain both instance fields and container-managed fields. However, both fields appear as instance fields in the CMP entity bean because nothing distinguishes a container-managed field from an instance field in the CMP entity bean. Container-managed fields are identified as such in the deployment descriptor.

A container-managed field must have a column in a table of a database that is of a like type. That is, an int container-managed field in a CMP entity bean must have a corresponding int or equivalent column in the database that is associated with the CMP entity bean.

One or more container-managed fields must be identified in the deployment descriptor as the primary key that is used to locate records in the database. Typically, the primary key for the database is also defined as the primary key for the CMP entity bean.

Listing 12-27
The Product object definition.

```
import java.io.Serializable;
public class Product implements Serializable
    {
    public String prodName, prodDescription;
    public Product(String prodName, String prodDescription)
    {
      this.prodName = prodName;
      this.prodDescription = prodDescription;
    }
  }
```

CMP Entity Bean Home Interface and Remote Interface

The CMP entity bean requires both home and remote interfaces. As described previously in this chapter, a client located on the same Java Virtual Machine (JVM) as the EJB uses a Local interface. A client on a different JVM interacts with the EJB by using the remote interface.

Listing 12-28 contains the home interface for the EJB defined in Listing 12-27, and Listing 12-29 contains the remote interface for this EJB. In this example, the home interface has one create() method that accepts the prodID as an argument. You can overload the create() method to have no arguments or more and/or different arguments than that shown in this example, depending on the functionality that you give to the EJB.

The create() method is used to initialize instance variables and objects prior to inserting a record into a database. The create() method is called by the EJB container and returns a null to the EJB container. It is the container's responsibility to insert a record into the database using the value of container-managed fields in the CMP bean. The insertion occurs while the create() method is invoked; afterwards, the CMP bean is said to exist. Other methods can be accessed once the CMP bean exists.

The home interface should contain one or more find methods that are used to retrieve information from a database. The way in which find methods are implemented is unique to each EJB container vendor. Vendors of EJB containers provide a tool that enables the developer to define the behavior of find methods. One of the two more common definitions is to require the developer to enter SQL commands that define the logic of a find method. The other is to require the developer to use an object-relational mapping tool to define the find methods.

The remote interface provides a definition for business methods available in the CMP bean. Each business method defined in the remote interface must have a matching business method defined in the CMP bean.

Once the CMP bean is defined, you must reference the CMP bean in the deployment descriptor as discussed previously in this chapter.

Listing 12-28
Home interface.

```
public interface myEJBHome extends javax.ejb.EJBHome {
public myEJB create (Integer prodID) throws RemoteException, CreateException;
public myEJB findByPrimaryKey(Integer prodID) throws RemoteException,
FinderException;
}
```

Listing 12-29
Remote interface.

```
import javax.ejb.EJBObject;
import java.rmi.RemoteException;

public interface myEJBRemote extends EJBObject {
public getProduct() throws RemoteException;
public setProduct(Product prod()) throws Remote Exception;
}
```

Accessing the CMP Bean

You can use the home interface or the remote interface to access the CMP bean. In both cases, the initial step is to get a reference to the CMP bean. In the home interface, an instance of the CMP bean is created by invoking the create() method, as illustrated in Listing 12-30. You can call methods of the CMP bean once the create() method returns an instance of the CMP Remote interface.

The remote interface directly calls methods of the CMP bean, as is illustrated in Listing 12-31. In this example, the getProduct() method of the CMP bean is called. This method returns an instance of the Product object.

Listing 12-30
Calling the CMP using the home interface.

```
javax.naming.Context jndiContext = new InitialContext();
Object obj = jndiContext.lookup("java:comp/env/ejb/myEJBHome");
myEJB mybean = obj.create(4321);
```

Listing 12-31
Calling the CMP using the remote interface.

```
javax.naming.Context jndiContext = new InitialContext();
Object obj = jndiContext.lookup("java:comp/env/ejb/myEJBHome");
Product prod = obj.getProduct();
```

Bean-Managed Persistence

A bean-managed persistence (BMP) bean uses the JDBC API or another appropriate database API to interface with the database. However, these interactions take place under the direction of the EJB container. That is, the EJB container tells the BMP bean when to insert a new record, retrieve data, modify data, or delete data. The developer of the BMP bean must define methods within the BMP bean that respond to requests received from the EJB container. You should use a BMP bean when you need complex relationship fields instead of simple persistence fields.

There are typically a minimum of five methods defined in a BMP bean, as illustrated in Listing 12-32. These are ejbLoad(), ejbStore(), ejbCreate(), ejbRemote(), and findXXX()

The ejbLoad() method must contain code that reads data from a database. Similarly, the ejbStore() method writes data to a database. The ejbCreate() method must have code that inserts a new record in a database and the ejbRemote() removes a record from the database. The findXXX() method contains code that locates one or more records in the database. The XXX identifies the kind of information the method locates. In this example there is one find method, which is findProduct(), and it requires the product identification number as an argument. You can have any number of findXXX() methods in a BMP bean, as required by the nature of the project.

The BMP bean uses the same home interface and remote interface as is used for the CMP bean. Once the BMP bean is defined, you must reference the BMP bean in the deployment descriptor, as discussed previously in this chapter.

Listing 12-32
A skeleton
of a bean-
managed
persistence
bean.

```
public class myBMPBean implements EntityBean
{
   public void ejbLoad()
   {
      //Read data from database
   }
   public void ejbStore()
   {
      //Save data to a database
   }
   public void ejbCreate()
   {
      //Insert a record into the database
   }
   public void ejbRemote()
   {
      //Remove a record from a database
   }
   public Product findProduct(Integer prod)
   {
      //Find the specified product
   }
}
```

Message-Driven Bean

A message-driven bean MDB is designed for clients to invoke server-side business logic using asynchronous communication, which is a special case of a stateless session bean, described previously in this chapter.

There isn't any home interface or remote interface for a MDB. Instead, a MDB monitors Java Message Service communications and reacts to messages sent by clients. Clients don't directly access a MDB. Instead, the MDB intercedes and processes requests anonymously. This is possible because a MDB is stateless. Therefore, the EJB container can begin a new instance of the MDB when the message is received or use an existing instance of the MDB from the instance pool. And unlike a session bean or entity bean, a client does not control the life of an MDB. The EJB container handles the responsibility for creating and removing an MDB.

Requests from clients are sent via JMS. The EJB container listens for messages in the JMS service that MDBs are registered to receive. The developer must provide all the logic to process a message in the onMessage() method. The JMS service enables the client and MDB to work independently and without having to wait until the other is finished processing. The MDB doesn't know anything about the client. You'll learn the details on how JMS works in Chapter 17.

An MDB processes a client request by using business methods defined in the MDB and by invoking business methods defined in other EJBs. This means an MDB is scalable, because an MDB is stateless and efficient by using asynchronous messaging while still maintaining functionality.

Before the introduction of MDBs, developers wrote their own queue processing code, which was not standardized. MDB introduced a standard way to process messages handled by the EJB container and JMS. Developers can focus on coding business logic rather than on queue processing.

Behind the Scenes

An advantage of using an MDB is that the EJB container does most of the work for you. As previously mentioned, clients send requests in the form of a JMS message to the JMS service. The EJB container acts as the intermediary between JMS service and the MDB.

The EJB container makes a connection to the JMS service and registers to receive JMS messages that have a particular JMS topic or that are on a particular JMS message queue (see Chapter 18), depending on if a client uses JMS topics or a JMS message queue to send a request for service.

The EJB container then creates a TopicSubscriber object or QueueReceiver object, depending on how JMS messages are handled by the JMS server. The TopicSubscriber object or QueueReceiver object is then used to receive JMS messages from clients. The EJB container knows which receiver object to create because the receiver object is specified in the MDB deployment descriptor.

The EJB container also registers the message listener and sets the message acknowledge mode to respond to the JMS server when a JMS message is received by the EJB container. All this occurs behind the scenes without the MDB developer needing to write additional code in the MDB.

Creating an MDB

An MDB must define four methods. These are ejbCreate(), ejbRemove(), setMessageDrivenContext(), and onMessage(), as illustrated in Listing 12-33. The ejbCreate() method is called when the MDB is created by the container first invoked by the EJB container, but not when a JMS message is received from a client. The ejbRemove() is called by the EJB container when the container terminates the instance of the MDB.

The setMessageDrivenContext() method creates the context for the MDB, which is similar to the session and entity context classes. And the onMessage() method is called each time the EJB container receives a JMS message from a client, as discussed previously in this chapter.

Listing 12-33
A skeleton of
an MDB.

```
import javax.ejb.MessageDrivenBean;
import javax.ejb.MessageDrivenContext;
import javax.jms.MessageListener;
import javax.jms.Message;
public class myMDB implements MessageListener, MessageDrivenBean {
  public void setMessageDrivenContext(MessageDrivenContext mdc)
  {
  }
  public void ejbCreate()
  {
  }
  public void ejbRemove()
  {
  }
  public void onMessage(Message clientMessage)
  {
  }
}
```

The onMessage() method is where the MDB processes messages received indirectly from a client. Any type of stateless process can be included in this method. The simplest form of processing is to display incoming messages on the screen. Listing 12-34 shows how this is done.

In this example, the message from the client is passed to the onMessage() method in the form of a Message object, which is called clientMessage in this sample code. The onMessage() method determines if the clientMessage is a TextMessage object. If so, the message is assigned to an instance TextMessage object called tmpMesg. The body of the message, if the type is a TextMessage object, is then retrieved using the getText() method and is displayed on the screen. If the clientMessage isn't a TextMessage object, the name of the class is retrieved and displayed on the screen. Any JMSException errors that are thrown are trapped by the catch { } block. Once the MDB bean is defined, you must reference the MDB bean in the deployment descriptor as discussed previously in this chapter.

Listing 12-34
An onMessage()
method
displays the
message
received from
a client.

```
public void onMessage(Message clientMessage) {
  TextMessage tmpMesg = null;
  try {
    if (clientMessage instanceof TextMessage) {
      tmpMesg = (TextMessage) clientMessage;
```

```
        System.out.println("Incoming Message: " + tmpMesg.getText());
    }
    else
    {
     System.out.println("Incorrect Message: "
        + clientMessage.getClass().getName());
    }
  }
  catch (JMSException error)
  {
   System.out.println("Error: " + error.getMessage());
  }
}
```

The JAR File

EJB classes and related files are packaged together into a Java Archive (JAR) file for deployment. The JAR file is a compressed file format that was originally designed to reduce the size of software so it could be easily be transported.

The JAR file used to package an EJB must contain the following; however, it is customary to keep dependent classes and dependent interfaces in different JAR files. In either case, the dependent classes and dependent interfaces must be in the runtime CLASSPATH.

- EJB classes
- Dependent classes
- Remote interface
- Home interface
- Dependent interfaces
- Primary key class
- Deployment descriptor

In addition, the deployment descriptor must be located in the META-INF/ejb-jar.xml path. This means that you place the deployment descriptor in the META-INF/ejb-jar.xml directory before archiving the EJB package. Classes must retain the directory structure associated with the package names.

You can use the JAR utility by entering **jar cf** followed by name of the JAR file, and then followed by the path and names of files that will be archived.

Quick Reference Guide

This Quick Reference Guide provides a brief overview of Java classes used with EJB. Full details of these classes and all Java classes and interfaces are available at java.sun.com.

Syntax	Descriptions
void ejbActivate()	Called when the instance is activated from its "passive" state.
void ejbPassivate()	Called before the instance enters the "passive" state.
void ejbRemove()	Called before the EJB container ends the session object.
void setSessionContext (SessionContext con)	Sets the associated session context.

Table 12-5.   *Public Interface Session Bean Extends Enterprise Bean*

Syntax	Descriptions
void ejbActivate()	Called when an instance is removed from the pool of instances to become associated with a specific EJB object.
void ejbLoad()	Instructs the instance to synchronize its state by loading its state from the underlying database.
void ejbPassivate()	Called by the EJB container before an instance becomes disassociated with an EJB object.
void ejbRemove()	Called before the EJB container removes the EJB object associated with the instance.
void ejbStore()	Instructs the instance to synchronize its state by storing it to the underlying database.
void setEntityContext (EntityContext ctx)	Sets the associated entity context.
void unsetEntityContext()	Unsets the associated entity context.

Table 12-6.   *Public Interface Entity Bean Extends Enterprise Bean*

Syntax	Descriptions
void ejbRemove()	This method is called before the EJB container ends the life of the message-driven object.
void setMessageDrivenContext (MessageDrivenContext con)	Sets the associated message-driven context.

Table 12-7. *Public Interface Message-Driven Bean Extends Enterprise Bean*

Syntax	Descriptions
EJBMetaData getEJBMetaData()	Obtains the EJB's EJBMetaData interface.
HomeHandle getHomeHandle()	Obtains a handle for the remote home object.
void remove(Handle handle)	Removes an EJB object identified by its handle.
void remove(Object primaryKey)	Removes an EJB object identified by its primary key.

Table 12-8. *Public Interface EJB Home Extends java.rmi.Remote*

Syntax	Descriptions
EJBHome getEJBHome()	Obtains the EJB remote home interface.
Class getHomeInterfaceClass()	Obtains the Class object for the EJB remote home interface.
Class getPrimaryKeyClass()	Obtains the Class object for the EJB primary key class.
Class getRemoteInterfaceClass()	Obtains the Class object for the EJB remote interface.
boolean isSession()	Tests if the EJB type is "session."
boolean isStatelessSession()	Tests if the EJB type is "stateless session."

Table 12-9. *Public Interface EJB Metadata*

The
Complete
Reference

J2EE

Part IV

J2EE Interconnectivity

The glue that holds J2EE technologies together is its interconnectivity ability. This ability fosters communication among server-side components and between server-side components and client applications. Interconnectivity is made possible through the use of Java APIs that have been incorporated into the J2EE specification.

These include Java Mail, Java IDL/CORBA, Java Remote Method Invocation, Java Message Service, Java Security, Java Naming and Directory Interface.

In Part IV of this book you'll explore these APIs and learn how to implement them in your J2EE component or client application.

The Complete Reference

J2EE

Chapter 13

JavaMail API

W eb services built using J2EE components fulfill a variety of services based on the needs of a J2EE application. One of those needs might be to send and receive email messages. Let's say that a J2EE application may want to send a personal email message to all customers who have purchased a particular product. Based on business rules, the J2EE application probably sends the request along with an email message and mailing list identifier to a JSP or Java servlet web services component for processing. It is the responsibility of the web services component to create and generate those email messages.

Likewise, a web services component might be required to automatically retrieve email messages and, based on business rules, those email messages are forwarded to a client or responded to automatically by the web services component.

You can develop web service components, using J2EE technology, that interact with email messages by using the JavaMail API. JavaMail API is one of the Java interconnectivity technologies that you'll learn in Part III. You'll begin by learning about JavaMail in this chapter. Forthcoming chapters in this part explore other Java interconnectivity technologies that can be used to communicate between web services.

JavaMail

Email is probably the most widely used method of communication. In the near future, more messages will be carried by email than by the postal service. A J2EE application is able to send and receive email messages through the use of the JavaMail API.

The JavaMail API is protocol independent and can send messages created by a J2EE application via email using existing email protocols. Likewise, the JavaMail API can receive email messages and make those messages available to a J2EE application for future processing, such as displaying the message on the screen.

A developer can create a Mail User Agent (MUA) as part of a J2EE application. A MUA is a program that enables a person or component to compose, send, and receive email messages. A Mail Transfer Agent (MTA) uses one of several email protocols to transport email messages. JavaMail API is used to create a MUA. Think of MUA as an email client such as Microsoft Outlook and MTA as an email server such as sendmail. The MUA composes, sends, and receives email from your local mail server or ISP and then the MTA, located on the server, transports the email message to its final destination.

JavaMail API and Java Activation Framework

The latest JavaMail API requires Java Activation Framework (JAF), which is downloaded separately from java.sun.com. JAF contains services to determine the type of data that is associated with an email. This enables the program to call the appropriate EJB to process the data. Let's say that an email attachment is a BMP image. JAF identifies it as such, enabling the program to display the BMP image.

Caution *JDK 1.4 throws compile errors when compiling JAF classes. This is a bug. Keep checking the Sun web site for patches to fix this problem.*

 Protocols

A protocol is a standard way of doing something. In the case of email, protocols provide a standard way to format an email message. There are four protocols used for emails. These are Multipurpose Internet Mail Extensions (MIME), Simple Mail Transfer Protocol (SMTP), Post Office Protocol (POP3), and Internet Message Access Protocol (IMAP).

MIME is the protocol used to send multipart emails where each part of the multipart email defines its own formatting such as an email message that contains an attachment. Similarly, the Secure Multipurpose Internet Mail Extensions (S/MIME) protocol is used to encode multipart email messages for secure transmission. The MUA determines which of these protocols to use.

The SMTP is the protocol used to deliver email messages. The MUA sends an email message to an SMTP server that is provided by an Internet service provider (ISP) or by the business that is using the J2EE application. The SMTP server is responsible for forwarding the message to the recipient's SMTP server.

The recipient's MUA retrieves the email message from the recipient's SMTP server and then processes the message by making the message available to the recipient the next time the email account (also known as a mailbox) is checked. Sometimes the email message must be sent to several SMTP servers before reaching the recipient's SMTP server. This is possible by using SMTP servers that are open relays to other SMTP servers.

POP3 is a store-and-forward service where email messages are stored on the mail server until the client logs in to receive them. The email messages are then downloaded to the client and deleted from the server. In contrast, IMAP functions similar to a remote file server where a client views email on the server. Deleting a local copy of the email message does not delete the email message from the server. Continuous interaction between client and server causes IMAP to require lots of overhead when compared to POP3.

 JavaMail API interacts with protocols that are available on clients and servers used to transport email messages. JavaMail API cannot change the protocols used by a client or server, nor can JavaMail API increase the capability of a protocol. Simply stated, JavaMail API cannot use a feature that isn't supported by a protocol.

Exceptions

In an effort to make the basic concepts of JavaMail easy to understand, exception handling is not included in examples in this chapter. However, a fully implemented JavaMail program must be prepared to handle each of the 11 commonly encountered exceptions that might be thrown by the program.

Three of these exceptions are related to the folder that is used to store the email message. These are the ReadOnlyFolderException, FolderClosedException, and FolderNotFoundException. The ReadOnlyFolderException is thrown when the program attempts to open a folder for read-write access, but the folder is marked for read only. The FolderClosedException is thrown whenever the Messaging object and the folder that owns the Messaging object are terminated and the program attempts to open the folder. And the FolderNotFoundException is thrown whenever a Folder method is called to interact with a folder that does not exist.

Next is a trio of general exceptions. These are the MessagingException, the AuthenticationFailedException, and the MethodNotSupportedException. The MessagingException is the base class for all exceptions that are thrown by the Messaging classes. The AuthenticationFailedException is thrown whenever authentication fails, usually due to a bad username or bad password. And the MethodNotSupportedException occurs whenever a method that is invoked by the program isn't supported by the implementation.

One of another trio of exceptions might be thrown while the program is sending an email message. These are the SendFailedException, the IllegalWriteException, and the NoSuchProviderException. The SendFailedException happens whenever the email message is unable to be set. The IllegalWriteException is thrown whenever the program attempts to write to a read-only messaging object. And the NoSuchProviderException is thrown when attempts are made to instantiate a provider that doesn't exist.

The final two exceptions happen during storage. These are the MessageRemovedException and the StoreClosedException. The MessageRemovedException is thrown whenever an invalid method is called to expunge a Message object. The StoreClosedException occurs when the store that owns a Messaging object is terminated, but a method is invoked to access the Messaging object.

Send Email Message

A J2EE component that provides email service to a client can send an email by using the JavaMail API. There are three steps required to send an email. These are to obtain a session, to create an email, and then to send the email.

However, one of the services provided by the EJB container is to create and manage a mail session. Therefore, you can use a JNDI lookup to retrieve a mail session created by the EJB container as an option to creating the email session.

Listing 13-1 illustrates how to send an email. In this example, three String objects are declared. These are host, which is assigned the smtp host; from, which is assigned the sender's email address; and to, which is assigned to the email address of the recipient.

Next, the getProperties() method is called to return the system's properties. The mail.smtp.host property is then changed to the new smtp host using the put() method. Once the smtp host is set, the program must open a session using the getDefaultInstance() method. The new session is called ses1 in this example.

The email message is formatted using MIME. Therefore, the program must create a new MimeMessage object, which is used to form the email. The MimeMessage object is called msg. The from and to String objects are then converted to InternetAddress objects, which are then passed as arguments to the setFrom() method and the addRecipient()

method, respectively. These set the Internet addresses for the email. The setSubject() method is passed the subject line of the email and the body of the email message is passed to the setText() method. The final step is to pass the MimeMessage object (msg) to the send() method of the Transport object, which transmits the email.

Listing 13-1
Sending an email using JavaMail.

```
import java.util.Properties;
import javax.mail.*;
import javax.mail.internet.*;
public class sendMail {
    public static void main (String args[]) throws Exception {
        String host = "smtp.mydomain.com";
        String from = "me@myweb.com";
        String to = "you@myweb.com";
        Properties prop = System.getProperties();
        prop.put("mail.smtp.host", host);
        Session ses1 = Session.getDefaultInstance(prop, null);
        MimeMessage msg = new MimeMessage(ses1);
        msg.setFrom(new InternetAddress(from));
        msg.addRecipient(Message.RecipientType.TO, new InternetAddress(to));
        msg.setSubject("Urgent Message");
        msg.setText("You won the lottery!");
        Transport.send(msg);
    }
}
```

Retrieving Email Messages

A J2EE component retrieves an email message by logging in to the SMTP host and then requesting reference to the INBOX folder that contains incoming email messages. Listing 13-2 illustrates how this is done.

In this example, the smtp host, username, and password are assigned to String objects. Next, the program creates an instance of a Property object, which is called prop. The Property object is passed to the getDefaultInstance() method of the Session object to create a new session.

The next step is to create a Store object using the getStore() method. The getStore() method requires one argument, which is the POP3 protocol that is used to store the email. The program then passes the host and login information to the connect() method of the Store object to log into the store.

Once logged in, the program retrieves reference to the INBOX folder using the getFolder() method. The INBOX folder is then opened for read only. The program creates an instance of the BufferedReader object called bReader, which is an input stream.

An array of messages called msg is then retrieved from the folder using the getMessage() method. Afterwards, the program steps through each message displaying the sender's name and subject line of each email message. These are retrieved using the getFrom() and getSubject() methods, respectively.

In this example, the sender's name and subject line of each email are displayed and the client is asked if he or she wants to read the email message. The response is assigned to the line1 String object and is evaluated by the if statement. The body of the email is retrieved and displayed if the response is yes.

Keep in mind that a J2EE component is not likely to interact directly with the end user. Instead, emails are likely to be returned to the requesting client or filtered for particular emails before they are returned to the requesting client.

Listing 13-2
Reading an email using JavaMail.

```
import java.io.*;
import java.util.Properties;
import javax.mail.*;
import javax.mail.internet.*;
public class retrieveEmail {
  public static void main (String args[]) throws Exception {
    String host = "smtp.mydomain.com";
    String username = "userName";
    String password = "password";
    Properties prop = new Properties();
    Session ses1 = Session.getDefaultInstance(prop, null);
    Store store1 = ses1.getStore("pop3");
    store1.connect(host, username, password);
    Folder folder1 = store1.getFolder("INBOX");
    folder1.open(Folder.READ_ONLY);
    BufferedReader bReader = new BufferedReader (new InputStreamReader(System.in));
    Message msg[] = folder1.getMessages();
    for (int i=0, n= msg.length; i<n; i++)
    {
      System.out.println(i + ": " + msg [i].getFrom()[0] "\t"
          + msg [i].getSubject());
      System.out.println("Do you want to read message? [Y/N]");
      String line1 = bReader.readLine();
      if ("Y".equals(line1))
      {
        System.out.println(msg [i].getContent());
      }
      else if ("N".equals(line1))
      {
        break;
      }
    }
    folder1.close(false);
    store1.close();
  }
}
```

Deleting Email Messages

A J2EE component requests that an email message be deleted by setting the delete flag that is associated with the message to true. Each email message has a variety of flags that are used to indicate the status of the email message. The commonly used flags are answered, draft, seen, and, of course, delete. Some flags are unique to a particular system and users define others. The JavaMail API has commonly used flags predefined in the Flags.Flag inner class.

Caution *Not all predefined flags are supported by all protocols. A good example is POP3. POP3 only supports the delete flag. You can retrieve the flags supported by a folder by calling the getPermanentFlag() method and then comparing elements of the String array returned by the getPermanentFlag() with the flag you want to set.*

Listing 13-3 illustrates how to have an email message deleted. You'll notice that this example is nearly identical to Listing 13-2. However, Listing 13-3 displays the sender and subject of the email message and then asks if the client wants to delete the email message.

Here's how this works. The Folder object called folder1 is opened in READ_WRITE mode. This is necessary because after the email message sender and subject are read, the program might change the setting of the delete flag, which is written to the folder.

Next, the program retrieves and displays the sender and subject of each email message and prompts the user to delete the email message. This is described in detail in the previous section of this chapter.

If the client selects Y, then the DELETE flag is set to true by calling the setFlag() method and passing it the name of the flag and the setting. Passing a false to the setFlag() method unsets a flag. You can determine if a flag is set to true by calling the isSet() method. Next, the deleteStatus boolean variable is set to true. The deleteStatus variable is passed to the close() method, which causes the email message to be deleted.

Caution *This technique may not be implemented by all mail server providers. Some require the use of the expunge() method of the Folder object instead of the close() method to delete an email message.*

Listing 13-3
Deleting an email using JavaMail.

```
import java.io.*;
import java.util.Properties;
import javax.mail.*;
import javax.mail.internet.*;
public class deleteEmail {
  public static void main (String args[]) throws Exception {
    String host = "pop3.mydomain.com";
    String username = "userName";
    String password = "password";
    boolean deleteStatus = false;
    Properties prop = new Properties();
```

JAVA INTERCONNECTIVITY

```
Session ses1 = Session.getDefaultInstance(prop, null);
Store store1 = ses1.getStore("pop3");
store1.connect(host, username, password);
Folder folder1 = store1.getFolder("INBOX");
folder1.open(Folder.READ_WRITE);
BufferedReader bReader = new BufferedReader (new InputStreamReader(System.in));
Message msg[] = folder1.getMessages();
for (int i=0, n= msg.length; i<n; i++)
{
  System.out.println(i + ": " + msg [i].getFrom()[0] + "\t"
      + msg [i].getSubject());
  System.out.println("Do you want to delete message? [Y/N]");
  String line1 = bReader.readLine();
  if ("Y".equals(line1))
  {
    msg[i].setFlag(Flags.Flag.DELETED, true);
    deleteStatus = true;
  }
}
folder1.close(deleteStatus);
store1.close();
}
}
```

Replying to and Forwarding an Email Message

A J2EE component can reply to an email by using the reply() method of the Message object. The reply() method copies the from address of the email message to the to address. You can indicate whether or not to reply to the sender or all recipients by passing the reply() method a boolean value where true replies to all recipients and false replies to the sender.

Listing 13-4 illustrates how to reply to an email message. This example is similar to other examples in this chapter. The program begins by initializing String objects with information needed to retrieve and reply to email messages.

Next, the program creates an instance of the Properties object called prop, by calling getProperties(). This object is passed to the getDefaultInstance() to return a Session object called session. The getStore() method is called and passed the protocol used to store email messages. In this example, the POP3 protocol is being used. The getStore() method returns a Store object called store1.

Login information is then passed to the connect() method to log into the mail server. Once the login is successful, the program calls the getFolder() method, passing the name of the folder that the program wants to reference. In this case, the INBOX folder is being retrieved. The getFolder() method returns a Folder object called folder1. The open() is then called to open the folder in READ_ONLY mode.

The program requires a buffered reader to read email messages from the INBOX folder and therefore creates an instance of the BufferedReader object, which is called reader. As described in Listing 13-2, the sender and the subject of each email message are retrieved and displayed, and the client is asked if a reply is necessary.

In this scenario, the reply is sent only to the sender by passing a boolean false to the reply() method. The program proceeds to set the from header of the reply using the setFrom() method. The original email message is retrieved as a MimeMessage object called body. Creating a StringBuffer object called buffer1, which is assigned the reply message, follows this.

Only if the original message is a MIME type, the program creates and sends the reply. In this case, the program retrieves the body of the original email message and assigns it to the String object content. Next, the String object is used to create a StringReader object, which is used to create a BufferedReader object.

The program then reads each line of the original email message and appends the line to the buffer1, which is the StringBuffer object that already contains the reply message. Notice that each line from the original email message begins with the "> ". This is a commonly used character to indicate that the line was from the original email message.

The full reply message is passed to the setText() method, which places the message in the reply object. The reply object is then passed to the send() method for transmission.

Listing 13-4
Replying to an email using JavaMail.

```
import java.io.*;
import java.util.Properties;
import javax.mail.*;
import javax.mail.internet.*;
public class replyEmail {
  public static void main (String args[]) throws Exception {
    String host = "pop3.mydomain.com";
    String sendHost = "smtp.mydomain.com";
    String username = "userName";
    String password = "password";
    String from = "me@myweb.com";
    Properties prop = System.getProperties();
    prop.put("mail.smtp.host", sendHost);
    Session session = Session.getDefaultInstance(prop, null);
    Store store1 = session.getStore("pop3");
    store1.connect(host, username, password);
    Folder folder1 = store1.getFolder("INBOX");
    folder1.open(Folder.READ_ONLY);
    BufferedReader reader = new BufferedReader (new InputStreamReader(System.in));
    Message msg[] = folder1.getMessages();
    for (int i=0, n= msg.length; i<n; i++)
    {
      System.out.println(i + ": " + msg[i].getFrom()[0]
        + "\t" + msg[i].getSubject());
      System.out.println("Do you want to reply to the message? [Y/N]");
```

```
        String line = reader.readLine();
        if ("Y".equals(line))
        {
          MimeMessage reply = (MimeMessage)msg[i].reply(false);
          reply.setFrom(new InternetAddress(from));
          MimeMessage body = (MimeMessage) msg[i];
          StringBuffer buffer1 = new StringBuffer("My reply goes here\n");
    if (body.isMimeType("text/plain"))
          {
            String content = (String)body.getContent();
            StringReader cReader = new StringReader(content);
            BufferedReader bReader = new BufferedReader(cReader);
            String cLine;
            while ((cLine = bReader.readLine()) != null)
            {
              buffer1.append("> ");
              buffer1.append(cLine);
              buffer1.append("\r\n");
            }
          }
          reply.setText(buffer1.toString());
          Transport.send(reply);
        }
        else if ("N".equals(line))
        {
          break;
        }
      }
      folder1.close(false);
      store1.close();
    }
}
```

Forwarding an Email Message

A J2EE component can forward an email message using the basic framework used to reply to an email; however, the J2EE component must build the forward email message from the original, which is illustrated in Listing 13-5.

This example is very similar to Listing 13-4. The difference is when the client responds positively to forwarding an email message. First the program creates an instance of the Message object called fwd, and then sets the subject line for the new email message. The subject begins with "Fwd:", which is the standard abbreviation used to indicate that the message is a forwarded message. The getSubject() method is called to retrieve the subject of the original email message.

The program proceeds to set the "from" and the "to" headers of the new email message. These use the from and to String objects declared at the beginning of the program. Next, the program adds a new part to the forwarded messages by creating a BodyPart object.

The setText() method is used to place the J2EE component-generated text that describes the forwarded message to the recipient. The program must create a Multipart object that will receive the parts of the forwarded email message. This is mPart. The text of the J2EE component's message is then added to the Multipart object by calling the addBodyPart() method.

Another part is created to contain the original message, which is set by calling the setDataHandler() method and passing the method to the DataHandler of the original message. The part is then added to the Multipart object by calling the addBodyPart() method. The Multipart object is then placed in the forward message by calling the setContent() method, which is then passed to the send() method for transmission.

Listing 13-5
Forwarding
to an email
using
JavaMail.

```
import java.io.*;
import java.util.Properties;
import javax.mail.*;
import javax.mail.internet.*;
public class forwardEmail {
  public static void main (String args[]) throws Exception {
    String host = "smtp host";
    String sendHost = "smtp host";
    String username = "userName";
    String password = "password";
    String from = "me@myweb.com";
    String to = "forward_to@myweb.com";
    Properties prop = System.getProperties();
    prop.put("mail.smtp.host", sendHost);
    Session session = Session.getDefaultInstance(prop, null);
    Store store1 = session.getStore("pop3");
    store1.connect(host, username, password);
    Folder folder1 = store1.getFolder("INBOX");
    folder1.open(Folder.READ_ONLY);
    BufferedReader reader = new BufferedReader (new InputStreamReader(System.in));
    Message msg[] = folder1.getMessages();
    for (int i=0; i<msg.length; i++)
    {
     System.out.println(i + ": " + msg[i].getFrom()[0]
        + "\t" + msg[i].getSubject());
     System.out.println("Do you want to forward to the message? [Y/N]");
     String line = reader.readLine();
     if ("Y".equals(line))
     {
       Message fwd = new MimeMessage(session);
       fwd.setSubject("Fwd: " + msg[i].getSubject());
       fwd.setFrom(new InternetAddress(from));
       fwd.addRecipient(Message.RecipientType.TO,new InternetAddress(to));
```

```
        BodyPart msgBP = new MimeBodyPart();
        msgBP.setText("Your message goes here. \n");
        Multipart mPart = new MimeMultipart();
        mPart.addBodyPart(msgBP);
        msgBP = new MimeBodyPart();
        msgBP.setDataHandler(msg[i].getDataHandler());
        mPart.addBodyPart(msgBP);
        fwd.setContent(mPart);
        Transport.send(fwd);
      }
     else if ("N".equals(line))
     {
      break;
     }
    }
    folder1.close(false);
    store1.close();
  }
}
```

Sending Attachments

An attachment is a resource, typically a file, that is external to the email message but is sent along with an email message. A J2EE component can send an email message with an attachment using basically the same technique that is used to forward an email message.

The J2EE component must build the email message from parts beginning with the body of the email message, and then the DataHandler for each attachment is appended to the email message. This technique is illustrated in Listing 13-6. In this example, one JPG file is attached to the email message.

The program is similar to the forward program and begins by assigning the host, to and from, and the attachment information to String objects that are later used to form the email message. Next, the program uses a Properties object called prop to set up the mail server for the email message by calling the put() method. The Properties object is also used to create an instance of the Session object, which is called ses1.

The email message called msg is then associated with the session. The setFrom(), addRecipient(), and setSubject() methods are called to set the sender, recipient, and subject of the email message.

As with the program that forwarded an email message, sending an email message with an attachment requires that the program create two message parts. The first message part is the body of the email message and the second is the attachment.

First, the setText() method is called and passed the text of the body of the email message. Next, the program needs to create the second part of the email message by initially creating a Multipart object call mPart, to which the BodyPart called msgBP is added by calling the addBodyPart() method.

The second Multipart object is created to create the second body for the email message. The data handler to the attachment must be associated with the second Multipart object. This is accomplished by creating a DataSource object called src and passing the DataSource object to the setDataHandler() method. And then the filename must be associated with the second Multipart object by calling the setFileName()method. The filename is displayed to the recipient, which is usually the original filename without the directory path—but the filename can be any string and doesn't have to match the original filename.

The parts are then combined by calling the addBodyPart() method, and the consolidated parts become the body of the email message when the setContent() is called and passed the Multipart object. The last step is to call the send() method to send the email message with the attachment.

Listing 13-6
Sending an email message with an attachment using JavaMail.

```
import java.util.Properties;
import javax.mail.*;
import javax.mail.internet.*;
import javax.activation.*;
public class sendAttachment {
  public static void main (String args[]) throws Exception {
    String host = "smtp.mydomain.com";
    String from = "me@myweb.com";
    String to = "you@myweb.com";
    String filename = "myPhoto.jpg";
    Properties prop = System.getProperties();
    prop.put("mail.smtp.host", host);
    Session ses1 = Session.getInstance(prop, null);
    Message msg = new MimeMessage(ses1);
    msg.setFrom(new InternetAddress(from));
    msg.addRecipient(Message.RecipientType.TO, new InternetAddress(to));
    msg.setSubject("Photo Attached");
    BodyPart msgBP = new MimeBodyPart();
    msgBP.setText("Take a look at this!");
    Multipart mPart = new MimeMultipart();
    mPart.addBodyPart(msgBP);
    msgBP = new MimeBodyPart();
    DataSource src = new FileDataSource(filename);
    msgBP.setDataHandler(new DataHandler(src));
    msgBP.setFileName(filename);
    mPart.addBodyPart(msgBP);
    msg.setContent(mPart);
    Transport.send(msg);
  }
}
```

Receiving Attachments

Whenever a J2EE component receives an email message that contains an attachment, the J2EE component must decompose the email message into parts and then save the part of the email message that contains the attachment.

This technique is illustrated in Listing 13-7. This example is similar to Listing 13-5 that is used to forward an email message. The difference between Listing 13-7 and Listing 13-5 is seen after the user decides to save the attachment to the email message.

The program creates a Multipart object called mPart, which is assigned the content of the email message by calling the getContent() method. Next, the program steps through the parts of the email message and extracts each part. The getDisposition() method is called to determine if the current part is an attachment or inline. If so, then the saveFile() method is called and passed the filename and the input stream. You create the saveFile() method using basic Java file I/O routines.

Listing 13-7
Receiving an email message with an attachment using JavaMail.

```java
import java.io.*;
import java.util.Properties;
import javax.mail.*;
import javax.mail.internet.*;
public class receiveAttachment{
  public static void main (String args[]) throws Exception {
    String host = "pop3.mydomain.com";
    String sendHost = "smtp.mydomain.com";
    String username = "userName";
    String password = "password";
    String from = "me@myweb.com";
    Properties prop = System.getProperties();
    prop.put("mail.smtp.host", sendHost);
    Session session = Session.getDefaultInstance(prop, null);
    Store store1 = session.getStore("pop3");
    store1.connect(host, username, password);
    Folder folder1 = store1.getFolder("INBOX");
    folder1.open(Folder.READ_ONLY);
    BufferedReader reader = new BufferedReader (new InputStreamReader(System.in));
    Message msg[] = folder1.getMessages();
    for (int i=0; i<msg.length; i++)
    {
     System.out.println(i + ": " + msg[i].getFrom()[0]
        + "\t" + msg[i].getSubject());
     System.out.println("Do you want to save attachment? [Y/N]");
     String line = reader.readLine();
     if ("Y".equals(line))
     {
       Multipart mPart = (Multipart)msg[i].getContent();
       for (int j=0; j<mPart.getCount(); j++)
       {
```

```
        Part part1 = mPart.getBodyPart(j);
        String disp1 = part1.getDisposition();
        if (disp1 != null && (disp1.equals(Part.ATTACHMENT) || disp1.equals(Part.INLINE)))
        {
          saveFile(part1.getFileName(), part1.getInputStream());
        }
      }
    }
  else if ("N".equals(line))
  {
    break;
  }
  }
  folder1.close(false);
  store1.close();
  }
}
```

Searching an Email Folder

A J2EE component is able to search an email folder for an email message that either contains or does not contain search criteria in any component of the email message. The J2EE component begins the search by creating a logical expression, called a search term, using predefined classes. The search term is then passed to the search() method for processing.

The following code segment illustrates how this is done. Assume in this example that folder1 is already identified using techniques shown in previous listings in this chapter. The code segment begins by creating a SearchTerm object call searchCriteria.

The SearchTerm object is assigned an expression that looks for matches to the subject or from headers of the email message. That is, all email messages that have "Welcome" as the subject or "personnel@mycompany.com" in the from header are considered a match.

Conditions are created within the SearchTerm object by using the AndTerm(), OrTerm(), and NotTerm() methods. In this example, the OrTerm() method is used to set the condition to OR. Components are identified in the SearchTerm by calling the appropriate method. In this example, the SubjectTerm() method is used to set the value of the subject header in the SearchTerm and the FromStringTerm() method is used to set the sender's address in the SearchTerm. You can also use the SentDateTerm(), BodyTerm(), RecipientStringTerm() methods to set the other search criteria. The Quick Reference Guide at the end of the chapter lists other commonly used objects for this purpose.

Once the SearchTerm object is assigned the search criteria, the code segment calls the search() method and passes the searchCriteria. The search() method returns an array of Message objects that meet the search criteria. You can then step through the array by using techniques illustrated previously in this chapter.

```
SearchTerm searchCriteria = new OrTerm( new SubjectTerm("Welcome"),
new FromStringTerm("personnel@mycompany.com"));
Message[] msg = folder1.search(searchCriteria);
```

Quick Reference Guide

This Quick Reference Guide provides a brief overview of Java classes used by JavaMail Full. details of these classes and all Java classes and interfaces are available at java.sun.com.

Syntax	Descriptions
BodyPart getBodyPart(int index)	Get the specified part.
int getCount()	Return the number of enclosed BodyPart objects.

Table 13-1. *public interface* MultipartDataSource *extends DataSource*

Syntax	Descriptions
void addHeader (String header_name, String header_value)	Adds this value to the existing values for the header.
Enumeration getAllHeaders()	Returns all the headers from the part as an enumeration of Header objects.
Object getContent()	Returns the content as a Java object.
String getContentType()	Returns the Content-Type of the content of the part.
DataHandler getDataHandler()	Returns a DataHandler for the content within the part.
String getDescription()	Returns a description String for the part.

Table 13-2. *public interface* Part

Syntax	Descriptions
String getDisposition()	Returns the disposition of the part.
String getFileName()	Gets the filename associated with this part.
String[] getHeader (String header_name)	Gets all the headers for the header name.
InputStream getInputStream()	Returns an input stream for the part's content.
int getLineCount()	Returns the number of lines in the content of this part.
Enumeration getMatchingHeaders (String[] header_names)	Returns matching headers from this part as an enumeration of Header objects.
Enumeration getNonMatchingHeaders (String[] header_names)	Returns nonmatching headers from the envelope as an enumeration of Header objects.
int getSize()	Returns the size of the content of the part in bytes.
boolean isMimeType (String mimeType)	Returns a true if this is part of the specified MIME type and a false if it is not part of the specified MIME type.
void removeHeader (String header_name)	Removes all headers with this name.
void setContent(Multipart mp)	Sets the Multipart object as the message's content.
void setContent (Object obj, String type)	Sets the part's content.
void setDataHandler (DataHandler dh)	Sets the part's content.
void setDescription (String description)	Sets a description String for the part.
void setDisposition (String disposition)	Sets the disposition of the part.
void setFileName (String filename)	Sets the filename associated with the part.

Table 13-2. *public interface* Part *(continued)*

Syntax	Descriptions
void setHeader (String header_name, String header_value)	Sets the value for the header.
void setText (java.lang.String text)	Sets the String as the part's content with a MIME type of "text/plain".
void writeTo(OutputStream os)	Outputs a bytestream for this part.

Table 13-2. *public interface* Part *(continued)*

Syntax	Descriptions
void addHeader(String name, String value)	Adds this value to the existing values for the header.
void addHeaderLine(String line)	Adds a header line to the part.
Enumeration getAllHeaderLines()	Gets all header lines as an enumeration of Strings.
Enumeration getAllHeaders()	Returns all the headers as an enumeration of Header objects.
Object getContent()	Returns the content as a Java object.
String getContentID()	Returns the value of the "Content-ID" header field.
String[] getContentLanguage()	Gets the languages specified in the Content-Language header of the MimePart.
String getContentMD5()	Returns the value of the "Content-MD5" header field.
protected InputStream getContentStream()	Produces the raw bytes of the content.
String getContentType()	Returns the value of the RFC 822 "Content-Type" header field.

Table 13-3. *public class* MimeBodyPart *extends BodyPart implements MimePart*

Syntax	Descriptions
DataHandler getDataHandler()	Returns a DataHandler for the part's content.
String getDescription()	Returns the "Content-Description" header field of the body part.
String getDisposition()	Returns the value of the "Content-Disposition" header field.
String getEncoding()	Returns the content transfer encoding from the "Content-Transfer-Encoding" header field.
String getFileName()	Gets the filename associated with the part.
String[] getHeader(String name)	Gets all the headers.
String getHeader(String name, String delimiter)	Gets all the headers separated by the delimiter for the header name.
InputStream getInputStream()	Returns a decoded input stream for the part's content.
int getLineCount()	Returns the number of lines for the content of this part.
Enumeration getMatchingHeaderLines (String[] names)	Gets matching header lines as an enumeration of Strings.
Enumeration getMatchingHeaders (String[] names)	Returns matching headers as an enumeration of Header objects.
Enumeration getNonMatchingHeaderLines (String[] names)	Gets nonmatching header lines as an enumeration of Strings.
Enumeration getNonMatchingHeaders (String[] names)	Returns nonmatching headers as an enumeration of Header objects.
int getSize()	Returns the size of the content of the body part in bytes.
boolean isMimeType (String mimeType)	Returns a true if this is part of the specified MIME type and a false if it is not part of the specified MIME type.
void removeHeader(String name)	Removes all headers with this name.

Table 13-3.   *public class* MimeBodyPart *extends BodyPart implements MimePart* (continued)

Syntax	Descriptions
void setContent(Multipart mp)	Sets the body part's content to a Multipart object.
void setContent (Object o, String type)	Sets the body part's content.
void setContentLanguage (String[] languages)	Sets the Content-Language header of the MimePart.
void setContentMD5(String md5)	Sets the "Content-MD5" header field of the body part.
public void setContentID (String cid)	Sets the content ID header field of the body part.
void setDataHandler (DataHandler dh)	Sets the body part's content.
void setDescription (String description)	Sets the "Content-Description" header field for the body part.
void setDescription(String description, String charset)	Sets the "Content-Description" header field for the body part.
void setDisposition (String disposition)	Sets the "Content-Disposition" header field of the body part.
void setFileName (String filename)	Sets the filename associated with this body part.
void setHeader(String name, String value)	Sets the value for the header.
void setText(String text)	Sets the part's content, with a MIME type of "text/plain".
void setText(String text, String charset)	Sets the part's content, with a MIME type of "text/plain" and the specified charset.
void updateHeaders()	Examines the content of this body part and updates MIME headers.
void writeTo(OutputStream os)	Outputs the body part as an RFC 822 format stream.

Table 13-3. *public class* MimeBodyPart *extends BodyPart implements MimePart* (continued)

Syntax	Descriptions
void addFrom(Address[] addresses)	Adds the specified addresses to the existing "From" field.
void addHeader(String name, String value)	Adds this value to the existing values for this header_name.
void addHeaderLine(String line)	Adds a raw RFC 822 header line.
void addRecipients(Message.RecipientType type, Address[] addresses)	Adds the given addresses to the specified recipient type.
Enumeration getAllHeaderLines()	Gets all header lines as an enumeration of Strings.
Enumeration getAllHeaders()	Returns all the headers as an enumeration of Header objects.
Address[] getAllRecipients()	Gets all the recipient addresses for the message.
Object getContent()	Returns the content as a Java object.
String getContentID()	Returns the value of the "Content-ID" header field.
String[] getContentLanguage()	Gets the languages specified in the "Content-Language" header field of this message.
String getContentMD5()	Returns the value of the "Content-MD5" header field.
protected InputStream getContentStream()	Produces the raw bytes of the content.
String getContentType()	Returns the value of the RFC 822 "Content-Type" header field.
DataHandler getDataHandler()	Returns a DataHandler for the content.
String getDescription()	Returns the "Content-Description" header field.
String getDisposition()	Returns the value of the "Content-Disposition" header field.
String getEncoding()	Returns the content transfer encoding from the "Content-Transfer-Encoding" header field.

Table 13-4.   *public class* MimeMessage *extends Message implements MimePart*

Syntax	Descriptions
String getFileName()	Gets the filename associated with this message.
Flags getFlags()	Returns a Flags object containing the flags for this message.
Address[] getFrom()	Returns the value of the RFC 822 "From" header fields.
String[] getHeader(String name)	Gets all the headers.
String getHeader(String name, String delimiter)	Gets all the headers separated by the delimiter for the header.
InputStream getInputStream()	Returns a decoded input stream for the content.
int getLineCount()	Returns the number of lines for the content of this message.
Enumeration getMatchingHeaderLines (String[] names)	Gets matching header lines as an enumeration of Strings.
Enumeration getMatchingHeaders (String[] names)	Returns matching headers as an enumeration of Header objects.
String getMessageID()	Returns the value of the "Message-ID" header field.
Enumeration getNonMatchingHeaderLines (String[] names)	Gets nonmatching header lines as an enumeration of Strings.
Enumeration getNonMatchingHeaders (String[] names)	Returns nonmatching headers as an enumeration of Header objects.
Date getReceivedDate()	Returns the date the message was received.
Address[] getRecipients (Message.RecipientType type)	Returns the recipients specified by the type.
Address[] getReplyTo()	Returns the value of the RFC 822 "Reply-To" header field.
Date getSentDate()	Returns the value of the RFC 822 "Date" field.
public Address getSender()	Returns the value of the RFC 822 sender header or null if header is absent.

Table 13-4. *public class* MimeMessage *extends Message implements MimePart* (continued)

Syntax	Descriptions
public void setSender (Address address)	Sets the RFC 822 sender header field at the specified address.
int getSize()	Returns the size of the content.
String getSubject()	Returns the value of the "Subject" header field.
boolean isMimeType(String mimeType)	Returns a true if this is part of the specified MIME type and a false if it is not part of the specified MIME type.
boolean isSet(Flags.Flag flag)	Checks whether the flag specified in the flag argument is set in this message.
void removeHeader(String name)	Removes all headers with this name.
Message reply(boolean replyToAll)	Gets a new message suitable for a reply to the message.
void saveChanges()	Updates the appropriate header fields to be consistent with the message's contents.
void setContent(Multipart mp)	Sets the message's content to a Multipart object.
void setContent(Object o, String type)	Sets the message's content.
void setContentID(String cid)	Sets the "Content-ID" header field.
void setContentLanguage (String[] languages)	Sets the "Content-Language" header.
void setContentMD5(String md5)	Sets the "Content-MD5" header field.
void setDataHandler(DataHandler dh)	Sets the part's content.
void setDescription(String description)	Sets the "Content-Description" header field.
void setDescription(String description, String charset)	Sets the "Content-Description" header field.
void setDisposition(String disposition)	Sets the "Content-Disposition" header field.

Table 13-4. *public class* MimeMessage *extends Message implements MimePart* (continued)

Syntax	Descriptions
void setFileName(String filename)	Sets the filename associated with the part.
void setFlags(Flags flag, boolean set)	Sets the flags for this message.
void setFrom()	Sets the RFC 822 "From" header field using the value of the InternetAddress.getLocalAddress() method.
void setFrom(Address address)	Sets the RFC 822 "From" header field.
void setHeader(String name, String value)	Sets the value for the named header.
void setRecipients(Message.RecipientType type, Address[] addresses)	Sets the recipient type to the addresses.
void setReplyTo(Address[] addresses)	Sets the RFC 822 "Reply-To" header field.
void setSentDate(Date d)	Sets the RFC 822 "Date" header field.
void setSubject(String subject)	Sets the "Subject" header field.
void setSubject(String subject, String charset)	Sets the "Subject" header field.
void setText(String text)	Sets the given String as this part's content, with a MIME type of "text/plain".
void setText(String text, String charset)	Sets String as this part's content, with a MIME type of "text/plain" and the specified charset.
void writeTo(OutputStream os)	Outputs the message as an RFC 822 format stream.
void writeTo(OutputStream os, String[] ignoreList)	Outputs the message as an RFC 822 format stream, without headers.

Table 13-4. *public class* MimeMessage *extends Message implements MimePart* (continued)

Syntax	Descriptions
BodyPart getBodyPart(int index)	Gets specified BodyPart.
BodyPart getBodyPart(String CID)	Gets MimeBodyPart referred to by ContentID (CID).
int getCount()	Returns the number of enclosed BodyPart objects.
void setSubType(String subtype)	Sets the subtype.
protected void updateHeaders()	Updates headers.
void writeTo(OutputStream os)	Iterates through all the parts and outputs each Mime part.

Table 13-5. *public class* MimeMultipart *extends Multipart*

Syntax	Descriptions
protected AddressStringTerm (String pattern)	Constructor. Implements string comparisons for message addresses.
protected AddressTerm (Address address)	Constructor. Implements message address comparisons.
AndTerm(SearchTerm[] t)	Constructor that takes array of SearchTerms and implements the logical AND operator on individual SearchTerms.
AndTerm(SearchTerm t1, SearchTerm t2)	Constructor. Implements the logical AND operator on individual SearchTerms.
BodyTerm(String pattern)	Constructor. Implements searches on message body.
public ComparisonTerm()	Constructor. Models the comparison operator.

Table 13-6. *javax.mail.search*

Syntax	Descriptions
protected DateTerm(int comparison, Date date)	Constructor. Implements comparisons for dates.
FlagTerm(Flags flags, boolean set)	Constructor. Implements comparisons for Message flags.
FromStringTerm(String pattern)	Constructor. Implements String comparisons for the From Address header.
FromTerm(Address address)	Constructor. Implements String comparisons for the From Address header.
HeaderTerm(String headerName, String pattern)	Constructor. Implements comparisons for Message headers.
protected IntegerComparisonTerm (int comparison, int number)	Constructor. Implements comparisons for integers.
MessageIDTerm(String msgid)	Constructor. Models the RFC 822 "MessageId" unique per message.
MessageNumberTerm(int number)	Constructor. Implements comparisons for message numbers.
NotTerm(SearchTerm t)	Constructor. Implements the logical NEGATION operator.
OrTerm(SearchTerm[] t)	Constructor. Takes an array of SearchTerms and implements the logical OR operator on individual SearchTerms.
OrTerm(SearchTerm t1, SearchTerm t2)	Constructor. Implements the logical OR operator on individual SearchTerms.
ReceivedDateTerm(int comparison, Date date)	Constructor. Implements comparisons for the message received date.
RecipientStringTerm(Message.Recipient Type type, String pattern)	Constructor. Implements String comparisons for the Recipient Address headers.
RecipientTerm(Message.RecipientType type, Address address)	Constructor. Implements comparisons for the Recipient Address headers.

Table 13-6. *javax.mail.search* (continued)

Syntax	Descriptions
SearchTerm()	Constructor. Search criteria expressed as a tree of search terms for the search expression.
SentDateTerm(int comparison, Date date)	Constructor. Implements comparisons for the Message SentDate.
SizeTerm(int comparison, int size)	Constructor. Implements comparisons for message sizes.
protected StringTerm(String pattern)	Constructor. Implements the match method for Strings.
protected StringTerm(String pattern, boolean ignoreCase)	Constructor. Implements the match method for Strings.
SubjectTerm(String pattern)	Constructor. Implements case-insensitive comparisons for the Message Subject header.

Table 13-6.   *javax.mail.search* (continued)

The
Complete
Reference

Chapter 14

Java Interface
Definition Language
and CORBA

A J2EE application is likely to require Web services that are provided by components written in other than the Java programming language such as in C and C++, and in COBOL, which was popular with legacy applications. These components are invoked by using the Java Interface Definition Language (IDL).

Java IDL is based on the Common Object Request Brokerage Architecture (CORBA), which is one of the original methods used to standardize the distribution of objects within a distributed environment.

Java IDL is an interconnectivity technology that can be used to link together web services to fulfill requests by J2EE components. In this chapter, you'll learn about Java IDL and how to integrate Java IDL into your J2EE application and J2EE components.

The Concept of Object Request Brokerage

CORBA is designed to enable clients to use a remote interface to access server-side components that adhere to the CORBA standards. A client invokes methods of objects by sending a request to the Object Request Brokerage (ORB), which is the hub of CORBA. The request must contain the stub method of the method requested by the client.

A stub method is an alias for the actual method, both of which are associated with each other in the ORB. The ORB acts as a local agent for the client and the object. A client sends a request directly to ORB, which receives the request on behalf of the object. The ORB then translates the request into the method call to the local object. Likewise, the ORB acts as the agent of the client by receiving responses from the object in the form of results or errors, which are then forwarded to the client for future processing.

Clients and objects communicate with ORB by using the Internet Inter-ORB Protocol (IIOP). IIOP, IDL, and CORBA are standards established by the Object Management Group (OMG). In addition to providing access to objects, ORB typically provides other services that include transaction processing, persistence, messaging, and object searches.

Java IDL and CORBA

The client's interface to a remote object is defined using the Interface Definition Language (IDL). The definition is placed in an interface definition file, which is then compiled using the idlj compiler that translates the IDL interface into a Java interface and generates other files that contain the class code for stubs and skeleton code that enables you to link your application into ORB.

You may not need to create the IDL interface if a client application is using an existing object. Instead, the person who implements the object will provide the IDL interface, which can be compiled into a Java interface.

The client uses the stubs generated by the idlj compiler. The ORB provides the name service that is necessary to locate the server and reference the object on the server. The client can then use the reference and the stub to called methods of the object.

On the server side, the skeleton code that is produced by the idlj compiler is used to implement the object's methods. The skeleton code is used to start ORB and wait for a request from a client.

The IDL Interface

The IDL interface is defined in a CORBA IDL module. The module is similar to a Java package and is a namespace container for interfaces and declarations, as is illustrated in Listing 14-1. In this example, the module declares myInterface that contains the declaration of myMethod, which returns a String.

The interface definition in the CORBA IDL module must map to a Java interface statement. Methods declared within the interface definition provide services that the object offers to a client that uses the interface.

Listing 14-1
An example of a CORBA IDL module.

```
module myApplication
{
  interface myInterface
  {
    string myMethod();
    oneway void shutdown();
  };
};
```

Save the module as myApplication.idl and then compile by entering

```
idlj -fall myApplication.idl
```

Caution   *The idlj compiler must be in your path; otherwise, you'll receive an error message.*

The compiler creates a directory called myApplication and generates a number of files, which is dependent on the options selected when compiling. The default is to produce client stubs as shown in the bullet list. The -fall option produces the server stubs, which generate the following files. Once these files are generated, you can implement the client that requests the object and the server that fulfills the request. During compiling, IDL conventions are mapped to Java conventions as shown in Table 14-1.

- **myApplicationPOA.java**   This is an abstract class that contains the server skeleton and is used to provide CORBA functionality to the server.

- **myApplicationStub.java**   This is the stub used by the client and implements the myApplication.java interface.

- **myApplication.java**   This is the Java interface of the IDL interface.

IDL	Java
module myApplication	package myApplication
interface myApplication	public interface myApplication
string myMethod()	String myMethod()
oneway void shutdown()	void Shutdown()

Table 14-1. *Mapping IDL to Java*

- **myApplicationHelper.java** This final class casts CORBA object references to their proper types.

- **myApplicationHolder.java** This final class provides public instance members for out and inout arguments.

- **myApplicationOperations.java** This file contains the mapping of operations that are defined in the IDL interface. In Listing 14-1, these operations are myMethod() and shutdown(). Stubs and skeletons share this file.

The Client Side

Once the CORBA IDL module is compiled, you can develop the client-side application that will request the services of the object. The client-side application is a class that is illustrated in Listing 14-2. This class requires that three packages be imported. These are the stubs package generated by the idlj compiler and two CORBA packages.

In this example, the myApplicationApp.* package contains the stubs. The org.omg .CosNaming.* package contains the naming services used by the class to call CORBA objects. And the org.omg.CORBA.* is the package that contains CORBA classes.

One of the first tasks for the application is to create and initialize a local ORB object. The local ORB object, called orb, handles IIOP operations. The init() method is passed any command-line arguments to set any properties at runtime based on the needs of the application. The parameters are required to define the IP address and port number for the ORB service.

Next, the program needs to locate the required service in order to obtain reference to the object that will fulfill the client's request. The program does this by calling the orb.resolve_initial_references() method to receive a reference to the name server. NameService is defined for ORB so the ORB knows to return the initial naming context of the object, referred to as name service. Using the object called obj references the name service.

However, obj is a generic CORBA object that must be narrowed to a specific proper type by calling the narrow() method, which is passed the obj reference and returns an instance of the NamingContext called nc1.

Names are complex and are handled by NameComponent objects. A NameComponent object references an element of a name and an array of NameComponent objects references all the elements of a name, including the path of the object that will provide services to the client.

The NameComponent constructor requires the name of the server and the kind field. In this example, the server name is myApplication and the kind is an empty String. This creates a NameComponent object called nc2.

In order for the program to receive a local reference to the myApplication object, the program needs to call the resolve_str() method. The resolve_str() method returns a generic CORBA object and must be narrowed to the myApplication object by calling the narrow() method of the myApplicationHelper object, which was generated by the idltojava compiler.

And finally, once the local reference to the object is obtained, the program can call methods of that object. In this example, reference to the instance is called myApp, which is used to call myMethod() to return a String object that is assigned to msg.

Listing 14-2
Client-side
* Code
already
fixed.

```java
import myApplication.*;
import org.omg.CosNaming.*;
import org.omg.CosNaming.NamingContextPackage.*;
import org.omg.CORBA.*;
public class myClient
{
  static myApplication myApp;
  public static void main(String args[])
  {
      try{
        ORB orb = ORB.init(args, null);
        org.omg.CORBA.Object nc1 =
orb.resolve_initial_references("NameService");
        NamingContextExt nc2 = NamingContextExtHelper.narrow(nc1);
        myInterface myInt =
myInterfaceHelper.narrow(nc2.resolve_str("myInterface"));insert this one
        System.out.println(myInt.myMethod());
        myInt.shutdown();
      }
      catch (Exception error) {
          System.out.println("ERROR: " + error.getMessage()) ;
      }
    }
}
```

The Server Side

The server-side program that responds to client requests is commonly referred to a CORBA server program, which is illustrated in Listing 14-3. You'll notice that this example contains may of the constructs found in the client-side program (Listing 14-2).

The CORBA server program begins by importing packages and creates an ORB object as discussed in the previous section. Three additional packages are imported. These are org.omg.PortableServer.*, org.omg.PortableServer.POA, and java.util .Properties. The first two packages contain classes used for the Portable Server Inheritance Model and the last package contains properties used to initiate the ORB.

Next, the program creates a Servant subclass called MyApplication that extends myApplicationPOA. Notice that the subclass is defined within the same file as the myServer class, although the subclass is defined outside of the myServer class. The Servant subclass inherits CORBA functionality.

Three methods are defined within the Servant subclass. These are setORB(), myMethod(), and shutdown(). The setORB() method is used to initialized the private variable called orb. The myMethod() returns a simple String, and the shutdown() method shuts down the service so no more requests are processed when the object is terminated by calling the org.omg.CORBA.ORB.shutdown() method. This is different than doing some cleanup when you're done using the object, which immediately terminates the object before any pending process is completed. Of course, such a class in a real-world application contains functional code that is required to fulfill requests from clients.

The program then defines the server class. The first steps within the server class definition is to create a local ORB object by calling the init() method, which returns an ORB object called orb in this example. The init() method is passed command-line arguments enabling the IP address and port to be set at runtime.

Next, the program obtains reference to the Name Service by calling the resolve_ initial_references() method, the results of which are passed to the narrow() method of the POAHelper to obtain reference to the root Portable Object Adapter (POA). The resolve_initial_references() returns a generic CORBA object that must be narrowed to its proper type by using the narrow() method.

POA provides variety of features, such as allowing the perception of persistent objects. That is, a server may restart an object several times, but the object seems to persist from the viewpoint of the client. POA also gives the object implementer control over the object's life cycle, state, identity, and storage, in addition to code that responds to requests for methods. And POA can be used with multiple ORB implementations to minimize the need to modify code based on different vendor's implementations.

The activate() method is called next to change the state of the POA manager to active, which causes the POA to begin to process requests. The program then creates a servant called myApps. The servant handles interface options with the interface. The servant is then passed to the setORB() method of the subclass, enabling the servant to be closed when the shutdown() method is called.

The program needs to obtain an object reference to the servant. This is accomplished by calling the servant_to_reference() method and the narrow() method. Although the program has an object reference to the servant, the servant is not available as yet to clients. Reference to the servant must be published using the Common Object Services (COS) Naming Service.

To do this, the program must obtain reference to the name server by calling the resolve_initial_references() and passing it the "NameService" String, which is defined for CORBA ORBs. The resolve_initial_references() method returns the Naming Context object. The Naming Context object is the reference for the name service. The Naming Context object must be narrowed to its proper type using the narrow() method.

The rebind() method requires an array of NameComponents, called path in this example. The path contains reference to the Servant object. However, the Servant object is identified by a String called "myInterface". Therefore, the program must convert the String to a reference using the to_name() method, which is then assigned to the NameComponent array.

The rebind() method can then be called to make the servant available to clients. A client can now call resolve("myInterface") to obtain a reference to the servant and then begin calling methods defined in the interface.

And finally, the program calls the run() method to start the server-side program and wait for client request.

Listing 14-3
Server side.

```
import myApplication.*;
import org.omg.CosNaming.*;
import org.omg.CosNaming.NamingContextPackage.*;
import org.omg.CORBA.*;
import org.omg.PortableServer.*;
import org.omg.PortableServer.POA;
import java.util.Properties;
class MyApplication extends myApplicationPOA {
  private ORB orb;
  public void setORB(ORB v) {
    orb = v;
  }
  public String myMethod() {
    return "I'm here to serve.";
  }
  public void shutdown() {
    orb.shutdown(false);
  }
}
public class myServer {
  public static void main(String args[]) {
    try{
      ORB orb = ORB.init(args, null);
      POA rpoa =
POAHelper.narrow(orb.resolve_initial_references("RootPOA"));
```

```
        rpoa.the_POAManager().activate();
        MyApplication myApp = new MyApplication();
        myApp.setORB(orb);
        org.omg.CORBA.Object rf = rpoa.servant_to_reference(myApp);
        myInterface hrf = myInterfaceHelper.narrow(rf);
        org.omg.CORBA.Object orf =
            orb.resolve_initial_references("NameService");
        NamingContextExt ncrf = NamingContextExtHelper.narrow(orf);
        NameComponent path[] = ncrf.to_name( "myInterface" );
        ncrf.rebind(path, hrf);
        System.out.println("myServer: Operational");
        orb.run();
    }
    catch (Exception error) {
      System.err.println("ERROR: " + error.getMessage());
    }
    System.out.println("myServer: Terminated ");
  }
}
```

Running the Code

You run the code by first starting the ORB service. On Windows NT, enter the following statement at the command prompt. The parameters are the IP address and the port for the service. You'll find the orbd executable in the bin directory along with java and javac.

```
start orbd -ORBInitialPort 1050 -ORBInitialHost localhost
```

Next, start the server by entering the following command at the command prompt. Be sure to enter the command-line parameters because they are passed to the init() method.

```
start java myApplicationServer -ORBInitialPort 1050 -ORBInitialHost localhost
```

Finally, you can run the client by entering the following command at the command prompt:

```
java myApplicationClient -ORBInitialPort 1050 -ORBInitialHost localhos
```

Chapter 15

Java Remote Method Invocation

A J2EE client is capable of receiving service from a server-side component regardless of their location and the language used to develop a component. This is made possible through interconnectivity used in J2EE technology to create an industrial-strength web service architecture.

Interconnectivity is at the heart of J2EE technology and provides the logical infrastructure that enables clients and server-side components to interact with each other either directly or indirectly.

In the previous chapter you learned how to develop a client- and server-side component that uses Java Interface Definition Language and CORBA for invocation of server-side objects that are not written in the Java programming language. In this chapter you'll learn to use Java Remote Method Invocation to invoke server-side objects that are written in Java.

Remote Method Invocation Concept

A Java object runs within a Java Virtual Machine (JVM), which you learned about in Part I. Likewise, a J2EE application runs within a JVM; however, objects used by a J2EE application do not need to run on the same JVM as the J2EE application. This is because a J2EE application and its components can invoke objects located on a different JVM by using the Java Remote Method Invocation (RMI) system. RMI is used for remote communication between Java applications and components, both of which must be written in the Java programming language.

RMI is used to connect together a client and a server. A client is an application or component that requires the services of an object to fulfill a request. A server creates an object and makes the object available to clients. A client contacts the server to reference and invoke the object by using RMI.

A client locates a remote object by either using the RMI naming registry or by passing a string that references the remote object. In either case, RMI returns a reference to the remote object, which is then invoked by the client as if the object was on the local JVM.

RMI handles transmission of requests and provides the facility to load the object's bytecode, which is referred to as *dynamic code loading*. This means that the behavior of an application can be dynamically extended by the remote JVM.

Remote Interface

Server-side objects that are invoked by remote clients must implement a remote interface and associated method definitions. The remote interface is used by clients to interact with the object using RMI communications. A remote interface extends java.rmi.Remote and each method must throw a RemoteException.

When a client references a remote object, the RMI passes a remote stub for the remote object. The remote stub is the local proxy for the remote object. The client calls the method on the local stub whenever the client wants to invoke one of the remote object's methods. The remote stub in turn invokes the actual remote object's method. A remote stub implements the set of remote interfaces that are implemented by the remote object.

Passing Objects

RMI passes objects as arguments and returns a value by reference. The reference is the stub of the remote object. Any changes made to an object's state by an invocation of a remote call affect the original remote object.

Object serialization is used to pass a local object by value. Serialization can override how static and transient fields are passed. Those fields are not passed by default. Any changes made to an object's state by the client are not reflected in the original object.

The RMI Process

There are three steps necessary to make an object available to remote clients. These are to design an object, to compile the object, and then to make the object accessible to remote clients over the network.

Besides defining the business logic of an object, the developer must define a remote interface for the object, which identifies methods that are available to remote clients. Likewise, those methods must be defined in the object. In addition to methods that can be invoked by remote clients, the developer must also define other methods that support the processing of client-invoked methods. These are referred to as *server methods*, while methods invoked by a client are called *client methods*.

Compilation of the object is a two-step process that begins by compiling the object using the javac compiler. The object must contain implementation of the remote interface, and server and client methods. Once the object is compiled, you must create a stub for the object. This is done by calling the RMI compiler called rmic.

The compiled object is then made accessible over the network by loading the object to a server. Make sure that the RMI remote object registry is running; otherwise, a remote client will be unable to access the object. To start the RMI registry on Windows NT, type the following at the command line:

```
C:\> start rmiregistry
```

Server Side

The server side of a remote object invocation consists of a remote interface and methods. The remote interface is at the center of every remote object because the remote interface defines how the client views the object. Methods provide the business logic that fulfills a client's request whenever the client remotely invokes the method.

JAVA INTERCONNECTIVITY

Listing 15-1 illustrates the remote interface definition and Listing 15-2 shows the server-side component. Listing 15-1 makes one method called myMethod() available to clients. This method doesn't require an argument and returns a String object. Of course, there would be many additional methods appearing in a remote interface in a real-world J2EE application. Only one method is shown here for illustrative purposes.

Listing 15-1
Remote interface.

```
import java.rmi.Remote;
import java.rmi.RemoteException;
public interface myApplication extends Remote {
    String myMethod() throws RemoteException;
}
```

Listing 15-2 shows the server-side program that contains the remote object's definition. The program begins by importing the necessary packages that are required to implement RMI and implements the myApplication remote interface defined in Listing 15-1.

Next, the program defines the constructor and myMethod, which is the only method contained in the object. This method simply returns the string "I'm here to serve.\n". You can modify the method as necessary based on the business rules that are implemented by the object.

The program proceeds to create and install a security manager. A security manager serves as a firewall and grants or rejects downloaded code access to the local file system and similar privileged operations. RMI requires that server-side applications install a security manager. In this example, the getSecurityManager() method creates a SecurityManager object and the setSecurityManager() method associates the server-side program with the SecurityManager object.

Then, the server-side program creates an instance of myApplication and makes the remote object myMethod available to remote clients by calling the rebind() method. The rebind() method registers the remote object with the RMI remote object registry or with another naming service. The object's name is "//host/myApplication" where host is the name or IP address of the server.

Caution *The port number on the server must be specified if port number 1099 is not used. Port number 1099 is the default port.*

The argument to the rebind() method is the URL that contains the location and name of the remote object and the server. Although the location and name of the remote object is registered, RMI returns to a remote client reference to the remote object's stub and not to the object itself.

Caution *Reference to a remote object can be bound, unbound, or rebound to the registry only if the object and registry are on the same host. This is a security restriction that prevents the registry from being deleted or modified by a remote client.*

JAVA INTERCONNECTIVITY

Listing 15-2
Implementing the remote interface.

```java
import java.rmi.*;
import java.rmi.server.*;
 public class myApplicationServer extends UnicastRemoteObject implements
myApplication
{
  public myApplicationServer() throws RemoteException {
    super();
  }
  public String myMethod()
  {
    return "I'm here to serve.\n";
  }
  public static void main(String[] args) {
    if (System.getSecurityManager() == null)
    {
      System.setSecurityManager(new RMISecurityManager());
    }
    String app = "//localhost/myApplication";
     try {
      MyApplicationServer server = new myApplicationServer();
      Naming.rebind(app, server);
    }
    catch (Exception error) {
      System.err.println("myApplicationServer exception: " +
      error.getMessage());
    }
  }
}
```

Client Side

The client-side program calls the remote object defined in Listing 15-2, which returns a String object that the client-side program displays. A real-world application requires the remote object to perform complicated operations that simply return a String object. However, those operations are application specific and you can easily modify code illustrated in this chapter to include complex operations.

Listing 15-4 illustrates the client-side program. This example begins by creating a security manager using the same method as described previously in the server-side program. Next, the lookup() method is used to locate the remote object, which is called myApplication. The lookup() method returns a reference to the object called mApp.

And the program calls the myMethod() method to invoke the myMethod of the remote object. The myMethod method returns a String object that is passed to the println() method, which displays the contents of the String object on the screen.

Any exceptions that are thrown while the client-side program runs are trapped by the catch() block. The catch() block calls the getMessage() method to retrieve the error message that is associated with the exception. The error message is then displayed on the screen.

Before running the client, you need to

- Compile the source code.
- Compile the server class using the rmic compiler, which produces the skeleton and stub classes.
- Start the rmiregistry.
- Start the server.
- Run the client.

You'll need to define the security properties as command-line arguments when running Listing 15-4. Here is the command line necessary to run the client program:

```
java -Djava.security.policy=c:/javacode/src/policy myApplicationServer
```

Here is the command line necessary to run the server program:

```
java -Djava.rmi.server.codebase=file:///c:/javacode/classes/ -
Djava.security.policy=c:/javacode/src/policy myApplicationServer
```

The Djava.rmi.server.codebase argument identifies the location of the class files. One or three forward slashes must precede the path depending on the operating environment. The Djava.security.policy argument identifies the location of the policy file. Listing 15-3 contains the policy file that grants all permissions.

Listing 15-3
The policy file.

```
grant {
  permission java.security.AllPermission;
};
```

Listing 15-4
Client-side application.

```
import java.rmi.*;
 public class myApplicationClient {
  public static void main(String args[]) {
    if (System.getSecurityManager() == null)
    {
      System.setSecurityManager(new RMISecurityManager());
    }
    try {
      String app = "//localhost/myApplication";
      myApplication mApp = (myApplication) Naming.lookup(app);
      System.out.println(mApp.myMethod());
    }
    catch (Exception error) {
      System.err.println("myApplicationClient exception: " + error.getMessage());
    }
  }
}
```

Quick Reference Guide

This Quick Reference Guide provides a brief overview of Java classes used by a Java servlet to interact with RMI that can be used. Full details of these classes and all Java classes and interfaces are available at java.sun.com.

Syntax	Descriptions
static void bind(String name, Remote obj)	Binds the specified name to a remote object.
static String[] list(String name)	Returns an array of the names bound in the registry.
static Remote lookup(String name)	Returns a reference for a remote object.
static void rebind(String name, Remote obj)	Rebinds the specified name to a new remote object.
static void unbind(String name)	Destroys the binding that is associated with a remote object.

Table 15-1. *public final class* naming *extends object*

Syntax	Descriptions
void bind(String name, Remote obj)	Binds a remote reference to the specified name in this registry.
String[] list()	Returns an array of the names bound in this registry.
Remote lookup(String name)	Returns the remote reference bound to the specified name in this registry.
void rebind(String name, Remote obj)	Replaces the binding for the specified name in this registry.
void unbind(String name)	Removes the binding for the specified name in this registry.

Table 15-2. *public interface* Registry *extends Remote*

Syntax	Descriptions
static Registry createRegistry (int port)	Creates and exports a registry on the local host.
static Registry createRegistry(int port, RMIClientSocketFactory csf, RMIServerSocketFactory ssf)	Creates and exports a registry on the local host.
static Registry getRegistry()	Returns the remote object registry.
static Registry getRegistry(int port)	Returns the remote object registry.
static Registry getRegistry(String host)	Returns a reference to the remote object registry.
static Registry getRegistry(String host, int port)	Returns a reference to the remote object registry.
static Registry getRegistry (String host, int port, RMIClientSocketFactory csf)	Returns a locally created remote reference to the remote object registry.

Table 15-3. *public final class* LocateRegistry *extends Object*

Syntax	Descriptions
String getRefClass(ObjectOutput out)	Returns the class name of the ref type to be serialized onto the stream 'out'.
boolean remoteEquals(RemoteRef obj)	Compares two remote objects for equality.
int remoteHashCode()	Returns a hashcode for a remote object.
String remoteToString()	Returns the reference of this remote object.

Table 15-4. *public interface* RemoteRef *extends Externalizable*

Syntax	Descriptions
Socket createSocket(String host, int port)	Creates a client socket connected to the specified host and port.

Table 15-5. *public interface* RMIClientSocketFactory

Syntax	Descriptions
boolean failure(Exception ex)	The failure is invoked when the RMI runtime is unable to create a ServerSocket via the RMISocketFactory.

Table 15-6. *public interface* RMIFailureHandler

Syntax	Descriptions
ServerSocket createServerSocket (int port)	Creates a server socket on the specified port.

Table 15-7. *public interface* RMIServerSocketFactory

Syntax	Descriptions
RemoteStub exportObject(Remote obj, Object data)	Creates a client stub object for a Remote object.
String getClientHost()	Returns the hostname of the current client.

Table 15-8. *public interface* ServerRef *extends RemoteRef*

Syntax	Descriptions
boolean equals(Object obj)	Compares two Remote objects.
RemoteRef getRef()	Returns the remote reference for the Remote object.
int hashCode()	Returns a hashcode for a Remote object
String toString()	Returns the value of a Remote object.
static Remote toStub(Remote obj)	Returns the stub for the Remote object obj.

Table 15-9. *public abstract class* RemoteObject *extends Object implements Remote, Serializable*

Syntax	Descriptions
static String getClientHost()	Returns the client host for the remote method invocation.
static PrintStream getLog()	Returns stream for the RMI call log.
static void setLog(OutputStream out)	Logs RMI calls to the output stream out.

Table 15-10. *public abstract class* RemoteServer *extends RemoteObject*

Syntax	Descriptions
static String getClassAnnotation (Class cl)	Returns a string RMI used to annotate the class descriptor when marshalling objects.
static ClassLoader getClassLoader(String codebase)	Returns a class loader that loads classes from the given codebase URL path.
static RMIClassLoaderSpi getDefaultProviderInstance()	Returns the canonical instance of the default provider for the service provider interface RMIClassLoaderSpi.

Table 15-11. *public class* RMIClassLoader *extends Object*

Syntax	Descriptions
static Class loadClass(String codebase, String name)	Loads a class from a codebase URL path.
static Class loadClass(String codebase, String name, ClassLoader defaultLoader)	Loads a class from a codebase URL path.
static Class loadClass(URL codebase, String name)	Loads a class from a codebase URL.
static Class loadProxyClass(String codebase, String[] interfaces, ClassLoader defaultLoader)	Loads a dynamic proxy class that implements a set of interfaces with the given names from a codebase URL path.

Table 15-11.   *public class RMIClassLoader extends Object* (Continued)

Syntax	Descriptions
abstract ServerSocket createServerSocket(int port)	Creates a server socket on the specified port.
abstract Socket createSocket(String host, int port)	Creates a client socket connected.
static RMISocketFactory getDefaultSocketFactory()	Returns a reference to the default socket.
static RMIFailureHandler getFailureHandler()	Returns the handler for socket creation failure set by the setFailureHandler method.
static RMISocketFactory getSocketFactory()	Returns the socket factory set by the setSocketFactory method.
static void setFailureHandler (RMIFailureHandler fh)	Sets the failure handler to be called by the RMI runtime if server socket creation fails.
static void setSocketFactory (RMISocketFactory fac)	Set the global socket factory from which RMI gets sockets.

Table 15-12.   *public abstract class RMISocketFactory extends Object implements RMIClientSocketFactory, RMIServerSocketFactory*

The Complete Reference

Chapter 16

Java Message Service

J2EE applications and components are loosely coupled. As you learned in previous chapters of the book, a component contains business logic to perform a task that may be required by multiple applications.

However, components are independent of applications. A component applies business logic to information received from an application and then returns the results of its processing to the application.

Java Message Service is the glue that links together J2EE applications with components by providing a means to transmit messages between them. You might think of Java Message Service as the postal system. You'll learn about the Java Message Service in this chapter and see how you can implement the Java Message Service with your J2EE application and components.

Messaging Service

You can imagine the J2EE environment as a large city composed of clients. Each client provides a service to other clients. And a client requires the services of other clients to provide its services. This is similar to how your grocery store provides services to your community. However, the grocery store requires the services of a food distributor to help it service the community. In the J2EE environment, clients are applications and components.

Clients require a means to communicate with each other to request services and to deliver services. This means is the messaging service. A messaging service is comprised of clients and a messaging agent. Clients are similar to houses and businesses within your community and the messaging agent is your local post office.

Every client connects to the messaging service. A client can create a message, send a message, receive a message, and read a message. The messaging service can forward messages received from a client to another client.

A key feature of a messaging service is that clients need only minimal information to communicate with another client. That is, a client must know the service another client provides, the information needed by the client to perform the service, and the client's address. The client doesn't need to know how the service is performed.

This is similar to you dealing with your tax accountant. The tax accountant is a messaging service client (that is, postal client) who prepares tax returns. The tax accountant requires your financial information to prepare your taxes. And you need to know the tax accountant's address so you can send the tax accountant your financial information.

Both clients are known to the messaging service, enabling the messaging service to deliver a message sent by one client to another, similar to you mailing your financial information to your tax accountant. Likewise, the recipient delivers the service by using the messaging service. This is like your tax accountant sending you your prepared tax forms in the return mail.

The messaging service uses a forward-storing architecture to deliver messages asynchronously. This means that the recipient does not have to be available to receive a message when the message is sent. Instead, the message is forwarded to the messaging service and stored until the recipient requests the message.

This is similar to your tax accountant having a post office box. You send your financial information to the postal service, which places your financial information into your accountant's post office box. Your financial information remains in the post office box until your tax accountant opens the post office box.

Java Messaging Service

The Java Message Service (JMS) was introduced in 1998 and designed to enable Java applications to communicate with a Messaging-Oriented Middleware (MOM) infrastructure. However, the industry soon embraced JMS as a full-service messaging service.

JMS is a messaging agent that delivers messages between J2EE applications and components. J2EE applications and components interact with JMS by using the JMS API. The JMS API defines common interfaces for communicating with any commercial messaging service that implements the JMS API.

JMS is the first messaging agent to standardize an interface to access messaging services, although messaging service products have been around for decades. For example, the MQSeries from IBM supports JMS and non-JMS APIs, including C, C++, and VB. An advantage of JMS is that a J2EE application can send a message to a message queue that can be retrieved and processed by a C++ object.

JMS enables requests for services to be processed without delaying the requestor. For example, an application can make a request for service and do something else until the service provider delivers results to the application.

This is a major advantage for JMS because the operation of the application is not hindered if the service provider (that is, component) is temporarily unavailable to provide service, which might occur if the component is processing a request from another application.

JMS Fundamentals

JMS consists of five elements. These are a provider, clients, messages, administered objects, and native clients. A provider is the messaging agent that is responsible for managing the messaging service. Clients are applications and components written in Java that use the provider for communication. Messages are objects transmitted between clients. Administered objects are JMS objects used in transmission. There are two such objects. These are the designation factory object and the connection object. These connections are used to connect to the message service and handle transmission between the sender and receiver, both of which are discussed in this section. And native clients are applications built before the introduction of JMS that use another messaging system's native client API. JMS is also used for applications that require better performance and send messages that are processed objects written in another language such as C++.

Flexibility

JMS is capable of interacting with two other kinds of messaging architectures besides the forward-storage architecture. Prior to the introduction of JMS, communications between clients were handled using point-to-point architecture or subscriber/publisher architecture.

Point-to-point architecture requires the synchronization of the sender client and the receiver client during transmission of messages. This means the receiver client must be available and connected to the sender before a message can be sent. Both clients cannot perform other tasks while transmission occurs. A queue is used in point-to-point messaging, where the message is stored on the queue until the receiver retrieves the message. It isn't unusual for the sender to know nothing about the receiver.

In the subscriber/publisher architecture, a sender forwards a message to the publisher who broadcasts the message to clients who have subscribed to receiving a particular message type. For example, say you are a baseball fan and coverage of all your favorite team's games is provided on a premium cable channel. You subscribe to the channel and the cable company (publisher) broadcasts information about the team over the premium cable channel.

The subscriber/publisher architecture requires that the subscriber be available to receive messages as they are published. However, JMS introduced the durable subscription feature that is less restrictive than the subscriber/publisher architecture. The durable subscription feature consists of forward storage. That is, a subscriber doesn't have to be available when a message is published in order to receive the message. Each message is temporarily stored when published until the client is back online. A queue can be durable, enabling persistent storage on a hard drive. This means messages and the queue can be restored if something happens (such as the computer crashes).

Components of a JMS Program

The five elements of JMS that are described in the previous section correspond to five JMS programming components. These components are administered objects, sessions, message producers, message consumers, and messages.

Two administered objects are the connection factory object and the session object. The connection factory object is used to create a session object. A session object is used to create a sender or receiver. Clients using a corresponding interface access both of these.

Low-level operations are hidden from clients and are handled by the JMS provider. This enables clients to use the same interface regardless of the JMS provider.

A client accesses the connection factory at the beginning of the program by using the lookup() method. There are two kinds of connection factory objects. These are the QueueConnectionFactory and the TopicConnectionFactory. QueueConnectionFactory is used to receive messages and the TopicConnectionFactory is used to receive messages by topic. Messages on a queue are arranged out of sequence based on priorities, rather than storing messages sequentially. Messages can be retrieved using message selectors, which are discussed later in this chapter.

Listing 16-1 illustrates how to access the connection factory. This example first creates an InitialContext object and then a TopicConnectionFactory object using the lookup() method of the InitialContext object. A QueueConnectionFactory object is created in a similar fashion by replacing occurrences of TopicConnectionFactory with QueueConnectionFactory. The TopicConnectionFactory is registered under the JNDI name TopicConnectionFactory in this example.

Listing 16-1
Accessing the connection factory.

```
InitialContext cx = new InitialContext();
TopicConnectionFactory tcf = (TopicConnectionFactory)
cx.lookup("TopicConnectionFactory");
```

A client accesses the destination interface by using the lookup() method of the InitialContext object. There are two ways to a retrieve the destination interface. These are by topic and by queue. The topic approach creates a Topic object and assigns reference to the topic to that object. Likewise, the queue approach creates a Queue object and assigns reference to a queue to that object.

Listing 16-2 illustrates how to create a Queue object. You create a Topic object by substituting Topic for Queue in this listing. The string passed to the lookup() method contains the name of the queue or the name of the topic that will receive messages sent by the program. The JNDI lookup name is configured in the JMS product.

Listing 16-2
Accessing the destination factory.

```
InitialContext cx = new InitialContext();
Queue mq = (Queue) cx.lookup("QueueName");
```

Once the program accesses the topic or queue to receive messages and to send messages, the program must open a connection with the JMS provider. This connection is then used to create a session.

The connection is made by using the connection factory. There are two kinds of connections that can be created. These are topic and queue, and they must coincide with the choice of connection factory used by the program.

Listing 16-3 illustrates how to create a connection using the TopicConnnectionFactory. The same technique is used to create a connection using the QueueConnectionFactory by replacing TopicConnnectionFactory with QueueConnectionFactory.

Listing 16-3
Creating a connection.

```
Context cx = new InitialContext();
TopicConnectionFactory tcf = (TopicConnectionFactory)
cx.lookup("TopicConnectionFactory");
TopicConnection tc= tcf.createTopicConnection();
```

Before the program receives, the connection's start() method must be called (tc.start()). Also, the connection's close() method must be called (tc.close()) to break the connection, which also terminates the session.

Sessions

A session is a transactional context that is used to create message producers, message consumers, and messages themselves. There are two forms of sessions. These are QueueSession interface or TopicSession interface. A QueueSession interface is created for a QueueConnection object. Likewise, a TopicSession interface is used for a TopicConnection object.

Listing 16-4 illustrates how to create both a QueueSession interface and TopicSession interface. In this example, the createQueueSession() method is called to create the QueueSession object. The first argument to the createQueueSession() method is a Boolean value indicating whether or not the QueueSession is transacted. The other argument is an integer that specifies that message acknowledgement is not used for transacted sessions. The integer values are Session.AUTO_ACKNOWLEDGE, Session.CLIENT_ACKNOWLEDGE, and Session.DUPS_OK_ACKNOWLEDGE

The createTopicSession() method is called to create a TopicSession object. Like the createQueueSession(), the first argument of the createTopicSession() is a Boolean value indicating whether or not the session is transacted. The second argument indicates whether or not the session automatically acknowledges incoming messages.

Listing 16-4
Creating two sessions.

```
QueueSession qs = queueConnection.createQueueSession(true, 0);
TopicSession ts = topicConnection.createTopicSession(false,
Session.AUTO_ACKNOWLEDGE);
```

Acknowledgement Modes

JMS uses an acknowledgement protocol to guarantee messaging. There are three acknowledgement modes used in the acknowledgement protocols. These are the AUTO_ACKNOWLEDGE, CLIENT_ ACKNOWLEDGE, and the DUPS_OK_ ACKNOWLEDGE modes. The acknowledgement mode is passed when the session is created.

Once a message sender sends a message to the message provider, the message sender waits for an acknowledgement from the message provider before continuing with another task. Any failed response causes an error to be thrown, which is handled by the message sender program.

The acknowledgement from a message provider only acknowledges that the message was received by the message provider and not that the message was delivered to the message receiver.

The AUTO_ACKNOWLEDGE acknowledgement mode specifies that the message provider automatically sends an acknowledgement each time a message receiver receives the message. Delivery of the message occurs only once to a destination. However, this might cause messages to be lost if failure occurs during transmission.

The DUPS_OK_ACKNOWLEDGE acknowledgement mode tells the message providers to redeliver a message should the message receiver fail to acknowledge delivery. Let's say that a message is lost if failure occurs while the message provider attempts to deliver a message to a non-durable message receiver. However, failure delivering a message to a durable message receiver can cause a duplicate message to be delivered.

After delivering a message to a durable message receiver, a message provider waits for an acknowledgement. The message is redelivered to the message receiver if the message receiver fails to acknowledge receipt of the message. In this case, the message provider automatically sets the JMSRedelivered flag to true and redelivers the message.

If the message is being distributed using the DUPS_OK_ACKNOWLEDGE acknowledgement mode, messages received must call the Message object's getJMSRedelivered() method to determine if the JMSRedelivered flag is set to true.

The CLIENT_ACKNOWLEDGE acknowledgement mode explicitly gives the message receiver control over acknowledging a message. Listing 16-5 illustrates how to acknowledge receipt of a message. In this example, the Message object's acknowledge() method is called once the incoming message is processed. The acknowledge() method notifies the message provider that the message was received.

Listing 16-5
Acknowledging that a message was received.

```
public void onMessage(Message msg) {
  try {
    //Process incoming message.
    msg.acknowledge();
  }
  catch {
    //Handle errors
  }
}
```

Message Transactions

A message transaction consists of a group of messages where either all messages within the group are sent or not sent to the message provider, which is similar in concept to SQL transactions discussed in Part II of this book.

Messages that are part of a transaction are sent from the message sender to the message provider, where the message provider caches them. The message sender calls the rollback() method if any failure occurs while the group of messages are being sent to the message provider. The message provider then discards those messages of the group that were successfully sent prior to the failure. Messages remain cached until the message sender calls the commit() method, at which time all the messages within the message group are made available to the message receiver.

A message transaction is created by passing a Boolean true as the first argument in the createTopicSession() method and createQueueSession() method. This is illustrated in Listing 16-6. In this example, tc is the TopicConnection and qs is the QueueConnection. The Session's commit() method is placed at the end of the try { } block following statements that send all the messages to the message provider. The Session's rollback() method is called in the associated catch { } block.

Listing 16-6 Creating a message transaction.	```TopicSession ts = tc.createTopicSession(true, Session.AUTO_ACKNOWLEDGE);``` ```QueueSession qs = qc.createQueueSession(true, Session.AUTO_ACKNOWLEDGE);```

Message Producer

A message producer is an object that sends messages and is created by a session. There are two interfaces used by a message producer, depending on the session object. These are the QueueSender interface and the TopicPublisher interface, and they correspond to the Queue and Topic session objects.

Listing 16-7 illustrates how to create a message producer. Two message producers are created in this example. The first is the QueueSender created by calling the createSender() method. The createSender() method requires one argument, which is a Queue object used by the message producer to send messages. The other message producer in this example is a TopicPublisher and is created by calling the createPublisher() method, which requires the Topic object as an argument.

Once a message producer is created, the message producer can transmit messages by calling either the send() method or the publish() method, which are illustrated in Listing 16-7. The send() method is called for a QueueSender object and the publish() method is called for a TopicPublisher. Both methods require one argument—the message object, which you'll learn how to create later in this chapter.

Listing 16-7
Create two
message
producers
and send two
messages.
	```QueueSender qSender = qs.createSender(mq);```
	```TopicPublisher tPublisher = ts.createPublisher(mt);```
	```qSender.send(msg);```
	```tPublisher.publish(msg);```

Message Consumer

A message consumer is an object that receives messages and is also created by a session object. Before any messages are received, the client must register with a JMS provider indicating interest in receiving messages. Once registered, the JMS provider is responsible for delivering messages to the client.

A message consumer, depending on the type of session that is created, uses one of two interfaces. These are the QueueReceiver interface and the TopicSubscriber interface. The QueueReceiver interface is used for a QueueSession and the TopicSubscriber interface is used for a TopicSession.

Listing 16-8 illustrates how both types of message consumers are created. A QueueReceiver message consumer is created by calling the createReceiver() method of the session object and passing the createReceiver() the Queue object that will be used to receive messages.

A TopicSubscriber message consumer is created by calling the createSubscriber() method of the session object. The createSubscriber() method requires one argument, which is the Topic object that will be sending messages to the message consumer.

Once a message consumer is created, the connection is started by calling the start() method, and the receive() method is called to begin receiving messages synchronously. The start() method is found in the QueueConnection object or TopicConnection object. The receive() method can accept an argument, which is the number of milliseconds that must pass before the message consumer times out. In this example, the TopicSubscriber message consumer times out after 1,500 milliseconds. If no parameter is passed or the parameter is 0, the call is blocked indefinitely until the message is received. The close() method can be called for both the QueueReceiver object and TopicSubscriber object to deactivate the object.

Listing 16-8
Creating two message consumers.

```
QueueReceiver qr = qs.createReceiver(mq);
TopicSubscriber tSubscriber = ts.createSubscriber(mt);
qc.start();
Message msg1 = qr.receive();
tc.start();
Message msg2 = tSubscriber.receive(1500);
```

The message consumer receives messages asynchronously by creating a message listener. A message listener is an object that reacts to events similar to an event handler.

Message Listener

A message listener implements the MessageListener interface that contains the onMessage() method. The onMessage() method contains actions that must occur whenever a message is received from the JMS provider. The onMessage() method requires one argument, which is the message received from the JMS provider.

Listing 16-9 illustrates how to create a message listener for a QueueReceiver and TopicSubscriber. The first statement in this example creates a QueueListener called ql, which is then registered with the JMS provider by calling the setMessageListener() method of the QueueReceiver object.

The third statement in the example creates a TopicListener that is also registered by calling the setMessageListener() of the TopicSubscriber. Both methods require that the listener object be passed to the setMessageListener() method. Once the message listener is registered, the onMessage() is automatically called whenever a message is received. You create the Listener object by implementing the MessageListener interface, which you'll learn how to do later in this chapter.

Listing 16-9
Creating two message listeners.

```
QueueListener ql = new QueueListener();
qr.setMessageListener(ql);
TopicListener tl = new TopicListener();
tSubscriber.setMessageListener(tl);
```

Messages

A message is comprised of three parts. These are a header, properties, and the body of the message. Only the header is required to be included on every message. Properties and the body are optional.

A message header consists of predefined fields that are shown next. Values are assigned to message header fields by using a setXXX() method and values of a message header field are read using a getXXX() method where XXX is the name of the field. Many message fields are automatically set by the send() method or publish() method, as discussed previously in this chapter. Other fields are set by the client or by the JMS provider.

- Set by the send() method or publish() method
  - JMSDestination
  - JMSDeliveryMode
  - JMSExpiration
  - JMSPriority
  - JMSMessageID
  - JMSTimestamp
  - JMSCorrelationID
  - JMSReplyTo
  - JMSType
  - JMSRedelivered

- Set by the client
  - JMSCorrelationID
  - JMSReplyTo
  - JMSType
- Set by the JMS provider
  - JMSRedelivered

The message header contains commonly used fields that are necessary to transmit and process a message. However, there might be occasions when additional information is required to assure the message is compatible with other messaging systems. A message property is a built-in facility to include application-defined values that are also used to filter messages.

The message body contains the message. JMS supports six message formats, called *message types*. These are TextMessage, MapMessage, BytesMessage, StreamMessage, ObjectMessage, and Message.

The TextMessage message type contains a String object consisting of text. The MapMessage message type is a pairing of name and values that can be accessed sequentially or randomly. The name component of the MapMessage message type is a String object and the value component is a primitive Java programming language type.

The BytesMessage message type consists of bytes of information that are not interpreted, such as a graphic. The StreamMessage message type contains a stream of values that are read sequentially. These values are of a primitive Java programming language type. The ObjectMessage message type contains a Serializable Java programming language object. And the Message message type is used when there is an empty message body.

Listing 16-10 illustrates how to create a JMS message. In this example, the createTextMessage() method of the QueueSession object qs is called to create a TextMessage object called msg. Next, the setText() method is called and passed the String myMessage, which contains the actual message. The TextMessage object is then passed to the send() method of the QueueSender object called qSender, which transmits the message.

Listing 16-10
Creating a
TextMessage
message.

```
TextMessage msg = qs.createTextMessage();
msg.setText(myMessage);
qSender.send(msg);
```

When the message is received, the message consumer must read the body of the message. Listing 16-11 illustrates how this is done. In this example, the receive() method of the QueueReceiver object qr is called to receive a Message object, which is identified as msg in this example. If the Message object is a TextMessage, the Message object is type cast to a TextMessage object and assigned to the TextMessage object called tMsg. The text of the message is retrieved by calling the getText() method, which is displayed on the screen in this example.

However, if the message isn't a TextMessage, the program should test for other message types within the else statement and process each one according to the message type.

Listing 16-11
Reading a
TextMessage
message.

```
Message msg = qr.receive();
if (msg instanceof TextMessage)
{
    TextMessage tMsg = (TextMessage) msg;
    System.out.println("Incoming message: " + tMsg.getText());
}
else
{
    // Handle error
}
```

Message Selector

A message consumer can choose messages received by using a message selector. A message selector uses a conditional expression as criteria to select a message based on a message property and message header.

The conditional expression used by a message selection must conform to a SQL-92 conditional expression used in a WHERE clause, as is described in Part II of this book. Listing 16-12 illustrates how to create and use a message selector.

This example is a code segment that can be used to replace the TopicSubscriber statement in Listing 16-16. First, the selection criteria is defined and assigned to a String object called criteria where the request is to receive messages where the value of the Customer property is equal to '1234'. Of course, this assumes a message has a Customer property. A message can have any number of properties created by the sender or publisher. Next, the createSubscriber() method is called and is passed the topic and criteria as arguments.

A message selector applies only to messages destined for the message consumer. This means that the message selector criterion for one message consumer doesn't affect messages destined for another message consumer.

Although Listing 16-12 uses the publisher/subscriber model, a message selector can also be used with the point-to-point model with a message queue when calling the createReceiver() method.

Messages that are not seen by a message consumer because of criteria set in a message selector remain available to other message consumers. That is, the message remains on the message queue and is delivered to subscribers to that particular topic, depending on if the point-to-point model or the publisher/subscriber model is being employed.

Listing 16-12
Creating and
using a
message
selector.

```
String criteria = "Customer = '1234'";
TopicSubscriber tSubscriber  = ts.createSubscriber(myTopic, criteria, false);
```

Sending Messages to a Queue

JMS messages can be transmitted by a message producer using a message queue, as described earlier in this chapter. Listing 16-13 illustrates how to send a message to a message queue. This example sends a short welcome statement to the message queue, which will be read from the message queue in Listing 16-14.

The name of the message queue and the number of messages to be sent to the message queue are passed to the program as command-line arguments. You'll see how this is done later in this chapter.

The name of the message queue is assigned to the String object qName and the number of messages to be sent to the message queue is assigned to the msgCount int. Next, the program creates a JNDI context called jc by calling the InitialContext() method.

The lookup() method is then used to create the QueueConnectionFactory object called qcf by passing the lookup() method to the QueueConnectionFactory string. This is followed by passing the queue name to the lookup() method to create the Queue object called q. Any errors are trapped by the associated catch {} block.

The program calls the createQueueConnection() method of the QueueConnectionFactory object to create a QueueConnection object, which is used to create a QueueSession object. The QueueSession object's createSender() method is called to create a QueueSender.

The QueueSession object is used to create a TextMessage object and to send the message using the QueueSender's send() method. This example creates and sends one message until the value of the msgCount is reached. Afterwards, the program terminates the QueueConnection by calling the close() method to close the sender and the session.

Listing 16-13
Sending
messages to
a queue.

```
import javax.jms.*;
import javax.naming.*;
public class Sender {
  public static void main(String[] args) {
    final int msgCount;
    if ( (args.length < 1) || (args.length > 2) )
    {
      System.out.println("Enter the message queue name and number of messages to
send.");
```

JAVA INTERCONNECTIVITY

```
   System.exit(1);
  }
  String qName = new String(args[0]);
  if (args.length == 2)
  {
    msgCount = (new Integer(args[1])).intValue();
  }
  else
  {
   msgCount = 1;
  }
  QueueConnection qc = null;
  try {
    InitialContext jc = new InitialContext();
    QueueConnectionFactory qcf = (QueueConnectionFactory)
jc.lookup("QueueConnectionFactory");
    Queue q = (Queue) jc.lookup(qName);
    qc = qcf.createQueueConnection();
    QueueSession qs = qc.createQueueSession(false, Session.AUTO_ACKNOWLEDGE);
    QueueSender qSender = qs.createSender(q);
    TextMessage msg = qs.createTextMessage();
    for (int i = 0; i < msgCount; i++)
    {
      msg.setText("Welcome number " + (i + 1));
      qSender.send(msg);
    }
    qSender.close();
    qs.close();
  }
  catch (Exception error) {
    System.out.println("Error: " + error.toString());
  }
  finally {
    if (qc != null)
    {
      try {
        qc.close();
      }
      catch (JMSException error) {
        System.out.println("Error: " + error.toString());
      }
    }
  }
 }
}
```

Receiving Messages from a Queue

A message consumer receives messages from a message queue by using a program similar to the program in Listing 16-14. This example retrieves messages sent to the message queue by the program in Listing 16-13.

Listing 16-14 requires that the name of the message queue be passed to the program as a command-line argument. The message queue name is then assigned to the String object qName. Next, the program must call the InitialContext() method to create a JNDI context, which is called jc. The lookup() method of the JNDI context is called and passed the string QueueConnectionFactory to return a QueueConnectionFactory object called qcf. The lookup() method is also invoked and passed the name of the queue to return a Queue object. In this example, the Queue object is simply called q.

The program must create a QueueConnection object by calling the createQueueConnection() method of the QueueConnectionFactory. The QueueConnection object's createQueueSession() method is invoked to create a QueueSession. And finally, the QueueSession object's createReceiver() method is invoked and passed the Queue object to create a QueueReceiver.

Once the QueueReceiver is created, the program tells the service to start serving received requests by calling the start() method. As long as the queue connection is alive, the program calls the receive() method of the QueueReceiver to retrieve one message from the message queue that is assigned to the Message object msg.

If a message is returned and that message is a TextMessage object, the program assigns the message to a TextMessage object called tmsg. The getText() method of the TextMessage object is called to retrieve and display the message on the screen.

Listing 16-14
Receiving
messages
from a
queue.

```
import javax.jms.*;
import javax.naming.*;
public class Receiver {
  public static void main(String[] args) {
    Message msg;
    TextMessage tmsg;
    if (args.length != 1)
    {
      System.out.println("Enter Message Queue Name: ");
      System.exit(1);
    }
    String qName = new String(args[0]);
    QueueConnection qc = null;
    try {
      InitialContext jc = new InitialContext();
      QueueConnectionFactory qcf = (QueueConnectionFactory)
jc.lookup("QueueConnectionFactory");
      Queue q = (Queue) jc.lookup(qName);
```

JAVA INTERCONNECTIVITY

```
qc = qcf.createQueueConnection();
QueueSession qs = qc.createQueueSession(false, Session.AUTO_ACKNOWLEDGE);
QueueReceiver qr = qs.createReceiver(q);
qc.start();
msg = qr.receive(10);
while (msg != null) {
    if (msg instanceof TextMessage)
    {
        tmsg = (TextMessage) msg;
        System.out.println("Message: " + tmsg.getText());
    }
    msg = qr.receive(10);
}
qr.close();
qs.close();
}
catch (Exception error) {
    System.out.println("Error: " + error.toString());
}
finally {
    if (qc != null)
    {
        try {
            qc.close();
        }
        catch (JMSException error) {
            System.out.println("Error: " + error.toString());
        }
    }
}
}
}
```

Compiling and Running Queue Programs

Instructions for compiling and running the queue programs are different for each vendor product. These instructions here work for the J2EE download from java.sun.com.

Make sure that your environment is set up properly before you attempt to compile and run the Sender and Receiver programs. If you're running Microsoft Windows, you will need to do the following:

1. Assign the directory that contains the J2SDK to the %JAVA_HOME% environment variable.

2. Assign the directory that contains the J2SDKEE to the %J2EE_HOME% environment variable.

3. The %CLASSPATH% environment variable must contain

```
.;%J2EE_HOME%\lib\j2ee.jar;
%J2EE_HOME%\lib\locale
```

4. The %PATH% environment variable must include %J2EE_HOME%\bin.

If you're running under UNIX, you need to do the following:

1. Assign the directory that contains the J2SDK to the $JAVA_HOME environment variable.

2. Assign the directory that contains the J2SDKEE to the $J2EE_HOME environment variable.

3. The $CLASSPATH environment variable must contain

```
.:$J2EE_HOME\lib\j2ee.jar:
$J2EE_HOME\lib\locale
```

4. The $PATH environment variable must include $J2EE_HOME\bin.

You compile the Sender and Receiver programs by entering the following commands at the command line:

```
javac Sender.java
javac Receiver.java
```

Next, start the J2EE server by entering the following command at the command line. Once you see the message display that confirms that the J2EE server is running, you can proceed to create the message queue that will be used by the Sender and Receiver programs.

```
j2ee -verbose
```

You create the message queue by using the j2eeadmin, as shown here. In this example, the msgQueue is created as a queue as indicated by the last command-line argument.

```
j2eeadmin -addJmsDestination msgQueue queue
```

Once the message queue is created, you can run the Sender program by executing the following command. The first argument is the jms_client.properties, which is followed by the name of the program, the name of the message queue, and the number of messages to create. The first example runs the program under Microsoft Windows and the second example runs the program under UNIX.

```
java -Djms.properties=%J2EE_HOME%\config\jms_client.properties Sender msgQueue 10
java -Djms.properties=$J2EE_HOME\config\jms_client.properties Sender msgQueue 10
```

You run the Receiver with similar commands to those used to run the Sender. The only difference is the Receiver doesn't require the number of messages as a command-line argument. Here's how to run the Receiver under Microsoft Windows and under UNIX:

```
java -Djms.properties=%J2EE_HOME%\config\jms_client.properties Receiver msgQueue
java -Djms.properties=$J2EE_HOME\config\jms_client.properties Receiver msgQueue
```

Make sure that you remove the message queue and stop the J2EE server after you are finished running the Receiver. You remove the message queue and terminate the J2EE server by running the following commands:

```
j2eeadmin -removeJmsDestination msgQueue
j2ee -stop
```

Creating a Publisher

The publisher illustrated in Listing 16-15 sends messages to a specified topic, as described previously in this chapter. Subscribers to the topic then receive those messages. Listing 16-16 illustrates how to construct a subscriber.

Listing 16-15 requires two command-line arguments. These are the name of the topic that will receive the message and the number of messages that will be sent to the topic. The topic name is assigned to the tName String and the number of messages is assigned the numMsg int.

Next, the program creates a JNDI context by creating an InitialContext object. The lookup() method of the JNDI context is used to retrieve the TopicConnectionFactory, which is called tcf. The lookup() method is also used to retrieve the Topic.

The program requires a TopicConnection in order to create a TopicSession. The TopicConnection is created by calling the createTopicConnection() method of the TopicConnectionFactory.

A TopicSession is necessary so the program can create a TopicPublisher by using the createPublisher() method. The createPublisher() method must be passed the Topic object, which is then associated with the TopicPublisher.

The TopicSession is also used to create the TextMessage object by calling the createTextMessage() method. The setText() method of the TextMessage object is invoked to assign the message to the TextMessage object. A simple welcome message is used in this example. The message is then passed to the publish() method to publish the message. The close() method of the TopicConnection is then called to terminate the topic connection, as are close() methods for the publisher and session.

Listing 16-15
Creating a publisher.

```java
import javax.jms.*;
import javax.naming.*;
public class Publisher {
  public static void main(String[] args) {
    final int numMsg;
    if ( (args.length < 1) || (args.length > 2) )
    {
     System.out.println("Enter: Topic Name and Number of Messages ");
     System.exit(1);
    }
    String tName = new String(args[0]);
    if (args.length == 2)
    {
     numMsg = (new Integer(args[1])).intValue();
    }
    else
    {
      numMsg = 1;
    }
    TopicConnection tc = null;
    try {
      InitialContext jc = new InitialContext();
      TopicConnectionFactory tcf = (TopicConnectionFactory)
jc.lookup("TopicConnectionFactory");
      Topic t = (Topic) jc.lookup(tName);
      tc = tcf.createTopicConnection();
      TopicSession ts = tc.createTopicSession(false, Session.AUTO_ACKNOWLEDGE);
      TopicPublisher tp = ts.createPublisher(t);
      TextMessage msg = ts.createTextMessage();
      for (int i = 0; i < numMsg; i++)
      {
        msg.setText("Welcome number " + (i + 1));
        tp.publish(msg);
       }
      tp.close();
      ts.close();
    }
    catch (Exception error) {
      System.out.println("Error: " + error.toString());
    }
    finally {
      if (tc != null)
```

```
        {
          try {
            tc.close();
          }
          catch (JMSException error) {
            System.out.println("Error: " + error.toString());
          }
        }
      }
    }
  }
```

Creating a Subscriber

Listing 16-16 illustrates how to construct a subscriber program. In this example, the program subscribes to the topic published to by the publisher shown in Listing 16-15. The subscriber program requires one command-line argument, which is the name of the topic to which the program subscribes. The topic name is assigned to a String called tName.

As with the publisher, the subscriber program creates a JNDI context by creating an InitialContext object and then uses the InitialContext's lookup() method to retrieve a TopicConnectionFactory and a Topic object.

The program then creates a TopicConnection and TopicSession using the same techniques to create these objects in the publisher program. The TopicSession is then used to create a TopicSubscriber.

Next the program creates a TextListener, which is passed to the setMessageListener() method of the TopicSubscriber. The message listener receives any messages sent to a specific topic when a message is published to the topic.

The start() method is called to begin listening for published messages on the topic. The program continues to run until the user enters the letter 'q' or 'Q', at which time the program calls the close() method to terminate the TopicConnection as well as the close() methods for the subscriber and the session.

Listing 16-16
Creating a
subscriber.

```
import javax.jms.*;
import javax.naming.*;
import java.io.*;
public class Subscriber {
  public static void main(String[] args) {
    char response = '\0';
    if (args.length != 1)
    {
      System.out.println("Enter: Topic Name " );
```

```
        System.exit(1);
      }
    String tName = new String(args[0]);
    TopicConnection tc = null;
    try {
        InitialContext jc = new InitialContext();
        TopicConnectionFactory tcf = (TopicConnectionFactory)
jc.lookup("TopicConnectionFactory");
        Topic t = (Topic) jc.lookup(tName);
        tc = tcf.createTopicConnection();
        TopicSession ts = tc.createTopicSession(false, Session.AUTO_ACKNOWLEDGE);
        TopicSubscriber tSubscriber = ts.createSubscriber(t);
        TextListener tListener = new TextListener();
        tSubscriber.setMessageListener(tListener);
        tc.start();
        System.out.println("Enter 'q' and press <return> to exit ");
        InputStreamReader isr = new InputStreamReader(System.in);
        while (!((response == 'q') || (response == 'Q')))
        {
          try {
            response = (char) isr.read();
          }
          catch (IOException error) {
            System.out.println("Error: " + error.toString());
          }
        }
        tSubscriber.close();
        ts.close();
    }
    catch (Exception error) {
      System.out.println("Error: " + error.toString());
    }
    finally {
      if (tc != null)
      {
        try {
          tc.close();
        }
        catch (JMSException error) {
          System.out.println("Error: " + error.toString());
        }
      }
    }
  }
}
```

Creating a Message Listener

Listing 16-17 illustrates the message listener for the subscriber program. This example defines the onMessage() method. The onMessage() method is called each time a message is published by a publisher to a specific topic.

If the incoming message is a TextMessage, the message is assigned to the TextMessage object and made available to the subscriber for further processing.

Listing 16-17
Creating a
message
listener.

```
import javax.jms.*;
public class TextListener implements MessageListener {
  public void onMessage(Message msg) {
    try {
      if (msg instanceof TextMessage)
      {
          TextMessage tMessage = (TextMessage) msg;
          System.out.println("Message: " + tMessage.getText());
      }
      else
      {
       System.out.println("Message type error: " + msg.getClass().getName());
      }
    }
    catch (JMSException error) {
      System.out.println("onMessage() error: " + error.toString());
    }
    catch (Throwable error) {
      System.out.println("onMessage() error:" + error.getMessage());
    }
  }
}
```

Compiling and Running the Publisher and Subscriber

Before you begin, be sure the environment variables are set up properly as described in the "Compiling and Running Queue Programs" section of this chapter. You need to compile the publisher, TextListener, and subscriber using the following commands:

```
javac Publisher.java
javac TextListener.java
javac Subscriber.java
```

Next, start the J2EE server using the following command. A message is displayed once the J2EE server is running.

```
j2ee -verbose
```

A topic must be created by running the j2eeadmin program, as shown here:

```
j2eeadmin -addJmsDestination msgTopic topic
```

Once the topic is created, you can run the Subscriber program by executing the following command. The first argument is the jms_client.properties, which is followed by the name of the program, the name of the topic, and the number of messages to create. The first example runs the program under Microsoft Windows and the second example runs the program under UNIX.

```
java -Djms.properties=%J2EE_HOME%\config\jms_client.properties Subscriber msgTopic
java -Djms.properties=$J2EE_HOME\config\jms_client.properties Subscriber msgTopic
```

Once the message queue is created, you can run the Sender program by executing the following command. The first argument is the jms_client.properties, which is followed by the name of the program and the name of the message topic. The first example runs the program under Microsoft Windows and the second example runs the program under UNIX.

```
java -Djms.properties=%J2EE_HOME%\config\jms_client.properties Sender msgQueue 10
java -Djms.properties=$J2EE_HOME\config\jms_client.properties Sender msgQueue 10
```

You run the Receiver with similar commands to those used to run the Sender. The only difference is the Receiver doesn't require the number of messages as a command-line argument. Here's how to run the Receiver under Microsoft Windows and under UNIX:

```
java -Djms.properties=%J2EE_HOME%\config\jms_client.properties Receiver
java -Djms.properties=$J2EE_HOME\config\jms_client.properties Receiver
```

You run the Publisher with similar commands to those used to run the Subscriber. The only difference is the Publisher requires the number of messages as a command-line argument. Here's how to run the Publisher under Microsoft Windows and under UNIX:

```
java -Djms.properties=%J2EE_HOME%\config\jms_client.properties Publisher msgTopic 10
java -Djms.properties=$J2EE_HOME\config\jms_client.properties Publisher msgTopic 10
```

Make sure that you remove the topic and stop the J2EE server after you are finished running the Publisher. You remove the topic and terminate the J2EE server by running the following commands:

```
j2eeadmin -removeJmsDestination msgTopic
j2ee -stop
```

JAVA INTERCONNECTIVITY

Quick Reference Guide

This Quick Reference Guide provides a brief overview of Java classes used by a Java servlet to interact with JMS. Full details of these classes and all Java classes and interfaces are available at java.sun.com.

Syntax	Descriptions
void acknowledge()	Acknowledges messages received.
void clearBody()	Removes the message body.
void clearProperties()	Removes a message's properties.
boolean getBooleanProperty(String name)	Returns the boolean property value.
byte getByteProperty(String name)	Returns the byte property value.
double getDoubleProperty(String name)	Returns the double property value.
float getFloatProperty(String name)	Returns the float property value.
int getIntProperty(String name)	Returns the integer property value.
String getJMSCorrelationID()	Gets the message correlation ID.
byte[] getJMSCorrelationIDAsBytes()	Gets the message correlation ID as an array of bytes.
int getJMSDeliveryMode()	Gets the message delivery mode.
Destination getJMSDestination()	Gets the message destination.
long getJMSExpiration()	Gets the message's expiration value.
String getJMSMessageID()	Gets the message ID.
int getJMSPriority()	Gets the message priority.
boolean getJMSRedelivered()	Returns a true if the message is being redelievered, otherwise a false is returned.
Destination getJMSReplyTo()	Gets the message reply information.

Table 16-1. *public interface **Message***

Syntax	Descriptions
long getJMSTimestamp()	Gets the message timestamp.
String getJMSType()	Gets the message type.
long getLongProperty(String name)	Returns the long property value.
Object getObjectProperty(String name)	Returns the Java object property.
Enumeration getPropertyNames()	Returns an enumeration of property names.
short getShortProperty(String name)	Returns the short property value.
String getStringProperty(String name)	Returns the String property value.
boolean propertyExists(String name)	Checks if a property value exists.
void setBooleanProperty(String name, boolean value)	Sets a boolean property value.
void setByteProperty(String name, byte value)	Sets a byte property value.
void setDoubleProperty(String name, double value)	Sets a double property value.
void setFloatProperty(String name, float value)	Sets a float property value.
void setIntProperty(String name, int value)	Sets an integer property value.
void setJMSCorrelationID (String correlationID)	Sets the correlation ID for the message.
void setJMSCorrelationIDAsBytes (byte[] correlationID)	Sets the correlation ID as an array of bytes for the message.
void setJMSDeliveryMode(int deliveryMode)	Sets the delivery mode for this message.
void setJMSDestination(Destination destination)	Sets the destination for this message.

Table 16-1.   *public interface **Message*** (continued)

Syntax	Descriptions
void setJMSExpiration(long expiration)	Sets the message's expiration value.
void setJMSMessageID(String id)	Sets the message ID.
void setJMSPriority(int priority)	Sets the priority for this message.
void setJMSRedelivered (boolean redelivered)	The message should be redelivered.
void setJMSReplyTo(Destination replyTo)	Sets reply information.
void setJMSTimestamp(long timestamp)	Sets the message timestamp.
void setJMSType(String type)	Sets the message type.
void setLongProperty(String name, long value)	Sets a long property value.
void setObjectProperty (String name, Object value)	Sets a Java object property value.
void setShortProperty (String name, short value)	Sets a short property value.
void setStringProperty (String name, String value)	Sets a String property value.

Table 16-1.   *public interface **Message** (continued)*

Syntax	Descriptions
String getQueueName()	Gets the name of this queue.
String toString()	Returns a printed version of the queue name.

Table 16-2.   *public interface **Queue extends Destination***

Syntax	Descriptions
Queue getQueue()	Gets the queue associated with sender.
void send(Message message)	Sends a message to the queue.
void send(Message message, int deliveryMode, int priority, long timeToLive)	Sends a message specifying delivery mode, priority, and time to live.
void send(Queue queue, Message message)	Sends a message to a queue for an unidentified message producer.
void send(Queue queue, Message message, int deliveryMode, int priority, long timeToLive)	Sends a message to a queue for an unidentified message producer, specifying delivery mode, priority, and time to live.

Table 16-3.   *public interface **QueueSender** extends MessageProducer*

Syntax	Descriptions
Topic getTopic()	Gets the topic.
void publish(Message message)	Publishes a message using the topic's default delivery mode, time to live, and priority.
void publish(Message message, int deliveryMode, int priority, long timeToLive)	Publishes a message specifying delivery mode, priority, and time to live to the topic.
void publish(Topic topic, Message message)	Publishes a message for an unidentified message producer.
void publish(Topic topic, Message message, int deliveryMode, int priority, long timeToLive)	Publishes a message for an unidentified message producer, specifying delivery mode, priority, and time to live.

Table 16-4.   *public interface **TopicPublisher** extends MessageProducer*

JAVA INTERCONNECTIVITY

Syntax	Descriptions
boolean getNoLocal()	Gets the NoLocal attribute.
Topic getTopic()	Gets the topic.

Table 16-5. *public interface **TopicSubscriber** extends MessageConsumer*

Chapter 17

Security

Security is a major consideration whenever any application is connected to a network. A network is the backbone to distributive computing and the road hackers use to invade a computer system. Sun Microsystems, Inc. and the Java community have taken steps to make the Java environment stable and thwart security violations by building security features into Java technology.

J2EE developers need to be overly concerned about security measures because the JVM and Java container vendors implement security. Therefore, it is important for the J2EE developer to have a firm understanding of Java security fundamentals, but the developer doesn't need to know how to implement security measures.

In this chapter, you'll be introduced to features of J2EE that protect the J2EE application and components from security violations.

J2EE Security Concepts

A J2EE application is made secure by features found within the core Java classes, within the JVM, and within the Java programming language. There are many levels of a J2EE application—from Java statements used within classes, to low-level programming that occurs at the JVM. Security features can be implemented at each level.

Security is a balance between ultimate protection and utilization. The more the security scale moves towards ultimate protection, the less utilization is realized. This theory holds true whether we're talking about security at the airport or security of a J2EE application.

An increase in airport security creates a delay for air travelers. An increase in the security levels of a J2EE application hinders the ease of using the J2EE application and slows the application's performance.

The proper amount of security to apply is determined by perceived risk/utilization factors. In a high-risk environment, users accept tighter security measures and less utilization. In a low-risk environment, users accept loose security measures and high utilization.

For example, air travelers accept delays at the airport caused by increased security measures whenever there is a perceived heightened security risk. However, such delays are intolerable in a perceived low security risk environment. The same concept holds true with users of J2EE applications.

The Java security model is an open specification, which is a major advantage that Java has over other languages and environments. Sun Microsystems, Inc. and the Java community realize that the Java security model isn't foolproof. However, security faults in the model are identified and corrected because the Java security model specification is available to the Java community to study and validate, and they are able to propose enhancements to make it more secure.

JVM Security

Security measures are strictly enforced by the JVM, as the JVM verifies incoming classes before classes are run and performs runtime checks to assure that classes perform only valid operations. The JVM prevents a Java program from executing operations that jeopardize the operating environment except for denial of service where operating resources such as the CPU are monopolized by a wayward Java program.

The JVM doesn't rely on security measures imposed by the Java programming language to assure that classes are safe to run. Instead, JVM examines bytecode contained in classes before running the classes.

Bytecode undergoes a three-step examination by the class loader component of the JVM before the bytecode is executed. As each class is loaded, the JVM conducts security checks that are possible to perform on the first reading of the class, such as verifying that the first four bytes are 0xCAFEBABE. Next, the JVM performs security validations that are possible only on a second pass through the bytecode, such as examining superclasses.

Still another security examination occurs at runtime, where the JVM performs type checking and examines array boundaries to assure no security violations exist because of late binding involving dynamic memory allocation. Late binding is not validated at compile time.

Security Management

As you learned in Chapter 15, a security manager object can be implemented within a J2EE application to take advantage of security features available from the security manager installed in the JVM. The purpose of a security manager is to control the operations of runtime programs on the JVM. In addition, a security manager enables a J2EE application to create a security policy that limits the operation of a J2EE application.

A security manager plays a crucial role in defending against security violations such as preventing a remotely loaded Java applet from accessing the local filing system. Likewise, a security manager requires that a remote connection from a Java applet be limited to the server that provided the Java applet.

A security manager contains default security rules that are enforced on every program that runs within the JVM. These rules are called permissions and are defined in the <java installation directory /jre/lib/security/java.policy file. Furthermore, each user has a .java.policy file in the user's home directory that contains permissions specific to the user.

Additional security policies can be inserted into either security policy file by using the policytool. The policytool is used to grant permissions to access a resource. Start the policytool by entering **policytool** at the command line.

The policytool modifies the .java.policy file in the home directory and displays an error if the .java.policy file isn't found. The Add Policy Entry is used once the policytool's screen is displayed to see existing policies and associated settings on the screen.

The Add Permission option is used to display a screen that contains three options. These are a drop-down list box that contains available permissions, the Property Permission box that contains specific properties to choose from (or you enter properties yourself depending if the setting is already defined), and there is a text field that contains the corresponding Java class name that is affected by the permission. The policytool automatically updates the .java.policy file when the new permission is saved.

Java API Security

There are several Java packages that are used to incorporate additional security measures within a J2EE application. These are the Java Cryptography Architecture (JCA) in the java.security.* package and the Java Cryptography Extension (JCE) found in the javax.crypto.* package. These are used to integrate cryptographic algorithms, ciphers, secure streams, key generation, certificates, digital fingerprints, and signatures.

Although these classes are typically implemented by container providers and other third-party vendors, it is worthwhile to review the features provided by these classes. A digital fingerprint, also known as a message digest, consists of a calculation (similar to a checksum) based on the content of the message. The message sender performs the calculation and the result is sent along with the message to the message receiver. The message receiver performs the same calculation and compares the result with the result received in the message.

A digital fingerprint isn't foolproof since the message can be intercepted and replaced with another message that has the same digital fingerprint. A digital signature is designed to plug this potential security breach. A digital signature requires that the digital fingerprint be encrypted by the message sender using the message sender's private key. The message receiver uses the message sender's public key to decipher the digital fingerprint. Certificates are used to manage the identities of message senders who use digital signatures.

The vulnerability of a digital signature is the public key that is used to decipher the digital fingerprint. The message sender sends the public key to the message receiver. However, the message receiver still must be authenticated for the message sender to be sure the message sender is the person who actually sent the message.

A certificate is used to address the vulnerability of a digital signature. A certificate contains the message sender's email address, name, and public key, along with other information used to uniquely identify the message sender. The integrity of the certificate is attested to by a well-known and trusted organization called a certification authority, such as VeriSign. The certification authority provides a message sender with a private key, used to encrypt the digital fingerprint. Likewise, the certification authority provides the message receiver with the certificate that contains the certification authority's public key.

Browser Security

By its nature, a Java applet is untrustworthy because a Java applet is downloaded from a remote computer. The Java applet's security manager restricts a Java applet to secure operations such as preventing access to the local computer's resources.

For example, a Java applet is prevented from accessing files on a local disk drive. Typically, local files contain passwords and other sensitive information, including emails and address books.

Likewise, a Java applet cannot open a socket to an IP address other than to the IP address from where the Java applet was downloaded, because hackers commonly use a local computer to launch an attack against other remote computers. The attack appears to be coming from the local computer when, in reality, the hacker's remote computer is using the local computer for misdirection.

Also, a Java applet is denied access to monitoring incoming ports on a local computer. An incoming port is used to receive transmissions such as email from a remote computer. A Java applet could intercept and redirect incoming communication if the Java applet security manager didn't plug this potential security gap.

This leaves the local computer vulnerable to a security violation by a Java applet by consuming too much CPU time, denying service to other programs.

A browser executes a plug-in whenever a browser encounters reference to the plug-in with an HTML page. This reference typically is in the form of a URL to a file that contains a file extension that is associated with a plug-in, such as PDF for an Acrobat file. A security manager does not restrain a plug-in, meaning the plug-in has all the capabilities of any executable program running locally on the computer.

The security manager informs the user when an untrusted Java applet generates a message on the screen. The warning message varies according to the browser that is used by the local computer.

Web Services Security

Security is vital to a J2EE application that is implemented in a web services environment, because requests for service and responses from components are vulnerable during transmission over a network. The Java community addresses security concerns with the introduction of the declarative security mechanism contained in the Java Web Services Development Pack (WSDP).

The declarative security mechanism requires application providers to declare the application's security requirements, so that the security requirements can be addressed when the application is configured.

The application provider uses a declarative syntax deployment descriptor to define the security requirements for the application. (You learned how to create a deployment descriptor and specify security requirements for an application in Chapter 12.)

The deployment descriptor is used by the application deployer to implement the security requirements of the application. This is accomplished by mapping the security requirements to the security features of the web services container using a tool provided by the container vendor.

As you learned in Chapter 2, web services is a multi-tier architecture where web services components can reside on different tiers and yet communicate with each other as if components were local to a computer.

WSDP is designed to address security concerns through the web services in a multi-tier architecture. You might say that WSDP provides a security blanket around every component regardless of the component's location on the tier structure.

Each tier contains components and resources used by components to respond to requests from a J2EE application. Resources are divided into two groups: protected and unprotected resources. Protected resources are those that require that a component be authorized before access is granted. No authorization is required for a component to use unprotected resources.

WSDP security requirements address authentication and access control to web services resources. An authentication process must verify the identity and access rights of a component that needs access to a protected resource before the component is granted access to the resource. Components seeking access to unprotected resources are granted anonymous access to the resource without having to undergo the authentication process.

Web Services Security Classifications

Web services security is similar to security found on many operating systems in that access rights can be assigned to an individual user ID, to a particular functional role performed by a user, or to a group of users.

Although web services security parallels security used in many operating systems, both security implementations are independent of each other. That is, both web services and an operating system used to run a J2EE application use different security managers to control access rights to users, roles, and groups. For example, changing a right to an operating system group doesn't have an effect on a related web services group.

A user is a person or application that is assigned a user ID and password that can be authenticated by the security manager. A user can be associated with a role, such as a system administrator. Also, a user can be associated with a group of users, such as the accounts payable department.

A role is a name that identifies a function that is performed by one or more users. One or more users are assigned to a role if they perform the same function. Let's say that a corporation has several employees who are responsible for approving travel advances. This role might be called "travel advance approver." A user who is assigned to this role has rights to use the J2EE application and indirectly related web services components that are used to approve travel advances.

A group is a name that identifies an association of users who have common characteristics. For example, employees of the East Coast division of a company are permitted to view the East Coast division's intranet page and associated applications. The group name might be "East Coast division." Employees who work in the East Coast division are members of the East Coast division group.

A user is assigned a user ID and password, which are used to authenticate the user to web services. The administrator of web services uses the web services server security management tool to register the user ID and password with the server. The security management tool is also used to assign a user ID to either a role or group.

Access rights to web services resources are the rights assigned directly to a user ID—or, more likely, to a role or group. Administrators find it more efficient to assign access rights to resources to a role or group rather than to each user ID, because a single change to access rights of a role or group affects multiple user IDs.

User IDs, roles, and groups, along with related access rights, are stored in a database—commonly referred to as a "realm." Refer to the web service server documentation of the server you are using for information about how to use the server's security manager's administrative tools to implement security classifications.

Security Within a Web Services Tier

Web services is organized into tiers, as you learned in Chapter 2. Each tier contains a web resource collection, which is a list of URL patterns and HTTP methods. A web resource collection is protected by security constraints that authorize access to members of a web resource collection. Security constraints are defined in the deployment discriptor, which was discussed earlier in this chapter.

Security constraints are used by the web container to authenticate a user who requests service from a member of the resource collection. The web container doesn't process a service request until the user is authenticated.

No further web container security measures are taken once a user is authenticated. This means that the user (that is, the J2EE application) can access any resource in the collection without requiring additional permissions.

There are four kinds of authentication that can be implemented to protect a resource collection: basic authentication, form-based authentication, client-certificate authentication, and digest authentication.

Basic authentication, also known as HTTP basic authentication, requires the web server to use the user ID and password to authenticate a user. Form-based authentication uses a customized login screen that is displayed by an HTTP browser and is used to capture a user ID and password.

Basic authentication and form-based authentication provide a low degree of security. This is because both authentication methods transmit a user ID and password as unencrypted text over the Internet. The customer form should be submitted using SSL. A hacker could intercept and modify the user ID and password.

Client-certificate authentication requires the use of a certificate, as described earlier in this chapter, to authenticate a requestor and web server. Transmission occurs over

Secure Sockets Layer (SSL), which encrypts data and uses a private and public key to hinder decoding if a hacker intercepts the transmission.

Digest authentication requires that the user password be encoded before the password is transmitted to a web server. Transmission occurs over non-SSL or SSL. A hacker can still intercept the transmission, but the hacker's attempt to penetrate the web services server is impeded by the ciphered password.

Avoid using non-SSL for transmissions during a session. As you learned in Chapter 12, a session consists of a series of web services requests made by the same client once the client is authenticated by the web services server. Each session is uniquely identified with a session ID, which is then used in each request to associate requests with a session.

Authentication occurs at the beginning of a session and does not continue with each request during the session. A session ID can be intercepted if the requests for the session are transmitted using non-SSL. It can then be used by a hacker in subsequent requests to spoof the web services server into thinking the hacker is the previously authenticated web services user.

Programmatic Security

J2EE applications that require a high level of security must implement programmatic security to embellish declarative security provided by the deployment descriptor. Programmatic security is implemented by using the getRemoteUser(), isUserInRole(), and getUserPrincipal() methods of the HttpServletRequest interface.

These methods provide the remote username (getRemoteUser()) and the security role of the user (isUserInRole()), and obtain a user principal object (getUserPrincipal()). You can apply business logic to this information to create your own security validation process.

Quick Reference Guide

This Quick Reference Guide provides a brief overview of Java classes used with Java security. Full details of these classes and all Java classes and interfaces are available at java.sun.com.

Syntax	Descriptions
ProtectionDomain[] combine(ProtectionDomain[] currentDomains, ProtectionDomain[] assignedDomains)	Modifies or updates a ProtectionDomain.

Table 17-1. *public interface* **DomainCombiner**

Syntax	Descriptions
void checkGuard(Object object)	Determines if access is allowed to the guarded object.

Table 17-2.   *public interface **Guard***

Syntax	Descriptions
String getAlgorithm()	Returns the algorithm name for a key.
byte[] getEncoded()	Returns a key in its encoding format, or a null indicating that encoding is not supported.
String getFormat()	Returns the name of the primary encoding format.

Table 17-3.   *public interface **Key** extends Serializable*

Syntax	Descriptions
boolean equals(Object another)	Compares a principal to an object.
String getName()	Returns principal name.
int hashCode()	Returns a hash code.
String toString()	Returns a string of a principal.

Table 17-4.   *public interface **Principal***

Syntax	Description
Object run()	Performs computation.

Table 17-5.   *public interface **PrivilegedAction***

Syntax	Description
Object run()	Performs computation.

Table 17-6. *public interface **PrivilegedExceptionAction***

Syntax	Descriptions
void checkPermission(Permission perm)	Determines whether the access request should be allowed or denied.
boolean equals(Object obj)	Compares AccessControlContext objects.
DomainCombiner getDomainCombiner()	Returns the DomainCombiner.
int hashCode()	Returns the hash code value.

Table 17-7. *public final class **AccessControlContext** extends Object*

Syntax	Descriptions
static void checkPermission(Permission perm)	Determines if access should be allowed or denied.
static Object doPrivileged(PrivilegedAction action)	Performs the PrivilegedAction.
static Object doPrivileged(PrivilegedAction action, AccessControlContext context)	Performs the PrivilegedAction.
static Object doPrivileged(PrivilegedExceptionAction action	Performs the PrivilegedExceptionAction.
static Object doPrivileged(PrivilegedExceptionAction action, AccessControlContext context)	Performs the PrivilegedExceptionAction.
static AccessControlContext getContext()	Takes a snapshot of the current calling context.

Table 17-8. *public final class **AccessController** extends Object*

Syntax	Descriptions
AlgorithmParameters generateParameters()	Generates parameters.
String getAlgorithm()	Returns the standard name of the algorithm.
static AlgorithmParameterGenerator getInstance(String algorithm)	Generates an AlgorithmParameterGenerator object.
static AlgorithmParameterGenerator getInstance(String algorithm, Provider provider)	Generates an AlgorithmParameterGenerator object.
static AlgorithmParameterGenerator getInstance(String algorithm, String provider)	Generates an AlgorithmParameterGenerator object.
Provider getProvider()	Returns the provider of an algorithm.
void init(AlgorithmParameterSpec genParamSpec)	Initializes a parameter generator.
void init(AlgorithmParameterSpec genParamSpec, SecureRandom random)	Initializes a parameter generator.
void init(int size)	Initializes a parameter generator.
void init(int size, SecureRandom random)	Initializes a parameter generator.

Table 17-9. *public class **AlgorithmParameterGenerator** extends Object*

Syntax	Descriptions
protected abstract AlgorithmParameters engineGenerateParameters()	Generates parameters.
protected abstract void engineInit (AlgorithmParameterSpec genParamSpec, SecureRandom random)	Initializes this parameter generator.
protected abstract void engineInit(int size, SecureRandom random)	Initializes this parameter generator.

Table 17-10. *public abstract class **AlgorithmParameterGeneratorSpi** extends Object*

Syntax	Descriptions
String getAlgorithm()	Returns the name of the algorithm.
byte[] getEncoded()	Returns the parameters in primary encoding format.
byte[] getEncoded(String format)	Returns the parameters.
static AlgorithmParameters getInstance(String algorithm)	Generates a parameter object.
static AlgorithmParameters getInstance(String algorithm, Provider provider)	Generates a parameter object.
static AlgorithmParameters getInstance(String algorithm, String provider)	Generates a parameter object.
AlgorithmParameterSpec getParameterSpec(Class paramSpec)	Returns a transparent specification of a parameter object.
Provider getProvider()	Returns the provider of a parameter object.
void init(AlgorithmParameterSpec paramSpec)	Initializes a parameter object.
void init(byte[] params)	Imports and decodes parameters.
void init(byte[] params, String format)	Imports and decodes the parameters.
String toString()	Returns description of parameters.

Table 17-11. *public class **AlgorithmParameters** extends Object*

Syntax	Descriptions
protected abstract byte[] engineGetEncoded()	Returns parameters in primary encoding format.
protected abstract byte[] engineGetEncoded(String format)	Returns the format of the parameter.
protected abstract AlgorithmParameterSpec engineGetParameterSpec(Class paramSpec)	Returns a transparent specification of a parameter object.
protected abstract void engineInit(AlgorithmParameterSpec paramSpec)	Initializes the parameter object.
protected abstract void engineInit(byte[] params)	Imports and decodes the parameters.
protected abstract void engineInit(byte[] params, String format)	Imports and decodes the parameters.
protected abstract String engineToString()	Returns description of parameters.

Table 17-12. *public abstract class **AlgorithmParametersSpi** extends Object*

Syntax	Descriptions
boolean equals(Object obj)	Compares AllPermission objects x.
String getActions()	Returns a string of the actions.
int hashCode()	Returns the hash code.
boolean implies(Permission p)	Determines if the permission is "implied."
PermissionCollection newPermissionCollection()	Returns a new PermissionCollection object.

Table 17-13. *public final class **AllPermission** extends Permission*

Syntax	Descriptions
boolean equals(Object obj)	Compares BasicPermission objects.
String getActions()	Returns a string of the actions.
int hashCode()	Returns the hash code value.
boolean implies(Permission p)	Determines if the permission is "implied."
PermissionCollection newPermissionCollection()	Returns a new PermissionCollection object.

Table 17-14. *public abstract class **BasicPermission** extends Permission implements Serializable*

Syntax	Descriptions
boolean equals(Object obj)	Compares objects.
Certificate[] getCertificates()	Returns certificates.
URL getLocation()	Returns location of CodeSource.
int hashCode()	Returns the hash code value.
boolean implies(CodeSource codesource)	Determines if the permission is "implied."
String toString()	Returns a string containing URL and certificates.

Table 17-15. *public class **CodeSource** extends Object implements Serializable*

Syntax	Descriptions
MessageDigest getMessageDigest()	Returns the message digest.
void on(boolean on)	Turns the digest function on or off.
int read()	Reads and updates the message digest.
int read(byte[] b, int off, int len)	Reads and updates the message digest.
void setMessageDigest (MessageDigest digest)	Associates a message digest with a stream.
String toString()	Prints a string of a digest input stream.

Table 17-16. *public class **DigestInputStream** extends FilterInputStream*

Syntax	Descriptions
MessageDigest getMessageDigest()	Returns a message digest.
void on(boolean on)	Turns the digest function on or off.
void setMessageDigest (MessageDigest digest)	Associates a message digest with a stream.
String toString()	Prints a string of a digest output stream.
void write(byte[] b, int off, int len)	Updates a message digest.
void write(int b)	Updates a message digest.

Table 17-17.   *public class **DigestOutputStream** extends FilterOutputStream*

Syntax	Description
Object getObject()	Returns a guarded object.

Table 17-18.   *public class **GuardedObject** extends Object implements Serializable*

Syntax	Descriptions
PrivateKey generatePrivate(KeySpec keySpec)	Generates a private key object.
PublicKey generatePublic(KeySpec keySpec)	Generates a public key object.
String getAlgorithm()	Returns the name of an algorithm.
static KeyFactory getInstance(String algorithm)	Generates a KeyFactory object.
static KeyFactory getInstance(String algorithm, Provider provider)	Generates a KeyFactory object.
static KeyFactory getInstance(String algorithm, String provider)	Generates a KeyFactory object.
KeySpec getKeySpec(Key key, Class keySpec)	Returns a key material of a key object.
Provider getProvider()	Returns the provider of a key factory object.
Key translateKey(Key key)	Translates a key object into a key object of a key factory.

Table 17-19.   *public class **KeyFactory** extends Object*

JAVA INTERCONNECTIVITY

Syntax	Descriptions
protected abstract PrivateKey engineGeneratePrivate(KeySpec keySpec)	Generates a private key object.
protected abstract PublicKey engineGeneratePublic(KeySpec keySpec)	Generates a public key object.
protected abstract KeySpec engineGetKeySpec(Key key, Class keySpec)	Returns key material of a key object.
protected abstract Key engineTranslateKey(Key key)	Translates a key object into a key object of a key factory.

Table 17-20. *public abstract class **KeyFactorySpi** extends Object*

Syntax	Descriptions
PrivateKey getPrivate()	Returns a reference to the private key component.
PublicKey getPublic()	Returns a reference to the public key component.

Table 17-21. *public final class **KeyPair** extends Object implements Serializable*

Syntax	Descriptions
KeyPair generateKeyPair()	Generates a key pair.
KeyPair genKeyPair()	Generates a key pair.
String getAlgorithm()	Returns the name of the algorithm.

Table 17-22. *public abstract class **KeyPairGenerator** extends KeyPairGeneratorSpi*

Syntax	Descriptions
static KeyPairGenerator getInstance (String algorithm)	Generates a KeyPairGenerator object.
static KeyPairGenerator getInstance (String algorithm, Provider provider)	Generates a KeyPairGenerator object.
static KeyPairGenerator getInstance (String algorithm, String provider)	Generates a KeyPairGenerator object.
Provider getProvider()	Returns the provider of a key pair generator object.
void initialize(AlgorithmParameterSpec params)	Initializes the key pair generator.
void initialize(AlgorithmParameterSpec params, SecureRandom random)	Initializes the key pair generator.
void initialize(int keysize)	Initializes the key pair generator.
void initialize(int keysize, SecureRandom random)	Initializes the key pair generator.

Table 17-24. *public abstract class* **KeyPairGenerator** *extends KeyPairGeneratorSpi* (continued)

Syntax	Descriptions
abstract KeyPair generateKeyPair()	Generates a key pair.
void initialize(AlgorithmParameterSpec params, SecureRandom random)	Initializes the key pair generator.
abstract void initialize(int keysize, SecureRandom random)	Initializes the key pair generator.

Table 17-23. *public abstract class* **KeyPairGeneratorSpi** *extends Object*

Syntax	Descriptions
void deleteEntry(String alias)	Deletes the entry identified.
String getCertificateAlias (Certificate cert)	Returns alias of the first keystore entry whose certificate matches the given certificate.
Date getCreationDate(String alias)	Returns the creation date of an entry identified.
Certificate getCertificate(String alias)	Returns a certificate.
static String getDefaultType()	Returns the default keystore type.
static KeyStore getInstance(String type)	Generates a Keystore object.
static KeyStore getInstance(String type, Provider provider)	Generates a Keystore object.
static KeyStore getInstance(String type, String provider)	Generates a Keystore object.
Key getKey(String alias, char[] password)	Returns the key.
Provider getProvider()	Returns the provider of a keystore.
String getType()	Returns the type of a keystore.
boolean isCertificateEntry(String alias)	Returns true if the entry is a trusted certificate entry.
boolean isKeyEntry(String alias)	Returns true if the entry is a key entry.
void load(InputStream stream, char[] password)	Loads this keystore from an input stream.
void setCertificateEntry(String alias, Certificate cert)	Assigns the given certificate.
void setKeyEntry(String alias, byte[] key, Certificate[] chain)	Assigns the given key.
void setKeyEntry(String alias, Key key, char[] password, Certificate[] chain)	Assigns the given key to a given alias.
int size()	Retrieves the number of entries in this keystore.
void store(OutputStream stream, char[] password)	Stores this keystore to an output stream.

Table 17-25. *public class **KeyStore** extends ObjectEnumeration aliases()*

Syntax	Descriptions
abstract Enumeration engineAliases()	Lists aliases of a keystore.
abstract boolean engineContainsAlias (String alias)	Determines the existence of an alias.
abstract void engineDeleteEntry(String alias)	Deletes an entry.
abstract Certificate engineGetCertificate (String alias)	Returns a certificate.
abstract String engineGetCertificateAlias (Certificate cert)	Returns an alias of the keystore entry.
abstract Certificate[] engineGetCertificateChain(String alias)	Returns a certificate chain.
abstract Date engineGetCreationDate (String alias)	Returns creation date of an entry.
abstract Key engineGetKey(String alias, char[] password)	Returns a key associated with an alias.
abstract boolean engineIsCertificateEntry (String alias)	Returns true if an entry of an alias is a trusted certificate entry.
abstract boolean engineIsKeyEntry(String alias)	Returns true if an entry of an alias is a key entry.
abstract void engineLoad(InputStream stream, char[] password)	Loads a keystore from an input stream.
abstract void engineSetCertificateEntry(String alias, Certificate cert)	Assigns a certificate to a given alias.
abstract void engineSetKeyEntry(String alias, byte[] key, Certificate[] chain)	Assigns a protected key to a given alias.
abstract void engineSetKeyEntry(String alias, Key key, char[] password, Certificate[] chain)	Assigns a key to a given alias.
abstract int engineSize()	Returns the number of entries in a keystore.
abstract void engineStore(OutputStream stream, char[] password)	Stores this keystore to an output stream.

Table 17-26.   *public abstract class **KeyStoreSpi** extends Object*

Syntax	Descriptions
Object clone()	Returns a clone.
byte[] digest()	Completes the hash computation.
byte[] digest(byte[] input)	Performs a final update on the digest.
int digest(byte[] buf, int offset, int len)	Completes the hash computation.
String getAlgorithm()	Returns the algorithm.
int getDigestLength()	Returns the length of the digest in bytes, or 0 if not supported.
static MessageDigest getInstance (String algorithm)	Generates a MessageDigest object.
static MessageDigest getInstance (String algorithm, Provider provider)	Generates a MessageDigest object.
static MessageDigest getInstance (String algorithm, String provider)	Generates a MessageDigest object.
Provider getProvider()	Returns the provider of a MessageDigest object.
static boolean isEqual(byte[] digesta, byte[] digestb)	Compares digests.
void reset()	Resets the digest.
String toString()	Returns a MessageDigest object.
void update(byte input)	Updates the digest.
void update(byte[] input)	Updates the digest.
void update(byte[] input, int offset, int len)	Updates the digest.

Table 17-27. *public abstract class **KeyStoreSpi** extends Object*

Syntax	Descriptions
Object clone()	Returns a clone.
protected abstract byte[] engineDigest()	Completes the hash computation.
protected int engineDigest(byte[] buf, int offset, int len)	Completes the hash computation.
protected int engineGetDigestLength()	Returns the digest length.
protected abstract void engineReset()	Resets the digest.
protected abstract void engineUpdate(byte input)	Updates the digest.
protected abstract void engineUpdate(byte[] input, int offset, int len)	Updates the digest.

Table 17-28.   *public abstract class **MessageDigestSpi** extends Object*

Syntax	Descriptions
void checkGuard(Object object)	Implements the Guard interface.
abstract boolean equals(Object obj)	Compares Permission objects.
abstract String getActions()	Returns the actions as a String.
String getName()	Returns the name of a Permission.
abstract int hashCode()	Returns the hash code value.
abstract boolean implies(Permission permission)	Determines if a permission's actions are "implied by."
PermissionCollection newPermissionCollection()	Returns an empty PermissionCollection.
object, or null if one is not defined. String toString()	Returns a string describing a Permission.

Table 17-29.   *public abstract class **Permission** extends Object implements Guard, Serializable*

Syntax	Descriptions
abstract void add(Permission permission)	Adds a Permission object.
abstract Enumeration elements()	Returns an enumeration of all Permission objects.
abstract boolean implies (Permission permission)	Determines if a permission is implied.
boolean isReadOnly()	Returns true if a PermissionCollection object is read only.
void setReadOnly()	Sets a PermissionCollection object as read only.
String toString()	Returns a string describing this PermissionCollection object.

Table 17-30. *public abstract class **PermissionCollection** extends Object implements Serializable*

Syntax	Descriptions
void add(Permission permission)	Adds a Permission object to the PermissionCollection.
Enumeration elements()	Returns an enumeration of all the Permission objects.
boolean implies(Permission permission)	Determines if permissions of a permission's type imply the permissions of a permission object.

Table 17-31. *public final class **Permissions** extends PermissionCollection implements Serializable*

Syntax	Descriptions
abstract PermissionCollection getPermissions(CodeSource codesource)	Returns a PermissionCollection object containing a set of permissions.
PermissionCollection getPermissions(ProtectionDomain domain)	Returns a PermissionCollection object containing a set of permissions.
static Policy getPolicy()	Returns an installed Policy object.
boolean implies(ProtectionDomain domain, Permission permission)	Tests whether the permission is granted.
abstract void refresh()	Refreshes/reloads a policy.
static void setPolicy(Policy policy)	Sets a Policy object.

Table 17-32. *public abstract class **Policy** extends Object*

Syntax	Descriptions
ClassLoader getClassLoader()	Returns a ClassLoader.
CodeSource getCodeSource()	Returns a CodeSource.
PermissionCollection getPermissions()	Returns static permissions.
Principal[] getPrincipals()	Returns an array of principals.
boolean implies(Permission permission)	Determines if a ProtectionDomain implies the permissions of a Permission object.
String toString()	Convert a ProtectionDomain to a String.

Table 17-33. *public class **ProtectionDomain** extends Object*

Syntax	Descriptions
void clear()	Clears properties used to look up facilities.
Set entrySet()	Returns an unmodifiable Set view of property entries.
String getInfo()	Returns description of a provider.
String getName()	Returns a provider's name.
double getVersion()	Returns a provider's version number.
Set keySet()	Returns an unmodifiable Set view of a property key.
void load(InputStream inStream)	Reads a property list.
Object put(Object key, Object value)	Sets the key property.
void putAll(Map t)	Copies all of the mappings from Map to provider.
Object remove(Object key)	Removes the key property.
String toString()	Returns a string with the name and version of a provider.
Collection values()	Returns an unmodifiable Collection view of the property values.

Table 17-34. *public abstract class **Provider** extends Properties*

Syntax	Descriptions
protected Class defineClass(String name, byte[] b, int off, int len, CodeSource cs)	Converts an array of bytes to an instance of class Class.
protected PermissionCollection getPermissions(CodeSource codesource)	Returns the permissions for a CodeSource object.

Table 17-35. *public class **SecureClassLoader** extends ClassLoader*

Syntax	Descriptions
byte[] generateSeed(int numBytes)	Returns seed bytes.
static SecureRandom getInstance (String algorithm)	Generates a SecureRandom object.
static SecureRandom getInstance (String algorithm, Provider provider)	Generates a SecureRandom object.
static SecureRandom getInstance (String algorithm, String provider)	Generates a SecureRandom object.
Provider getProvider()	Returns the provider of a SecureRandom object.
static byte[] getSeed(int numBytes)	Returns the given number of seed bytes.
protected int next(int numBits)	Generates an integer of pseudo-random bits that are right-justified, with leading zeros.
void nextBytes(byte[] bytes)	Generates a user-specified number of random bytes.
void setSeed(byte[] seed)	Reseeds a random object.
void setSeed(long seed)	Reseeds a random object.

Table 17-36.   *public class **SecureRandom** extends Random*

Syntax	Descriptions
protected abstract byte[] engineGenerateSeed(int numBytes)	Returns seed bytes.
protected abstract void engineNextBytes(byte[] bytes)	Generates a user-specified number of random bytes.
protected abstract void engineSetSeed(byte[] seed)	Reseeds a random object.

Table 17-37.   *public abstract class **SecureRandomSpi** extends Object implements Serializable*

JAVA INTERCONNECTIVITY

Syntax	Descriptions
Object clone()	Returns a clone.
String getAlgorithm()	Returns the name of the algorithm for a Signature object.
static Signature getInstance(String algorithm)	Generates a Signature object.
static Signature getInstance(String algorithm, Provider provider)	Generates a Signature object.
static Signature getInstance(String algorithm, String provider)	Generates a Signature object.
AlgorithmParameters getParameters()	Returns parameters used with a Signature object.
Provider getProvider()	Returns the provider of a Signature object.
void initSign(PrivateKey privateKey)	Initialize an object for signing.
void initSign(PrivateKey privateKey, SecureRandom random)	Initialize an object for signing.
void initVerify(Certificate certificate)	Initializes an object for verification.
void initVerify(PublicKey publicKey)	Initializes an object for verification.
void setParameter(AlgorithmParameterSpec params)	Initializes a signature engine.
byte[] sign()	Returns the signature bytes.
int sign(byte[] outbuf, int offset, int len)	Stores the resulting signature bytes.
String toString()	Returns a string of a Signature object.
void update(byte b)	Updates the data to be signed or verified.
void update(byte[] data)	Updates the data to be signed or verified.

Table 17-38.   *public abstract class* **Signature** *extends SignatureSpi*

Syntax	Descriptions
void update(byte[] data, int off, int len)	Updates the data to be signed or verified.
boolean verify(byte[] signature)	Verifies the passed-in signature.
boolean verify(byte[] signature, int offset, int length)	Verifies the passed-in signature specified in the array starting at the offset.

Table 17-37.   *public abstract class* **Signature** *extends SignatureSpi* (continued)

Syntax	Descriptions
Object clone()	Returns a clone.
protected abstract void engineInitSign (PrivateKey privateKey)	Initializes this Signature object.
protected void engineInitSign(PrivateKey privateKey, SecureRandom random)	Initializes this Signature object and specifies source of randomness.
protected abstract void engineInitVerify (PublicKey publicKey)	Initializes this Signature object.
protected abstract byte[] engineSign()	Returns the signature bytes.
protected int engineSign(byte[] outbuf, int offset, int len)	Stores the signature bytes.
protected abstract void engineUpdate (byte b)	Updates data to be signed or verified where data is array of bytes.
protected abstract void engineUpdate (byte[] b, int off, int len)	Updates data to be signed or verified where data is array of bytes starting at the offset.
protected abstract boolean engineVerify(byte[] sigBytes)	Verifies a passed-in signature.
protected boolean engineVerify(byte[] sigBytes, int offset, int length)	Verifies a passed-in signature.

Table 17-38.   *public abstract class* **SignatureSpi** *extends Object*

Syntax	Descriptions
String getAlgorithm()	Returns the name of a signature algorithm.
Object getObject()	Returns an encapsulated object.
byte[] getSignature()	Returns the signature on the signed object.
boolean verify(PublicKey verificationKey, Signature verificationEngine)	Verifies valid signature.

Table 17-39.   *public final class **SignedObject** extends Object implements Serializable*

Syntax	Descriptions
boolean equals(Object obj)	Compares UnresolvedPermission objects.
String getActions()	Returns actions.
int hashCode()	Returns the hash code value.
boolean implies(Permission p)	Returns false for unresolved permissions.
PermissionCollection newPermissionCollection()	Returns a new PermissionCollection object.
String toString()	Returns a description of the UnresolvedPermission.

Table 17-40.   *public final class **UnresolvedPermission** extends Permission implements Serializable*

The
Complete
Reference

Chapter 18

Java Naming and Directory Interface API

A J2EE application is an assemblage of objects that are located either on a local computer or on remote computers that are accessible over a network. Programmers implement objects by referencing the name of the object within the application.

Keeping track of the location of objects could be a maintenance nightmare, because the location of each object must be known to every program that implements the object. However, this task is handled by the Java Naming and Directory facility that enables a program to retrieve an object. You do need to be concerned about the location of the JNDI service, however. The JNDI service typically is located on the same physical machine as the object. The Java Naming and Directory Interface API is used to access objects controlled by the Java Naming and Directory facility.

In this chapter you'll learn about the Java Naming and Directory concept and how to utilize the Java Naming and Directory Interface API from within your program.

Naming and Directories

Although we tend to associate the name of an object with the object itself, these are actually two separate entities. An object is a Java Object class that might be stored on a server's secondary storage unit or might reside only in memory. The name of an object is a string of characters that are associated with the location of the object, and this name is the key used to retrieve the object.

A naming service is used to relate an object's name to an object's location and enable a program to access the object by referencing the object's name. The Domain Name System (DNS) is a good example of a naming service. DNS is used on Internets and intranets to relate a domain name such as www.jimkeogh.com to the Internet Protocol (IP) address of the computer, such as 155.23.23.41. Likewise, a file system is a naming service that is used by computers to associate a filename with the location of the file on a computer's secondary storage unit.

The programmer who creates the object determines the object name. Any name can be used as long as the name conforms to the naming convention of the naming service. The naming convention specifies the structure and form of the name and any restrictions on character usage within the name. The process of associating the location of an object with the object's name is referred to as "binding the object."

A naming service does not store objects. Instead, a naming service stores object names and reference to the location of an object, which is also known as a pointer and an object handle, to the object.

A program must create a context to use a naming service. A context is an object name and object reference and contains methods such as lookup(), used by the programmer to access objects in the naming service. You can say that a naming service consists of a set of contexts. Object names of a naming service are called *namespaces*.

Associating a naming service with a directory service enhances a naming service. A directory service relates object names with attributes. An attribute is additional information about the object that is associated with the object name that can be accessed through the directory service without having to access the object itself.

A company's online employee telephone directory is a good example of a naming service that has been enhanced by a directory server. An employee in this example is an object. The employee's name in the telephone directory is similar to an object's name in a naming service. And the employee's telephone number is like the address of an object.

Typically, an online employee telephone directory contains other information about an employee, such as the employee's office location and department. These are attributes of an employee who is listed in the online employee telephone directory.

Attributes are identified by name and are assigned a value. For example, an employee's location is the name of an attribute and the actual location of the employee is the attribute's value. In a directory service, an object's attribute might be named access rights and the attribute value might be read or read and write. A programmer uses a directory service's interface to insert, modify, and delete an attribute.

There are two methods used to find objects in a naming service and directory service: by referencing the object's name or by using a search filter. A search filter is a query that identifies an object according to the object's attribute identifiers and attribute values. This is referred to as a reverse lookup. The directory service then returns objects that meet the criteria specified in the query.

Java Naming and Directory Interface

The Java Naming and Directory Interface (JNDI) is an API that enables Java programs to interact with any naming service and directory service that implements JNDI. This means that a Java program can utilize a naming service and directory service without explicitly knowing anything about them.

Listing 18-1 illustrates how to look up an object using JNDI. In this example, the program is searching for the object named MyObject. After assigning the name to the myObject String, the program specifies the service provider to use for the initial context. This is accomplished by placing the name of the service provider class in the environment properties using a HashTable object. This example uses the service provider from Sun Microsystems, Inc. called com.sun.jndi.fscontext.RefFSContextFactory, which is passed as the second argument to the put() method.

The HashTable object called ep is then passed as an argument to the InitialContext constructor, which returns the initial context called ct. The lookup() method of the InitialContext object is passed the search criteria—the name of the object. The program then displays the object returned by the lookup() method. Afterwards, the context is closed. Any errors that occur during this process are caught and displayed on the screen.

```
import javax.naming.Context;
import javax.naming.InitialContext;
import javax.naming.NamingException;
import java.util.Hashtable;
class MyLookupClass {
  public static void main(String[] args) {
    String myObject = "MyObject";
    Hashtable ep = new Hashtable(1);
    ep.put(Context.INITIAL_CONTEXT_FACTORY,
      "com.sun.jndi.fscontext.RefFSContextFactory");
    try {
      InitialContext ct = new InitialContext(ep);
      Object obj = ct.lookup(myObject);
      System.out.println("Object: " + obj);
      ct.close();
    }
    catch (NamingException error) {
      System.err.println("Error:" + error.getMessage());
    }
  }
}
```

Compile and Run the Listing

Before compiling Listing 18-1, you'll need to make sure that the CLASSPATH contains the path to the jndi.jar, fscontext.jar, and providerutil.jar, and the path to the MyLookupClass.class file. Otherwise, you'll experience a compiler error when compiling the listing.

Listing 18-1 searches for an object called MyObject. Make sure that you replace the name MyObject with the name of an object that is already bound and available on the file system provided by the service provider.

Compile the listing by executing the following command at the command line:

```
javac MyLookupClass.java
```

Run the listing by entering the following at the command line:

```
java MyLookupClass
```

Retrieving Attributes from an Object Using Directory Services

Attributes of a file can be retrieved using directory services, as is illustrated in Listing 18-2. This example creates a class called MyGetAttributeClass, the purpose of which is to retrieve and display on the screen attributes that are associated with the object MyObject.

The program begins within the main() function with the creation of a Hashtable object called ep. The program calls the put() method twice, the first time to place the directory service provider into the hash table and the second call to the put() method is to place the URL of the directory service into the hash table.

The put() methods in this example are used to place the minimum information into the hash table that is necessary to access directory services. Sometimes you'll be required to include a user ID and password in the hash table before the directory service provider returns an object's attribute.

In this situation you will need to call put() two additional times and pass the user ID and password to put(), as illustrated here:

```
ep.put(Context.SECURITY_PRINCIPAL, "MyID");
ep.put(Context.SECURITY_CREDENTIALS, "MyPassword");
```

Next the Hashtable object is passed to the constructor of the InitialDirContext object to create an InitialDirContext object called ct. The getAttributes() method is then called to return the Attributes object. Once the Attributes object is created, the get() method is called to retrieve and display attributes of MyObject; afterwards, the InitialDirContext is closed.

Errors that are thrown during the execution of statements in the try { } block are caught by the catch { } block and displayed on the screen.

Listing 18-2
Retrieving attributes of an object using a directory service.

```
import javax.naming.Context;
import javax.naming.directory.InitialDirContext;
import javax.naming.directory.DirContext;
import javax.naming.directory.Attributes;
import javax.naming.NamingException;
import java.util.Hashtable;
class MyGetAttributeClass {
  public static void main(String[] args) {
    Hashtable ep = new Hashtable(2);
    ep.put(Context.INITIAL_CONTEXT_FACTORY, "com.sun.jndi.ldap.LdapCtxFactory");
ep.put(Context.PROVIDER_URL, "ldap://127.0.0.1:389");
    try {
```

```
        InitialDirContext ct = new InitialDirContext(ep);
        Attributes attr = ct.getAttributes("MyObject");
        System.out.println(attr.get("MyObject").get());
        ct.close();
    }
    catch (NamingException error) {
        System.err.println("Error: " + error.getmessage());
    }
    }
}
```

Before you compile and run Listing 18-2, make sure that you substitute your directory service provider's information into the put() methods and also change the name of the MyObject to an object that exists in your directory service. The JNDI and the LDAP service provider classes must appear in the CLASSPATH before you compile the program.

Once you complete these preparations, enter the following command at the command line:

```
javac MyGetAttributeClass.java
```

The compiler generates the MyGetAttributeClass.java bytecode file in the same directory as the MyGetAttributeClass.java source code file. Run the program by entering the following command at the command line:

```
java MyGetAttributeClass
```

Naming Operations

Objects can be retrieved and modified within a directory by using the namespace feature of JNDI. The namespace feature enables you to manipulate an object's name within a directory service. You'll find this useful whenever an object's name or attribute requires modification.

Among the manipulations that you can perform using the JNDI namespace feature is to search for an object within the directory, display the context contents of an object, modify binding, and change an object's name.

Listing 18-3 illustrates how to retrieve multiple objects at the same time by using an enumeration of a name class pair. In this example, the main() method of the MyNameClassPair creates a Hashtable object called ep and uses the put() method to identify the directory service provider and the directory service URL parameters, as you saw in previous listings in this chapter.

Next, the Hashtable object is passed to the constructor of the InitialContext object, which returns the InitialContext object called ct. The list() method of the InitialContext object is passed the name of the directory that contains the namespace that we want to retrieve.

You should use the list() method whenever you want to display object names. You don't need to access all the objects in such an application, because typically object names are displayed on a screen that prompts the user to select one of those names for future processing. You can use the listBindings() method as an alternative to the list() method The listBindings() method returns a list of Binding objects.

Once Listing 18-3 retrieves the enumeration of names from the directory, the program calls the hasMore() method to determine if the enumeration has more names. If so, then the program calls the next() method to retrieve a NameClassPair object from the enumeration, which is then displayed on the screen. This process continues until the program is at the end of the enumeration; afterwards, the InitialContext object is closed.

Before compiling and running Listing 18-3, make sure that you create a directory and the necessary namespace within the directory. Modify the listing to reflect your directory service provider, the directory service server URL, and directory name. The JNDI and the LDAP service provider classes must appear in the CLASSPATH before you compile the program.

Once you complete these preparations, enter the following command at the command line:

```
javac MyNameClassPair.java
```

The compiler generates the MyNameClassPair.java bytecode file in the same directory as the MyNameClassPair.java source code file. Run the program by entering the following command at the command line:

```
java MyNameClassPair
```

Listing 18-3
Retrieving an enumeration of an object and class name.

```
import javax.naming.*;
import java.util.Hashtable;
class MyNameClassPair {
  public static void main(String[] args) {
    Hashtable ep = new Hashtable(2);
    ep.put(Context.INITIAL_CONTEXT_FACTORY,
        "com.sun.jndi.fscontext.RefFSContextFactory");
    ep.put(Context.PROVIDER_URL, "locahost:1099");
    try {
      InitialContext ct = new InitialContext(ep);
      NamingEnumeration ne = ct.list("MyDirectory");
      while (ne.hasMore()) {
```

```
        NameClassPair ncp = (NameClassPair) ne.next();
        System.out.println(ncp);
      }
      ct.close();
    }
    catch (NamingException error) {
      System.out.println("List failed: " + error);
    }
  }
}
```

Add Binding to a Directory Service

A value can be bound to a name in a directory service by using the bind() method of the InitialContext class. This technique is illustrated in Listing 18-4. This example creates a class called MyAddBinding. The class begins by creating a definition for the main() method and initially creates an instance of a Hashtable object called ep. The hash table contains properties that are bound to the name in the directory service.

There are two properties set in this example: the name of the directory service provider and the URL of the directory service server. Of course, you'll need to replace the value of these properties with the directory service provider and directory service server URL used in your J2EE application. Values are assigned to properties in the hash table by calling the put() method.

Next, the example creates an InitialContext called ct by passing the Hashtable object to the InitialContext constructor. Once the InitialContext object is created, a User object is created. The User class is a class that you define that will be associated with a name in the directory service. For this example, assume that an attribute of the User class is username and the constructor assigns the username passed to the constructor to the attribute. Although the class is called User in this example, you can replace the User class with any class that you want to be associated with a name in the directory service.

The User object is then bound to the name UserName by calling the bind() method and passing this method the name within the directory service and the object that is to be bound to the name. The lookup() method is then called to retrieve the object that is associated with the UserName in the directory service.

Listing 18-4
Adding a
binding to a
directory
service.

```
import javax.naming.*;
import java.util.Hashtable;
class MyAddBinding {
  public static void main(String[] args) {
    Hashtable ep = new Hashtable(2);
```

```
        ep.put(Context.INITIAL_CONTEXT_FACTORY,
            "com.sun.jndi.fscontext.RefFSContextFactory");
        ep.put(Context.PROVIDER_URL, "localhost:1099");
        try {
            InitialContext ct = new InitialContext(ep);
            User newUser = new User("John Smith");
            ct.bind("UserName", newUser);
            Object obj = ct.lookup("UserName");
            System.out.println(obj);
            ct.close();
        }
        catch (NamingException error) {
            System.out.println("Error: " + error.getMessage());
        }
    }
}
```

Remove Binding to a Directory Service

An object bound to a name in the directory service can be unbound from that name by calling the unbind() method, which is shown in Listing 18-5 where the object bound to the UserName name in the directory service is disassociated from the name.

Listing 18-5 begins similar to Listing 18-4 that originally bound the object to the UserName name. The program creates a hash table of properties and then uses the put() method to assign the directory service provider and directory service server URL to the hash table.

The program then creates an InitialContext and calls the unbind() method. The unbind() method requires that you pass the name contained in the directory service that is to be unbound. Next, the program attempts to retrieve the object that is associated with the UserName name. However, before doing so, the program creates a null Object object that is used to verify that the object was unbound from the UserName name.

The program calls the lookup() method and passes it the UserName name. The lookup() method returns the object associated with the UserName name. An error is thrown if there isn't an object bound to the name. This error is caught by the first catch { } block where a message is displayed on the screen indicating that the binding was previously removed from the UserName name.

However, a different message is displayed on the screen if the lookup() method returns an object because the unbind() method failed to disassociate the object from the UserName name. The InitialContext is then terminated by calling the close() method.

Errors occurring when terminating the InitialContext are trapped by the second catch { } block.

```
import javax.naming.*;
import java.util.Hashtable;
class MyRemoveBinding {
  public static void main(String[] args) {
    Hashtable ep = new Hashtable(2);
    ep.put(Context.INITIAL_CONTEXT_FACTORY,
      "com.sun.jndi.fscontext.RefFSContextFactory");
    ep.put(Context.PROVIDER_URL, "localhost:1099");
    try {
      InitialContext ct = new InitialContext(ep);
      ct.unbind("UserName");
      Object obj = null;
      try {
        obj = ct.lookup("UserName");
      }
      catch (NameNotFoundException error) {
        System.out.println("Binding removed");
        return;
      }
      System.out.println("Remove binding failed");
      ct.close();
    }
    catch (NamingException error) {
      System.out.println("Error: " + error.getMessage());
    }
  }
}
```

Replace Binding to a Directory Service

You can rebind an object that is bound to a name in the directory service with another object without having to call the unbind() method to unbind the existing object from the name. This is done by calling the rebind() method, which is illustrated in Listing 18-6.

You'll notice that this example is similar to Listing 18-4. Both programs create a hash table to store properties of the name in the directory service. And both programs use the put() method to set the values of the directory service provider and the URL of the directory service server.

Once an instance of the InitialContext is created, the program creates an instance of the User class. As mentioned in Listing 18-4, the User class is a class that you define. In this example, assume that the constructor of the User class assigns the name Mary Jones to an attribute of the class. You can replace the User class with any class that you want to bind to the name in the directory service.

Next, the program calls the rebind() method and passes it the name in the directory service to which the object will be bound and the name of the object. In this example, the newUser object is bound to the UserName name. The rebind() method replaces any existing object bound to the UserName with the newUser object.

Once the object is bound to the UserName name, the program calls the lookup() method and passes the method the UserName name to retrieve the object bound to the UserName name. The object returned by the lookup program is then displayed on the screen.

<table>
<tr><td>

Listing 18-6

Replace a binding in a directory service.

</td><td>

```java
import javax.naming.*;
import java.io.File;
import java.util.Hashtable;
class MyReplaceBinding {
  public static void main(String[] args) {
    Hashtable ep = new Hashtable(2);
    ep.put(Context.INITIAL_CONTEXT_FACTORY,
       "com.sun.jndi.fscontext.RefFSContextFactory");
    ep.put(Context.PROVIDER_URL, "localhost:1099");
    try {
      InitialContext ct = new InitialContext(ep);
      User newUser = new User("Mary Jones");
      ct.rebind("UserName", newUser);
      Object obj = ct.lookup("UserName");
      System.out.println(obj);
      ct.close();
    }
    catch (NamingException error) {
      System.out.println("Error: " + error.getMessage());
    }
  }
}
```

</td></tr>
</table>

Renaming a Name in the Directory Service

Any name in the directory service can be renamed without affecting the object bound to the name in the directory service by calling the rename() method. The rename()

method is used in Listing 18-7 to rename the name OldName to NewName in the directory service. Although the name is changed, the object bound to the name in the directory service remains unchanged.

Listing 18-7 is nearly identical to Listing 18-6 except for the call to the rename() method. The rename() method requires two arguments. The first argument is the current name in the directory service, which is called OldName. The other argument is the new name, which is NewName.

Once the name is changed, the program calls the lookup() method to retrieve the object that is bound to the new name. The object returned by the lookup() method should be the same object that was bound to the previous name. The object is then displayed on the screen.

Listing 18-7
Rename a name in the directory service.

```
import javax.naming.*;
import java.util.Hashtable;
class MyRenameObject {
  public static void main(String[] args) {
  Hashtable ep = new Hashtable(2);
  ep.put(Context.INITIAL_CONTEXT_FACTORY,
    "com.sun.jndi.fscontext.RefFSContextFactory");
  ep.put(Context.PROVIDER_URL, "localhost:1099");
  try {
    InitialContext ct = new InitialContext(ep);
    ct.rename("OldName", "NewName");
    Object obj = ct.lookup("NewName");
    System.out.println(obj);
    ct.close();
  }
  catch (NamingException error) {
    System.out.println("Error: " + error.getMessage());
  }
  }
}
```

Quick Reference Guide

This Quick Reference Guide provides a brief overview of Java classes used with JNDI. Full details of these classes and all Java classes and interfaces are available at java.sun.com.

Syntax	Descriptions
Object addToEnvironment(String propName, Object propVal)	Adds a new environment property.
void bind(Name name, Object obj)	Binds a name to an object.
void bind(String name, Object obj)	Binds a name to an object.
void close()	Closes a context.
Name composeName(Name name, Name prefix)	Composes a context name.
String composeName(String name, String prefix)	Composes a context name.
Context createSubcontext(Name name)	Creates and binds a context.
Context createSubcontext(String name)	Creates and binds a context.
void destroySubcontext(Name name)	Removes a named context from a namespace.
void destroySubcontext(String name)	Removes a named context from a namespace.
Hashtable getEnvironment()	Returns an environment.
String getNameInNamespace()	Returns the name of a context.
NameParser getNameParser(Name name)	Returns the parser associated with a context.
NameParser getNameParser(String name)	Returns the parser associated with a context.
NamingEnumeration list(Name name)	Enumerates the names and objects bound in a context.
NamingEnumeration list(String name)	Enumerates the names and objects bound in a context.
NamingEnumeration listBindings (Name name)	Enumerates the names and objects bound in a context.

Table 18-1.   *public interface* `Context`

Syntax	Descriptions
NamingEnumeration listBindings (String name)	Enumerates the names and objects bound in a context.
Object lookup(Name name)	Returns an object.
Object lookup(String name)	Returns an object.
Object lookupLink(Name name)	Returns an object except for the terminal component of the name.
Object lookupLink(String name)	Returns an object except for the terminal component of the name.
void rebind(Name name, Object obj)	Binds a name to an object.
void rebind(String name, Object obj)	Binds a name to an object.
Object removeFromEnvironment (String propName)	Removes an environment property.
void rename(Name oldName, Name newName)	Binds a new name to an object.
void rename(String oldName, String newName)	Binds a new name to an object.
void unbind(Name name)	Unbinds an object.
void unbind(String name)	Unbinds a named object.

Table 18-1.   *public interface* **Context** (continued)

Syntax	Descriptions
void close()	Closes an enumeration.
boolean hasMore()	Determines if the enumeration has additional elements.
Object next()	Retrieves the next element in the enumeration.

Table 18-2.   *public interface* **NamingEnumeration** *extends Enumeration*

Syntax	Descriptions
Name add(int posn, String comp)	Adds a component at a specified position within a name.
Name add(String comp)	Adds a component to the end of a name.
Name addAll(int posn, Name n)	Adds the components of a name at a specified position within a name in order.
Name addAll(Name suffix)	Adds components of a name to the end of this name in order.
Object clone()	Creates a copy of a name.
int compareTo(Object obj)	Compares names for order.
boolean endsWith(Name n)	Determines if a name ends with this suffix.
String get(int posn)	Returns a component of this name.
Enumeration getAll()	Returns the components as an enumeration of strings.
Name getPrefix(int posn)	Creates a name having a prefix.
Name getSuffix(int posn)	Creates a name having a suffix.
boolean isEmpty()	Determines if name is empty.
Object remove(int posn)	Removes a component from a name.
int size()	Returns the number of components in this name.
boolean startsWith(Name n)	Determines if a name starts with this prefix.

Table 18-3. *public interface* Name *extends Cloneable, Serializable*

Syntax	Descriptions
Name parse(String name)	Parses a name.

Table 18-4. *public interface* **NameParser**

Syntax	Descriptions
void add(int ix, Object attrVal)	Adds an attribute value to an order of values.
boolean add(Object attrVal)	Adds a new value to an attribute.
void clear()	Removes values from an attribute.
Object clone()	Copies an attribute.
boolean contains(Object attrVal)	Determines if an attribute has a value.
Object get()	Returns an attribute value.
Object get(int ix)	Returns an attribute value from the ordered list.
NamingEnumeration getAll()	Returns an enumeration of attribute values.
DirContext getAttributeDefinition()	Returns an attribute's schema definition.
DirContext getAttributeSyntaxDefinition()	Returns the syntax definition of an attribute.
String getID()	Returns an attribute ID.
boolean isOrdered()	Determines if attribute values are ordered.
Object remove(int ix)	Removes an attribute value from an ordered list.
boolean remove(Object attrval)	Removes an attribute.
Object set(int ix, Object attrVal)	Sets an attribute value.
int size()	Returns the number of values of an attribute.

Table 18-5. *public interface* **Attribute** *extends Cloneable, Serializable*

Syntax	Descriptions
Object clone()	Copies the attribute set.
Attribute get(String attrID)	Returns specified attribute ID.
NamingEnumeration getAll()	Returns an enumeration of attributes.
NamingEnumeration getIDs()	Returns an enumeration of attribute IDs.
boolean isCaseIgnored()	Determines if the search ignores the case of attribute identifiers.
Attribute put(Attribute attr)	Adds a new attribute.
Attribute put(String attrID, Object val)	Adds a new attribute.
Attribute remove(String attrID)	Removes the specified attribute.
int size()	Retrieves the number of attributes.

Table 18-6.   *public interface* **Attributes** *extends Cloneable, Serializable*

Syntax	Descriptions
void bind(Name name, Object obj, Attributes attrs)	Binds a name and attributes to an object.
void bind(String name, Object obj, Attributes attrs)	Binds a name and attributes to an object.
DirContext createSubcontext(Name name, Attributes attrs)	Creates and binds a new context and attributes.
DirContext createSubcontext(String name, Attributes attrs)	Creates and binds a new context and attributes.

Table 18-7.   *public interface* **DirContext** *extends Context*

Syntax	Descriptions
Attributes getAttributes(Name name)	Returns all of the attributes associated with a named object.
Attributes getAttributes(Name name, String[] attrIds)	Returns selected attributes associated with a named object.
Attributes getAttributes(String name)	Returns all attributes.
Attributes getAttributes(String name, String[] attrIds)	Returns selected attributes.
DirContext getSchema(Name name)	Returns a schema.
DirContext getSchema(String name)	Returns a schema.
DirContext getSchemaClassDefinition (Name name)	Returns a context containing the named object's class definitions.
DirContext getSchemaClassDefinition (String name)	Returns a context containing the named object's class definitions.
void modifyAttributes(Name name, int mod_op, Attributes attrs)	Modifies attributes.
void modifyAttributes(Name name, ModificationItem[] mods)	Modifies attributes of an order of values.
void modifyAttributes(String name, int mod_op, Attributes attrs)	Modifies attributes.
void modifyAttributes(String name, ModificationItem[] mods)	Modifies attributes using an ordered list.
void rebind(Name name, Object obj, Attributes attrs)	Binds a name and attributes to an object overwriting the existing binding.
void rebind(String name, Object obj, Attributes attrs)	Binds a name and attributes to an object overwriting the existing binding.
NamingEnumeration search(Name name, Attributes matchingAttributes)	Searches a context for objects for an attribute set.
NamingEnumeration search(Name name, Attributes matchingAttributes, String[] attributesToReturn)	Searches a context for objects for an attribute set and returns selected attributes.

Table 18-7. *public interface* **DirContext** *extends Context* (continued)

Syntax	Descriptions
NamingEnumeration search(Name name, String filterExpr, Object[] filterArgs, SearchControls cons)	Searches a context or object for search criteria.
NamingEnumeration search(Name name, String filter, SearchControls cons)	Searches a context or object for search criteria.
NamingEnumeration search(String name, Attributes matchingAttributes)	Searches a context for objects for an attribute set.
NamingEnumeration search(String name, Attributes matchingAttributes, String[] attributesToReturn)	Searches a context for objects for an attribute set and returns selected attributes.
NamingEnumeration search(String name, String filterExpr, Object[] filterArgs, SearchControls cons)	Searches a context or object for search criteria.
NamingEnumeration search (String name, Strinkg filter, SearchControls cons)	Searches a context or object for search criteria.

Table 18-7.   *public interface* **DirContext** *extends Context* (continued)

The Complete Reference

J2EE

Part V

Web Services

Web services is a technology that allows programmers to create large-scale distributive systems efficiently. These web services, which serve as building blocks, can be written in a number of computer languages, and include the J2EE components that you learned about throughout this book.

With the introduction of J2EE 1.4, the Java community program merged J2EE technology with Web services technology. This enables programmers to use J2EE to develop Web services applications.

Five new standards were developed with the introduction of web services. These are Service Oriented Architecture Protocol (SOAP), Universal Description, Discovery, Electronic Business XML (EbXML), and Web Services Description Language (WSDL).

In Part V, you'll learn about these standards and you'll also learn about the Java API for XML Registries (JAXR), which is used to access Web services within a J2EE Application.

Chapter 19

SOAP

E ver since corporations moved to distributive systems, there has been a growing demand for interoperability among applications—and this need has become critical with the onset of web services. As you learned in Part I, web services technology enables application programmers to assemble components called web services into a distributive application. Interoperability is a crucial element in web services technology since web services can be built using dissimilar programming languages and can reside on remote, dissimilar computers.

Industry leaders have long sought an efficient and reliable mechanism for distributive applications and components existing on dissimilar remote computers to interact with each other. A solution to this problem is the Simple Object Access Protocol, commonly referred to as SOAP.

SOAP is a communications protocol that facilitates the interaction between applications and web services located on remote computers. You'll be introduced to SOAP in this chapter and learn how to incorporate SOAP into your J2EE application using the Java API for XML Messaging (JAXM), which adheres to the SOAP standards.

SOAP Basics

Simple Object Access Protocol (SOAP) began in 1997 by three players in the industry: Microsoft, a small software company called Userland Software, and DevelopMentor, which is a Lucent spin-off. Together they set out to develop a communications protocol that was easy to use and flexible enough to apply to changes in the industry, and that could provide the ever-elusive interoperability.

Soon after the project began, they focused their attention on XML as the basis for the new communications protocol. XML is a markup language, as you learned in Chapter 8, and is straightforward to implement and extensible, providing a structure for flexibility.

XML is the ideal language to use to implement the new communication protocol because XML has built-in data types defined in the XML Schema. Data types are used by a communication protocol to define data transmissions. This meant that the team developing SOAP didn't have to reinvent data typing. Instead, they could adopt data types defined in XML. XML defined all by the array data type.

It took the team a year to flush out the details of the new communications protocol, and internal squabbles at Microsoft hampered development. Delays frustrated some of the team and resulted in a defection by Dave Winer. Winer created his own communication protocol called XML-Remote Procedure Call (XML-RPC), which gained popularity until the release of SOAP 1.0 in 2000.

SOAP 1.0 used HTTP as the transport protocol for transmitting messages sent using SOAP. Although HTTP is a widely used transport protocol, specifying HTTP as the transport protocol violated one of the key objectives of SOAP, which was interoperability. SOAP shouldn't be dependent on one transport protocol. SOAP became fully independent with the introduction of SOAP 1.1. This meant that SOAP messages can use any transport protocol, such as SMTP and FTP, as well as HTTP.

SOAP 1.1 is a communications protocol that addresses the concerns of the web services industry. However, it wasn't until the end of 2000 that the SOAP team caught the industry's attention when Microsoft adopted SOAP as the communications protocol used with .NET technology.

The SOAP team submitted SOAP 1.1 to the World Wide Web Consortium (W3C). W3C is the organization that adopts standards for the World Wide Web community. W3C formed their own committee that included Sun Microsystems, Inc., and set out to develop specifications for a communications protocol based on SOAP 1.1 They adopted a working draft for the new specification, called SOAP 1.2.

SOAP Functionality

SOAP is a specification for a messaging system where data is represented as text and defined as a data type. The text that contains this data is called a *SOAP message*, which is written in XML. Besides transmitting data, SOAP also transmits metadata in the SOAP message header.

Anyone familiar with HTML and XML can read and understand a SOAP message and, if necessary, use XML to modify the SOAP message. As you learned in Chapter 8, tags are used in XML to define data elements. Unlike HTML, XML enables you to create your own XML tags. This is referred to as extensibility, which is critical for implementing future developments in SOAP technology.

SOAP is a stateless communications protocol. That is, data and the SOAP message aren't saved during the course of the transmission. For example, SOAP transmits a request to invoke a remote procedure call to the service provider. The service provider responds to the request in a return SOAP message to the calling party. The relationship between the sender and receiver no longer exists once the client receives the response.

SOAP cannot reference objects because all data must be explicitly contained in a SOAP message. This means that a SOAP message cannot contain a reference to data that is external from the message.

Let's say that you want to transmit data contained on a remote computer. You cannot include code in the SOAP message that tells SOAP to get this data. Instead, you must invoke a remote procedure by making a remote procedure call within the SOAP message. The remote procedure must then get data from the remote computer. Each SOAP message can contain one remote procedure call.

The SOAP Message and Delivery Structure

There are three parts to a SOAP message: the envelope, the header, and the body. The SOAP envelope is a required XML tag that contains the SOAP header and body. The header is an optional XML tag in the SOAP message that contains metadata. The body of the SOAP message is a required part of the SOAP message and contains the text of the message. The Java API for XML Messaging (JAXM) generates the SOAP message for you based on the JAXM code in your J2EE application, which you'll learn about later in this chapter.

The SOAP envelope is used to contain the SOAP message, similar to an envelope used to post a letter. The header contains additional information and sometimes instructions for use by the SOAP processor to transmit the SOAP message. For example, the body of the SOAP message might have data that is defined in the header as metadata.

Any number of intermediate computers might process a SOAP message between the requestor, who generates the SOAP message, and the receiver, who responds to the request. Intermediate computers are called *SOAP nodes*, which receive and forward a SOAP message until the message reaches the receiver.

Some SOAP nodes simply relay the SOAP message to the next SOAP node or directly to the receiver. A SOAP message might need to be processed a particular way, based on the needs of the SOAP node or the receiver, before the SOAP message is relayed to the next SOAP node or receiver. Such processing instructions are generally contained in the SOAP message header, which is read and processed by the SOAP node.

The process performed on the SOAP message by a SOAP node before the SOAP message is relayed is called a SOAP actor. A SOAP node can have multiple SOAP actors and each SOAP actor might involve processing that occurs simultaneously on different machines.

There are three kinds of SOAP message bodies: a request, a response, and a fault. A request message body contains the name of the remote procedure and serialized input parameters, if any, that are passed to the remote procedures when the remote procedure is invoked.

The response message body contains the name of the remote procedure and output parameter, if any, that are returned by the remote procedure to the requestor. The fault message body contains fault codes and fault messages, known as the fault string, that describes failure of the message to be successfully distributed. A fault code is an abbreviation indicating the fault. A fault message is text that describes the fault.

The SOAP specification defines four kinds of faults: VersionMismatch, MustUnderstand, Client, and Server. The VersionMismatch is sent when an invalid namespace is detected in the envelope. MustUnderstand is generated when the receiving SOAP processor is unable to process the SOAP message header. The Client fault occurs when a client incorrectly formed the SOAP message. The SOAP server sends the Client fault. The Server fault is sent when the SOAP server cannot process the SOAP message, although the SOAP message is not at fault. A SOAP actor can also generate one of the four SOAP faults.

Java API for XML Messaging

A J2EE application that uses web services requests service from a component by referencing the component's URL in a request sent using SOAP, which is typically transmitted using the HTTP transmission protocol. The web services component replies to the request using SOAP and HTTP once the request has been processed.

The Java API for XML Messaging (JAXM) is used to create a JAXM message by making Java API calls. JAXM creates a message that conforms to the SOAP 1.1 standard and the SOAP with attachments specifications.

There are two types of SOAP messages: SOAP messages without attachments and SOAP messages with attachments. Both types of SOAP messages contain one or multiple parts. The first part of both types of SOAP messages is called the *SOAP Part*. The SOAP Part contains a SOAP envelope that is divided into an optional SOAP header and a required SOAP body as described in the previous section of this chapter.

JAXM has classes that create each part of a SOAP message. All the parts of a SOAP message are created once an instance of the SOAPMessage class is created in a J2EE application. The SOAPHeader object is automatically created as part of the SOAPMessage class; however, this can be deleted since the header is an optional part of a SOAP message.

The other type of SOAP message is a SOAP message with attachments. An attachment is a file that is not in the XML format but is part of the message, such as an image file. The attachment is transmitted along with the SOAP message. All messages that are not in the XML format must be sent as an attachment to a SOAP message.

The SOAP messages with attachments have a SOAP Part of the message and also one or more attachment parts. The AttachmentPart class creates attachments. You must instantiate the AttachmentPart class to create attachments and add attachments to a SOAP message.

The Connection

A JAXM message is sent over a connection either directly to the receiver or to a messaging provider that forwards the message to the receiver. A messaging provider is an intermediary process that transmits and routes messages.

There are two kinds of connection classes available in JAXM. These are the SOAPConnection class and the ProviderConnection class. The SOAPConnection class is used in a point-to-point connection between the requestor and the receiver. A SOAPConnection does not need to run in a container, such as the J2EE container, and is used whenever a messaging provider is unavailable to handle transmissions. The ProviderConnection class is used to connect to a messaging provider.

A SOAPConnection requires that messages be sent using a method call. A method call is a form of request-response messaging where the requestor is blocked until the response is received from the receiver. All receivers are required to respond to a request, even if a request does not warrant a response; otherwise, the requestor remains blocked.

The ProviderConnection class is used to connect to a messaging provider. A J2EE application that uses a messaging provider sends messages to the messaging provider, who then forwards the message to the receiver. The requestor does not pause until a response is received from a receiver. Instead, the messaging provider makes replies available to the requestor when responses are received by the messaging provider from the receiver. A messaging provider is transparent to a J2EE application.

SOAP messages can be placed within other protocols that add features to the messaging capabilities of SOAP. JAXM has classes that enable you to wrap such protocols around a SOAP message that is generated by your J2EE application. This technique is called a profile.

Typically, messaging providers support several profiles. However, a J2EE application can use one profile that both the requestor and the receiver agree to. Profile information is usually contained in the message header.

WEB SERVICES

A messaging provider uses store-forwarding technology that enables requests to be sent even if the receiver is not connected to the messaging provider. Likewise, the requestor does not need to be connected to the messaging provider after sending the message.

A messaging provider attempts to redeliver a message any time a message doesn't reach the receiver. Attempts end after the attempts exceed the limit for resending a message. The messaging provider stores all messages until the receiver reconnects with the messaging provider and retrieves messages.

Create, Send, and Receive a Point-to-Point SOAP Message

JAXM classes facilitate sending and receiving SOAP messages by formatting all messages. This means that you need to create an instance of the appropriate class and call related methods, passing it header and body text. These methods then insert header and body information into the appropriate XML tag within the SOAP message.

Listing 19-1 illustrates how to create and send a point-to-point SOAP message. This example requests a price for a product identified in the request. The price is then retrieved for a SOAP message sent by the receiver. Listing 19-2 contains the actual SOAP message that is generated by Listing 19-1.

The program begins within the main() function by creating a SOAPConnectionFactory called sf, which is used to create a SOAPConnection called sct. Next, a MessageFactory is created and is used to create a SOAPMessage.

Once the SOAPMessage is created, the program creates parts of the message as described previously in this chapter. These include SOAPPart, SOAPEnvelope, SOAPHeader, and SOAPBody. By default, every SOAPMessage has a SOAPHeader. However, you can remove the header by calling the detachNode() method, as shown in Listing 19-2.

The program must create a new element within the body of the message that is used to request the product price. Before a new element is created, you must create a fully qualified name for the element by calling the createName() method.

The createName() method requires three parameters. The first parameter is the name of the new element, which is GetProductPrice in Listing 19-2. The second parameter is the Namespace prefix, and the last parameter is the namespace URL. You'll need to replace the NamespacePrefix and Namespace URL with the corresponding values for the element when you run this example.

The new element must now be inserted into the body of the message by calling the addBodyElement() method and passing it the name of the new element. The new element in this example also has a child element that contains the product identification of the product whose price is being retrieved. Therefore, you'll need to create another name by calling the createName() method and adding the child element to the element by calling the addChildElement() method, passing it the name of the child element. In this example, the child element is called productID.

The final component that must be inserted into the message is the value of the child element, which is the value of the product identifier of the product whose price is being retrieved. You insert the value by calling the addTextNode() method and passing it the value, which in this case is 1234.

At this point in the program, you opened a connection and created the SOAP message. You now must identify where the message is being sent. You do this by creating an instance of the URLEndpoint class and passing its constructor the receiver's URL, as is shown in this example.

You are ready to send the SOAP message by calling the call() method and passing it the URLEndpoint instance and the message. The program then pauses until a response is received from the receiver, because the program does not use a messaging provider in this example.

Once the response is received, the program closes the connection by calling the close() method and then proceeds to access the SOAP message sent by the receiver. The program creates parts of the SOAP message, as described previously in this section, each of which is used to store parts of the incoming SOAP message.

The getChildElements() method of the SOAPBody is called to retrieve an iterator of child elements from the body of the incoming message. The program then steps through each iteration, calling the getValue() method to retrieve the value of the child element, which in this example contains the price of the product that is identified in the SOAP message sent previously to the receiver. This value is then displayed on the screen.

This program assumes that the receiver is a remote method that performs a price lookup. You probably don't have such a remote method available to you, therefore you should have little difficulty modifying the receiver URL, the body element and the child element in this program to related URL and elements needed for your program.

Listing 19-1
Using the SOAP Connection class to send and receive a SOAP message.

```
<SOAP-ENV:Envelope
   xmlns:SOAP-ENV="http://schemas.xmlsoap.org/soap/envelope/"
   <SOAP-ENV:Body>
   <NamespacePrefix:GetProductPrice xmlns:NamespacePrefix="
    http://namespace.mydomain.com">
   <productID>1234</productID>
   </NamespacePrefix:GetProductPrice>
   </SOAP-ENV:Body>
</SOAP-ENV:Envelope>
```

Listing 19-2
The SOAP message generated by Listing 19-1.

```
import javax.xml.soap.*;
import javax.xml.messaging.*;
import java.io.*;
import java.util.*;
public class MyPointToPoint {
  public static void main(String[] args)    {
     try {
```

```
        SOAPConnectionFactory sf = SOAPConnectionFactory.newInstance();
        SOAPConnection sct = sf.createConnection();
        MessageFactory mf = MessageFactory.newInstance();
        SOAPMessage smsg = mf.createMessage();
        SOAPPart sp1 = smsg.getSOAPPart();
        SOAPEnvelope env = sp1.getEnvelope();
        SOAPHeader hd = env.getHeader();
        SOAPBody bd1 = env.getBody();
        hd.detachNode();
        Name bName = env.createName(
                "GetProductPrice", "NamespacePrefix",
    "http://namespace.mydomain.com/");
        SOAPBodyElement sbe1 = bd1.addBodyElement(bName);
        Name name = env.createName("productID");
        SOAPElement se1 = sbe1.addChildElement(name);
        se1.addTextNode("1234");
        URLEndpoint ep = new URLEndpoint("ReceiverURL");
        SOAPMessage response = sct.call(smsg, ep);
        sct.close();
        SOAPPart sp2 = response.getSOAPPart();
        SOAPEnvelope se2 = sp2.getEnvelope();
        SOAPBody sb2 = se2.getBody();
        Iterator itr = sb2.getChildElements(bName);
        while (itr.hasNext()) {
          SOAPBodyElement sbe2 = (SOAPBodyElement)itr.next();
          String rValue = sbe2.getValue();
          System.out.print("Price:" + rValue);
        }
      }
    catch (Exception error) {
      System.out.print("Error:" + error.getMessage());
      }
    }
  }
}
```

Create and Send a SOAP Message Using a Messaging Provider

Sending a SOAP message using a messaging provider instead of point-to-point communication with the receiver is accomplished using a technique similar to that used in point-to-point communication. The program initially connects to the messaging provider, creates the SOAP message and then sends the message to the message provider.

Listing 19-3 demonstrates this technique and creates the same SOAP message, as shown in Listing 19-2. This example begins by creating an InitialContext called ct that is used to look up the message provider's name, using the lookup() method. Of course, you'll need to replace the MsgProviderName in this example with the name of your message provider.

The lookup() method returns a ProviderConnectionFactory that is used to create a ProviderConnection by calling the createConnection() method. Once the connection is made, the program calls getMetaData() to create the ProviderMetaData object called md.

The metadata contains profiles that are supported by the message provider. The program must determine if the message provider supports the profile used by the program. This is accomplished by calling the getSupportedProfiles() method of the ProviderMetaData object, which returns a String array that contains profiles supported by the message provider.

The program uses the ebXML protocol that is discussed in Chapter 22. A for loop is used to step through elements of the array in order to locate the ebXML profile. Once found, the value of the String is assigned to the profile2 String, which is passed to the constructor of the createMessageFactory() method. The createMessageFactory() method returns an instance of a MessageFactory that is used to create an ebXML message by calling the createMessage() method.

Next, the program sets the sender and receiver URL for the message. You need to replace the SenderURL with the URL of the machine that is sending the message. Likewise, replace the ReceiverURL with the message provider.

The program then creates the SOAP message by calling createMessage(), which returns an instance of a SOAPMessage object called smsg. Next, the program accesses components of the SOAP message by the getSOAPPart(), getEnvelope(), getHeader(), and getBody() methods.

The program continues by calling the detachNode() to remove the header from the SOAP message since this message doesn't use a header. The program creates the name for the body element by calling the createName() method. You'll need to replace the GetProductPrice with the name of your element and replace NamespacePrefix and Namespace URL with the namespace prefix and namespace URL required by your J2EE application.

Next, the program creates the name for a child element that is called productID, by calling the createName() method. This name is passed to the addChildElement() method to insert the child element into the SOAP message.

The addTextNode() method is called and passed the value that will appear in the child element part of the SOAP message. The message is then sent by calling the send() message; afterwards, the connection is closed by the close().

Listing 19-3
Using the messaging provider to send a SOAP message.

```
import javax.xml.soap.*;
import javax.xml.messaging.*;
import java.io.*;
import java.util.*;
public class MyMessageProvider {
  public static void main(String[] args)    {
    try {
      InitialContext ct = new InitialContext();
      ProviderConnectionFactory pcf
          =(ProviderConnectionFactory)ct.lookup("MsgProviderName");
```

```
     ProviderConnection pc = pcf.createConnection();
     ProviderMetaData md = pc.getMetaData();
     String[]profile1 = md.getSupportedProfiles();
     String profile2 = null;
     for (int i=0; i < profile1.length; i++)
     {
       if (profile1 [i].equals("ebxml"))
       {
         profile2 = profile1 [i];
         break;
       }
     }
     if(profile2 == null)
     {
      System.out.println("profile not supported");
      exit(1);
     }
     MessageFactory mf = pc.createMessageFactory(profile2);
     EbXMLMessageImpl msg = (EbXMLMessageImpl) mf.createMessage();
     msg.setSender(new Party("SenderURL"));
     msg.setReceiver(new Party("ReceiverURL"));
     SOAPMessage smsg = mf.createMessage();
     SOAPPart sp1 = smsg.getSOAPPart();
     SOAPEnvelope env = sp1.getEnvelope();
     SOAPHeader hd = env.getHeader();
     SOAPBody bd1= env.getBody();
     hd.detachNode();
     Name bName = env.createName("GetProductPrice", "NamespacePrefix",
       "Namespace URL");
     SOAPBodyElement sbe1 =bd1.addBodyElement(bName);
     Name name = env.createName("productID");
     SOAPElement se1 = sbe1.addChildElement(name);
     se1.addTextNode("1234");
     pc.send(msg);
     pc.close();
   }
 catch (Exception error) {
   error.getMessage();
   }
  }
}
```

Creating a SOAP Attachment

An attachment is a file that is sent along with a message, similar to attachments that you send with an email message. An attachment is part of a SOAP message that you create within your program.

Listing 19-4 illustrates how to create an attachment and attach it to a SOAP message. You can place this code segment beneath the child element section of previous listings that create a SOAP message.

This example begins by creating an instance of the AttachmentPart object by calling the createAttachmentPart() method of the SOAPMessage object. Next, the program sets the ContentID of the attachment by invoking the setContentID() and passing it the ID NewLogo. Of course, you need to replace NewLogo with an appropriate ID for your attachment.

The attachment in this example is a GIF file called logo.gif. This must be an array of bytes that is called logo in this example. The byte array is coming from an input stream; therefore, you must create a ByteArrayInputStream object used by the program to copy the logo.gif file into the message envelope. The constructor of the ByteArrayInputStream object is passed the byte array called logo.

Next, the program must set the content of the attachment. This is accomplished by calling the setContent() method and passing it the stream that contains reference to the attachment and the image/gif identifier. The addAttachmentPart() method is then called and passed the AttachmentPart object.

Listing 19-4
Creating an attachment to a SOAP message.

```
AttachmentPart attm = smsg.createAttachmentPart();
attm.setContentID("NewLogo");
byte[] logo = "logo.gif";
ByteArrayInputStream stream = new ByteArrayInputStream(logo);
attm.setContent(stream, "image/gif");
smsg.addAttachmentPart(attm);
```

Accessing a SOAP Attachment

An attachment to a SOAP message can be accessed by calling the getAttachments() methods of the SOAPMessage object, as illustrated in Listing 19-5. In this example, attachments are returned as an iterator and then are extracted and displayed within the while loop.

If there is at least one attachment, the program enters the while loop where reference to the next attachment is in the iterator. The getContent() and getContentID() methods are called to return the content and the content ID of the message, which are then displayed on the screen.

WEB SERVICES

Listing 19-5
Accessing an
attachment
to a SOAP
message.

```
java.util.Iterator itr = smsg.getAttachments();
while (itr.hasNext()) {
    AttachmentPart attm = itr.next();
    Object content = attm.getContent();
    String cID = attm.getContentId();
    System.out.print(cID + ": " + content);
}
```

Quick Reference Guide

This Quick Reference Guide provides a brief overview of Java classes used with SOAP. Full details of these classes and all Java classes and interfaces are available at java.sun.com.

Syntax	Descriptions
DetailEntry addDetailEntry (Name name)	Creates a new DetailEntry object.
Iterator getDetailEntries()	Returns detail entries in a Detail object.

Table 19-1.   *public interface* Detail *extends SOAPFaultElement*

Syntax	Descriptions
String getLocalName()	Returns the local name part of the XML name.
String getPrefix()	Returns the prefix associated with the namespace.
String getQualifiedName()	Returns the namespace-qualified name of a Name object.
String getURI()	Returns the URI of a namespace.

Table 19-2.   *public interface* Name

Syntax	Descriptions
void detachNode()	Removes a Node object.
SOAPElement getParentElement()	Returns the parent element of a Node object.
String getValue()	Returns the value of the child of a Node object.
void recycleNode()	Notifies that a Node object is no longer being used by an application.
void setParentElement (SOAPElement parent)	Sets the parent of a Node object.

Table 19-3. *public interface* Node

Syntax	Descriptions
SOAPBodyElement addBodyElement(Name name)	Creates a new SOAPBodyElement object.
SOAPFault addFault()	Creates and inserts a new SOAPFault object.
SOAPFault getFault()	Returns the SOAPFault object for a SOAPBody object.
boolean hasFault()	Determines if a SOAPFault object exists in a SOAPBody object.

Table 19-4. *public interface* SOAPBody *extends SOAPElement*

Syntax	Descriptions
static String URI_NS_SOAP_ENCODING	The encoding namespace identifier.
static String URI_NS_SOAP_ENVELOPE	The envelope namespace identifier.
static String URI_SOAP_ACTOR_NEXT	The URI for the first application processing a SOAP request intended for an actor identified in a header entry.

Table 19-5. *public interface SOAPConstants*

Syntax	Descriptions
SOAPElement addAttribute (Name name, String value)	Inserts an attribute.
SOAPElement addChildElement (Name name)	Creates and initializes a new SOAPElement object.
SOAPElement addChildElement (SOAPElement element)	Inserts a child SOAPElement.
SOAPElement addChildElement (String localName)	Creates and initializes a new SOAPElement object.
SOAPElement addChildElement (String localName, String prefix)	Creates and initializes a new SOAPElement object.
SOAPElement addChildElement (String localName, String prefix, String uri)	Creates and initializes a new SOAPElement object.
SOAPElement addNamespaceDeclaration (String prefix, String uri)	Adds a namespace declaration.
SOAPElement addTextNode (String text)	Creates and initializes a new Text object.
Iterator getAllAttributes()	Returns an iterator of attribute names.
String getAttributeValue(Name name)	Returns an attribute's value.

Table 19-6. *public interface SOAPElement extends Node*

Syntax	Descriptions
Iterator getChildElements()	Returns an iterator of an element's content.
Iterator getChildElements (Name name)	Returns an iterator of child elements.
Name getElementName()	Returns the name of a SOAPElement object.
String getEncodingStyle()	Returns an encoding style.
Iterator getNamespacePrefixes()	Returns an iterator of a namespace prefix.
String getNamespaceURI (String prefix)	Returns the URI of a namespace.
boolean removeAttribute(Name name)	Deletes an attribute.
boolean removeNamespace Declaration(String prefix)	Deletes a namespace declaration.
void setEncodingStyle (String encodingStyle)	Sets the encoding style.

Table 19-6.   *public interface* SOAPElement *extends Node* (continued)

Syntax	Descriptions
SOAPBody addBody()	Creates a SOAPBody object.
SOAPHeader addheader()	Creates a SOAPHeader object.
Name createName(String localName)	Creates and initializes a new Name object.
Name createName(String localName, String prefix, String uri)	Creates and initializes a new Name object.
SOAPBody getBody()	Returns a SOAPBody object.
SOAPHeader getheader()	Returns a SOAPHeader.

Table 19-7.   *public interface* SOAPEnvelope *extends SOAPElement*

Syntax	Descriptions
Detail addDetail()	Creates a Detail object.
Detail getDetail()	Returns the detail element of a SOAPFault object.
String getFaultActor()	Returns the fault actor.
String getFaultCode()	Returns the fault code.
String getFaultString()	Returns the fault string.
void setFaultActor(String faultActor)	Sets a fault actor for a SOAPFault object.
void setFaultCode(String faultCode)	Sets a fault code for a SOAPFault object.
void setFaultString(String faultString)	Sets the fault string for a SOAPFault object.

Table 19-8. *public interface* SOAPFault *extends* **SOAPBodyElement**

Syntax	Descriptions
SOAPHeaderElement addheaderElement(Name name)	Creates and initializes a new SOAPHeaderElement object.
Iterator examineheaderElements (String actor)	Returns a list of SOAPHeaderElement objects that have the specified actor.
Iterator extractheaderElements (String actor)	Returns a list of SOAPHeaderElement objects that have this actor and detaches the actor from a SOAPHeader object.

Table 19-9. *public interface* SOAPHeader *extends* **SOAPElement**

Syntax	Descriptions
String getActor()	Returns the URI of the actor.
boolean getMustUnderstand()	Returns the status of the mustUnderstand attribute.
void setActor(String actorURI)	Sets the actor of the SOAPHeader Element object.
void setMustUnderstand(boolean mustUnderstand)	Sets the mustUnderstand attribute to on or off.

Table 19-10.   *public interface* SOAPHeaderElement *extends SOAPElement*

Syntax	Description
boolean isComment()	Returns if Text object is a comment.

Table 19-11.   *public interface* Text *extends Node*

Syntax	Descriptions
abstract void addMimeheader (String name, String value)	Inserts a MIME header.
abstract void clearContent()	Deletes the content of an AttachmentPart object.
abstract Iterator getAllMimeheaders()	Returns headers for an AttachmentPart object as an iterator.
abstract Object getContent()	Returns the content of an AttachmentPart object.
String getContentId()	Returns the value of the Content-Id MIME header.
String getContentLocation()	Returns the value of the Content-Location MIME header.

Table 19-12.   *public abstract class* AttachmentPart *extends Object*

Syntax	Descriptions
String getContentType()	Returns the value of the Content-Type MIME header.
abstract DataHandler getDataHandler()	Returns the DataHandler object.
abstract Iterator getMatchingMimeheaders (String[] names)	Returns Mimeheader objects found in an array.
abstract String[] getMimeheader (String name)	Returns values of a header identified by name.
abstract Iterator getNonMatchingMimeheaders (String[] names)	Returns Mimeheader objects not found in the array.
abstract int getSize()	Returns bytes of the AttachmentPart object.
abstract void removeAllMimeheaders()	Deletes all the MIME headers.
abstract void removeMimeheader (String header)	Deletes specified MIME headers.
abstract void setContent(Object object, String contentType)	Sets attachment part to an Object and sets the Content-Type header to contentType.
void setContentId(String contentId)	Sets the Content-Id MIME header.
void setContentLocation (String contentLocation)	Sets the Content-Location MIME header.
void setContentType (String contentType)	Sets the Content-Type MIME header.
abstract void setDataHandler (DataHandler dataHandler)	Sets a DataHandler object as the data handler.
abstract void setMimeheader (String name, String value)	Modifies the name header entry with the specified value. A new header is inserted if name is not found.

Table 19-12.   *public abstract class* AttachmentPart *extends Object* (continued)

Syntax	Descriptions
abstract SOAPMessage createMessage()	Creates a new SOAPMessage object.
abstract SOAPMessage createMessage (Mimeheaders headers, InputStream in)	Internalizes the contents of an InputStream object.
static MessageFactory newInstance()	Creates a new MessageFactory object.

Table 19-13.   *public abstract class* MessageFactory *extends Object*

Syntax	Descriptions
String getName()	Returns the name of a Mimeheader object.
String getValue()	Returns the value of a Mimeheader object.

Table 19-14.   *public class* MimeHeader *extends Object*

Syntax	Descriptions
void addheader(String name, String value)	Inserts a Mimeheader object.
Iterator getAllheaders()	Returns all the headers.
String[] getheader(String name)	Returns values of a header.
Iterator getMatchingheaders (String[] names)	Returns Mimeheader objects that are in the array.
Iterator getNonMatchingheaders (String[] names)	Returns Mimeheader objects that are not in the array.
void removeAllheaders()	Removes header entries.
void removeheader(String name)	Removes Mimeheader objects that match name matches.
void setheader(String name, String value)	Replaces the current header value.

Table 19-15.   *public class* MimeHeaders *extends Object*

Syntax	Descriptions
abstract SOAPMessage call (SOAPMessage request, Endpoint endpoint)	Sends a message, then pauses until a response is received.
abstract void close()	Closes this SOAPConnection object.

Table 19-16. *public abstract class* SOAPConnection *extends Object*

Syntax	Descriptions
abstract SOAPConnection createConnection()	Creates a new SOAPConnection object.
static SOAPConnectionFactory newInstance()	Creates an instance of the SOAPConnectionFactory object.

Table 19-17. *public abstract class* SOAPConnectionFactory *extends Object*

Syntax	Descriptions
abstract SOAPElement create (Name name)	Creates a SOAPElement object initialized with object name.
abstract SOAPElement create (String localName)	Creates a SOAPElement object initialized with localName.
abstract SOAPElement create(String localName, String prefix, String uri)	Creates a new SOAPElement object.
static SOAPElementFactory newInstance()	Creates an instance of SOAPElementFactory.

Table 19-18. *public abstract class* SOAPElementFactory *extends Object*

Syntax	Descriptions
abstract void addAttachmentPart (AttachmentPart AttachmentPart)	Inserts an AttachmentPart object into a SOAPMessage object.
abstract int countAttachments()	Returns the number of attachments in a message.
abstract AttachmentPart createAttachmentPart()	Creates a new AttachmentPart object.
AttachmentPart createAttachmentPart (DataHandler dataHandler)	Creates an AttachmentPart object and populates it using the given DataHandler object.
AttachmentPart createAttachmentPart (Object content, String contentType)	Creates and populates an AttachmentPart object.
abstract Iterator getAttachments()	Returns AttachmentPart objects that are part of this SOAPMessage object.
abstract Iterator getAttachments (Mimeheaders headers)	Returns AttachmentPart objects that match these headers.
abstract String getContentDescription()	Returns a description of a SOAPMessage object's content.
abstract Mimeheaders getMimeheaders()	Returns the transport MIME headers for a SOAPMessage object.
abstract SOAPPart getSOAPPart()	Returns the SOAP part of a SOAPMessage object.
abstract void removeAllAttachments()	Deletes AttachmentPart objects.
abstract void saveChanges()	Updates a SOAPMessage object.
abstract boolean saveRequired()	Returns whether a SOAPMessage object's saveChanges method was called.
abstract void setContentDescription (String description)	Sets the description of a SOAPMessage object's content.
abstract void writeTo(OutputStream out)	Writes a SOAPMessage object to an output stream.

Table 19-19.   *public abstract class* SOAPMessage *extends Object*

WEB SERVICES

Syntax	Descriptions
abstract void addMimeheader (String name, String value)	Creates a Mimeheader object.
abstract Iterator getAllMimeheaders()	Returns headers for this SOAPPart object as an iterator.
abstract Source getContent()	Returns the content of the SOAPenvelope.
String getContentId()	Returns the value of the Content-Id MIME header.
String getContentLocation()	Returns the value of the Content-Location MIME header.
abstract SOAPenvelope getenvelope()	Returns a SOAPenvelope object.
abstract Iterator getMatching Mimeheaders(String[] names)	Returns Mimeheader objects that match an array element.
abstract String[] getMimeheader (String name)	Returns values of the Mimeheader object in a SOAPPart object.
abstract Iterator getNonMatching Mimeheaders(String[] names)	Returns Mimeheader objects whose names do not appear in the array.
abstract void removeAllMimeheaders()	Removes the Mimeheader objects for a SOAPenvelope object.
abstract void removeMimeheader (String header)	Removes MIME headers of the specified name.
abstract void setContent(Source source)	Sets the content of the SOAPenvelope object.
void setContentId(String contentId)	Sets the value of the Content-Id MIME header.
String void setContentLocation (String contentLocation)	Sets the value of the Content-Location MIME header.
abstract void setMimeheader (String name, String value)	Changes header identified by name to the value specified by value. If name not found, then new header is added.

Table 19-20.   *public abstract class* SOAPPart *extends java.lang.Object*

The Complete Reference

Chapter 20

Universal Description, Discovery, and Integration (UDDI)

Throughout this book you learned that web services technology provides an infrastructure over which clients can request services from service providers, and what service providers use to service clients. Clients and service providers can be different in many ways and still be able to interact with each other. For example, they can be written using different programming languages, or running on different operating systems, or affiliated with different businesses.

Business partners can exchange data by using web services technology to connect together each other's systems, if both partners are exposed to web services. For example, an online retailer might link its inventory control system directly to a vendor's ordering system. The inventory control system automatically places orders whenever inventory becomes low.

The Universal Description, Discovery, and Integration is a database of web services providers that is accessible from within a program and supplies information about the web services available from the provider, including information about interfaces to web services. You'll learn how to interact with the Universal Description, Discovery, and Integration in this chapter.

Inside the Universal Description, Discovery, and Integration

A group of companies, including Microsoft and IBM, launched an effort in late 2000 to create a community of organizations that provide web services. The web services community centers around a group of web-based registries that contain information about each member, their web services, and the application programming interfaces used to access those services. This group of registries is called the *Universal Description, Discovery, and Integration (UDDI)*. UDDI registries are available on public operator sites and there are no access charges for using the UDDI registries.

A key benefit of UDDI is the way it accommodates electronic interaction among businesses. Prior to the introduction of web services and UDDI, the electronic exchange of information among companies was cumbersome to implement. Typically, a team of programmers from each company had to customize each implementation, which was time-consuming and costly.

Web services and UDDI set out to simplify this process by making available the information needed to access a business's web service in a standardized entry in the UDDI. Information a programmer requires to access a web service is obtained by retrieving the UDDI entry for the web service. The programmer still must obtain rights to use the web service and invoke the web service's interface from within a program.

A UDDI entry is called a *tModel* and contains

■ The name of the business
■ Contact information

- Industry codes
- Product classification
- A description of the web service
- Requirements for rights to access the web service
- Technical reference to the interface and properties

A Look at tModels

A tModel is metadata describing specifications about a UDDI registry and is used as a way to share UDDI registry specifications amongst programs. Prior to the introduction of UDDI, organizations that wanted to share information had to agree upon specifications used for the exchange of information. However, UDDI altered this philosophy by creating a facility for organizations to publish their specifications.

A tModel contains specifications for interfaces and other technical information about a web service provider that a client needs to know to access the web service. Let's see how this works in the real world.

Many online retailers are capable of displaying online catalog pages of products as long as vendors send raw product information electronically to the retailer's catalog program. A retailer facilitates this business data interchange by registering the catalog program's tModel with public UDDI sites. The tModel contains the interface to the catalog program's data input routine used to receive product information from vendors. The registration process results in a tModelKey being assigned to the tModel, which is used to look up the tModel information by vendors who want to send the retail product information.

The registration process binds a particular web service to a tModelKey. This is a critical factor in a UDDI registry because some organizations might use the same commercial software to provide a web service. Let's say that two online retailers use the same catalog program to generate online catalogs. In this case, both retailers have the identical interface for their web service. The tModelKey uniquely identifies the interface and the retailer within the UDDI registry.

After a vendor and online retailer agree to do business with each other, software used by the vendor to transmit product information can look up the interface to the retailer's catalog program on the UDDI registry using the tModelKey. Once the interface is found, the vendor's program can use the interface to transmit product information to the retailer's catalog program.

Besides using the tModelKey, web services are also found using other commonly used identification taxonomies such as industry codes, product codes, geographical codes, and business codes, all of which can be included in the organization's UDDI registration.

UDDI version 2 supports two types of taxonomies: unchecked and checked. Unchecked taxonomies are used without UDDI performing validation by registering a tModel as a taxonomy identifier. Checked taxonomies require the UDDI to assure that a registered taxonomy identifier is validated. Validation is performed by UDDI by calling a web service that validates a taxonomy entry.

UDDI Architecture

UDDI is accessible by using the UDDI API. There are two kinds of APIs: the publisher API and the inquiry API. The publisher API is used by a web services provider to register a web service with the UDDI registry. The publisher API is also used to modify an existing registry. The inquiry API is used by a web services client to locate a web service in a UDDI registry.

A publisher must sign up with each UDDI site where the publisher receives the necessary publisher credentials to register its web services. Each UDDI site imposes its own authentication protocol, and credentials are necessary for a publisher to create new entries in the UDDI registry and to modify existing entries. No signup is required for a web services client to use the UDDI registry since UDDI does not authenticate web services clients.

An API is version stamped to avoid conflicts with incompatible API versions. The version stamp is the value of an XML attribute. The version attribute name is generic, and its value is the version number. All UDDI sites support the UDDI API version 1.

Web services are registered with the UDDI registry and requested from the UDDI registry by using SOAP messaging, which you learned about in Chapter 19. Both UDDI API version 1 and version 2 use SOAP and HTTP-POST protocols to interconnect between a client and a web services provider. Errors that occur during processing are returned in the SOAP fault report. The entire request for web services becomes invalidated when an error occurs. Only the first detected error is reported in the SOAP fault report. Table 20-1 contains UDDI error codes that are reported in the SOAP fault report.

Error Code	Description
30000 E_assertionNotFound	A publisher of businessKey values and a keyed reference cannot be identified.
10110 E_authTokenExpired	Authentication token timed out.
10120 E_authTokenRequired	Invalid authentication token passed to an API.
10160 E_accountLimitExceeded	A save request exceeded the data type quantity limits.
10400 E_busy	Request cannot be processed at the current time.

Table 20-1.   *UDDI Errors Reported by SOAP*

Error Code	Description
10500 E_fatalError	Serious technical error has occurred.
10210 E_invalidKeyPassed	The uuid_key value passed did not match with any known key values.
20230 E_invalidProjection	An attempt made to save a businessEntity containing a service projection that does not match the projected businessService.
30100 E_invalidCompletionStatus	An assertion status value passed is unrecognized.
20200 E_invalidValue	A value passed in a keyValue attribute did not pass validation.
10060 E_languageError	An error detected while processing elements that were annotated with xml:lang qualifiers.
30100 E_messageTooLarge	Message is too large.
10020E_nameTooLong	Partial name value passed exceeds the maximum name length.
30220 E_publisherCancelled	Publisher cancelled custody transfer operation.
30210 E_requestDenied	Custody transfer request refused.
30230 E_secretUnknown	Publisher unable to match the shared secret and attempt limit was exhausted.
0 E_success	No failure occurred.
10030 E_tooManyOptions	Too many or incompatible arguments passed.
30200 E_transferAborted	A custody transfer request will not succeed.
10040 E_unrecognizedVersion	The generic attribute value passed is unsupported by the operator instance.
10150 E_unknownUser	Unknown user ID and password.
10050 E_unsupported	The implementer does not support a feature or API.
10140 E_userMismatch	Publishing API controlled by another party.
20210 E_valueNotAllowed	Value did not pass validation because of contextual issues.

Table 20-1.   *UDDI Errors Reported by SOAP* (continued)

The UDDI site modifies entries in two ways. First, the UDDI site assigns keys to the entry. The UDDI site also removes leading and trailing whitespace characters from fields, elements, and attributes, including carriage returns, line feeds, and tabs. In addition, all entities that are named must not be empty.

UDDI Application Programming Interface

The UDDI API is divided into two components: the inquiry API and the publisher API. Clients access information contained in the UDDI registry using the inquiry API. Publishers of web services use the publisher API to enter and modify publisher information in the UDDI registry.

Both the inquiry API and the publisher API take the form of an XML message that is placed within the body of a SOAP message envelope, as you learned in Chapter 19. The receiver URL of the SOAP message is the UDDI site.

Once the UDDI site receives an inquiry SOAP message from a client, the UDDI site retrieves the requested information from the UDDI registry, which is returned to the client in the form of a SOAP message. The client retrieves the SOAP message, as shown in Chapter 19, and retrieves the response from the body of the SOAP message.

There are three patterns in which a client can query a UDDI site: the browser pattern, the drill-down pattern, and the invocation pattern. The browser pattern is where a search begins by seeking general information, the results of which are used to narrow the scope of further searches.

Browser pattern inquiries use the find_xx API calls, where xx is a type of information contained in the UDDI registry. For example, a client may want to search for businesses whose names begin with a sequence of characters.

The drill-down pattern is used once a client narrows choices to a selected group of candidates. Let's say that the browser pattern search returned all businesses whose names begin with ABC. The drill-down pattern is used to search businesses whose names begin with ABC. The drill-down pattern uses the get_xx API calls where xx represents a specific kind of information about a particular business.

The invocation pattern is the third inquiry pattern. The invocation pattern is used to prepare the client application to use the web services found by inquiring the UDDI site. This process is called binding and requires the client application to bind data obtained from the UDDI registry for a particular web service.

Inquiry Application Programming Interface

There are ten inquiry API calls that are used in searching the UDDI registry for information about web services. Each of these is discussed in this section, along with examples that illustrate how you invoke the inquiry API call from within a SOAP message.

find_binding

The find_binding API call is invoked whenever a client wants to locate details on how to bind to a particular web service. Listing 20-1 illustrates how to call find_binding. This example (as will all UDDI API calls) uses XML format, which is discussed in Chapters 8 and 9. The find_binding API can contain up to six arguments, depending on whether you want all related rows returned from the UDDI site or a subset of rows returned.

The first argument is the serviceKey. The serviceKey specifies a particular instance of a businessService element within the UDDI registry. Only rows pertaining to the serviceKey are returned as a result of the inquiry. The value of the serviceKey is the access key that is a universal unique identifer formatted using an algorithm adopted by the UDDI Operator council.

The second argument is maxRows and specifies the maximum number of rows that the UDDI site should return as a result of the inquiry. The maxRows argument is optional. All rows associated with the serviceKey are returned if the maxRows argument is omitted from the API call. However, the UDDI site operator may limit the number of rows returned should the maxRows argument be omitted.

The third argument is generic and is the version used to format the SOAP message when invoking the find_binding API call. In this case, version 2.0 is necessary.

The fourth argument is xmlns, which is the namespace qualifier whose value is the universal resource name that is reserved for reference to the schema.

The fifth argument is findQualifiers. The findQualifiers argument contains search criteria the UDDI site will use to narrow the number of rows that are returned to the client. You'll learn more about findQualifiers in the "Search Qualifiers" section of this chapter. findQualifiers is an optional argument. If omitted, all rows related to the serviceKey are returned. If included, a subset of rows that relate to the serviceKey and match the findQualifiers argument value are returned to the client.

The tModelBag argument is the sixth argument to the findBinding API call. The value of the tModelBag argument is the unique identifier of the bindingTemplate structure of the web service. Only bindingTemplates that contain all of the listed tModels keys will be returned (logical AND operation).

The findBinding API call returns the bindingDetail message that contains information necessary to bind the client application to the web service. This information is contained in the bindingDetail structure. However, an empty bindingDetail structure is returned if the web service is not found in the UDDI site. In the event of an overly large number of matches, or if the number of matches exceeds the maxRows attribute, the response will include the "truncated" attribute with the value set to "true."

A dispositionReport element is returned when processing errors are detected. This element will contain one of two error messages: E-invalidKeyPassed and E_unsupported. E_invalidKeyPassed indicates that the serviceKey could not be found in the UDDI registry.

The E_unsupported error indicates that the findQualifier is invalid, which will be clearly indicated in the dispositionReport.

Listing 20-1
Invoking the
find_binding
API call.

```
<find_binding serviceKey="UUID:CD157937-096B-4437-B336-6BCDBDCC7635"
maxRows="100" generic="2.0" xmlns="urn:uddi-org:api_v2" >
  <findQualifiers/>
  <tModelBag/>
</find_binding>
```

find_business

The find_business API call is used to find information about one or more businesses that are registered in the UDDI registry. Listing 20-2 illustrates how to invoke the find_business API call. The find_business API call arguments are listed here.

The first argument is maxRows, which specifies the number of rows the UDDI site is to return to the client. This is an optional argument, and if omitted, the UDDI site operator determines the maximum number of rows to return.

The second argument is generic and is the version used to format the SOAP message when invoking the find_business API call. In this case, version 2.0 is necessary.

The third argument is xmlns, which is the namespace qualifier whose value is the universal resource name that is reserved for reference to the schema.

The fourth argument is findQualifiers, which contains search criteria used to narrow the number of rows that are returned to the client (see the "Search Qualifiers" section of this chapter). This is an optional argument and all rows are returned if omitted.

The fifth argument is name and contains a string value that represents all or part of the business name that is being searched. The % wildcard character is used to represent unknown characters if a partial name is used in the argument. You can specify up to five name arguments. The UDDI site returns information structures of businesses whose names match these arguments. The names are evaluated using a logical OR basis.

The sixth argument is discoveryURLs, which is a list of URLs that are to be matched to the discoveryURL contained in a business' businessEntity information with the UDDI registry. The UDDI site returns a businessList containing a business' businessInfo structure whenever there is a match of the discoveryURLs.

The seventh argument is identifierBag. The identifierBag is a list of business identifiers that tell the UDDI site to return business information structures for businesses whose business identifiers are contained in the identifierBag. The identifierBag argument is optional.

The eighth argument is categoryBag. The categoryBag is a list of category identifiers used to identify categories of businesses to the UDDI site. The UDDI site then returns businesses associated with each category. The categoryBag argument is optional.

The ninth argument is tModelBag. The tModelBag argument is the unique identifier of the bindingTemplate structure of the web service.

The information returned by the UDDI site in response to the find_business API call is dependent on the arguments used in the call. Generally, the UDDI site returns a businessList that contains information about businesses whose criteria match that of the arguments in the find_business API call.

However, the UDDI site returns information about businesses that contain a matching bindingTemplate if the tModelBag argument is used in the find_business API call. An empty businessList is returned should no entries in the UDDI registry match values of arguments to the find_business API call.

Be sure to examine the truncated attribute of the returned businessList. If this attribute is set to true, then a subset of rows were returned. This is because the full complement of rows exceeds the value of the maxRow argument or were truncated automatically by the UDDI site operator because of the exceedingly large number of rows that met the search criteria for the query.

A dispositionReport element is returned if the UDDI site encountered errors when processing the inquiry. This element will contain one of three error messages: E_nameTooLong, E_unsupported, and E_tooManyOptions. The E_nameTooLong message indicates that the name passed as the value to an argument exceeds the maximum length for a name field. The E_unsupported error indicates that the findQualifier is invalid, which will be clearly indicated in the dispositionReport. The E_tooManyOptions message is returned if more than five name arguments are included in the inquiry.

Listing 20-2
Invoking the
find_business
API call.

```
<find_business maxRows="100" generic="2.0" xmlns="urn:uddi-org:api_v2" >
   <findQualifiers/>
   <name/>
   <discoveryURLs/>
   <identifierBag/>
   <categoryBag/>
   <tModelBag/>
</find_business>
```

find_relatedBusinesses

The find_relatedBusinesses API call, illustrated in Listing 20-3, is used to retrieve information about one or more registrations that are related to the same business entity. For example, some businesses are comprised of multiple business units as related to its organizational hierarchy. Each business unit might have its own entry in the UDDI registry. The find_relatedBusinesses API call returns a relatedBusinessList that contains information about all the business units of a specified business.

There are five arguments to the find_relatedBusinesses API call. The first two arguments are generic, which is the version used to format the SOAP message, and xmlns, which is the namespace qualifier whose value is the universal resource name that is reserved for reference to the schema.

The third argument is findQualifiers, which contains search criteria used to narrow the number of rows that are returned to the client (see the "Search Qualifiers" section of this chapter). This is an optional argument, and all rows are returned if omitted. The fourth argument is businessKey. The businessKey specifies a particular businessEntity that is the target of the request.

The last argument is keyedReference. The keyedReference argument is optional and specifies that the results should include only businesses that are related to the businessEntity in a specific way.

The UDDI site returns a relatedBusinessesList that contains businesses that relate to the businessEntity. However, the relatedBusinessesList contains an empty relatedBusinessInfos element if the UDDI registry does not contain any businesses that match the search criteria.

Sometimes the UDDI site operator limits the number of rows that are returned in order to provide efficient service to clients requesting registry information. Be sure to examine the truncated attribute of the returned relatedBusinessesList. If this attribute is set to true, a subset of rows was returned.

A dispositionReport element is returned if the UDDI site encountered errors when processing the inquiry. This element will contain one of two error messages: E_invalidKeyPassed and E_unsupported. The E_invalidKeyPassed error indicates that the businessKey wasn't found in the UDDI registry. The E_unsupported error indicates that the findQualifier is invalid, which will be clearly indicated in the dispositionReport.

Listing 20-3
Invoking the find_related Businesses API call.

```
<find_relatedBusinesses generic="2.0" xmlns="urn:uddi-org:api_v2" >
   <findQualifiers/>
   <businessKey/>
   <keyedReference/>
</find_relatedBusinesses>
```

find_service

The find_service API call, shown in Listing 20-4, is used to find one or more services of a businessEntity in the UDDI register. The UDDI site returns a serviceList that contains available services from a businessEntity.

Here are the arguments used with the find_service API call. The first argument is the businessKey, which specifies a particular businessEntity that is the target of the request. Next is maxRows, which is an optional argument indicating the maximum number of rows the UDDI site is to return to the client.

The next two arguments are generic, which is the version used to format the SOAP message, and xmlns, which is the namespace qualifier whose value is the universal resource name that is reserved for reference to the schema.

The fifth argument is findQualifiers, which contains search criteria used to narrow the number of rows that are returned to the client (see the "Search Qualifiers" section of this chapter). This is an optional argument, and all rows are returned if omitted.

The next argument is name and contains a string value that represents all or part of the business name that is being searched. The % wildcard character is used to represent unknown characters if a partial name is used in the argument. You can specify up to five name arguments. The UDDI site returns information structures of businesses whose names match these arguments.

The two final arguments are categoryBag and tModelBag. The categoryBag argument is a list of category identifiers used to identify categories of businesses to the UDDI site. The tModelBag argument is the unique identifier of the bindingTemplate structure of the web service.

The UDDI site returns a serviceList that contains services available from a businessEntity. However, the serviceList contains an empty businessServices element if the UDDI registry does not match the search criteria.

The UDDI site operator can limit the number of rows that are returned to clients. Be sure to examine truncated attribute of the returned serviceList. If this attribute is set to true, a subset of rows was returned.

A dispositionReport element is returned if the UDDI site encountered errors when processing the inquiry. This element will contain one of three error messages: E_invalidKeyPassed, E_nameTooLong, and E_unsupported. The E_invalidKeyPassed error indicates that the businessKey wasn't found in the UDDI registry. The E_nameTooLong indicates that the name passed as the value to an argument exceeds the maximum length for a name field. The E_unsupported error indicates that the findQualifier is invalid, which will be clearly indicated in the dispositionReport.

Listing 20-4
Invoking the
find_service
API call.

```
<find_service businessKey="UUID:CD157937-096B-4437-B336-6BCDBDCC7635" "
maxRows="100" generic="2.0
xmlns="urn:uddi-org:api_v2" >
   <findQualifiers/>
   <name/>
   <categoryBag/>
   <tModelBag/>
</find_service>
```

find_tModel

Listing 20-5 illustrates the find_tModel API call, which is used to find one or more tModel information structures in the UDDI registry. The UDDI site returns a tModelList that contains tModel information structures.

Here are the arguments used with the find_tModel API call. The first argument is maxRows, which specifies the number of rows the UDDI site is to return to the client. This is an optional argument, and if omitted, the UDDI site operator determines the maximum number of rows returned.

The next argument is generic, which is the version used to format the SOAP message. This is followed by xmlns, which is the namespace qualifier whose value is the universal resource name that is reserved for reference to the schema.

The fourth argument is findQualifiers. The findQualifiers argument contains search criteria used to narrow the number of rows that are returned to the client (see the "Search Qualifiers" section of this chapter). This is an optional argument, and all rows are returned if omitted.

WEB SERVICES

The fifth argument is name and contains a string value that represents all or part of the business name that is being searched. The % wildcard character is used to represent unknown characters if a partial name is used in the argument. You can specify one name argument.

The next argument is identifierBag. The identifierBag argument is a list of business identifiers that tell the UDDI site to return business information structures for businesses whose business identifiers are contained in the identifierBag.

The last argument is categoryBag. The categoryBag argument is a list of category identifiers used to identify categories of businesses to the UDDI site.

The UDDI site returns a tModelList. The tModelList contains an empty tModelInfo element if the UDDI registry does not contain any businesses that match the search criteria. Be sure to examine the truncated attribute of the returned tModelList. If this attribute is set to true, a subset of rows was returned.

A dispositionReport element is returned if the UDDI site encountered errors when processing the inquiry. This element will contain one of two error messages: E_nameTooLong and E_unsupported. The E_nameTooLong message indicates that the name passed as the value to an argument exceeds the maximum length for a name field. The E_unsupported error indicates that the findQualifier is invalid, which will be clearly indicated in the dispositionReport.

Listing 20-5
Invoking the
find_tModel
API call.

```
<find_tModel maxRows="100" generic="2.0" xmlns="urn:uddi-org:api_v2" >
   <findQualifiers/>
   <name/>
   <identifierBag/>
   <categoryBag/>
</find_tModel>
```

get_bindingDetail

The get_bindingDetail API call is used to retrieve the full runtime bindingTemplate information from the UDDI registry. This is illustrated in Listing 20-6. The UDDI site returns bindingDetail, which is used to request service from the targeted businessEntity.

The get_bindingDetail API call has three arguments. These are generic, xmlns, and bindingKey. The generic argument is the version used to format the SOAP message, and the xmlns argument is the namespace qualifier whose value is the universal resource name that is reserved for reference to the schema. The bindingKey argument is the key value of the bindingTemplate data registered in the UDDI registry.

The UDDI site returns the bindingDetail elements that match bindingKeys contained in the API call. The bindingDetail elements are returned in the order in which bindingKeys appear in the API call. Sometimes the UDDI site operator limits the number of rows that are returned in order to provide efficient service to clients requesting registry information. Be sure to examine the truncated attribute of the returned bindingDetail elements. If this attribute is set to true, a subset of rows was returned.

A dispositionReport element is returned if the UDDI site encountered errors when processing the inquiry. This element will contain one error message, which is E_invalidKeyPassed. The E_invalidKeyPassed error indicates that the businessKey wasn't found in the UDDI registry.

Listing 20-6
Invoking the get_binding tail API call.

```
<get_bindingDetail generic="2.0" xmlns="urn:uddi-org:api_v2" >
  <bindingKey/>
</get_bindingDetail>
```

get_businessDetail

Listing 20-7 illustrates how to invoke the get_businessDetail API call to retrieve full businessEntity information from businesses that are registered in the UDDI registry. The UDDI returns businessDetail elements related to those businesses.

The get_businessDetail API call has one argument, which is businessKey. The businessKey argument specifies a particular businessEntity that is the target of the request. The UDDI site returns businessDetail elements in the order in which businessKey arguments are passed to the UDDI site. Be sure to examine the truncated attribute of the returned businessDetail. If this attribute is set to true, a subset of rows was returned.

A dispositionReport element is returned if the UDDI site encountered errors when processing the inquiry. This element will contain one error message, which is E_invalidKeyPassed. The E_invalidKeyPassed error indicates that the businessKey wasn't found in the UDDI registry.

Listing 20-7
Invoking the get_business Detail API call.

```
<get_businessDetail generic="2.0" xmlns="urn:uddi-org:api_v2" >
  <businessKey/>
</get_businessDetail>
```

get_businessDetailExt

The get_businessDetailExt API call is used to retrieve extended information about a businessEntity from the UDDI registry. The UDDI site returns the businessDetailExt. Listing 20-8 illustrates how to make the get_businessDetailExt API call.

The get_businessDetailExt API call requires the businessKey argument. The businessKey argument specifies a particular businessEntity that is the target of the request. The UDDI site returns businessDetailExt elements in the order in which businessKey arguments are passed to the UDDI site. Be sure to examine the truncated attribute of the returned businessDetail. If this attribute is set to true, a subset of rows was returned.

A dispositionReport element is returned if the UDDI site encountered errors when processing the inquiry. This element will contain one of two possible error messages: E_invalidKeyPassed error, which indicates that the businessKey wasn't found in the

UDDI registry, and E_unsupported, indicating that the UDDI site does not support extended detail function.

Listing 20-8
Invoking the
get_business
DetailExt
API call.

```
<get_businessDetailExt generic="2.0" xmlns="urn:uddi-org:api_v2" >
    <businessKey/>
</get_businessDetailExt>
```

get_serviceDetail

The get_serviceDetail API call is used to retrieve all the details related to a businessService registered in a UDDI registry. This is illustrated in Listing 20-9. The get_serviceDetail API call returns serviceDetail.

There is one argument required by the get_serviceDetail API call. This is serviceKey. The serviceKey argument is the key that identifies businessService data in a UDDI registry. There can be multiple serviceKey arguments, and the UDDI site returns serviceDetail elements in the order in which serviceKey arguments appear in the API call. Be sure to examine the truncated attribute of the returned serviceDetail. If this attribute is set to true, a subset of rows was returned.

A dispositionReport element is returned if the UDDI site encountered errors when processing the inquiry. This element will contain one error message, which is E_invalidKeyPassed. The E_invalidKeyPassed error indicates that the serviceKey wasn't found in the UDDI registry.

Listing 20-9
Invoking the
get_service
Detail API call.

```
<get_serviceDetail generic="2.0" xmlns="urn:uddi-org:api_v2" >
    <serviceKey/>
</get_serviceDetail>
```

get_tModelDetail

Listing 20-10 demonstrates how to invoke the get_tModelDetail API call in order to retrieve full details for a specified tModel from the UDDI registry. The get_tModelDetail API call requires one argument, which is tModelKey. The tModelKey argument is the key that uniquely identifies a tModel in the UDDI registry.

Multiple tModelKey arguments can be passed to the get_tModelDetail API call. The UDDI site returns tModel information in the order in which the tModelKey arguments appear in the API call. Be sure to examine the truncated attribute of the returned tModelDetail. If this attribute is set to true, a subset of rows was returned.

A dispositionReport element is returned if the UDDI site encountered errors when processing the inquiry. This element will contain one error message, which is E_invalidKeyPassed. The _invalidKeyPassed error indicates that the serviceKey wasn't found in the UDDI registry.

```
<get_tModelDetail generic="2.0" xmlns="urn:uddi-org:api_v2" >
  <tModelKey/>
</get_tModelDetail>
```

Search Qualifiers

Some inquiry API calls enable you to identify types of UDDI registry entries by specifying a search qualifier as an argument of an API call. A search qualifier overrides the default search method used by the UDDI site operator.

A search qualifier is placed within the search qualifier findQualifiers element name within the API call, as described in the previous section of this chapter. The value of a findQualifiers element (see Listing 20-11) can be one of the values shown in Table 20-2.

```
<findQualifiers>
  <findQualifier>exactNameMatch</findQualifier>
  <findQualifier>sortByNameDesc</findQualifier>
</findQualifers>
```

Search Qualifier Values	Description
exactNameMatch	Only entries that exactly match the argument are returned.
caseSensitiveMatch	Only entries that match the case of the argument are returned.
sortByNameAsc	Results sorted on the name field in ascending alphabetic sort order prior to any truncation of the return values.
sortByNameDesc	Results sorted on the name field in descending alphabetic sort order prior to any truncation of the return values.
sortByDateAsc	Results sorted on the date last updated in ascending chronological sort order (earliest returns first).
sortByDateDesc	Results sorted on the date last updated in descending chronological sort order (most recent change returns first).

Table 20-2.   *Search Qualifier Values*

WEB SERVICES

Search Qualifier Values	Description
orLikeKeys	Used in a categoryBag or identifierBag that contains multiple keyedReference elements to indicate to match any value from the namespace in the argument (version 2.0).
orAllKeys	Matches at least one key specified in the argument (version 2.0).
combineCategoryBags	Used with the find_business API call and returns results where the categoryBag elements are found in the full businessEntity element and a UDDI entry (version 2.0).
serviceSubset	Used with the find_business API call and in conjunction with a passed categoryBag argument. Limits search to the businessService elements within the registry (version 2.0).
andAllKeys	Matches all keys specified in the argument (default search, version 2.0).
soundex	Performs sound-alike searches using the argument value and searches the businessEntity and businessService entities. Used with find_business, find_service, and find_tModel API calls (version 2.0).

Table 20-2. *Search Qualifier Values* (continued)

Response Messages

An inquiry is created by calling the appropriate API call using search qualifiers, if necessary, and is placed within the body of a SOAP message. The SOAP message is sent to a UDDI site, where the inquiry is removed from the body of the SOAP message and processed by the UDDI site.

After processing is completed, the UDDI site creates a response and places the response in the body of another SOAP message, which is then returned to the client. The client then extracts the message body, as described in Chapter 19, and processes the response.

The type of process the client uses to process a response is dependent on the nature of the client's application. For example, a client may require binding information that contains the interface to a service provider's service. The client sends a UDDI inquiry to the UDDI site to retrieve binding information, which is then used within the client's application to access the service provider's service.

The UDDI site responds to an inquiry with possibly 14 response messages that appear as elements of the return message. These response messages are contained in Table 20-3.

Response Message	Description
assertionStatusReport	Returned in response to the get_assertionStatusReport API call. Determines the status of assertions made by either the publisher or by other parties.
authToken	Returned in response to the get_authToken API call. Returns authentication information and is used in subsequent calls that require an authInfo value.
bindingDetail	Returned in response to the get_bindingDetail API call. Returns technical information needed to access a web service.
businessDetail	Returned in response to the get_businessDetail API call and the save_business API call. Returns full details for businessEntity elements.
businessDetailExt	Returned in response to the get_businessDetailExt API call. Returns businessEntityExt elements.
businessList	Returned in response to the find_business API call. Returns abbreviated information about registered businessEntity information in businessInfo elements.
dispositionReport	Returns errors discovered during processing.
publisherAssertions	Returned in response to the get_publisherAssertions API call. Returns a publisher's assertion collection.
registeredInfo	Returned in response to the get_registeredInfo API call. Returns abbreviated information about all registered businessEntity and tModel information of a businessEntity specified in the argument of the API call as businessInfo elements and tModelInfo elements.
RelatedBusinessesList	Returned in response to the find_relatedBusinesses API call. Returns publicly visible business relationships.

Table 20-3.   *Response Messages*

Response Message	Description
serviceDetail	Returned in response to the get_serviceDetail API call. Returns full details for businessService elements.
serviceList	Returned in response to the find_service API call. Returns abbreviated information about registered businessService information in the form of serviceInfo elements.
tModelList	Returned in response to the find_tModelDetail API call. Returns abbreviated information about registered tModelDetail information in the form of tModel elements.
tModelDetail	Returned in response to the get_tModelDetail API call and the save_tModel API call. Returns full details for tModel elements.

Table 20-3. *Response Messages* (continued)

Publishing Application Programming Interface

A service provider can make services available to clients by publishing services on a UDDI site using publishing API calls. Typically, a service provider selects a UDDI operator site to publish its services and must use the UDDI operator site to publish new services and update registered services. The reason for limiting a service provider to a UDDI operator is because UDDI entries are not automatically duplicated on other UDDI sites or reconciled with manually duplicated entries on other UDDI sites.

Services are registered in a UDDI registry by invoking a publisher API call. A publisher API call is similar in concept to the inquiry API call discussed previously in this chapter in that a publisher API call is formatted using XML and is placed in the body of a SOAP message. The SOAP message is then transmitted to a UDDI site for processing. Afterwards, a response is returned in the body of another SOAP message. Responses are discussed in an earlier section of this chapter.

The follow sections describe each publisher API calls.

add_publisherAssertions

The add_publisherAssertions API call is used to publish the publisher's assertion collection. Listing 20-12 illustrates how to invoke the add_publisherAssertions API call.

The add_publisherAssertions API call contains several arguments. These are generic, xmlns, authInfo, publisherAssertion, fromKey, toKey, and keyedReference.

The generic argument is the version used to format the SOAP message and the xmlns argument is the namespace qualifier whose value is the universal resource name that is reserved for reference to the schema.

The authInfo argument contains an authentication token that is obtained by invoking the get_authToken API call. The publisherAssertion argument consists of relationship assertions that reference two businessEntity key values. The fromKey and toKey arguments contain businessEntity key values that define the publisherAssertion. The keyedReference argument defines the direction of the relationship.

The UDDI site returns a dispositionReport that contains either a success indicator or one of four error messages: E_invalidKeyPassed, E_authTokenExpired, E_authTokenRequired, or E_userMismatch.

The E_invalidKeyPassed error indicates that the businessKey or tModelKey wasn't found in the UDDI registry. The E_authTokenExpired error indicates that the authentication token has expired. The E_authTokenRequired error indicates that the authentication token is missing or invalid. Finally, the E_userMismatch error indicates that the authentication token isn't associated with the publisher account as indicated by the fromKey and toKey arguments.

Listing 20-12
Invoking the add_publisher Assertions API call.

```
<add_publisherAssertions generic="2.0" xmlns="urn:uddi-org:api_v2" >
  <authInfo/>
  <publisherAssertion>
    <fromKey/>
    <toKey/>
    <keyedReference/>
  </publisherAssertion>
</add_publisherAssertions>
```

delete_binding

The delete_binding API call is used to remove a bindingTemplate from a UDDI registry. Listing 20-13 illustrates how to call the delete_binding API call. The delete_binding API call has four arguments: generic, xmlns, authInfo, and bindingKey.

The generic argument is the version used to format the SOAP message, and the xmlns argument is the namespace qualifier whose value is the universal resource name that is reserved for reference to the schema. The authInfo argument contains an authentication token that is obtained by invoking the get_authToken API call. The bindingKey argument contains the key that identifies the bindingTemplate.

The UDDI site returns a dispositionReport that contains either a success indicator or one of four error messages: E_invalidKeyPassed, E_authTokenExpired, E_authTokenRequired, or E_userMismatch.

The E_invalidKeyPassed error indicates that the businessKey wasn't found in the UDDI registry. The E_authTokenExpired error indicates that the authentication token

WEB SERVICES

has expired. The E_authTokenRequired error indicates that the authentication token is missing or invalid. The E_userMismatch error indicates the bindingKey doesn't match the bindingTemplate that is associated with the authentication token.

```
<delete_binding generic="2.0" xmlns="urn:uddi-org:api_v2" >
  <authInfo/>
  <bindingKey/>
</delete_binding>
```

delete_business

The delete_business API call is used to delete a business registration from the UDDI registry. This includes businessEntity and all related entries. Listing 20-14 illustrates how to call the delete_business API.

The delete_business API call has four arguments: generic, xmlns, authInfo, and businessKey. The generic argument is the version used to format the SOAP message, and the xmlns argument is the namespace qualifier whose value is the universal resource name that is reserved for reference to the schema. The authInfo argument contains an authentication token that is obtained by invoking the get_authToken API call. The businessKey argument contains the key that identifies the businessEntity.

The UDDI site returns a dispositionReport that contains either a success indicator or one of four error messages: E_invalidKeyPassed, E_authTokenExpired, E_authTokenRequired, or E_userMismatch.

The E_invalidKeyPassed error indicates that the businessKey wasn't found in the UDDI registry. The E_authTokenExpired error indicates that the authentication token has expired. The E_authTokenRequired error indicates that the authentication token is missing or invalid. The E_userMismatch error indicates the businessKey doesn't match the businessEntity that is associated with the authentication token.

```
<delete_business generic="2.0" xmlns="urn:uddi-org:api_v2" >
  <authInfo/>
  <businessKey/>
</delete_business>
```

delete_publisherAssertions

The delete_publisherAssertions API call deletes publisherAssertion from a publisher's assertion collection. This is illustrated in Listing 20-15. The delete_publisherAssertions API contains several arguments: generic, xmlns, authInfo, publisherAssertion, fromKey, toKey, and keyedReference.

The generic argument is the version used to format the SOAP message, and the xmlns argument is the namespace qualifier whose value is the universal resource name that is reserved for reference to the schema.

The authInfo argument contains an authentication token that is obtained by invoking the get_authToken API call. The publisherAssertion argument consists of relationship assertions that reference two businessEntity key values. The fromKey and toKey arguments contain businessEntity key values that define the publisherAssertion. The keyedReference argument defines the direction of the relationship. More than one publisherAssertion may be specified.

The UDDI site returns a dispositionReport that contains either a success indicator or one of four error messages: E_assertionNotFound, E_authTokenExpired, E_userMismatch, or E_authTokenRequired.

The E_assertionNotFound error indicates that the assertion wasn't found in the UDDI registry. The E_authTokenExpired error indicates that the authentication token has expired. The E_authTokenRequired error indicates that the authentication token is missing or invalid. Finally, the E_userMismatch error indicates that the authentication token isn't associated with the publisher account as indicated by the fromKey and toKey arguments.

Listing 20-15
Invoking the
delete_publisher
Assertions
API call.

```
<delete_publisherAssertions generic="2.0" xmlns="urn:uddi-org:api_v2" >
  <authInfo/>
  <publisherAssertion>
    <fromKey/>
    <toKey/>
    <keyedReference/>
  </publisherAssertion>
</delete_publisherAssertions>
```

delete_service

The delete_service API call is used to remove a businessService from a UDDI registry, as illustrated in Listing 20-16. The delete_service API call requires four arguments: generic, xmlns, authInfo, and serviceKey.

The generic argument is the version used to format the SOAP message, and the xmlns argument is the namespace qualifier whose value is the universal resource name that is reserved for reference to the schema.

The authInfo argument contains an authentication token that is obtained by invoking the get_authToken API call. The serviceKey argument is the key that identifies the businessService. More than one serviceKey may be specified.

The UDDI site returns a dispositionReport that contains either a success indicator or one of four error messages: E_invalidKeyPassed, E_authTokenExpired, E_authTokenRequired, or E_userMismatch.

The E_invalidKeyPassed error indicates that the serviceKey wasn't found in the UDDI registry. The E_authTokenExpired error indicates that the authentication token has expired. The E_authTokenRequired error indicates that the authentication token is missing or invalid. Finally, the E_userMismatch error indicates that the authentication token isn't associated with the serviceKey.

Listing 20-16
Invoking the
delete_service
API call.

```
<delete_service generic="2.0" xmlns="urn:uddi-org:api_v2" >
  <authInfo/>
  <serviceKey/>
</delete_service>
```

delete_tModel

The delete_tModel API call is used to remove a tModel from a UDDI registry, as illustrated in Listing 20-17. The delete_tModel API call requires four arguments: generic, xmlns, authInfo, and tModelKey.

The generic argument is the version used to format the SOAP message, and the xmlns argument is the namespace qualifier whose value is the universal resource name that is reserved for reference to the schema. The authInfo argument contains an authentication token that is obtained by invoking the get_authToken API call. The tModelKey argument is the key that identifies the tModel. More than one tModelKey may be specified.

The UDDI site returns a dispositionReport that contains either a success indicator or one of four error messages: E_invalidKeyPassed, E_authTokenExpired, E_authTokenRequired, or E_userMismatch.

The E_invalidKeyPassed error indicates that the tModelKey wasn't found in the UDDI registry. The E_authTokenExpired error indicates that the authentication token has expired. The E_authTokenRequired error indicates that the authentication token is missing or invalid. Finally, the E_userMismatch error indicates that the authentication token isn't associated with the tModelKey.

Listing 20-17
Invoking the
delete_tModel
API call.

```
<delete_tModel generic="2.0" xmlns="urn:uddi-org:api_v2" >
  <authInfo/>
  <tModelKey/>
</delete_tModel>
```

discard_authToken

The discard_authToken API call tells the UDDI site to discard the authentication token and end the session. This is illustrated in Listing 20-18. The discard_authToken API call has three arguments: generic, xmlns, and authInfo.

The generic argument is the version used to format the SOAP message, and the xmlns argument is the namespace qualifier whose value is the universal resource name that is reserved for reference to the schema. The authInfo argument contains an authentication token that is obtained by invoking the get_authToken API call.

The UDDI site returns a dispositionReport that contains either a success indicator or the E_authTokenRequired error, which indicates that the authentication token has expired.

Listing 20-18
Invoking the discard_ authToken API call.

```
<discard_authToken generic="2.0" xmlns="urn:uddi-org:api_v2" >
  <authInfo/>
</discard_authToken>
```

get_assertionStatusReport

The get_assertionStatusReport API call is used to determine the current status of a publisher's assertions, as shown in Listing 20-19. The get_assertionStatusReport API call has four arguments: generic, xmlns, authInfo, and completionStatus.

The generic argument is the version used to format the SOAP message, and the xmlns argument is the namespace qualifier whose value is the universal resource name that is reserved for reference to the schema. The authInfo argument contains an authentication token that is obtained by invoking the get_authToken API call. The completionStatus argument must be one of the values listed in Table 20-4.

The UDDI site returns a dispositionReport that contains either a success indicator or one of three error messages: E_invalidCompletionStatus, E_authTokenExpired, or E_authTokenRequired.

The E_invalidCompletionStatus error indicates that the completionStatus value is unrecognized by the UDDI site. The E_authTokenExpired error indicates that the authentication token has expired. The E_authTokenRequired error indicates that the authentication token is missing or invalid.

Listing 20-19
Invoking the get_assertio nStatusRepo rt API call.

```
<get_assertionStatusReport generic="2.0" xmlns="urn:uddi-org:api_v2" >
  <authInfo/>
  <completionStatus/>
</get_assertionStatusReport>
```

Value	Description
status:complete	Return only the publisher assertions that are complete.
status:toKey_incomplete	Return only the publisher assertions that don't match assertions referenced by the toKey value.
status:fromKey_ incomplete	Return only the publisher assertions that don't match assertions referenced by the fromKey value.

Table 20-4.   *Values for the completionStatus Argument*

get_authToken

The get_authToken API call is used to retrieve an authentication token that is used in other publisher API calls, as is illustrated in Listing 20-20. The get_authToken API call has four arguments: generic, xmlns, userID, and cred.

The generic argument is the version used to format the SOAP message, and the xmlns argument is the namespace qualifier whose value is the universal resource name that is reserved for reference to the schema. The userID argument contains the user ID required to access the UDDI site, and the cred argument contains the password associated with the user ID.

The UDDI site returns a dispositionReport that contains either a success indicator and the token or E_unknownUser, which indicates that the UDDI site does not recognize the login information supplied by the get_authToken API call.

Listing 20-20
Invoking the
get_authToken
API call.

```
<get_authToken generic="2.0" xmlns="urn:uddi-org:api_v2" userID="user ID" cred="
password" />
</get_authToken>
```

get_publisherAssertions

The get_publisherAssertions API call is used to retrieve all the assertions associated with a publisher that are contained on the UDDI registry. This is illustrated in Listing 20-21. The get_publisherAssertions API call requires three arguments: generic, xmlns, and authInfo.

The generic argument is the version used to format the SOAP message, and the xmlns argument is the namespace qualifier whose value is the universal resource name that is reserved for reference to the schema. The authInfo argument contains an authentication token that is obtained by invoking the get_authToken API call.

The UDDI site returns a dispositionReport that contains either a success indicator and the publisher assertions or one of two error messages: E_authTokenExpired or E_authTokenRequired. The E_authTokenExpired error indicates that the authentication token has expired. The E_authTokenRequired error indicates that the authentication token is missing or invalid.

Listing 20-21
Invoking the
get_publisher
Assertions
API call.

```
<get_publisherAssertions generic="2.0" xmlns="urn:uddi-org:api_v2" >
  <authInfo/>
</get_publisherAssertions>
```

get_registeredInfo

The get_registeredInfo API call is used to retrieve the abbreviated list of businessEntity and tModel information, as shown in Listing 20-22. The get_registeredInfo API call requires three arguments: generic, xmlns, and authInfo.

The generic argument is the version used to format the SOAP message, and the xmlns argument is the namespace qualifier whose value is the universal resource name that is reserved for reference to the schema. The authInfo argument contains an authentication token that is obtained by invoking the get_authToken API call.

The UDDI site returns a dispositionReport that contains either a success indicator and the registeredInfo or one of two error messages: E_authTokenExpired or E_authTokenRequired. The E_authTokenExpired error indicates that the authentication token has expired. The E_authTokenRequired error indicates that the authentication token is missing or invalid.

Listing 20-22
Invoking the
et_registeredI
nfo API call.

```
<get_registeredInfo generic="2.0" xmlns="urn:uddi-org:api_v2" >
  <authInfo/>
</get_registeredInfo>
```

save_binding

The save_binding API call is used to save a bindingTemplate, as is illustrated in Listing 20-23. The save_binding API call requires four arguments: generic, xmlns, authInfo, and bindingTemplate.

The generic argument is the version used to format the SOAP message, and the xmlns argument is the namespace qualifier whose value is the universal resource name that is reserved for reference to the schema. The authInfo argument contains an authentication token that is obtained by invoking the get_authToken API call. The bindingTemplate argument is the bindingTemplate that is being saved. More than one bindingTemplate may be listed.

The UDDI site returns a dispositionReport that contains either a success indicator and the bindingDetail or one of five error messages: E_authTokenExpired, E_authTokenRequired, E_invalidKeyPassed, E_userMismatch, or E_accountLimitExceeded.

The E_authTokenExpired error indicates that the authentication token has expired. The E_authTokenRequired error indicates that the authentication token is missing or invalid. The E_invalidKeyPassed error indicates an invalid key was passed to the UDDI site. The E_userMismatch error indicates that the authentication token is not authorized to access the bindingTemplate. Finally, the E_accountLimitExceeded error indicates that the business has reached its bindingTemplate limits on the UDDI site.

Listing 20-23
Invoking the
save_binding
API call.

```
<save_binding generic="2.0" xmlns="urn:uddi-org:api_v2" >
  <authInfo/>
  <bindingTemplate/>
</save_binding>
```

WEB SERVICES

save_business

The save_business API call is used to save a businessEntity, and is shown in Listing 20-24. The save_business API call has four arguments: generic, xmlns, authInfo, and businessEntity.

The generic argument is the version used to format the SOAP message, and the xmlns argument is the namespace qualifier whose value is the universal resource name that is reserved for reference to the schema. The authInfo argument contains an authentication token that is obtained by invoking the get_authToken API call. The businessEntity argument is the businessEntity that is being saved. More than one businessEntity may be listed.

The UDDI site returns a dispositionReport that contains either a success indicator and the businessDetail or one of seven error messages: E_authTokenExpired, E_authTokenRequired, E_invalidKeyPassed, E_userMismatch, E_invalidValue, E_valueNotAllowed, or E_accountLimitExceeded.

The E_authTokenExpired error indicates that the authentication token has expired. The E_authTokenRequired error indicates that the authentication token is missing or invalid. The E_invalidKeyPassed error indicates an invalid key was passed to the UDDI site. The E_userMismatch error indicates that that authentication token is not authorized to access the bindingTemplate. The E_invalidValue error indicates that the key passed as an argument is not within the taxonomy specified by the tModelKey value in the categoryBag. The E_valueNotAllowed error indicates that the businessEntity failed the UDDI site's validation routine. Finally, the E_accountLimitExceeded error indicates that the business has reached its businessEntity limits on the UDDI site.

<table>
<tr>
<td>

Listing 20-24
Invoking the
save_business
API call.
</td>
<td>

```
<save_business generic="2.0" xmlns="urn:uddi-org:api_v2" >
    <authInfo/>
    <businessEntity/>
</save_business>
```
</td>
</tr>
</table>

save_service

The save_service API call inserts or updates a businessService based on whether or not the businessService specified in the save_service API call already exists in the UDDI registry. This is illustrated in Listing 20-25. The save_service API call has four arguments: generic, xmlns, authInfo, and businessService.

The generic argument is the version used to format the SOAP message, and the xmlns argument is the namespace qualifier whose value is the universal resource name that is reserved for reference to the schema. The authInfo argument contains an authentication token that is obtained by invoking the get_authToken API call. The businessEntity argument is the businessService that is being inserted or updated.

The UDDI site returns a dispositionReport that contains either a success indicator and the serviceDetail or one of seven error messages: E_authTokenExpired, E_authTokenRequired, E_invalidKeyPassed, E_userMismatch, E_invalidValue, E_valueNotAllowed, or E_accountLimitExceeded.

The E_authTokenExpired error indicates that the authentication token has expired. The E_authTokenRequired error indicates that the authentication token is missing or invalid. The E_invalidKeyPassed error indicates an invalid key was passed to the

UDDI site. The E_userMismatch error indicates that that authentication token is not authorized to access the businessEntity. The E_invalidValue error indicates that the key passed as an argument is not within the taxonomy specified by the tModelKey value in the categoryBag. The E_valueNotAllowed error indicates that the businessEntity failed the UDDI site's validation routine. Finally, the E_accountLimitExceeded error indicates that the business has reached its businessEntity limits on the UDDI site.

Listing 20-25
Invoking the
save_service
API call.

```
<save_service generic="2.0" xmlns="urn:uddi-org:api_v2" >
  <authInfo/>
  <businessService/>
</save_service>
```

save_tModel

The save_tModel API call inserts or updates a tModel based on whether or not the tModel specified in the save_tModel API call already exists in the UDDI registry. This is illustrated in Listing 20-26. The tModel API call has four arguments: generic, xmlns, authInfo, and tModel.

The generic argument is the version used to format the SOAP message, and the xmlns argument is the namespace qualifier whose value is the universal resource name that is reserved for reference to the schema. The authInfo argument contains an authentication token that is obtained by invoking the get_authToken API call. The tModel argument is the tModel that is being inserted or updated. More than one tModel may be listed.

The UDDI site returns a dispositionReport that contains either all relationship assertions for the publisher or one of seven error messages: E_authTokenExpired, E_authTokenRequired, E_invalidKeyPassed, E_userMismatch, E_invalidValue, E_valueNotAllowed, or E_accountLimitExceeded.

The E_authTokenExpired error indicates that the authentication token has expired. The E_authTokenRequired error indicates that the authentication token is missing or invalid. The E_invalidKeyPassed error indicates an invalid key was passed to the UDDI site. The E_userMismatch error indicates that the authentication token is not authorized to access the tModel. The E_invalidValue error indicates that the key passed as an argument is not within the taxonomy specified by the tModelKey value in the categoryBag. The E_valueNotAllowed error indicates that the tModel failed the UDDI site's validation routine. Finally, the E_accountLimitExceeded error indicates that the business has reached its businessEntity limits on the UDDI site.

Listing 20-26
Invoking the
save_tModel
API call.

```
<save_tModel generic="2.0" xmlns="urn:uddi-org:api_v2" >
  <authInfo/>
  <tModel/>
</save_tModel>
```

set_publisherAssertions

The set_publisherAssertions API call is used to replace a full set of publisher assertions, as shown in Listing 20-27. The set_publisherAssertions API call has seven arguments: generic, xmlns, authInfo, publisherAssertion, fromKey, toKey, and keyedReference.

The generic argument is the version used to format the SOAP message, and the xmlns argument is the namespace qualifier whose value is the universal resource name that is reserved for reference to the schema. The authInfo argument contains an authentication token that is obtained by invoking the get_authToken API call. The publisherAssertion argument consists of relationship assertions that reference two businessEntity key values. More than one publisherAssertion may be listed. The fromKey and toKey arguments contain businessEntity key values that define the publisherAssertion. The keyedReference argument defines the direction of the relationship.

The UDDI site returns a dispositionReport that contains either a success indicator and the tModelDetail or one of four error messages: E_authTokenExpired, E_authTokenRequired, E_invalidKeyPassed, and E_userMismatch.

The E_authTokenExpired error indicates that the authentication token has expired. The E_authTokenRequired error indicates that the authentication token is missing or invalid. The E_invalidKeyPassed error indicates an invalid key was passed to the UDDI site. The E_userMismatch error indicates that the authentication token is not authorized to access the tModel.

Listing 20-27
Invoking the
set_publisher
Assertions
API call.

```
<set_publisherAssertions generic="2.0" xmlns="urn:uddi-org:api_v2" >
  <authInfo/>
  <publisherAssertion>
    <fromKey/>
    <toKey/>
    <keyedReference/>
  </publisherAssertion>
</set_publisherAssertions>
```

Chapter 21

Electronic Business XML

Electronic commerce made its debut in the late 1990s with the successful launch of Amazon.com and a host of other successful electronic commerce web sites— and hundreds of thousands of unsuccessful ones.

It was during this period that representatives from some of the world's most important international corporations launched a global effort to create a framework within which consumers and businesses of any size could participate in electronic commerce.

That framework became the Electronic Business XML standard. In this chapter, you'll learn about the Electronic Business XML standard and how the international community is adopting this standard to open electronic commerce to all sizes of corporations.

Electronic Data Interchange

Electronic commerce had been around for decades prior to what many believe was the electronic commerce revolution of the late 1990s. Electronic commerce is the exchange of goods and services between trading partners, using technology. Trading partners can be two or more businesses, referred to as business-to-business (B2B) or business to end consumers—called business-to-consumer (B2C).

The late 1990s saw a surge in B2C activity led by Amazon.com, which opened a floodgate of B2C ventures—most of which failed. However, B2B electronic commerce flourished long before "B2C businesses" became household words.

Businesses have been interacting with trading partners electronically by using electronic data interchange (EDI). EDI is a technology that enables the effective exchange of information between trading partners, resulting in increased efficiencies in operations of both trading partners.

The automotive industry is a good example of the benefits of EDI. An automobile is comprised of thousands of parts and subassemblies. Automobile manufacturers have thousands of trading partners, each of which is responsible for building an automobile part to specifications and delivering the part to the automobile assembly plant just in time for the part to be installed on the new automobile.

Prior to the introduction of EDI, there was a mountain of paperwork backed up by an army of employees at both the automobile manufacturer and supplier to control the manufacturing and delivery of parts.

However, EDI practically eliminated the need for paperwork. The automobile manufacturer used a computer system to control the manufacturing and assembly of automobiles. Likewise, suppliers also used computer systems to control the manufacturing and delivery process of parts to the automobile manufacturer.

EDI is used to link together both the automobile manufacturer's computer system and the supplier's computer system so that information required by both systems to manage the manufacturing and delivery of parts, and assembly of those parts into an automobile, are exchanged electronically instead of using paperwork.

The success of EDI in the automobile industry was soon adopted by other industries to link together computer systems operated by trading partners. While EDI provided a framework for businesses to exchange information, there was a steep threshold a business had to reach before being able to participate in EDI.

EDI requires participants to invest heavily in technology and have a systems staff who would link together their company's systems with those of trading partners. The threshold presented a challenging obstacle for small and intermediate-size businesses that lacked the technological foundation required by EDI.

It is difficult to appreciate this challenge today considering that the majority of homes in the United States have the technology to conduct electronic commerce. But in the heyday of EDI, computer technology was an expensive asset whose benefits were not necessary to conduct business.

Electronic Business XML

By the mid-1990s, the cost of using technology to conduct business dramatically decreased to a level where consumers even had the technology to purchase goods and provide services to their trading partners. Consumers could order merchandise over the Internet from the comfort of their home or office. And some employees could perform their duties for their employer without leaving the comfort of their homes.

Although technological developments dramatically lowered the threshold for small and medium-size companies to participate in EDI, there remained another formidable obstacle—the data exchanged between business partners. Conceptually, each business partner required the same information to conduct business, but each required the information to be in a unique format.

Let's say that a business wanted to place electronic orders for various supplies with 20 suppliers. The technology is available to transmit the order, but each of the 20 suppliers has its own order format. This means the systems staff of the business had to write programs to extract from the appropriate database information that was reformatted and transmit 20 different order formats.

Extensible Markup Language Arrives

Extensible Markup Language (XML), as you learned in Chapters 8 and 9, provides a straightforward way for businesses to describe information by using metadata called elements. XML is an outgrowth of the Hypertext Markup Language (HTML) that is used to describe to web browsers and other programs how information is to be displayed.

An XML document type definition (DTD, see Chapter 8) defines HTML. XML is the generic markup language that allows you to define specific formats and elements using a DTD, which provides a framework for industries to standardize on elements that are used to described information that is necessary to conduct electronic commerce.

WEB SERVICES

The electronic component industry was one of the first business groups to develop a set of XML elements used to define components of an electronic component catalog. This set of XML elements is called *Information and Content Exchange (ICE)* and is considered a syndication protocol because they're using XML messages transmitted over existing protocols like HTTP, much like how SOAP works.

Electronic Business XML Arrives

The concept of a syndication protocol soon evolved into other industries and the creation of nearly a thousand XML-based vocabularies, each of which had its own set of elements that represented types of information needed by trading partners to effect electronic commerce.

The propagation of XML-based vocabularies led to groups of trading partners being able to use a syndication protocol to conduct business, but members of a group could not interact with members of another syndicate group without having to modify their systems to use a different XML-based vocabulary.

Let's say that a business wanted to place an electronic order with a vendor who is outside the syndicate group of trading partners. The business must modify its systems to generate the order, using the syndicate protocol recognized by the vendor.

The incompatibility of various syndicate protocols has led to the Electronic Business XML (ebXML) initiative. The ebXML consortium of world businesses and technology organizations realized that a new framework was necessary for electronic commerce to flourish worldwide, and set out to build that framework building on existing technology.

The ebXML initiative created new specifications that make electronic commerce ubiquitous by using XML. The initiative enables cross-industry transactions by defining an XML-based vocabulary that can be used by all syndicate groups and by members of those groups to conduct B2C business.

The ebXML consortium isn't reinventing EDI. In a sense, they are reinventing EDI because they're taking all the flat file formats defined in EDI and redefining them using XML. In addition to data files, EDI uses flat files to send responses and confirmations. These flat files are being replaced by XML messages inside the communications protocol. EDI is used extensively with legacy systems. The flat files typically map directly onto a pre-staging table of a mainframe computer. Much of the expense of implementing EDI is the software to do the mapping. Converting EDI to XML still requires mapping to a mainframe.

Instead, the consortium is consolidating existing EDI standards and XML syndicate protocols into an ebXML standard. For example, every business requires certain information when receiving an order from a customer. An industry group might have developed an XML syndicate protocol that defines XML elements for order information. Likewise, a different industry group might have adopted a similar but different set of XML elements for the same purpose. Both industry groups probably require the same order information, but use different XML elements to define the information. The ebXML consortium has set out to resolve those differences into a single standard that can be easily adopted by all industry groups.

At the heart of the ebXML initiative is the objective to avoid requiring proprietary software or specialized systems needed to implement the ebXML standards and thereby minimize expense for any size business to participate in electronic commerce. However, most of the expense in EDI is mapping legacy systems. Mapping an XML file to a legacy system is still an expense. In some situations, the expense of mapping an XML file to a legacy system outweighs the benefits.

In addition, the ebXML initiative has set a far-reaching and sometimes elusive goal to develop a standard that supports multiple written languages and adheres to rules of national and international trade.

The Technology of ebXML

The ebXML initiative is founded on an architecture that uses existing standards to build the foundation of the ebXML standard. The key to the ebXML architecture is modularization. Rather than using a one-size-fits-all approach to establishing an ebXML specification, the ebXML consortium grouped the ebXML specification into modules, each of which could be implemented or ignored by industry groups that apply the ebXML specification to their industry.

There are five modules to the ebXML specification: messaging, business processes, trading partner profiles and agreement, registries and repositories, and core components.

The Messaging module is a specification that defines the technology and format businesses use to exchange information. The ebXML consortium standardized on SOAP, which you learned about in Chapter 19.

The Business Processes module is a specification that defines how a business describes its business processes to its trading partners. Understanding the business process of a trading partner enables technologists to determine the kind of information a trading partner requires to conduct electronic commerce.

Let's say that a business wants to send an electronic invoice to a trading partner. In the EDI environment, technologists from both businesses meet to understand each other's needs and then use this information to reprogram their individual systems to send and receive electronic invoices. There are hundreds of standardized EDI formats. Trading partners agree on existing formats that contain all fields needed to conduct business. However, only a handful of formats are commonly used.

A drawback of EDI is that modification of an EDI format has the potential to negatively impact existing systems. Let's say that trading partners want to include a mother's maiden name into an existing specification. Programs that parse the flat file that contains data in the existing specification format must be modified to accommodate the new maiden name field.

In contrast, an existing program that parses an ebXML document doesn't have to be modified when a new field is introduced into the document, unless the existing program needs to access that field. This is because a program that parses an ebXML document searches the document for specific XML tags. Therefore, inserting an XML tag that identifies a new field in the ebXML document is skipped by the program that parses the ebXML document.

The ebXML consortium adopted Unified Modeling Language (UML) as the modeling language used to convey business processes to trading partners. UML is used to describe the flow of information that is necessary to conduct and process electronic commerce within a trading partner organization.

UML is an ideal choice as the standard modeling language of ebXML because UML constructs can be implemented in every industry group and can be used to systematically define details of any business process. Furthermore, UML isn't dependent on technology used by any industry.

The Trading Partner Profiles and Agreement module is a specification referred to as a *collaboration protocol profile (CPP),* which defines the capabilities of a trading partner to conduct electronic commerce.

Electronic commerce capabilities of a trading partner are identified as XML elements that describe the trading partner as to industry, messaging supported, business processes, and data-exchange technologies used by the trading partner.

The CPP is consulted before prospective trading partners agree to conduct electronic commerce with each other. Realistically, the CPP of each trading partner might have opposing profiles. The ebXML consortium anticipated such conflicts and established the collaboration protocol agreement (CPA) as an XML document that specifies the resolution of any conflicts between trading partners.

Technologists can identify potential conflicts by referencing the CPP and then personally resolving those differences, which is recorded as a CPA and made available on the ebXML repository.

The Registries and Repositories module is a specification that defines an ebXML registry of information about trading partners and an ebXML repository used to store the ebXML registry and related information.

The ebXML registry is used by a business to list its CPP so that the business can be considered a potential trading partner by other businesses. Businesses seeking a trading partner search CPPs stored in the registry and review the prospective trading partner's business processes and other ebXML modules stored in the registry. A potential trading partner is then contacted, and if agreeable, both businesses enter a CPA.

The Core Components module is a specification that defines data items most often used by businesses and industries. Data items are defined as XML elements that enable a business to easily identify information supplied by a trading partner. This is especially beneficial when electronic commerce crosses industry boundaries where it is common for each industry to refer to the same data element by different names.

The ebXML consortium resolves such conflicts with the Core Components specification. Finalizing the Core Components specification is a daunting task, but the EDI standards bodies are relating the Core Components specification to EDI data dictionaries.

The Inner Workings of ebXML

At this writing, the ebXML consortium is actively working to establish a completed set of specifications for ebXML. Therefore, it is premature to present ebXML as a finished work. Instead, we'll take a closer look at some key ebXML modules to acquire a better understanding of ebXML operations. You can receive the latest update on the ebXML consortium's work by visiting www.ebxml.org.

Message Service

The ebXML message service is a specification that defines a namespace-qualified SOAP header and SOAP body within the SOAP envelope. The SOAP envelope is combined within a MIME multipart message envelope to form a message package.

The message package (see Listing 21-1) consists of two components. These are the communications protocol envelope and the SOAP with attachments MIME envelope. The communications protocol identifies the content by content ID and content type. The content ID is a specific message package located at a specified site. In Listing 21-1, the message package is identified by xxx, where xxx is a placeholder for an integer that represents a specific message package. The SOAP envelope follows the communication protocol within the message package, which is described in detail in Chapter 19.

Within the SOAP body is the application payload container. An application payload container contains that application payload, which is information necessary to transact business. Listing 21-2 illustrates an application payload container. The application payload container in this example is divided into two parts. First there is descriptive information about the payload identified as content. This is followed by information about an order.

Listing 21-1
The ebXML message package.

```
Content-ID: <messagepackage-xxx@mySite.com>
Content-Type: text/xml; charset="UTF-8"

<SOAP:Envelope xmlns:SOAP="http://schemas.xmlsoap.org/soap/envelope/">
  <SOAP:Header>
  </SOAP:Header>
  <SOAP:Body>
  </SOAP:Body>
</SOAP:Envelope>
```

Listing 21-2
Payload container.

```
Content-ID: <myBusiness.mySite.com>
Content-Type: application/xml

<Order>
```

```
<Orderdata>
</Orderdata>
</Order >
```

Business Processes

Business processes describe the flow of information within a trading partner's system by using UML concepts and terminology. UML concepts and terminology are defined by UML classes. The ebXML consortium specified XML elements with the ebXML standard that correspond to UML classes.

Table 21-1 contains ebXML business process elements and the corresponding UML class. The relationship between ebXML business process elements and UML classes is nearly identical, although not all UML classes have a corresponding ebXML business process element as yet. The Quick Reference Guide at the end of this chapter provides more information about ebXML business processing elements and related information.

Listing 21-3 illustrates a segment of an ebXML business process model. An actual ebXML business process model is lengthy and contains many components that are not illustrated in this segment. You can view complete illustrations of ebXML business process models at www.ebxml.org.

This example describes a sale. A sale is a multiparty collaboration that consists of two parties: the customer and the retailer. The name attribute of the MultiPartyCollaboration element identifies the business process as a unit.

The BusinessPartnerRole elements define each trading partner in the business process. The first BusinessPartnerRole element is called Customer and the other is called Retailer. Each BusinessPartnerRole element is further defined by the Performs element and the Transition element. The Performs element describes the behavior of a trading partner. The Transition element describes transitions between business processes that are participated in by a trading partner.

For example, the Customer BusinessPartnerRole performs the role of a prospective customer, a buyer, and a payee as the customer moves from the process of browsing merchandise in the store to placing an order.

Likewise, the Retailer BusinessPartnerRole performs the role of a seller and a payor as the transaction moves from the creation of an order to the process of consummating the transaction.

Listing 21-3
A segment of a business process.

```
<MultiPartyCollaboration name="Sale">
  <BusinessPartnerRole name="Customer">
    <Performs initiatingRole="prospect"/>
    <Performs initiatingRole="buyer"/>
    <Performs initiatingRole="Payee"/>
    <Transition fromBusinessState="Browse Store" toBusinessState="Place Order"/>
  </BusinessPartnerRole>
  <BusinessPartnerRole name="Retailer">
```

```
   <Performs respondingRole="seller"/>
   <Performs respondingRole="Payor"/>
   <Transition fromBusinessState="Create Order" toBusinessState="Consumate
Transaction"/>
  </BusinessPartnerRole>
</MultiPartyCollaboration>
```

ebXML Business Processes Element	UML Class
Attachment	Attachment
Binary Collaboration	Binary Collaboration
Business Transaction	Business Transaction
Business Transaction Activity	Business Transaction Activity
BusinessPartner Role	BusinessPartner Role
Collaboration Activity	Collaboration Activity
DocumentEnvelope	DocumentEnvelope
Failure	Failure
Fork	Fork
InitiatingRole	AuthorizedRole
Join	Join
MultiParty Collaboration	MultiParty Collaboration
Performs	Performs
Requesting BusinessActivity	Requesting BusinessActivity
Responding BusinessActivity	Responding BusinessActivity
RespondingRole	AuthorizedRole
Schema	Schema
Start	Start
Success	Success
Transition	Transition

Table 21-1. *ebXML Business Processes Element and UML Class Conversions*

CPP

A business announces to potential trading partners that it is available to participate in electronic commerce by registering its CPP with an ebXML site, as discussed previously in this chapter. The ebXML site then assigns a globally unique identifier (GUID) as part of the CPP's metadata that distinguishes the CPP from other registry items.

Besides announcing that availability of the business for entering into electronic commerce, the CPP also defines the technological and business capabilities of the business. Technological capabilities include support for various messaging protocols, and business capabilities include business collaborations that the business can participate in.

Listing 21-4 illustrates the structure of a CPP. All CPPs begin with the CollaborationProtocolProfile root element. The CollaborationProtocolProfile element specifies the default namespace, the digital signature namespace (ds), and the XLINK namespace (xlink). The CollaborationProtocolProfile element also specifies the version of the CPP. This example contains version 2.0 of the CPP. This value changes each time the CPP is updated.

The CollaborationProtocolProfile element contains child elements. These are the PartyInfo element, Packaging element, ds:Signature element, and Comment element. The PartyInfo element and the Packaging element are required.

PartyInfo

The PartyInfo element contains information that identifies the business that published the CPP. There can be multiple PartyInfo elements, each representing a subdivision of the business and having its own characteristics.

The PartyInfo element has its own child elements, as shown in Listing 21-4. The PartyId element is the business' identifier. The PartyRef is a pointer to additional information about the business. This requires an xlink:type attribute set to "simple" indicating an XLINK, the xlink:href attribute that contains the URI of the external information about the business, and the type attribute that identifies the type of the external business information. The CollaborationRole element specifies roles the business can play in an electronic commerce transaction.

The Certificate element identifies security certificates recognized by the business. The DeliveryChannel element contains the transport level and messaging protocol the business uses to receive messages. These are identified in the Transport element and the DocExchange element.

The CollaborationRole element relates the business with a role contained in the BusinessCollaboration. The BusinessCollaboration is defined in the Process-Specification document.

The PartyInfo element can have a CollaborationRole element that indicates the roles that can be played by the party. In addition, within the CollaborationRole element are a ProcessSpecification element and a Role element, both of which are illustrated in Listing 21-4. In addition to these elements, the CollaborationRole element also contains a CertificateRef element and a ServiceBinding element.

ProcessSpecification

The ProcessSpecification element is used to define the role of the party. Although a role is defined in the ProcessSpecification element, the party may not support that role. The Role element is used to identify roles supported by the party. The CertificateRef element specifies the certificate that is to be used for transactions with the party. The ServiceBinding element relates the role to a DeliveryChannel that specifies the channel used by the party to receive messages.

The ProcessSpecification element has a name attribute that uniquely identifies the ProcessSpecification element and a version attribute that indicates the version number of the ProcessSpecification and the xlink:type attribute and the xlink:href attribute. The xlink:type attribute is set to "simple" indicating an XLINK, the xlink:href attribute contains the URI of the external information about the business.

Within the ProcessSpecification element, there are a number of child elements that describe the digital signature used by the party. The first of these child elements is the ds:Reference element that indicates the XML Digital Signature specification supported by the party. The ds:URI attribute of the ds:Reference element indicates the URI of the XML Digital Signature specification, which is the same URI as the xlink:href attribute.

The ds:Reference element contains child elements. This includes the ds:Transforms element that contains a ds:Transform element that specifies the algorithm to sequence transformation.

The Role element of the CPP defines the role the business supports within the CollaborationRole element. With the ServiceBinding element there is an Override element that is used to identify an alternative to the default delivery channel used by the business to receive messages from trading partners. The CPP can have multiple Override elements, each defining a different alternative delivery channel and an associated action. In Listing 21-4, the Override element is implemented whenever a message is received to place an order. The other attributes identify various elements that are associated with the Override element.

Certificate

The Certificate element defines the certificate that is supported by the business to conduct secured transactions. Within the Certificate element there is the ds:KeyInfo child element that identifies information related to the certificate. Each Certificate element is uniquely identified by the certId attribute, which is referenced in the CertificateRef element, as discussed previously in this section.

Business Delivery Channel

A business' delivery channel is comprised of three elements. These are the DeliveryChannel element, the Transport element, and the DocExchange element. The DeliveryChannel element specifies the characteristics supported by a business for incoming messages and includes three attributes that identify the delivery channel, the Transport element, and the DocExchange element that is associated with the DeliveryChannel.

The channelId attribute is a unique value that identifies the DeliveryChannel. The transportID attribute and the docExchangeId attribute contain values that uniquely identify the Transport element and DocExchange element that are associated with the DeliveryChannel.

The Characteristics element is the only child element of the DeliveryChannel element. The Characteristics element contains attributes that define characteristics of the delivery channel. These are syncReplyMode, nonrepudiationOfOrigin, nonrepudiationOfReceipt, secureTransport, confidentiality, authenticated, and authorized.

The syncReplyMode attribute indicates what the business expects as a response while communicating synchronously with a trading partner during a transaction. The value of the syncReplyMode attribute can be signalsOnly, responseOnly, signalsAndResponse, or none.

The signalsOnly value means the response will include business signals defined in the process specification and not include the business-response message. The responseOnly value means the response includes only the business-response message. The signalsAndResponse value means that the response includes both business signals and the business-response message. Finally, the none value means that no synchronous response will be returned. All responses are returned asynchronously. This is the default value of the syncReplyMode attribute.

The syncReply attribute indicates whether or not the business replies using synchronous or asynchronous responses. The syncReply attribute value is set to true when the business replies asynchronously.

The nonrepudiationOfOrigin attribute indicates whether or not the business requires that incoming messages must be digitally signed using a certificate. A true value requires a digital signature and a false value doesn't require a digital signature.

The nonrepudiationOfReceipt attribute is similar to the nonrepudiationOfOrigin attribute, except the nonrepudiationOfReceipt attribute specifies whether or not the business requires acknowledgements to be digitally signed using a certificate.

The secureTransport attribute indicates whether or not the business uses a secure transport protocol for transactions. A true value indicates the delivery channel must be secured; otherwise, a false value specifies that an unsecured delivery channel is used for transmissions.

The confidentiality attribute indicates whether or not the business requires that messages be encrypted above the transport level and delivered encrypted to the application. A true value indicates encryption is required; otherwise, a false value indicates messages need not be encrypted.

The authenticated attribute indicates whether or not the business requires the trading partner to authenticate messages sent by the business before the trading partner delivers the message to the trading partner's application. A true value indicates authentication is required; otherwise, a false value doesn't require the trading partner to authenticate the message.

The authorized attribute indicates whether or not the business requires the trading partner to receive authorization from the trading partner's application before delivering the message to the application. A true value indicates authorization is required; otherwise, a false value does not require authorization before the message is delivered to the application.

Transport

The Transport element specifies the communication protocol and encoding supported by the business and information about the business's transport security. The Transport element is uniquely identified using the transportId attribute, which is referred to by the DeliveryChannel element discussed previously in this chapter.

The SendingProtocol element within the Transport element specifies the communications protocol supported by the business for sending messages. There are three communications protocols that can be used in the SendingProtocol element: HTTP, SMTP, and FTP. However, other protocols are likely to be included as they become widely used in communications.

The ReceivingProtocol element is similar to the SendingProtocol element, except the ReceivingProtocol element specifies the communication protocol used when receiving messages.

The Endpoint element is used to provide a prospective trading partner with communication information about the business. The Endpoint element has two attributes. The first attribute is the uri attribute, whose value is the business' electronic communication address. The value of the uri attribute must be in the form of the communication protocol specified by the ReceivingProtocol element.

The other Endpoint element attribute is the type attribute, which describes the purpose of the end point. The type attribute value can be login, request, response, error, or allPurpose. The login value indicates that the end point is used for the initial message between the business and a trading partner. The request value indicates the end point is used by a trading partner to make a request of the business. The response value indicates the end point is used by the business to respond to a trading partner. The error value indicates the end point is used for communicating error messages from the messaging service. Finally, the allPurpose value indicates that the end point is used for any communication.

The TransportSecurity element specifies a business's security specifications that are necessary for the ReceivingProtocol element. The TransportSecurity element contains two child elements: the Protocol element and the CertificateRef element.

The Protocol element specifies the transport security protocol supported by the business, where the value of the version attribute indicates the version of the transport security protocol that the business supports. In Listing 21-4, the SSL transport security protocol is used and encrypts the certificate and uses an authentication certificate.

The CertificateRef element identifies the Certificate element of the PartyInfo element that is to be used with the TransportSecurity element. The Certificate element is identified by the value of the certId attribute of the CertificateRef element.

DocExchange

The DocExchange element specifies information that the business and the trading partner require to exchange documents. The DocExchange element is uniquely identified by the value of the docExchangedId attribute. Within the DocExchange element are several child elements: the ebXMLBinding element, the Retries element, the RetryInterval element, the PersistDuration element, the Protocol element, the HashFunction element, the SignatureAlgorithm element, EncryptionAlgorithm element, and the CertificateRef element.

The ebXMLBinding element specifies the properties of the ebXML message service used by the business. The ebXMLBinding element contains several child elements. The first child element is the ReliableMessaging element that defines the characteristics of reliable messaging required by the ebXML message exchange. Next there is the NonRepudiation element, which identifies requirements for signing a message.

The DigitalEnvelope child element identifies requirements for encrypting the digital envelope. The NamespaceSupported element specifies namespace extensions required by the messaging service.

The DocExchange element also has a ReliableMessaging element that contains several child elements. The first child element is the Retries element, which identifies the number of retries in seconds before an exchange timeout. There is also a RetryInterval element that identifies the number of seconds that must pass before another attempt is made to establish communications between the business and a trading partner.

Next is the PersistDuration element, which specifies the minimum duration a message will be kept in persistent storage by the ebXML message service.

The ReliableMessaging element also has three attributes, the first of which is the deliverySemantics attribute. The value of the deliverySemantics attribute identifies the reliability of the message delivered and can have one of the following attribute values: OnceAndOnlyOnce or BestEffort. The OnceAndOnlyOnce value indicates that the message is delivered once, and the BestEffort value indicates that reliable messaging isn't to be used for exchanging documents.

There is also the idempotency attribute that indicates whether the business requires that messages undergo the idempotency test. The idempotency test determines if a message is duplicated. The value of the idempotency attribute is either true or false, where a true value requires that the idempotency test be performed.

The last attribute of the ReliableMessaging element is the messageOrderSemantics attribute, whose value controls the order in which messages are received when messages are transmitted OnceAndOnlyOnce. The value of the messageOrderSemantics attribute can be either Guaranteed or NotGuaranteed, where Guaranteed indicates that messages are passed to the receiving application in the order the messages are received. The NotGuaranteed value indicates that the receiving application can receive messages in any order. NotGuaranteed is the default value.

There is also a NonRepudiation element that specifies who sent a message based on the digital signature. The NonRepudiation element has several child elements, beginning with the Protocol element. The Protocol element specifies the protocol used to digitally sign a message as specified in the Protocol element's version attribute.

Next is the HashFunction element that specifies the algorithm used to compute the digitally signed message. The SignatureAlgorithm element specifies the algorithm used to compute the digital signature. There is also a CertificateRef element, used to reference a Certificate element based on the value of the CertificateRef element's certId attribute.

The DigitalEnvelope element specifies the encryption procedure, where the shared secret key encryption key and the private encryption key are sent to the recipient of the message.

The Protocol element specifies the security protocol used for the communication. The EncryptionAlgorithm element specifies the encryption algorithm used by both the business and a trading partner.

The NamespaceSupported element specifies the namespace extensions that the messaging service supports.

Packaging

The Packaging element contains information that describes the packaging of the message header and message payload of messages that are exchanged between the business and a trading partner. The Packaging element consists of a subtree that specifies the organization of a message that includes MIME context types and data structure, namespaces, and security parameters.

The Packaging element is uniquely identified by the id attribute, which is used in the ServiceBinding element and the Override element as described previously in this chapter. In addition, the Packaging element has three child elements: ProcessingCapabilities, SimplePart, and CompositeList.

The ProcessingCapabilities element identifies the processing supported by the business. The ProcessingCapabilities element has two attributes: the parse attribute and the generate attribute. Both have either true or false values. A true parse attribute value indicates that the business supports parsing; otherwise, a false parse attribute value indicates parsing isn't supported. Likewise, a true generate attribute indicates that the business can generate messages and a false value indicates generation is not supported.

The SimplePart element specifies a list of MIME content type values. The SimplePart element has two attributes. These are id and mimetype. The id attribute uniquely identifies the SimplePart element for use elsewhere in the CPP. The mimetype attribute contains the content-type value for the message part.

Within the SimplePart element, there can be the NamespaceSupported element. The NamespaceSupported element specifies the namespace extension supported for the simple body part of the message.

The CompositeList element is the last child element and specifies the manner in which simple parts are organized into MIME multiparts and grouped into MIME content types if security encapsulation is used in the message.

The CompositeList element has three attributes: mimetype, id, and mimeparameters. The mimetype attribute identifies the MIME content-type value for the message part. The id attribute uniquely identifies the CompositeList element, which is used to reference the CompositeList element elsewhere in the CPP. The mimeparameters attribute identifies parameters required to understand how to process the content type.

The CompositeList element also has two child elements. The first is the Constituent element. The Constituent element specifies the order of the contents in the composition or encapsulation of the message. The Constituent element has an attribute called idref that is used to identify the value of the associated Composite, Encapsulation, or SimplePart element. The other child element is the ds:Signature element, which indicates the digital signature supported by the business.

The Encapsulation element specifies the MIME security structure. The Encapsulation element has three attributes: mimetype, id, and mimeparameters. The mimetype attribute identifies the MIME content type for the message. The id attribute uniquely identifies the Encapsulation element. Finally, the mimeparameters attribute identifies MIME parameters required to process the content type. The Encapsulation element has one child element, which is the ds:Signature element as described in the Composite element.

Comment

The Comment element contains any textual comments about the CPP. The Comment element has an xml:lang attribute that identifies the language used to create the comment.

Listing 21-4
The structure
of a CPP.

```
<CollaborationProtocolProfile
    xmlns="http://www.ebxml.org/namespaces/tradePartner"
    xmlns:ds="http://www.w3.org/2000/09/xmldsig#"
    xmlns:xlink="http://www.w3.org/1999/xlink"
    version="2.0">
<PartyInfo>
  <PartyId type="ABCD">123</PartyId>
  <PartyRef xlink:type="simple", xlink:
     href="http://my.com/businessInfo.xml" type="uri-reference"/>
  <CollaborationRole id="M31" >
    <ProcessSpecification name="BuySell" version="1.0" xlink:type="simple"
       xlink:href="http://www.ebxml.org/services/my.com/businessInfo.xml">
       <ds:Reference ds:URI="http://www.ebxml.org/services/my.com/businessInfo.xml ">
         <ds:Transforms>
           <ds:Transform ds:Algorithm=
"http://www.w3.org/TR/2000/CR-xml-c14n-20001026"/>
         </ds:Transforms>
         <ds:DigestMethod ds:Algorithm=
"http://www.w3.org/2000/09/xmldsig#dsa-sha1"> String</ds:DigestMethod>
         <ds:DigestValue>j6lwx3rvEPO0vKtMup4NbeVu8nk</ds:DigestValue>
       </ds:Reference>
```

```
      </ProcessSpecification>
      <Role name="buyer" xlink:href="http://my.com/businessInfo.xml"/>
      <CertificateRef certId = "M23"/>
      <ServiceBinding name="MyProcess" channelId="N02"  packageId="M26">
        <Override action="OrderPlaced" channelId="M25" packageId="M29"
        xlink:type="simple" xlink:href="http://my.com/businessInfo.xml"/>
        </ServiceBinding>
    </CollaborationRole>
    <Certificate certId = "M23">
            <ds:KeyInfo>... </ds:KeyInfo>
    </Certificate>
    <DeliveryChannel channelId="M25">
      <Characteristics syncReplyMode =
"responseOnly" nonrepudiationOfOrigin =
"true" nonrepudiationOfReceipt = "true" secureTransport =
"true" confidentiality = "true" authenticated = "true" authorized = "true"/>
    </DeliveryChannel>
    <Transport transportId = "M25">
      <SendingProtocol version = "2.0">HTTP</SendingProtocol>
      <ReceivingProtocol version = "2.0">HTTP</ReceivingProtocol>
      <Endpoint uri="http://my.com/requesthandler" type = "request"/>
      <TransportSecurity>
        <Protocol version="2.0">SSL</Protocol>
        <CertificateRef certId = "M23"/>
      </TransportSecurity>
    </Transport>
    <DocExchange docExchangeId = "M26">
      <ebXMLBinding version = "0.92">
        <ReliableMessaging
              deliverySemantics="OnceAndOnlyOnce" idempotency="true"
              messageOrderSemantics="Guaranteed">
          <Retries>5</tp:Retries>
          <RetryInterval>30</RetryInterval>
          <PersistDuration>P1D</PersistDuration>
        </ReliableMessaging>
        <NonRepudiation>
          <Protocol>http://www.w3.org/2000/09/xmldsig#</Protocol>
          <HashFunction>http://www.w3.org/2000/09/xmldsig#sha1</HashFunction>
          <SignatureAlgorithm>
            http://www.w3.org/2000/09/xmldsig#dsa-sha1
          </SignatureAlgorithm>
          <CertificateRef certId="N03"/>
        </NonRepudiation>
        <DigitalEnvelope>
          <Protocol version="3.1">S/MIME</Protocol>
          <EncryptionAlgorithm>DES-CBC</EncryptionAlgorithm>
          <CertificateRef tp:certId="M23"/>
```

```
        </DigitalEnvelope>
          <NamespaceSupported location=
http://www.my.com/ messageService.xsd" version="0.98b">
            http://www.my.com/messageService
          </NamespaceSupported>
      </ebXMLBinding>
    </DocExchange>
  </PartyInfo>
  <Packaging id="M29">
      <ProcessingCapabilities parse="true" generate="true"/>
      <SimplePart id="M21" mimetype="text/xml">
        <NamespaceSupported location="http://my.com/buysell.xsd"
 version="2.1">http://my.com/buysell.xsd
        </NamespaceSupported>
      </SimplePart>
      <CompositeList>
        <Composite id="M22" mimetype="multipart/related"
            mimeparameters="type=text/xml;">
          <Constituent idref="M21"/>
        </Composite>
      </CompositeList>
  </Packaging>
  <Comment xml_lang="en-us">>Enter comments here</Comment>
</CollaborationProtocolProfile>
```

CPA

A business's CPP contains information that prospective trading partners need to know before both parties enter into electronic commerce, which you learned about previously in this chapter. Once a business and a trading partner agree to enter into electronic commerce, they created a collaboration protocol agreement (CPA).

The CPA consists of a set of agreed-upon capabilities that both the business and the trading partner use when conducting electronic commerce. The CPA is very similar in design to the CPP, and in fact contains nearly all the elements found in the CPP. The CPP contains all the electronic commerce capabilities supported by a business and the CPA contains those electronic commerce capabilities that both the business and the trading partner agree to use in electronic commerce.

Listing 21-5 illustrates the structure of the CPA. The root element of the CPA is the CollaborationProtocolAgreement element, which contains child elements—most of which have been explained in the CPP section. The CollaborationProtocolAgreement element is uniquely identified by the cpaid attribute. The cpaid attribute value is assigned an identifying value that is used by both the business and the trading partner. Typically, the cpaid attribute value is a URI that is accessible by both parties.

The CollaborationProtocolAgreement element also has a version attribute whose value identifies the version of the CollaborationProtocolAgreement. In addition, both parties must agree on the procedure for tracking versions of the CollaborationProtocolAgreement.

The CollaborationProtocolAgreement element has child elements that are unique to the CollaborationProtocolAgreement element and many other elements that are in common with the CPP. In this section, you'll learn about the unique child elements, because the other child elements are covered in the CPP section.

The Status element specifies the status of the negotiation process between the business and a prospective trading partner. The Status element has a value attribute whose value indicates the current status of the CPA. The value attribute has one of three values: proposed, agreed, or signed.

The proposed value implies that both parties continue to negotiate the CPA. The agreed value indicates that the business and the prospective trading partner have settled on the contents of the CPA. Finally, the signed value states that both parties have officially signed the agreement, usually with a digital signature.

The Start element and the End element are used to specify the term of the CPA, similar to the duration of any agreement. The Start element defines the date and time that the CPA takes effect using the coordinated universal time (UTC). The End element defines the termination date and time after which the terms of the CPA are no longer binding on either party to the CPA. Transactions that are in progress when the CPA terminates continue to process. The End element also uses the UTC.

The ConversationConstraints element defines the maximum number of conversations that can be conducted using the CPA. The ConversationConstraints element has two attributes: invocationLimit and concurrentConversations. The value of the invocationLimit attribute establishes the maximum number of conversations that can be processed under the CPA. Once this value is reached, the CPA automatically terminates and both parties must renegotiate a new CPA. The value of the concurrentConversations attribute sets the number of conversations that can occur simultaneously.

The PartyInfo element is the same as the PartyInfo element in the CPP. However, the value of the PartyId attribute of the PartyInfo element must be agreed upon by both the business and the prospective trading partner because both organizations will refer to the same PartyInfo element.

The ProcessSpecification element is the same as the ProcessSpecification element of the CPP, except that information contained within the CPA ProcessSpecification element represents information agreed to by both parties.

The digital signature elements of the CPA have the same definition as described in the CPP. Likewise, the Comment element and other elements in the CPA are identical to the CPP, except that both parties to the CPA agreed on capabilities defined within those elements.

Listing 21-5
The structure
of the CPA.

```
<CollaborationProtocolAgreement
    xmlns="http://www.ebxml.org/namespaces/tradePartner"
    xmlns:bpm="http://www.ebxml.org/namespaces/businessProcess"
    xmlns:ds = "http://www.w3.org/2000/09/xmldsig#"
    xmlns:xlink = "http://www.w3.org/1999/xlink" cpaid="M52" version="3.1">
```

```
    <Status value = "agreed"/>
    <Start>2005-04-07T12:00:00</Start>
    <End>2006-04-07T12:00:00</End>
    <ConversationConstraints invocationLimit = "365" concurrentConversations = "6"/>
  <PartyInfo>
    <!--See CPP -->
  </PartyInfo>

  <Packaging id="N35">
    <!--See CPP -->
  </Packaging>
  <ds:Signature>
    <!--See CPP -->
  </ds:Signature>
  <Comment>
   <!--See CPP -->
  </Comment>
</CollaborationProtocolAgreement>
```

Quick Reference Guide

This Quick Reference Guide provides a brief overview of ebXML business procedures.
Full details of these procedures are available at www.ebxml.org.

Element	Description	Attribute(s)
BusinessDocument	A generic name of a document.	name: Defines the generic name of the business document conditionExpression: Evaluates if it is a valid business document for an envelope; one conditionExpression permitted
AttributeSubstitution	Substitutes one attribute value for another attribute value.	attributeName: CDATA value: CDATA

Table 21-2. *Business Process Elements*

Element	Description	Attribute(s)
BinaryCollaboration	Defines an interaction protocol between two roles.	name: CDATA nameID: ID pattern: CDATA beginsWhen: CDATA endsWhen: CDATA precondition: CDATA postCondition: CDATA timeToPerform: CDATA
BusinessDocument	A generic document name.	name: CDATA nameID: ID specificationLocation: CDATA specificationElement: CDATA
BusinessPartnerRole	A role played by a business partner in a MultiPartyCollaboration.	name: CDATA nameID: ID
BusinessTransaction	A set of business information and business exchanges amongst two trading partners that occur in an agreed format, sequence, and time period.	name: CDATA nameID: ID pattern: CDATA beginsWhen: CDATA endsWhen: CDATA isGuaranteedDelivery Required true/false Default: false precondition: CDATA postCondition: CDATA

Table 21-2.   *Business Process Elements* (continued)

Element	Description	Attribute(s)
BusinessTransactionActivity	Defines a business activity that executes a specified business transaction within a binary collaboration.	name: CDATA nameID: ID businessTransaction: CDATA businessTransaction IDRef: IDREF fromAuthorizedRole: CDATA fromAuthorizedRoleID Ref: IDREF toAuthorizedRole: CDATA toAuthorizedRoleIDRef: IDREF isConcurrent: true/false Default: false isLegallyBinding: true/false Default: false timeToPerform: CDATA
CollaborationActivity	An activity performed by a binary collaboration within another binary collaboration.	name: CDATA nameID: ID fromAuthorizedRole: CDATA fromAuthorizedRoleID Ref: CDATA toAuthorizedRole: CDATA toAuthorizedRoleIDRef: CDATA binaryCollaboration: CDATA binaryCollaboration IDRef: CDATA

Table 21-2. *Business Process Elements* (continued)

Element	Description	Attribute(s)
Documentation	Defines user documentation for an element and can be an inline PCDATA and/or a URI pointing to complete documentation.	uri: CDATA
DocumentEnvelope	Conveys business information between the two roles in a business transaction.	businessDocument: CDATA businessDocumentID Ref: IDREF isPositiveResponse: CDATA isAuthenticated: true/false Default: false isConfidential: true/false Default: false isTamperProof: true/false Default: false
DocumentSubstitution	Identifies a document that should be substituted for another document.	originalBusiness Document: CDATA originalBusiness DocumentID: IDREF substituteBusiness Document: CDATA substituteBusiness DocumentId: IDREF

Table 21-2.   *Business Process Elements* (continued)

Element	Description	Attribute(s)
Failure	Defines failure of a binary collaboration.	fromBusinessState: CDATA fromBusinessStateIDRef: IDREF conditionGuard: Success/BusinessFailure /TechnicalFailure/Any Failure
Fork	A state with one inbound transition and multiple outbound transitions.	name: CDATA nameID: ID
Include	Merges that specification with the current specification.	name: CDATA version: CDATA uuid: CDATA uri: CDATA
InitiatingRole	A role authorized to send the first request.	name: CDATA nameID: ID
Join	The point where previously forked activities join again.	name: CDATA nameID: ID waitForAll: true/false Default: true
MultiPartyCollaboration	Business partner roles; each playing roles in binary collaborations.	name: CDATA nameID: ID
Package	Defines a container of reusable elements.	name: CDATA nameID: ID
Performs	The relationship between a BusinessPartnerRole and the roles played by the business partner.	initiatingRole: CDATAinitiating RoleIDRef: IDREFrespondingRole: CDATArespondingRoleI DRef: IDREF

Table 21-2. *Business Process Elements* (continued)

Element	Description	Attribute(s)
ProcessSpecification	Root element of a process specification document.	name:ID version: CDATA uuid: CDATA
RequestingBusinessActivity	A business action performed by a requesting role within a business transaction.	name: CDATA nameID: ID isAuthorizationRequired : true/false Default: falseisIntelligibleCheck Required: true/false Default: false isNonRepudiation ReceiptRequired true/false Default: false isNonRepudiation Required: true/false Default: false timeToAcknowledge Acceptance: CDATA timeToAcknowledge Receipt: CDATA

Table 21-2.   *Business Process Elements* (continued)

Element	Description	Attribute(s)
RespondingBusinessActivity	A business action performed by a role within a business transaction.	name:CDATA nameID: ID isAuthorizationRequired: true/false Default: false isIntelligibleCheck Required: true/false Default: false isNonRepudiation ReceiptRequired true/false Default: false isNonRepudiation Required: true/false Default: false timeToAcknowledge Receipt: CDATA
RespondingRole	A role authorized to send the first response.	name: CDATA nameID: ID
Start	The starting state for a binary collaboration.	toBusinessState: CDATA toBusinessStateIDRef: IDREF
SubstitutionSet	A container for an AttributeSubstitution and/or DocumentSubstitution elements.	name: CDATA nameID: ID applyToScope: CDATA
Success	Defines the successful conclusion of a binary collaboration.	fromBusinessState: CDATA conditionGuard: Success/ BusinessFailure/ TechnicalFailure/ AnyFailure

Table 21-2. *Business Process Elements* (continued)

Element	Description	Attribute(s)
Transition	A transition between two business states in a binary collaboration.	onInitiation: true/false Default: false fromBusinessState: CDATA fromBusinessStateIDRef: IDREF toBusinessState: CDATA toBusinessStateIDRef: IDREF conditionGuard: Success/ BusinessFailure/ TechnicalFailure/ AnyFailure

Table 21-2.   *Business Process Elements* (continued)

The
Complete
Reference

Chapter 22

The Java API for XML
Registries (JAXR)

The keystone of web services is the XML registry that is the repository for information about the availability of web services and information necessary to access web services. The XML registry is the mechanism for organizations to make available web services to other organizations and to avail themselves of another organization's web services.

An XML registry adheres to a standardized format that is created by a consortium and adopted by multiple organizations that use the standard to interact with each other electronically. Two important XML registry standards are the Universal Description, Discovery, and Integration (UDDI) created by a consortium of vendors, and the ebXML Registry and Repository standard developed by the Organization for the Advancement of Structured Information Standards (OASIS) and the United Nations.

You learned about UDDI in Chapter 20 and ebXML in Chapter 21. In this chapter, you'll learn about the Java API for XML Registries (JAXR) API that is used to access an XML registry.

Inside JAXR

The JAXR architecture is organized into two groups: the JAXR client and the JAXR provider. The JAXR client is a Java program that accesses information contained in an XML registry by interacting with a JAXR provider. A JAXR provider implements the RegistryService interface, giving a JAXR client registry access.

There are two packages that are necessary to implement JAXR: the javax.xml.registry package and the javax.xml.registry.infomodel package. The javax.xml.registry package contains the interface to access the registry. The javax.xml.registry.infomodel package contains interfaces that define registry objects and how those objects are interrelated.

JAXR Client

A JAXR client is any program that interacts with an XML registry to locate web services that are registered with an XML registry; to publish a client's own web services, making them available to other clients; and to remove a web service that a client previously published on the XML registry.

The JAXR client API is designed to access any XML registry. However, you'll find using one of the four most popular public XML registries operated by Microsoft and IBM enables you to test JAXR client programs if you don't have an XML registry available to you. Anyone can query a public XML registry. However, permission is required from the operator of the registry site to publish a web service or modify an existing web service. Table 22-1 lists the URLs for the four most popular public XML registries and the URL used to request permission to publish web services on those directories.

Public XML Registry	Owner	Permission Requests
http://www-3.ibm.com/services/uddi/testregistry/inquiryapi	IBM	http://www-3.ibm.com/services/uddi/
http://uddi.microsoft.com/inquire	Microsoft	http://uddi.microsoft.com/
http://test.uddi.microsoft.com/inquire	Microsoft	http://uddi.microsoft.com/
https://test.uddi.microsoft.com/publish	Microsoft	http://uddi.microsoft.com/

Table 22-1. *Public XML Registries*

The Process

The JAXR client program must implement routines in sequence in order to utilize an XML registry. The first routine is to connect to the registry using a connection factory. In many cases, the JAXR provider makes available configured connection factories that a JAXR client can use to connect to a registry. These are available by following the directions supplied by the JAXR provider and using the Java Naming and Directory Interface (JNDI) API (see Chapter 18) to search the JAXR provider directory for the connection factory.

Alternatively, you can create your own connection factory by implementing an instance of the ConnectionFactory class that is contained in the javax.xml.registry package. Listing 22-1 shows how a ConnectionFactory is created:

Listing 22-1
Creating an instance of the Connection Factory.

```
ConnectionFactory cf = ConnectionFactory.newInstance();
```

After the instance of the ConnectionFactory is created, the JAXR client needs to create a set of properties that are required to make the connection to the XML registry. The set of properties specifies the information required to make a connection to the XML registry. These include the queryManagerURL and factoryClass.

You set the properties by first creating an instance of the Properties class and then setting each of the properties by invoking the setProperty() method of the Properties class. The setProperty() method requires two arguments. The first argument when setting the value of a property is the name of the property that is to be set, and the other argument is value that will be assigned to that property. The nature of each property depends on requirements of the XML registry site operator.

Listing 22-2 illustrates how to set properties for connecting to the IBM public registry and querying the registry. Once properties are set, the instance of the Properties class is passed as an argument to the setProperties() method and then the createConnection() method is called to connect to the XML registry. The createConnection() method returns an instance of a Connection object, as shown in Listing 22-2.

Once connection is made to the XML registry, the JAXR client must create an instance of the RegistryService object, which is then used to interact with the XML registry. The RegistryService object is created by calling the getRegistryService() method of the Connection object. The getRegistryService() method returns a RegistryService object.

Next, the client must create an instance of the BusinessQueryManager object, which is used to query the registry. You create a BusinessQueryManager object by calling the getBusinessQueryManager() method of the RegistryService object.

If you intend to insert a new entry into the registry or modify an existing entry, you also need to create an instance of the BusinessLifeCycleManager object. The BusinessLifeCycleManager object facilitates the publishing of services and maintaining the existing service. You create an instance of the BusinessLifeCycleManager object by calling the getBusinessLifeCycleManager() method of the RegistryService object. Listing 22-2 illustrates how to create these instances.

Making a Query

Once connection is made to the registry and the instance of the BusinessQueryManager object is created, a client is able to inquire about information stored in the registry. There are three common queries performed by clients: locating businesses that have published services on the registry, locating services of a particular business, and retrieving information on how to bind to a particular service. Binding to a service is the way in which a client avails itself of the service offered by a business.

The BusinessQueryManager object contains interfaces for each type of query. These are findOrganization(), findServices(), and findServiceBindings(). Each of these returns a BulkResponse object that contains a collection of objects containing the requested information.

The findOrganization() method is used to locate one or more organizations by name that are contained within the XML registry. The findOrganization() method requires six arguments. The first argument is a Collection consisting of an ArrayList that specifies a qualifier for the search such as sorting and case-sensitive searches (see the Quick Reference Guide). The second argument is another Collection consisting of an ArrayList that contains the organization's name that is being sought as a String. The % wildcard character can be used to search for partial organization names. The remaining arguments can be null.

The findOrganization() method returns a BulkResponse object that contains the getCollection() method used to retrieve organizations that match the search criteria.

The getCollection() method returns a Collection object that can then be used by the client. This is illustrated in Listing 22-2 where the program searches for any organization that has MyBusiness in its name.

Alternatively, a client can search an XML registry based on industry classifications. Organizations within an XML registry are assigned an industry classification based on the North American Industry Classification System (NAICS). Industry classification codes can be found at www.census.gov/epcd/naics/naicscod.txt.

Here's how this is done. First, create a BusinessLifeCycleManager by invoking the getBusinessLifeCycleManager() of the RegistryService object. Next, create a ClassificationScheme object by calling the findClassificationSchemeByName() method of the BusinessQueryManager object. The findClassificationSchemeByName() method requires one argument that is the name of the industry code classification system, which is ntis-gov:naics. The findClassificationSchemeByName() method returns an instance of the ClassificationScheme object.

Next, the program must identify the classification that will be sought in the registry. This is done by calling the createClassification() method, which returns an instance of the Classification object. The createClassification() method requires three arguments. The first argument is the ClassificationScheme. The second argument is the name of the industry classification that is being sought. And the third argument is the industry code.

A Collection object is then created consisting of an ArrayList, and the Classification returned by the createClassification() method is added to the Collection. The findOrganizations() method is then called and the Collection is passed as the third argument to the findOrganizations() method. The other arguments are null. The findOrganization() returns a BulkResponse object whose getCollection() method is invoked to retrieve information about organizations that are in the industry group.

Listing 22-2 illustrates the routine required to search an XML registry by industry code. In this example, the program is searching the XML registry for businesses that are in the Software Reproducing industry. The Software Reproducing industry is assigned the industry code 334611.

Listing 22-2
Search an XML registry by industry code.

```
BusinessLifeCycleManager blcmgr = rs1.getBusinessLifeCycleManager();
ClassificationScheme cs1 = bqManager.findClassificationSchemeByName
("ntis-gov:naics");
Classification clsf1 = (Classification) blcmgr.createClassification(cs1,
"Software Reproducing", "334611");
Collection clsf2 = new ArrayList();
clsf2.add(clsf1);
BulkResponse br = bqManager.findOrganizations(null, null, clsf2, null, null,
null);
Collection org1 = br.getCollection();
```

Once the organization is retrieved from the XML registry, you can access individual pieces of information about the organization by invoking the appropriate method of the Collection. In Listing 22-3, a variety of methods are used to retrieve information about the organization. Although the information in this example is displayed on the screen, the program can utilize this information for any purpose.

Since the inquiry is a Collection that is likely to contain multiple organizations that meet the search criteria, the program must loop through the Collection in order to retrieve information elements from each organization.

Listing 22-3
Querying an
XML registry.

```
import javax.xml.registry.*;
import javax.xml.registry.infomodel.*;
import java.net.*;
import java.util.*;
public class xmlQuery {
  public static void main(String[] args) {
    String qs1 = new String("%MyBusiness%");
    xmlQuery q1 = new xmlQuery ();
    q1.inquire(qs1);
  }
  public void inquire(String qs2) {
    Connection con1 = null;
    Properties prop1 = new Properties();
    prop1.setProperty("javax.xml.registry.queryManagerURL",
      "http://www-3.ibm.com/services/uddi/testregistry/inquiryapi");
    prop1.setProperty("javax.xml.registry.factoryClass",
      "com.sun.xml.registry.uddi.ConnectionFactoryImpl");
    try {
      ConnectionFactory cf = ConnectionFactory.newInstance();
      cf.setProperties(prop1);
      con1 = cf.createConnection();
      RegistryService rs1 = con1.getRegistryService();
      BusinessQueryManager bqmgr = rs1.getBusinessQueryManager();
      Collection fqs1 = new ArrayList();
      fqs1.add(FindQualifier.CASE_SENSITIVE_MATCH);
      Collection c1 = new ArrayList();
      c1.add(qs2);
      BulkResponse br = bqmgr.findOrganizations
          (fqs1, c1, null, null, null, null);
      Collection c2 = br.getCollection();
      Iterator itr1 = c2.iterator();
      while (itr1.hasNext()) {
        Organization org1 = (Organization) itr1.next();
        System.out.println("Name: " + org1.getName().getValue());
        System.out.println("Desc.: " + org1.getDescription().getValue());
        System.out.println("Id: " + org1.getKey().getId());
        User pcontact = org1.getPrimaryContact();
        if (pcontact!= null)
        {
          PersonName pname = pcontact.getPersonName();
          System.out.println("Name: " + pname.getFullName());
```

```
        Collection c3 = pcontact.getTelephoneNumbers(pcontact.getType());
        Iterator itr2 = c3.iterator();
        while (itr2.hasNext()) {
          TelephoneNumber tnum = (TelephoneNumber) itr2.next();
          System.out.println("Telephone: " + tnum.getNumber());
        }
        Collection c4 = pcontact.getEmailAddresses();
        Iterator itr3 = c4.iterator();
        while (itr3.hasNext()) {
          System.out.println("Email: " + (EmailAddress) itr3.next());
        }
      }
    Collection c5 = org1.getServices();
    Iterator itr4 = c5.iterator();
    while (itr4.hasNext()) {
      Service serv = (Service) itr4.next();
      System.out.println("Service: " + serv.getName().getValue());
      System.out.println(" Service description: " +
        serv.getDescription(). getValue());
      System.out.println("ID: " + serv.getKey().getId());
      Collection c6 = serv.getServiceBindings();
      Iterator itr5 = c6.iterator();
      while (itr5.hasNext()) {
        ServiceBinding sb1 = (ServiceBinding) itr5.next();
        System.out.println("Binding " + sb1.getDescription());
        System.out.println("URI: " + sb1.getAccessURI());
      }
    }
   }
  }
}
catch (Exception error)
{
 System.out.println("Error: " + error.getMessage());
}
finally
{
  if (con1 != null)
  {
    try {
      con1.close();
    }
    catch (JAXRException error)
    {
    }
  }
 }
}
}
```

Publishing a Service to an XML Registry

A business can make web services available to other organizations by inserting new information into an XML registry. This process is referred to as "publishing a web service." A business must provide an XML registry with specific information in order to register a web service with the XML registry. This information consists of

- The name of the organization
- The name of the primary contact
- The primary contact's telephone number and email address
- The industry classification and code of the business
- The name and description of the web service supported by the business
- The Binding description and binding URI

Listing 22-4 illustrates the technique used to publish a web service on an XML registry using the JAXR API. This example contains three methods. These are the main() method, the connect() method, and the publish() method. The connect() method and the publish() method are optional and are used to group related activities. The connect() method contains routines necessary to connect to the XML registry, and the publish() method contains routines to insert new information into the XML registry. Although you can combine these methods into the main() method, it is advisable to maintain three separate methods to facilitate maintenance of the code.

Prior to calling the main() method, the program creates a Connection object, a RegistryService object, a BusinessLifeCycleManager object, and a BusinessQueryManager object, all of which are used throughout the program. These objects are initialized to null.

The main() method begins by creating two String objects. The first String object is assigned the URL used to query the XML registry. The other String object is assigned the URL used to publish new information to the XML registry.

Next, you must create an instance of the program class, which is called xmlPublish, and then invoke the connect() method followed by the publish() method. The connect() method requires two arguments. The first argument is the URL used to query the XML registry and the other argument is the URL used to publish new information to the XML registry.

The connect() Method

The connect() method contains statements that open a connection to the XML registry. The connect() method begins by creating an instance of the Properties object and then calling the setProperty() method to set individual property values.

The URL used to query the XML registry is the first property set, followed by setting the URL used to publish new information to the XML registry. The last property is a reference to the ConnectionFactory that is provided by the XML registry operator.

An instance of a ConnectionFactory object is created by calling the newInstance() method, and the Property object is passed as an argument to the setProperties() method of the ConnectionFactory. The createConnection() is then invoked to open the connection to the XML registry. Any errors that occur are caught by the catch() blocks.

The publish() Method

Once the connection to the XML registry is successfully opened, the publish() method is called. The publish() method begins by assigning objects to the RegistryService object, the BusinessLifeCycleManager object, and the BusinessQueryManager object that were created previously in the program.

The RegistryService object is returned by the getRegistryService() of the Connection object. The getBusinessLifeCycleManager() and the getBusinessQueryManager() methods of the RegistryService object are invoked to return the BusinessLifeCycleManager object and the BusinessQueryManager object.

Next, the program creates two String objects that are used to store the userID and password necessary for the program to log into the XML registry as a publisher. These String objects are referred to as "credentials" and are passed to the PasswordAuthentication object that is created by the program.

Credentials must be contained in a HashSet. Therefore, the program creates a HashSet and then calls the add() method to insert the PasswordAuthentication object into the HashSet. The add() method requires one argument, which is the PasswordAuthentication object. Once the PasswordAuthentication object is inserted into the HashSet, the HashSet is passed to the setCredentials() method of the Connection object.

Information about the web service that is being published must be associated with an Organization object. Therefore, the program creates an instance of the Organization object and initializes the Organization object with the name of the business, which is MyCompany in this example.

Each entry into the XML registry must have a description in the form of an InternationalString object. The InternationalString object is created by calling the createInternationalString() method of the BusinessLifeCycleManager object and passing the method the description of the business. Once the InternationalString object is created, the setDescription() method of the Organization object is invoked, passing the method the InternationalString object.

Next, you must create a primary contact within the business that potential trading partners will contact whenever a potential trading partner wants to use the business' web service. You create a primary contact by calling the createUser() object that returns a User object.

There are three pieces of information needed for the primary contact: the name of the primary contact, the primary contact's phone number, and the contact's email address. The name of the primary contact takes the form of a PersonName object that is created by calling the createPersonName() method and the primary contact's name as an argument to the method. The PersonName object is then passed to the setPersonName() of the User object to assign the primary contact's name to the User object.

The createTelephoneNumber() method of the BusinessLifeCycleManager object is called to create a TelephoneNumber object, and the setNumber() method of the TelephoneNumber object is called to set the telephone number value.

The User object expects to receive telephone numbers in an ArrayList. Therefore, the program creates an ArrayList and calls the add() method of the ArrayList to insert the TelephoneNumber object into the ArrayList. The add() method requires one argument, which is the TelephoneNumber object. The setTelephoneNumbers() method of the User object is then called and passed the ArrayList of telephone numbers.

Next, the program creates an EmailAddress object by calling the createEmailAddress() method of the BusinessLifeCycleManager object. The EmailAddress object is initialized with the primary contact's email address.

The User object requires email addresses to be inserted as an ArrayList. The program creates an ArrayList and invokes the add() method, passing the add() method the EmailAddress object as an argument. The ArrayList is then passed to the setEmailAddresses() method of the User object.

At this point in the program, all information about the primary contact has been assigned to the User object. The User object is then passed as an argument to the setPrimaryContact() method of the Organization object.

You must now assign the industry classification to the business. This is accomplished by first creating a ClassificationScheme object. A ClassificationScheme object is created by calling the findClassificationSchemeByName() method of the BusinessQueryManager and passing the method name of the industry classification that you want to reference.

Next, a Classification object is created. The Classification object is created by calling the createClassification() method of the BusinessLifeCycleManager object. The createClassification() method requires three arguments. The first argument is the ClassificationScheme object. The second argument is the description of the industry classification, and the last argument is the industry code.

The Organization object expects that classifications take the form of an ArrayList, so you must create an ArrayList and use the add() method to insert the Classification object into the ArrayList. The addClassifications() method of the Organization object is then invoked and passed the ArrayList.

The Organization object requires an ArrayList that contains the name of the service, the service description, the Binding description, and the binding access URI. Therefore, the program creates an ArrayList.

The first item in the ArrayList is the Service object. The object is created by invoking the createServer() method of the BusinessLifeCycleManager object. The createServer() method requires one argument, which is the name of the service.

The service description is used to initialize an InternationalString and is associated with the service name by passing the InternationalString object to the setDescription() method of the Service object.

Another ArrayList is necessary to store the Binding description and the access URI. The Binding description is passed as the argument to the createInternationalString object(). The Binding description is then passed to the setDescription() method of the ServiceObject.

The next piece of information is the Binding description. You create a ServiceBinding object by calling the createServerBinding() method of the BusinessLifeCycleManager object. The ServiceBinding expects an InternationalString; therefore, the program calls the createInternationalString object and initializes the createInternationalString object with the Binding description, which is passed to the setDescription() method of the ServiceBinding object.

The final piece of information required to publish a web service is the access URI. The access URI is created by calling the setAccessURI() method of the ServiceBinding object and passing the setAccessURI() the URI. The ServiceBinding object is the ArrayList by calling the add() method and passing the add() method the ServiceBinding object.

The addServiceBindings() method of the Service object is called and is passed the ArrayList that contains the ServiceBinding object. The Service object is then the ArrayList, which in turn is added to the Organization object by calling the addServices() method, passing the ArrayList to the addServices() method.

The Organization object now contains all the information required to publish the web service to the XML registry. However, the Organization object must be inserted into an ArrayList before publishing occurs. This is because the saveOrganizations() method of the BusinessLifeCycleManager object expects to be passed an ArrayList() that contains the Organization object.

Therefore, the program creates an ArrayList() and invokes the add() method, passing the add() method the Organization object. Next, the saveOrganizations() method is called and is passed the ArrayList. The saveOrganizations() method returns a BulkResponse object that contains the response to inserting the web service into the XML registry.

You must determine if any errors occurred while inserting the web service into the XML registry. You do this by calling the getException() method of the BulkResponse object. The getException() method returns a Collection of exceptions.

If the Collection is null, no errors occurred and the web service is published. This program displays notification on the screen. If the Collection is not null, one or more errors occurred. The program needs to retrieve each error and display the error on the screen. This is accomplished by creating an Iterator for the Collection and then stepping through the Collection, retrieving and displaying each error.

Statements within the try{ } block can throw an exception. The catch{ } block traps those exceptions and displays the appropriate error message on the screen.

Listing 22-4
Inserting information into an XML registry.

```
import javax.xml.registry.*;
import javax.xml.registry.infomodel.*;
import java.net.*;
import java.security.*;
```

```java
import java.util.*;
public class xmlPublish {
  Connection con1 = null;
  RegistryService rs1 = null;
  BusinessLifeCycleManager blcmgr = null;
  BusinessQueryManager bqmgr = null;
  public static void main(String[] args) {
    String qURL = "http://www-3.ibm.com/services/uddi/
        testregistry/inquiryapi";
    String pURL = "https://www
3.ibm.com/services/uddi/testregistry/protect/publishapi";
    xmlPublish xPub = new xmlPublish ();
    xPub.connect(qURL, pURL);
    xPub.publish();
  }
  public void connect(String qUrl, String pUrl) {
    Properties prop1 = new Properties();
    prop1.setProperty("javax.xml.registry.queryManagerURL", qUrl);
    prop1.setProperty("javax.xml.registry.lifeCycleManagerURL", pUrl);
    prop1.setProperty("javax.xml.registry.factoryClass",
        "com.sun.xml.registry.uddi.ConnectionFactoryImpl");
    try {
      ConnectionFactory cf1 = ConnectionFactory.newInstance();
      cf1.setProperties(prop1);
      con1 = cf1.createConnection();
    }
    catch (Exception error) {
      System.out.println("Error: " + error.getMessage());
      if (con1 != null) {
      try {
        con1.close();
      }
      catch (JAXRException jaxr)
      {
        System.out.println("Error: " + jaxr.getMessage());
      }
    }
    }
  }
}
public void publish() {
  try {
    rs1 = con1.getRegistryService();
    blcmgr = rs1.getBusinessLifeCycleManager();
    bqmgr = rs1.getBusinessQueryManager();
```

```
    String userID = "myID";
    String pw = "myPassword";
    PasswordAuthentication pa = new PasswordAuthentication(userID,
        pw.toCharArray());
    Set hs= new HashSet();
    hs.add(pa);
    con1.setCredentials(hs);
    Organization org1 = blcmgr.createOrganization("My Company");
    InternationalString istr =
        blcmgr.createInternationalString("My Business");
    org1.setDescription(istr);
    User contact = blcmgr.createUser();
    PersonName person = blcmgr.createPersonName("Jim Keogh");
    contact.setPersonName(person);
    TelephoneNumber phone = blcmgr.createTelephoneNumber();
    phone.setNumber("617-555-1234");
    Collection phns = new ArrayList();
    phns.add(phone);
    contact.setTelephoneNumbers(phns);
    EmailAddress email = blcmgr.createEmailAddress("jk@MyCompany.com");
    Collection eas = new ArrayList();
    eas.add(email);
    contact.setEmailAddresses(eas);
    org1.setPrimaryContact(contact);
    ClassificationScheme cs = bqmgr.findClassificationSchemeByName("ntis
gov:naics");
    Classification cf1 = (Classification)
    blcmgr.createClassification(cs, "Software Reproducing", "334611");
    Collection cf2 = new ArrayList();
    cf2.add(cf1);
    org1.addClassifications(cf2);
    Collection serv1 = new ArrayList();
    Service serv2 = blcmgr.createService("Name of Service");
    InternationalString istr2 = blcmgr.createInternationalString("Service
Description");
    serv2.setDescription(istr2);
    Collection sb1 = new ArrayList();
    ServiceBinding sb2 = blcmgr.createServiceBinding();
    istr2 = blcmgr.createInternationalString("Binding Description");
    sb2.setDescription(istr2);
    sb2.setAccessURI("http://MyCompany.com:8080/sb/");
    sb1.add(sb2);
    serv2.addServiceBindings(sb1);
    serv1.add(serv2);
```

```
      org1.addServices(serv1);
      Collection org2 = new ArrayList();
      org2.add(org1);
      BulkResponse br1 = blcmgr.saveOrganizations(org2);
      Collection error1 = br1.getException();
      if (error1 == null)
      {
        System.out.println("Information Published");
      }
      else
      {
        Iterator iter2 = error1.iterator();
        Exception error3 = null;
        while (iter2.hasNext()) {
          error3 = (Exception) iter2.next();
          System.err.println("Error: " + error3.getMessage());
        }
      }
    }
    catch (Exception error) {
      System.err.println("Error: " + error.getMessage());
      if (con1 != null)
      {
        try {
         con1.close();
        }
        catch (JAXRException jaxr) {
          System.err.println("Error: " + jaxr.getMessage());
        }
      }
    }
  }
}
```

Removing a Published Service from an XML Registry

A business can delete its web service from an XML registry by invoking the deleteOrganization() method, as is illustrated in Listing 22-5. The deleteOrganization() method instructs the XML registry site to remove all information from the XML registry that is associated with the key that uniquely identifies the web service.

Before removing information about the web service from the XML registry, your program needs to perform several routines. First, your program must connect to the XML registry and log in using a userID and password that were assigned to the business by the XML registry. This is the same userID and password used when publishing the web service.

Next, your program must be assured that the web service being deleted actually exists in the XML registry. This is accomplished by searching the XML registry for the web service. Once the web service is located on the XML registry, your program can proceed to delete the web service.

Listing 22-5 groups each of these routines into separate methods. The first method is called connect(). This is followed by the inquire() method and then concludes with the delete() method. You don't need to separate these routines in your program, but you'll find that the program is easier to write and maintain by creating a method for each routine.

The program begins by setting initial values to several String objects that are used throughout the program. The first two String objects are the query URL and the publishing URL. The user ID and password String objects follow these. And the last two String objects are the search criteria, which are the organization's name and the key to the web service that is being deleted.

Once String objects are created and initialized, the program creates an instance of the program class called xmlDelete and then calls the connect() method. The connect() method is designed to receive two arguments: the query URL and the publishing URL.

The connect() method performs the same routine as described in the connect() method section of the "Publishing a Service to an XML Registry" section of this chapter.

The inquire() Method

The purpose of the inquire() method is to use the search criteria of the organization's name and web service key value to locate the web service in the XML registry. The delete() method is then invoked once the web service is found in the XML registry.

The inquire() method begins by creating a RegistryService object, by calling the getRegistryService() method of the Connection object. The inquire() method also creates a BusinessQueryManager object by calling the getBusinessQueryManager() method of the RegistryService object.

There are two search routines that are implemented in the inquire() method. The first search routine invokes the findOrganizations() method of the BusinessQueryManager object to retrieve all web services from the XML registry that are associated with the organization's name. Once these web services are returned, the second search routine begins and compares the key of each web service for the organization against the key of the web service that is being deleted.

The findOrganizations() method requires six arguments, all but two of which are null. The first argument is an ArrayList object that contains search qualifiers, and the second argument is an ArrayList object that contains the names of the organization.

Before the findOrganizations() method is invoked, the program must create two ArrayList objects, one for the search qualifier and the other for the organization's name. Once these objects are created, the add() method is called to insert the search qualifier and the organization's name into their respective ArrayList objects.

The inquire() method in Listing 22-5 qualifies the search by sorting names in descending order. The Quick Reference Guide at the end of this chapter contains other types of search qualifiers. The business name is inserted into the second ArrayList object and both objects are passed to the findOrganization() method.

The findOrganization() method returns a BulkResponse object that contains all the web services that match the business name. The returned web services must be placed into a Collection object in order for the inquire() method to implement the second search routine using the key.

The inquire() method creates the Collection by calling the getCollection() method of the BulkResponse object. The inquire() method also creates an Iterator object in order to move through the Collection of web services.

Next, a boolean value and a String object are created and initialized. These are used in the second search routine. The second search routine is implemented within the while loop. The second search routine interacts with an Organization object that contains web services retrieved from the XML registry.

Therefore, the inquire() method must create an Organization object within the while loop and initialize the Organization object with the current web service in the iterator. A different web service is assigned to the Organization object as the inquire() method moves through the iterator.

The inquire() method retrieves the key of the current web service by calling the getKey() method of the Organization object. Next, the getId() method is called to extract the key ID from the web service key. The equals() method is called and passed the search criteria that contains the key ID of the web service that is being deleted. The equals() method returns a boolean value indicating whether or not both key IDs are the same value. If they are the same value, a message is displayed on the screen and the inquire() method returns the key ID back to the main() method. If they are not the same value, the key ID is set to null and returned to the main() method where a message is displayed stating that the web services was not located in the XML registry.

The delete() Method

The delete() method is called from the main() method if the inquire() method returned a key ID that matched the search criteria. The delete() method requires three arguments. The first argument is the key ID, and the other arguments are the user ID and password.

Before the XML registry permits the removal of a web service, the publisher must provide the XML registry with a HashSet that contains a PasswordAuthentication object. Therefore, the delete() method begins by creating a PasswordAuthentication object and initializing it with the userID and password.

Next, the delete() method creates a HashSet and invokes the add() method to insert the PasswordAuthentication object into the HashSet. The HashSet is then passed as an argument to the setCredentials() method of the Connection object.

The delete() method is also ready to invoke the deleteOrganizations() method. However, the deleteOrganizations() method requires that the key ID of the web service that is being deleted be contained within an ArrayList. Therefore, the delete() method creates an ArrayList and inserts the key ID into the ArrayList by calling the add() method.

Since the deleteOrganizations() method is a member of the BusinessLifeCycleManager object, the delete() method must create a BusinessLifeCycleManager by calling the getBusinessLifeCycleManager() method from the RegistryService object.

The deleteOrganizations() method is then invoked and passed the ArrayList that contains the key ID of the web service that is being deleted. The deleteOrganizations() method returns a BulkResponse object that may contain errors should the XML registry site be unable to remove the web service.

An if statement is used to determine if an error occurred during the deletion process. If there aren't any errors, a message is displayed indicating that the web service was removed from the XML registry.

If there is an error when the delete() method attempts to remove the web service from the XML registry, the delete() method creates an iterator and proceeds to step through all the errors, displaying each on the screen.

Any errors that occur within the try{ } block throw an exception that is trapped by the catch{ } block where they are appropriately handled.

Listing 22-5
Removing information from an XML registry.

```
import javax.xml.registry.*;
import javax.xml.registry.infomodel.*;
import java.net.*;
import java.security.*;
import java.util.*;
public class xmlDelete {
  Connection con1 = null;
  RegistryService rs1 = null;
  BusinessLifeCycleManager blcmgr = null;
  BusinessQueryManager bqmgr = null;
  public static void main(String[] args) {
    String qURL = "http://www-3.ibm.com/services/uddi/
testregistry/inquiryapi";
    String pURL ="https://www
3.ibm.com/services/uddi/testregistry/protect/publishapi";
    String userID = "MyID";
    String pw = "MyPassword";
    String bName = "My Company";
    String ks1 = "MyKey";
    xmlDelete del = new xmlDelete();
    del.connect(qURL, pURL);
    javax.xml.registry.infomodel.Key imkey1 = del.inquire(ks1, bName);
    if (imkey1!= null)
    {
     del.delete(imkey1, userID, pw);
    }
```

```
       else
       {
         System.out.println("Not Found");
       }
    }
    public void connect(String qUrl, String pUrl) {
      Properties prop1 = new Properties();
      prop1.setProperty("javax.xml.registry.queryManagerURL", qUrl);
      prop1.setProperty("javax.xml.registry.lifeCycleManagerURL", pUrl);
      prop1.setProperty("javax.xml.registry.factoryClass",
        "com.sun.xml.registry.uddi.ConnectionFactoryImpl");
      try {
        ConnectionFactory cf1 = ConnectionFactory.newInstance();
        cf1.setProperties(prop1);
        con1 = cf1.createConnection();
      }
      catch (Exception error) {
        System.out.println("Error: " + error.getMessage());
        if (con1!= null)
        {
          try {
            con1.close();
          }
          catch (JAXRException jaxr)
          {
            System.out.println("Error: " + jaxr.getMessage());
          }
        }
      }
    }
    public javax.xml.registry.infomodel.Key inquire(String ks1, String bName) {
      javax.xml.registry.infomodel.Key imKey = null;
      try {
        rs1 = con1.getRegistryService();
        bqmgr = rs1.getBusinessQueryManager();
        Collection fq1 = new ArrayList();
        fq1.add(FindQualifier.SORT_BY_NAME_DESC);
        Collection np1 = new ArrayList();
        np1.add(bName);
        BulkResponse br1 = bqmgr.findOrganizations(fq1, np1, null, null, null,
          null);
        Collection org2 = br1.getCollection();
        Iterator iter1 = org2.iterator();
        boolean found = false;
        String id = null;
        while (!found && iter1.hasNext()) {
          Organization org3 = (Organization) iter1.next();
          imKey = org3.getKey();
```

```
        id = imKey.getId();
        found = id.equals(ks1);
      }
      if (found)
      {
        System.out.println("Found");
      }
      else
      {
        imKey = null;
      }
    }
    catch (Exception error) {
      System.err.println("error: " + error.getMessage());
      if (con1 != null)
      {
        try {
          con1.close();
        }
        catch (JAXRException jaxr) {
          System.err.println("error: " + jaxr.getMessage());
        }
      }
    }
    return imKey;
  }
  public void delete(javax.xml.registry.infomodel.Key imKey1, String userID,
String pw) {
    try {
      PasswordAuthentication pa1 = new PasswordAuthentication(userID,
      pw.toCharArray());
      Set hs1 = new HashSet();
      hs1.add(pa1);
      con1.setCredentials(hs1);
      String id = imKey1.getId();
      Collection imKey2= new ArrayList();
      imKey2.add(imKey1);
      blcmgr = rs1.getBusinessLifeCycleManager();
      BulkResponse br1 = blcmgr.deleteOrganizations(imKey2);
      Collection error = br1.getException();
      if (error == null)
      {
        System.out.println("Information Deleted");
      }
      else
      {
        Iterator iter2 = error.iterator();
        while (iter2.hasNext()) {
```

```
          Exception e = (Exception) iter2.next();
          System.err.println("Error: " + e.getMessage());
        }
      }
    }
    catch (Exception error) {
      System.err.println("Error: " + error.getMessage());
    }
    finally {
      if (con1 != null)
      {
        try {
          con1.close();
        }
        catch (JAXRException error) {
          System.err.println("Error: " + error.getMessage());
        }
      }
    }
  }
}
```

Quick Reference Guide

This quick reference guide provides a brief overview of Java classes used with JAXR.
Full details of these classes, and all Java classes and interfaces, are available at
java.sun.com.

Syntax	Descriptions
Collection getCollection()	Returns a Collection of objects.
Collection getException()	Returns a JAXRException Collection.
boolean isPartialResponse()	Returns true if a partial response caused by the large size of the result set.

Table 22-2.   *public interface BulkResponse **extends JAXRResponse***

Syntax	Descriptions
BulkResponse deleteAssociations (Collection schemeKeys)	Delete Associations of schemeKeys.
BulkResponse deleteClassificationSchemes (Collection schemeKeys)	Delete ClassificationSchemes of schemeKeys.
BulkResponse deleteConcepts (Collection conceptKeys)	Delete Concepts of conceptKeys.
BulkResponse deleteOrganizations (Collection organizationKeys)	Delete organization of organizationKeys.
BulkResponse deleteServiceBindings (Collection bindingKeys)	Delete ServiceBindings of bindingKeys.
BulkResponse deleteServices (Collection serviceKeys)	Delete services of serviceKeys.
BulkResponse saveAssociations(Collection associations, boolean replace)	Saves Association.
BulkResponse saveClassificationSchemes (Collection schemes)	Saves ClassificationScheme.
BulkResponse saveConcepts (Collection concepts)	Saves Concepts.
BulkResponse saveOrganizations (Collection organizations)	Saves Organizations.
BulkResponse saveServiceBindings (Collection bindings)	Saves ServiceBindings.
BulkResponse saveServices (Collection services)	Saves Services.

Table 22-3. *public interface BusinessLifeCycleManager* **extends LifeCycleManager**

Syntax	Descriptions
BulkResponse findAssociations(Collection findQualifiers, Collection associationTypes, boolean sourceObjectConfirmed, boolean targetObjectConfirmed)	Returns Associations matching the parameter list.
ClassificationScheme findClassificationSchemeByName (String namePattern)	Returns a ClassificationScheme by name.
BulkResponse findClassificationSchemes(Collection findQualifiers, Collection namePatterns, Collection classifications, Collection externalLinks)	Returns ClassificationSchemes matching the parameter list.
Concept findConceptByPath(String path)	Returns a Concept using a parameter.
BulkResponse findConcepts(Collection findQualifiers, Collection namePatterns, Collection classifications, Collection externalIdentifiers, Collection externalLinks)	Returns Concepts matching the parameter list.
BulkResponse findOrganizations(Collection findQualifiers, Collection namePatterns, Collection classifications, Collection specifications, Collection externalIdentifiers, Collection externalLinks)	Returns Organizations matching the parameter list.
BulkResponse findRegistryPackages (Collection findQualifiers, Collection namePatterns, Collection classifications, Collection externalLinks)	Returns RegistryPackages matching the parameter list.
BulkResponse findServiceBindings(Key serviceKey, Collection findQualifiers, Collection classifications, Collection specifications)	Returns ServiceBindings matching the parameter list.
BulkResponse findServices(Key orgKey, Collection findQualifiers, Collection namePatterns, Collection classifications, Collection specifications)	Returns Services matching the parameter list.

Table 22-4. *public interface BusinessQueryManager* **extends QueryManager**

Syntax	Descriptions
int getCapabilityLevel()	Returns the JAXR provider capability level supported.
String getVersion()	Returns the JAXR provider JAXR specification version.

Table 22-5. *public interface CapabilityProfile*

Syntax	Descriptions
RegistryEntry getRegistryEntry()	Returns the registry entry.
Object getRepositoryItem()	Returns the optional repository item.

Table 22-6. *public interface CataloguedObject*

Syntax	Descriptions
void close()	Closes a connection.
Set getCredentials()	Returns client credentials.
RegistryService getRegistryService()	Returns the RegistryService interface.
boolean isClosed()	Returns true if Connection is closed.
boolean isSynchronous()	Returns true if client uses synchronous communication.
void setCredentials(Set credentials)	Sets client's Credentials.
void setSynchronous(boolean sync)	Sets whether a client uses synchronous communication.

Table 22-7. *public interface Connection*

WEB SERVICES

Syntax	Descriptions
Query createQuery(int queryType, String queryString)	Creates a Query object.
BulkResponse executeQuery(Query query)	Executes a query.

Table 22-8. *public interface DeclarativeQueryManager* **extends QueryManager**

Syntax	Descriptions
static String AND_ALL_KEYS	Includes search criteria and all keys.
static String CASE_SENSITIVE_MATCH	Activates case sensitive matching.
static String COMBINE_CLASSIFICATIONS	Indicates a combine classification is being used.
static String EXACT_NAME_MATCH	Indicates an exact name must be matched.
static String OR_ALL_KEYS	Includes search criteria or all keys.
static String OR_LIKE_KEYS	Includes search criteria or like keys.
static String SERVICE_SUBSET	Indicates a subset is used.
static String SORT_BY_DATE_ASC	Indicates the sort is by date in ascending order.
static String SORT_BY_DATE_DESC	Indicates the sort is by date in decending order.
static String SORT_BY_NAME_ASC	Indicates the sort is by name in ascending order.
static String SORT_BY_NAME_DESC	Indicates the sort is by name in decending order.
static String SOUNDEX	Allows matching strings by their sounds.

Table 22-9. *public interface FindQualifier*

Syntax	Descriptions
String getRequestId()	Returns a unique ID for a request.
int getStatus()	Returns the status for a response.
boolean isAvailable()	Returns true if a response is available; otherwise, false is returned if a response is unavailable.
Association createAssociation (RegistryObject targetObject, Concept associationType)	Create an Association using parameter list.
Classification createClassification (ClassificationScheme scheme, String name, String value)	Create a Classification using parameter list.
Classification createClassification (Concept concept)	Create a Classification using parameter list.
ClassificationScheme createClassificationScheme (Concept concept)	Create a ClassificationScheme where the Concept ClassificationScheme doesn't exist and where the Concept isn't a child Concept.
ClassificationScheme createClassificationScheme (String name, String description)	Create a scheme given using parameter list.
Concept createConcept(RegistryObject parent, String name, String value)	Create a Concept using parameter list.
void createConceptEquivalence (Concept concept1, Concept concept2)	Create an equivalence between Concepts.
EmailAddress createEmailAddress (String address)	Create an EmailAddress using parameter list.
EmailAddress createEmailAddress (String address, java.lang.String type)	Create an EmailAddress using parameter list.

Table 22-10. *public interface LifeCycleManager*

Syntax	Descriptions
ExternalIdentifier createExternalIdentifier (ClassificationScheme identificationScheme, String name, String value)	Create an ExternalIdentifier using parameter list.
ExternalLink createExternalLink(String externalURI, String description)	Create an ExternalLink using parameter list.
ExtrinsicObject createExtrinsicObject()	Create an ExtrinsicObject using parameter list.
InternationalString createInternationalString()	Create an InternationalString using parameter list.
InternationalString createInternationalString (Locale l, String s)	Create an InternationalString using parameter list.
InternationalString createInternationalString(String s)	Create an InternationalString using parameter list.
Key createKey(String id)	Create a Key instance using parameter list.
LocalizedString createLocalizedString(Locale l, java.lang.String s)	Create a LocalizedString using parameter list.
Object createObject(String className)	Create an information model interface.
Organization createOrganization (String name)	Create an Organization using parameter list.
PersonName createPersonName (String fullName)	Create a PersonName using parameter list.
PersonName createPersonName (String firstName, String middleName, String lastName)	Create a PersonName using parameter list.
PostalAddress createPostalAddress(String streetNumber, String street, String city, String stateOrProvince, String country, String postalCode, String type)	Create a PostalAddress using parameter list.

Table 22-10.   *public interface LifeCycleManager* (continued)

Syntax	Descriptions
RegistryPackage createRegistryPackage (String name)	Create a RegistryPackage using parameter list.
Service createService(String name)	Create a Service using parameter list.
ServiceBinding createServiceBinding()	Create a ServiceBinding using parameter list.
Slot createSlot(String name, Collection values, String slotType)	Create a Slot using parameter list.
Slot createSlot(String name, String value, String slotType)	Create a Slot using parameter list.
SpecificationLink createSpecificationLink()	Create a SpecificationLink using parameter list.
TelephoneNumber createTelephoneNumber()	Create a TelephoneNumber using parameter list.
User createUser()	Create a User using parameter list.
void deleteConceptEquivalence (Concept concept1, Concept concept2)	Deletes an equivalence between Concepts.
BulkResponse deleteObjects (Collection keys)	Deletes objects from a registry.
BulkResponse deprecateObjects (Collection keys)	Deprecates previously submitted objects.
BulkResponse saveObjects (Collection objects)	Saves an Object to a registry.
BulkResponse unDeprecateObjects (Collection keys)	Undeprecates previously deprecated objects.
boolean isAvailable()	Returns true if a response is available; otherwise, false is returned if a response is unavailable.

Table 22-10. *public interface LifeCycleManager* (continued)

Syntax	Descriptions
int getType()	Returns the type of a Query.
String toString()	Print the query.

Table 22-11. *public interface Query*

Syntax	Descriptions
CataloguedObject getCataloguedObject (String id)	Returns the CataloguedObject specified by the parameter list.
BulkResponse getCataloguedObjects (Collection objectKeys)	Returns the specified CataloguedObjects specified by the parameter list.
RegistryObject getRegistryObject(String id)	Returns the RegistryObject specified by the parameter list.
BulkResponse getRegistryObjects()	Returns the RegistryObjects.
BulkResponse getRegistryObjects (Collection objectKeys)	Returns the RegistryObjects.
BulkResponse getRegistryObjects (String objectType)	Returns the RegistryObjects specified by the parameter list.

Table 22-12. *public interface QueryManager*

Syntax	Descriptions
BulkResponse getBulkResponse (String requestId)	Returns the BulkResponse specified by the parameter list.
BusinessLifeCycleManager getBusinessLifeCycleManager()	Returns the JAXR provider's BusinessLifeCycleManager interface.
BusinessQueryManager getBusinessQueryManager()	Returns the JAXR provider's BusinessQueryManager interface.
CapabilityProfile getCapabilityProfile()	Returns the JAXR provider's CapabilityProfile.
DeclarativeQueryManager getDeclarativeQueryManager()	Returns the JAXR provider's DeclarativeQueryManager interface.
ClassificationScheme getDefaultPostalScheme()	Returns the default user-defined postal scheme.
LifeCycleManager getLifeCycleManager()	Returns the JAXR provider's basic LifeCycleManager interface.
String makeRegistrySpecificRequest (String request)	Returns a String object that is in the registry format.

Table 22-13.   *public interface RegistryService*

The Complete Reference

Chapter 23

Web Services Description Language (WSDL)

Organizations are able to offer web services to other organizations through the use of a set of standards that are based on XML. Throughout Part V you learned about web services and how to implement web services within your J2EE application.

A key component of web services is SOAP (see Chapter 19), which is a standard that defines the electronic message structure used by organizations to interact with each other when either offering or utilizing web services.

Information about web services is contained within an XML registry that adheres to the Universal Description, Discovery, and Integration (UDDI). UDDI is a database of web services providers (see Chapter 20).

And enhancing the capabilities of SOAP and UDDI is the Electronic Business XML (ebXML, see Chapter 21) standard that defines the way web services designed for electronic commerce are offered to prospective trading partners and provides a means for trading partners to agree to enter into electronic commerce.

Your J2EE application is able to interact with an XML registry of web services by implementing the Java API for XML Registries (JAXR) API (see Chapter 22). JAXR contains all the classes and interfaces necessary to query an XML registry and to publish a web service on an XML registry.

The backbone of web services is communication used to transmit between web services providers to an XML registry and from an XML registry to a web services consumer. The Web Service Description Language (WSDL) is a standard used to describe network services used to facilitate the interaction between web services providers and consumers. You'll learn how to implement WSDL in this chapter.

Inside WSDL

Organizations that either publish web services or consume web services must be able to communicate with each other using an agreed upon protocol. Protocols supported by an organization are described using WSDL.

WSDL standardizes XML elements that describe a collection of communication endpoints. A communication endpoint is a port that sends and receives messages. Web services providers and web services consumers are endpoints in communication each of which has one or multiple ports. Each port is associated with a network address. Collectively ports of a web services provider or web services consumer is called a *network service*.

WSDL defines a network service using seven XML elements. These are type, message, operation, port type, binding, port, and service. The type element contains data type definitions. The message element contains the data type of the data that is being transmitted. The operation element describes an action supported by the network service. The port type element defines operations supported by the web services provider. The binding element specifies the protocol and data format for a port type.

And the service element contains other ports associated with the web services provider. Each WSDL element is discussed in detail later in this chapter.

WSDL has binding extensions for popular protocols and message formats that are positioned on top of the network service definition. These include SOAP 1.1, HTTP GET/POST, and MIME. Other binding extensions can also be used with WSDL.

The WSDL Document

The WSDL document should be organized into a set of three documents so that the WSDL document can be easily maintained and reused as necessary. The first document contains the data type definition (DTD), which is shown in Listing 23-1. The next document contains abstract definitions and is shown in Listing 23-2. The third document identifies service bindings and is illustrated in Listing 23-3.

This example illustrates a WSDL document set that is used to provide a product pricing service to a trading partner. The DTD in Listing 23-1 identifies the target namespace schemas located at mycompany.com/pricing.

The first element defined in the DTD is ProductPriceRequest, which is a complex type that contains the child element called ProductID. ProductID is a string. The other element defined in the DTD is called ProductPrice. ProductPrice is also a complex type and has one child element called UnitPrice. UnitPrice is a float.

The next document in the set is the abstract definition called Pricing. The document begins by identifying namespaces. You'll notice that the DTD is incorporated into the abstract definition document by using the import element. The import element enables you to divide the WSDL document into a set of three documents and then combine the set into one WSDL document by importing the other documents of the set.

The abstract definition document creates two message elements. The first message element is called GetProductPriceInput, and the body of this message is the ProductPriceRequest element. The other message element is called GetProductPriceOutput, and the body of this message is the ProductPrice element. Both the ProductPriceRequest element and the ProductPrice element are defined in the DTD.

Next, the abstract definition document creates the portType element called ProductPricePortType that contains one child element, which is called operation. The operation element contains two child elements: the input element and the output element. The input element message is the GetProductPriceInput element and the output element message is the GetProductPriceOutput element. Both of these elements are defined in the message elements of the abstract definition document.

The last document in the WSDL document set is the service bindings, which is shown in Listing 23-3. This document begins by identifying namespaces and imports the DTD and the abstract definition documents.

Next, the document creates the ProductPriceSoapBinding element that is a ProductPricePortType. ProductPricePortType is defined in the abstract definition document. Within the binding element is the operations element that identifies the location of GetProductPrice, which is used by the trading partner to obtain product pricing. The document also creates a service element that identifies information about the product pricing service offered by the business.

```
<?xml version="1.0"?>
<schema targetNamespace="http://mycompany.com/pricing/schemas"
        xmlns="http://www.w3.org/2000/10/XMLSchema">
    <element name="ProductPriceRequest">
        <complexType>
            <all>
                <element name="ProductID" type="string"/>
            </all>
        </complexType>
    </element>
    <element name="ProductPrice">
        <complexType>
            <all>
                <element name="UnitPrice" type="float"/>
            </all>
        </complexType>
    </element>
</schema>
```

```
<?xml version="1.0"?>
<definitions name="Pricing"
targetNamespace="http://mycompany.com/pricing/definitions"
        xmlns:tns="http://mycompany.com/pricing/definitions"
        xmlns:xsd1="http://mycompany.com/pricing/schemas"
        xmlns:soap="http://schemas.xmlsoap.org/wsdl/soap/"
        xmlns="http://schemas.xmlsoap.org/wsdl/">
    <import namespace="http://mycompany.com/pricing/schemas"
            location="http://mycompany.com/pricing/pricing.xsd"/>
    <message name="GetProductPriceInput">
        <part name="body" element="xsd1:ProductPriceRequest"/>
    </message>
    <message name="GetProductPriceOutput">
        <part name="body" element="xsd1:ProductPrice"/>
    </message>
    <portType name="ProductPricePortType">
        <operation name="GetProductPrice">
            <input message="tns:GetProductPriceInput"/>
```

```
                <output message="tns:GetProductPriceOutput"/>
            </operation>
        </portType>
</definitions>
```

Listing 23-3
Service
bindings.

```xml
<?xml version="1.0"?>
<definitions name="pricing"
targetNamespace="http://mycompany.com/pricing/service"
xmlns:tns="http://mycompany.com/pricing/service"
        xmlns:soap="http://schemas.xmlsoap.org/wsdl/soap/"
        xmlns:defs="http://example.com/stockquote/definitions"
        xmlns="http://schemas.xmlsoap.org/wsdl/">
    <import namespace="http://mycompany.com/pricing/definitions"
            location="http://mycompany.com/pricing/pricing.wsdl"/>
    <binding name="ProductPriceSoapBinding" type="defs:ProductPricePortType">
        <soap:binding style="document"
transport="http://schemas.xmlsoap.org/soap/http"/>
        <operation name="GetProductPrice">
            <soap:operation soapAction="http://mycompany.com/GetProductPrice"/>
            <input>
                <soap:body use="literal"/>
            </input>
            <output>
                <soap:body use="literal"/>
            </output>
        </operation>
    </binding>
    <service name="ProductPriceService">
        <documentation>Product pricing service</documentation>
        <port name="ProductPricePort" binding="tns:ProductPriceBinding">
            <soap:address location="http://mycompany.com/pricing"/>
        </port>
    </service>
</definitions>
```

Type Element

The Type element of the WSDL document contains definitions of data types used within the WSDL document message. WSDL uses XSD as the canonical type system, so data types are independent of wire format.

WSDL also introduces flexibility when it comes to data type systems, through the use of extensibility elements. An extensibility element functions similar to the XML schema element in that the extensibility element identifies both the type definition system and the XML container element for the type definition.

Message Element

The message element identifies the body of the WSDL document and is divided into multiple sections where each section is typed using an extensible message attribute. Two of the commonly used message attributes are element and type. The element attribute identifies the unique name of the message. The type is either simpleType or complexType (see Chapter 8). You can create your own attributes, as necessary. However, your attributes must use a namespace other than the WSDL namespace.

A message is identified by a unique name that is assigned to the name attribute. The message name must be unique among all messages within the same document. A message can be divided into logical components where each component is referred to as a message part. Message parts are identified with the part element. Each part element must have a unique name within the message. The name of the part element is identified by the part element's name attribute.

PortType Element

The portType element is used to describe abstract operations and messages. The portType element has a name attribute whose value uniquely identifies the portType element within all the portTypes of the WSDL XML document.

The portType element has a child element called operation, which also has a name attribute used to uniquely identify the operation within the portType element. The portType uses one of four transmission primitives supported by an endpoint.

The first transmission primitive is one way that indicates that the endpoint supports receiving a message. This is identified by using the wsdl:input element, as shown in Listing 23-4. In this example, GetPricing is the name of the wsdl:input operation and ProductPricing is the message associated with this operation.

Listing 23-4
One-way transmission primitive.

```
<wsdl:operation name="GetProductPricing">
    <wsdl:input name="GetPricing"? message="InputProductPricing"/>
</wsdl:operation>
```

Next is the request-response transmission primitive that states the endpoint receives and sends a responding message. This is illustrated in Listing 23-5. The operation is called GetProductPricing, and ProductID is the parameterOrder.

The parameterOrder attribute is used with the request-response and solicit-response transmission primitives to capture the function signature of the remote procedure call that made the request. Although this example shows one parameter, there can be other parameters—each separated by a space. Parameters do not need to be used by the operation.

There are three child elements within the operation: wsdl:input, wsdl:output, and wsdl:fault. The wsdl:input element called GetPricing indicates that the endpoint receives messages. The InputProductPricing message is the message associated with the input operation. Next is the wsdl:output operation called SendPricing that indicates the endpoint supports sending a reply message. OutputProductPricing is the message associated with the output operation. The last operation is the wsdl:fault element that sets the default. The default is used if the name attribute is not specified. The wsdl:fault element is called DefaultPricing and is associated with the DefaultProductPricing message.

Listing 23-5
Request-response transmission primitive.

```
<wsdl:operation name=" GetProductPricing " parameterOrder="ProductID">
   <wsdl:input name=" GetPricing "? message="InputProductPricing"/>
   <wsdl:output name="SendPricing "? message="OutputProductPricing"/>
   <wsdl:fault name="DefaultPricing" message="DefaultProductPricing"/>*
</wsdl:operation>
```

The third transmission primitive is solicit-response. The solicit-response transmission primitive indicates that the endpoint sends a message and then receives a responding message and is structured the same as the request-response transmission primitive.

The final transmission primitive is a notification that states that the endpoint sends a message. Listing 23-6 illustrates this structure. In this example, the wsdl:output element called GetPricing is used and is associated with the OutputProductPricing message.

Listing 23-6
Notification transmission primitive.

```
<wsdl:operation name=" SendProductPricing ">
    <wsdl:output name="GetPricing"? message="OutputProductPricing"/>
</wsdl:operation>
```

WSDL defines bindings for two of the four transmission primitives: the one-way transmission primitive and the request-response transmission primitive.

Binding Element

The purpose of the binding element is to define details of protocols and the message format that are referenced in a portType element. Since a portType can have many operations, there can be multiple binding elements for each portType described in the WSDL XML document.

The binding element requires a name attribute whose value uniquely identifies the binding in the WSDL XML document. The binding element is associated with a portType through the binding element's type attribute.

Within the binding element is the wsdl:operation child element. The wsdl:operation element contains information necessary for binding operations specified in the portType. Listing 23-7 illustrates how operations are specified in the wsdl:operation element of the binding element.

WEB SERVICES

You'll notice that there are three operations: input, output, and the default operation. Each operation is identified with the appropriate child element of the operation element. You place the necessary information needed to bind each operation within its operation element.

Listing 23-7
The binding element.

```
<wsdl:binding name="ProductPriceSoapBinding" type="ProductPricePortType">
   <wsdl:operation name="GetProductPrice">
     <wsdl:input name="GetProductPriceInput"? > ?
     </wsdl:input>
     <wsdl:output name="GetProductPriceOutput"? > ?
     </wsdl:output>
     <wsdl:fault name="GetProductPriceDefault">
     </wsdl:fault>
   </wsdl:operation>
</wsdl:binding>
```

Port Element

Endpoints are identified by the wsdl:port element in the WSDL XML document. The wsdl:port element is a child element of the wsdl:service element and each port element contains the URL of a binding. The wsdl:port element requires two attributes: the name attribute and the binding attribute.

The value of the name attribute uniquely identifies the wsdl:port element within the WSDL XML document. The value of the binding attribute identifies the binding that is associated with the wsdl:port element.

Listing 23-8 illustrates the wsdl:port element. This example identifies the location for the ProductPriceBinding at the URL mycompany.com/pricing.

Listing 23-8
The wsdl:port element.

```
< wsdl:port name="ProductPricePort" binding="tns:ProductPriceBinding">
    wsdl:<soap:address location="http://mycompany.com/pricing"/>
</wsdl:port>
```

Service Element

The wsdl:port element is a child element of the wsdl:service element, as discussed in the previous section. The wsdl:service element is used within a WSDL document that has grouped together related wsdl:port elements. The wsdl:service element is the child element of the wsdl:definitions element.

The wsdl:definitions element can have multiple wsdl:service elements, each associated with a group of ports. Therefore, you'll need to use the name attribute to uniquely identify each wsdl:service element contained within the wsdl:definitions element.

A port within a wsdl:service element is restricted from communicating with other ports contained in the same wsdl:service element. Ports within a wsdl:service element that share the same port type and have a different binding URL are semantically similar. A trading partner can choose the appropriate port within the wsdl:service using a port's communication characteristics as criteria for the selection.

Listing 23-9 illustrates the use of the wsdl:service element within a WSDL document. This example defines the wsdl:service called ProductPriceService that contains the wsdl:port ProductPricePort, which was presented in the previous section.

Listing 23-9
The
wsdl:service
element.

```
<wsdl:service name="ProductPriceService">
   <wsdl:port name="ProductPricePort" binding="tns:ProductPriceBinding">
      <soap:address location="http://mycompany.com/pricing"/>
   </wsdl:port>
</wsdl:service>
```

WSDL and SOAP

Simple Object Access Protocol (SOAP) is a communications protocol that facilitates the interaction between applications and web services located on remote computers, which you learned about in Chapter 19. WSDL can be used to describe network services used with SOAP by including a binding for SOAP 1.1 protocol endpoints.

There are two commonly used transmission primitives for SOAP: a one-way transmission primitive using SMTP, and a request-response transmission primitive using HTTP. Listing 23-10 illustrates the one-way transmission primitive and Listing 23-11 shows the request-response transmission primitive.

SOAP One-Way Transmission Primitive

The SOAP one-way transmission primitive is similar in design to the one-way transmission primitive described earlier in this chapter for the WSDL document. A one-way transmission primitive consists of only an input operation. There isn't an output operation.

Listing 23-10 shows how to construct a one-way transmission primitive using SMTP within a SOAP binding. You'll notice that this listing begins (similar to previous listings in this chapter) by identifying the namespaces.

The document is divided into WSDL document components such as message, portType, binding, operation, service, port, and types, all of which are described in the previous discussion about WSDL.

SOAP elements are placed within the appropriate elements of the WSDL document. The first SOAP element used in the WSDL document is the soap:binding element. The soap:binding element has two attributes that describe the SOAP binding: style and transport.

WEB SERVICES

The value of the style attribute describes the type of binding. There are two types: document and rpc, which is used for a remote procedure call. This example uses the document type. Listing 23-11 uses rpc. The value of the transport attribute is the URI of the SMTP server.

The next two SOAP elements used in the WSDL document appear as child elements of the input element. These are the soap:body element and the soap:header element, each of which describe components of the SOAP message (see Chapter 19) that will be received from a trading partner.

The last SOAP element to appear within this WSDL document is the soap:address element. The soap:address element is a child element of the port element. The soap:address element has one attribute called location. The value of the location attribute is the port binding used to receive requests from potential trading partners.

Listing 23-10
SOAP
one-way
transmission
primitive
using SMTP.

```xml
<?xml version="1.0"?>
<definitions name="pricing" targetNamespace=
    "http://mycompany.com/pricing.wsdl"
    xmlns:tns="http://mycompany.com/pricing.wsdl"
    xmlns:xsd1="http://mycompany.com/pricing.xsd"
    xmlns:soap="http://schemas.xmlsoap.org/wsdl/soap/"
    xmlns="http://schemas.xmlsoap.org/wsdl/">
  <message name="ProductPricing">
    <part name="body" element="xsd1:ProductPricing"/>
    <part name="productheader" element="xsd1:ProductHeader"/>
  </message>
  <portType name="ProductPricePortType">
    <operation name="GetProductPricing">
      <input message="tns:GetProductPricingInput"/>
    </operation>
  </portType>
  <binding name="ProductPriceSoapBinding" type="tns:ProductPricePortType">
    <soap:binding style="document" transport="http://mycompany.com/smtp"/>
      <operation name="GetProductPricing">
        <input message="tns:GetProductPricing">
          <soap:body parts="body" use="literal"/>
          <soap:header message="tns:GetProductPricing" part="productheader"
use="literal"/>
        </input>
      </operation>
  </binding>
  <service name="ProductPricingService">
    <port name="ProductPricingPort" binding="tns:ProductPricingSoap">
      <soap:address location="mailto:customer@mycompany.com"/>
    </port>
  </service>
  <types>
  <schema targetNamespace="http://mycompany.com/ProductPrice.xsd"
```

```
      xmlns="http://www.w3.org/2000/10/XMLSchema">
    <element name="ProductPrice">
      <complexType>
        <all>
          <element name="ProductID" type="string"/>
        </all>
      </complexType>
    </element>
    <element name="ProductPriceHeader" type="uriReference"/>
  </schema>
  </types>
</definitions>
```

SOAP Request-Response Transmission Primitive

The SOAP request-response transmission primitive is used whenever a web service is designed to receive requests from potential trading partners and is designed to respond to such a request. The request-response transmission primitive is very similar in concept to the WSDL request-response transmission primitive described previously in this chapter.

Listing 23-11 illustrates the SOAP request-response transmission primitive. This example begins by specifying namespaces used in the document. And, as with the SOAP one-way transmission primitive, the structure of the document is similar to the WSDL document that uses the request-response transmission primitive.

Within the WSDL elements are SOAP elements, the first of which is the soap:binding element. The soap:binding element, as discussed in the previous section, is a child element within the binding element. In this example, the soap:binding element uses rpc as the value of the style attribute. This means binding is designed for a remote procedure call. The value of the transport attribute references HTTP as the protocol used for transmission.

The next SOAP element appears within the operation element. This is the soap:operation element. The soap:operation element requires one attribute, which is the soapAction attribute. The soapAction attribute contains the URI of the operation. In this example, GetProductPrice is the operation.

Within the input element is the soap:body element. The soap:body requires three attributes: use, namespace, and encodingStyle. The value of the use attribute specifies if the soap:body is encoded or not. The namespace attribute identifies the namespacing used in the SOAP body, and the encodingStyle attribute specifies the URI of the encoding style if the soap:body is encoded. Likewise, another soap:body element is included in the WSDL document. This one is within the output element and describes the SOAP body of the output.

The last SOAP element in the example is soap:address and is contained within the port element. The soap:address identifies the URI used for the binding.

Listing 23-11
The request-
response
transmission
primitive.

```xml
<?xml version="1.0"?>
<definitions name="pricing" targetNamespace=
    "http://mycompany.com/pricing.wsdl"
        xmlns:tns="http://mycompany.com/pricing.wsdl"
        xmlns:xsd="http://www.w3.org/2000/10/XMLSchema"
        xmlns:xsd1="http://mycompany.com/pricing.xsd"
        xmlns:soap="http://schemas.xmlsoap.org/wsdl/soap/"
        xmlns="http://schemas.xmlsoap.org/wsdl/">
    <message name="ProductPricingInput">
        <part name="ProductID" element="xsd:string"/>
    </message>
    <message name="ProductPricingOutput">
      <part name="price" type="xsd:float"/>
    </message>
    <portType name="ProductPricePortType">
      <operation name="GetProductPricing">
        <input message="tns:GetProductPricingInput"/>
        <output message="tns:GetProductPricingOutput"/>
      </operation>
    </portType>
    <binding name="ProductPriceSoapBinding" type="tns:ProductPricePortType">
      <soap:binding style="rpc" transport=
"http://schemas.xmlsoap.org/soap/http"/>
     <operation name="GetProductPrice">
       <soap:operation soapAction="http://mycompany/GetProductPrice"/>
        <input>
          <soap:body use="encoded" namespace="http://mycompany.com/pricing"
             encodingStyle="http://schemas.xmlsoap.org/soap/encoding/"/>
        </input>
        <output>
          <soap:body use="encoded" namespace="http://mycompany.com/pricing"
             encodingStyle="http://schemas.xmlsoap.org/soap/encoding/"/>
        </output>
     </operation>
    </binding>
    <service name="ProductPricingService">
      <documentation>My first service</documentation>
      <port name="ProductPricePort" binding="tns:ProductPriceBinding"
        <soap:address location="http://mycompany.com/pricing"/>
      </port>
    </service>
</definitions>
```

SOAP Binding Element

The soap:binding element represents that the WSDL document is bound to the SOAP
1.1 protocol. As you'll recall from Chapter 19, the SOAP protocol defines a SOAP
message as having an envelopee, a header, and a body.

There are two attributes required by the soap:binding element: the style attribute, which has a value of either document or rpc (as described previously in this chapter), and the transport attribute. The transport attribute contains the URI of the SOAP transport used for the binding. SOAP transports include HTTP, SMTP, and FTP among others (see Chapter 19).

Both of these attributes are necessary whenever you need to use a SOAP binding to a WSDL document. However, the value of the style attribute defaults to document if the style attribute is excluded from the soap:binding.

SOAP Operation Element

The soap:operation element supplies information about the operation and contains two attributes: the style attribute and the soapAction attribute. The style attribute states if the message contains a document or parameters and return values. The value of the style attribute is document if the message contains a document; otherwise, the value of the style attribute is rpc. As discussed previously in this chapter, rpc implies a remote procedure call, which uses parameters and return values. The default value of the style attribute is document.

The style attribute is important to the SOAP binding because the value of the style attribute determines the structure of the message body and determines the programming model that will be used to access the message.

The soapAction attribute is used to identify the contents of the SOAPAction header. The content of the SOAPAction header is specific to an operation. The value of the soapAction attribute is the URI of the SOAPAction header content.

SOAP Body Element

The soap:body element defines the organization of message parts within the SOAP body element and provides information on how message parts are assembled. Message parts fall into two categories: abstract type definitions and concrete schema definitions. An abstract type definition defines types that are serialized based on rules of an encoding style. The encoding style is identified by a URI.

An encoding style sets rules that enable the message to be formatted in various ways, which requires the message recipient to interpret all the variations in the message format. An alternative to the abstract type definition is the concrete schema definition, which avoids the use of various message formats. Therefore, the message recipient needs to be able to interpret one message format as specified in the schema definition.

The soap:body element contains four attributes: parts, user, encodingStyle, and namespace. The parts attribute specifies that the SOAP message parts are contained in the body of the message. The parts attribute defaults to all parts of a SOAP message if the parts attribute is omitted.

The use attribute specifies whether parts of the message use an abstract type definition and concrete schema definition. The value encoded indicates that an abstract type definition is being used, and the value literal implies use of a concrete schema definition.

The encodingStyle attribute contains the URI of the abstract type definition and is required only if the use attribute is assigned the encoded value. The encodingStyle attribute value can contain multiple URIs, each representing a different abstract type definition supported by the message. Each URI assigned to the encodingStyle attribute must be separated by a space.

The namespace attribute identifies the URI of the namespace used by the encodingStyle and is applied to content that isn't defined by the abstract type definition.

SOAP Fault Element

The soap:fault element defines SOAP fault details and follows the style of the soap:body element. The soap:fault has four attributes: name, use, encodingStyle, and namespace. The value of the name attribute associates the soap:fault element with the wsdl:fault element that is used for the same operation. The other attributes have the same functionality as they do within the soap:body element.

SOAP Header Element

The SOAP header element actually consists of two elements: the soap:header and the soap:headerfault. Both elements define the header for the SOAP Envelope Header element. The soap:headerfault is the default definition for the header element.

Both the soap:header element and the soap:headerfault element contain five attributes: message, part, use, encodingStyle, and namespace. The value of the message attribute identifies the SOAP message whose header is being defined. The value of the part attribute identifies the message part that defines the header type. The other attributes function the same as they do in the soap:body element.

SOAP Address Element

The soap:address element is used to identify the address that is to be used for binding the SOAP message. The soap:address element contains one attribute called location. The location attribute is assigned the URI of the port used for binding.

WSDL and HTTP Binding

Typically a web browser is used to interact with a web site, although there are other programmatic ways of achieving the same interaction. WSDL contains specifications for binding to a web site by using GET and POST, which are components of the HTTP 1.1 protocol.

Let's see how this works in Listing 23-12. This example defines two messages. The first message has three parts, where the first and third parts are of xsd:string types and the second part is an xsd:int type. The second message has one part that is of an xsd:binary type.

The portType called FirstPort defines two operations. The first operation is input and receives the FirstMessage and the second operation is output, which is the SecondMessage. This means that the web service receives a three-part message that consists of a xsd:string, xsd:int, and xsd:string. When this message is received, the web service replies with a message that contains an xsd:binary type. As you'll see later in this example, the output operation returns a JPEG file containing an image.

The service element assigns an http:address to each port and associates ports with related bindings. These bindings are defined in subsequent binding elements. You'll notice that both the FirstBinding and SecondBinding use GET and output mime:content. However, input to the FirstBinding is http:urlReplacement and input to the SecondBinding is http:urlEncoded. The ThirdBinding uses POST and inputs and outputs mime:content.

The http:address element requires one attribute, which is location. The value of the location attribute is the base address for the element.

The http:operation element contains a location attribute. The value of the location attribute is the URI that is specific for the operation and is combined with the URI of the http:address to become the URI used for the HTTP request.

The http:urlEncoded element signifies that the standard URI-encoding rules are used to encode parts of the message. The URI-encoding rule uses a name=value pair where each pair is separated with an ampersand (&) such as fname="Bob"&lname= "Smith" (see Chapter 8).

The http:urlReplacement element specifies that a replacement algorithm is used to encode parts of the message. The replacement algorithm contains steps used to search for a set of patterns in the http:operation element URI. This search occurs prior to the http:operation and http:address values being joined. When a match occurs, the related part of the message replaces the part matching the pattern.

Listing 23-12
WSDL HTTP
binding.

```
<definitions>
  <message name="FirstMessage">
    <part name="FirstPart" type="xsd:string"/>
    <part name="SecondPart" type="xsd:int"/>
    <part name="ThirdPart" type="xsd:string"/>
  </message>
  <message name="SecondMessage">
    <part name="FirstPart" type="xsd:binary"/>
  </message>
  <portType name="FirstPort">
    <operation name="FirstOperation">
      <input message="tns:FirstMessage"/>
      <output message="tns:SecondMessage"/>
    </operation>
  </portType>
  <service name="FirstService">
    <port name="FirstPort" binding="tns:FirstBinding">
      <http:address location="http://mycompany.com/"/>
    </port>
```

WEB SERVICES

```xml
      <port name="SecondPort" binding="tns:SecondBinding">
        <http:address location="http://mycompany.com/"/>
      </port>
      <port name="ThirdPort" binding="tns:ThirdBinding">
        <http:address location="http://mycompany.com/"/>
      </port>
  </service>
  <binding name="FirstBinding" type="FirstPart">
    <http:binding verb="GET"/>
    <operation name="FirstOperation">
      http:operation location="FirstOperation/A(part1)B(part2)/(part3)"/>
        <input>
          <http:urlReplacement/>
        </input>
        <output>
          <mime:content type="image/jpeg"/>
        </output>
    </operation>
  </binding>
  <binding name="SecondBinding" type="FirstPart">
    <http:binding verb="GET"/>
     <operation name="FirstOperation">
       <http:operation location="FirstOperation"/>
       <input>
         <http:urlEncoded/>
       </input>
       <output>
         <mime:content type="image/jpeg"/>
       </output>
     </operation>
  </binding>
  <binding name="ThirdBinding" type="FirstPart">
    <http:binding verb="POST"/>
      <operation name="FirstOperation">
        <http:operation location="FirstOperation"/>
        <input>
          <mime:content type="application/x-www-form-urlencoded"/>
        </input>
        <output>
          <mime:content type="image/jpeg"/>
        </output>
      </operation>
    </binding>
</definitions>
```

WSDL and MIME Binding

In addition to binding SOAP and HTTP, a WSDL document is also capable of binding MIME. Listing 23-13 illustrates how to implement this binding. This example sends a product price and a JPEG image of the product.

The example begins with a schema definition that defines two elements: ProductPrice and GetProductPrice. The ProductPrice element has one complex type that is a string. The GetProductPrice element is a float type. The complexType defines the ProductImageArray type, which is an array of binary values used to store the image of the product that is associated with the product price.

Two messages are defined outside of the schema. The first message is named FirstMessage and has one part consisting of the ProductPrice. The other message is called SecondMessage and consists of two parts, the first being the GetProductPrice element and the other being ProductImage. ProductImage is of the ProductImageArray type.

Next, the portType element called FirstPort is defined. This has two operations—the first of which is the input operation, followed by the output operation. The input operation uses the FirstMessage and the output operation uses the SecondMessage.

The port is then bound using the binding element. The soapAction attribute identifies the URI for the binding. The input is expected to be a literal and the output is a multipart MIME document that consists of two parts. These are the body and the JPEG of the product. In addition, the service element identifies the URI for the service.

The mime:content element is used whenever the only information that is necessary is a MIME string type. The mime:content element has two attributes: the part and the type. The part attribute identifies the part that is associated with the mime:content element and the type attribute specifies the type of the mime:content. The mime:multipartRelated element is used to combine MIME-formatted parts into one message.

Listing 23-13
WSDL MIME
binding.

```
<definitions>
  <types>
   <schema>
    <element name="ProductPrice">
      <complexType>
        <all>
          <element name="ProductPrice " type="string"/>
        </all>
      </complexType>
    </element>
    <element name="GetProductPrice">
      <complexType>
        <all>
          <element name="Price" type="float"/>
        </all>
```

```
          </complexType>
        </element>
        <complexType name="ProductImageArray">
          <complexContent>
            <restriction base="soapenc:Array">
              <attribute ref="soapenc:arrayType" wsdl:arrayType="xsd:binary[]"/>
            </restriction>
          <complexContent>
        </complexType>
      </schema>
    </types>
    <message name="FirstMessage">
      <part name="body" element="tns:ProductPrice"/>
    </message>
    <message name="SecondMessage">
      <part name="body" element="tns:GetProductPrice"/>
      <part name="ProductImage" type="tns:ArrayOfBinary"/>
    </message>
    <portType name="FirstPort">
      <operation name="ProductPrice">
        <input message="FirstMessage"/>
        <output message="SecondMessage"/>
      </operation>
    </portType>
    <binding name="FirstBinding" type="tns:FirstPort">
      <operation name="ProductPrice">
        <soap:operation soapAction="http://mycompany.com/ProductPrice"/>
          <input>
            <soap:body use="literal"/>
          </input>
          <output>
            <mime:multipartRelated>
              <mime:part>
                <soap:body parts="body" use="literal"/>
              </mime:part>
              <mime:part>
                <mime:content part="ProductImage" type="image/jpeg"/>
              </mime:part>
            </mime:multipartRelated>
          </output>
      </operation>
    </binding>
    <service name="ProductPriceService">
      <port name="FirstPort"binding="tns:FirstBinding">
        <soap:address location="http://mycompany.com/ProductPrice"/>
      </port>
    </service>
</definitions>
```

The Complete Reference

J2EE

Part VI

Appendixes

There always a time during development of a J2EE application when you need to quickly locate a class or method that enables your program to perform a unique task. But, you might not have the time or inclination to sift through hundreds of pages of theory and real world solutions to find it.

I've been in such situations countless times and instead of fumbling through manuals and various online help sites, I created my own guide to J2EE classes, methods, and interfaces, along with those of related technologies that are discussed in this book. The following appendixes contain information that a will help a developer get back on track fast.

Furthermore, the following J2EE classes, methods, and interfaces are organized in a way that enables you to glance through available solutions without having to read the theory that you already learned in previous sections of this book.

I'm sure you'll find this just as handy as I have.

Appendix A

HTTP References

H TTP is a protocol that defines a message specification that can be used to exchange information between two applications. A message consists of data sent by an application and other information, called a request header, sent by the browser that makes the request on behalf of the application. Here are the HTTP references used when sending and receiving an HTTP request:

- HTTP request headers
- MIME types
- HTTP 1.1 status codes
- HTTP 1.1 response headers
- Java servlet request

HTTP Request Headers

HTTP Request Header	Description
Accept	Identifies the Multipurpose Internet Mail Extension (MIME) type (see Table 10-2) of data that can be handled by the browser that made the request. The Java servlet can read the Accept HTTP request header and avoid returning data in a data format that cannot be processed by the browser. Table 10-1 contains a list of MIME types. Some browsers such as Explorer 5 send the Accept header correctly for the original request, but incorrectly when the request is reloaded by the browser.

MIME Types

MIME Types	Description
application/msword	Microsoft Word file
application/octet-stream	Unrecognized or binary data

MIME Types	Description
application/pdf	Acrobat file
application/postscript	PostScript file
application/vnd.lotus-notes	Lotus Notes file
application/vnd.ms-excel	Microsoft Excel file
application/vnd.ms-powerpoint	Microsoft PowerPoint file
application/x-gzip	Gzip archive
application/x-java-archive	JAR file
application/x-java-serialized-object	Serialized Java object
applciation/x-java-vm	Java bytecode (.class) file
application/zip	Zip file
audio/basic	Sound file in .au or .snd format
audio/mdid	MIDI sound file
audio/x-aiff	AIFF sound file
audio/x-wav	MS Windows sound file
image/gif	GIF image
image/jpeg	JPEG
image/png	PNG image
image/tiff	TIFF image
image/x-xbitmap	X Windows bitmap image
text/css	HTML Cascading Style Sheet
text/html	HTML document
text/plain	Plain text
text/xml	XML
video/mpeg	MPEG video clip
video/quicktime	QuickTime video clip

HTTP 1.1 Status Codes

Status Code	Short Message	Constant	Description
100	Continue	SC_CONTINUE	Can the client send an attached document in a follow-up request? Respond with a status 100 if the answer is yes, or 417 Expectation Failed if the answer is no.
200	OK	SC_OK	Means everything is fine.
202	Accepted	SC_ACCEPTED	The request is being acted upon, but processing is not yet complete.
204	No Content	SC_NO_CONTENT	Continue to display the previous document because no new document is available.
205	Reset Content	SC_RESET_CONTENT	No new document. Reset the document view.
301	Moved Permanently	SC_MOVED_PERMANENTLY	The document is elsewhere. Supply new URL for the document in the Location HTTP response header.

Status Code	Short Message	Constant	Description
302	Found	SC_FOUND	Interpret the URL given in the Location HTTP response header as a temporary replacement—not a permanent replacement.
303	See Other	SC_SEE_OTHER	Similar to 301 and 302 if the original request is POST; retrieve the new document with GET.
304	Not Modified	SC_NOT_MODIFIED	The client should use the cached version.
307	Temporary Redirect	No constant defined	The client is temporarily redirected to another URL.
400	Bad Request	SC_BAD_REQUEST	Bad syntax in the client request.
401	Unauthorized	SC_UNAUTHORIZED	Attempt to access a password-protected page without identifying information in the Authorization HTTP response header.

Status Code	Short Message	Constant	Description
403	Forbidden	SC_FORBIDDEN	Server refused the resource, usually because of bad file or directory permissions on the server.
404	Not Found	SC_NOT_FOUND	Resource not found.
405	Method Not Allowed	SC_METHOD_NOT_ ALLOWED	Request method not allowed for resource.
415	Unsupported Media Type	SC_UNSUPPORTED_ MEDIA_TYPE S	Server doesn't know how to handle attached document type.
500	Internal Server Error	SC_INTERNAL_ SERVER_ERROR	Generic error caused by CGI programs or servlets failure.
501	Not Implemented	SC_NOT_ IMPLEMENTED	The server cannot respond because of maintenance or overloading.
503	Service Unavailable	SC_SERVICE_UNAVAIL ABLE	The server is unable to process the request.
505	HTTP Version Not Supported	SC_HTTP_VERSION_ NOT_SUPPORTED HTTP	Version not supported by server.

HTTP 1.1 Response Headers

Allow	Specifies the request method (that is, GET or POST) supported by the server.

Cache-Control	Identifies conditions when the response document can safely be cached. One of the following possible values must be used:
	public - Document is cacheable.
	private - Store in private nonshared caches.
	no-cache - Do not cache.
	no-store - Do not cache. Do not store in a temporary location on disk.
	must-revalidate - Revalidate document with original server.
	proxy-revalidates - Same as must-revalidate. Applies only to shared caches.
	max-age=xxx - Document is stale after xx seconds.
	s-max-age=xxx - Shared caches consider the document stale after xxx seconds.
Connection	Instructs to use or not to use persistence.
Close	This is a parameter for the Connection header. If you don't want persistent connection, then you tell the server http1.0.
Content-Encoding	Indicates page encoding.
Content-Language	Indicates the language of the document.
Content-Length	Indicates the number of bytes in the message before any character encoding is applied.
Content-Type	Indicates the MIME type of the response document.
Expires	Specifies the time in milliseconds when document is out of date (long tenMinutes = 18*60*1000).
Last-Modified	Indicates the last time the document was changed.
Location	The location of the document. This gets sent with sendRedirect().
Refresh	Indicates the number of seconds to wait before asking for a page update.
Retry-After	Indicates the number of seconds to wait before requesting service, if the service is unavailable.

Set-Cookie	Identifies the cookie for the page.
WWW-Authenticate	Indicates the authorization type (that is, GASIC, DIGEST).

Java Servlet Request

Syntax	Descriptions
String getAuthType()	Returns the name of the authentication scheme.
String getContextPath()	Returns the context of the request.
Cookie[] getCookies()	Returns an array containing all of the cookies sent with this request.
long getDateHeader(String name)	Returns the value of the request header as a long value that represents a Date object.
String getHeader(String name)	Returns the value of the s request header as a String.
Enumeration getHeaderNames()	Returns an enumeration of all the header names.
Enumeration getHeaders(String name)	Returns all the values of the request header as an Enumeration.
int getIntHeader(String name)	Returns the value of the specified request header as an int.
String getMethod()	Returns the HTTP method (GET, POST, or PUT).
String getPathInfo()	Returns any extra path.
String getPathTranslated()	Returns any extra path information after the servlet name.

Table A-1.   *javax.servlet.http HttpServletRequest Class*

Syntax	Descriptions
String getQueryString()	Returns the query string in the request URL after the path.
String getRemoteUser()	Returns the user login if authenticated, or null if not authenticated.
String getRequestedSessionId()	Returns the session ID.
String getRequestURI()	Returns the URI of the URL.
StringBuffer getRequestURL()	Reconstructs the URL.
String getServletPath()	Returns the path of the URL.
HttpSession getSession()	Returns the current session or creates a session if there isn't a session.
HttpSession getSession(boolean create)	Returns the current HttpSession. If there is no session, a new session is created if the parameter is true; otherwise, returns null.
Principal getUserPrincipal()	Returns a Principal object containing the current authenticated user.
boolean isRequestedSessionIdFromCookie()	Determines if the session ID is part of a cookie.
boolean isRequestedSessionIdFromURL()	Determines if the session ID is part of the request URL.
boolean isRequestedSessionIdValid()	Determines if session ID is valid.
boolean isUserInRole(String role)	Returns a boolean indicating whether the authenticated user is specified.

Table A-1.   *javax.servlet.http HttpServletRequest Class* (continued)

The
Complete
Reference

J2EE

Appendix B

Cookie References

Y our application can save a small amount of data on a client's machine in the form of a cookie that can be referenced by a Java servlet using the Java Servlet Cookie API. Cookies have attributes and values. Here are references that you'll find useful when writing and reading cookies:

- Cookie attributes
- Java cookie

Cookie Attributes

Attribute	Description
Comment	The comment about a cookie
Domain	The domain of a cookie
MaxAge	The maximum length of time the cookie remains valid
Name	The name of the cookie
Path	The path of the cookie
Secure	The boolean value that indicates whether or not the cookie should be transmitted only over an encrypted connection
Value	The value of the cookie
Version	The version of the cookie

Java Cookie

Syntax	Descriptions
Object clone()	Overrides the standard clone method to return a copy of this cookie.
String getComment()	Returns the comment for the cookie.
String getDomain()	Returns the domain name set for this cookie.
int getMaxAge()	Returns the maximum age of the cookie, specified in seconds. By default, a -1 cookie persists until the browser shuts down.

Table B-1. *javax.servlet.http Cookie class*

Syntax	Descriptions
String getName()	Returns the name of the cookie.
String getPath()	Returns the path on the server to which the browser returns this cookie.
boolean getSecure()	Returns true if the cookie must be sent by (unspecified) secure means, or false if it is not required to be sent over (unspecified) secure means.
String getValue()	Returns the value of the cookie.
int getVersion()	Returns the version of the protocol of the cookie.
void setComment(String purpose)	Specifies a comment of a cookie.
void setDomain(String pattern)	Specifies the domain of the cookie.
void setMaxAge(int expiry)	Sets the maximum age of the cookie in seconds.
void setPath(String uri)	Specifies a path for the cookie.
void setSecure(boolean flag)	Indicates the cookie should only be sent using secure means.
void setValue(String newValue)	Assigns a new value to a cookie.
void setVersion(int v)	Sets the version of the cookie protocol.

Table B-1.   *javax.servlet.http Cookie class* (continued)

The
Complete
Reference

J2EE

Appendix C

Enterprise JavaBeans
References

717

usiness logic for a Java 2 Enterprise Edition application is coded into an Enterprise JavaBean, which interacts with other server-side J2EE components. Here are references that you'll need when writing an Enterprise JavaBean:

- Enterprise JavaBeans subelements for the <ejb-jar> element
- Enterprise JavaBeans subelements for <session> subelement and <entity> subelement
- Enterprise JavaBeans subelements for <session>, <entity> sub-<message-driven> elements
- Enterprise JavaBeans subelements for <session>, <entity> subelements for the <message-driven> element transaction
- Enterprise JavaBeans session bean
- Enterprise JavaBeans entity bean
- Enterprise JavaBeans message-driven bean
- Enterprise JavaBeans home
- Enterprise JavaBeans metadata

Enterprise JavaBeans Subelements for the <ejb-jar> Element

Subelement	Required/ Optional	Description
<description>	Optional	Describes the deployment descriptor.
<display-name>	Optional	Describes the JAR file and individual EJB components.
<small-icon>	Optional	Describes a small icon within the JAR file that is used to represent the JAR file.
<large-icon>	Optional	Describes a large icon within the JAR file that is used to represent the JAR file.
<enterprise-beans>	Required	Describes one or more Enterprise JavaBean contained in a JAR file. Only one <enterprise-beans> element is permitted in a deployment descriptor.
<ejb-client-jar>	Optional	Describes the path of the client JAR and is used by the client to access EJBs described in the deployment discriptor.
<assembly-descriptor>	Optional	Describes how EJBs are used in the J2EE application.

Enterprise JavaBeans Subelements for <session> and <entity> Subelements

Subelement	Required/Optional	Description
<description>	Optional	Describes the session or entity EJB.
<display-name>	Optional	Describes the JAR file and individual EJB components.
<small-icon>	Optional	Describes a small icon within the JAR file that is used to represent the session or entity EJB.
<large-icon>	Optional	Describes a large icon within the JAR file that is used to represent the session or entity EJB.
<ejb-name>	One required	Describes the name of the session or entity EJB.
<home>	EJB 1.1 - one required EJB 2.0 - optional	Describes the fully qualified class name of the session or entity EJB remote home interface.
<remote>	EJB 1.1 - one required EJB 2.0 - optional	Describes the fully qualified class name of the session or entity EJB remote interface.
<local-home)	EJB 2.0 - optional	Describes the fully qualified class name of the session or entity EJB local home interface.
<local>	EJB 2.0 - optional	Describes the fully qualified class name of the session or entity EJB local interface.

Subelement	Required/Optional	Description
<ejb-class>	One required	Describes the fully qualified class name of the session or entity EJB class.
<primkey-field>	Entity bean only - optional	Describes the primary key field for entity beans that use container-managed persistence.
<prim-key-class>	Entity bean only - one required	Describes the primary key class for entity beans.
<persistence-type>	Entity bean only - one required Value: Container or Bean	Specifies either container-managed persistence or bean-managed persistence.
<reentrant>	Entity bean only - one required Values: True or False	Specifies whether back (reentrant invocations) is allowed or not.
<cmp-version>	EJB 2.0 - optional EJB containers must support both EJB 2.0 CMP and EJB 1.1	Specifies the version of container-managed persistence.
<abstract-schema-name>	EJB 2.0 - optional	Specifies entity beans in a JAR file.
<cmp-field>	Entity bean only - zero or more Must exist for each container-managed field in the entity EJB class Must include a <field-name> element	For entity beans with container-managed persistence.
<env-entry>	Optional - zero or more	Specifies an environment entry available through JNDI ENC.
<ejb-ref>	Optional - zero or more	Specifies a remote EJB reference available through the JNDI NEC.

Subelement	Required/Optional	Description
<ejb-local-ref>	Optional - zero or more - EJB 2.0	Specifies a local EJB reference available through the JNDI ENC.
<resource-ref>	Optional - zero or more	Specifies reference to connection factory available through the JNDI ENC.
<resource-env-ref>	Optional - zero or more - EJB 2.0	Specifies required administered objects.
<security-role-ref>	Optional - zero or more	Specifies security roles.
<security-identity>	EJB 2.0 - optional	Describes the principal for a method.
<session-type>	One required - session bean Value: Stateful or Stateless	Specifies a session bean is either stateful or stateless.
<transaction-type>	One required - session bean Value: Bean or Container	Specifies that a session bean manages transactions or the container manages transactions.
<query>	Optional - zero or more - EJB 2.0	Specifies that it contains an EJB QL statement bound to a find or select method.

Enterprise JavaBeans Subelements for <session>, <entity> sub?- <message-driven> Elements

Subelement	Required/Optional	Description
<description>	Optional	Describes the session or entity EJB.
<display-name>	Optional	Describes the JAR file and individual EJB components.
<small-icon>	Optional	Describes a small icon within the JAR file that is used to represent the message-driven bean EJB.
<large-icon>	Optional	Describes a large icon within the JAR file that is used to represent the message-driven bean EJB.

Subelement	Required/Optional	Description
<ejb-name>	One required	Describes the name of the message-driven bean EJB.
<ejb-class>	One required	Describes the fully qualified class name of the message-driven bean EJB class.
<transaction-type>	One required - session bean Value: Bean or Container	Specifies that a message-driven bean manages transactions or the container manages transactions.
<security-identity>	EJB 2.0 - optional	Describes the principal for a method.
<env-entry>	Optional - zero or more	Specifies an environment entry available through JNDI ENC.
<ejb-ref>	Optional - zero or more	Specifies a remote EJB reference available through the JNDI NEC.
<ejb-local-ref>	Optional - zero or more - EJB 2.0	Specifies a local EJB reference available through the JNDI ENC.
<resource-ref>	Optional - zero or more	Specifies reference to the connection factory available through the JNDI ENC.
<resource-env-ref>	Optional - zero or more - EJB 2.0	Specifies required administered objects.
<message-selector>	Optional Caution: Can cause problems with XML process. See CDATA.	Specifies a conditional expression using boolean logic to choose messages that are received from a topic or queue and delivered to a client.
<acknowledge-mode>	Required Only if EJB manages transactions Value: Auto-acknowledge or Dups-ok-acknowledge	Specifies the type of acknowledgement that is used when a message is received.
<message-driven-destination>	Required Value: jacax.jms.Queue or javax.jms.Topic	Specifies the type of destination subscribed or listened to by the message-driven bean.

Enterprise JavaBeans Subelements for <session>, <entity> Subelements for the <message-driven> Element Transaction

Transaction Attribute	Client	Associated with Business Method	Associated with Resource Managers
NotSupported	None	None	None
NotSupported	Passed with client request	None	None
Required	None	Initiated by container	Initiated by container
Required	Passed with client request	Passed with client request	Passed with client request
Supports	None	None	None
Supports	Passed with client request	Passed with client request	Passed with client request
RequiresNew	None	Initiated by container	Initiated by container
RequiresNew	Passed with client request	Initiated by container	Initiated by container
Mandatory	None	Error	Not available
Mandatory	Passed with client request	Passed with client request	Passed with client request
Never	None	None	None
Never	Passed with client request	Error	Not available

Enterprise JavaBeans Session Bean

Syntax	Descriptions
void ejbActivate()	Called when the instance is activated from its "passive" state.

Table C-1. *public interface SessionBean extends EnterpriseBean*

Syntax	Descriptions
void ejbPassivate()	Called before the instance enters the "passive" state.
void ejbRemove()	Called before the EJB container ends the session object.
void setSessionContext (SessionContext con)	Set the associated session context.

Table C-1. *public interface SessionBean extends EnterpriseBean* (continued)

Enterprise JavaBeans Entity Bean

Syntax	Descriptions
void ejbActivate()	Called when an instance is removed from the pool of instances to become associated with a specific EJB object.
void ejbLoad()	Instructs the instance to synchronize its state by loading its state from the underlying database.
void ejbPassivate()	Called by the EJB container before an instance becomes disassociated with an EJB object.
void ejbRemove()	Called before the EBJ container removes the EJB object associated with the instance.
void ejbStore()	Instructs the instance to synchronize its state by storing it to the underlying database.
void setEntityContext (EntityContext ctx)	Set the associated entity context.
void unsetEntityContext()	Unset the associated entity context.

Table C-2. *public interface EntityBean extends EnterpriseBean*

Enterprise JavaBeans Message-Driven Bean

Syntax	Descriptions
void ejbRemove()	This method is called before the EJB container ends the life of the message-driven object.
void setMessageDrivenContext (MessageDrivenContext con)	Set the associated message-driven context.

Table C-3.   *public interface MessageDrivenBean extends EnterpriseBean*

Enterprise JavaBeans Home

Syntax	Descriptions
EJBMetaData getEJBMetaData()	Obtain the EJB's EJBMetaData interface.
HomeHandle getHomeHandle()	Obtain a handle for the remote home object.
void remove(Handle handle)	Remove an EJB object identified by its handle.
void remove(Object primaryKey)	Remove an EJB object identified by its primary key.

Table C-4.   *public interface EJBHome extends java.rmi.Remote*

Enterprise JavaBeans Metadata

Syntax	Descriptions
EJBHome getEJBHome()	Obtain the EJB remote home interface.
Class getHomeInterfaceClass()	Obtain the Class object for the EJB remote home interface.

Table C-5.   *public interface EJBMetaData*

Syntax	Descriptions
Class getPrimaryKeyClass()	Obtain the Class object for the EJB primary key class.
Class getRemoteInterfaceClass()	Obtain the Class object for the EJB remote interface.
boolean isSession()	Test if the EJB type is "session."
boolean isStatelessSession()	Test if the EJB type is "stateless session."

Table C-5. *public interface EJBMetaData* (continued)

Appendix D

JavaMail References

A Java 2 Enterprise Edition application is capable of interacting with other applications and Java 2 Enterprise Edition service-side components in a number of ways. One common way of communication is by using JavaMail. Here are references that you'll need when communicating via JavaMail:

- JavaMail 1.3 specifications
- JavaMail multipart data source
- JavaMail part
- JavaMail MIME body part
- JavaMail MIME message
- JavaMail MIME multipart
- JavaMail search

JavaMail 1.3 Specifications

Syntax	Descriptions
public Address getSender() throws MessagingException	Returns the value of the RFC 822 sender head field or a null if the sender head field is not contained in the email message.
public void setSender(Address address) throws MessagingException	Sets the value of the RFC 822 sender head field.
public void setContentID(String cid) throws MessagingException	Sets the content ID of an email message.
mail.mime.charset	A system property used for default charset used by JavaMail. The standard J2EE file.encoding System property is used if this is not set.
public int getDeletedMessageCount() throws MessagingException	Returns the count of the number of deleted messages in a folder.

Table D-1.   *JavaMail 1.3 Specifications Additions*

Syntax	Descriptions
public static InternetAddress[] parseHeader(String s, boolean strict) throws AddressException	Parse addresses into InternetAddress object. If strict is true, many but not all of the RFC 822 syntax rules are enforced. If strict is false, the full syntax rules for individual addresses are not enforced. The mail.mime.address.strict property is a new JavaMail 1.3 addition.
public InternetAddress(String address, boolean strict) throws AddressException	Validates that the address conforms to the syntax rules of RFC 822. The mail.mime.address.strict property is a new JavaMail 1.3 addition.
public boolean isGroup()	Indicates whether the address is an RFC 822 group address.
public InternetAddress[] getGroup(boolean strict) throws AddressException	Returns members of a group address.

Table D-1. *JavaMail 1.3 Specifications Additions* (continued)

JavaMail Multipart Data Source

Syntax	Descriptions
BodyPart getBodyPart(int index)	Get the specified part.
int getCount()	Return the number of enclosed BodyPart objects.

Table D-2. *public interface MultipartDataSource extends DataSource*

JavaMail Part

Syntax	Descriptions
void addHeader(String header_name, String header_value)	Add this value to the existing values for the header.
Enumeration getAllHeaders()	Return all the headers from the part as an enumeration of Header objects.
Object getContent()	Return the content as a Java object.
String getContentType()	Returns the Content-Type of the content of the part.
DataHandler getDataHandler()	Return a DataHandler for the content within the part.
String getDescription()	Return a description String for the part.
String getDisposition()	Return the disposition of the part.
String getFileName()	Get the filename associated with this part.
String[] getHeader(String header_name)	Get all the headers for the header name.
InputStream getInputStream()	Return an input stream for the part's content.
int getLineCount()	Return the number of lines in the content of this part.
Enumeration getMatchingHeaders (String[] header_names)	Return matching headers from this part as an enumeration of Header objects.
Enumeration getNonMatchingHeaders (String[] header_names)	Return nonmatching headers from the envelope as an enumeration of Header objects.
int getSize()	Return the size of the content of the part in bytes.
boolean isMimeType(String mimeType)	Is this part of the specified MIME type?

Table D-3.   *public interface Part*

Syntax	Descriptions
void removeHeader(String header_name)	Remove all headers with this name.
void setContent(Multipart mp)	Set the Multipart object as the message's content.
void setContent(Object obj, String type)	Set the part's content.
void setDataHandler(DataHandler dh)	Set the part's content.
void setDescription(String description)	Set a description String for the part.
void setDisposition(String disposition)	Set the disposition of the part.
void setFileName(String filename)	Set the filename associated with the part.
void setHeader(String header_name, String header_value)	Set the value for the header.
void setText(java.lang.String text)	Set the String as the part's content with a MIME type of "text/plain".
void writeTo(OutputStream os)	Output a bytestream for this part.

Table D-3. *public interface Part* (continued)

JavaMail MIME Body Part

Syntax	Descriptions
void addHeader(String name, String value)	Add this value to the existing values for the header.
void addHeaderLine(String line)	Add a header line to the part.
Enumeration getAllHeaderLines()	Get all header lines as an enumeration of Strings.
Enumeration getAllHeaders()	Return all the headers as an enumeration of Header objects.

Table D-4. *public class MimeBodyPart extends BodyPart implements MimePart*

Syntax	Descriptions
Object getContent()	Return the content as a Java object.
String getContentID()	Return the value of the "Content-ID" header field.
String[] getContentLanguage()	Get the languages specified in the Content-Language header of the MimePart.
String getContentMD5()	Return the value of the "Content-MD5" header field.
protected InputStream getContentStream()	Produce the raw bytes of the content.
String getContentType()	Return the value of the RFC 822 "Content-Type" header field.
DataHandler getDataHandler()	Return a DataHandler for the part's content.
String getDescription()	Return the "Content-Description" header field of the body part.
String getDisposition()	Return the value of the "Content-Disposition" header field.
String getEncoding()	Return the content transfer encoding from the "Content-Transfer-Encoding" header field.
String getFileName()	Get the filename associated with the part.
String[] getHeader(String name)	Get all the headers.
String getHeader(String name, String delimiter)	Get all the headers separated by the delimiter for the header name.
InputStream getInputStream()	Return a decoded input stream for the part's content.
int getLineCount()	Return the number of lines for the content of this part.

Table D-4.   *public class MimeBodyPart extends BodyPart implements MimePart (continued)*

Syntax	Descriptions
Enumeration getMatchingHeaderLines (String[] names)	Get matching header lines as an enumeration of Strings.
Enumeration getMatchingHeaders (String[] names)	Return matching headers as an enumeration of Header objects.
Enumeration getNonMatching HeaderLines(String[] names)	Get nonmatching header lines as an enumeration of Strings.
Enumeration getNonMatchingHeaders (String[] names)	Return nonmatching headers as an enumeration of Header objects.
int getSize()	Return the size of the content of the body part in bytes.
boolean isMimeType(String mimeType)	Is this part of the specified MIME type?
void removeHeader(String name)	Remove all headers with this name.
void setContent(Multipart mp)	Set the body part's content to a Multipart object.
void setContent(Object o, String type)	Set the body part's content.
void setContentLanguage(String[] languages)	Set the Content-Language header of the MimePart.
void setContentMD5(String md5)	Set the "Content-MD5" header field of the body part.
void setDataHandler(DataHandler dh)	Set the body part's content.
void setDescription(String description)	Set the "Content-Description" header field for the body part.
void setDescription(String description, String charset)	Set the "Content-Description" header field for the body part.
void setDisposition(String disposition)	Set the "Content-Disposition" header field of the body part.
void setFileName(String filename)	Set the filename associated with this body part.

Table D-4.   *public class MimeBodyPart extends BodyPart implements MimePart (continued)*

Syntax	Descriptions
void setHeader(String name, String value)	Set the value for the header.
void setText(String text)	Set the part's content, with a MIME type of "text/plain".
void setText(String text, String charset)	Set the part's content, with a MIME type of "text/plain" and the specified charset.
void updateHeaders()	Examine the content of this body part and update MIME headers.
void writeTo(OutputStream os)	Output the body part as an RFC 822 format stream.

Table D-4.   *public class MimeBodyPart extends BodyPart implements MimePart* (continued)

JavaMail MIME Message

Syntax	Descriptions
void addFrom(Address[] addresses)	Add the specified addresses to the existing "From" field.
void addHeader(String name, String value)	Add this value to the existing values for this header_name.
void addHeaderLine(String line)	Add a raw RFC 822 header line.
void addRecipients (Message.RecipientType type, Address[] addresses)	Add the given addresses to the specified recipient type.
Enumeration getAllHeaderLines()	Get all header lines as an enumeration of Strings.

Table D-5.   *public class MimeMessage extends Message implements MimePart*

Syntax	Descriptions
Enumeration getAllHeaders()	Return all the headers as an enumeration of Header objects.
Address[] getAllRecipients()	Get all the recipient addresses for the message.
Object getContent()	Return the content as a Java object.
String getContentID()	Return the value of the "Content-ID" header field.
String[] getContentLanguage()	Get the languages specified in the "Content-Language" header field of this message.
String getContentMD5()	Return the value of the "Content-MD5" header field.
protected InputStream getContentStream()	Produce the raw bytes of the content.
String getContentType()	Return the value of the RFC 822 "Content-Type" header field.
DataHandler getDataHandler()	Return a DataHandler for the content.
String getDescription()	Return the "Content-Description" header field.
String getDisposition()	Return the value of the "Content-Disposition" header field.
String getEncoding()	Return the content transfer encoding from the "Content-Transfer-Encoding" header field.
String getFileName()	Get the filename associated with this message.
Flags getFlags()	Return a Flags object containing the flags for this message.
Address[] getFrom()	Return the value of the RFC 822 "From" header fields.

Table D-5. *public class MimeMessage extends Message implements MimePart* (continued)

Syntax	Descriptions
String[] getHeader(String name)	Get all the headers.
String getHeader(String name, String delimiter)	Get all the headers separated by the delimiter for the header.
InputStream getInputStream()	Return a decoded input stream for the content.
int getLineCount()	Return the number of lines for the content of this message.
Enumeration getMatchingHeaderLines(String[] names)	Get matching header lines as an enumeration of Strings.
Enumeration getMatchingHeaders(String[] names)	Return matching headers as an enumeration of Header objects.
String getMessageID()	Return the value of the "Message-ID" header field.
Enumeration getNonMatchingHeaderLines(String[] names)	Get nonmatching header lines as an enumeration of Strings.
Enumeration getNonMatchingHeaders(String[] names)	Return nonmatching headers as an enumeration of Header objects.
Date getReceivedDate()	Return the date the message was received.
Address[] getRecipients(Message.RecipientType type)	Return the recipients specified by the type.
Address[] getReplyTo()	Return the value of the RFC 822 "Reply-To" header field.
Date getSentDate()	Return the value of the RFC 822 "Date" field.
int getSize()	Return the size of the content.

Table D-5. *public class MimeMessage extends Message implements MimePart* (continued)

Syntax	Descriptions
String getSubject()	Return the value of the "Subject" header field.
boolean isMimeType(String mimeType)	Is this part of the specified MIME type?
boolean isSet(Flags.Flag flag)	Check whether the flag specified in the flag argument is set in this message.
void removeHeader(String name)	Remove all headers with this name.
Message reply(boolean replyToAll)	Get a new message suitable for a reply to the message.
void saveChanges()	Updates the appropriate header fields to be consistent with the message's contents.
void setContent(Multipart mp)	Set the message's content to a Multipart object.
void setContent(Object o, String type)	Set the message's content.
void setContentID(String cid)	Set the "Content-ID" header field.
void setContentLanguage(String[] languages)	Set the "Content-Language" header.
void setContentMD5(String md5)	Set the "Content-MD5" header field.
void setDataHandler(DataHandler dh)	Set the part's content.
void setDescription(String description)	Set the "Content-Description" header field.
void setDescription(String description, String charset)	Set the "Content-Description" header field.
void setDisposition(String disposition)	Set the "Content-Disposition" header field.
void setFileName(String filename)	Set the filename associated with the part.

Table D-5.   *public class MimeMessage extends Message implements MimePart* (continued)

Syntax	Descriptions
void setFlags(Flags flag, boolean set)	Set the flags for this message.
void setFrom()	Set the RFC 822 "From" header field using the value of the InternetAddress.getLocalAddress() method.
void setFrom(Address address)	Set the RFC 822 "From" header field.
void setHeader(String name, String value)	Set the value for the named header.
void setRecipients (Message.RecipientType type, Address[] addresses)	Set the recipient type to the addresses.
void setReplyTo(Address[] addresses)	Set the RFC 822 "Reply-To" header field.
void setSentDate(Date d)	Set the RFC 822 "Date" header field.
void setSubject(String subject)	Set the "Subject" header field.
void setSubject(String subject, String charset)	Set the "Subject" header field.
void setText(String text)	Set the given String as this part's content, with a MIME type of "text/plain".
void setText(String text, String charset)	Set String as this part's content, with a MIME type of "text/plain" and the specified charset.
void writeTo(OutputStream os)	Output the message as an RFC 822 format stream.
void writeTo(OutputStream os, String[]ignoreList)	Output the message as an RFC 822 format stream, without headers.

Table D-5. *public class MimeMessage extends Message implements MimePart* (continued)

JavaMail MIME Multipart

Syntax	Descriptions
BodyPart getBodyPart(int index)	Get specified BodyPart.
BodyPart getBodyPart(String CID)	Get MimeBodyPart referred to by ContentID (CID).
int getCount()	Return the number of enclosed BodyPart objects.
void setSubType(String subtype)	Set the subtype.
protected void updateHeaders()	Update headers.
void writeTo(OutputStream os)	Iterates through all the parts and outputs each Mime part.

Table D-6.   *public class MimeMultipart extends Multipart*

JavaMail Search

Syntax	Descriptions
protected AddressStringTerm (String pattern)	Constructor. Implements string comparisons for message addresses.
protected AddressTerm(Address address)	Constructor. Implements message address comparisons.
AndTerm(SearchTerm[] t)	Constructor. Takes an array of search terms and implements the logical AND operator on individual search terms.

Table D-7.   *javax.mail.search*

Syntax	Descriptions
AndTerm(SearchTerm t1, SearchTerm t2)	Constructor. Implements the logical AND operator on individual search terms.
BodyTerm(String pattern)	Constructor. Implements searches on message body.
public ComparisonTerm()	Constructor. Models the comparison operator.
protected DateTerm(int comparison, Date date)	Constructor. Implements comparisons for dates.
FlagTerm(Flags flags, boolean set)	Constructor. Implements comparisons for message flags.
FromStringTerm(String pattern)	Constructor. Implements string comparisons for the From address header.
FromTerm(Address address)	Constructor. Implements string comparisons for the From address header.
HeaderTerm(String headerName, String pattern)	Constructor. Implements comparisons for message headers.
protected IntegerComparisonTerm (int comparison, int number)	Constructor. Implements comparisons for integers.
MessageIDTerm(String msgid)	Constructor. Models the RFC 822 "MessageId" unique per message.
MessageNumberTerm(int number)	Constructor. Implements comparisons for message numbers.
NotTerm(SearchTerm t)	Constructor. Implements the logical NEGATION operator.
OrTerm(SearchTerm[] t)	Constructor. Takes an array of search terms and implements the logical OR operator on individual SearchTerms.

Table D-7.   *javax.mail.search* (continued)

Syntax	Descriptions
OrTerm(SearchTerm t1, SearchTerm t2)	Constructor. Implements the logical OR operator on individual search terms.
ReceivedDateTerm(int comparison, Date date)	Constructor. Implements comparisons for the Message Received date.
RecipientStringTerm (Message.RecipientType type, String pattern)	Constructor. Implements string comparisons for the Recipient address headers.
RecipientTerm(Message.RecipientType type, Address address)	Constructor. Implements comparisons for the Recipient address headers.
SearchTerm()	Constructor. Search criteria expressed as a tree of search terms for the search expression.
SentDateTerm(int comparison, Date date)	Constructor. Implements comparisons for the Message Sent date.
SizeTerm(int comparison, int size)	Constructor. Implements comparisons for message sizes.
protected StringTerm(String pattern)	Constructor. Implements the match method for Strings.
protected StringTerm(String pattern, boolean ignoreCase)	Constructor. Implements the match method for Strings.
SubjectTerm(String pattern)	Constructor. Implements case-insensitive comparisons for the Message Subject header.

Table D-7.   *javax.mail.search* (continued)

Appendix E

Java Interface Definition Language and CORBA

Java Interface Definition Language (IDL) is based on the Common Object Request Brokerage Architecture (CORBA), which is one of the original methods used to standardize the distribution of objects within a distributed environment. Your Java 2 Enterprise Edition application is likely to interact with web services written in other popular languages such as C, C++, and COBOL that require you to use IDL. Here are references that you'll need to interact with these Web services.

Mapping IDL to Java

IDL	Java
module myApplication	package myApplication
interface myApplication	public interface myApplication
string myMethod()	String myMethod()
oneway void shutdown()	void Shutdown()

Appendix F

Java Remote Method Invocation

A Java 2 Enterprise Edition application can communicate with other Java applications that run on a different Java Virtual Machine by using the Java Remote Method Invocation system. Here are references that you'll need when writing a Java application to interact with another Java application running on a different Java Virtual Machine:

- Java Remote Method Invocation Naming
- Java Remote Method Invocation Registry
- Java Remote Method Invocation Locate Registry
- Java Remote Method Invocation Remote Referencing
- Java Remote Method Invocation Client Sockets
- Java Remote Method Invocation Failure Handler
- Java Remote Method Invocation Server Sockets
- Java Remote Method Invocation Server References
- Java Remote Method Invocation Remote Object
- Java Remote Method Invocation Remote Server
- Java Remote Method Invocation Class Loader
- Java Remote Method Invocation Sockets

Java Remote Method Invocation Naming

Syntax	Descriptions
static void bind(String name, Remote obj)	Binds the specified name to a remote object.
static String list(String name)	Returns an array of the names bound in the registry.
static Remote lookup(String name)	Returns a reference for a remote object.
static void rebind(String name, Remote obj)	Rebinds the specified name to a new remote object.
static void unbind(String name)	Destroys the binding that is associated with a remote object.

Table F-1.   *public final class Naming* ***extends Object***

Java Remote Method Invocation Registry

Syntax	Descriptions
void bind(String name, Remote obj)	Binds a remote reference to the specified name in this registry.
String[] list()	Returns an array of the names bound in this registry.
Remote lookup(String name)	Returns the remote reference bound to the specified name in this registry.
void rebind(String name, Remote obj)	Replaces the binding for the specified name in this registry.
void unbind(String name)	Removes the binding for the specified name in this registry.

Table F-2.   *public interface Registry* ***extends Remote***

Java Remote Method Invocation Locate Registry

Syntax	Descriptions
static Registry createRegistry(int port)	Creates and exports a Registry on the local host.
static Registry createRegistry (int port, RMIClientSocketFactory csf, RMIServerSocketFactory ssf)	Creates and exports a Registry on the local host.
static Registry getRegistry()	Returns the remote object Registry.
static Registry getRegistry(int port)	Returns the remote object Registry.
static Registry getRegistry (String host)	Returns a reference to the remote object Registry.
static Registry getRegistry (String host, int port)	Returns a reference to the remote object Registry.
static Registry getRegistry(String host, int port, RMIClientSocketFactory csf)	Returns a locally created remote reference to the remote object Registry.

Table F-3.   *public final class LocateRegistry* ***extends Object***

Java Remote Method Invocation Remote Referencing

Syntax	Descriptions
String getRefClass (ObjectOutput out)	Returns the class name of the ref type to be serialized onto the stream "out."
boolean remoteEquals (RemoteRef obj)	Compares two remote objects for equality.
int remoteHashCode()	Returns a hash code for a remote object.
String remoteToString()	Returns the reference of this remote object.

Table F-4.   *public interface RemoteRef **extends Externalizable***

Java Remote Method Invocation Client Sockets

Syntax	Description
Socket createSocket (String host, int port)	Create a client socket connected to the specified host and port.

Table F-5.   *public interface RMIClientSocketFactory*

Java Remote Method Invocation Failure Handler

Syntax	Description
boolean failure (Exception ex)	The failure is invoked when the RMI runtime is unable to create a ServerSocket via the RMISocketFactory.

Table F-6.   *public interface RMIFailureHandler*

Java Remote Method Invocation **Server Sockets**

Syntax	Description
ServerSocket createServerSocket (int port)	Create a server socket on the specified port.

Table F-7.   *public interface RMIServerSocketFactory*

Java Remote Method Invocation **Server References**

Syntax	Descriptions
RemoteStub exportObject (Remote obj, Object data)	Creates a client stub object for a remote object.
String getClientHost()	Returns the hostname of the current client.

Table F-8.   *public interface ServerRef* **extends RemoteRef**

Java Remote Method Invocation **Remote Object**

Syntax	Descriptions
boolean equals(Object obj)	Compares two remote objects.
RemoteRef getRef()	Returns the remote reference for the remote object.
int hashCode()	Returns a hash code for a remote object.
String toString()	Returns the value of a remote object.
static Remote toStub(Remote obj)	Returns the stub for the remote object obj.

Table F-9.   *public abstract class RemoteObject extends Object implements Remote, Serializable*

Java Remote Method Invocation Remote Server

Syntax	Descriptions
static String getClientHost()	Returns the client host for the remote method invocation.
static PrintStream getLog()	Returns stream for the RMI call log.
static void setLog(OutputStream out)	Log RMI calls to the output stream out.

Table F-10. *public abstract class RemoteServer* ***extends RemoteObject***

Java Remote Method Invocation Class Loader

Syntax	Descriptions
static String getClassAnnotation (Class cl)	Returns a string RMI used to annotate the class descriptor when marshalling objects.
static ClassLoader getClassLoader (String codebase)	Returns a class loader that loads classes from the given code base URL path.
static RMIClassLoaderSpi getDefaultProviderInstance()	Returns the canonical instance of the default provider for the service provider interface RMIClassLoaderSpi.
static Class loadClass (String codebase, String name)	Loads a class from a code base URL path.
static Class loadClass (String codebase, String name, ClassLoader defaultLoader)	Loads a class from a code base URL path.
static Class loadClass (URL codebase, String name)	Loads a class from a code base URL.
static Class loadProxyClass (String codebase, String[] interfaces, ClassLoader defaultLoader)	Loads a dynamic proxy class that implements a set of interfaces with the given names from a code base URL path.

Table F-11. *public class RMIClassLoader* ***extends Object***

Java Remote Method Invocation Sockets

Syntax	Descriptions
abstract ServerSocket createServerSocket(int port)	Creates a server socket on the specified port.
abstract Socket createSocket (String host, int port)	Creates a client socket connection.
static RMISocketFactory getDefaultSocketFactory()	Returns a reference to the default socket.
static RMIFailureHandler getFailureHandler()	Returns the handler for socket creation failure set by the setFailureHandler() method.
static RMISocketFactory getSocketFactory()	Returns the socket factory set by the setSocketFactory() method.
static void setFailureHandler (RMIFailureHandler fh)	Sets the failure handler to be called by the RMI runtime if server socket creation fails.
static void setSocketFactory (RMISocketFactory fac)	Set the global socket factory from which RMI gets sockets.

Table F-12.   *public abstract class RMISocketFactory extends Object implements RMIClientSocketFactory, RMIServerSocketFactory*

The
Complete
Reference

Appendix G

Java Message Service

ommunication between Java 2 Enterprise Edition applications is handled by the Java postal system, technically called the Java Message Service. Here are references that you'll need when writing communications routines in your Java 2 Enterprise Edition application to communicate with other Java applications:

- Java Message Service Message
- Java Message Service Queue
- Java Message Service Queue Sender
- Java Message Service Topic Publisher
- Java Message Service Topic Subscriber

Java Message Service Message

Syntax	Descriptions
void acknowledge()	Acknowledge messages received.
void clearBody()	Remove the message body.
void clearProperties()	Remove a message's properties.
boolean getBooleanProperty (String name)	Return the boolean property value.
byte getByteProperty(String name)	Return the byte property value.
double getDoubleProperty (String name)	Return the double property value.
float getFloatProperty(String name)	Return the float property value.
int getIntProperty(String name)	Return the integer property value.
String getJMSCorrelationID()	Get the message correlation ID.
byte[] getJMSCorrelationIDAsBytes()	Get the message correlation ID as an array of bytes.
int getJMSDeliveryMode()	Get the message delivery mode.
Destination getJMSDestination()	Get the message destination.
long getJMSExpiration()	Get the message's expiration value.
String getJMSMessageID()	Get the message ID.

Table G-1. *public interface Message*

Syntax	Descriptions
int getJMSPriority()	Get the message priority.
boolean getJMSRedelivered()	The message is being redelivered.
Destination getJMSReplyTo()	Get the message reply information.
long getJMSTimestamp()	Get the message timestamp.
String getJMSType()	Get the message type.
long getLongProperty(String name)	Return the long property value.
Object getObjectProperty(String name)	Return the Java object property.
Enumeration getPropertyNames()	Return an enumeration of property names.
short getShortProperty(String name)	Return the short property value.
String getStringProperty(String name)	Return the String property value.
boolean propertyExists(String name)	Check if a property value exists.
void setBooleanProperty (String name, boolean value)	Set a boolean property value.
void setByteProperty (String name, byte value)	Set a byte property value.
void setDoubleProperty (String name, double value)	Set a double property value.
void setFloatProperty (String name, float value)	Set a float property value.
void setIntProperty (String name, int value)	Set an integer property value.
void setJMSCorrelationID (String correlationID)	Set the correlation ID for the message.
void setJMSCorrelationIDAsBytes (byte[] correlationID)	Set the correlation ID as an array of bytes for the message.
void setJMSDeliveryMode (int deliveryMode)	Set the delivery mode for this message.

Table G-1. *public interface Message* (continued)

Syntax	Descriptions
void setJMSDestination(Destination destination)	Set the destination for this message.
void setJMSExpiration(long expiration)	Set the message's expiration value.
void setJMSMessageID(String id)	Set the message ID.
void setJMSPriority(int priority)	Set the priority for this message.
void setJMSRedelivered(boolean redelivered)	The message should be redelivered.
void setJMSReplyTo (Destination replyTo)	Set reply information.
void setJMSTimestamp (long timestamp)	Set the message timestamp.
void setJMSType(String type)	Set the message type.
void setLongProperty (String name, long value)	Set a long property value.
void setObjectProperty (String name, Object value)	Set a Java object property value.
void setShortProperty (String name, short value)	Set a short property value.
void setStringProperty (String name, String value)	Set a String property value.

Table G-1.   *public interface Message* (continued)

Java Message Service Queue

Syntax	Descriptions
String getQueueName()	Get the name of this queue.
String toString()	Return a printed version of the queue name.

Table G-2.   *public interface Queue* ***extends Destination***

Java Message Service Queue Sender

Syntax	Descriptions
Queue getQueue()	Get the queue associated with sender.
void send(Message message)	Send a message to the queue.
void send(Message message, int deliveryMode, int priority, long timeToLive)	Send a message specifying delivery mode, priority, and time to live.
void send(Queue queue, Message message)	Send a message to a queue for an unidentified message producer.
void send(Queue queue, Message message, int deliveryMode, int priority, long timeToLive)	Send a message to a queue for an unidentified message producer, specifying delivery mode, priority, and time to live.

Table G-3.   *public interface QueueSender* **extends MessageProducer**

Java Message Service Topic Publisher

Syntax	Descriptions
Topic getTopic()	Get the topic.
void publish(Message message)	Publish a message using the topic's default delivery mode, time to live, and priority.
void publish(Message message, int deliveryMode, int priority, long timeToLive)	Publish a message specifying delivery mode, priority, and time to live to the topic.
void publish(Topic topic, Message message)	Publish a message for an unidentified message producer.
void publish(Topic topic, Message message, int deliveryMode, int priority, long timeToLive)	Publish a message for an unidentified message producer, specifying delivery mode, priority, and time to live.

Table G-4.   *public interface TopicPublisher* **extends MessageProducer**

Java Message Service Topic Subscriber

Syntax	Descriptions
boolean getNoLocal()	Get the NoLocal attribute.
Topic getTopic()	Get the topic.

Table G-5. *public interface TopicSubscriber* **extends MessageConsumer**

Appendix H

Java Security

You must make your Java 2 Enterprise Edition application secure in a web services environment, and Sun Microsystems, Inc. and the Java community have developed ways of making the Java environment stable in order to thwart attempts to violate security. Here are references used to secure a Java 2 Enterprise Edition application:

- Java Security Domain Combiner
- Java Security Guard
- Java Security Key
- Java Security Principal
- Java Security Privilege
- Java Security Access Control
- Java Security Algorithm Parameter
- Java Security Permissions
- Java Security Code Source
- Java Security Streams
- Java Security Message
- Java Security Domain Protection
- Java Security Provider
- Java Security Secure Class Loader
- Java Security Randomizer
- Java Security Signature

Java Security Domain Combiner

Syntax	Description
ProtectionDomain[] combine(ProtectionDomain[] currentDomains, ProtectionDomain[] assignedDomains)	Modify or update a ProtectionDomain.

Table H-1. *public interface DomainCombiner*

Java Security Guard

Syntax	Description
void checkGuard(Object object)	Determines if access is allowed to the guarded object.

Table H-2.   *public interface Guard*

Syntax	Description
Object getObject()	Returns a guarded object.

Table H-3.   *public class GuardedObject extends Object, implements Serializable*

Java Security Key

Syntax	Descriptions
String getAlgorithm()	Returns the algorithm name for a key.
byte[] getEncoded()	Returns a key in its encoding format, or null if encoding is not supported.
String getFormat()	Returns the name of the primary encoding format.

Table H-4.   *public interface Key extends Serializable*

Syntax	Descriptions
PrivateKey generatePrivate(KeySpec keySpec)	Generates a private key object.
PublicKey generatePublic(KeySpec keySpec)	Generates a public key object.
String getAlgorithm()	Returns the name of an algorithm.
static KeyFactory getInstance(String algorithm)	Generates a KeyFactory object.
static KeyFactory getInstance(String algorithm, Provider provider)	Generates a KeyFactory object.
static KeyFactory getInstance(String algorithm, String provider)	Generates a KeyFactory object.
KeySpec getKeySpec(Key key, Class keySpec)	Returns a key material of a key object.
Provider getProvider()	Returns the provider of a key factory object.
Key translateKey(Key key)	Translates a key object into a key object of a key factory.

Table H-5.   *public class KeyFactory extends Object*

Syntax	Descriptions
protected abstract PrivateKey engineGeneratePrivate(KeySpec keySpec)	Generates a private key object.
protected abstract PublicKey engineGeneratePublic(KeySpec keySpec)	Generates a public key object.
protected abstract KeySpec engineGetKeySpec(Key key, Class keySpec)	Returns key of a key object.
protected abstract Key engineTranslateKey(Key key)	Translates a key object into a key object of a key factory.

Table H-6.   *public abstract class KeyFactorySpi extends Object*

Syntax	Descriptions
PrivateKey getPrivate()	Returns a reference to the private key component.
PublicKey getPublic()	Returns a reference to the public key component.

Table H-7. *public final class KeyPair extends Object, implements Serializable*

Syntax	Descriptions
KeyPair generateKeyPair()	Generates a key pair.
KeyPair genKeyPair()	Generates a key pair.
String getAlgorithm()	Returns the name of the algorithm.
static KeyPairGenerator getInstance(String algorithm)	Generates a KeyPairGenerator object.
static KeyPairGenerator getInstance(String algorithm, Provider provider)	Generates a KeyPairGenerator object.
static KeyPairGenerator getInstance(String algorithm, String provider)	Generates a KeyPairGenerator object.
Provider getProvider()	Returns the provider of a key pair generator object.
void initialize(Algorithm ParameterSpec params)	Initializes the key pair generator.
void initialize(Algorithm ParameterSpec params, SecureRandom random)	Initializes the key pair generator.
void initialize(int keysize)	Initializes the key pair generator.
void initialize(int keysize, SecureRandom random)	Initializes the key pair generator.

Table H-8. *public abstract class KeyPairGenerator extends KeyPairGeneratorSpi*

Syntax	Descriptions
abstract KeyPair generateKeyPair()	Generates a key pair.
void initialize(AlgorithmParameterSpec params, SecureRandom random)	Initializes the key pair generator.
abstract void initialize(int keysize, SecureRandom random)	Initializes the key pair generator.

Table H-9.   *public abstract class KeyPairGeneratorSpi extends Object*

Syntax	Descriptions
void deleteEntry(String alias)	Deletes the entry identified.
String getCertificateAlias (Certificate cert)	Returns alias of the first keystore entry whose certificate matches the given certificate.
Date getCreationDate(String alias)	Returns the creation date of an identified entry.
Certificate getCertificate(String alias)	Returns a certificate.
static String getDefaultType()	Returns the default KeyStore type.
static KeyStore getInstance(String type)	Generates a KeyStore object.
static KeyStore getInstance(String type, Provider provider)	Generates a KeyStore object.
static KeyStore getInstance(String type, String provider)	Generates a keystore object.
Key getKey(String alias, char[] password)	Returns the key.
Provider getProvider()	Returns the provider of a keystore.
String getType()	Returns the type of a keystore.
boolean isCertificateEntry(String alias)	Returns true if the entry is a trusted certificate entry.

Table H-10.   *public class KeyStore extends ObjectEnumeration aliases()*

Syntax	Descriptions
boolean isKeyEntry(String alias)	Returns true if the entry is a key entry.
void load(InputStream stream, char[] password)	Loads this KeyStore from an input stream.
void setCertificateEntry(String alias, Certificate cert)	Assigns the given certificate.
void setKeyEntry(String alias, byte[] key, Certificate[] chain)	Assigns the given key.
void setKeyEntry(String alias, Key key, char[] password, Certificate[] chain)	Assigns the given key to a given alias.
int size()	Retrieves the number of entries in this keystore.
void store(OutputStream stream, char[] password)	Stores this keystore to an output stream.

Table H-10. *public class KeyStore extends ObjectEnumeration aliases()* (continued)

Syntax	Descriptions
abstract Enumeration engineAliases()	Lists aliases of a keystore.
abstract boolean engineContainsAlias(String alias)	Determines the existence of an alias.
abstract void engineDeleteEntry (String alias)	Deletes an entry.
abstract Certificate engineGetCertificate(String alias)	Returns a certificate.
abstract String engineGetCertificateAlias (Certificate cert)	Returns an alias of the keystore entry.

Table H-11. *public abstract class KeyStoreSpi extends Object*

Syntax	Descriptions
abstract Certificate[] engineGetCertificateChain(String alias)	Returns a certificate chain.
abstract Date engineGetCreationDate(String alias)	Returns creation date of an entry.
abstract Key engineGetKey(String alias, char[] password)	Returns a key associated with an alias.
abstract boolean engineIsCertificateEntry(String alias)	Returns true if an entry of an alias is a trusted certificate entry.
abstract boolean engineIsKeyEntry(String alias)	Returns true if an entry of an alias is a key entry.
abstract void engineLoad(InputStream stream, char[] password)	Loads a keystore from an input stream.
abstract void engineSetCertificateEntry(String alias, Certificate cert)	Assigns a certificate to a given alias.
abstract void engineSetKeyEntry(String alias, byte[] key, Certificate[] chain)	Assigns a protected key to a given alias.
abstract void engineSetKeyEntry(String alias, Key key, char[] password, Certificate[] chain)	Assigns a key to a given alias.
abstract int engineSize()	Returns the number of entries in a keystore.
abstract void engineStore (OutputStream stream, char[] password)	Stores this keystore to an output stream.

Table H-11. *public abstract class KeyStoreSpi extends Object* (continued)

Java Security Principal

Syntax	Descriptions
boolean equals(Object another)	Compares a principal to an object.
String getName()	Returns principal name.
int hashCode()	Returns a hash code.
String toString()	Returns a string of a principal.

Table H-12. *public interface Principal*

Java Security Privilege

Syntax	Description
Object run()	Performs computation.

Table H-13. *public interface PrivilegedAction*

Syntax	Description
Object run()	Performs computation.

Table H-14. *public interface PrivilegedExceptionAction*

Java Security Access Control

Syntax	Descriptions
void checkPermission (Permission perm)	Determines whether the access request should be allowed or denied.
boolean equals(Object obj)	Compares AccessControlContext objects.
DomainCombiner getDomainCombiner()	Returns the domain combiner.
int hashCode()	Returns the hash code value.

Table H-15.   *public final class AccessControlContext extends Object*

Syntax	Descriptions
static void checkPermission (Permission perm)	Determines if access should be allowed or denied.
static Object doPrivileged (PrivilegedAction action)	Performs the privileged action.
static Object doPrivileged (PrivilegedAction action, AccessControlContext context)	Performs the privileged action.
static Object doPrivileged (PrivilegedExceptionAction action	Performs the privileged exception action.
static Object doPrivileged (PrivilegedExceptionAction action, AccessControlContext context)	Performs the privileged exception action.
static AccessControlContext getContext()	Takes a snapshot of the current calling context.

Table H-16.   *public final class AccessController extends Object*

Java Security Algorithm Parameter

Syntax	Descriptions
AlgorithmParameters generateParameters()	Generates parameters.
String getAlgorithm()	Returns the standard name of the algorithm.
static AlgorithmParameterGenerator getInstance(String algorithm)	Generates an AlgorithmParameter Generator object.
static AlgorithmParameterGenerator getInstance(String algorithm, Provider provider)	Generates an AlgorithmParameter Generator object.
static AlgorithmParameterGenerator getInstance(String algorithm, String provider)	Generates an AlgorithmParameter Generator object.
Provider getProvider()	Returns the provider of an algorithm.
void init(AlgorithmParameterSpec genParamSpec)	Initializes a parameter generator.
void init(AlgorithmParameterSpec genParamSpec, SecureRandom random)	Initializes a parameter generator.
void init(int size)	Initializes a parameter generator.
void init(int size, SecureRandom random)	Initializes a parameter generator.

Table H-17.   *public class AlgorithmParameterGenerator extends Object*

Syntax	Descriptions
protected abstract AlgorithmParameters engineGenerateParameters()	Generates parameters.
protected abstract void engineInit(AlgorithmParameterSpec genParamSpec, SecureRandom random)	Initializes this parameter generator.
protected abstract void engineInit (int size, SecureRandom random)	Initializes this parameter generator.

Table H-18.   *public abstract class AlgorithmParameterGeneratorSpi extends Object*

Syntax	Descriptions
String getAlgorithm()	Returns the name of the algorithm.
byte[] getEncoded()	Returns the parameters in primary encoding format.
byte[] getEncoded(String format)	Returns the parameters.
static AlgorithmParameters getInstance(String algorithm)	Generates a parameter object.
static AlgorithmParameters getInstance(String algorithm, Provider provider)	Generates a parameter object.
static AlgorithmParameters getInstance(String algorithm, String provider)	Generates a parameter object.
AlgorithmParameterSpec getParameterSpec(Class paramSpec)	Returns a transparent specification of parameter object.

Table H-19.   *public class AlgorithmParameters extends Object*

Syntax	Descriptions
Provider getProvider()	Returns the provider of a parameter object.
void init(AlgorithmParameterSpec paramSpec)	Initializes a parameter object.
void init(byte[] params)	Imports and decodes parameters.
void init(byte[] params, String format)	Imports and decodes the parameters.
String toString()	Returns a description of parameters.

Table H-19.   *public class AlgorithmParameters extends Object* (continued)

Syntax	Descriptions
protected abstract byte[] engineGetEncoded()	Returns parameters in primary encoding format.
protected abstract byte[] engineGetEncoded(String format)	Returns parameters format.
protected abstract AlgorithmParameterSpec engineGetParameterSpec (Class paramSpec)	Returns a transparent specification of a parameter object.
protected abstract void engineInit(Algorithm ParameterSpec paramSpec)	Initializes a parameter object.
protected abstract void engineInit(byte[] params)	Imports and decodes the parameters.
protected abstract void engineInit(byte[] params, String format)	Imports and decodes the parameters.
protected abstract String engineToString()	Returns a description of parameters.

Table H-20.   *public abstract class AlgorithmParametersSpi extends Object*

Java Security Permissions

Syntax	Descriptions
boolean equals(Object obj)	Compares AllPermission objects.
String getActions()	Returns a string of the actions.
int hashCode()	Returns the hash code.
boolean implies(Permission p)	Determines if the permission is "implied."
PermissionCollection newPermissionCollection()	Returns a new PermissionCollection object.

Table H-21.   *public final class AllPermission extends Permission*

Syntax	Descriptions
boolean equals(Object obj)	Compares BasicPermission objects.
String getActions()	Returns a string of the actions.
int hashCode()	Returns the hash code value.
boolean implies(Permission p)	Determines if the permission is "implied."
PermissionCollection newPermissionCollection()	Returns a new PermissionCollection object.

Table H-22.   *public abstract class BasicPermission extends Permission, implements Serializable*

Syntax	Descriptions
void checkGuard(Object object)	Implements the guard interface.
abstract boolean equals (Object obj)	Compares Permission objects.
abstract String getActions()	Returns the actions as a String.
String getName()	Returns the name of a permission.

Table H-23.   *public abstract class Permission extends Object, implements Guard, Serializable*

Syntax	Descriptions
abstract int hashCode()	Returns the hash code value.
abstract boolean implies (Permission permission)	Determines if a permission's actions are "implied by."
PermissionCollection newPermissionCollection()	Returns an empty permission collection.
object, or null if one is not defined. String toString()	Returns a String describing a permission.

Table H-23. *public abstract class Permission extends Object, implements Guard, Serializable* (continued)

Syntax	Descriptions
abstract void add(Permission permission)	Adds a Permission object.
abstract Enumeration elements()	Returns an enumeration of all Permission objects.
abstract boolean implies (Permission permission)	Determines if a permission is implied.
boolean isReadOnly()	Returns true if a PermissionCollection object is read only.
void setReadOnly()	Sets a PermissionCollection object as read only.
String toString()	Returns a string describing this PermissionCollection object.

Table H-24. *public abstract class PermissionCollection extends Object, implements Serializable*

Syntax	Descriptions
void add(Permission permission)	Adds a Permission object to the permission collection.
Enumeration elements()	Returns an enumeration of all the Permission objects.
boolean implies (Permission permission)	Determines if permissions of a permission's type implies the permissions of a Permission object.

Table H-25. *public final class Permissions extends PermissionCollection, implements Serializable*

Syntax	Descriptions
abstract PermissionCollection getPermissions(CodeSource codesource)	Returns a PermissionCollection object containing a set of permissions.
PermissionCollection getPermissions(ProtectionDomain domain)	Returns a PermissionCollection object containing a set of permissions.
static Policy getPolicy()	Returns the installed Policy object.
boolean implies(ProtectionDomain domain, Permission permission)	Tests whether the permission is granted.
abstract void refresh()	Refreshes/reloads a policy.
static void setPolicy(Policy policy)	Sets a Policy object.

Table H-26. *public abstract class Policy extends Object*

Syntax	Descriptions
boolean equals(Object obj)	Compares UnresolvedPermission objects.
String getActions()	Returns actions.
int hashCode()	Returns the hash code value.
boolean implies(Permission p)	Returns false for unresolved permissions.
PermissionCollection newPermissionCollection()	Returns a new PermissionCollection object.
String toString()	Returns a description of the unresolved permission.

Table H-27. *public final class UnresolvedPermission extends Permission, implements Serializable*

Java Security Code Source

Syntax	Descriptions
boolean equals(Object obj)	Compares objects.
Certificate[] getCertificates()	Returns certificates.
URL getLocation()	Returns location of code source.
int hashCode()	Returns the hash code value.
boolean implies(CodeSource codesource)	Determines if the permission is "implied."
String toString()	Returns a string containing URL and certificates.

Table H-28.   *public class CodeSource extends Object, implements Serializable*

Java Security Streams

Syntax	Descriptions
MessageDigest getMessageDigest()	Returns the message digest.
void on(boolean on)	Turns the digest function on or off.
int read()	Reads and updates the message digest.
int read(byte[] b, int off, int len)	Reads and updates the message digest.
void setMessageDigest (MessageDigest digest)	Associates a message digest with a stream.
String toString()	Prints a string of a digest input stream.

Table H-29.   *public class DigestInputStream extends FilterInputStream*

Syntax	Descriptions
MessageDigest getMessageDigest()	Returns a message digest.
void on(boolean on)	Turns the digest function on or off.
void setMessageDigest (MessageDigest digest)	Associates a message digest with a stream.
String toString()	Prints a string of a digest output stream.
void write(byte[] b, int off, int len)	Updates a message digest.
void write(int b)	Updates a message digest.

Table H-30.   *public class DigestOutputStream extends FilterOutputStream*

Java Security Message

Syntax	Descriptions
Object clone()	Returns a clone.
byte[] digest()	Completes the hash computation.
byte[] digest(byte[] input)	Performs a final update on the digest.
int digest(byte[] buf, int offset, int len)	Completes the hash computation.
String getAlgorithm()	Returns the algorithm.
int getDigestLength()	Returns the length of the digest in bytes, or 0 if not supported.
static MessageDigest getInstance(String algorithm)	Generates a MessageDigest object.
static MessageDigest getInstance (String algorithm, Provider provider)	Generates a MessageDigest object.

Table H-31.   *public abstract class MessageDigest extends MessageDigestSpi*

Syntax	Descriptions
static MessageDigest getInstance (String algorithm, String provider)	Generates a MessageDigest object.
Provider getProvider()	Returns the provider of a MessageDigest object.
static boolean isEqual(byte[] digesta, byte[] digestb)	Compares digests.
void reset()	Resets the digest.
String toString()	Returns a MessageDigest object.
void update(byte input)	Updates the digest.
void update(byte[] input)	Updates the digest.
void update(byte[] input, int offset, int len)	Updates the digest.

Table H-31. *public abstract class MessageDigest extends MessageDigestSpi (continued)*

Syntax	Descriptions
Object clone()	Returns a clone.
protected abstract byte[] engineDigest()	Completes the hash computation.
protected int engineDigest(byte[] buf, int offset, int len)	Completes the hash computation.
protected int engineGetDigestLength()	Returns the digest length.
protected abstract void engineReset()	Resets the digest.
protected abstract void engineUpdate (byte input)	Updates the digest.
protected abstract void engineUpdate (byte[] input, int offset, int len)	Updates the digest.

Table H-32. *public abstract class MessageDigestSpi extends Object*

Java Security Domain Protection

Syntax	Descriptions
ClassLoader getClassLoader()	Returns a class loader.
CodeSource getCodeSource()	Returns a code source.
PermissionCollection getPermissions()	Returns static permissions.
Principal[] getPrincipals()	Returns an array of principals.
boolean implies (Permission permission)	Determines if a protection domain implies the permissions of a Permission object.
String toString()	Converts a protection domain to a String.

Table H-33.   *public class ProtectionDomain extends Object*

Java Security Provider

Syntax	Descriptions
void clear()	Clears properties used to look up facilities.
Set entrySet()	Returns an unmodifiable Set view of property entries.
String getInfo()	Returns description of a provider.
String getName()	Returns a provider.
double getVersion()	Returns a provider version number.
Set keySet()	Returns an unmodifiable Set view of a property key.
void load(InputStream inStream)	Reads a property list.
Object put(Object key, Object value)	Sets the key property.
void putAll(Map t)	Copies all of the mappings from map to provider.
Object remove(Object key)	Removes the key property.

Table H-34.   *public abstract class Provider extends Properties*

Syntax	Descriptions
String toString()	Returns a String with the name and version of a provider.
Collection values()	Returns an unmodifiable Collection view of the property values.

Table H-34.   *public abstract class Provider extends Properties* (continued)

Java Security Secure Class Loader

Syntax	Descriptions
protected Class defineClass(String name, byte[] b, int off, int len, CodeSource cs)	Converts an array of bytes to an instance of class Class.
protected PermissionCollection getPermissions(CodeSource codesource)	Returns the permissions for a CodeSource object.

Table H-35.   *public class SecureClassLoader extends ClassLoader*

Java Security Randomizer

Syntax	Descriptions
byte[] generateSeed(int numBytes)	Returns seed bytes.
static SecureRandom getInstance (String algorithm)	Generates a SecureRandom object.
static SecureRandom getInstance (String algorithm, Provider provider)	Generates a SecureRandom object.
static SecureRandom getInstance (String algorithm, String provider)	Generates a SecureRandom object.
Provider getProvider()	Returns the provider of a SecureRandom object.

Table H-36.   *public class SecureRandom extends Random*

Syntax	Descriptions
static byte[] getSeed(int numBytes)	Returns the given number of seed bytes.
protected int next(int numBits)	Generates an integer of pseudorandom bits that are right-justified, with leading zeros.
void nextBytes(byte[] bytes)	Generates a user-specified number of random bytes.
void setSeed(byte[] seed)	Reseeds a random object.
void setSeed(long seed)	Reseeds a random object.

Table H-36.   *public class SecureRandom extends Random* (continued)

Syntax	Descriptions
protected abstract byte[] engineGenerateSeed(int numBytes)	Returns seed bytes.
protected abstract void engineNextBytes(byte[] bytes)	Generates a user-specified number of random bytes.
protected abstract void engineSetSeed(byte[] seed)	Reseeds a random object.

Table H-37.   *public abstract class SecureRandomSpi extends Object, implements Serializable*

Java Security Signature

Syntax	Descriptions
Object clone()	Returns a clone.
String getAlgorithm()	Returns the name of the algorithm for a Signature object.

Table H-38.   *public abstract class Signature extends SignatureSpi*

Syntax	Descriptions
static Signature getInstance(String algorithm)	Generates a Signature object.
static Signature getInstance(String algorithm, Provider provider)	Generates a Signature object.
static Signature getInstance(String algorithm, String provider)	Generates a Signature object.
AlgorithmParameters getParameters()	Returns parameters used with a Signature object.
Provider getProvider()	Returns the provider of a Signature object.
void initSign(PrivateKey privateKey)	Initialize an object for signing.
void initSign(PrivateKey privateKey, SecureRandom random)	Initialize an object for signing.
void initVerify(Certificate certificate)	Initializes an object for verification.
void initVerify(PublicKey publicKey)	Initializes an object for verification.
void setParameter (AlgorithmParameterSpec params)	Initializes a signature engine.
byte[] sign()	Returns the signature bytes.
int sign(byte[] outbuf, int offset, int len)	Stores the resulting signature bytes.
String toString()	Returns a String of a signature object.
void update(byte b)	Updates the data to be signed or verified.
void update(byte[] data)	Updates the data to be signed or verified.
void update(byte[] data, int off, int len)	Updates the data to be signed or verified.
boolean verify(byte[] signature)	Verifies the passed-in signature.
boolean verify(byte[] signature, int offset, int length)	Verifies the passed-in signature specified in the array starting at the offset.

Table H-38.   *public abstract class Signature extends SignatureSpi* (continued)

Syntax	Descriptions
Object clone()	Returns a clone.
protected abstract void engineInitSign(PrivateKey privateKey)	Initializes this Signature object.
protected void engineInitSign(PrivateKey privateKey, SecureRandom random)	Initializes this Signature object and specifies source of randomness.
protected abstract void engineInitVerify(PublicKey publicKey)	Initializes this Signature object.
protected abstract byte[] engineSign()	Returns the signature bytes.
protected int engineSign(byte[] outbuf, int offset, int len)	Stores the signature bytes.
protected abstract void engineUpdate(byte b)	Updates data to be signed or verified where data is array of bytes.
protected abstract void engineUpdate(byte[] b, int off, int len)	Updates data to be signed or verified where data is array of bytes starting at the offset.
protected abstract boolean engineVerify(byte[] sigBytes)	Verifies a passed-in signature.
protected boolean engineVerify(byte[] sigBytes, int offset, int length)	Verifies a passed-in signature.

Table H-39. *public abstract class SignatureSpi extends Object*

Syntax	Descriptions
String getAlgorithm()	Returns the name of a signature algorithm.
Object getObject()	Returns an encapsulated object.
byte[] getSignature()	Returns the signature on the signed object.
boolean verify(PublicKey verificationKey, Signature verificationEngine)	Verifies valid signature.

Table H-40. *public final class SignedObject extends Object, implements Serializable*

Appendix I

Java Naming and Directory Interface

The Java Naming and Directory facility is used to locate objects required by a Java 2 Enterprise Edition application, which can be located on a local computer or a remote computer. You can locate these objects by using the Java Naming and Directory Interface. Here are references that you need to use when locating an object from within your Java 2 Enterprise Edition application:

- Java Naming and Directory Context
- Java Naming and Directory Naming
- Java Naming and Directory Attributes
- Java Naming and Directory Directory Context

Java Naming and Directory Context

Syntax	Descriptions
Object addToEnvironment(String propName, Object propVal)	Adds a new environment property.
void bind(Name name, Object obj)	Binds a name to an object.
void bind(String name, Object obj)	Binds a name to an object.
void close()	Closes a context.
Name composeName(Name name, Name prefix)	Composes a context name based on a String prefix.
String composeName(String name, String prefix)	Composes a context name based on a String prefix.
Context createSubcontext(Name name)	Creates and binds a context.
Context createSubcontext(String name)	Creates and binds a context.
void destroySubcontext(Name name)	Removes a named context from a namespace.
void destroySubcontext(String name)	Removes a named context from a namespace.
Hashtable getEnvironment()	Returns an environment.

Table I-1. *public interface Context*

Syntax	Descriptions
String getNameInNamespace()	Returns the name of a context.
NameParser getNameParser (Name name)	Returns the parser associated with a context.
NameParser getNameParser (String name)	Returns the parser associated with a context.
NamingEnumeration list(Name name)	Enumerates the names and objects bound in a context.
NamingEnumeration list(String name)	Enumerates the names and objects bound in a context.
NamingEnumeration listBindings (Name name)	Enumerates the names and objects bound in a context.
NamingEnumeration listBindings (String name)	Enumerates the names and objects bound in a context.
Object lookup(Name name)	Returns an object.
Object lookup(String name)	Returns an object.
Object lookupLink(Name name)	Returns an object except for the terminal component of the name.
Object lookupLink(String name)	Returns an object except for the terminal component of the name.
void rebind(Name name, Object obj)	Binds a name to an object.
void rebind(String name, Object obj)	Binds a name to an object.
Object removeFromEnvironment (String propName)	Removes an environment property.
void rename(Name oldName, Name newName)	Binds a new name to an object.
void rename(String oldName, String newName)	Binds a new name to an object.
void unbind(Name name)	Unbinds an object.
void unbind(String name)	Unbinds a named object.

Table I-1.   *public interface Context* (continued)

Java Naming and Directory Naming

Syntax	Descriptions
void close()	Closes an enumeration.
boolean hasMore()	Determines if the enumeration has additional elements.
Object next()	Retrieves the next element in the enumeration.

Table I-2.   *public interface NamingEnumeration* **extends Enumeration**

Syntax	Descriptions
Name add(int posn, String comp)	Adds a component at a specified position within a name.
Name add(String comp)	Adds a component to the end of a name.
Name addAll(int posn, Name n)	Adds the components of a name at a specified position within a name, in order.
Name addAll(Name suffix)	Adds components of a name to the end of this name, in order.
Object clone()	Creates a copy of a name.
int compareTo(Object obj)	Compares names for order.
boolean endsWith(Name n)	Determines if a name ends with this suffix.
String get(int posn)	Returns a component of this name.
Enumeration getAll()	Returns the components as an enumeration of strings.
Name getPrefix(int posn)	Creates a name having a prefix.
Name getSuffix(int posn)	Creates a name having a suffix.
boolean isEmpty()	Determines if a name is empty.
Object remove(int posn)	Removes a component from a name.

Table I-3.   *public interface Name* **extends Cloneable, Serializable**

Syntax	Descriptions
int size()	Returns the number of components in this name.
boolean startsWith(Name n)	Determines if a name starts with this prefix.

Table I-3. *public interface Name **extends Cloneable, Serializable*** (continued)

Syntax	Descriptions
Name parse(String name)	Parses a name.

Table I-4. *public interface NameParser*

Java Naming and Directory Attributes

Syntax	Descriptions
void add(int ix, Object attrVal)	Adds an attribute value to an ordered list.
boolean add(Object attrVal)	Adds a new value to an attribute.
void clear()	Removes values from an attribute.
Object clone()	Copies an attribute.
boolean contains(Object attrVal)	Determines if an attribute has a value.
Object get()	Returns an attribute value.
Object get(int ix)	Returns an attribute value from the ordered list.
NamingEnumeration getAll()	Returns an enumeration of attribute values.

Table I-5. *public interface Attribute **extends Cloneable, Serializable***

Syntax	Descriptions
DirContext getAttributeDefinition()	Returns an attribute's schema definition.
DirContext getAttribute SyntaxDefinition()	Returns the syntax definition of an attribute.
String getID()	Returns an attribute ID.
boolean isOrdered()	Determines if attribute values are ordered.
Object remove(int ix)	Removes an attribute value from an ordered list.
boolean remove(Object attrVal)	Removes an attribute.
Object set(int ix, Object attrVal)	Sets an attribute value.
int size()	Returns the number of values of an attribute.

Table I-5. *public interface Attribute* ***extends Cloneable, Serializable*** (continued)

Syntax	Descriptions
Object clone()	Copies the attribute set.
Attribute get(String attrID)	Returns specified attribute ID.
NamingEnumeration getAll()	Returns an enumeration of attributes.
NamingEnumeration getIDs()	Returns an enumeration of attribute's IDs.
boolean isCaseIgnored()	Determines if the search ignores the case of attribute identifiers.
Attribute put(Attribute attr)	Adds a new attribute.
Attribute put(String attrID, Object val)	Adds a new attribute.
Attribute remove(String attrID)	Removes the specified attribute.
int size()	Retrieves the number of attributes.

Table I-6. *public interface Attributes* ***extends Cloneable, Serializable***

Java Naming and Directory Directory Context

Syntax	Descriptions
void bind(Name name, Object obj, Attributes attrs)	Binds a name and attributes to an object.
void bind(String name, Object obj, Attributes attrs)	Binds a name and attributes to an object.
DirContext createSubcontext (Name name, Attributes attrs)	Creates and binds a new context and attributes.
DirContext createSubcontext (String name, Attributes attrs)	Creates and binds a new context and attributes.
Attributes getAttributes (Name name)	Returns all of the attributes associated with a named object.
Attributes getAttributes (Name name, String[] attrIds)	Returns selected attributes associated with a named object.
Attributes getAttributes (String name)	Returns all attributes.
Attributes getAttributes (String name, String[] attrIds)	Returns selected attributes.
DirContext getSchema (Name name)	Returns a schema.
DirContext getSchema (String name)	Returns a schema.
DirContext getSchema ClassDefinition (Name name)	Returns a context containing the named object's class definitions.
DirContext getSchema ClassDefinition (String name)	Returns a context containing the named object's class definitions.
void modifyAttributes (Name name, int mod_op, Attributes attrs)	Modifies attributes.

Table I-7.   *public interface DirContext* ***extends Context***

Syntax	Descriptions
void modifyAttributes(Name name, ModificationItem[] mods)	Modifies attributes using an ordered list.
void modifyAttributes (String name, int mod_op, Attributes attrs)	Modifies attributes.
void modifyAttributes(String name, ModificationItem[] mods)	Modifies attributes using an ordered list.
void rebind(Name name, Object obj, Attributes attrs)	Binds a name and attributes to an object, overwriting the existing binding.
void rebind(String name, Object obj, Attributes attrs)	Binds a name and attributes to an object, overwriting the existing binding.
NamingEnumeration search(Name name, Attributes matchingAttributes)	Searches a context for objects for an attribute set.
NamingEnumeration search(Name name, Attributes matchingAttributes, String[] attributesToReturn)	Searches a context for objects for an attribute set and returns selected attributes.
NamingEnumeration search(Name name, String filterExpr, Object[] filterArgs, SearchControls cons)	Searches a context or object for search criteria.
NamingEnumeration search(Name name, String filter, SearchControls cons)	Searches a context or object for search criteria.
NamingEnumeration search(String name, Attributes matchingAttributes)	Searches a context for objects for an attribute set.
NamingEnumeration search(String name, Attributes matchingAttributes, String[] attributesToReturn)	Searches a context for objects for an attribute set and returns selected attributes.

Table I-7. *public interface DirContext **extends Context*** (continued)

Syntax	Descriptions
NamingEnumeration search(String name, String filterExpr, Object[] filterArgs, SearchControls cons)	Searches a context or object for search criteria.
NamingEnumeration search(String name, String filter, SearchControls cons)	Searches a context or object for search criteria.

Table I-7.   *public interface DirContext **extends Context*** (continued)

Appendix J

Simple Object Access Protocol

A Java 2 Enterprise application can communicate with web services located on a remote computer by using the Simple Object Access Protocol, commonly referred to as SOAP. SOAP is an efficient and reliable mechanism for distributive applications where a component that must interact with other components exists on dissimilar remote computers. Here are references that you'll need when communicating using the Simple Object Access Protocol:

- Simple Object Access Protocol detail
- Simple Object Access Protocol name
- Simple Object Access Protocol node
- Simple Object Access Protocol body
- Simple Object Access Protocol constants
- Simple Object Access Protocol element
- Simple Object Access Protocol envelope
- Simple Object Access Protocol fault
- Simple Object Access Protocol header
- Simple Object Access Protocol text
- Simple Object Access Protocol attachment
- Simple Object Access Protocol message
- Simple Object Access Protocol MIME header
- Simple Object Access Protocol connection
- Simple Object Access Protocol Part

Simple Object Access Protocol Detail

Syntax	Descriptions
DetailEntry addDetailEntry(Name name)	Creates a new DetailEntry object.
Iterator getDetailEntries()	Returns detail entries in a Detail object.

Table J-1.   *public interface Detail extends SOAPFaultElement*

Simple Object Access Protocol Name

Syntax	Descriptions
String getLocalName()	Returns the local name part of the XML name.
String getPrefix()	Returns the prefix associated with the namespace.
String getQualifiedName()	Returns the namespace-qualified name of an Name object.
String getURI()	Returns the URI of a namespace.

Table J-2.   *public interface Name*

Simple Object Access Protocol Node

Syntax	Descriptions
void detachNode()	Removes a Node object.
SOAPElement getParentElement()	Returns the parent element of a Node object.
String getValue()	Returns the value of the child of a Node object.
void recycleNode()	Notifies that a Node object is no longer being used by an application.
void setParentElement (SOAPElement parent)	Sets the parent of a Node object.

Table J-3.   *public interface Node*

Simple Object Access Protocol Body

Syntax	Descriptions
SOAPBodyElement addBodyElement(Name name)	Creates a new SOAPBodyElement object.
SOAPFault addFault()	Creates and inserts a new SOAPFault object.
SOAPFault getFault()	Returns the SOAPFault object for a SOAPBody object.
boolean hasFault()	Determines if a SOAPFault object exists in a SOAPBody object.

Table J-4. *public interface SOAPBody extends SOAPElement*

Simple Object Access Protocol Constants

Syntax	Descriptions
static String URI_NS_SOAP_ENCODING	The encoding namespace identifier.
static String URI_NS_SOAP_ENVELOPE	The envelope namespace identifier.
static String URI_SOAP_ACTOR_NEXT	The URI for the first application processing a SOAP request intended for an actor identified in a header entry.

Table J-5. *public interface SOAPConstants*

Simple Object Access Protocol Element

Syntax	Descriptions
SOAPElement addAttribute(Name name, String value)	Inserts an attribute.
SOAPElement addChildElement (Name name)	Creates and initializes a new SOAPElement object.
SOAPElement addChildElement (SOAPElement element)	Inserts a child SOAPElement.
SOAPElement addChildElement (String localName)	Creates and initializes a new SOAPElement object.
SOAPElement addChildElement (String localName, String prefix)	Creates and initializes a new SOAPElement object.
SOAPElement addChildElement (String localName, String prefix, String uri)	Creates and initializes a new SOAPElement object.
SOAPElement addNamespaceDeclaration (String prefix, String uri)	Adds a namespace declaration.
SOAPElement addTextNode (String text)	Creates and initializes a new Text object.
Iterator getAllAttributes()	Returns an iterator of attribute names.
String getAttributeValue(Name name)	Returns an attribute's value.
Iterator getChildElements()	Returns an iterator of an element's content.
Iterator getChildElements(Name name)	Returns an iterator of child elements.
Name getElementName()	Returns the name of a SOAPElement object.
String getEncodingStyle()	Returns an encoding style.
Iterator getNamespacePrefixes()	Returns an iterator of a namespace prefix.

Table J-6.   *public interface SOAPElement extends Node*

Syntax	Descriptions
String getNamespaceURI(String prefix)	Returns the URI of a namespace.
boolean removeAttribute(Name name)	Deletes an attribute.
boolean removeNamespaceDeclaration (String prefix)	Deletes a namespace declaration.
void setEncodingStyle (String encodingStyle)	Sets the encoding style.

Table J-6. *public interface SOAPElement extends Node* (continued)

Syntax	Descriptions
abstract SOAPElement create (Name name)	Create a SOAPElement object initialized with object Name.
abstract SOAPElement create (String localName)	Create a SOAPElement object initialized with localName.
abstract SOAPElement create (String localName, String prefix, String uri)	Create a new SOAPElement object.
static SOAPElementFactory newInstance()	Creates an instance of SOAPElementFactory.

Table J-7. *public abstract class SOAPElementFactory extends Object*

Simple Object Access Protocol Envelope

Syntax	Descriptions
SOAPBody addBody()	Creates a SOAPBody object.
SOAPHeader addHeader()	Creates a SOAPHeader object.

Table J-8. *public interface SOAPEnvelope extends SOAPElement*

Syntax	Descriptions
Name createName(String localName)	Creates and initializes a new Name object.
Name createName(String localName, String prefix, String uri)	Creates and initializes a new Name object.
SOAPBody getBody()	Returns a SOAPBody object.
SOAPHeader getHeader()	Returns a SOAPHeader object.

Table J-8.   *public interface SOAPEnvelope extends SOAPElement* (continued)

Simple Object Access Protocol Fault

Syntax	Descriptions
Detail addDetail()	Creates a Detail object.
Detail getDetail()	Returns the detail element of a SOAPFault object.
String getFaultActor()	Returns the fault actor.
String getFaultCode()	Returns the fault code for the SOAP message
String getFaultString()	Returns the fault string.
void setFaultActor (String faultActor)	Sets a fault actor for a SOAPFault object.
void setFaultCode (String faultCode)	Sets a fault code for a SOAPFault object.
void setFaultString (String faultString)	Sets the fault string for a SOAPFault object.

Table J-9.   *public interface SOAPFault extends SOAPBodyElement*

Simple Object Access Protocol Header

Syntax	Descriptions
SOAPHeaderElement addHeaderElement(Name name)	Creates and initializes a new SOAPHeaderElement object.
Iterator examineHeaderElements (String actor)	Returns a list of SOAPHeaderElement objects that have the specified actor.
Iterator extractHeaderElements (String actor)	Returns a list of SOAPHeaderElement objects that have this actor and detaches the actor from a SOAPHeader object.

Table J-10. *public interface SOAPHeader extends SOAPElement*

Syntax	Descriptions
String getActor()	Returns the URI of the actor.
boolean getMustUnderstand()	Returns the status of the mustUnderstand attribute.
void setActor(String actorURI)	Sets the actor of the SOAPHeaderElement object.
void setMustUnderstand (boolean mustUnderstand)	Sets the mustUnderstand attribute to on or off.

Table J-11. *public interface SOAPHeaderElement extends SOAPElement*

Simple Object Access Protocol Text

Syntax	Description
boolean isComment()	Returns if Text object is a comment.

Table J-12. *public interface Text extends Node*

Simple Object Access Protocol Attachment

Syntax	Descriptions
abstract void addMimeHeader (String name, String value)	Inserts a MIME header.
abstract void clearContent()	Deletes the content of an AttachmentPart object.
abstract Iterator getAllMimeHeaders()	Returns headers for an AttachmentPart object as an iterator.
abstract Object getContent()	Returns the content of an AttachmentPart object.
String getContentId()	Returns the value of the Content-Id MIME header.
String getContentLocation()	Returns the value of the Content-Location MIME header.
String getContentType()	Returns the value of the Content-Type MIME header.
abstract DataHandler getDataHandler()	Returns the DataHandler object.
abstract Iterator getMatchingMimeHeaders (String[] names)	Returns MimeHeader objects found in an array.
abstract String[] getMimeHeader (String name)	Returns values a header identified by name.
abstract Iterator getNonMatchingMimeHeaders (String[] names)	Returns MimeHeader objects not found in the array.
abstract int getSize()	Returns bytes of AttachmentPart object.
abstract void removeAllMimeHeaders()	Deletes all the MIME headers.
abstract void removeMimeHeader (String header)	Deletes specified MIME headers.

Table J-13. *public abstract class AttachmentPart extends Object*

Syntax	Descriptions
abstract void setContent(Object object, String contentType)	Sets attachment part to an object and sets the Content-Type header to contentType.
void setContentId(String contentId)	Sets the Content-Id MIME header.
void setContentLocation(String contentLocation)	Sets the Content-Location MIME header.
void setContentType(String contentType)	Sets the Content-Type MIME header.
abstract void setDataHandler (DataHandler dataHandler)	Sets a DataHandler object as the data handler.
abstract void setMimeHeader(String name, String value)	Modifies the name header entry with the specified value. A new header is inserted if name is not found.

Table J-13. *public abstract class AttachmentPart extends Object* (continued)

Simple Object Access Protocol Message

Syntax	Descriptions
abstract SOAPMessage createMessage()	Creates a new SOAPMessage object.
abstract SOAPMessage createMessage (MimeHeaders headers, InputStream in)	Internalizes the contents of an InputStream object.
static MessageFactory newInstance()	Creates a new MessageFactory object.

Table J-14. *public abstract class MessageFactory extends Object*

Syntax	Descriptions
abstract void addAttachmentPart (AttachmentPart AttachmentPart)	Inserts an AttachmentPart object to a SOAPMessage object.
abstract int countAttachments()	Returns the number of attachments in a message.
abstract AttachmentPart createAttachmentPart()	Creates a new AttachmentPart object.
AttachmentPart createAttachmentPart (DataHandler dataHandler)	Creates an AttachmentPart object and populates it using the given DataHandler object.
AttachmentPart createAttachmentPart (Object content, String contentType)	Creates and populates an AttachmentPart object.
abstract Iterator getAttachments()	Returns AttachmentPart objects that are part of this SOAPMessage object.
abstract Iterator getAttachments (MimeHeaders headers)	Returns AttachmentPart objects that match these headers.
abstract String getContentDescription()	Returns a description of a SOAPMessage object's content.
abstract MimeHeaders getMimeHeaders()	Returns the transport MIME headers for a SOAPMessage object.
abstract SOAPPart getSOAPPart()	Returns the SOAP part of a SOAPMessage object.
abstract void removeAllAttachments()	Delete AttachmentPart objects.
abstract void saveChanges()	Updates a SOAPMessage object.
abstract boolean saveRequired()	Returns whether a SOAPMessage object's saveChanges method was called.
abstract void setContentDescription (String description)	Sets the description of a SOAPMessage object's content.
abstract void writeTo (OutputStream out)	Writes a SOAPMessage object to an output stream.

Table J-15.   *public abstract class SOAPMessage extends Object*

Syntax	Descriptions
String getName()	Returns the name of a MimeHeader object.
String getValue()	Returns the value of a MimeHeader object.

Table J-16. *public class MimeHeader extends Object*

Simple Object Access Protocol MIME Header

Syntax	Descriptions
void addHeader(String name, String value)	Inserts a MimeHeader object.
Iterator getAllHeaders()	Returns all the headers.
String[] getHeader(String name)	Returns values of a header.
Iterator getMatchingHeaders (String[] names)	Returns MimeHeader objects that are in the array.
Iterator getNonMatchingHeaders (String[] names)	Returns MimeHeader objects that are not in the array.
void removeAllHeaders()	Removes header entries.
void removeHeader(String name)	Removes MimeHeader objects that match name matches.
void setHeader(String name, String value)	Replaces the current header value.

Table J-17. *public class MimeHeaders extends Object*

Simple Object Access Protocol Connection

Syntax	Descriptions
abstract SOAPMessage call(SOAPMessage request, Endpoint endpoint)	Sends a message and pauses until a response is received.
abstract void close()	Closes this SOAPConnection object.

Table J-18. *public abstract class SOAPConnection extends Object*

Syntax	Descriptions
abstract SOAPConnection createConnection()	Creates a new SOAPConnection object.
static SOAPConnectionFactory newInstance()	Creates an instance of the SOAPConnectionFactory object.

Table J-19. *public abstract class SOAPConnectionFactory extends Object*

Simple Object Access Protocol Part

Syntax	Descriptions
abstract void addMimeHeader(String name, String value)	Creates a MimeHeader object.
abstract Iterator getAllMimeHeaders()	Returns headers for this SOAPPart object as an iterator.
abstract Source getContent()	Returns the content of the SOAPEnvelope.

Table J-20. *public abstract class SOAPPart extends java.lang.Object*

Syntax	Descriptions
String getContentId()	Returns the value of the Content-Id MIME header.
String getContentLocation()	Returns the value of the Content-Location MIME header.
abstract SOAPEnvelope getEnvelope()	Returns a SOAPEnvelope object.
abstract Iterator getMatchingMimeHeaders (String[] names)	Returns MimeHeader objects that match an array element.
abstract String[] getMimeHeader (String name)	Returns values of the MimeHeader object in a SOAPPart object.
abstract Iterator getNonMatchingMimeHeaders (String[] names)	Returns MimeHeader objects whose names do not appear in the array.
abstract void removeAllMimeHeaders()	Removes the MimeHeader objects for a SOAPEnvelope object.
abstract void removeMimeHeader (String header)	Removes MIME headers of the specified name.
abstract void setContent(Source source)	Sets the content of the SOAPEnvelope object.
void setContentId(String contentId)	Sets the value of the Content-Id MIME header.
String void setContentLocation (String contentLocation)	Sets the value of the Content-Location MIME header.
abstract void setMimeHeader (String name, String value)	Changes header identified by name to the value specified by value. If name not found, then new header is added.

Table J-20.   *public abstract class SOAPPart extends java.lang.Object* (continued)

Appendix K

Universal Description, Discovery, and Integration

807

The Universal Description, Discovery, and Integration (UDDI) is a database of web services that business partners can use to exchange data about each other's web services offerings. A business refers to UDDI whenever it wants its systems to interface with a business partner's system. UDDI contains all the information necessary to carry out the interface between systems. Here are references that you need whenever your Java 2 Enterprise Edition application either publishes information to or accesses information from a UDDI database:

- Universal Description, Discovery, and Integration SOAP errors
- Universal Description, Discovery, and Integration search qualifier values
- Universal Description, Discovery, and Integration response messages
- Universal Description, Discovery, and Integration values for the completionStatus argument

Universal Description, Discovery, and Integration SOAP Errors

Error Code	Description
30000 E_assertionNotFound	A publisher of businessKey values and a keyed reference cannot be identified.
10110 E_authTokenExpired	Authentication token timed out.
10120 E_authTokenRequired	Invalid authentication token passed to an API.
10160 E_accountLimitExceeded	A save request exceeded the data type quantity limits.
10400 E_busy	Request cannot be processed at the current time.
10500 E_fatalError	Serious technical error has occurred.
10210 E_invalidKeyPassed	The uuid_key value passed did not match any known key values.
20230 E_invalidProjection	An attempt was made to save a businessEntity containing a service projection that does not match the projected businessService.

Error Code	Description
30100 E_invalidCompletionStatus	An assertion that status values passed are unrecognized.
20200 E_invalidValue	A value passed in a keyValue attribute did not pass validation.
10060 E_languageError	An error was detected while processing elements that were annotated with xml:lang qualifiers.
30100 E_messageTooLarge	Message is too large.
10020E_nameTooLong	Partial name value passed exceeds the maximum name length.
30220 E_publisherCancelled	Publisher cancelled custody transfer operation.
30210 E_requestDenied	Custody transfer request refused.
30230 E_secretUnknown	Publisher unable to match the shared secret and attempt limit was exhausted.
0 E_success	No failure occurred.
10030 E_tooManyOptions	Too many or incompatible arguments passed.
30200 E_transferAborted	A custody transfer request will not succeed.
10040 E_unrecognizedVersion	The generic attribute value passed is unsupported by the Operator instance.
10150 E_unknownUser	Unknown user ID and password.
10050 E_unsupported	The implementer does not support a feature or API.
10140 E_userMismatch	Publishing API controlled by another party.
20210 E_valueNotAllowed	Value did not pass validation because of contextual issues.

Universal Description, Discovery, and Integration Search Qualifier Values

Search Qualifier Values	Description
exactNameMatch	Only entries that exactly match the argument are returned.
caseSensitiveMatch	Only entries that match the case of the argument are returned.
sortByNameAsc	Results sorted on the name field in ascending alphabetic sort order prior to any truncation of the return values.
sortByNameDesc	Results sorted on the name field in descending alphabetic sort order prior to any truncation of the return values.
sortByDateAsc	Results sorted on the date last updated in ascending chronological sort order (earliest returns first).
sortByDateDesc	Results sorted on the date last updated in descending chronological sort order (most recent changed returns first).
orLikeKeys	Used in a categoryBag or identifierBag that contains multiple keyedReference elements to indicate to match any value from the namespace in the argument (version 2.0).
orAllKeys	Matches at least one key specified in the argument (version 2.0).
combineCategoryBags	Used with the find_business API call and returns results where the categoryBag elements are found in the full businessEntity element and a UDDI entry (version 2.0).
serviceSubset	Used with the find_business API call and in conjunction with a passed categoryBag argument. Limits search to the businessService elements within the registry (version 2.0).

Search Qualifier Values	Description
andAllKeys	Matches all keys specified in the argument (default search, version 2.0).
soundex	Performs sound-alike searches using the argument value and searches the businessEntity and businessService entities. Used with find_business, find_service, and find_tModel API calls (version 2.0).

Universal Description, Discovery, and Integration Response Messages

Response Message	Description
assertionStatusReport	Returned in response to the get_assertionStatusReport API call. Determines the status of assertions made by either the publisher or by other parties.
authToken	Returned in response to the get_authToken API call. Returns authentication information and is used in subsequent calls that require an authInfo value.
bindingDetail	Returned in response to the get_bindingDetail API call. Returns technical information needed to access a web service.
businessDetail	Returned in response to the get_businessDetail API call and the save_business API call. Returns full details for businessEntity elements.
businessDetailExt	Returned in response to the get_businessDetailExt API call. Returns businessEntityExt elements.

Response Message	Description
businessList	Returned in response to the find_business API call. Returns abbreviated information about registered businessEntity information in businessInfo elements.
dispositionReport	Returns errors discovered during processing.
publisherAssertions	Returned in response to the get_publisherAssertions API call. Returns a publisher's assertion collection.
registeredInfo	Returned in response to the get_registeredInfo API call. Returns abbreviated information about all registered businessEntity and tModel information of a businessEntity specified in the argument of the API call as businessInfo elements and tModelInfo elements.
RelatedBusinessesList	Returned in response to the find_relatedBusinesses API call. Returns publicly visible business relationships.
serviceDetail	Returned in response to the get_serviceDetail API call. Returns full details for businessService elements.
serviceList	Returned in response to the find_service API call. Returns abbreviated information about registered businessService information in the form of serviceInfo elements.

Response Message	Description
tModelList	Returned in response to the find_tModelDetail API call. Returns abbreviated information about registered tModelDetail information in the form of tModel elements.
tModelDetail	Returned in response to the get_tModelDetail API call and the save_tModel API call. Returns full details for tModel elements.

Universal Description, Discovery, and Integration Values for the completionStatus Argument

Value	Description
status:complete	Return only the publisher assertions that are complete.
status:toKey_incomplete	Return only the publisher assertions that don't match assertions referenced by the toKey value.
status:fromKey_incomplete	Return only the publisher assertions that don't match assertions referenced by the fromKey value.

The Complete Reference

J2EE

Appendix L

Electronic Business XML

lectronic Business XML (ebXML) is a framework that is used by some of the world's important international corporations, within which all sizes businesses and consumers can participate in electronic commerce. Here are references that you'll need when writing a Java 2 Enterprise Edition application that interacts with the Electronic Business XML standards.

- Electronic Business XML business processes element and UML class conversion table
- Electronic Business XML business process elements

Electronic Business XML Business Processes Element and UML Class Conversion Table

ebXML Business Processes Element	UML Class
Attachment	Attachment
Binary collaboration	Binary collaboration
Business transaction	Business transaction
Business transaction activity	Business transaction activity
BusinessPartner role	BusinessPartner role
Collaboration activity	Collaboration activity
DocumentEnvelope	DocumentEnvelope
Failure	Failure
Fork	Fork
InitiatingRole	AuthorizedRole
Join	Join
Multiparty collaboration	Multiparty collaboration
Performs	Performs
Requesting BusinessActivity	Requesting BusinessActivity
Responding BusinessActivity	Responding BusinessActivity
RespondingRole	AuthorizedRole
Schema	Schema
Start	Start
Success	Success
Transition	Transition

Electronic Business XML Business Process Elements

Element	Description	Attribute(s)
BusinessDocument	A generic name of a document.	name: Defines the generic name of the business document. conditionExpression: Evaluates if it is a valid business document for an envelope (one conditionExpression permitted).
AttributeSubstitution	Substitutes one attribute value for another attribute value.	attributeName: CDATA value: CDATA
BinaryCollaboration	Defines an interaction protocol between two roles.	name: CDATA nameID: ID pattern: CDATA beginsWhen: CDATA endsWhen: CDATA precondition: CDATA postCondition: CDATA timeToPerform: CDATA
BusinessDocument	A generic document name.	name: CDATA nameID: ID specificationLocation: CDATA specificationElement: CDATA
BusinessPartnerRole	A role played by a business partner in a MultiPartyCollaboration.	name: CDATA nameID: ID
BusinessTransaction	A set of business information and business exchanges amongst two trading partners that occur in an agreed format, sequence, and time period.	name: CDATA nameID: ID pattern: CDATA beginsWhen: CDATA endsWhen: CDATA isGuaranteedDeliveryRequired: true/false Default: false precondition: CDATA postCondition: CDATA

Element	Description	Attribute(s)
BusinessTransactionActivity	Defines a business activity that executes a specified business transaction within a binary collaboration.	name: CDATA nameID: ID businessTransaction: CDATA businessTransactionIDRef: IDREF fromAuthorizedRole: CDATA fromAuthorizedRoleIDRef: IDREF toAuthorizedRole: CDATA toAuthorizedRoleIDRef: IDREF isConcurrent: true/false Default: false isLegallyBinding: true/false Default: false timeToPerform: CDATA
CollaborationActivity	An activity performed by a binary collaboration within another binary collaboration.	name: CDATA nameID: ID fromAuthorizedRole: CDATA fromAuthorizedRoleIDRef: CDATA toAuthorizedRole: CDATA toAuthorizedRoleIDRef: CDATA binaryCollaboration: CDATA binaryCollaborationIDRef: CDATA
Documentation	Defines user documentation for an element and can be an inline PCDATA and/or a URI pointing to complete documentation.	uri: CDATA
DocumentEnvelope	Conveys business information between the two roles in a business transaction.	businessDocument: CDATA businessDocumentIDRef: IDREF isPositiveResponse: CDATA isAuthenticated: true/false Default: false isConfidential: true/false Default: false isTamperProof: true/false Default: false

Element	Description	Attribute(s)
DocumentSubstitution	Identifies a document that should be substituted for another document.	originalBusinessDocument: CDATA originalBusinessDocumentID: IDREF substituteBusinessDocument: CDATA substituteBusinessDocumentId: IDREF
Failure	Defines failure of a binary collaboration.	fromBusinessState: CDATA fromBusinessStateIDRef: IDREF conditionGuard: Success/ BusinessFailure/TechnicalFailure/ AnyFailure
Fork	A state with one inbound transition and multiple outbound transitions.	name: CDATA nameID: ID
Include	Merges that specification with the current specification.	name: CDATA version: CDATA uuid: CDATA uri: CDATA
InitiatingRole	A role authorized to send the first request.	name: CDATA nameID: ID
Join	The point where previously forked activities join again.	name: CDATA nameID: ID waitForAll: true/false Default: true
MultiPartyCollaboration	Business partner roles, each playing roles in binary collaborations.	name: CDATA nameID: ID
Package	Defines a container of reusable elements.	name: CDATA nameID: ID
Performs	The relationship between a business partner role and the roles played by the business partner.	initiatingRole: CDATAinitiatingRoleIDRef: IDREFrespondingRole: CDATArespondingRoleIDRef: IDREF

Element	Description	Attribute(s)
ProcessSpecification	Root element of a process specification document.	name: ID version: CDATA uuid: CDATA
RequestingBusinessActivity	A business action performed by a requesting role within a business transaction.	name: CDATA nameID: ID isAuthorizationRequired: true/false Default: false isIntelligibleCheckRequired: true/false Default: false isNonRepudiationReceiptRequired: true/false Default: false isNonRepudiationRequired: true/false Default:false timeToAcknowledgeAcceptance: CDATA timeToAcknowledgeReceipt: CDATA
RespondingBusinessActivity	A business action performed by a role within a business transaction.	name: CDATA nameID: ID isAuthorizationRequired: true/false Default: false isIntelligibleCheckRequired: true/false Default: false isNonRepudiationReceiptRequired: true/false Default: false isNonRepudiationRequired: true/false Default: false timeToAcknowledgeReceipt: CDATA
RespondingRole	A role authorized to send the first response.	name: CDATA nameID: ID
Start	The starting state for a binary collaboration.	toBusinessState: CDATA toBusinessStateIDRef: IDREF

Element	Description	Attribute(s)
SubstitutionSet	A container for an AttributeSubstitution and/or DocumentSubstitution elements.	name: CDATA nameID: ID applyToScope: CDATA
Success	Defines the successful conclusion of a binary collaboration.	fromBusinessState: CDATA conditionGuard: Success/ BusinessFailure/TechnicalFailure/ AnyFailure
Transition	A transition between two business states in a binary collaboration.	onInitiation: true/false Default: false fromBusinessState: CDATA fromBusinessStateIDRef: IDREF toBusinessState: CDATA toBusinessStateIDRef: IDREF conditionGuard: Success/ BusinessFailure/TechnicalFailure/ AnyFailure

The
Complete
Reference

Appendix M

The Java API for
XML Registries

Java API for XML Registries (JAXR) is used to access XML web services registries from within a Java 2 Enterprise Edition application, which is used to make web services available to your application. Here are references that you'll need whenever you use JAXR to access web services:

- Java API for XML Registries Public XML Registries
- Java API for XML Registries Responses
- Java API for XML Registries Business Life Cycle Manager
- Java API for XML Registries Query
- Java API for XML Registries Profile
- Java API for XML Registries Catalogue
- Java API for XML Registries Connection
- Java API for XML Registries Response
- Java API for XML Registries Service

Java API for XML Registries Public XML Registries

Public XML Registry	Owner	Permission Requests
http://www-3.ibm.com/services/uddi/testregistry/inquiryapi	IBM	http://www-3.ibm.com/services/uddi/
http://uddi.microsoft.com/inquire	Microsoft	http://uddi.microsoft.com/
http://test.uddi.microsoft.com/inquire	Microsoft	http://uddi.microsoft.com/
https://test.uddi.microsoft.com/publish	Microsoft	http://uddi.microsoft.com/

Java API for XML Registries Responses

Syntax	Descriptions
Collection getCollection()	Returns a collection of objects.
Collection getException()	Returns a JAXRException collection.
boolean isPartialResponse()	Returns true if there is a partial response, caused by the large size of the result set.

Table M-1.   *public interface BulkResponse extends JAXRResponse*

Java API for XML Registries Business Life Cycle Manager

Syntax	Descriptions
BulkResponse deleteAssociations (Collection schemeKeys)	Delete associations of scheme Keys.
BulkResponse deleteClassificationSchemes (Collection schemeKeys)	Delete classification schemes of schemeKeys.
BulkResponse deleteConcepts (Collection conceptKeys)	Delete concepts concept of Keys.
BulkResponse deleteOrganizations (Collection organizationKeys)	Delete organization of organizationKeys.
BulkResponse deleteServiceBindings (Collection bindingKeys)	Delete service bindings of bindingKeys.
BulkResponse deleteServices (Collection serviceKeys)	Delete services of serviceKeys.
BulkResponse saveAssociations(Collection associations, boolean replace)	Saves association.
BulkResponse saveClassificationSchemes (Collection schemes)	Saves classification scheme.
BulkResponse saveConcepts (Collection concepts)	Saves concepts.
BulkResponse saveOrganizations(Collection organizations)	Saves organizations.
BulkResponse saveServiceBindings (Collection bindings)	Saves service bindings.
BulkResponse saveServices(Collection services)	Saves services.

Table M-2. *public interface **BusinessLifeCycleManager** extends LifeCycleManager*

Syntax	Descriptions
Association createAssociation(RegistryObject targetObject, Concept associationType)	Create an association using a parameter list.
Classification createClassification (ClassificationScheme scheme, String name, String value)	Create a classification using a parameter list.
Classification createClassification (Concept concept)	Create a classification using a parameter list.
ClassificationScheme createClassificationScheme (Concept concept)	Create a classification scheme where the concept ClassificationScheme doesn't exist and where the concept isn't a child concept.
ClassificationScheme createClassificationScheme(String name, String description)	Create a scheme using a parameter list.
Concept createConcept(RegistryObject parent, String name, String value)	Create a concept using a parameter list.
void createConceptEquivalence(Concept concept1, Concept concept2)	Create an equivalence between concepts.
EmailAddress createEmailAddress (String address)	Create an email address using a parameter list.
EmailAddress createEmailAddress (String address, java.lang.String type)	Create an email address using a parameter list.
ExternalIdentifier createExternalIdentifier(ClassificationScheme identificationScheme, String name, String value)	Create an external identifier using a parameter list.
ExternalLink createExternalLink(String externalURI, String description)	Create an external link using a parameter list.
ExtrinsicObject createExtrinsicObject()	Create an extrinsic object using a parameter list.
InternationalString createInternationalString()	Create an international string using a parameter list.

Table M-3. *public interface LifeCycleManager*

Syntax	Descriptions
InternationalString createInternationalString (Locale l, String s)	Create an international string using a parameter list.
InternationalString createInternationalString (String s)	Create an international string using a parameter list.
Key createKey(String id)	Create a key instance using a parameter list.
LocalizedString createLocalizedString(Locale l, java.lang.String s)	Create a localized string using a parameter list.
Object createObject(String className)	Create an information model interface.
Organization createOrganization(String name)	Create an organization using a parameter list.
PersonName createPersonName(String fullName)	Create a PersonName using a parameter list.
PersonName createPersonName(String firstName, String middleName, String lastName)	Create a person's name using a parameter list.
PostalAddress createPostalAddress(String streetNumber, String street, String city, String stateOrProvince, String country, String postalCode, String type)	Create a postal address using a parameter list.
RegistryPackage createRegistryPackage (String name)	Create a registry package using a parameter list.
Service createService(String name)	Create a service using a parameter list.
ServiceBinding createServiceBinding()	Create a service binding using a parameter list.
Slot createSlot(String name, Collection values, String slotType)	Create a slot using a parameter list.
Slot createSlot(String name, String value, String slotType)	Create a slot using a parameter list.
SpecificationLink createSpecificationLink()	Create a specification link using a parameter list.

Table M-3.   *public interface LifeCycleManager* (continued)

Syntax	Descriptions
TelephoneNumber createTelephoneNumber()	Create a telephone number using a parameter list.
User createUser()	Create a user using a parameter list.
void deleteConceptEquivalence(Concept concept1, Concept concept2)	Deletes an equivalence between concepts.
BulkResponse deleteObjects(Collection keys)	Deletes objects from a registry.
BulkResponse deprecateObjects(Collection keys)	Deprecates previously submitted objects.
BulkResponse saveObjects(Collection objects)	Saves an object to a registry.
BulkResponse unDeprecateObjects (Collection keys)	Undeprecates previously deprecated objects.

Table M-3.   *public interface LifeCycleManager* (continued)

Java API for XML Registries Query

Syntax	Descriptions
BulkResponse findAssociations(Collection findQualifiers, Collection associationTypes, boolean sourceObjectConfirmed, boolean targetObjectConfirmed)	Returns associations matching the parameter list.
ClassificationScheme findClassificationSchemeByName (String namePattern)	Returns a classification scheme by name.
BulkResponse findClassificationSchemes (Collection findQualifiers, Collection namePatterns, Collection classifications, Collection externalLinks)	Returns classification schemes matching the parameter list.

Table M-4.   *public interface BusinessQueryManager* **extends QueryManager**

Syntax	Descriptions
Concept findConceptByPath(String path)	Returns a concept using a parameter.
BulkResponse findConcepts(Collection findQualifiers, Collection namePatterns, Collection classifications, Collection externalIdentifiers, Collection externalLinks)	Returns concepts matching the parameter list.
BulkResponse findOrganizations(Collection findQualifiers, Collection namePatterns, Collection classifications, Collection specifications, Collection externalIdentifiers, Collection externalLinks)	Returns organizations matching the parameter list.
BulkResponse findRegistryPackages (Collection findQualifiers, Collection namePatterns, Collection classifications, Collection externalLinks)	Returns registry packages matching the parameter list.
BulkResponse findServiceBindings(Key serviceKey, Collection findQualifiers, Collection classifications, Collection specifications)	Returns service bindings matching the parameter list.
BulkResponse findServices(Key orgKey, Collection findQualifiers, Collection namePatterns, Collection classifications, Collection specifications)	Returns services matching the parameter list.

Table M-4.   *public interface BusinessQueryManager* **extends QueryManager**
(continued)

Syntax	Descriptions
int getType()	Returns the type of a query.
String toString()	Print the query.

Table M-5.   *public interface* Query

Syntax	Descriptions
CataloguedObject getCataloguedObject (String id)	Returns the catalogued object specified by the parameter list.
BulkResponse getCataloguedObjects (Collection objectKeys)	Returns the specified catalogued objects specified by the parameter list.
RegistryObject getRegistryObject (String id)	Returns the registry object specified by the parameter list.
BulkResponse getRegistryObjects()	Returns the registry objects.
BulkResponse getRegistryObjects (Collection objectKeys)	Returns the registry objects.
BulkResponse getRegistryObjects (String objectType)	Returns the registry objects specified by the parameter list.

Table M-6.   *public interface* QueryManager

Syntax	Descriptions
Query createQuery(int queryType, String queryString)	Creates a query object.
BulkResponse executeQuery(Query query)	Execute a query.

Table M-7.   *public interface* DeclarativeQueryManager *extends QueryManager*

Syntax	Descriptions
static String AND_ALL_KEYS	Match using specified key and all keys
static String CASE_SENSITIVE_MATCH	Match case of search criteria

Table M-8.   *public interface* FindQualifier

Syntax	Descriptions
static String COMBINE_CLASSIFICATIONS	Search using combine classifications.
static String EXACT_NAME_MATCH	Use exact match.
static String OR_ALL_KEYS	Match using specified key or all keys.
static String OR_LIKE_KEYS	Match using specified key or like keys.
static String SERVICE_SUBSET	Match using a service subset.
static String SORT_BY_DATE_ASC	Sort by date in ascending order.
static String SORT_BY_DATE_DESC	Sort by date in descending order.
static String SORT_BY_NAME_ASC	Sort by name in ascending order.
static String SORT_BY_NAME_DESC	Sort by name in descending order
static String SOUNDEX	Allows matching strings by their sounds.

Table M-8.   *public interface* FindQualifier (continued)

Java API for XML Registries Profile

Syntax	Descriptions
int getCapabilityLevel()	Returns the JAXR provider capability level supported.
String getVersion()	Returns the JAXR provider JAXR specification version.

Table M-9.   *public interface* CapabilityProfile

Java API for XML Registries Catalogue

Syntax	Descriptions
RegistryEntry getRegistryEntry()	Returns the registry entry.
Object getRepositoryItem()	Returns the optional repository item.

Table M-10. *public interface* CataloguedObject

Java API for XML Registries Connection

Syntax	Descriptions
void close()	Closes a connection.
Set getCredentials()	Returns client credentials.
RegistryService getRegistryService()	Returns the registry service interface.
boolean isClosed()	Returns true if connection is closed.
boolean isSynchronous()	Returns true if client uses synchronous communication.
void setCredentials(Set credentials)	Sets client's credentials.
void setSynchronous(boolean sync)	Sets whether a client uses synchronous communication.

Table M-11. *public interface* Connection

Java API for XML Registries Response

Syntax	Descriptions
String getRequestId()	Returns a unique ID for a request.
int getStatus()	Returns the status for a response.
boolean isAvailable()	Returns true if a response is available; otherwise, a false is returned if a response is unavailable.

Table M-12.   *public interface* JAXRResponse

Java API for XML Registries Service

Syntax	Descriptions
BulkResponse getBulkResponse (String requestId)	Returns the bulk response specified by the parameter list.
BusinessLifeCycleManager getBusinessLifeCycleManager()	Returns the JAXR provider's BusinessLifeCycleManager interface.
BusinessQueryManager getBusinessQueryManager()	Returns the JAXR provider's BusinessQueryManager interface.
CapabilityProfile getCapabilityProfile()	Returns the JAXR provider's capability profile.
DeclarativeQueryManager getDeclarativeQueryManager()	Returns the JAXR provider's DeclarativeQueryManager interface.
ClassificationScheme getDefaultPostalScheme()	Returns the default user-defined postal scheme.
LifeCycleManager getLifeCycleManager()	Returns the JAXR provider's basic LifeCycleManager interface.
String makeRegistrySpecificRequest (String request)	Returns a String object that's in the registry format.

Table M13.   *public interface* RegistryService

Index

J

K

L

T

INTERNATIONAL CONTACT INFORMATION

AUSTRALIA
McGraw-Hill Book Company Australia Pty. Ltd.
TEL +61-2-9415-9899
FAX +61-2-9415-5687
http://www.mcgraw-hill.com.au
books-it_sydney@mcgraw-hill.com

CANADA
McGraw-Hill Ryerson Ltd.
TEL +905-430-5000
FAX +905-430-5020
http://www.mcgrawhill.ca

GREECE, MIDDLE EAST,
NORTHERN AFRICA
McGraw-Hill Hellas
TEL +30-1-656-0990-3-4
FAX +30-1-654-5525

MEXICO (Also serving Latin America)
McGraw-Hill Interamericana Editores S.A. de C.V.
TEL +525-117-1583
FAX +525-117-1589
http://www.mcgraw-hill.com.mx
fernando_castellanos@mcgraw-hill.com

SINGAPORE (Serving Asia)
McGraw-Hill Book Company
TEL +65-863-1580
FAX +65-862-3354
http://www.mcgraw-hill.com.sg
mghasia@mcgraw-hill.com

SOUTH AFRICA
McGraw-Hill South Africa
TEL +27-11-622-7512
FAX +27-11-622-9045
robyn_swanepoel@mcgraw-hill.com

UNITED KINGDOM & EUROPE
(Excluding Southern Europe)
McGraw-Hill Education Europe
TEL +44-1-628-502500
FAX +44-1-628-770224
http://www.mcgraw-hill.co.uk
computing_neurope@mcgraw-hill.com

ALL OTHER INQUIRIES Contact:
Osborne/McGraw-Hill
TEL +1-510-549-6600
FAX +1-510-883-7600
http://www.osborne.com
omg_international@mcgraw-hill.com